Sol y viento
beginning spanish

Second Edition

Bill VanPatten
Texas Tech University

Michael J. Leeser
Florida State University

Gregory D. Keating
San Diego State University

McGraw-Hill
Higher Education

Boston   Burr Ridge, IL   Dubuque, IA   New York   San Francisco   St. Louis
Bangkok   Bogotá   Caracas   Kuala Lumpur   Lisbon   London   Madrid   Mexico City
Milan   Montreal   New Delhi   Santiago   Seoul   Singapore   Sydney   Taipei   Toronto

 **McGraw-Hill**
Higher Education

Sol y viento
Beginning Spanish

Published by McGraw-Hill, an imprint of The McGraw-Hill Companies, Inc., 1221 Avenue of the Americas, New York, NY 10020. Copyright © 2009 by The McGraw-Hill Companies, Inc. All rights reserved. No part of this publication may be reproduced or distributed in any form or by any means, or stored in a database or retrieval system, without the prior written consent of The McGraw-Hill Companies, Inc., including, but not limited to, in any network or other electronic storage or transmission, or broadcast for distance learning.

This book is printed on acid-free paper.

1 2 3 4 5 6 7 8 9 0 QPD QPD 0 9 8

MHID: 0-07-334287-4 (Instructor's Edition)
ISBN: 978-0-07-334287-0 (Instructor's Edition)

Editor-in-chief: *Michael J. Ryan*
Publisher: *William R. Glass*
Executive editor: *Christa Harris*
Director of development: *Scott Tinetti*
Marketing manager: *Jorge Arbujas*
Senior production editor: *Mel Valentín*
Lead production supervisor: *Randy Hurst*
Senior production supervisor: *Richard DeVitto*
Senior supplements producer: *Louis Swaim*
Photo research coordinator: *Nora Agbayani*
Freelance photo researcher: *Judy Mason*
Art director: *Jeanne M. Schreiber*
Design manager: *Violeta Díaz/Andrei Pasternak*
Interior designer: *Amanda Kavanaugh*
Cover designer: *Violeta Díaz*
Art editor: *Emma Ghiselli*
Illustrators: *Kathryn Rathke, Diane Dempsey*
Compositor: *Aptara-York*
Typeface: *10/12 Bookman*
Printer and binder: *Quebecor World*

Because this page cannot legibly accommodate all the copyright notices, credits are listed after the Index and constitute an extension of the copyright page.

Library of Congress Cataloging-in-Publication Data

VanPatten, Bill.
   Sol y viento : beginning Spanish / Bill VanPatten, Michael Leeser, Gregory
D. Keating. — 2nd ed.
      p. cm.
   Includes index.
   ISBN-13: 978-0-07-351312-6 (alk. paper)
   ISBN-10: 0-07-351312-1 (alk. paper)
   1. Spanish language—Textbooks for foreign speakers—English. I. Leeser,
Michael J. II. Keating, Gregory D. III. Sol y viento. IV. Title.
PC4129.E5S64 2008
468.2'421—dc22
                                                    2007046247

Contents

Episodio 1: La llegada   18

Episodio 2: El encuentro 78

Episodio 3: A la viña   138

Episodio 4: Otro encuentro   198

Episodio 5: Un día perfecto   258

Episodio 6: Confrontación   318

Episodio 7: Bajo el sol   378

Episodio 8: Sin alternativa   438

Episodio 9: Un brindis por el futuro   498

Preface

Sol y viento: The Film

A successful young businessman gets orders to travel abroad to secure a land deal. Occupied with other matters and unwilling to go at first, he finally accepts the assignment and soon finds himself in Chile, a country far from his native California. Here, in this Andean nation—land of fertile valleys and soaring mountains, home to the condor, a place exotic and familiar all at once—this young man regains and embraces values he had set aside years ago. He rediscovers the importance of loyalty to family and friends and learns that a person's past is part of his or her soul. He rediscovers the meaning of community and how people and their land may share a bond as strong as that between any two people. Most importantly, he comes to understand that from love, forgiveness is possible—but it is not easily dispensed. Forgiveness must be earned.

Such is the story of the exciting new movie, *Sol y viento*. Follow Jaime "James" Talavera on his unexpected journey of self-discovery. Along the way meet Mario, the talkative personal driver who becomes Jaime's first friend in a new land. Meet Carlos, the secretive administrator of the winery who is eager to sell his family's lands—and those of others. Meet doña Isabel, the matriarch of the Sol y viento winery, and don Paco, the friend of the family who travels from Mexico to aid doña Isabel as she faces a crisis that threatens to alter an entire community's way of life. Finally, meet the high-spirited María, the young woman who captures Jaime's heart and mind. However, their mutual attraction may prove to be fleeting if Jaime does not grapple with the moral issues that confront him. As events unfold and the forces of nature conspire to draw the characters together, Jaime is forced to make the most difficult decision of his life.

Dramatic and engaging, the *Sol y viento* film serves as the centerpiece for the textbook of the same name. Divided into ten episodes, consisting of a prologue and nine segments of approximately ten minutes each, the movie is easily managed for viewing in class and is fully integrated into the textbook. Students see each episode multiple times with varied accompanying activities, thus maximizing their exposure to language and greatly increasing their comprehension skills. Language is taken directly from the movie to illustrate grammar points, and the movie also provides points of departure for readings and discussions on cultural themes. In the Instructional Version of the film, approximately five hours long, on-screen activities facilitate instruction and learning.

Sol y viento: The Textbook

Equally innovative and as interesting as the movie, the *Sol y viento* textbook, now in its Second Edition, is firmly framed in communicative-oriented language teaching. Completely meaning-based and drill-free, it presents the grammatical points that most instructors expect to cover in a first-year college-level Spanish course. How does it do this? *Sol y viento* borrows from the most recent innovations and research in instructed second language acquisition. Using an input-to-output approach for the presentation of vocabulary and grammar, *Sol y viento* provides instructors and students with a clear focus on the language without sacrificing meaning; or, to look at it another way, it provides a clear focus on meaning without sacrificing a focus on the language.

In short, *Sol y viento* provides the instructor with a refreshing approach to grammar instruction and practice that fits well within the tenets of communicative language teaching. The materials allow instructors to maintain a simultaneous focus on both meaning and formal properties of language as students are engaged in learning about their classmates, their instructor, and the world around them. Paired with an exciting movie, the *Sol y viento* textbook provides students with a complete and effective beginning Spanish course that will lead them to higher levels of proficiency in comprehension and production than they might achieve with other materials. However, *Sol y viento* is not a set of learning materials focused on vocabulary and grammar alone. As a complete learning package, it presents abundant information on cultural topics relevant to the Spanish-speaking world, as well as opportunities for students to develop their reading and writing abilities.

For a more detailed description on using the film and textbook together, please refer to the Instructor's Manual and Testing Program on the Online Learning Center Website at **www.mhhe.com/solyviento2.**

New to the Second Edition

Based on user feedback, we have made the following changes in the new edition of the textbook:

- activities are now clearly marked as input or output activities in the annotations of the Instructor's Edition;

- more pair-work activities have been included to allow students to communicate with each other in Spanish;
- we've developed a new activity type called **¿Qué leíste?** and **¿Qué escuchaste?** in which students work in small groups to recreate a short narration that focuses on a particular grammar point;
- we have added **Una historia** activities in which students make up a story based on four or five cartoon-like drawings;
- some larger vocabulary presentations have been pared down to a more manageable size;
- we have revised several grammar presentations to make them clearer and more concise, and some grammar points have been relocated in the text (see the Instructor's Manual for details);
- for a number of complicated grammar points, we have added an appendix in the Instructor's Manual, along with student self-tests;
- we have revised and updated many **Vistazo cultural** readings and have added instructor annotations for use in class (see the Instructor's Manual for details);
- we have written all new **Entremés cultural** sections with shorter, more manageable readings that present interesting facts about the Spanish-speaking world.

Cast of Characters

Jaime
A successful businessman from San Francisco, California, who travels to Chile to finalize a deal with the Sol y viento winery

María
A Chilean university professor and anthropologist, who has always let her head rule over her heart

Carlos
Proprietor and administrator of the Sol y viento winery, who is working on the deal with Jaime's company

Isabel
Carlos' ailing mother and, with her now-deceased husband, original proprietor of Sol y viento

Paco
An old family friend of Isabel's, who is called away from his native Mexico to help his friend in a time of need

Mario
A taxi driver in Jaime's employ during his stay in Chile

Traimaqueo
The longtime foreman of the Sol y viento winery

Yolanda
Traimaqueo's wife and Isabel's primary caregiver

Diego
María's student assistant at both the university and at anthropological dig sites

Who are the Mapuches?

Throughout the course of the film, *Sol y viento* touches upon the plight of the Mapuche people and their struggle to retain their ancestral lands and maintain harmony with the Earth. The Mapuches are an indigenous people whose roots are found in southern and south central Chile and date back to thousands of years before the Europeans' arrival in the western hemisphere. In Quechua, the language of the Mapuche, **mapu** means *land* and **che** means *people*, essentially making them "people of the land." This connection to the Earth is deeply rooted in the spirit and culture of the Mapuche people.

Since the 1880's, when the nations of Chile and Argentina began to appropriate ancestral Mapuche lands, the Mapuches have strived to retain these lands and, later, to make their struggles known to the world at large. In *Sol y viento*, this struggle is shown by the attempt of outsiders to purchase

Mapuche lands in order to build a large dam to flood the region and produce cheap hydroelectric power.

In her book *Mi país inventado*, the acclaimed Chilean writer Isabel Allende relates a real-life struggle that echoes this theme in the film:

Nuestros indios no pertenecían a una cultura espléndida, como los aztecas, mayas o incas; eran hoscos, primitivos, irascibles y poco numerosos, pero tan corajudos, que estuvieron en pie de guerra durante trescientos años, primero contra los colonizadores españoles y luego contra la república. Fueron pacificados en 1880 y no se oyó hablar mucho de ellos por más de un siglo, pero ahora los mapuches —«gente de la tierra»— han vuelto a la lucha para defender las pocas tierras que les quedan, amenazadas por la construcción de una represa en el río Bío Bío.*

One of the Mapuche characters in the film, the **machi,** is a spiritual leader of her tribe. At the beginning of the film, we see her telling a tale to a group of adults and children. As her tale unfolds, we witness how the lives of Jaime, María, and others are intricately woven into her story and how the forces of nature conspire to bring resolution to the conflicts with which they are faced.

The figurine seen here is a representation of a protective spirit in the beliefs of the Mapuche people. This spirit also plays an important role in the film, as you will see.

---

*Our Indians didn't belong to a grand culture, like the Aztecs, Mayas, or Incas; they were gruff, primitive, irritable, and few in number, but so brave that they waged war for 300 years, first against the Spanish settlers and then against the republic. They were pacified in 1880, and for more than a century you didn't hear a lot about them. But now the Mapuches —"people of the earth"— have renewed their fight in order to defend the few lands they have left, threatened by the construction of a dam on the Bío Bío River.
(Isabel Allende, *Mi país inventado* [Buenos Aires: Sudamericana, 2003], p. 56.)

Sol y viento

A Guided Tour of the Textbook

Episode Opener

The text is divided into nine units (**Episodios**) with two lessons each (**A** and **B**), for a total of 18 regular lessons. Thus, **Lecciones 1A** and **1B** correspond to **Episodio 1** of the film, **Lecciones 2A** and **2B** correspond to **Episodio 2,** and so forth.

Lesson Opener

Lesson openers provide a list of goals that prepare students for what they will learn in the lesson.

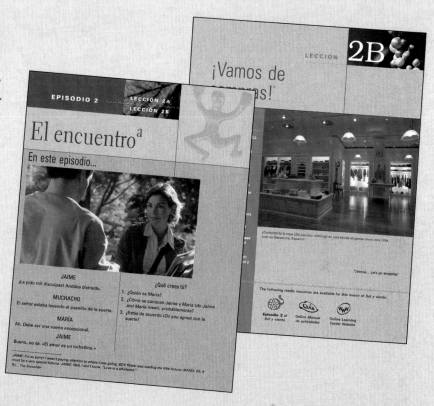

Lesson Organization

Each lesson is organized into three parts (**Primera parte, Segunda parte, Tercera parte**),* each of which contains a **Vocabulario** and **Gramática** presentation and accompanying activities. An audio recording of the **Vocabulario** presentations can be found on the Online Learning Center.

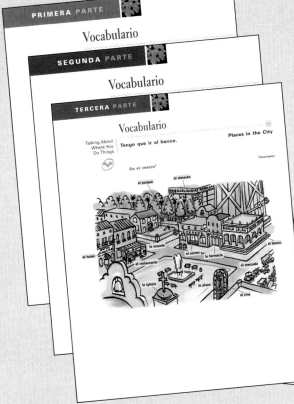

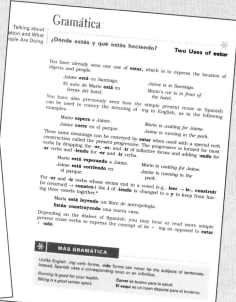

*__Lecciones 9A__ and __9B__ contain just the **Primera parte** and **Segunda parte.**

Sol y viento

Every lesson concludes with a two-page *Sol y viento* section that focuses on the story line and characters of the film with pre- and post-viewing activities. "A" lessons contain the section *Sol y viento:* **A primera vista,** for a first viewing of each episode. "B" lessons contain *Sol y viento:* **A segunda vista,** in which students watch the episode again for review and further exploration of the plot, characters, and themes of the film.

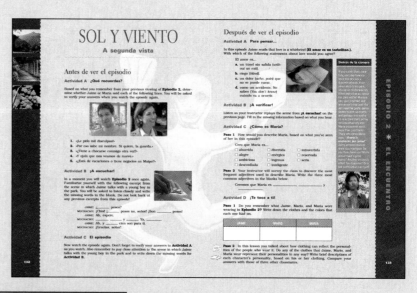

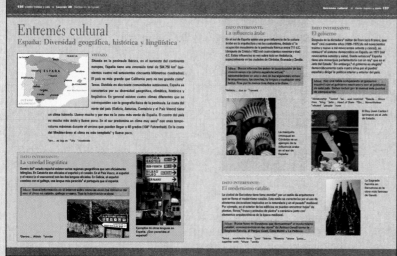

Entremés cultural

New to the Second Edition are completely revised **Entremés cultural** sections. Each set of brief readings focuses on a country or region of the Spanish-speaking world, presenting interesting information on history, geography, the people, personalities, and other aspects of that place. Each reading is accompanied by **Idea,** an optional research-based project that encourages students to find out more about that country or region and to report their findings to the class.

Other Cultural Features

- Each regular lesson contains three **Vistazo cultural** sections that focus on a cultural topic of interest related to the lesson theme. Topics range from "big C" culture (art, literature, and so forth) to "little c" culture (everyday life, customs, and so forth).
- *Sol y viento:* **Enfoque cultural** sections explore a cultural point illustrated in the *Sol y viento* film.

Additional Features

- **De *Sol y viento*** boxes highlight portions of dialogue from the film that illustrate grammar points presented in the text. In this way, students are able to view the grammar in context in the film. In addition, they offer "previews" of scenes that will aid student comprehension of the episode.
- **Enfoque lingüístico** features help students understand the nature of language in general. Although Spanish and English are often compared, for students to fully capture how languages work, contrasts with languages such as Chinese, Arabic, and Nahuatl also appear.
- **Más vocabulario** and **Más gramática** boxes are found in **Vocabulario** and **Gramática** sections, respectively, and present additional vocabulary and grammar that students need to know to complete the accompanying activities.
- **¡Exprésate!** boxes highlight a key element of language, whether vocabulary, useful phrases, or structures, that students will need to complete accompanying activities.
- **Comunicación útil** features present useful phrases and other tips for successfully communicating in Spanish.
- **Detrás de la cámara** boxes are found in *Sol y viento* sections and provide additional information not presented in the film, such as the characters' background, motivation, personalities, and so forth.
- **Icons** highlight partner/pair or group work, activities that require listening to the instructor for information, writing activities that require an additional sheet of paper, and content provided on the Online Learning Center.

Vistazo cultural

Diseñadores hispanos

For decades, a number of Hispanic des[igners] for their elegant, high-end fashion de[signs] created a world-renowned fashion hous[es] success on both sides of the Atlantic. Ven[ezuelan] can Óscar de la Renta have been at the f[orefront] than two decades. In addition to creating [fashion] known for creating designs described a[s] Cuban-American Narciso Rodríguez gaine[d fame] for Carolyn Bessette Kennedy in 1996. Hi[s clients] such as Salma Hayek and Sarah Jessica [Parker].

In terms of popular fashion, perhaps th[e most famous] born entrepreneur Amancio Ortega. Wha[t began] in provincial Galicia in the early sixties has turned into an empire of more than one thousand stores worldwide and the third-largest clothing company in the world (after Gap and the Swedish HM). Ortega's flagship store is Zara, which can be found in many Spanish cities, as well as in major cities in Europe, the United [States]

SOL Y VIENTO: Enfoque cultural

City parks abound in Spanish-speaking countries, as they do in this country. However, they are often used in different ways. In **Episodio 2** you will watch Jaime as he jogs through the Parque Forestal in Santiago. However, using a public park as a place to exercise is not the norm for most Spanish-speaking people. Instead, parks are often places to socialize, and on Sundays they may flourish with couples and families of all ages out for an old-fashioned Sunday afternoon stroll (**el paseo**). It is also typical to find vendors of all types in these parks selling everything from cotton candy to balloons, as well as entertainers working for donations, such as the organ-grinding fortune teller with his parrot that you will see in this episode. Some well-known parks in Spanish-speaking cities include the Retiro (Madrid), Lazema (Buenos Aires), and Chapultepec (Mexico City), among others.

▲ El parque Chapultepec (México, D.F.)

DE SOL Y VIENTO

Remember the scene from **Episodio 2** of *Sol y viento* in which Jaime returns a business card that María has dropped? Part of their exchange appears in the dialogue.

JAIME
¡Señorita Sánchez!

MARÍA
¿Viene a chocarse conmigo[a] [...]

JAIME
Eh, no. Creo que _____

MARÍA
¡Ah! Por eso sabe[c] mi nombre. [...] la guarda.[d]

Selecting from the following [...] demonstrative pronoun belongs [...]

1. esto   2. eso   3. a[quello]

[a]chocarse... *bump into me*   [b]*yours*

Enfoque lingüístico

Más sobre las inflexiones

You may recall that *inflections* are forms that are added to words that provide the listener with certain information. For example, you learned in **Lección 1A** that one way in which Spanish is an inflectionally rich language is that its verb inflections are unique for each person (e.g., *I, you, he/she, we,* and *they*). In the last few lessons, you've learned the present-tense inflections for Spanish **-ar, -er,** and **-ir** verbs. Later in *Sol y viento* you will learn other verb inflections to express various meanings and speaker perspectives. All of the Spanish verb inflections that you will learn are *suffixes*; that is, they are forms that are attached to the *end* of a word or stem. (Remember in **Lección 1A** you read that you will have to get used to listening to the ends of verbs to find out who is being talked about.)

However, not all languages use suffixes for verbal inflections. Some Native American languages like Navajo use *prefixes* (forms attached to the *beginning* of a word or [...] **naal** (roughly equivalent [...] to form **naalnish**. Instead [...] inserted in the *middle* of [...]ines, uses infixes to form

MÁS VOCABULARIO

buscar	to look for	de compras	shopping
comprar	to buy	la marca	brand name
encontrar (ue)	to find	el precio (fijo)	(fixed) price
gastar	to spend	la talla	size
quedar bien/mal	to fit well/poorly	grande	large
regatear	to bargain	mediano/a	medium
vender	to sell	pequeño/a	small
barato/a	inexpensive		
caro[...]			

¡Exprésate!

You can use the preposition **para** plus an infinitive to express "in order to (*do something*)".

Para comprar ropa de última moda, necesitas mucho dinero.

In order to buy the latest fashions, you need lots of money.

MÁS GRAMÁTICA

Although **bien** is usually translated into English as *well* when used with the [...] it is usually translated as *to be OK/fine*.

Está bien.	*It's OK. / That's fine.*
Estoy bien, gracias.	*I'm fine, thanks.*
¿Necesitan algo más?	*Do you all need anything else?*
No, gracias. **Estamos bien.**	*No, thank you. We're fine.*

COMUNICACIÓN ÚTIL

To say *to get dressed* or *to dress oneself,* use the verb **vestir** with reflexive pronouns, just like the verbs **despertarse** and **acostarse** that you learned in Lecc[...] learn more about reflexive pronouns and verbs in **Lección 5A.** For now, [...] common expressions with **vestirse.**

Me visto rápidamente.	*I get dressed quickly.*
¡Vístete!	*Get dressed!*
¿Cómo **nos vestimos?**	*How do/should we dress?*

Detrás de la cámara

If you watch María carefully, you may have noticed that she has a determined walk. Even when she's in the park, she never strolls leisurely. What might that say about her personality? María is very goal-oriented, and

Supplements

As a full-service publisher of quality educational products, McGraw-Hill does much more than just sell textbooks to your students. We create and publish an extensive array of print, video, and digital supplements to support instruction on your campus. Orders of new (versus used) textbooks help us to defray the cost of developing such supplements, which is substantial. Please consult your local McGraw-Hill representative to learn about the availability of the supplements that accompany *Sol y viento,* Second Edition.

For Students and Instructors

- Available for purchase in VHS or DVD formats, the *Instructional Version* of the *Sol y viento* film contains on-screen pre- and post-viewing activities for each episode (written by Isabel Anievas-Gamallo and Scott Tinetti). The DVD version also contains film clips of the **De Sol y viento** features in the text, as well as additional features such as interviews with the cast and crew, a behind-the-scenes look at the filming of *Sol y viento,* and much more.

- The *Director's Cut* is also available for those who wish to purchase it. This version of the film (in VHS or DVD formats) contains the complete, uninterrupted movie, with or without Spanish subtitles (DVD only). The DVD also contains individual episodes of the film, without any on-screen activities, as well as special features.

- Introducing the new *Sol y viento* Learning Management System with integrated digital textbook, powered by Quia™. McGraw-Hill has partnered with Quia™, the leading developer of online tools for foreign language instruction and learning, to create a comprehensive learning management system that allows you to manage your course with robust communication tools, record keeping that can be imported to Blackboard and other CMS platforms, integration of instructor resources such as digital transparencies and PowerPoint slides, as well as the ability to customize or add your own content. Last but certainly not least, it includes a fully interactive digital version of the textbook that has a real-time voice chat feature, integrated audio and video, and many other resources that make this a truly integrated online system for the teaching and learning of Spanish. Please contact your local McGraw-Hill sales representative for more information.

- The *Manual de actividades,* Volumes 1 and 2, offers additional practice with vocabulary, grammar, and listening comprehension. Two distinguishing features of the *Manual* are the **¡A escuchar!** section at the end of every "A" lesson and the **Para escribir** section at the end of every "B" lesson. **¡A escuchar!** provides in-depth listening comprehension practice, accompanied by listening strategies. **Para escribir** guides students through the process of writing, from jotting down ideas, to creating outlines and rough drafts, and finally to the reviewing and editing of the final written piece. Verb charts and an Answer Key provide excellent reference materials for students.

- McGraw-Hill is also proud to partner with Quia™ in the development of the *Online Manual de actividades,* Volumes 1 and 2. Carefully integrated with the textbook, this robust digital version of the printed *Manual* is easy for students to use and great for instructors who want to manage students' coursework online. Identical in practice material to the print version, the *Online Manual* contains the complete audio program and provides students with automatic feedback and scoring of their work. The Instructor Workstation contains an easy-to-use gradebook and class roster system that facilitates course management.

- The *Audio Program* to accompany the *Manual* provides additional listening comprehension practice outside of the classroom.

- The Student Edition of the Online Learning Center Website (**www.mhhe.com/solyviento2**) provides even more practice with the vocabulary and grammar presented in the textbook. It also contains useful resources such as interactive verb charts, grammar tutorials, and the laboratory audio program.

- The *Student Viewer's Guide* is ideal for those courses in which the *Sol y viento* film is used as a supplement to another core text. The *Student Viewer's Guide* offers a variety of pre- and post-viewing activities for use with the film, as well as cultural information and a process writing activity that accompanies each episode of the film.

For Instructors Only

- The annotated *Instructor's Edition* contains detailed suggestions for carrying out activities in class. It also offers options for expansion and follow-up.

- The instructor's section of the Online Learning Center Website (**www.mhhe.com/solyviento2**) contains many digital resources to assist instructors in getting the most out of the *Sol y viento* program. Such resources include:

  - The combined *Instructor's Manual and Testing Program* expands on the methodology of the *Sol y viento* materials. Among other things, it offers suggestions for carrying out the activities in the textbook. It also contains the complete script of the *Sol y viento* film and information on using *Sol y viento* for distance learning courses. The *Testing Program* includes sample quizzes for each lesson and a comprehension quiz for each episode, as well as quarter and semester final exams.

  - The *Audioscript* contains the transcript of the material on the *Audio Program* that accompanies the *Manual.*

- The *Picture File* contains fifty images from the film that may be used as a springboard for student discussion about the film or related topics.

- *Digital Transparencies* include vocabulary presentation art from the textbook as well as many of the art pieces that accompany textbook activities.

- New cultural PowerPoint™ presentations, available on the Online Learning Center, cover all of the Spanish-speaking countries in the world, including Equatorial Guinea. Each individual photo-based slideshow provides a visual introduction to the country and presents cultural information ranging from festivals and holidays to art, dance, and musical traditions. Presentation notes for the instructor are included in each slideshow.

- *EZ Test,* McGraw-Hill's own test generator, provides a wealth of testing questions that instructors can use to create customized and randomly-generated tests to suit their needs.

Because the instructor's side of the Online Learning Center is password-protected, please contact your local McGraw-Hill sales representative to obtain a login name and password.

- Available for instructors only, a brand new music CD titled *Ritmos y sonidos* is a collection of contemporary music from around the Spanish-speaking world. The music showcases a wide variety of styles, from traditional salsa, merengue, and son, to today's Latin-influenced pop. Featuring a variety of well-known and lesser-known artists and groups, *Ritmos y sonidos* is a great resource for instructors who want to bring the musical traditions of the Spanish-speaking world into the language classroom.

Acknowledgments

The authors and the publisher wish to express their gratitude to the following instructors across the country, whose valuable suggestions contributed to the preparation of this program. Special thanks are due to our Advisory Panel members, who provided us valuable feedback at every step of the way, from the writing of the film's script to the development of the print and media materials. The appearance of their names in this list does not necessarily constitute their endorsement of the text or its methodology.

Advisory Panel

Barbara Gatski, The Millbrook School
Kathy O'Connor, Tidewater Community College
Jeff Stevenson, University of Washington
Miguel Verano, United States Air Force Academy
Joseph Weyers, College of Charleston

Reviewers

Kimberly K. Arzate, Cabrillo College
Robert Baah, Seattle Pacific University
Lomalyn Bement, Shenandoah University
Anja Bernardy, Kennesaw State University
Patrick Brady, Tidewater Community College
Peggy Buckwater, Black Hills State University
Irena Cajkova, The School of the Art Institute of Chicago
Ramiro Canto-Lugo, Yuba Community College
Thomas Capuano, Truman State University
Samira Chater, Valencia Community College
Donald Clymer, Eastern Mennonite University
Marci S. Cobo, Cabrillo College
Michelle Connolly, Community College of Rhode Island
Connie Curtis, Bethune-Cookman College
Mary Ann Dellinger, Virginia Military Institute
Donion Doman, Truman State University
Mary Ebuna, Colorado Mountain College
Jennifer Ewald, Saint Joseph University
Ana Fernández, Clemson University
Claudia Fernández, DePaul University
John Finan, William Rainey Harper College

Yolanda González, Valencia Community College
Miriam Gorriaran, Rhode Island College
Richard Heath, Kirkwood Community College, Iowa City Campus
Elissa Heil, University of the Ozarks
Yolanda Hernández, Community College of Southern Nevada
Laurie Huffman, Los Medanos College
Casilde Isabelli, University of Nevada–Reno
Elizabeth Kissling, Virginia Commonwealth University
M. Phillip Kristiansen, University of the Ozarks
Jared Larson, Emporia State University
Chang Lee, Azusa Pacific University
Lora Looney, University of Portland
Rebecca Marquis, Dickinson College
Monica Massei, Clemson University
Elaine McArthur, Brigham Young University–Hawaii
Shannon McBurnette-Argüelles, Texas A & M International University
Victor McFarlane, Kennedy-King College
Mary Yetta McKelva, Grayson County College
John Meredith, Northern Virginia Community College, Manassas Campus
Lourdes Michalak, Seattle Pacific University
Barbara Mitchell, Plymouth State University
Jeanne Mullaney, Community College of Rhode Island
Katie Nielson, University of Maryland, University College
Luisa Pérez, Emporia State University
Harland Rall, Abilene Christain University
Janice Randle, St. Edward's University
Rita Ricaute, Nebraska Wesleyan University
Cristina Sáenz de Tejada, Goucher College
José Sainz, University of Mary Washington
Jorge Salvo, University of South Carolina Upstate
Jeffrey Samuels, Goucher College
Leon Schultz, Rhode Island College
Paul Siegrist, Fort Hays State University
Jeff Stevenson, Seattle Pacific University
Cristina Szterensus, Rock Valley College

Enrique Torner, Minnesota State University, Mankato

Yvonne Unnold, University of Southern Mississippi

Marcela Valencia, Stephen F. Austin State University

Debra Vedder, Ohio Wesleyan University

Eric Vogt, Seattle Pacific University

Marilyn Walker, Emory and Henry College

Caroline White, College of St. Catherine

Jaime Zambrano, University of Central Arkansas

Leticia Zervas-Gaytán, College of Mount Saint Vincent

Judith Zinszer, Anderson University

Course Survey Participants

We would like to thank the 558 instructors who participated in a general course survey conducted by McGraw-Hill. The results of this survey helped shape and form the Second Edition and provided timely and useful information for other projects currently in development.

Symposia Attendees

We are grateful to the following instructors who recently attended McGraw-Hill symposia on introductory Spanish. These two-day, in-depth round table symposia provided the authors and editors of *Sol y viento* with invaluable feedback and suggestions and helped shape this edition and all of its ancillaries.

Claudia Acosta, *College of the Canyons*

Esther Aguilar, *San Diego State University*

Carlos Arce, *Cerritos College*

Luis Belaustegui, *University of Missouri, Kansas City*

Marla Calico, *Georgia Perimeter College*

Carmen Chávez, *Florida Atlantic University*

Eliud Chuffe, *University of Arizona*

Alicia Cipria, *University of Alabama*

Xuchitl Coso, *Georgia Perimeter College*

Richard Curry, *Texas A&M University*

Alicia de la Torre Falzón, *Northern Virginia Community College*

Beatrice DeAngelis, *University of Pittsburgh*

Annette Dunzo, *Howard University*

Ronna Feit, *Nassau Community College*

Neysa Figueroa, *Kennesaw State University*

Joan Fox, *University of Washington*

Marianne Franco, *Modesto Junior College*

Grant Goodall, *University of California, San Diego*

Sue Griffin, *Boston University*

Sergio Guzmán, *Community College of Southern Nevada*

Lucía Harrison, *Southeastern Louisiana University*

Casilde Isabelli, *University of Nevada, Reno*

Adam Karp, *American River College*

Linda Jane Keown, *University of Missouri, Columbia*

Ruth Fátima Konopka, *Grossmont College*

Josefa Lindquist, *University of North Carolina at Chapel Hill*

Lydia Llerena, *Rio Hondo College*

Jeff Longwell, *New Mexico State University*

Nuria López-Ortega, *University of Cincinnati*

Pedro Maligo, *Coastal Carolina University*

Laura Manzo, *Modesto Junior College*

Lois Mignone, *Suffolk County Community College*

M. Cristina Moreno, *De Anza College*

José Ramón Núñez, *Long Beach City College*

Ana Oskoz, *University of Maryland Baltimore County*

Marilyn Palatinus, *Pellissippi State Technical College*

Yanira Paz, *University of Kentucky*

Michelle Petersen, *Arizona State University*

Luisa Piemontese, *Southern Connecticut State University*

Comfort Pratt, *Texas Tech University*

Anne Prucha, *University of Central Florida*

Mónica Rojas de Massei, *Clemson University*

Amy Rossomondo, *University of Kansas*

Marcella Ruiz-Funes, *East Carolina University*

Theresa Ruiz-Velasco, *College of Lake County*

Maritza Salguiero-Carlisle, *Bakersfield College*
Robert Sanders, *Portland State University*
Carmen Schlig, *Georgia State University*
Louis Silvers, *Monroe Community College*
Mercedes Thompson, *El Camino College*

We owe a ton of thanks to lots of people. First, to everyone at McGraw-Hill who saw this project from start to finish: Christa Harris, Scott Tinetti, Jorge Arbujas, Mel Valentín, Violeta Díaz, and Laura Chastain. Extra thanks to Christa, who was our sponsoring editor and helped us shape this project; and other extra thanks to Scott, our development editor—always a pleasure! We would also like to thank Steve Debow, who was behind this project 100 percent and who is such an avid supporter of languages. And no less enthusiastic are our thanks to our publisher, Bill Glass. We can think of no publishing team better to work with than the people at McGraw-Hill.

A round of thanks to all the folks at Truth-Function who were involved with the filming of the movie: David Murray (our great director), Hugo Kryspin (our second unit director), Rocío Barajas (producer), Lamar Owen (director of photography), and Tom Sherer (associate producer, still photography), among others. Of course, many thanks to the local production crew in Chile, headed by Rodrigo Fernández of RF Films, as well as all of the talented actors, most notably Frank Lord (Jaime) and Javiera Contador (María). Such great professionals. Thanks also to the Gil family of the Miraflores winery in the Maipo Valley who so graciously let us film in their home and on their land. Thanks to Carlos Barón for his work on the screenplay and for being such a great source of information. Big thanks to María A. Pérez and Robert D. Cameron for their excellent work on the Testing Program.

Finally, thanks to all our loved ones who put up with overcommitted authors and academics. We think we can do it all, but in reality we can only do it because of your patience.

¡Aquí estamos![a]

OBJETIVOS

IN THIS PRELIMINARY LESSON, YOU WILL:

- learn how to greet people and make introductions in Spanish
- learn the verb **ser** and some of its basic uses
- talk about courses and majors
- learn about articles and the gender and number of nouns
- name common objects and people in the classroom
- learn the verb **estar** and one of its basic uses

In addition, you will prepare for and watch the **Prólogo** of the film *Sol y viento*.

This woman is a **machi,** a spiritual leader within the Mapuche tribe of Chile. What do you think she is doing? Is she telling a tale? Leading a group in song? Warning of an impending danger?

[a]¡Aquí... *Here we are!*

The following media resources are available for this lesson of *Sol y viento:*

Prólogo of *Sol y viento*

Online *Manual de actividades*

Online Learning Center Website

Vocabulario

Meeting and Greeting People

Me llamo...

Introductions

Note: These vocabulary items can be heard in this lesson's Textbook Audio section of the Online Learning Center Website.

Más vocabulario, **Note:** Use and nonuse of subject pronouns will be presented in *Lección 1A,* along with regular *-ar* verbs. If students ask about *¿Cómo se llama (él/ella)?,* just explain to them the meaning of each pronoun and that they are optional in Spanish, except where clarification or emphasis is needed.

INPUT
Act. A, Note: You will note that in *Sol y viento* all initial activities for vocabulary and grammar are input, or comprehension, activities that allow students to hear and begin to internalize new material. Input activities are clearly marked as such in the instructor's annotations. Production and pair work activities (also called output activities) are also clearly indicated. Thus, in each vocabulary and grammar string, you will see both input- and output-oriented activities. Please see the Instructor's Manual for additional information on input (comprehension) and output (production). See especially the section called "Making Input Activities Come Alive."

—¡Hola! **Soy** Tomás Villa.
—¡Hola! **Me llamo** Jorge. Jorge Mateos.
—**¿Cómo se llama él?**
—**No sé.**

The most common way to greet someone in Spanish is to say **hola,** equivalent to *hello* in English. Note the following exchange in Spanish.

¡Hola! Me llamo Paco.	*Hi! My name is Paco.*
¡Hola! Soy Elena. **Mucho gusto.**	*Hi! I'm Elena. Pleased to meet you.*
Igualmente.	*Likewise.*

✳ **MÁS VOCABULARIO**

¿Cómo te llamas?	What's your name?
Mi nombre es Paula.*	My name is Paula.
¿Cuál es tu apellido?	What's your last name?
Mi apellido es González.	My last name is González.
¿Cómo se llama (él/ella)?	What's his/her name?
¿Cuál es su apellido?	What's his/her last name?
No sé.	I don't know.

Actividad A   En orden

Put the following phrases in the order in which two speakers would most likely say them.

_3_ Mucho gusto.   _1_ ¡Hola! Soy Pablo. ¿Cómo te llamas?

_2_ Mi nombre es Adriana.   _4_ Igualmente.

---

*In Spanish, **mi nombre es** is a word-for-word equivalent of the English *my name is.* However, **me llamo** is literally translated as *I call myself.* When you ask **¿Cómo te llamas?** you are actually saying *How do you call yourself?* So don't make the mistake of thinking **me** means *my* and **llamo** means *name.* In Spanish *my* is **mi** and *name* is **nombre.**

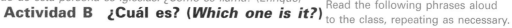

Actividad B ¿Cuál es? (*Which one is it?*)

Listen as your instructor says a phrase. Then select the phrase that would most logically follow it.

1. **a.** Soy Alfredo. **b.** Mucho gusto. **c.** ¡Hola!
2. **a.** Me llamo Paula. **b.** Es Rodríguez. **c.** ¿Cómo te llamas?
3. **a.** Igualmente. **b.** ¿Cuál es tu apellido? **c.** ¡Hola!

Actividad C Algunas (*Some*) personas famosas

Answer the question your instructor asks about each of these photos.

▲ 1.   ▲ 2.   ▲ 3.   ▲ 4.

Actividad D ¡A conocernos! (*Let's get acquainted!*)

Move around the room, greeting and introducing yourself to at least four people. Write down their first and last names.

NOMBRE APELLIDO

1. _____ _____
2. _____ _____
3. _____ _____
4. _____ _____

¡Exprésate!

In addition to **hola**, you might want to use the following greetings. In Hispanic cultures, these expressions are typical when meeting and greeting people. Try using them as you complete **Actividad D.**

Buenos días.
  Good morning.

Buenas tardes.
  Good afternoon/evening.

The expression **Buenas noches** (*Good night*) is used when saying good-bye in the evening.

▒〰 Vistazo cultural

Los saludos[a]

In the Spanish-speaking world, when people first meet it is customary for them to shake hands, no matter their age or sex. When friends greet each other, men generally shake hands and women kiss each other on the cheek. In Spain, a kiss on each cheek is the norm, whereas a kiss on one cheek is customary elsewhere. Kissing on the cheek between male and female friends varies from country to country but is fairly typical, especially among younger friends. As you watch the episodes of *Sol y viento*, pay attention to the ways in which people greet each other.

Un saludo entre (*between*) amigos hispanos. ▶

[a]Los... *Greetings*

Gramática

Expressing
Origin

Soy de México.

Introduction to ser

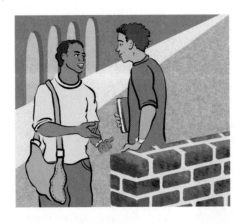

—**¿De dónde eres,** Jorge?
—**De** Nueva York. ¿Y tú?
—**Soy de** Puerto Rico, de San Juan.

Spanish has two verbs that mean *to be.* In this section, you will focus on the verb **ser.** One very common use of **ser** is to express one's place of origin. In this case, it is used with the preposition **de,** which means *from* in this particular expression.

Jennifer López **es de** Nueva York.   *Jennifer López is from New York.*

Antonio Banderas **es de** España.   *Antonio Banderas is from Spain.*

All Spanish verbs have endings that express the English equivalents of subject pronouns (**los pronombres personales**) *I, you, he/she, we,* and so on. Spanish also uses formal and informal ways to address people. When talking to someone whom you don't know well, who is older, or who is in a position of respect, use the **usted** form. When talking to a friend, family member, or a person younger than you, use the **tú** form.* Here are the forms for **ser.**

ser *(to be)*			
(yo) **soy**	I am	(nosotros/as) **somos**	we are
(tú) **eres**	you (*informal, singular*) are	(vosotros/as) **sois**	you (*informal, plural, Spain*) are
(usted) **es**	you (*formal, singular*) are	(ustedes) **son**	you (*formal, plural*) are
(él/ella) **es**	he/she is	(ellos/ellas)† **son**	they are

✳ MÁS GRAMÁTICA

¿De dónde eres?	Where are you from?
¿Y él?	And him?
Es de Guatemala **también.**	He's from Guatemala too.

---

*You will learn more about these distinctions later. For now, you should use **tú** with your classmates; your instructor will tell you what to use with him or her.
†The issue of when to use **ellos** and when to use **ellas** is dealt with later in this book.

INPUT

Act. E, Suggestions
Paso 1: Allow 1 minute for students to complete sentences.
Paso 2: Allow 2 more minutes, then ask several students *¿De dónde eres?* using the question with at least 3 students. Also, be sure to ask *Y tus padres, ¿de dónde son? Y ella* (pointing to student next to him), *¿de dónde es?* The idea here is for 2–3 students to express real information and for the rest of the class to hear you ask the questions a number of times.

INPUT/OUTPUT

Act. F, Suggestions
Paso 1: The Spanish alphabet is presented on the inside front cover of the textbook. Pronounce each letter several times as students listen.
Paso 2: Spell each of the following place names, then review before going on to the next one. (Note: Write "*nueva palabra =* new word" on the board, for use with multiple words in a name.) 1. *Rusia* 2. *Grecia* 3. *Italia* 4. *Estados Unidos* 5. *Londres* 6. *Quito* 7. *Sevilla*
Paso 3: Spell each of the following names, then review before going on to the next one. (Note: Write "*con acento =* with an accent mark" on the board, for use with diacritical marks on vowels.) 1. *José* 2. *Roberto* 3. *Patricia* 4. *Enrique* 5. *Isabel* 6. *Verónica* 7. *Cristina*

OUTPUT

Act. G, Suggestion:
Briefly model if you think it's necessary. Then allow about 5 minutes.

Actividad E ¿De dónde eres?

Paso (*Step*) **1** Complete each sentence with correct information for you. Your instructor will then call on some of you to present your information. How many of your classmates are from the same city or state as you? How many of you are from the same city or state as your parents? (If you opted to talk about your children, are you from the same place as they are?)

1. Soy de _____ (*city/state/country*).
2. Mis padres (*My parents*) son de _____.
3. **(Optativo)** Mis hijos (*children*) son de _____.

Paso 2 Now ask two people next to you where they are from. Are they from the same place as you? If you want to ask about a person's parents or children you should ask **¿De dónde son tus padres (hijos)?**

Actividad F ¿Cómo se escribe? (*How is it spelled?*)

Paso 1 You may have to spell your name or the name of the place you are from often in Spanish. Listen as your instructor reviews the Spanish alphabet, presented on the inside front cover of your textbook.

Paso 2 Listen as your instructor spells the names of some countries and cities. Write down what you hear. Do you know what their English equivalents are?

1. ...   2. ...   3. ...   4. ...   5. ...   6. ...   7. ...

Paso 3 Now listen as your instructor spells some names in Spanish. Write down what you hear. Do you know what their English equivalents are?

1. ...   2. ...   3. ...   4. ...   5. ...   6. ...   7. ...

Actividad G ¡A conocernos mejor (*better*)!

Introduce yourself to four more people in the classroom and find out the following information about each one. You may have to spell your name or place of origin (**lugar de origen**). Be prepared to present the information to the rest of the class afterward.

	NOMBRE	APELLIDO	LUGAR DE ORIGEN
1.	_____	_____	_____
2.	_____	_____	_____
3.	_____	_____	_____
4.	_____	_____	_____

Follow-up: Have students present whom they met, but do not call on the same people from previous activities.

SEGUNDA PARTE

Vocabulario

Talking About Majors and Classes

Note: These vocabulary items can be heard in this lesson's Textbook Audio section of the Online Learning Center Website.

Vocabulario, **Suggestion:** Briefly introduce students to the nature of cognates (*los cognados*), telling them that a cognate is a word that sounds like or is spelled similarly in two or more languages. Then read the following out loud to see if students can deduce the English equivalents: *el diccionario, el doctor, la secretaria, la tecnología, la medicina, la instrucción.* Remind students to deduce the meaning of cognates in context. Students must also watch out for false cognates, such as *pariente,* which does not mean *parent,* but rather *relative.*

Las materias

las humanidades y las artes*
>   **el arte**
>   **la filosofía**
>   **los idiomas / las lenguas**
>   (*languages*)
>>   **el alemán** (*German*)
>>   **el español**
>>   **el francés**
>>   **el inglés**
>   **la literatura**
>   **la música**

las ciencias sociales
>   **la antropología**
>   **las ciencias políticas**
>   **la historia**
>   **la psicología**
>   **la sociología**

las ciencias naturales
>   **la astronomía**
>   **la biología**
>   **la física**
>   **la química** (*chemistry*)

School Subjects

el comercio (*business*)
>   **la administración de empresas**
>   (*business administration*)
>   **la contabilidad** (*accounting*)
>   **la economía** (*economics*)

los estudios interdepartamentales
>   **los estudios latinos** (*Latino studies*)
>   **los estudios sobre el género**
>   (*gender studies*)

más (*more*) **materias**
>   **las comunicaciones**
>   **la informática** (*computer science*)
>   **la ingeniería (civil, eléctrica, mecánica)**
>   **las matemáticas**

❋ MÁS VOCABULARIO

¿Cuál es tu campo? ⎱	What's your major?
¿Qué carrera haces? ⎰	
¿Qué estudias?	What are you studying?
Estudio...	I'm studying . . .
Todavía no sé.	I still don't know.
¿Qué clases tienes este semestre/trimestre?	What classes do you have this semester/quarter?
Tengo una clase de...	I have a . . . class.

---

*When used in the singular, **el arte** takes the masculine article **el.** When pluralized, the feminine article **las** is used: **las artes.** You will learn more about gender and articles in **Segunda parte: Gramática.**

INPUT
Act. A, *Paso 1,*
Statements: 1. *la
biología* 2. *la música* 3. *la
literatura* 4. *la economía*
5. *la contabilidad* 6. *las
matemáticas*
Paso 2, **Suggestion:** Here
are some suggested asso-
ciations for the unchosen
objects/people, though
students may have other
associations: 1. *las guerras mundiales = la historia, las ciencias políticas*
2. *Hillary Clinton = las
ciencias políticas, la historia* 3. *los chimpancés = la
antropología, la biología*
4. *el Museo del Prado =
las artes* 5. *Friedrich
Nietzsche = la filosofía*
6. *España = el español, la
historia*

INPUT/OUTPUT
Act. C, Suggestion:
Remind students to
deduce the meaning of
cognates. Read each
statement once. Students
may ask for repetition.
Statements:
1. *Me llamo Juana. Tengo
una clase de lógica, una
de cálculo
avanzado y una
sobre geometría
multidimensional. (las
matemáticas)* 2. *¡Hola!
Soy Paco. Yo tengo una
clase sobre la evolución,
otra sobre la estructura
celular, una de anatomía y
dos laboratorios.
(la biología)*
3. *Mi nombre es
Ramón. Mis clases son: la
novela mexicana contem-
poránea, literatura
española, gramática
avanzada y otra sobre
Cervantes. (el español)*
4. (Note: This one is chal-
lenging!) *¡Hola! Me llamo
Lucía. Tengo unas clases
muy interesantes. Tengo
una sobre la memoria,
otra sobre la investigación,
otra sobre la cognición y
un laboratorio. (la
psicología)*

Actividad A Asociaciones

Paso 1 Indicate the item you associate with the subject matter your instructor mentions.

1. **a.** el microscopio   **b.** las guerras mundiales (*world wars*)
2. **a.** Mozart   **b.** Hillary Clinton
3. **a.** los chimpancés   **b.** las novelas
4. **a.** la Bolsa (*stock market*)   **b.** el Museo (*Museum*) del Prado
5. **a.** Friedrich Nietzsche   **b.** la calculadora
6. **a.** España   **b.** la geometría

Paso 2 Go back to the items you didn't choose. Can you give a subject matter association for each one?

Actividad B Uno estudia... (*One studies . . .*)

INPUT
Actividad B

Using the following columns, make logical sentences according to the model.

MODELO: En economía uno estudia la Bolsa.

En...	...uno estudia...
1. __d__ historia	**a.** las reacciones nucleares.
2. __a__ física	**b.** la lógica.
3. __f__ arte	**c.** el comportamiento (*behavior*) de las personas.
4. __e__ química	**d.** las causas y consecuencias de las guerras.
5. __b__ filosofía	**e.** las propiedades de los elementos.
6. __c__ psicología	**f.** el uso (*use*) del color y de la luz (*light*).

Actividad C ¿Cuál es su (*his/her*) campo?

Listen as your instructor reads statements from several people. Can you guess what that person's major is? Note: The word **sobre** means *about* (**una clase sobre Shakespeare**).

OUTPUT
Act. D, Suggested follow-up: Have several people report on what they learned.

1. ...   2. ...   3. ...   4. ...

Write the following models on the board while students are interviewing each other. Students
haven't yet learned the third-person plural form *tienen*. Write "*tienen* = (they) have" on the board.

Actividad D ¿Qué clases tienes?

*Modelo: Claudia, Robert y Jennifer tienen
clases de historia.*

Following the model, interview three people to find out what classes they are taking and what they think of them. Be sure to jot down the information.

MODELO: E1*: ¿Qué clases tienes este semestre/trimestre?
     E2*: Tengo una clase de biología, una de historia y una de
        español.
     E1: ¡Gracias! (*Thanks!*)
     E2: De nada. (*You're welcome.*)

*Sally, Carlos y Michael no tienen
clases en común.*

Additional suggested follow-up: Tabulate the
common classes on the board. Then say once
or twice: *Muchos tienen una clase de* _____. *¿Por qué? ¿Es un requisito o es una clase
electiva?* (If
someone says *clase electiva* you can follow up with *¿Hay otras clases electivas populares?*) Students
should be able to deduce meaning. (Note: At this stage, ask only yes/no and either/or questions.)

*E1 and E2 will be used throughout *Sol y viento* to represent **Estudiante 1 (uno)** and **Estudiante 2 (dos),** respectively.

Gramática

Naming Things | **El cálculo y las matemáticas**

En el escritorio de la profesora hay (*there are*) **un libro, un bolígrafo** y **una mochila.**

Unlike English, Spanish has grammatical gender. Every Spanish noun (a person, a place, a thing, or an idea) is classified as being either masculine or feminine. The two categories distinguish animate beings on the basis of biological gender: **el hombre** (*the man*), **la mujer** (*the woman*). However, their application to inanimate things is arbitrary; chairs, tables, and books, for example, have no biological gender, but they have grammatical gender in Spanish.

Gender is expressed not only in the noun but in the article that accompanies it. Spanish also expresses number (singular versus plural) with its articles.

Suggestion: You may wish to explain what an article is. Suggested explanation: There are two types of articles: definite and indefinite. In English, there is only one definite article: *the.* There are two indefinite articles in English: *a, an.* The chart shows the Spanish definite and indefinite articles as well as the noun endings that typically indicate gender and number.

ARTICLES, GENDER, AND NUMBER		
	MASCULINO	FEMENINO
Singular	**un** libro (*a book*)	**una** pizarra (*a chalkboard*)
	el libro (*the book*)	**la** pizarra (*the chalkboard*)
	un profesor (*a male professor*)	**una** profesora (*a female professor*)
	el profesor (*the male professor*)	**la** profesora (*the female professor*)
Plural	**unos** libros (*some books*)	**unas** pizarras (*some chalkboards*)
	los libros (*the books*)	**las** pizarras (*the chalkboards*)
	unos profesores (*some professors*)	**unas** profesoras (*some professors [female only]*)
	los profesores (*the professors*)	**las** profesoras (*the professors [female only]*)

INPUT

Act. E, Suggestion: Use objects and people in the classroom in either/or questions to get students used to hearing and responding with correct indefinite articles. For example, point to a book and say: *¿Es un libro o es una mochila?* Point to a male student and say: *¿Es una estudiante o un estudiante?* and so on. Do approximately 7–8 such either/or questions.

INPUT

Act. F, Suggestion: Allow about 1 minute for students to complete their sentences. Then call on students to provide completed statements, e.g.: *Número uno. En una mochila hay unos libros.*

¡Exprésate!

To express *there is* or *there are* and to ask *Is there . . . ?* or *Are there . . . ?*, Spanish uses the verb **hay** (pronounced similar to English *eye*): **Hay unas mochilas en la clase. ¿Hay profesores excelentes en la universidad?**

Act. F, Suggested follow-up: Select 2 volunteers who will reveal the contents of their backpacks. Ask each student questions such as: *¿Hay unos libros en tu mochila?* The student may respond *Sí* and then show the item(s), or *No.* **Alternative:** If you have a backpack, have students ask you the questions about what's in it, using the items from *Actividad F.*

OUTPUT

Act. G, Suggestion: Allow about 4 minutes. After 2 minutes, have students switch roles.

In general, nouns ending in **-o** or in most consonants are masculine. Most nouns ending in **-a** are feminine. However, biological gender takes precedence over any ending as in **una mujer** (*a woman*) versus **un señor** (*a man*), which both end in a consonant. You will continue to learn the gender of nouns throughout your study of Spanish. For now, here is a list to help you get started.

un chico	a boy	**un bolígrafo**	a pen
una chica	a girl	**un escritorio**	a desk
un estudiante	a (male) student	**un lápiz**	a pencil
una estudiante	a (female) student	**un libro**	a book
un hombre	a man	**una mochila**	a backpack
una mujer	a woman	**una silla**	a chair

Actividad E   ¿Qué es? (*What is it?*)

Listen to and answer the questions your instructor asks. Note that the verb **ser** is used to identify people, objects, and things as in *It's a pencil* = **Es un lápiz.**

MODELO: PROFESOR(A): ¿Es una mochila o (*or*) un lápiz?
                    TÚ: Es un lápiz.

Actividad F   ¿Qué hay en una mochila típica?

Complete each statement to talk about what you might find in a typical student's backpack. Note: Your completed sentences must be both grammatical and logical, so pay attention to gender and number as well as meaning!

En una mochila hay...

1. unos...
   a. estudiantes   b. sillas   (c.) libros   d. escritorios
2. unas...
   (a.) calculadoras   b. sillas   c. lápices*   d. hombres
3. un...
   a. cartera (*wallet*)   b. cajita (*box*) de Tic-Tacs   (c.) teléfono celular   d. profesor
4. una...
   a. mujer   (b.) revista (*magazine*)   c. cuaderno (*notebook*)   d. disco compacto

Actividad G   En la sala de clase (*classroom*)

With a partner, take turns pointing to two items in the room that are far away. The other should see if he or she can guess which items the first student is referring to. How many did you both guess correctly? (Note: **sí** = *yes*.)

MODELO: E1: (points to two items)
                E2: ¿Son una mochila y una estudiante?
                E1: No, son una silla y una estudiante.

---

*Nouns ending in **-z** must change this letter to a **c** when adding the plural suffix **-es.**

Vocabulario

Talking About
Things in the
Classroom and on
Campus

En la sala de clase

Classroom Objects

Note: These
vocabulary items
can be heard in
this lesson's Text-
book Audio section of the
Online Learning Center
Website.

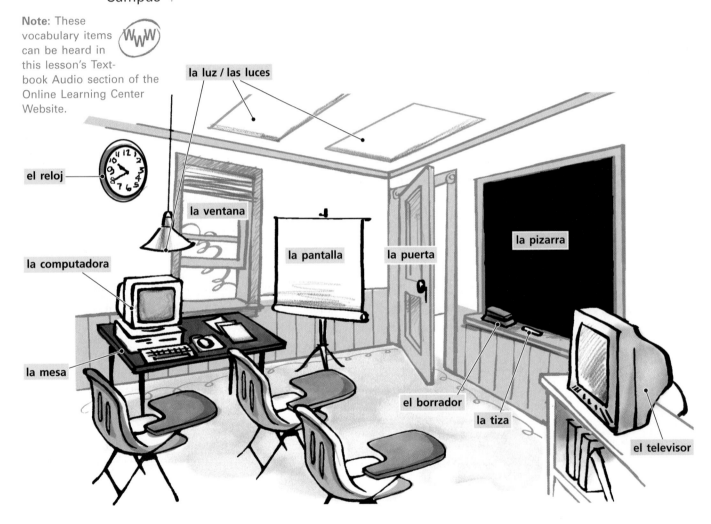

la luz / las luces

el reloj

la ventana

la computadora

la pantalla

la puerta

la pizarra

la mesa

el borrador

la tiza

el televisor

En la universidad

el auditorio	auditorium
la biblioteca	library
la cafetería	cafeteria
el edificio	building
la facultad	department
la librería	bookstore
la oficina	office
la residencia estudiantil	dormitory
el teléfono público	public phone

Actividad A ¿Sí o no?

Listen as your instructor names a classroom object. Does the object named fit the description given?

	SÍ	NO
1. Indica la hora. (*It tells the time.*)	☑	☐
2. Limpia (*It cleans*) la pizarra.	☐	☑
3. Deja entrar (*It lets in*) mucha (*lots of*) luz.	☑	☐
4. Es blanca (*white*).	☑	☐
5. Hay dos (*two*) en la sala de clase.	☐	☐

Actividad B Asociaciones

Match each item in the first column with an appropriate action from the second.

1. __e__ la librería
2. __a__ la cafetería
3. __b__ la residencia estudiantil
4. __f__ la biblioteca
5. __c__ la oficina del profesor (de la profesora)
6. __d__ el teléfono público

a. comer (*to eat*)
b. vivir (*to live*)
c. hacer una cita (*to make an appointment*)
d. hacer una llamada (*to make a call*)
e. comprar (*to buy*) libros
f. sacar (*to check out*) libros

Actividad C La sala de clase y la universidad

Paso 1 Answer each question about what is in your Spanish classroom.

MODELO: ¿Hay una computadora? →
Sí, hay una computadora Mac. (No, no hay computadora.)

1. ¿Hay un reloj? ¿Es digital?
2. ¿Hay un televisor? ¿Con (*With*) vídeo? ¿con DVD?
3. ¿Hay una pantalla? ¿Hay un proyector (*projector*)?
4. ¿Hay una pizarra con tiza y borrador?
5. ¿Hay muchas (*many*) ventanas?

Paso 2 What do you know about your university or college? With a partner, read each question, then answer as best as you can. Prepare a brief statement to present your answers to your classmates. If you don't know the answer to a question, respond with **No sé** (*I don't know*).

MODELO: ¿Hay una Facultad de Español? →
No, no hay una Facultad de Español, pero (*but*) sí hay una Facultad de Lenguas Extranjeras.

1. ¿Cómo se llama la biblioteca?
2. ¿Cómo se llama el edificio donde tienes la clase de español?
3. ¿Hay una Facultad de Lenguas Extranjeras?
4. ¿Hay una oficina de servicios estudiantiles?
5. ¿Hay teléfonos públicos en todos (*all*) los edificios? Da (*Give*) un ejemplo.
6. ¿Hay residencias estudiantiles? ¿Cómo se llaman?

Gramática

Expressing Location

¡Están aquí!

Introduction to estar

—¿Dónde **está** la biblioteca?
—**Está** enfrente de (*in front of*) este edificio.

De *Sol y viento*, Purpose: This recurring feature focuses on language from the film that can be used to illustrate a grammatical concept in context. In most cases, a small portion of the script is reproduced in the text, sometimes as a cloze activity. In subsequent chapters, the first grammar activity following this feature will focus on the characters or situations from the film as related to the current grammar topic.

Note: You can access this film clip from a special menu section on Disc 5 of the Instructional Version on DVD.

Suggestion: Review the photo and script with the class, asking students to explain briefly (in English) what someone might mean when they say *Nuestros espíritus están aquí.* Who are these spirits? Then read each of the 3 statements out loud, asking after each how many students agree with the statement.

You have already learned the verb **ser** and some of its uses. Here is a review of the uses you have studied so far.

1. to indicate where someone or something is from: **Soy de Chicago.** **¿De dónde *eres* tú?**

2. to say what someone or something is: **Soy estudiante.** *Es* **una mochila.**

Estar is another Spanish verb that is translated as *to be.* However, its uses are very different from those of **ser.** One important use of **estar** is to express location.

El libro **está** en el escritorio.   *The book is on the desk.*

Juan y Diego no **están** en clase.   *Juan and Diego are not in class.*

Here are the forms of **estar.**

estar (*to be*)			
yo	**estoy**	nosotros/as	**estamos**
tú	**estás**	vosotros/as	**estáis**
usted	**está**	ustedes	**están**
él/ella	**está**	ellos/ellas	**están**

🎞 DE SOL Y VIENTO

In the prologue of *Sol y viento* that you will soon watch, a character talks about the presence of certain beings. Here are some lines of dialogue from the prologue. Notice the use of **estar** to express location.

MACHI
¡Nuestros[a] espíritus **están** aquí! **Están** con nosotros —¡siempre[b]!

What do you think is always with us? Do you agree with the following three statements?

1. Nuestros antepasados (*ancestors*) siempre están con nosotros.

2. El pasado (*The past*) siempre está con nosotros.

3. Nuestros hechos (*deeds*) siempre están con nosotros.

[a]*Our*   [b]*always*

Actividad D ¿Dónde está?

Listen to your instructor's questions. Answer them with one of the following phrases:

- en el escritorio / en la mesa
- en la silla
- en el suelo (*floor*)

1. ... **2.** ... **3.** ... **4.** ... **5.** ... **6.** ... **7.** ... **8.** ...

Actividad E ¿Quiénes (*Who*) están en el grupo?

Your instructor will ask several students to form a group in front of the class. Can you say who is in the group?

◉ Enfoque lingüístico

¿Dos verbos que significan lo mismo?[a]

You may wonder why Spanish needs two verbs that mean *to be* whereas English has only one. Simply put, languages vary widely. In this case, Spanish seems more complex to an English speaker. In Chinese, however, there is no verb *to be;* you would simply say something like "John here." In Arabic, the verb *to be* is used only in certain contexts and not in all tenses (e.g., present, past, future). As you continue your studies, you will see that Spanish expresses some subtle and somewhat abstract notions through the use of the two verbs that mean *to be.* Here's a sneak preview. In English, if one says "The apple is green," this could mean it isn't ripe or it could refer to its color (such as a Pippin or Granny Smith). In Spanish, the verb indicates which meaning is intended: **La manzana está verde** can only mean the apple isn't ripe, and **la manzana es verde** can only mean the apple is a green one, like a Pippin.

¿Dos... *Two verbs that mean the same thing?*

▲ ¿Dónde está esta (*this*) persona? ¿Está en una oficina o en una sala de clase?

SOL Y VIENTO

Antes de ver, Suggestion: Before beginning this section, you may want to review (with your students) the *Intro-ducción* at the beginning of the Instructional Version of the film. It contains much useful information about how to use the textbook and film together, including a visual demonstration of the "Arc of Activities," a description

Antes de ver[a] el episodio

of which can also be found in the Instructor's Manual. [a]*Antes... Before watching*

You are about to watch the prologue of *Sol y viento.* In this brief episode, you will meet several principal characters, and a major plot line will be established. Before watching the episode, complete the activities in **Antes de ver el episodio.**

Actividad A   Dos personajes (*characters*)

These are the two main characters you will meet in this episode. Try to determine which of the sentences for each character strikes you as true or likely based on a first impression from the photos.

▲ María Sánchez

1. Es profesora de economía.
2. Es española.
3. Es inteligente y dedicada.

▲ Jaime (James) Talavera

1. Es hombre de negocios (*businessman*).
2. Es español.
3. Es inteligente y sensible (*sensitive*).

Actividad B   Un diálogo

Act. B, Suggestion: Don't reveal answer to students, as they will verify it in *Después de ver el episodio.*

In one scene, María speaks to her assistant. Read the dialogue and then select the word that you think best completes it.

MARÍA: ¿Qué quieres,[b] Diego?

DIEGO: Sólo quiero decirle[c] que _____ es _____ muy tarde.[d] Ya terminamos,[e] profesora.

[b]*¿Qué... What do you want*   [c]*Sólo... I just want to tell you*   [d]*late*   [e]*Ya... We're finished*

1. es   2. tienes   3. hay

Actividad C   El episodio

Act. C, Suggestion: Tell students they may want to watch the entire episode once to get a feel for it, then go back and watch it again or any parts in particular that they might like to review.

Now watch the episode. Don't worry if you don't understand everything in Spanish; just try to get the gist of what is going on.

Después de ver[a] el episodio

Después... *After watching*

Actividad A   ¿Qué recuerdas? (*What do you remember?*)

Answer each item based on what you remember from watching the **Prólogo.**

1. ¿Cómo se llama el hombre que necesita viajar (*needs to travel*) a Chile?
   a. Andy   **b.** John   **c.** James

2. El hombre está muy contento (*The man is very happy*) con la idea de viajar (*traveling*) a Chile. ¿Cierto (*True*) o falso?
   a. cierto   **b.** falso

3. ¿Cuál es la relación entre (*between*) María y Diego?
   a. Ella es estudiante y él es profesor.
   b. Él es estudiante y ella es profesora.

4. Probablemente, la especialización (*specialty*) de María es...
   a. contabilidad.   **b.** ingeniería.   **c.** antropología.

Actividad B   Verificación

Go back to **Actividad B** of **Antes de ver el episodio** and verify your answer. Remember: If it helps, watch the corresponding section of the episode again.

Actividad C   Pistas (*Clues*) lingüísticas

One skill you will want to develop as you study Spanish is guessing the meaning of language from context. Here are the first lines of the scene between María and Diego:

DIEGO: Es lindo, ¿no?
MARÍA: Sí. Es muy lindo.

Go back and watch this scene again without looking up any words. What are they talking about and what do you think **lindo** means?

Actividad D   Descripciones

Make statements about the following characters using the verb **ser** and the adjectives listed. For adjectives ending in **-o/a,** use **-o** with males and **-a** with females.

1. bilingüe
2. chileno/a (*Chilean*)
3. sabio/a (*wise*)
4. persistente
5. guapo/a (*good-looking*)

You have been exposed to a number of question words. You can now understand them in context and use them in some expressions you have learned.

¿cómo?	how?
¿cuál?	which?/ what?
¿dónde?	where?
¿por qué?	why?
¿qué?	what?
¿quién(es)?	who?

Notice how many of these are used in **Actividad A.**

Detrás de la cámara, **Purpose:** This recurring feature gives additional information not presented in the film about the *Sol y viento* characters. It also poses questions for students to think about in greater depth regarding the characters: their personalities, their motivations, their pasts. Some sections will also give students cues on what to watch for in upcoming episodes.

Act. C, Suggestion: Ask students the meaning of *¿no?* at the end of Diego's sentence. Did they figure out it is similar to English "isn't it?" in this context? Suggest that, as students watch future episodes, they write down unfamiliar expressions and try to guess their meaning in context.

Act. D, Suggestion: Model examples for students, using cognates: *Jaime es inteligente. Jaime es norteamericano. María no es norteamericana.*

Detrás de[b] la cámara

One of the main characters is addressed in the **Prólogo** as "James." However, his given name (and the name with which he grew up) is "Jaime." Why do you suppose he goes by James, the English equivalent of Jaime? What might this tell you about his character?

Keep this in mind as you watch future episodes of *Sol y viento*. In what other ways may Jaime/James have left his past behind?

[b] Detrás... *Behind*

PRÓLOGO * LOS ESPÍRITUS

▲ María

▲ Jaime (James)

▲ Andy   ▲ la machi

15

RESUMEN DE VOCABULARIO

Las presentaciones

¿Cómo te llamas?	What's your name?
Me llamo…	My name is . . .
Mi nombre es…	
Soy…	I'm . . .
¿Cuál es tu apellido?	What's your last name?
Mi apellido es…	My last name is . . .
¿Cómo se llama (él/ella)?	What's his/her name?
¿Cuál es su apellido?	What's his/her last name?
¡Hola!	Hello! Hi!
Mucho gusto.	Pleased to meet you.
Igualmente.	Likewise.
Buenos días.	Good morning.
Buenas tardes.	Good afternoon/evening.
Buenas noches.	Good night.
¿De dónde eres?	Where are you from?
Soy de…	I'm from . . .

Las materias

la administración de empresas	business administration
la antropología	anthropology
el arte (*pl.* **las artes**)	art
la astronomía	astronomy
la biología	biology
las ciencias naturales	natural sciences
las ciencias políticas	political science
las ciencias sociales	social sciences
el comercio	business
las comunicaciones	communications
la contabilidad	accounting
la economía	economics
los estudios interdepartamentales	interdisciplinary studies
los estudios latinos	Latino studies
los estudios sobre el género	gender studies
la filosofía	philosophy
la física	physics
la historia	history
las humanidades	humanities

los idiomas / las lenguas	languages
el alemán	German
el español	Spanish
el francés	French
el inglés	English
la informática	computer science
la ingeniería (civil, eléctrica, mecánica)	(civil, electrical, mechanical) engineering
la literatura	literature
las matemáticas	mathematics
la música	music
la psicología	psychology
la química	chemistry
la sociología	sociology
¿Cuál es tu campo?	What's your major?
¿Qué carrera haces?	
¿Qué estudias?	What are you studying?
Estudio…	I'm studying . . .
Todavía no sé.	I still don't know.
¿Qué clases tienes este semestre/trimestre?	What classes do you have this semester/quarter?
Tengo una clase de…	I have a(n) . . . class.

Verbos

estar (*irreg.*)	to be
hay	there is / there are
ser (*irreg.*)	to be

En la sala de clase

el bolígrafo	pen
el borrador	eraser
el/la chico/a	boy/girl
la computadora	computer
el escritorio	desk
el/la estudiante	student
el hombre	man
el lápiz (*pl.* **lápices**)	pencil
el libro	book
la luz (*pl.* **luces**)	light
la mesa	table
la mochila	backpack

la mujer	woman
la pantalla	screen
la pizarra	chalkboard
el/la profesor(a)	professor
la puerta	door
el reloj	clock; watch
la silla	chair
el televisor	TV (set)
la tiza	chalk
la ventana	window

En la universidad

el auditorio	auditorium
la biblioteca	library
la cafetería	cafeteria
el edificio	building
la facultad	department
la librería	bookstore
la oficina	office
la residencia estudiantil	dormitory
el teléfono público	public telephone

Los pronombres personales

yo	I
tú	you (*inf., sing.*)
usted	you (*form., sing.*)

él	he
ella	she
nosotros/as	we
vosotros/as	you (*inf., pl., Sp.*)
ustedes	you (*form., pl.*)
ellos	they (*m. pl.*)
ellas	they (*f. pl.*)

Palabras y expresiones adicionales

con	with
de	of; from
más	more
mucho/a/os/as	much, a lot; many
No sé.	I don't know.
o	or
pero	but
sí	yes
también	too, also
y	and

EPISODIO 1

LECCIÓN 1A
LECCIÓN 1B

La llegadaᵃ

Notes
• Each episode opener contains material similar to that found on this page. The intent is to let students read the excerpt from the film and to ponder the questions provided. For subsequent episode openers, you may wish to conduct a whole-class question and answer activity. Or you may wish to have them get in groups of 3 to discuss responses, then have them present to the class.
• For this first episode, students do not have the language skills to work in small groups and discuss the questions in Spanish. You may wish to have them read the excerpt and then conduct a whole-class discussion as they answer in English. You can recast their responses in Spanish to provide more input.

En este episodio...

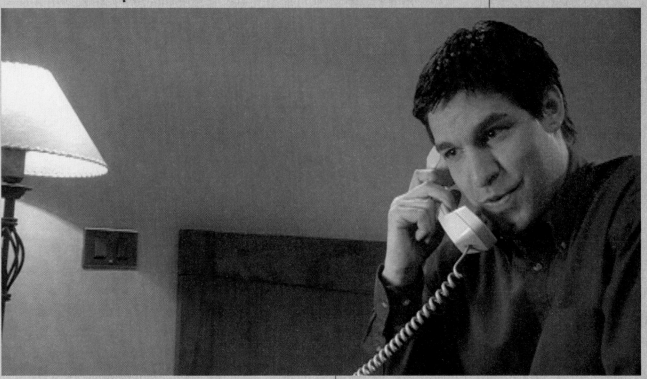

JAIME

¿Aló, la viña «Sol y viento»?... Don Carlos Sánchez... Ah, con él. Bien. Soy Jaime Talavera, de los Estados Unidos. Compañía Bartel Aquapower... Sí, claro que hablo español. Ya estoy aquí... No, en Santiago. Mañana voy a verlo, como a mediodía.

¿Qué crees tú? (*What do you think?*)

1. ¿Quién (*Who*) es el Sr. Sánchez?
2. ¿Dónde está Jaime en este (*this*) momento?
3. ¿Qué necesita hacer Jaime (*does Jaime need to do*) en la viña?

Hello? Sol y viento Winery? . . . Mr. Carlos Sánchez . . . Oh, it's you. Great. This is Jaime Talavera, from the United States. From Bartel Aquapower . . . Yes, of course I speak Spanish. I'm here now . . . No, in Santiago. I'm coming to see you tomorrow, around noon.

ᵃLa... *The Arrival*

Sobre los horarios[a]

OBJETIVOS

IN THIS LESSON, YOU WILL LEARN:

- the numbers 0–30
- about regular -ar verbs to talk about daily schedules
- the days of the week
- how to express the need or desire to do something
- how to talk about time
- about possessive adjectives

In addition, you will prepare for and watch **Episodio 1** of the film *Sol y viento*.

El señor tiene una cita (*has an appointment*). ¿Llega tarde? (*Is he arriving late?*)

[a]Sobre... *About schedules*

The following media resources are available for this lesson of *Sol y viento*:

Episodio 1 of *Sol y viento*

Online *Manual de actividades*

Online Learning Center Website

Vocabulario

Talking About Your Course Load

Llevo quince créditos.

Numbers 0–30

Note: These vocabulary items can be heard in this lesson's Textbook Audio section of the Online Learning Center Website.

Los números 0–30

0 cero		
1 uno	11 once	21 veintiuno
2 dos	12 doce	22 veintidós
3 tres	13 trece	23 veintitrés
4 cuatro	14 catorce	24 veinticuatro
5 cinco	15 quince	25 veinticinco
6 seis	16 dieciséis	26 veintiséis
7 siete	17 diecisiete	27 veintisiete
8 ocho	18 dieciocho	28 veintiocho
9 nueve	19 diecinueve	29 veintinueve
10 diez	20 veinte	30 treinta

In Spanish, most numbers greater than fifteen are actually combinations of two numbers, but they are generally spelled as one. For example, **dieciséis** is actually **diez y seis, veintidós** is actually **veinte y dos,** and so forth.

✳ MÁS VOCABULARIO

¿Cuántos créditos llevas?	How many credits are you taking?
En total tengo veintiún* créditos.	I have twenty-one credits altogether.
Este semestre/trimestre llevo dieciocho créditos.	This semester/quarter I'm taking eighteen credits.
Llevo doce créditos de ciencias.	I am taking twelve credits of science.
¿Tienes/Llevas muchas clases?	Do you have / Are you taking a lot of classes?
¿Tienes/Llevas muchos créditos?	Do you have / Are you taking a lot of credits?
Esteban lleva quince créditos.	Esteban is taking fifteen credits.

Vistazo cultural

Vistazo cultural, **Suggestion:** Have students read quickly. Then tell them you will read several statements. After each, they should indicate whether the statement refers to the Spanish-speaking system or the U.S. system. (Say: *Se refiere al sistema hispano o al sistema norteamericano?* 1. *El estudiante recibe la nota aprobado.* (*sistema hispano*) 2. *El estudiante lleva 18 créditos.* (*sistema norteamericano*) 3. *El estudiante está en su segundo año.* (*sistema hispano*)

Optional: Bring to class the academic program from a Hispanic university that you've found online or assign students to find one and bring to class. Review the curriculum for a student in that program. Find out which courses resemble those that students in your university take and which do not.

Los cursos y los créditos

Courses and grading in Spanish-speaking countries not only vary from systems used in this country, but they often vary from each other as well. Transcripts don't normally list credit hours, only classes. In Spain, grades are assigned using the terms **sobresaliente** (*excellent*), **notable** (*good*), **aprobado** (*passed*), and **suspendido** (*failed*). Based on this system, then, a Spanish student would never have a "G.P.A." as an American student would.

In universities throughout Latin America a numerical system is used, generally 0–10, with 10 being the highest possible grade. Unless you're in Puerto Rico, which uses a U.S.-based system, it doesn't make sense to ask someone from a Spanish-speaking country: **¿Cuántos créditos llevas?** Instead, you would simply ask students what year of university studies they are in and which classes they have, as in the following scene.

CLAUDIA: Manuel, ¿en qué año estás?[a]
MANUEL: Estoy en mi segundo.[b] ¿Y tú?
CLAUDIA: Igual. También estoy en mi segundo.
MANUEL: ¡Ah! Entonces tomas[c] Filosofía II, como[d] yo.
CLAUDIA: Exactamente.

[a]¿en... *what year are you in?*   [b]*second*   [c]*you're taking*   [d]*like*

***Veintiuno** shortens to **veintiún** when followed by a masculine noun; for example, **Tengo veintiún créditos.**

INPUT
Act. A,
Suggestion: Read each number once followed by the responses: *Número uno. Quince. ¿Qué número sigue: seis, dieciséis o veintiséis?* (b. 16) *Correcto. Vamos al número dos,* and so forth.
Statements: 1. 15 2. 24 3. 12 4. 18 5. 7 6. 3
Suggested follow-up: Say any number from 0–29 to see if students can come up with the number that follows.

INPUT/OUTPUT
Act. B, *Paso 1,* **Note:** Numbers will need to be read individually (i.e., *seis, cuatro, dos...*) since students don't know numbers beyond 30.
Suggestion: Have a different student write each phone number on the board.
Statements:
1. 642-9131
2. 334-2150
3. 996-5218
4. 769-1516
Paso 2, **Suggestion:** Students will learn numbers 31–99 in *Lección 2A* and 100–1000 in *Lección 2B.* But have them scan the ad to see if they can recognize any cognates (e.g., *¡Suscríbete!, recibe, electrónica, suscripción, precio*).

Actividad A   ¿Qué número sigue (*follows*)?

Listen as your instructor says a number. Select the number that follows it.

1. **a.** 6   **(b.)** 16   **c.** 26
2. **a.** 15   **(b.)** 25   **c.** 5
3. **(a.)** 13   **b.** 3   **c.** 23
4. **a.** 7   **b.** 20   **(c.)** 19
5. **(a.)** 8   **b.** 11   **c.** 26
6. **a.** 2   **(b.)** 4   **c.** 14

Actividad B   Números de teléfono

Paso 1   Listen as your instructor reads some telephone numbers, then write down what you hear. Can you get them all correct?

1. _____
2. _____
3. _____
4. _____

Paso 2   Look at the following ad for the Spanish magazine *Quo.* Can you say the phone number out loud? What do you think the number in parentheses is?

Paso 3   In Spanish, ask for the phone numbers of two classmates and write them down. Use the phrase **¿Cuál es tu número de teléfono?** (*What is your phone number?*) Keep the numbers in case one day you are absent and need to find out something about class.

¡Suscríbete!
(55)9177 4342

SUSCRÍBETE y recibe 12 números de **Quo** por **$179** y te regalamos **$100** en una tarjeta electrónica para comprar lo que quieras en **Mixup**

Con tu suscripción sólo pagas **$14.90** por ejemplar y te ahorras **$121.00** sobre el precio de portada

ahorra 40%

INPUT
Act. C, Suggestion:
Read once and tell
students to pay careful
attention. *Marcos es un
estudiante de química y
lleva muchos créditos este
semestre. Tiene dos clases
de química. También tiene
una clase de historia y otra
de español. Finalmente,
lleva dos sesiones de
laboratorio. En total lleva
18 créditos.*
Answers: 1. *Marcos
lleva dieciocho
créditos en total.*
2. *Tiene cuatro
clases y dos sesiones de
laboratorio.* 3. *Cada clase
lleva cuatro créditos (cuatro
clases × cuatro
créditos = 16 créditos),
más dos sesiones de
laboratorio de un crédito
cada una = 18 créditos.*

OUTPUT
Act. D,
Suggestion: Allow about 4
minutes. If you are short on
time, limit to 2 interviews.
Then call on several
students to report. Model
for them: *Esta persona es
Christa. Lleva muchos créditos: 18 en total.* You can follow up by asking questions
such as *¿Cuántas clases
lleva?* See if you can find
out the average number of
credits and if anyone is taking more than the average.

Enfoque cultural, **Note:** This
recurring feature of the text
uses a scene or quote from
the current episode of the
film to focus on a cultural
aspect of the Spanish-
speaking world. Annotations
in this Instructor's Edition
will contain follow-up activities that students can do in
class or out of class as
research assignments.
Point out: Explain to
students that most large
cities also have some kind
of subway or other train
service to provide
transportation options.

Actividad C   Una deducción

Listen as your instructor describes Marcos' schedule and total credits. Then answer these questions.

1. ¿Cuántos créditos lleva Marcos en total?
2. ¿Cuántas clases tiene (*does he have*)? ¿Y cuántas sesiones de laboratorio tiene?
3. Sabiendo (*Knowing*) la respuesta al número 1, ¿cuántos créditos lleva cada (*each*) clase, probablemente? ¿y las sesiones de laboratorio?

Actividad D   ¿Cuántos créditos?

Find three people to interview. Using the **Más vocabulario** from p. 21, find out what their class loads and credits are this term. Jot the information down because your instructor may call on you to present it to the rest of the class.

SOL Y VIENTO: Enfoque cultural

In **Episodio 1** of *Sol y viento*, you will see Jaime's arrival at the airport in Santiago, where he is greeted by an enthusiastic driver, Mario. Santiago, like any major city in the Spanish-speaking world, offers both private drivers like Mario as well as regular public taxis. However, taxi systems and taxi drivers vary from city to city. In Santiago, they are safe, clean, and convenient, and as in any great city there are many of them. As in this country, in Chile the fare is calculated by taximeters, and there is no need to negotiate a price (unless you use a private taxi). In Mexico City, in contrast, you generally have to ask how much it will cost to get to your destination before getting in the taxi. If not, you may wind up paying much more than you should, as those taxis may not use meters. Nonetheless, in most Spanish-speaking countries outside of Spain, taxi rides tend to be less expensive than they are in this country.

▲ Hay muchos taxis en México, D.F.*

Suggested follow-up: Provide students with a photocopy or show an overhead of the subway system of a large city in a Spanish-speaking country and ask which line(s) to take to get from one point to another.

*__D.F.__ = **Distrito Federal,** much like Washington, D.C. (District of Columbia)

Gramática

Talking About Activities | **Estudio y trabajo.**

Regular -ar Verbs

REGULAR *-ar* VERBS			
llevar (*to take; to carry*)			
yo	llev**o**	nosotros/as	llev**amos**
tú	llev**as**	vosotros/as	llev**áis**
usted (Ud.)*	llev**a**	ustedes (Uds.)*	llev**an**
él/ella	llev**a**	ellos/ellas	llev**an**

You will remember from the **Lección preliminar** that verb forms in Spanish can vary depending on the subject. The chart summarizes the forms that belong to what are called regular **-ar** verbs.

Present-tense verbs in Spanish can have three different meanings in English. For example, **llevo** can mean *I take* (simple present tense), *I am taking* (present progressive, indicating an action in progress), or *I will take* (near future). You will learn more about tense as you continue your studies in Spanish.

Since the verb ending expresses the subject, the subject pronoun is generally not necessary in Spanish except for emphasis or clarity. For example, it is sufficient to say **Llevo muchos créditos** without using **yo,** unless you are contrasting what you are saying with what someone else is saying, or you are emphasizing something. Note the following exchange in which Manolo contrasts what he says with what Marcos says.

> MARCOS: Llevo dieciséis créditos.
> MANOLO: Pues (*Well*), *yo* llevo veinte.
> MARCOS: ¡Uf! Es mucho.

An important thing to note is that the use of **nosotros, vosotros, ellos,** and **ellas** as pronouns depends on who is included in that particular group. **Nosotros, vosotros,** and **ellos** are used if the group is all male or of mixed sexes. **Nosotras, vosotras,** and **ellas** are used only if the group contains only females.

---

*The subject pronouns **usted** and **ustedes** are often abbreviated as **Ud.** and **Uds.,** respectively.

MÁS VOCABULARIO

Here are some common regular **-ar** verbs that you will use in this lesson.

charlar	to chat
estudiar	to study
hablar	to speak; to talk
llamar (por teléfono)	to call (on the phone)
llevar	to take; to carry
navegar la red	to surf the Web
pagar (el alquiler)	to pay (the rent)
practicar (un deporte)	to practice (a sport)
preparar	to prepare
regresar (a casa)	to return (home)
tocar (la guitarra, el piano)	to play (the guitar, the piano)
tomar* (café, cerveza)	to drink (coffee, beer)
tomar* (una clase)	to take (a class)
trabajar	to work
visitar (a† la familia)	to visit (one's family)

De *Sol y viento,* Note: You can access this film clip from a special menu section on Disc 5 of the Instructional Version on DVD.

DE SOL Y VIENTO

In **Episodio 1** of *Sol y viento* you will watch a scene in which Mario, a taxi driver eagerly waiting for a fare, rushes up to Jaime at the airport. Part of their exchange appears here.

MARIO
¡Para servirlo,ᵃ señor! ¡El mejor choferᵇ de Chile! ¿—————, señor?

JAIME
Al Hotel Bonaparte. ¿A cuánto sale?ᶜ

MARIO
Eh, um, unos diez milᵈ pesos, más o menos.ᵉ

Selecting from the list below, what do you think Mario asks in the phrase that's missing from the dialogue?

1. ¿De dónde es Ud.?
2. ¿Adónde lo llevo? (*Where shall I take you?*)
3. ¿Necesita ayuda con las maletas? (*Do you need help with your luggage?*)

ᵃ¡Para... *At your service* ᵇ¡El... *The best driver* ᶜ¿A... *How much is it?* ᵈ*thousand*
ᵉmás... *more or less*

---

*You will learn that, like English, Spanish also contains words that have more than one meaning. Think of the word *run* in English. How many different meanings can you come up with? (Hint: run a mile, a run in your hose, run for office . . .)

†The **a** used in this phrase is called the **a personal** and has no direct equivalent in English. You will learn more about the **a personal** in subsequent lessons.

INPUT

Act. E, Note: Refer to the Instructor's Manual regarding input activities for grammar. See especially the section "Making Input Activities Come Alive." **Suggestion:** There may be more than one possible response for each item. As students read their finished sentences out loud, ask the class: *¿Qué creen? ¿Es cierto para Jaime o es falso?*

Actividad E ¿Cierto o falso?

Match each phrase in column A with one from column B to make a logical statement. Then, speculate whether each sentence is true for the *Sol y viento* character, Jaime.

	A		**B**	CIERTO	FALSO
Jaime...					
1.	_c_ estudia	**a.**	la cena (*dinner*) cada noche.	☐	☐
2.	_e_ habla	**b.**	en un restaurante o bar.	☐	☐
3.	_b_ trabaja	**c.**	cuatro horas cada noche.	☐	☐
4.	_a_ prepara	**d.**	la guitarra en una banda.	☐	☐
5.	_d_ toca	**e.**	dos idiomas.	☐	☐
6.	_f_ toma	**f.**	café cada mañana.	☐	☐

INPUT/OUTPUT
Actividad F

Actividad F ¿Cuándo? (*When?*)

Paso 1 Indicate whether you do each activity daily (**cada día**), weekly (**cada semana**), monthly (**una vez al mes**), or never (**nunca**) on a normal basis.

	CADA DÍA	CADA SEMANA	UNA VEZ AL MES	NUNCA
1. Trabajo.	☐	☐	☐	☐
2. Regreso a la residencia / a casa.	☐	☐	☐	☐
3. Llamo a un amigo por teléfono.	☐	☐	☐	☐
4. Estudio español.	☐	☐	☐	☐
5. Pago el alquiler.	☐	☐	☐	☐
6. Charlo con mis amigos por correo electrónico (*e-mail*).	☐	☐	☐	☐
7. Navego la red.	☐	☐	☐	☐
8. Visito a mi familia.	☐	☐	☐	☐

Paso 2 Now form questions using the **tú** form of the verbs, and interview someone in class to see if that person does the same thing as you. Jot down his or her responses.

MODELOS: Estudio español. → ¿Estudias español cada día?

  Pago el alquiler. → ¿Pagas el alquiler una vez al mes?

Paso 3 Report to the class one thing you and your classmate do that's similar. Then indicate something the two of you do differently.

MODELOS: John y yo estudiamos español cada día.

  Yo trabajo, pero John no trabaja.

INPUT
Act. G,
Suggested follow-up: Ask students questions about what these famous people do or do not do. 1. *¿Cantan José Carreras y Plácido Domingo la música rock o la ópera?* (la ópera) 2. *¿Bailan Jennifer López y Shakira bien o mal?* (use thumbs up to model *bien* and thumbs down to model *mal*) (*bien*) 3. *¿Hablan inglés o alemán Matt Damon y Cate Blanchett?* (*inglés*) 4. *¿Practican Tiger Woods y Sergio García el fútbol o el golf?* (*el golf*)

INPUT/OUTPUT
Act. H, *Paso 3*,
Suggestion:
Time permitting, skim the descriptions quickly and then read one aloud, correcting any errors as you go. Ask the class to decide if that schedule is accurate or not based on what they learned. Have them correct any false statements or statements they think are false. In the end, tell them what is accurate and what is not in the schedule. Do one more if time allows.

Actividad G Personas célebres (*Famous people*)

For each statement, name at least two famous people who do the activity with some regularity.

MODELO: Tocan la guitarra. → Sting y Carlos Santana tocan la guitarra.

1. Tocan el piano.
2. Cantan (*They sing*) en público.
3. Bailan (*They dance*) en público.
4. Hablan español.
5. Hablan francés.
6. Practican el tenis.
7. Charlan con el presidente de los Estados Unidos.
8. Critican las películas (*movies*).

Actividad H El horario del profesor (de la profesora)

Paso 1 With a partner, use everything you've learned so far to create at least six sentences about what you think your instructor's schedule is like.

MODELO: El profesor (La profesora) enseña tres clases. También...

Vocabulario útil

pero	but
solamente	only
también	also, in addition to
y	and
desayunar	to eat breakfast
enseñar	to teach
viajar	to travel

Paso 2 Members of the class should begin asking questions of the instructor to see if their schedules are accurate. Note: Each group may only ask one question so that all groups get to ask questions. Jot down your instructor's responses.

MODELO: ¿Cuántas clases enseña Ud.?

Vocabulario útil

¿cuándo?	when
¿cuánto/a/os/as?	how much/many?
¿dónde?	where?

Paso 3 Working with your partner, revise your instructor's schedule based on the information you received in **Paso 2** and turn it in.

Vocabulario

More About
Schedules

Note: These vocabulary items can be heard in this lesson's Textbook Audio section of the Online Learning Center Website.

Los días de la semana

Days of the Week

lunes	Monday
martes	Tuesday
miércoles	Wednesday
jueves	Thursday
viernes	Friday
sábado	Saturday
domingo	Sunday

■ Note that the first day of the week is Monday (instead of Sunday) in most calendars from the Spanish-speaking world. You will read more about this in the **Vistazo cultural** in this section.

■ Note too that the days of the week are not capitalized in Spanish as they are in English.

✳ MÁS VOCABULARIO

el fin de semana	weekend
el horario	schedule
el (los) lunes	on Monday(s)
por la mañana	in the morning
por la tarde	in the afternoon
por la noche	in the evening / at night
todos los días	every day
todas las noches	every night
¿Qué día es hoy?	What day is it today?

Origen de los nombres de los días

Como el español se deriva del latín, los nombres de los días son de origen latino.

lunes: día de la luna [a]

martes: día de Marte, el dios de la guerra [b]

miércoles: día de Mercurio, el dios mensajero [c]

jueves: día de Júpiter, padre y jefe [d] de los dioses

viernes: día de Venus, la diosa del amor [e]

sábado: del latín **sabbatum,** día de descanso [f]

domingo: del latín **dominicus,** día del Señor [g]

Los nombres de los días, en inglés, tienen un origen un poco diferente. Algunos [h] son de la mitología vikinga (*Thursday*, por ejemplo, se deriva del día de Thor).

▲ *Mercury,* por Simeon Solomon (inglés, 1840–1905)

[a]*moon*   [b]*dios... god of war*   [c]*messenger*
[d]*boss*   [e]*love*   [f]*rest*   [g]*Lord*   [h]*Some*

agosto	1:00	2:00	3:00	4:00
14 lunes				
15 martes				
16 miércoles				
17 jueves				
18 viernes				
19 sábado				
20 domingo				

¿Puedes nombrar (*Can you name*) las fechas (*dates*) en este calendario?

INPUT/OUTPUT
Act. A, *Paso 1*,
Statements:
1. *Roberto tiene tres clases los martes.* (falso)
2. *No tiene clases los lunes.* (falso) 3. *Tiene tres clases los viernes.* (cierto)
4. *Roberto tiene un laboratorio los jueves.* (cierto) 5. *Tiene una clase de filosofía los miércoles.* (cierto, y también los lunes y viernes) 6. *Tiene una clase de español todos los días.* (falso)
Paso 2, **Suggested follow-up:** Ask some volunteers to make statements similar to those in *Paso 1*. Call on a total of 5 volunteers to make 1 statement each.

Actividad A Las clases de Roberto

Paso 1 Listen as your instructor makes a series of statements about Roberto's class schedule. Indicate whether the statements are **cierto** (*true*) or **falso** based on his schedule, provided in the following table.

1. ...   **2.** ...   **3.** ...   **4.** ...   **5.** ...   **6.** ...

LUNES	MARTES	MIÉRCOLES	JUEVES	VIERNES
Química II		Química II	Laboratorio de Química II	Química II
	Español III	Español III	Español III	Español III
	Historia de la Norteamérica colonial		Historia de la Norteamérica colonial	
Filosofía I		Filosofía I		Filosofía I

Paso 2 With a partner, take turns making statements about Roberto's schedule using the models below. See if each of you can make five different statements.

MODELOS: Roberto tiene una clase de química los lunes, miércoles y viernes.

Tiene dos clases los lunes.

INPUT
Act. B, **Suggested follow-up:** Ask different students: *¿Cuál es el peor día de la semana para ti?* See how many agree by raising hands. Continue by asking some students: *Para ti, ¿es mejor estudiar por la mañana, por la tarde o por la noche?*, again seeing how many agree by a show of hands. Avoid open-ended questions at this point, and stick to yes/no, either/or questions, or questions that can be answered with 1 or 2 words.

Actividad B ¿Estás de acuerdo? (*Do you agree?*)

Indicate whether you agree or disagree with each statement.

	ESTOY DE ACUERDO.	NO ESTOY DE ACUERDO.
1. Es buena idea estudiar todas las noches.	☐	☐
2. No es buena idea estudiar los fines de semana.	☐	☐
3. Para mí (*For me*), es mejor (*better*) estudiar por la mañana.	☐	☐
4. Para mí, es mejor tomar las clases por la tarde, si (*if*) es posible.	☐	☐
5. Los mejores (*best*) programas de televisión se presentan (*are aired*) los jueves por la noche.	☐	☐
6. El peor (*worst*) día de la semana para mí es el lunes.	☐	☐

Actividad C Un horario

Using the grid that follows as a guide, interview a classmate to find out what days of the week he or she has classes and what those classes are. Also indicate whether the classes are **por la mañana, por la tarde,** or **por la noche.** Turn in the schedule to your instructor with the student's name on it.

MODELO: E1: ¿Qué clase tienes los lunes por la mañana?
E2: Tengo dos. Una clase de química y una de historia.

	LUNES	MARTES	MIÉRCOLES	JUEVES	VIERNES
por la mañana					
por la tarde					
por la noche					

≋ Vistazo cultural

Los calendarios

Although calendars in this country list Sunday as the first day of the week, in the Spanish-speaking world, Monday is traditionally shown as the first day of the week. This difference reflects the Latinate and Judeo-Christian background of the Spanish system rather than the Germanic and Scandinavian influences in English. The Romans imported the idea of a seven-day week from Jewish tradition and named the days accordingly. When the Roman empire converted to Christianity, Sunday became the last day of the week and the official "day of rest" or, as Emperor Constantine declared, "the Christian sabbath." As part of the Roman empire and as a country that emerged as strongly Catholic, Spain kept this system and took it to its empire in Africa (Equatorial Guinea), the Philippines, and the Americas.

However, due to globalization, Anglo influence has started to creep into some Hispanic cultures, and it is possible to find calendars whose first day of the week is **domingo** rather than the traditional **lunes.** But Hispanic countries still consider **domingo** the "day of rest," and many businesses (including shops and restaurants) are closed on this day. In rural areas of Mexico, Chile, and Colombia, for example, as well as in many cities, you will still find couples and families strolling through parks and plazas on Sundays.

Gramática

Talking About
Needing or Wanting
to Do Something

Necesito estudiar.

Verb + *infinitive*

EXPRESSING THE NEED OR DESIRE TO DO SOMETHING	
necesidad	deseo
necesitar + *infinitive* **Necesito estudiar** para un examen. *I need to study for a test.* **¿Necesitas comprar** un libro? *Do you need to buy a book?*	**desear** + *infinitive* **Deseo visitar** Madrid. *I want to visit Madrid.* **¿Desean** los estudiantes **hablar** bien el español? *Do the students want to speak Spanish well?*
es necesario + *infinitive* **Es necesario escuchar** bien en clase. *It's necessary to listen well in class.*	

As you saw in the previous grammar section, Spanish has verb forms that end in **-r.** These forms indicate the same thing that *to* indicates in front of an English verb (for example, *to talk* = **hablar** and *to need* = **necesitar**). These verb forms are called *infinitives.* To express the need to do something, Spanish does not require a word equivalent to the English word *to,* since it is implied in the Spanish infinitive.

> **Necesito viajar** al Valle del Maipo.   *I need to travel to the Maipo Valley.*

In addition to using the verb **necesitar,** you can also use certain "impersonal expressions" in Spanish to convey general necessity to do something. Again, there is no word added to express English *to.*

> **Es necesario** practicar mucho.   *It's necessary to practice a lot.*

The verb **desear** (*to desire, want*) can be combined with infinitive verb forms to talk about what people want to do. Again, no equivalent word for *to* is used.

> **Deseo visitar** Buenos Aires.   *I want to visit Buenos Aires.*
>
> **¿Desean** muchos estudiantes **estudiar** otro idioma?   *Do a lot of students want to study another language?*

The chart summarizes how to express necessity and desire to do something.

✳ MÁS VOCABULARIO

Here are some other regular **-ar** verbs and expressions that you will want to use in this lesson.

bailar	to dance	**mirar**	to watch
buscar	to look for	**pasar (mucho)**	to spend
cantar	to sing	**tiempo**	(a lot of) time
descansar	to rest	**repasar**	to review
escuchar	to listen (to)	**tomar apuntes**	to take notes
memorizar	to memorize		

De *Sol y viento,* Note: You can access this film clip from a special menu section on Disc 5 of the Instructional Version on DVD.

DE SOL Y VIENTO

In **Episodio 1** of *Sol y viento,* you will watch a scene in which Jaime and his taxi driver, Mario, discuss the possibility of a trip outside the city of Santiago. Part of their exchange appears here.

JAIME
¿Ud. hace viajes fuera de Santiago?[a]

MARIO
Pero, ¡claro que sí![b]... ¿Qué se le ofrece?[c]

JAIME
Necesito _____ mañana[d]...

Selecting from the following list, what verb or activity do you think Jaime mentions in this scene?

1. viajar   2. visitar   3. charlar

[a]¿Ud.... *Do you take trips outside of Santiago?*   [b]Pero... *But of course!*   [c]¿Qué... *What can I do for you?*   [d]*tomorrow*

Enfoque lingüístico

Enfoque lingüístico, Point out: Tell students that the point of these brief readings is to give them a picture of the diversity among languages and to compare English and Spanish with each other as well as with other languages.

Suggestion: After they read this Enfoque, ask them to define inflections ("endings on nouns and verbs that add information other than the basic meaning of the word"). Then ask them if inflections exist on nouns in Spanish and English. What are these inflections and what do they represent? English: number, that is, singular vs. plural (dog/dogs), possession (dog's); Spanish: number (*chico/chicos*), and with certain animate nouns biological gender (*chico/chica, profesor/profesora*). Thus, Spanish and English typically only overlap in the use of inflections to indicate number.

La importancia (o no) de las inflexiones

Some languages are "inflectionally rich." This means that they add endings (called *inflections*) to either nouns or verbs (or both) that provide the listener with information. English is inflectionally poor. For any regular verb, there are only two forms in the present tense: one with the inflection *-s* to talk about someone else (e.g., *John studies a lot*) and one "common" verb with no following *-s* to talk about everyone else (e.g., *You/We/I/They study a lot*). Some languages, such as Chinese, have no verb inflections for person, so you might consider these languages "inflectionless." Spanish, as you are beginning to learn, is inflectionally rich. Verb endings tend to be unique for each person, *person* being a term that refers to the meaning contained in the subject pronouns *I, you, he/she, they,* and *we.* A Spanish verb ending in **-o,** for example, will always refer to **yo,** a verb ending in **-mos** will always mean **nosotros/as,** and so forth.

Estudio química.	(No need to say **yo estudio** because the verb indicates who studies.)
¿Llevas muchos créditos?	(No need to say **llevas tú** because the verb indicates **tú**).
Trabajamos mucho en la clase de español.	(No need to say **nosotros** because **-mos** can only refer to *we*).

For infinitives, **-r** is the inflection that means "to" (as in the English verbs *to work, to take,* and so forth). This is why Spanish does not need another word for *to* in constructions with **necesitar** and **desear:** the **-r** at the end of the second verb indicates this meaning. Learning Spanish, then, requires paying attention to the ends of verbs as you listen and read.

INPUT/OUTPUT
Act. D, Point out: *¿Qué leíste?* is an input activity called a **dictogloss**, which will appear once every lesson. The purpose is to have students work together to recreate a short paragraph they have just read, and then compare what they remember with the original version.
Paso 1: Display the following paragraph using an overhead projector or by other means so that all class members can see it. Remove it after 1 minute (do not let students memorize the paragraph by giving them too much time). Alternatively, read the paragraph twice, at slightly less than conversational speed: *Jaime necesita viajar al Valle del Maipo. Desea hablar con el Sr. Sánchez mañana. Pero necesita descansar ahora. Por la tarde necesita llamar a la oficina en San Francisco.*
Paso 2: Allow approximately 5 minutes. Expect students to say such things as "Wasn't there something about *necesita hablar con el Sr. Sánchez?*" "No, I think it was *desea, desea hablar.*" Using English at this stage to recreate the paragraph is normal and necessary given they are trying to recall the input they were just exposed to. See the Instructor's Manual for information on dictogloss activities.
Follow-up: Call on one group to present its final version. Ask another group if it has the exact same wording. Finally, display the original so all groups can compare. How close did everyone come to the original? Ask

Actividad D ¿Qué leíste? (*What did you read?*)

Paso 1 Quickly read the paragraph that your instructor displays to the class. Try to remember as much of the information as possible, but do not take notes.

Paso 2 In groups of three, recreate the paragraph as best as you can remember, writing out a final version to share with the class.

Actividad E ¿Qué necesitamos hacer (*to do*)?

Paso 1 On your own, decide which of the following you think are true for studying Spanish.

	ES CIERTO	NO ES CIERTO
1. Uno necesita estudiar todas las noches.	☐	☐
2. Uno necesita escuchar música en español.	☐	☐
3. Uno necesita tomar apuntes en clase.	☐	☐
4. Uno necesita memorizar el vocabulario.	☐	☐
5. No es necesario pasar mucho tiempo estudiando (*studying*) la gramática.	☐	☐
6. Es necesario hablar un poco (*a little bit*) en español con otra persona todos los días.	☐	☐
7. Uno necesita mirar programas de televisión en español.	☐	☐
8. No es necesario pasar mucho tiempo en el laboratorio de lenguas.	☐	☐

Paso 2 Compare your responses to **Paso 1** with those of two other people. Together, present a final list of the statements that you all agree are true.

COMUNICACIÓN ÚTIL

Another handy expression to talk about what you like to do is **me gusta** + *infinitive*. What you are saying literally is "(*something*) is pleasing to me."

> **Me gusta estudiar** por la mañana.
> **No me gusta pagar** el alquiler.

To ask a classmate if he or she likes to do something, use **te gusta** + *infinitive*.

> **¿Te gusta navegar** la red?

a few content questions to keep focus on meaning. For example, *¿Con quién viaja al Valle del Maipo? ¿Con quién necesita hablar en la oficina en San Francisco?* Total time for dictogloss: 15–20 minutes. You may wish to shorten or skip another activity to allow time for the dictogloss.

INPUT
Act. E, *Paso 1*, Point out: Use of impersonal *uno necesita* to describe what "one needs (you need)" to do.
***Paso 2,* Suggested follow-up:** Have 1 group present its statements to the class and see if the others agree.
Additional follow-up: Tell students to return to *Paso 1* but this time to think about the statements in terms of passing this course.

INPUT

Act. F, Suggested follow-up: After students mark their responses, call on some individuals to make a statement from the list. Follow up using *¿Te gusta... ?* questions. For example, Student: *Esta noche deseo quemar unos discos compactos.* Instructor: *¿Sí? ¿Te gusta quemar discos? ¿Qué música te gusta escuchar? ¿la clásica? ¿el rock? ¿el hip hop?* etc.

Actividad F   Lo que (*What*) deseamos hacer

In the previous activity, you talked about what you need to do to learn Spanish. But suppose you don't have to do any of those things tonight. What do you *want* to do instead? Check each item that applies to you.

Esta noche...	SÍ	NO
1. deseo descansar.	☐	☐
2. deseo bailar.	☐	☐
3. deseo mirar una película.	☐	☐
4. deseo tomar cerveza con mis amigos.	☐	☐
5. deseo limpiar (*to clean*) la casa (el apartamento).	☐	☐
6. deseo quemar (*to burn*) unos discos compactos.	☐	☐
7. deseo ¿ ?	☐	☐

OUTPUT

Act. G, Suggestion: Tell students to switch roles when 1 interview is completed.

Suggested follow-up: Collect the schedules and read 1 or 2 out loud. Students respond by saying *Es cierto para mí también* or *Yo necesito _____ los martes, no los jueves,* etc. You may need to prod with questions, for example: *Y tú, ¿también necesitas trabajar los fines de semana? ¿Te gusta estudiar los fines de semana?* etc. Again, keep questions simple, to yes/no or either/or questions.

Actividad G   Entrevista (*Interview*)

Interview a classmate about what days of the week he or she needs, wants, or likes to do particular activities. Find out about at least seven activities. Then list a series of complete sentences, as in the model.

MODELO: Susie necesita trabajar en Blockbuster los martes y jueves por la noche.

	LUNES	MARTES	MIÉRCOLES	JUEVES	VIERNES
por la mañana					
por la tarde					
por la noche					

▲ ¿Qué necesita hacer mañana Jaime? ¿Recuerdas? (*Do you remember?*)

TERCERA PARTE

Note: These vocabulary items can be heard in this lesson's Textbook Audio section of the Online Learning Center Website.

Vocabulario

Talking About When You Do Things | **¿A qué hora?**

Telling Time

Es la una de la tarde.

Son las cinco **y cuarto de la mañana.**

Son las siete **y media de la noche.**

Son las once **menos** veinte de la mañana.

Although you may encounter regional variation in how Spanish speakers talk about the time, you will always be understood if you use the following guidelines.

- To tell what time it is, use forms of the verb **ser,** either **es** or **son,** depending on whether the hour is one o'clock or some other hour.

  Es la una.   *It's one o'clock.*
  Son las dos.   *It's two o'clock.*
  Son las seis de la tarde.   *It's six o'clock in the evening.*

- To add minutes, use **y** as in the expressions below.

  Es la una **y diez.**   *It's 1:10.*
  Son las tres **y veinte.** *It's 3:20.*

- Note that special words are used to mean quarter of the hour or half-hour.

  Es la una **y cuarto.**   *It's 1:15.*
  Son las ocho **y media.** *It's 8:30.*

- For a time that is approaching an hour, Spanish uses the expression **menos** (*less*).

  Es la una **menos cuarto.**   *It's a quarter to one.*
  Son las cinco **menos veinte.** *It's twenty to five.*

EL HORARIO DE JULIA RAMÍREZ					
	LUNES	MARTES	MIÉRCOLES	JUEVES	VIERNES
9:00	Biología II		Biología II		Biología II
10:00		Inglés III	Inglés III	Inglés III	Inglés III
11:00		Historia mexicana contemporánea		Historia mexicana contemporánea	
12:00	Filosofía I		Filosofía I		Filosofía I
2:00	trabaja en la biblioteca		trabaja en la biblioteca		trabaja en la biblioteca

Julia tiene una clase **a las nueve** de la mañana.

Necesita llegar (*to arrive*) a la biblioteca **a las dos menos cinco.**

When talking about schedules and at what time you do things, use the phrases **a la** or **a las,** again depending on whether you are talking about one o'clock or some other hour.

Necesito regresar a mi casa **a la una.**

I need to return home at one o'clock.

Necesito llamar a mi mamá **a las tres.**

I need to call my mom at three.

✳ MÁS VOCABULARIO

¿A qué hora... ?	At what time . . . ? / When . . . ?
¿Qué hora es?	What time is it?
¡Uy! Es muy tarde/temprano.	Oh! It's very late/early.
llegar a tiempo	to arrive on time
ser (*irreg.*) **puntual**	to be punctual
a la misma hora	at the same time
de la mañana	in the morning, A.M.
de la tarde/noche	in the afternoon/evening, P.M.
de las dos y cuarto hasta las tres y media	from 2:15 until 3:30
en punto	on the dot, exactly
mediodía (*m.*)	noon
medianoche (*f.*)	midnight

One potential problem when listening to others talk about time is hearing the difference between **dos** and **doce**. For example:

Necesitamos llegar a las dos y media.

Necesitamos llegar a las doce y media.

At first, these may sound the same to you. To request clarification, you might say:

Perdón. ¿A qué hora?

Perdón. ¿A las dos o a las doce y media?

INPUT
Act. A, Statements:
1. *Son las cinco de la tarde.* 2. *Es la una menos cuarto de la mañana.* 3. *Son las once y media.* 4. *Son las seis.* 5. *Son las dos menos diez de la mañana.* 6. *Son las tres y veinte de la tarde.* 7. *Es medianoche.*
Suggested follow-up:
Invent 3 or 4 more times, including some that require *Es la una...*

Actividad A ¿Qué hora es?

Write down each time of day your instructor reads aloud in the spaces provided. Be sure to include A.M. or P.M. if specified.

MODELOS: *Instructor says:* Son las dos.
You write: 2:00

Instructor says: Es mediodía.
You write: noon

1. 5:00 P.M. **2.** 12:45 A.M. **3.** 11:30 **4.** 6:00
5. 1:50 A.M. **6.** 3:20 P.M. **7.** midnight

INPUT/OUTPUT
Act. B,
Suggestion: Read each statement once. Students may ask for repetition if needed.
1. *Enrique tiene clase de literatura a las once.* (cierto) 2. *Regresa a casa a las seis menos quince.* (cierto) 3. *Tiene laboratorio de biología a las diez en punto.* (cierto) 4. *Estudia en la biblioteca a las dos y media.* (falso) 5. *Estudia con unos amigos de las siete menos cuarto hasta las nueve y cuarto.* (falso)

Actividad B ¿Cierto o falso?

Paso 1 Your instructor will read a series of statements about what Enrique does on Mondays. Based on his schedule, which follows, indicate whether each statement is true (**cierto**) or false (**falso**).

Este lunes

8:30 clase de biología

10:00 laboratorio de biología

11:00 clase de literatura

12:30 estudiar en la biblioteca

2:30–5:30 trabajar en la librería

5:45 regresar a casa

7:15–9:45 reunión para estudiar

1. ...
2. ...
3. ...
4. ...
5. ...

Paso 2 With a partner, indicate what you typically do at each time in Enrique's schedule.

MODELO: A las 8:30, tengo una clase de biología. A las 10:00, ...

Vocabulario útil

almuerzo	I eat lunch
desayuno	I eat breakfast
duermo	I sleep
ceno	I eat dinner

Actividad C Comparación de horarios

Paso 1 Write at least two things you do in the morning, in the afternoon, and at night for each day, including the time at which you do them.

MODELOS: (*under* lunes, miércoles, viernes) 10:00 clase de español

(*under* martes *and* jueves) 12:00 clase de química

(*under* sábado) trabajo de 1:00 a 9:00

	LUNES	MARTES	MIÉRCOLES	JUEVES	VIERNES	SÁBADO	DOMINGO
por la mañana yo mi compañero/a							
por la tarde yo mi compañero/a							
por la noche yo mi compañero/a							

OUTPUT
Act. C, *Paso 1*, Suggestion: Allow 5 minutes.
***Paso 2*, Suggestion:** Allow 5–6 minutes.
***Paso 3*, Suggestion:** Ask several students to present the results of *Paso 3* and to offer 1 or 2 statements that support their conclusion. You may need to prod with leading questions. For example: *¿Cuándo trabajas tú y cuándo trabaja Luis? ¿Estudian Uds. a la misma hora?*

***Vistazo cultural*, Suggestion:** Have students quickly read the text. Then see if they can give the non-24 hour equivalent of the following times: 1. *las 22:00 horas (10:00)* 2. *las 19:30 (7:30)* 3. *las 21:00 horas (las 9:00).* Ask them a few questions about arriving on time. *Si tienes una cita con un amigo a las 2:00, ¿llegas tú en punto? ¿Crees que llegar a*

Paso 2 Now ask a partner what he or she does at the times and days you've written down in your schedule.

MODELOS: ¿Qué haces (*do you do*) los lunes a las diez?

¿Tienes clase a las doce los martes y jueves?

Paso 3 With the information you have obtained in **Paso 2,** indicate which of the following is true. Be able to say at least two things that support your choice.

☐ Tenemos (*We have*) actividades y horarios parecidos (*similar*).

☐ Tenemos actividades y horarios diferentes.

≋ Vistazo cultural

De 0:00 a 24:00

Although people talk about time as you have learned in this lesson, the twenty-four hour clock is used in most Spanish-speaking countries for schedules, in the news, and in other types of official reporting. Thus, you will see train schedules with departures at 14:30 (2:30 P.M.), for example, and movie times at 22:00 (10:00 P.M.). Store hours may be given the same way: **abierto**ᵃ **de 10:00 a 21:00.**

In the business world, people in Spanish-speaking countries are as punctual when keeping appointments as are people in this country. On the other hand, the concept of **en punto** is relatively flexible for social occasions. For example, when two friends from Venezuela, Argentina, or Costa Rica say they'll meet **a las dos,** neither one would normally expect the other to be there right at 2:00. In fact, arriving at 2:30 would not be considered rude in some of these contexts.

las 2:15 es muy tarde? ¿a las 2:30? ¿Qué haces si no puedes llegar a las 2:00? (llamar
ᵃ*open   al amigo por celular may be a typical answer) Si tu amigo no llega para las 2:30 y no llama por teléfono, ¿esperas más o no? (write esperar = "to wait" on the chalkboard).*

Gramática

Es mi libro.   **Unstressed Possessive Adjectives**

Gramática, **Note:** This is
the first time students
have had to work with
gender and number
agreement with adjectives.
Descriptive adjectives will
be introduced in *Lección
1B,* where students will
continue to reinforce their
knowledge of the concept
of gender and number
agreement.

POSSESSIVE ADJECTIVES			
mi(s) libro(s)	my book(s)	**nuestro(s) libro(s)** **nuestra(s) vida(s)**	our book(s) our life (lives)
tu(s) libro(s)	your (*informal*) book(s)	**vuestro(s) libro(s)** **vuestra(s) vida(s)**	your (*informal, Spain*) book(s) your life (lives)
su(s) libro(s)	your (*formal*) book(s)	**su(s) libro(s)**	your (*formal*) book(s)
su(s) libro(s)	his/her book(s)	**su(s) libro(s)**	their book(s)

There are a variety of ways to talk about what is yours, someone else's, theirs, and so forth in Spanish. Unstressed possessive adjectives are simple possessive adjectives that precede nouns and are equivalent to *my, your, his, her,* and so forth in English. The chart contains the Spanish equivalents.

Note that the one word **su** can mean a variety of possessors, so context will determine who is the owner.

In the next lesson you will learn about something called *adjective agreement,* but you need to know a bit about it here for possessive adjectives. Remember that nouns have gender (e.g., **el libro, la mochila**). In Spanish, adjectives must agree in gender with the nouns they modify. Fortunately in the case of possessive adjectives, only **nuestro** and **vuestro** show this agreement. So, if a noun is feminine, you must use **nuestra** or **vuestra: nuestra/vuestra clase** (*our/your class*).

But adjectives must also agree in number (singular versus plural) with the nouns they modify. This is true for all possessive adjectives in the chart. Thus, an **-s** is added to the adjective if the noun is plural.

nuestra clase	*our class* →	nuestra**s** clase**s**	*our classes*
mi clase	*my class* →	mi**s** clase**s**	*my classes*
su estudiante	*his (her or their) student* →	su**s** estudiante**s**	*his (her or their) students*

DE SOL Y VIENTO

In an earlier **De *Sol y viento*** activity, you saw part of an exchange between Jaime and Mario regarding a trip that Jaime wants to take out of Santiago. Here is the entire exchange.

JAIME
¿Ud. hace viajes fuera de Santiago?

MARIO
Pero, ¡claro que sí! Es _____ mi _____ autito, soy _____ mi _____ propio jefe[a]...
¿Qué se le ofrece?

JAIME
Necesito viajar mañana, como a las diez de la mañana.

MARIO
¡Perfecto! ¿Adónde desea ir?[b]

JAIME
Al... al Valle del Maipo.

MARIO
¿Valle del Maipo? ¡Fantástico! Muy, muy lindo.[c] A propósito:[d] me llamo Mario Verdejo. «Verdejín» para _____ mis _____ amigos.

What forms of the possessive adjective do you think Mario is using in the blanks above?

[a]propio... *own boss* [b]*to go* [c]*pretty* [d]A... *By the way*

Actividad D   ¿Mario o Jaime?

Which of the two characters would most likely make each statement below?

	MARIO	JAIME
1. Mi compañía paga bien.	☐	☑
2. Necesito trabajar todos los días para mantener (*support*) a mi familia.	☑	☐
3. Nuestro país es lindo (*pretty*), ¿no?	☑	☐
4. Nuestros vinos son excelentes.	☑	☑
5. ¿Su señora (*wife*) también es de Santiago?	☐	☑

Actividad E ¿Cierto o falso?

Listen to the statements your instructor makes about the people and things in your class. Then decide if each statement is true or not.

1. ...
2. ...
3. ...
4. ...
5. ...
6. ...
7. ...

Actividad F ¿Cómo es nuestra universidad?

Paso 1 Select the response that best reflects your reaction to each statement. Note: **más o menos** = *more or less.*

	SÍ	MÁS O MENOS	NO
1. Nuestros edificios son bonitos (*pretty*).	☐	☐	☐
2. Nuestra biblioteca es grande (*big*).	☐	☐	☐
3. Nuestro equipo (*team*) de fútbol americano es excelente.	☐	☐	☐
4. Nuestras residencias son cómodas (*comfortable*).	☐	☐	☐
5. Nuestra matrícula (*tuition*) es cara (*expensive*).	☐	☐	☐
6. Nuestros profesores son buenos.	☐	☐	☐
7. Nuestro auditorio es moderno.	☐	☐	☐
8. Nuestra clase de español es interesante.	☐	☐	☐

Paso 2 Compare your responses with those of three other people. Then prepare a statement to share with the class about something you all agree upon.

MODELO: Pensamos que (*We think that*) nuestra biblioteca es grande.

Paso 3 Based on everyone's statements, what is the overall attitude (**actitud**) about the university?

☐ Nuestra actitud es buena.

☐ Nuestra actitud es más o menos buena.

☐ Nuestra actitud es bastante (*rather*) negativa.

Paso 4 (Optativo) Listen as your instructor gives his or her reactions to the statements in **Paso 1.** What can you say about your instructor's attitude about the university?

Su actitud es buena / más o menos buena / bastante negativa.

OUTPUT
Act. G,
Suggestion:
Instead of having
students make statements
about their partners, they
could write down their
statements on a separate
sheet of paper and turn it
in. You could then redis-
tribute the statements and
have students read the
descriptions (or read
them yourself) without
saying the name of the
student. Students could
guess either the name of
the person or guess the
gender by saying *Es un
chico* or *Es una chica.*

Actividad G   Algunas (*Some*) de nuestras cosas (*things*) favoritas

Paso 1   First answer each of the questions in the **yo** column in the chart. Then interview a partner, asking him or her the same questions, jotting down each response under the column **mi compañero/a.**

	YO	MI COMPAÑERO/A
1. ¿Cuál es tu clase favorita?		
2. ¿Cuáles son dos de tus artistas (*performers*) favoritos?		
3. ¿Cuál es tu auto favorito?		
4. ¿Cuáles son dos de tus programas de televisión favoritos?		
5. ¿Cómo se llama tu actor favorito (actriz favorita)?		
6. ¿Cómo se llama tu profesor favorito (profesora favorita)?		
7. ¿Cuál es tu película (*movie*) favorita?		

Paso 2   Prepare three to four statements about your classmate to share with the class.

MODELO: Hablé (*I spoke*) con _____. Su auto favorito es _____. Sus programas de televisión favoritos son _____…

*Navegando la
red,* Purpose:
This recurring
optional feature
offers suggested Web-
based research topics.
Most of these features
require students to locate
a specific type of
information and to later
share their findings with
the class.

NAVEGANDO LA RED

Find a university's website in a Spanish-speaking country and locate *one* of the following to report on in class: (1) a schedule of classes on English literature or (2) a professor's office hours.

SOL Y VIENTO

A primera vista

Antes de ver el episodio

Actividad A ¿Qué recuerdas? (*What do you remember?*)

Think briefly about what you know regarding the movie *Sol y viento* thus far. Which of the following are true?

1. ☐ Jaime desea ir (*to go*) a Chile.
2. ☑ Jaime habla inglés y español.
3. ☑ Jaime trabaja para una compañía norteamericana.
4. ☑ María es antropóloga y profesora.
5. ☑ La machi habla de un conflicto.

Act. B, Suggestions
Paso 1: Don't reveal answers, as students will verify their choices later.
Paso 2: Students will probably say something like "Hold on" or "Wait." Tell them that *¡Oiga!* is literally "Hear!" (formal form) and is used throughout the Spanish-speaking world to get someone's attention. The colloquial translation is "Hey!"

Actividad B ¿Qué falta? (*What's missing?*)

Paso 1 Here is part of the exchange between Mario and Jaime in the hotel lobby that you haven't yet seen or read. Select from the choices below to fill in each blank.

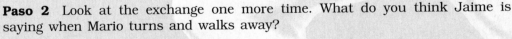

MARIO: _____¹ diez mil pesos, señor.

JAIME: Aquí tiene. _____.² (*Mario turns and walks away. Jaime calls to him.*) ¡Oiga! ¡Espere!

MARIO: ¿Sí, señor? Diga, nomás.ᵃ

JAIME: ¿Ud. hace viajes fuera de Santiago?

ᵃDiga... *Just say the word.*

1. **a.** Es
   b. Hay
   c. Son
   d. Están

2. **a.** Por favor (*Please*)
   b. Gracias (*Thank you*)
   c. De nada (*You're welcome*)

Paso 2 Look at the exchange one more time. What do you think Jaime is saying when Mario turns and walks away?

Actividad C El episodio

Now watch the episode. Remember that it's OK to let some words and expressions slip by you, especially since this is the first time you are watching the episode. You should be able to follow along without understanding every single word. You will watch the episode again in **Lección 1B,** by which time you will understand more.

Después de ver el episodio

Actividad A ¿Qué recuerdas?

Answer each item according to what you remember from the episode.

1. Cuando Jaime llega a su habitación (*room*), está cansado (*tired*). ¿Sí o no? Sí.
2. ¿Cómo se llama el hotel donde se queda (*is staying*) Jaime? el Hotel Bonaparte
3. Mañana Jaime necesita ir al Valle del ___Maipo___.
4. ¿Cuál es el apellido de Jaime? ¿Y el de Mario? Talavera, Verdejo
5. En su habitación, Jaime habla por teléfono con...
   a. Andy, de Bartel Aquapower (b.) Carlos Sánchez, de «Sol y viento»
6. ¿Qué palabra describe mejor (*best*) la expresión de Carlos al final?
   (a.) preocupación (*worry*) b. alegría (*happiness*) c. indiferencia

Actividad B ¿Lo captaste? (*Did you get it?*)

Go back to **Actividad B** of **Antes de ver el episodio** to verify your answers. If you need to, watch that particular section of the episode again.

Actividad C Utilizando (*Using*) el contexto

Paso 1 You have already begun to learn the skill of guessing the meaning of language in context. Did you deduce the meanings of the following phrases in italics? Watch this scene in the episode again if it helps.

> JAIME: Al Hotel Bonaparte. *¿A cuánto sale?*
> MARIO: Eh, um, unos 10.000 (diez mil) pesos, más o menos. *¿Le parece bien?*
> JAIME: Sí. Vamos.

Paso 2 Another skill you have begun to work on is noting that a word or phrase can have multiple meanings. For example, Jaime says **Sí. Vamos.** in response to Mario. **Vamos** means *we go* or *we are going*, but does that make sense in this context? What do you think is the equivalent of **vamos** in this context?

Actividad D Primeras (*First*) impresiones

Paso 1 You have now been introduced to Jaime and Mario. How would you describe their personalities, based on your initial impressions? Using what you have learned in this lesson, describe each in several sentences.

Paso 2 Share your descriptions with two other people. Decide what you all agree on and present your descriptions to the class. Does everyone else agree?

RESUMEN DE VOCABULARIO

Verbos

bailar	to dance
buscar	to look for
cantar	to sing
charlar	to chat
descansar	to rest
desear	to desire, want
enseñar	to teach
escuchar	to listen (to)
hablar	to speak; to talk
llamar (por teléfono)	to call (on the phone)
llegar a tiempo	to arrive on time
llevar	to take; to carry
mirar	to watch
navegar la red	to surf the Web
necesitar	to need
pagar (el alquiler)	to pay (the rent)
pasar (mucho) tiempo	to spend (a lot of) time
practicar (un deporte)	to practice (a sport)
regresar (a casa)	to return (home)
repasar	to review
ser (*irreg.*) **puntual**	to be punctual
tocar (la guitarra, el piano)	to play (the guitar, the piano)
tomar (apuntes, una clase)	to take (notes, a class)
tomar (café, cerveza)	to drink (coffee, beer)
trabajar	to work
viajar	to travel
es necesario + *infin.*	it's necessary to (*do something*)
tiene	he/she has; you (*form.*) have

Cognados: estudiar, memorizar, preparar, visitar (a la familia)

¿Qué día es hoy?

lunes, martes, miércoles, jueves, viernes, sábado, domingo

el fin de semana	weekend
el (los) lunes	on Monday(s)

Los números del 0 al 30

cero, uno, dos, tres, cuatro, cinco, seis, siete, ocho, nueve, diez, once, doce, trece, catorce, quince, **dieciséis, diecisiete, dieciocho, diecinueve, veinte, treinta**

¿Qué hora es?

Es la una.	It's one o'clock.
Son las dos (tres, cuatro,…)	It's two (three, four, . . .) o'clock.
¿A qué hora… ?	At what time . . . ? / When . . . ?
A la una.	At one o'clock.
A las dos (tres, cuatro,…)	At two (three, four, . . .) o'clock.
de la mañana	in the morning (A.M.)
de la tarde/noche	in the afternoon/ evening (P.M.)
y cuarto	quarter past
y media	half past
menos cuarto	quarter to
a la misma hora	at the same time
de la(s)… hasta la(s)	from (*hour*) to (*hour*)
en punto	on the dot, exactly
mañana	tomorrow
medianoche (*f.*)	midnight
mediodía (*m.*)	noon
por la mañana (tarde, noche)	in the morning (afternoon, evening / at night)
tarde	late
temprano	early
todos los días / todas las noches	every day / every night

Adjetivos posesivos

mi(s), tu(s), su(s), nuestro/a/os/as, vuestro/a/os/as

Otras palabras y expresiones

el crédito	credit (*school*)
el día	day
el horario	schedule
la película	movie
ahora	now
cada	each
mucho (*adv.*)	a lot
muy	very
solamente	only

1B

Más sobre las actividades

OBJETIVOS

IN THIS LESSON, YOU WILL:

- review interrogative (question) words
- learn to use regular **-er** and **-ir** verbs to talk about activities
- talk about the months, seasons, and the weather
- express immediate and planned future events with **ir**
- describe people using adjectives
- learn about adjective agreement

In addition, you will watch **Episodio 1** of the film *Sol y viento* again.

Santiago, la capital de Chile, es una ciudad (*city*) grande y cosmopolita.

The following media resources are available for this lesson of *Sol y viento*:

Episodio 1 of *Sol y viento*

Online *Manual de actividades*

Online Learning Center Website

Vocabulario

Asking Questions

¿Cuándo?

Summary of Interrogative Words

¿Adónde?	¿Adónde vas (*are you going*)?
¿Cómo?	¿Cómo te llamas?
¿Cuál(es)?	¿Cuál es tu apellido?
¿Cuándo?	¿Cuándo estudias?
¿Cuánto/a/os/as?	¿Cuántos estudiantes hay en la clase?
¿Dónde?	¿De dónde eres?
¿Por qué?	¿Por qué estudias español?
¿Qué?	¿Qué clase te gusta más?
¿Quién(es)?	¿Quién llama?

▲ **¿Quién** es esta (*this*) persona? **¿Cómo** se llama? **¿Dónde** vive (*does he live*)?

By now you have seen and heard many of these basic interrogative words in Spanish. Here are a few things to keep in mind when using them to ask questions.

■ Prepositions always stay with question words. They cannot be left alone as in English.

¿De dónde eres?	Where are you from? (the English preposition *from* can be left alone at the end of the sentence)
¿Con quién hablas?	Whom are you speaking with? (the English preposition *with* can be left alone at the end of the sentence)

■ You may be fooled if you rely on English translations, especially with **cómo, cuál,** and **qué.** Note the following.

¿Cómo te llamas?	In English we say "What's your name?" but **cómo** actually means *how.* So what you are asking literally means "How do you call yourself?" Compare with **¿Cómo se dice... ?,** which in English *does* translate as "How do you say . . . ?"
¿Cuál es tu apellido?	In English we say "What's your last name?" but **cuál** literally means *which.* So you are actually asking "Which is your last name?" Contrast with the phrase **¿Cuál de los tres desea Ud.?,** which *does* translate as "Which of the three do you want?"
¿Qué clases tienes por la tarde?	In English we can say either "Which classes" or "What classes do you have in the afternoon?" But in Spanish, **qué** literally means *what* as in **¿Qué necesitas?** ("What do you need?")

■ Although you will study adjective agreement later in this lesson, note that **cuánto** and **cuál** are adjectives and will agree with the noun they modify or refer to.

¿**Cuáles** son **los nombres** de los días de la semana?

¿**Cuántas clases** tienes este semestre?

■ To answer a question with ¿**por qué?**, you respond with **porque** (*because*), written as a single word and no accent mark.

—¿**Por qué** estudias español?

—**Porque** me gusta.

COMUNICACIÓN ÚTIL

In English, when requesting repetition, we often say "What did you say?" or, depending on the context, simply "What?" In Spanish, however, a very typical way of asking for repetition or clarification is to use ¿**cómo?***

| ¿**Cómo?** | What? (lit: How?) |
| ¿**Cómo dices?** | What are you saying? (lit: How are you saying it?) |

With added emphasis, ¿**cómo?** can also be used to express surprise at what someone says.

¿Cómo? ¡Es imposible!

〰 Vistazo cultural

Vistazo cultural, **Suggestion**: Have students read quickly. Ask them if they are familiar with any other dialectal differences. Then ask them to make similar comparisons and provide specific examples with English, such as pronunciation (e.g., dialects in the U.S., U.S. vs. Australian English, etc.); vocabulary, again providing specific examples; grammar (this may be harder for them; some examples include "y'all," "youse guys," "Have you any?," which is used in formal situations in the U.K. whereas in the U.S. "Do you have any?" is used in all situations).

Los dialectos

Spanish, like other languages, exhibits dialectal variation. For a native speaker of Spanish, it is often easy to determine what country or region another speaker is from. Dialects are based on various features of language:

• Pronunciation: In Mexico, you would hear **estás,** but in Cuba, Puerto Rico, and other Caribbean countries you are likely to hear **ehtáh** or even **etá.**

• Vocabulary: In Spain, the word **el bebé** is used, but in Chile you would likely hear **la guagua** when the speaker refers to an infant or small child.

• Grammar: In much of Spain, **vosotros** and **ustedes** are used, whereas in Spanish-speaking America **ustedes** is used for both formal and informal situations.

As you watch *Sol y viento,* take note of differences in pronunciation and other aspects of language as you hear characters from different regions and countries interact.

*There are dialectical differences for expressing *what?* in the Spanish-speaking world, but you will always be understood if you use ¿**cómo?** in this way.

INPUT

Act. A, Suggested follow-up: Follow up with real questions that utilize the same question words, e.g.: *¿Quién es tu actor favorito?* (student responds) *¿Todos están de acuerdo? ¿Cuántos dicen que _____ es su actor favorito?;* (to a new student) *¿Cuál es tu clase favorita? ¿Cuántas horas lleva la clase?;* (to a new student) *¿Quién llama a tu casa con frecuencia?,* etc.

INPUT/OUTPUT

Act. B, Note: This activity is designed to help students get used to using a form of **ser** with the interrogative *¿cuál?* There may be some information that students don't exactly know, but they should be able to deduce from each pair of choices that one of the answers is clearly incorrect and thereby select the correct one.

Actividad A   Correspondencias

Choose the most logical match between the question word and a possible response.

1. _e_ ¿Cuándo?   **a.** En Europa.
2. _a_ ¿Dónde?   **b.** José.
3. _b_ ¿Quién?   **c.** Tres.
4. _c_ ¿Cuántos?   **d.** La clase de historia.
5. _d_ ¿Cuál?   **e.** A las tres de la tarde.

Actividad B   ¿Cuál es la diferencia entre (*between*)... ?

Paso 1   See if you can answer each question by selecting the appropriate answer.

1. ¿Cuál es una diferencia entre el Brasil y la Argentina?
    a. El producto principal del Brasil es el chocolate. El producto principal de la Argentina es el vino.
    (b.) En la Argentina, hablan español. En el Brasil, hablan portugués.
2. ¿Cuál es una diferencia entre los Estados Unidos y el Canadá?
    a. En los Estados Unidos juegan al (*they play*) fútbol americano, pero en el Canadá no.
    (b.) El francés es una lengua oficial en el Canadá, pero en los Estados Unidos no.
3. ¿Cuál es una diferencia entre Chile y la Guinea Ecuatorial?
    (a.) Chile está en Sudamérica y la Guinea Ecuatorial está en África.
    b. La Guinea Ecuatorial es más grande que (*bigger than*) Chile.

Paso 2   Make up at least two questions about *Sol y viento* using **cuál.** Do your classmates know the answer?

MODELO: ¿Cuál es el apellido de Mario?

▲ ¿Cuál es una diferencia entre Jaime y Mario? Jaime es estadounidense y Mario es chileno.

INPUT/OUTPUT
Act. C, *Paso 1,* **Suggestion:** Do as a whole class. Students provide preposition and then you read entire sentence out loud.
Paso 2, **Alternative:** You may ask the questions, asking each question of several students. Tell students to take notes. Then come back at end and ask, e.g., *¿Con quién habla Susie si tiene problemas?* This reinforces the students' need to pay attention during whole-class activities.

Actividad C Las preposiciones

Paso 1 Remembering that prepositions cannot be left alone in Spanish, insert the preposition from the list that makes the most sense for each question.

a	to	**de**	of; from
con	with	**para**	for

1. ¿___Con___ quién hablas si (*if*) tienes problemas?
2. ¿___A___ cuál de los dos países (*countries*) deseas viajar, Chile o México?
3. ¿___De___ dónde es tu mejor (*best*) amigo/a?
4. ¿___Para___ qué clase pasas mucho tiempo estudiando (*studying*)?
5. ¿___Con___ cuáles de tus amigos de la secundaria (*high school*) te mantienes (*do you maintain*) en contacto?
6. ¿___De___ qué país o países hispanos importamos mucho vino?

Paso 2 With a partner, take turns asking the questions of each other. But don't ask them in the order they are listed. Make sure to pay attention to your partner!

OUTPUT
Act. D, Suggested follow-up: Ask 2 or 3 students to report 2 or 3 pieces of information about the person they interviewed.

Actividad D Otra (*Another*) entrevista

What can you find out about someone with all the question words you know now? Using the hints that follow as a guide, interview someone in the class. Jot down any information that you receive. Your instructor may call on you to make a brief presentation to the class.

- the person's favorite class
- the person's favorite professor
- where the person studies and how many hours per day/night
- how many classes the person has
- where and when the person works
- ¿ ?

▲ ¿Dónde está Mario? ¿Con quién habla?

Gramática

More on Activities
and Schedules

¿Dónde vives? **Present Tense of Regular -er and -ir Verbs**

REGULAR *-er/-ir* VERBS					
	comer (*to eat*)	**vivir** (*to live*)		**comer**	**vivir**
yo	com**o**	viv**o**	nosotros/as	com**emos**	viv**imos**
tú	com**es**	viv**es**	vosotros/as	com**éis**	viv**ís**
Ud.	com**e**	viv**e**	Uds.	com**en**	viv**en**
él/ella	com**e**	viv**e**	ellos/ellas	com**en**	viv**en**

In addition to regular verbs that end in **-ar,** Spanish has two other classes of verbs that have regular, or easily predictable, forms in the present tense, as the chart shows. Note the following:

- The endings for **-er** and **-ir** verbs are the same except for the **nosotros/as** and **vosotros/as** forms.

- The endings that mark person (the subject) are the same for **-ar, -er,** and **-ir** verbs in the present tense. In other words, **-o** always means **yo, -s** always means **tú, -mos** always means **nosotros/as,** some form of **-is** always means **vosotros/as, -n** always means **Uds.** or **ellos/ellas,** and a plain vowel other than **-o** with no following consonant always means **Ud.** or **él/ella.**

✳ MÁS VOCABULARIO

Here are some common verbs ending in **-er** and **-ir** that you will use in this lesson:

abrir	to open
aprender	to learn
asistir (a)	to attend (*a class*)
beber	to drink
comer	to eat
comprender	to understand
correr	to run
creer (que)	to think, believe (that)
escribir	to write
leer	to read
recibir	to receive
ver (*irreg.*)*	to see; to watch
vivir	to live

*Note that regular verbs drop the **-er** and add **-o: bebo, corro. Ver,** however, keeps an **e** as part of the stem of the verb in the **yo** form. Thus, the **yo** form of **ver** is **veo** and not **vo. Ver** has irregularities in other tenses as well, which is why it's often classified as an irregular verb.

De *Sol y viento,* **Note**: You can access this film clip from a special menu section on Disc 5 of the Instructional Version on DVD.

DE SOL Y VIENTO

By now you are somewhat familiar with the scene between Jaime and Mario in the hotel lobby. Examine the exchange that follows and see if you can select the correct verb to fit in the blank.

MARIO
A propósito,ᵃ me llamo Mario Verdejo.
«Verdejín» para mis amigos.

JAIME
Yo soy Jaime. Jaime Talavera. Bueno, Mario. Lo* __veo__ mañana. Hasta luego.

MARIO
Hasta mañana.

Is the missing verb **creo, veo,** or **leo?**

ᵃ*A... By the way*

Enfoque lingüístico, **Point out**: The purpose of this reading is to let students know how important tense is as a concept in Spanish, that they are learning verb forms because they are crucial to communication.
Suggestion: Have students read quickly. If you want, point out that, technically, there are three time frames: past, present, and future, and all verb tenses are related to one of these time frames. Ask students the possible meanings of the following sentence: *¿Qué comes?* (What are you eating? / What do you [normally] eat? / What do you [like to] eat?) All of these relate to the present time frame in some way, even though the meanings are not equivalent.

 # Enfoque lingüístico

El tiempo verbal

What does the term *tense* mean? *Tense* refers to the general time frame in which something happens, such as the present, the past, or the future. English distinguishes all three (*I eat / I am eating, I ate / I was eating, I will eat / I will be eating*) as does Spanish, but differently, as you will learn later. Some languages do not mark tense at all; they let other words such as *right now, later today,* and *last week* carry the full responsibility of indicating tense.

Languages also vary as to the functions assigned to verb inflections that indicate tense. For example, in Spanish, **¿Qué lees?** can mean any one of the following English equivalents: *What are you reading* (*at this moment*)*?, What are you reading* (*these days*)*?,* and *What do you read* (as in "What do you like to read?")*?* Another way to think of this is that Spanish is less restrictive than English in the possible interpretations of a present-tense verb form. For example, to which of the following English statements could you add the phrase *this week?:* a. *John is running a lot.* b. *John runs a lot.* The answer, of course, is that only sentence **a** lets you add *this week.* In Spanish, however, you could add **esta semana** to the sentence **Juan corre mucho** to mean the same as *Juan is running a lot this week.* Context, then, is important to determine the function of a present-tense verb form. If someone interviews you and asks **¿Qué estudias?,** you will know that the meaning is something like "What's your major?" If someone walks in on you while you have a book open and asks the very same question, you will understand that the person means "What are you studying (at this moment)?" What is more, Spanish present-tense verb forms can also take on a future meaning, as in the following: **Mañana escribo la carta** (*Tomorrow I'll write the letter*).

*****Lo** is what is called an *object pronoun,* something you will study in a later lesson. Here it means formal *you* as in "I'll _____ *you* tomorrow."

INPUT

Act. E, Suggestion: After the students finish describing Jaime, have them compare him to Mario by changing the introductory phrase to *Probablemente, Mario...*

Actividad E ¿Cómo es Jaime Talavera?

Complete each sentence as best as you can to describe Jaime and his life. How many different responses can you and your classmates think of?

Probablemente, Jaime...

1. lee el _____ todos los días.
2. ve _____ en la televisión cada semana.
3. vive en _____.
4. come en _____ por lo menos (*at least*) una vez (*once*) a la semana.
5. bebe _____ casi todos los días.
6. recibe muchos mensajes (*messages*) por correo electrónico (*e-mail*) de _____.

▲ Jaime corre para hacer ejercicio (*to exercise*).

INPUT

Act. F, Suggestion: Call on individual students to answer each item. Then ask the class whether students agree with each statement made or not.

Actividad F Los animales

For each statement, indicate whether it applies to dogs (**los perros**), cats (**los gatos**), or both (**los perros y los gatos**). If you disagree with what someone says, speak up!

MODELO: Aprenden fácilmente (*easily*). →

TÚ: Los perros aprenden fácilmente, pero los gatos no.
OTRO/A ESTUDIANTE: No, no. Los gatos también aprenden fácilmente.

1. Aprenden fácilmente.
2. Viven dentro de (*inside*) la casa.
3. Comen de todo (*everything*).
4. Beben agua del inodoro (*toilet*).
5. Asisten a clases de obediencia.
6. Creen que son humanos.
7. Comprenden todo lo que decimos (*everything we say*).

Actividad G ¿Cuándo?

Paso 1 Indicate the frequency with which you do each activity listed. Note: **una vez al mes** = *once a month.*

	CADA DÍA	CADA SEMANA	UNA VEZ AL MES	NUNCA
1. Escribo una carta (*letter*).	☐	☐	☐	☐
2. Como en un restaurante.	☐	☐	☐	☐
3. Bebo cerveza en un bar.	☐	☐	☐	☐
4. Aprendo algo nuevo (*something new*).	☐	☐	☐	☐
5. Abro el libro de español.	☐	☐	☐	☐
6. Asisto a clase por la tarde.	☐	☐	☐	☐
7. Corro para no llegar tarde a clase.	☐	☐	☐	☐
8. Leo el periódico (*newspaper*).	☐	☐	☐	☐

Paso 2 Now, form questions using the **tú** form and interview someone in class to see the frequency with which that person completes these activities. Jot down his or her responses.

MODELO: Bebo cerveza en un bar. → ¿Con qué frecuencia bebes cerveza en un bar?

Paso 3 Report to the class one thing you and your classmate do the same. Then report something you two do differently.

MODELOS: Jeff y yo leemos el periódico cada día.

Yo como en un restaurante cada semana, pero John no.

Actividad H El profesor (La profesora)

Paso 1 Using the verbs and phrases you have learned so far, create at least six questions to use in an interview with your instructor about his or her activities.

Paso 2 A volunteer will interview your instructor using his or her questions. Jot down all information obtained. If the volunteer does not ask any of the questions you created in **Paso 1,** then ask them yourself, taking turns with other students. Again, jot down all information.

Paso 3 Write a short paragraph in which you summarize four to five points about your instructor's activities. At the same time, indicate what you think other instructors do. The model shows some useful words.

MODELO: La profesora lee mucho. Lee revistas (*magazines*), novelas (*novels*) y otras cosas. Otros profesores también leen mucho, pero creo que no leen novelas.

Vocabulario

Talking About Times
of the Year | **¡Hace calor en junio!** | **Months, Weather, and Seasons**

Note: These vocabulary
items can be heard in
this lesson's Textbook
Audio section of the
Online Learning Center
Website.

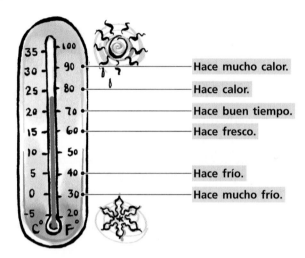

Hace mucho calor.

Hace calor.

Hace buen tiempo.

Hace fresco.

Hace frío.

Hace mucho frío.

Hace sol. Hace muy buen tiempo. **Está
despejado** (*clear*), no **nublado** (*cloudy*). Es
un día perfecto para **tomar el sol** (*sunbathe*).

Llueve. (Está lloviendo.) Hace mal tiempo.
Es un día perfecto para leer una novela o ver
una película en casa.

Hace mucho viento. No es buen tiempo
para los peinados (*hairdos*).

Nieva. (Está nevando.) No es un buen día
para muchas actividades afuera (*outdoors*).

Los meses y las estaciones del año

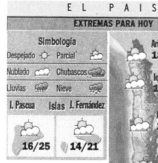

el invierno { diciembre / enero / febrero

la primavera { marzo / abril / mayo

el verano { junio / julio / agosto

el otoño { septiembre / octubre / noviembre

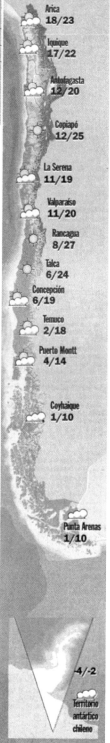

EL PAIS
EXTREMAS PARA HOY

Simbología
Despejado ☼ Parcial ☁
Nublado ☁ Chubascos ☁
Lluvias ☁ Nieve ☁

I. Pascua 16/25 Islas J. Fernández 14/21

Arica 18/23
Iquique 17/22
Antofagasta 12/20
Copiapó 12/25
La Serena 11/19
Valparaíso 11/20
Rancagua 8/27
Talca 6/24
Concepción 6/19
Temuco 2/18
Puerto Montt 4/14
Coyhaique 1/10
Punta Arenas 1/10
-4/-2
Territorio antártico chileno

COMUNICACIÓN ÚTIL

The phrases **está nevando** (*it's snowing*) and **está lloviendo** (*it's raining*) are in the *present progressive tense.* The present progressive indicates that something is happening *right now* and is formed by using **estar** + *gerund.* In English, gerunds end in *-ing.* In Spanish, gerunds are formed by adding **-ando** to the stem of **-ar** verbs and **-iendo** to the stem of **-er** and **-ir** verbs.

nevar (*to snow*) → **nev-** + **-ando** = **nevando** (*snowing*)

llover (*to rain*) → **llov-** + **-iendo** = **lloviendo** (*raining*)

You will formally study the present progressive later in the text. For now, just learn to recognize the forms when you see them.

El pronóstico (*forecast*) del tiempo en Chile se da (*is given*) en grados centígrados (*Celsius*). ▶

Actividad A ¿Qué actividad?

Listen as your instructor makes a statement about the weather. Select from the activities that follow to describe what the day is good for and what it is not good for. More than one response may be possible.

Es / No es un buen día para...

1. ...   **2.** ...   **3.** ...   **4.** ...

    a. abrir las ventanas de la casa.

    b. beber algo (*something*) muy frío.

    c. comer en el patio.

    d. correr.

    e. lavar (*wash*) el auto.

    f. manejar (*drive*) un auto descapotable (*convertible*).

    g. asistir a clase.

Actividad B Los hemisferios

Did you know that the seasons are reversed in the northern and southern hemi-spheres? Listen to each statement your instructor makes about the weather. Then respond by selecting elements from each of the following columns to cre-ate your own sentence. You will hear the following unfamiliar words: **las hojas** (*leaves*), **cambian** ([*they*] *change*), **el sur** (*south*).

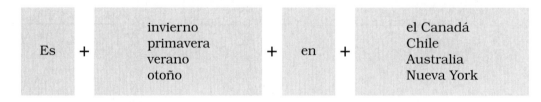

| Es | + | invierno
primavera
verano
otoño | + | en | + | el Canadá
Chile
Australia
Nueva York |

Actividad C ¿Cuándo es tu cumpleaños (*birthday*)?

Find five people with birthdays in five different months. Jot down the informa-tion below. Then listen to your instructor.

MODELO: E1: ¿Cuándo es tu cumpleaños?

            E2: Es el diecinueve de febrero.

NOMBRE   FECHA (*DATE*) DE SU CUMPLEAÑOS

_____   _____

_____   _____

_____   _____

_____   _____

_____   _____

Vistazo cultural,
Suggestion: Have students read quickly. Then ask them: *¿Cuándo es la fiesta de San Fermín? ¿Dónde es? ¿Y la fiesta de San José?*

Suggested follow-up: Have students do a quick Internet search and come to class with a holiday (not Christmas, Easter, etc.) in a Spanish-speaking city during which banks and other places are closed. This can be a national holiday. They must present the country, the city, the date, and the name of the holiday. Example: *En México, el cinco de febrero es un día festivo nacional. Es el Aniversario de la Constitución. Las personas no trabajan este día.* Note: To assure variety, assign countries to particular students or pairs of students.

COMUNICACIÓN ÚTIL

To ask the date, you can say **¿A cuánto estamos?** To reply and say what day it is, use **Estamos al*** + *date* + **de** + *month* or simply **al** + *date* + **de** + *month.*

—¿A cuánto estamos?

—Estamos al 20 de septiembre. /
—Al 20 de septiembre.

Actividad D   ¿Cuál es tu estación favorita?

Paso 1   Think about your favorite season and months. Write a short description of them, according to the model.

MODELO: Me gusta (*I like*) el invierno. Hace frío, pero me gusta el frío. También me gusta el mes de diciembre porque hay vacaciones.

Paso 2   Interview a classmate, using the following questions as a guide. Then determine if you have the same ideas in common. Your instructor may call on you to present what you've found out.

- ¿Cuál es tu estación favorita? ¿y tu mes favorito?
- ¿Te gusta (*Do you like*) el calor? ¿Te gusta el frío? ¿Qué tiempo te gusta?

≈ Vistazo cultural

Los días festivos[a]

In the United States there are few official holidays, such as New Year's Day, Presidents' Day, Easter, Memorial Day, the Fourth of July, Labor Day, Thanksgiving, and Christmas. In contrast, in many Spanish-speaking countries, many more days are celebrated—although with increasing globalization there is change and variety among Hispanic countries. In addition to national holidays (such as independence day in countries other than Spain), many local holidays are also celebrated. In Spain, it is typical to find towns closed on patron saint days. For example, almost everyone has heard of the running of the bulls in Pamplona, officially known as **la fiesta de San Fermín,** or **los sanfermines,** which takes place the second week of July. In Valencia, for the day of **San José,** the locals celebrate **las fallas,** which consist of huge *papier-mâché* caricatures that are then set ablaze on the last evening of the festival. Also, August is a popular vacation month for Spaniards, as many head out for vacation homes at the coasts and close their local businesses. In Mexico and other parts of Spanish-speaking America, similar local holidays are observed in addition to national holidays. Before you travel to a Spanish-speaking country, be sure to find out if any holidays occur during your stay and plan accordingly!

[a]Los... *Holidays*

▲ La celebración de las fallas en Valencia, España

---

*Note that the preposition **a** contracts with **el** to make the word **al. De** and **el** also contract to form **del.** You may have noticed this elsewhere in the film and in the text.

Gramática

Expressing Future
Events
¿**Vas a estudiar esta noche?** **Ir + a +** *infinitive*

ir *(to go)*			
yo	**voy**	nosotros/as	**vamos**
tú	**vas**	vosotros/as	**vais**
Ud.	**va**	Uds.	**van**
él/ella	**va**	ellos/ellas	**van**

One way to express future intent is by using the verb **ir** (*to go*), plus the preposition **a,** plus an infinitive, as in **Voy a ver una película esta noche** (*tonight*). The verb **ir,** however, is rather irregular. The **yo** form ends in **-oy** instead of **-o,** and all the other forms use the **-ar** endings!

Unlike **necesitar** and **desear, ir** requires **a** when followed by an infinitive.

Vamos a viajar a México en el verano.	*We're going to travel to Mexico in the summer.*
¿**Deseas visitar** un país de habla española?	*Do you want to visit a Spanish-speaking country?*
Necesito estudiar esta noche.	*I need to study tonight.*

Another way to express future intent, as you may recall from the previous **Enfoque lingüístico,** is with the present tense. This use is less frequent, often used with verbs that express movement or going from one place to another, and it is generally used when the event is to happen very soon.

Mañana voy a España.	*Tomorrow I'm going to Spain.*
Esta noche vamos todos a una fiesta. ¿Deseas ir?	*Tonight we're all going to party. Do you want to go?*
Pasado mañana llegan mis padres.	*My parents arrive the day after tomorrow.*

✳ MÁS VOCABULARIO

esta noche	tonight
(pasado) mañana	(the day after) tomorrow
la semana entrante	next week
el próximo verano (invierno, mes,...)	next summer (winter, month, . . .)
en unos (cuantos) días	in a few days
dentro de poco	soon
en un (dos, tres) año(s)	in one (two, three) year(s)

De *Sol y viento,* **Note:** You can access this film clip from a special menu section on Disc 5 of the Instructional Version on DVD.

Suggestions

- Tell class the suspension points in the dialogue mean that the person on the other end of the phone is saying something. Based on what Jaime says, can students figure out what that person might be saying? Here are the answers, in the order in which they appear: *Sí, ¿con quién desea hablar?; Ud. habla con él.; ¿Ud. habla español?; ¿Cómo? ¿Está aquí en el Valle del Maipo?*
- Point out that the verb *esperar* can mean *to wait (for)* or *to expect.* Here the meaning is *to expect,* and although in the present tense, the meaning intended is future, e.g., "I'll be expecting you

Enfoque lingüístico, **Point out**: In English, contractions are a regular feature: *want to* becomes *wanna, going to* becomes *gonna.* In Spanish, the only contractions are *al* and *del.* However, sometimes students may not hear the *a* in *ir a* + infinitive, such as in the cases when the infinitive begins with *a* or when *ir* is just *va: van a abrir* will sound like *vanabrir; va a llegar* may sound like *vallegar.* Contrast with *van a cantar* and *¿Vas a llegar tarde?*

DE SOL Y VIENTO

When Jaime finally gets to his hotel room, he needs to make a phone call to the winery that is the object of his company's acquisition bid. Read what he says here. What verb is missing?

JAIME

¿Aló, la viña «Sol y viento»?... Don* Carlos Sánchez... Ah, con él. Bien. Soy Jaime Talavera, de los Estados Unidos. Compañía Bartel Aquapower... Sí, claro que[a] hablo español. Ya estoy aquí... No, en Santiago. Mañana ___voy___ a verlo, como a mediodía.

CARLOS

Muy bien, señor Talavera. Lo espero[b] mañana. Hasta entonces. Chau.

[a]claro... *of course*   [b]Lo... *I'll be expecting you*

 ## Enfoque lingüístico

Las frases verbales

As you have probably guessed, there are basically four ways in which a speaker may indicate that an event will take place in the future. The first is with words that signal a future event, such as *tomorrow* and *next week,* with no verb inflection. The second is with verb inflection, as you will see later in your studies. The third is with what are called *modals,* small words that accompany verbs, such as English *will,* as in *I will arrive tomorrow at 8:00.* The fourth is with what are called *paraphrastic phrases,* such as *going to.* These phrases combine verbs in particular ways to express a meaning that is normally not part of the verb's function. For example, *go* normally means "to get from place X to place Y," but when combined with verbs it expresses some kind of future event. So, technically what you are learning in this lesson is called the "Paraphrastic Future with **ir** + **a** + infinitive"—quite a mouthful for something so simple as saying *going to,* right? Spanish has a variety of paraphrastic phrases that express different meanings and grammatical concepts. See if you can spot them as you continue your studies.

*In Spanish, the words **don** and **doña** are terms of respect used in front of a man's and a woman's name, respectively. There is no direct equivalent in English.

Actividad E ¿Qué leíste?

Paso 1 Quickly read the paragraph that your instructor displays to the class. Try to remember as much of the information as possible, but do not take notes.

Paso 2 In groups of three, recreate the paragraph as best as you can remember, writing out a final version to share with the class.

Actividad F ¿Qué vamos a hacer?

Paso 1 Do you know what you and your Spanish classmates are going to do during the next class session? Select a possibility for each item below.

1. Vamos a...
   a. aprender algo nuevo.
   b. ver un episodio de *Sol y viento.*
2. Vamos a...
   a. tomar un examen.
   b. trabajar en grupos.
3. Vamos a...
   a. hablar y escuchar mucho.
   b. leer un **Vistazo cultural.**

Paso 2 Now answer the following questions about your class, depending on what you know. Report your answers to the class. Does everyone agree?

1. ¿Van (Uds.) a tomar un examen final? ¿Cuándo?
2. ¿Van a escribir una composición? ¿Cuándo?
3. ¿Van a necesitar más/otros libros para la clase de español el próximo semestre/trimestre?
4. ¿Cuántos episodios de *Sol y viento* van a ver este semestre/trimestre?

Actividad G Lo que (*What*) voy a hacer esta noche

Think about what you are going to do tonight and mark a check next to any items from the list that apply to you. Then find different people who are going to do the same things as you and write their names in the appropriate spaces. Can you find someone different for each item? Note: The last item is for you to fill in your own activity.

MODELO: E1: ¿Vas a estudiar con un amigo? [E1 *has this item checked off*]
E2: No. Voy a estudiar a solas (*alone*). [E1 *does not write the name down.*]
E1: ¿Vas a estudiar con un amigo?
E3: Sí. [E1 *writes the person's name down.*]

1. ☐ Voy a estudiar con un amigo (una amiga).   _____
2. ☐ Voy a llamar a mi familia por teléfono.   _____
3. ☐ Voy a escribir algo.   _____
4. ☐ Voy a leer algo.   _____
5. ☐ Voy a salir (*go out*) con mis amigos.   _____
6. ☐ Voy a correr.   _____
7. ☐ Voy a _____.   _____

OUTPUT

Act. H, *Paso 1,*
Suggestion: Allow
about 6 minutes
for students to
interview and be
interviewed.
Suggested alternative:
Alter instructions so that
students have to
interview 3–4 people.
Their conclusions in *Paso
2* might then be compara-
tive.
Paso 2, **Suggested
follow-up:** Select 2
students to present what
they find. But first, model
for class. *Bueno. Susie
tiene planes muy fijos. Va
a comprar un auto nuevo
el próximo año. Va a ter-
minar los estudios en dos
años. También va a hacer
un viaje a Nueva York el
próximo verano,* etc.

Actividad H En el futuro

Paso 1   Review the expressions in the **Más vocabulario** section on p. 60. Then interview someone about his or her future plans. Jot down what he or she says. Here are some questions to ask.

1. ¿Cuándo vas a terminar (*finish*) los estudios en la universidad?
2. ¿Cuándo vas a hacer tu próximo viaje (*take your next trip*)? ¿Adónde vas?
3. ¿Cuándo vas a comprar (*buy*) un auto nuevo?
4. ¿Cuándo vas a ver una película en el cine (*movie theater*)?

Paso 2   Based on how the person responded, which of the following seems true for that person? Be prepared to present your findings to the class.

☐ Tiene muchos planes fijos (*fixed plans*).
☐ Tiene unos planes fijos.
☐ No tiene planes fijos.

▲ ¿Cuándo van a ir a la viña «Sol y viento» Jaime y Mario? ¿Qué van a hacer allí (*do there*)?

NAVEGANDO LA RED ⌇⌇⌇⌇⌇⌇⌇⌇⌇⌇⌇⌇⌇⌇⌇

Find a Spanish-speaking country's tourism website and report on the average weather conditions for each of the four seasons. Report on whether it mentions a rainy season or not. (Remember that the seasons in the northern hemisphere are reversed from those in the southern hemisphere.)

TERCERA PARTE

Note: These vocabulary items can be heard in this lesson's Textbook Audio section of the Online Learning Center Website.

Describing
Personalities

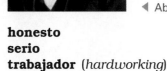

Vocabulario

Es un hombre serio.

Adjectives*

La personalidad

◀ Abraham Lincoln

honesto
serio
trabajador (*hardworking*)

◀ Robin Williams

cómico
enérgico
caótico

Note: The list of words presented on these two pages may seem daunting to students. Point out that nearly half (43%) are very close cognates (for example, *cómico, caótico, ambicioso*) and that students just need to work on pronunciation. Tell them that a good way to work on this vocabulary is to study it by associating it with famous people, as on this page. Suggest that they list a famous man or character (we are limited to masculine nouns for the time being) and find the traits on the list and write them below the name, saying the word out loud. For example, *Yoda* (*de* Star Wars): *humilde, sabio, serio.*

◀ Salvador Dalí

excéntrico
extrovertido
egoísta

◀ Bill Gates

ambicioso
astuto
cerebral

◀ Thomas Edison

inteligente
creador (*creative*)
imaginativo

◀ Don Quijote

soñador (*dreamer*)
sencillo (*simple*)
confiado (*confident*)

*In this section, you will just describe males for now. In the next **Gramática** section, you will learn about adjective placement and agreement and about describing females.

MÁS VOCABULARIO

aburrido (*boring*)	frente a (*versus*)	**interesante, estimulante** o **divertido** (*fun*)
alegre (*happy*)	frente a	**triste** (*sad*)
apasionado (*passionate*)	frente a	**indiferente**
arrogante	frente a	**humilde** (*humble*)
calmado	frente a	**explosivo**
conservador	frente a	**liberal**
caótico	frente a	**metódico, organizado, preciso**
discreto	frente a	**indiscreto** o **chismoso** (*gossipy*)
gregario	frente a	**introvertido, tímido, reservado**
leal (*loyal*)	frente a	**desleal**
malicioso	frente a	**simpático** (*nice*), **agradable** (*pleasant*)
pesimista	frente a	**optimista**
sabio (*wise*)	frente a	**ingenuo** (*naive*)
sospechoso, desconfiado (*untrusting*)	frente a	**confiado**
tonto (*dumb, foolish*)	frente a	**listo** (*clever*)
era	he/she was	
parece ser	he/she seems to be	

COMUNICACIÓN ÚTIL

You can use adjectives with **qué** to express either surprise or a reaction to how extreme something or someone is.

    ¡Qué interesante!   How interesting!

    ¡Qué desconfiado!   How untrusting!

¿Qué adjetivos describen a estos personajes (*these characters*) de *Sol y viento*? ¿Cómo es Jaime? ¿y Mario? ¿y Carlos?

INPUT

Act. A, Statements:
1. *Es cómico y pes-imista.*
2. *Es serio y muy honesto.* 3. *Es conservador y religioso.*
4. *Es excéntrico, pero tímido e introvertido.*
5. *Era metódico y apasionado, pero también malicioso y cruel.*
Suggested follow-up: Select an adjective and see what male celebrity or public figure students associate with that adjective. Example: You say *astuto,* students might say *General MacArthur* or *Yoda.* Do 3 or 4.

INPUT

Act. B, Note: If you are unfamiliar with the film characters mentioned in the activity, select some others with which you are familiar, using the same adjectives mentioned.

OUTPUT

Act. C, Suggestion: Allow about 5 minutes for students to work in pairs. Then, have at least 3 pairs present their ideas to the class. Ask if the class agrees. Ask if they know someone (famous or not) in which those two traits go together: *¿Están de acuerdo? Nombren un hombre famoso que es X y también Y. ¿Conocen a algún hombre que no es así?*

Actividad A ¿De quién hablamos?

Listen as your instructor describes some well-known men. Select the person you think is being described. Note: You may hear some new adjectives, but they are cognates, and you should be able to deduce their meanings.

1. **a.** Harrison Ford
    (b.) Woody Allen
    c. Mark Wahlberg
2. **(a.)** Harry Potter
    b. Elmer Fudd
    c. Darth Vader
3. **a.** Ralph Nader
    b. Bill Clinton
    (c.) Pat Robertson
4. **a.** David Letterman
    (b.) Prince
    c. Tom Hanks
5. **a.** Franklin D. Roosevelt
    (b.) Adolph Hitler
    c. Winston Churchill

Actividad B ¿Qué adjetivo?

Select the adjectives you think match the personality of each film character.

1. Darth Vader: ¿agradable o malicioso? ¿astuto o tonto?
2. Terminator: ¿calmado o explosivo? ¿apasionado o indiferente?
3. Forrest Gump: ¿sabio o tonto? ¿discreto o indiscreto?
4. Frodo Baggins: ¿arrogante o humilde? ¿pesimista u* optimista?
5. Shrek: ¿listo o ingenuo? ¿organizado o caótico?

Actividad C Dios los cría y ellos se juntan†

The expression **Dios los cría y ellos se juntan** refers to the fact that like tends to group with like ("Birds of a feather flock together"). With a partner, decide which personality traits tend to group together. Come up with at least five pairings. Then share with the class. Note: For the time being, you will have to limit yourselves to talking about men. In the next grammar section you will learn about an important concept in Spanish: adjective agreement of gender and number.

MODELO: El hombre soñador muchas veces (*often*) es ingenuo también.

---

*The word **u** (*or*) is substituted for **o** when the word immediately following it begins with an **o** or **ho**.
†This saying is literally as "God creates them and they get together."

COMUNICACIÓN ÚTIL

To talk about what sign of the zodiac you are, you use the verb **ser.**

—¿Qué signo **eres?**

—¿Yo? **Soy** Acuario. Somos muy cerebrales.

Here are the names of the signs of the zodiac in Spanish:

Capricornio	Tauro	Virgo
Acuario	Géminis	Libra
Piscis	Cáncer	Escorpio
Aries	Leo	Sagitario

Actividad D Personas famosas

Paso 1 In groups of three, select a famous male celebrity, politician, or character from a movie or book. Using the adjectives you have learned so far, describe him in three to four sentences, without mentioning who it is.

MODELO: Este (*This*) hombre es... y... También...

Paso 2 Present your description to the class. Can everyone guess who it is? If not, provide three possibilities for them to choose from.

Vistazo cultural, **Suggestion:** After students read the paragraph, ask several questions about speaking one's mind: *¿Quién no tiene pelos en la lengua? ¿Alguien famoso? ¿Alguien en la clase? Da ejemplos en español o en inglés de cosas que dice una persona que no tiene pelos en la lengua.* Students should not confuse the concept with such things as swearing or cursing. Instead, the idea is that people are frank, don't hold back on opinions, ask questions they have on their minds, maybe offer advice that's unsolicited. So, students should offer examples in these kinds of categories.

 # Vistazo cultural

La personalidad y la cultura

It is often said that people from various regions display certain characteristics. These trait descriptions may not necessarily be true. However, sometimes stereotypes are a matter of degree: We may all be hardworking people, but perhaps one group is even more so. For example, the stereotype of people from Great Britain is that they are reserved, whereas the typical American is considered to be much more outgoing or simply less reserved. In the Spanish-speaking world, various regions also carry stereotypes. People from Spain are often said to be more outspoken and less guarded in what they say compared to those from Latin America, the U.S., and other places where Spanish is spoken. In fact, there is an expression used to describe this: **no tener pelos en la lengua** (lit.: *to not have hairs on your tongue*). What this expression means is that people will say what they are thinking or feeling. As one example, although we might not want to comment on someone's recent weight gain or appearance, it would not be unusual for someone in Spain to do exactly that. A relative or friend might say right to your face, **¡Hombre! ¡Qué gordo estás! ¿Qué te pasa?** (*Man! You're fat! What's going on?*). Again, this does not mean that every Spaniard would be so frank with others, nor does it mean that there aren't people in other parts of the Spanish-speaking world who are equally frank. But perhaps there is a grain of truth in the statement that the typical Spaniard **no tiene pelos en la lengua.**

Gramática

More on Describing People

Es una mujer seria.   Adjective Placement and Agreement

As you may know, adjectives are words used to describe people, places, things, and ideas: *intelligent woman, wise old man.* Spanish is a language in which verbs must not only agree with subjects, but adjectives must also agree with the noun or pronoun they modify. This means that they must agree in gender and number, just as articles (**el, la, los, las**) do. Also note the following.

- Agreement is relatively straightforward with adjectives that end in **-o.** Change the **-o** to **-a** for agreement with a feminine noun and add **-s** if the noun is plural. However, not all adjectives end in **-o.** For example, adjectives that end in **-e** do not change the vowel to **-a.** And most that end in **-l** do not add an **-a,** but do add **-es** if the noun is plural.

- However, adjectives that end in **-r** (and other consonants) do add an **-a** for agreement with feminine nouns. Adjectives ending in **-ista** do not mark gender, just number.

The preceding explanation is summarized in the chart. Here are some additional points regarding adjective use.

- Adjectives normally follow the noun they modify.

  un **libro cómico**   una **mujer trabajadora**

- The adjectives **bueno** and **malo** can appear before nouns, but they are shortened in the masculine form.

  Es un **chico** muy **bueno.**   Es muy **buen chico.**

  Es una **chica** muy **buena.**   Es muy **buena chica.**

  Es un **administrador malo.**   Es **mal administrador.**

  Es una **administradora mala.**   Es **mala administradora.**

- The adjectives **grande** and **pobre** (*poor*) can be placed in front of nouns, but the meaning for each changes. Note that **grande** shortens to **gran** when placed in front of a noun, whether masculine or feminine.

  un **señor grande** (**grande** = physical stature)

  un **gran señor,** una **gran mujer** (**gran** = great)

  un **chico pobre** (**pobre** = broke, without money)

  un **pobre chico** (**pobre** = unfortunate)

- The words **alguien** (*someone*) and **persona** are masculine and feminine, respectively. When using adjectives with these nouns, remember that the adjective modifies these words and not a particular person you have in mind.

  alguien simpátic**o**

  una **persona** simpátic**a**

  Juan es una **persona** gregaria, pero no muy trabajador**a.**

- When gender is mixed (that is, men and women), use masculine agreement.

  Héctor y Mariela son muy **serios,** pero también son **simpáticos.**

NOUN AND ADJECTIVE AGREEMENT		
	MASCULINO	FEMENINO
para los adjetivos que terminan en -*o*		
singular	un señor ambicios**o**	una mujer ambicios**a**
plural	unos señores ambicios**os**	unas mujeres ambicios**as**
para los adjetivos que terminan en -*e*		
singular	un señor inteligent**e**	una mujer inteligent**e**
plural	unos señores inteligent**es**	unas mujeres inteligent**es**
para los adjetivos que terminan en -*l*		
singular	un señor libera**l**	una mujer libera**l**
plural	unos señores libera**les**	unas mujeres libera**les**
para los adjetivos que terminan en -*r*		
singular	un señor conservado**r**	una mujer conservado**ra**
plural	unos señores conservado**res**	unas mujeres conservado**ras**
para los adjetivos que terminan en -*ista*		
singular	un señor pesim**ista**	una mujer pesim**ista**
plural	unos señores pesim**istas**	unas mujeres pesim**istas**

De *Sol y viento,* **Note:** You can access this film clip from a special menu section on Disc 5 of the Instructional Version on DVD.

DE SOL Y VIENTO

At one point in **Episodio 1,** Mario implies that he knows Jaime's desired destination well:

> MARIO
> ¿Valle del Maipo? ¡Fantástico! Muy, muy
> _____. A propósito: me llamo Mario
> Verdejo. «Verdejín» para mis amigos.

Do you remember the word that Mario used to describe the valley?

1. lindo
2. grande
3. turístico

Actividad E ¿Qué tipo de mujer necesita Jaime?

By now you have a first impression of Jaime, but did you know he's single? What kind of person would be a good match for him? Number the descriptive adjectives in the order of importance you think they would be for him (**1** = most important, **5** = least important). Then share with the class.

Jaime necesita una mujer...

a. ＿＿ activa y enérgica.
b. ＿＿ inteligente y ambiciosa.
c. ＿＿ seria y trabajadora.
d. ＿＿ apasionada y confiada.
e. ＿＿ honesta y discreta.

Actividad F Mujeres famosas

For each person or persons listed, select the description you think fits. More than one may be possible. In some cases, none may fit!

1. Hillary Clinton
  a. Es ambiciosa.
  b. Es conservadora.
  c. Es honesta.
2. Madonna
  a. Es extrovertida.
  b. Es creadora.
  c. Es humilde.
3. Oprah Winfrey
  a. Es cerebral.
  b. Es trabajadora.
  c. Es organizada.
4. Madame Curie
  a. Era inteligente.
  b. Era imaginativa.
  c. Era caótica.
5. Paris Hilton y Nicole Richie
  a. Son gregarias.
  b. Son enérgicas.
  c. Son cerebrales.

6. Salma Hayek y Jennifer López
  a. Son inteligentes y listas.
  b. Son confiadas.
  c. Son cómicas.
7. Joan y Melissa Rivers
  a. Son cómicas.
  b. Son chismosas.
  c. Son discretas.

¡Exprésate!

To indicate that someone is *very, fairly,* or *not very* (*adjective*), use **muy, bastante,** and **poco,** respectively. To say *just a little* (*adjective*), use **un poco.**

• Miguel es **muy activo.**

• Tonya es **poco liberal.**

• Mis amigos son **bastante conservadores.**

• La profesora es **un poco generosa** con las notas (*grades*), ¿no?

Actividad G   Parejas (*Couples*) famosas

Paso 1 With a partner, select two famous couples. Then describe them as a couple, using at least two adjectives each.

MODELO: Bill y Melinda Gates son generosos y astutos.

Paso 2 Various groups should present their couples' names to the class. The class should use adjectives to describe them. Does everyone use the same adjectives as you and your partner?

Actividad H   ¿Cómo somos?

Paso 1 From the adjectives you've learned so far, select five that you think describe you (or don't!) and write out five sentences.

MODELOS: Soy bastante organizado.
Soy poco optimista.

Paso 2 Get together with another classmate and read him or her each adjective without revealing the sentences that you wrote. Can the other person deduce what you have said about yourself? Afterward, rate the person on the following scale (remembering that you have been in class together for only several weeks).

MODELO: E1: organizado, optimista.
E2: Eres organizado y optimista.
E1: Sí, soy organizado, pero no soy muy optimista.

Mi compañero/a es...

☐ muy observador(a).

☐ bastante observador(a).

☐ observador(a).

☐ poco observador(a).

Esta mujer es muy trabajadora y bastante organizada.

SOL Y VIENTO

A segunda vista

Antes de ver el episodio

Actividad A ¿Qué recuerdas?

Based on what you remember from the previous viewing of **Episodio 1**, determine whether Jaime, Mario, or Carlos said each of the lines below. You will be asked to verify your answers when you watch the episode again.

		JAIME	MARIO	CARLOS
1.	«Soy mi propio jefe.»	☐	☑	☐
2.	«¿A cuánto sale?»	☑	☐	☐
3.	«Son 10.000 (diez mil) pesos, señor.»	☐	☑	☐
4.	«¿Adónde desea ir?»	☐	☑	☐
5.	«Sí, claro que hablo español.»	☑	☐	☐
6.	«Lo espero mañana.»	☐	☐	☑

Act. B, Suggestion: Have students read the exchange before watching the episode. They do not need to write anything at this point. Do not reveal answers.
Alternative: Have the class brainstorm possible answers for each blank but do not have them write anything down.

Actividad B ¡A escuchar! (*Let's listen!*)

In a moment you will watch **Episodio 1** once again. But first, familiarize yourself with the following excerpt from the episode in which Jaime calls Carlos at the winery. You will be asked to listen closely and write the missing words in the blanks. Do not look back at any previous excerpts from this episode!

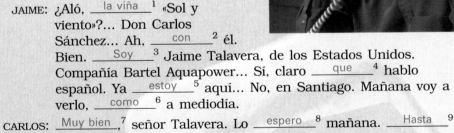

JAIME: ¿Aló, __la viña__ ¹ «Sol y viento»?... Don Carlos Sánchez... Ah, __con__ ² él. Bien. __Soy__ ³ Jaime Talavera, de los Estados Unidos. Compañía Bartel Aquapower... Sí, claro __que__ ⁴ hablo español. Ya __estoy__ ⁵ aquí... No, en Santiago. Mañana voy a verlo, __como__ ⁶ a mediodía.

CARLOS: __Muy bien__,⁷ señor Talavera. Lo __espero__ ⁸ mañana. __Hasta__ ⁹ entonces. Chau.

Actividad C El episodio

Now watch the episode again. Don't forget to verify your answers to **Actividad A** as you watch. Also remember to pay close attention to the scene in which Jaime calls Carlos on the phone and to write down the missing words for **Actividad B**.

Después de ver el episodio

Actividad A Para pensar... (*Something to think about . . .*)

Offer your opinion in English on the following questions. In later chapters you'll be able to offer such opinions in Spanish.

1. How would you describe Carlos' expression at the end of the episode?
2. Why does he have this expression?

Hint: Keep in mind the boardroom scene from the **Prólogo** when the three men discuss the situation in Chile.

If you need to, watch this scene again and see if you can determine anything by the way Carlos talks as well.

Actividad B ¡A verificar! (*Let's verify!*)

Listen as your instructor replays the scene from **¡A escuchar!** on the previous page. Fill in the missing information based on what you hear.

Actividad C ¿Cómo es Carlos Sánchez?

Paso 1 Although you have only seen Carlos Sánchez in a small portion of **Episodio 1,** you may have a few first impressions about him. The photo at the bottom of the page is from an upcoming episode. Does it give you any more ideas about Carlos? Using some of the adjectives you know, describe Carlos in a few brief sentences.

Paso 2 Share your descriptions with two other people. Decide what you all agree on and present your descriptions to the class. Does everyone else agree?

Act. B, Suggestion: Replay the scene once for students. Replay a second time if needed. Then ask for volunteers to provide answers for each blank. Verify using the instructor notes from *Act. B* on the previous page. **Alternative:** After students complete the conversation, have 2 students act it out.

Detrás de la cámara

Mario seems eager to help Jaime at the airport and even boasts by saying that he is **el mejor** (*best*) **chofer de Chile.** If you've taken cabs in this country, you may think he is overly zealous. But Mario is typical of many cab drivers in other countries who hustle to earn a living. Mario works hard to help support a wife and children. He spots Jaime coming out of the airport terminal and realizes, "This could be a good gig." He also knows that business travelers like Jaime often tip well.

RESUMEN DE VOCABULARIO

Verbos

abrir	to open
aprender	to learn
asistir (a)	to attend (*a class*)
beber	to drink
comer	to eat
comprender	to understand
correr	to run
creer (que)	to think, believe (that)
escribir	to write
ir (*irreg.*)	to go
ir a + *infin.*	to be going to (*do something*)
leer	to read
recibir	to receive
tomar el sol	to sunbathe
ver (*irreg.*)	to see; to watch
vivir	to live

Los meses y las estaciones del año

enero, febrero, marzo, abril, mayo, junio, julio, agosto, septiembre, octubre, noviembre, diciembre

el invierno	winter
el otoño	autumn
la primavera	spring
el verano	summer

Para hablar del tiempo

Está despejado.	It's clear.
Está nublado.	It's cloudy.
Hace buen/mal tiempo.	It's good/bad weather.
Hace (mucho) calor.	It's (very) hot.
Hace fresco.	It's cool.
Hace (mucho) frío.	It's (very) cold.
Hace sol.	It's sunny.
Hace (mucho) viento.	It's (very) windy.
Llueve. / Está lloviendo.	It's raining.
Nieva. / Está nevando.	It's snowing.

Para describir la personalidad

aburrido/a	boring
agradable	pleasant
alegre	happy
apasionado/a	passionate
chismoso/a	gossipy
confiado/a	confident
creador(a)	creative
desconfiado/a	untrusting
desleal	disloyal
divertido/a	fun
enérgico/a	energetic
gregario/a	gregarious
humilde	humble
ingenuo/a	naive
leal	loyal
listo/a	clever
sabio/a	wise
sencillo/a	simple
simpático/a	nice
soñador(a)	dreamer
sospechoso/a	untrusting
tonto/a	dumb, foolish
trabajador(a)	hardworking
triste	sad

era	he/she was
parece ser	he/she seems to be

Cognados: ambicioso/a, arrogante, astuto/a, calmado/a, caótico/a, cerebral, cómico/a, conservador(a), discreto/a, egoísta, estimulante, excéntrico/a, explosivo/a, extrovertido/a, honesto/a, imaginativo/a, indiferente, indiscreto/a, inteligente, interesante, introvertido/a, liberal, malicioso/a, metódico/a, optimista, organizado/a, pesimista, preciso/a, reservado/a, serio/a, tímido/a

Las palabras interrogativas

¿Adónde?	Where (*to*)?
¿Cómo?	How? What?
¿Cuál(es)?	Which?
¿Cuándo?	When?
¿Cuánto/a/os/as?	How much? How many?
¿Dónde?	Where?
¿Por qué?	Why?
¿Qué?	What?
¿Quién(es)?	Who? Whom?

Otras palabras y expresiones

alguien	someone, anyone
el año	year
la novela	novel
el periódico	newspaper
la persona	person
la revista	magazine

bueno/a (buen)	good
grande (gran)	large, big; great
malo/a (mal)	bad
otro/a	other, another
pobre	poor; unfortunate
próximo/a	next

a solas	alone
bastante	rather
dentro de poco	soon

en unos (cuantos) días	in a few days
esta noche	tonight
mañana	tomorrow
pasado mañana	the day after tomorrow
poco (*adv.*)	not very
un poco	a little
la semana entrante	next week
una vez al mes	once a month

a	to
entre	between
para	for
porque	because

Repaso (*Review*): **con, de, muy, pero**

lo que	what, that which
si	if

Entremés cultural
México: Nuestro vecino al sur[a]

VISTAZO

México tiene mucho en común con los Estados Unidos (EE.UU.), su vecino al norte.[b] Una nación de muchos contrastes, México está dividido en 31 (treinta y un) estados y un distrito federal (México, D.F.). En el oeste[c] de México corren[d] la Sierra Madre Occidental y la Sierra Madre del Sur, extensiones de la gran cordillera[e] del oeste de los EE.UU. —las Montañas Rocosas. El clima varía mucho. En el lado[f] pacífico, predomina un clima templado,[g] pero en el este[h] predomina un clima tropical, sobre todo[i] en los estados de Veracruz, Tabasco, Campeche, Yucatán y Quintana Roo. En el centro, el clima es más árido y en Durango y Sonora existen grandes desiertos que continúan en los estados de California, Arizona y Nuevo México.

[a]Nuestro... *Our neighbor to the south* [b]*north* [c]*west* [d]*extend* [e]*mountain range* [f]*side* [g]*moderate* [h]*east* [i]sobre... *above all*

DATO[a] INTERESANTE:
México, D.F.

La Ciudad[b] de México (México, D.F.), la capital, es una de las ciudades más grandes[c] del mundo.[d] Su población sobrepasa[e] 20 millones de personas. También tiene la distinción de ser la ciudad capital más alta[f] del mundo a unos 7.300 (siete mil trescientos) pies sobre el mar.[g]

> **IDEA:** Busca información sobre la Ciudad de México, concentrándote en los siguientes[h] temas: el transporte, los problemas urbanos como la contaminación,[i] atracciones turísticas y cualquier[j] otro tema. Trae[k] la información a la clase.

[a]*Fact* [b]*City* [c]más... *largest* [d]*world* [e]*exceeds* [f]más... *highest* [g]pies... *feet above sea level* [h]*following* [i]*pollution* [j]*any* [k]*Bring*

México, D.F.

DATO INTERESANTE:
Las lenguas indígenasª

En México se hablan[b] más de 62 (sesenta y dos) lenguas diferentes, como el náhuatl (lengua de los aztecas), el maya, el zapoteco, el mixteco, el otomí y muchas más. Para muchos de los hablantes[c] de estas lenguas, el español es una segunda[d] lengua y la educación bilingüe es un asunto[e] socio-político de mucha importancia en el país.[f]

IDEA: Como clase, decidan si las lenguas indígenas de los Estados Unidos tienen tanta importancia como[g] las de México hoy en día.[h] ¿Qué información necesitan Uds. para hacer esta comparación?

[a]lenguas... *indigenous (native) languages* [b]se... *are spoken*
[c]*speakers* [d]*second* [e]*matter* [f]*country* [g]tanta... *as much importance as* [h]hoy... *nowadays*

Benito Juárez es el único (*only*) presidente mexicano de ascendencia (*heritage*) indígena.

Estos niños (*These children*) de ascendencia (*heritage*) indígena reciben instrucción especial en español.

DATO INTERESTANTE:
El gobiernoª

México tiene un gobierno democrático con un congreso, un presidente, y una rama[b] judicial. El presidente de México sirve[c] por seis años —lo que se llama un sexenio— y no puede servir[d] más de una vez. Así que,[e] cada seis años los mexicanos eligen[f] un presidente diferente.

IDEA: Haz[g] una tabla comparando el gobierno mexicano con el gobierno de este país. Pon en letra azul las semejanzas[h] y en letra roja[i] los contrastes. Debes incluir por lo menos[j] cinco puntos de comparación.

[a]*government* [b]*branch* [c]*serves* [d]no... (*the president*) *can't serve* [e]Así... *Thus* [f]*elect* [g]*Make* [h]Pon... *Put the similarities in blue lettering* [i]*red* [j]por... *at least*

DATO INTERESANTE:
Las diferencias regionales

Hay mucha variación de cultura y tradiciones que se refleja[a] en las costumbres[b] locales. Así que la gente[c] de Sonora, la gente de Veracruz y la gente de Oaxaca muestran[d] diferencias en su artesanía[e] y gastronomía.[f]

IDEA: Busca información sobre la comida[g] regional en México. Por ejemplo, ¿hay diferencias entre la comida típica de Veracruz y la de[h] Jalisco?

[a]se... *is reflected* [b]*customs, traditions* [c]*people* [d]*display* [e]*arts and crafts* [f]*gastronomy, food* [g]*food* [h]la... *that of*

Los chapulines fritos (*fried grasshoppers*) es un plato (*dish*) regional de Oaxaca.

El encuentro^a

En este episodio...

JAIME

¡Le pido mil disculpas! Andaba distraído.

MUCHACHO

El señor estaba leyendo el papelito de la suerte.

MARÍA

Ah. Debe ser una suerte excepcional.

JAIME

Bueno, no sé. «El amor es un torbellino.»

¿Qué crees tú?

1. ¿Quién es María?
2. ¿Cómo se conocen Jaime y María (*do Jaime and María meet*), probablemente?
3. ¿Estás de acuerdo (*Do you agree*) con la suerte?

JAIME: I'm so sorry! I wasn't paying attention to where I was going. BOY: Mister was reading the little fortune. MARÍA: Oh. It must be a very special fortune. JAIME: Well, I don't know. "Love is a whirlwind."

^a*El... The Encounter*

En la universidad y la ciudad

2A

IN THIS LESSON, YOU WILL LEARN:

- the numbers 31–100 and how to express age

- more on talking about activities using verbs that end in **-go** (**yo** forms, present tense)

- prepositions of location to express where things and places are

- more on expressing location and actions using the verb **estar**

- names of places in a university and city

- more on talking about activities using stem-changing verbs

In addition, you will prepare for and watch **Episodio 2** of the film *Sol y viento*.

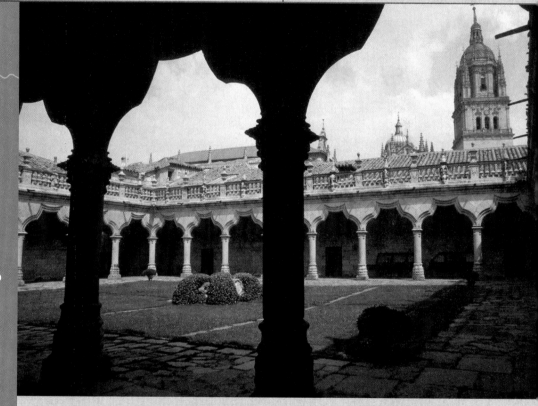

La Universidad de Salamanca (España) es una de las más antiguas (*oldest*) y más importantes de Europa.

The following media resources are available with this lesson of *Sol y viento*:

Episodio 2 of *Sol y viento*

Online *Manual de actividades*

Online Learning Center Website

PRIMERA PARTE

Vocabulario

Note: These vocabulary items can be heard in this lesson's Textbook Audio section of the Online Learning Center Website.

¿Cuántos años tiene? Numbers 31–100

In **Lección 1A** you learned that most numbers between 16 and 29 are combinations of two numbers but are generally spelled as one. For example, you learned that **veintiséis** is actually **veinte y seis.** For numbers 31–99, the numbers are written separately: **cuarenta y dos, cincuenta y tres,** and so forth.

Los números 31–100

31 treinta y uno	37 treinta y siete	70 setenta
32 treinta y dos	38 treinta y ocho	80 ochenta
33 treinta y tres	39 treinta y nueve	90 noventa
34 treinta y cuatro	40 cuarenta	100 cien
35 treinta y cinco	50 cincuenta	
36 treinta y seis	60 sesenta	

✳ MÁS VOCABULARIO

la edad	age
¿Cuántos años tienes?	How old are you?
Tengo… años.	I am . . . years old.
¿Cuántos años tiene… ?	How old is . . . ?

ANTONIO: ¡Feliz cumpleaños (*Happy birthday*), papá! **¿Cuántos años tienes?**

JOSÉ LUIS: **Cincuenta y dos.**

ANTONIO: ¡Uy! ¡Qué viejo (*old*) eres!

JOSÉ LUIS: Pero, recuerda (*remember*): ¡todavía soy más fuerte (*stronger*) y más guapo (*more handsome*) que tú!

Vistazo cultural, **Suggestion:** Ask students questions about the life expectancy table, such as: *¿En qué país(es) es de _____ años la esperanza de vida para los hombres / las mujeres?* and *¿Cuál es la esperanza de vida en _____ para los hombres / las mujeres?* As a follow-up ask: *En general, ¿quiénes viven más años, los hombres o las mujeres?*

 # Vistazo cultural

La esperanza de vida[a] en los países[b] hispanohablantes

How long can people from different countries expect to live? The following table shows the life expectancies for women and men in Spanish-speaking countries. What trends do you notice?

PAÍS	ESPERANZA DE VIDA (AÑOS)		PAÍS	ESPERANZA DE VIDA (AÑOS)	
	MUJERES	HOMBRES		MUJERES	HOMBRES
la Argentina	78	71	la Guinea Ecuatorial	44	43
Bolivia	66	62	Honduras	70	66
Chile	81	75	México	77	72
Colombia	75	69	Nicaragua	72	67
Costa Rica	81	76	Panamá	77	72
Cuba	79	75	el Paraguay	73	69
el Ecuador	77	71	el Perú	72	67
El Salvador	74	68	Puerto Rico	80	72
España	83	76	la República Dominicana	71	64
los Estados Unidos	80	75	el Uruguay	79	72
Guatemala	71	63	Venezuela	76	70

Source: United Nations Statistics, 2005.

[a]La... *Life expectancy* [b]*countries*

INPUT/OUTPUT
Act. B,
Suggestions:
Paso 1: Point out that in English we say "Is he that old?" but in Spanish the equivalent would be "Does he have that many years?" Read the following statements once. To remind students of certain characters (such as the Machi and Andy), you may wish to direct their attention to the photos on pages 14–15.
1. *La machi tiene 72 años.*
2. *María tiene 46 años.*
3. *Mario tiene 38 años.*
4. *Jaime tiene 32 años.*
5. *Carlos Sánchez tiene 89 años.*
6. *Diego tiene 75 años.*
7. *Andy tiene 40 años.*
Paso 2: Give students 1–2 minutes to decide if the statements are correct or not. Call on a variety of students to express their opinions about the ages of the people mentioned. Whenever they answer *No,...* either provide more possible ages until the students think the age is about right or have students (cont. p. 83)

¡Exprésate!

To say that someone is between certain ages, is approximately a certain age, or is older or younger than a certain age, Spanish uses the following expressions.

- **tiene entre veinte y treinta años** (*between 20 and 30*)
- **tiene aproximadamente cincuenta años** (*approximately 50*)
- **tiene más/menos de cuarenta años** (*older/younger than 40*)

Actividad A ¿Qué número es?

INPUT
Act. A, Statements: 1. *cincuenta y tres* 2. *ochenta y uno* 3. *sesenta y cuatro* 4. *treinta y nueve* 5. *cuarenta y seis* 6. *noventa y dos* 7. *setenta y cinco*

Listen as your instructor says some numbers. Write down what you hear.

1. _53_ **2.** _81_ **3.** _64_ **4.** _39_ **5.** _46_ **6.** _92_ **7.** _75_

Actividad B ¿Tienen tantos (*so many*) años?

Paso 1 Listen as your instructor gives you the approximate ages of various characters from *Sol y viento*, then jot down the names and the ages that you hear.

			CREO QUE SÍ.	NO, TIENE MÁS AÑOS.	NO, NO TIENE TANTOS AÑOS.
1. La machi	tiene	72 años.	☑	☐	☐
2. María	tiene	46 años.	☐	☐	☑
3. Mario	tiene	38 años.	☐	☑	☐
4. Jaime	tiene	32 años.	☑	☐	☐
5. Carlos Sánchez	tiene	89 años.	☐	☐	☑
6. Diego	tiene	75 años.	☐	☐	☑
7. Andy	tiene	40 años.	☑	☐	☐

Paso 2 Now decide whether you think the age of each person is correct by selecting the appropriate column for each, listed in **Paso 1.** If you disagreed with your instructor, how old do you think the person is?

Actividad C ¿Edades típicas?

Paso 1 Decide whether you think the ages shown are typical or not for the following events.

En tu opinión, ¿es típico en este país...

	SÍ	NO
1. casarse (*to get married*) a los treinta años?	☐	☐
2. graduarse (*to graduate*) de la universidad a los veintitrés años?	☐	☐
3. vivir hasta los noventa y cinco años?	☐	☐
4. tener el primer hijo (*child*) a los veintiún años?	☐	☐
5. tener nietos (*grandchildren*) a los cuarenta y seis años?	☐	☐
6. jubilarse (*to retire*) a los cincuenta y cinco años?	☐	☐

Paso 2 If you checked "no" for any of the above items, write out in Spanish the age that you think is typical for that event.

Paso 3 Compare your answers with those of three other classmates. Do you all agree about what are typical ages for those events? Be prepared to share your answers with the class.

MODELO: Creemos que es típico casarse a los treinta años.

Actividad D ¿Cuántos años tienen?

Paso 1 Fill out the **yo** line of the chart below for yourself, then indicate the ages of your parents and grandparents. If someone has died, you may either write the age that person would be today or write **ya murió** (*he/she already died*).

NOMBRE	EDAD DE LA MADRE (*mother*)	EDAD DEL PADRE (*father*)	EDAD DE LA(S) ABUELA(S) (*grandmother[s]*)	EDAD DEL ABUELO / DE LOS ABUELOS (*grandfather[s]*)
yo				
(compañero/a 1)				
(compañero/a 2)				
(compañero/a 3)				

Paso 2 Now complete the chart by talking with three other classmates.

MODELO: E1: ¿Cuántos años tiene tu _____?
E2: Tiene _____ años.

Paso 3 Based on the information you gathered, calculate the following average ages. Be prepared to share your answer with the class.

la edad media (*average age*) de las madres _____
la edad media de los padres _____
la edad media de las abuelas _____
la edad media de los abuelos _____

En general, ¿son mayores (*older*) las mujeres (las madres y las abuelas) o los hombres (los padres y los abuelos)?

Paso 4 Compare the average age of your parents and grandparents with those of your classmates. Then prepare one statement based on the clues below that describes the age of either your parents or your grandparents.

Mi _____ tiene una edad típica.
Mi _____ es joven (*young*) en comparación con (los/las _____) de mis compañeros.
Mi _____ es viejo/a (*old*) en comparación con (los/las _____) de mis compañeros.

Margin notes

come up with an appropriate age. **Suggested follow-up:** Have students come up with 3 true or false statements about the ages of different famous people. In groups of 3–4, they can share their statements and have the other members of the group decide if they agree (*Creo que sí*), or not (*No, tiene más / no tiene tantos años. Creo que tiene... años.*).

INPUT/OUTPUT
Act. C, *Paso 3,* **Suggested follow-up:** Find out if there are items about which students are not in agreement for typical ages and ask yes/no questions to find out why. For example: *¿Depende de la salud* (health) *de una persona? ¿Depende de donde vive una persona?* etc.

OUTPUT
Act. D, Suggestions:
Paso 1: Allow about 1 minute for students to complete.
Paso 2: Model questions if necessary, e.g.: *¿Cuántos años tiene tu madre?* Allow students about 5 minutes to complete.
Paso 3: Ask several groups the average ages they show in their charts, to find out if each group had more or less the same average, and also if the men or the women in the family are older.
Paso 4: Call on a variety of students to share their statements. If students respond that the age of a family member is typical, ask how old the family member is and see if the class agrees whether the age is typical or not.

Gramática

More on Talking
About Activities

Vengo de los Estados Unidos.   **Verbs that End in -go**

✳

A number of common verbs in Spanish end in **-go** in the first-person singular (**yo**). Among these are **hacer** (*to do; to make*), **poner** (*to put, place*), **salir** (*to leave; to go out*), **traer** (*to bring*). The rest of the verb forms follow the normal pattern of using the stem of the infinitive. Other verbs also end in **-go** in the **yo** form, but they have changes in the stem of some forms. Pay careful attention to the pattern of these *stem-changing verbs.*

VERBS THAT END IN *-go*
hacer (*to do; to make*): ha**go**, haces, hace, hace, hacemos, hacéis, hacen, hacen
poner (*to put, place*): pon**go**, pones, pone, pone, ponemos, ponéis, ponen, ponen
salir (*to leave; to go out*): sal**go**, sales, sale, sale, salimos, salís, salen, salen
traer (*to bring*): tra**igo***, traes, trae, trae, traemos, traéis, traen, traen

venir (*to come*) e → ie		tener (*to have*) e → ie	
ven**go**	venimos	ten**go**	tenemos
vienes	venís	tienes	tenéis
viene	vienen	tiene	tienen
viene	vienen	tiene	tienen

oír (*to hear*) i → y		decir (*to say; to tell*) e → i	
oi**go**	oímos	di**go**	decimos
oyes	oís	dices	decís
oye	oyen	dice	dicen
oye	oyen	dice	dicen

*Note that the **yo** form of **traer** contains another irregularity: An **i** is added as part of the stem: **traigo.**

De *Sol y viento,* Note: You can access this film clip from a special menu section on Disc 5 of the Instructional Version on DVD.

DE SOL Y VIENTO

In **Episodio 2** of *Sol y viento* you will watch a scene in which Jaime meets María, an anthropologist at a local university. Part of their exchange appears in the dialogue.

JAIME
¡Perdón! Soy Jaime Talavera. **Vengo** de los Estados Unidos.

MARÍA
Encantada. _____... señor Talavera. ¿O prefiere «Míster Talavera»?

JAIME
Prefiero «Jaime». Y ojalá que nos veamos de nuevo.[a]

Selecting from the following list, what do you think María says in the missing phrase?

1. Yo vengo del Perú.
2. Tengo que irme (*I have to leave*).
3. Tengo ganas de (*I feel like*) visitar los Estados Unidos.

[a]ojalá... *I hope that we see each other again*

***Enfoque lingüístico,* Point out:** Other similarities: *old = alt, years = Jahre* (English-German), similar word for *years* in Romance languages. Word order is also similar within each language group.

Enfoque lingüístico

¿*Tener* años?

You may wonder why Spanish uses the verb **tener** (*to have*) to express age (***Tengo diecioucho años***), whereas English uses *to be* (*I am* eighteen years old). The literal translation is, of course, *I have eighteen years.* Spanish is not the only language that does this. Other Romance languages (languages that have evolved from Latin) also use the verb *to have* to express age, including Catalan, Italian, French, and Portuguese. Although English has some Latin influences, English belongs to a family of Germanic languages. Modern German also comes from this same language family, and both English and German use the verb *to be* to express age. Look at the translations of *I am eighteen years old* in these languages, and see if you can notice other similarities among languages in the same family in addition to the use of *to have* or *to be.*

Spanish	**Tengo diecioucho años.**	Portuguese	**Tenho dezoito anos.**
Catalan	**Tinc divuit anys.**	English	**I am eighteen years old.**
French	**J'ai dix-huit ans.**	German	**Ich bin achtzehn Jahre alt.**
Italian	**Ho diciotto anni.**		

INPUT
Act. E,
Statements:
1. *Sale con Mario para el Valle del Maipo.* 2. *Tiene un auto.* 3. *Dice que es el mejor chofer de Chile.* 4. *Viene de los Estados Unidos.* 5. *Dice que un artefacto es muy lindo.* 6. *Tiene que ir a la viña «Sol y viento».*

Actividad E ¿Quién es?

Listen as your instructor reads statements about the characters from *Sol y viento* pictured below. Then match each statement with the appropriate character.

▲ **a.** Jaime

▲ **b.** María

▲ **c.** Mario

1. _a_ **2.** _c_ **3.** _c_ **4.** _a_ **5.** _b_ **6.** _a_

INPUT
Act. F, Statements:
1. *Vengo de un país africano donde hablamos español. Vengo de...*
2. *Vengo de un país muy pequeño en Centroamérica. Vengo de...*
3. *Vengo de un país que ahora no es muy amigo de los Estados Unidos. Vengo de...* 4. *Vengo de un país sudamericano donde hablamos portugués; no hablamos español. Vengo de...* 5. *Vengo de un país donde hace mucho calor en los meses de diciembre, enero y febrero, pero hace mucho frío en los meses de junio, julio y agosto. Vengo de...*

INPUT/OUTPUT
Actividad G

Actividad F ¿De dónde vengo?

Listen as your instructor reads statements made by students from various Spanish-speaking countries. Then decide where you think each one comes from.

1. (**a.**) la Guinea Ecuatorial **b.** Bolivia **c.** España
2. (**a.**) El Salvador **b.** México **c.** Bolivia
3. **a.** el Perú (**b.**) Cuba **c.** el Ecuador
4. **a.** el Uruguay **b.** Nicaragua (**c.**) el Brasil
5. **a.** México **b.** Venezuela (**c.**) la Argentina

Actividad G ¿Con qué frecuencia?

Paso 1 Indicate the frequency with which you do the following activities related to your Spanish class.

	SIEMPRE (*always*)	MUCHAS VECES	A VECES	NUNCA (*never*)
1. Vengo a la clase de español preparado/a.	☐	☐	☐	☐
2. Salgo de la clase de español confundido/a (*confused*).	☐	☐	☐	☐
3. Hago la tarea (*homework*) para la clase de español.	☐	☐	☐	☐
4. Oigo a mi profesor(a) y comprendo bien lo que dice.	☐	☐	☐	☐
5. Traigo comida (*food*) a la clase.	☐	☐	☐	☐

¡Exprésate!

Note the following common expressions with the verb **tener.**

• **tener que** + *infin.* = to have to (*do something*)
Tengo que hacer más ejercicio.

• **tener ganas de** + *infin.* = to feel like (*doing something*)
No tengo ganas de estudiar más.

	SIEMPRE (*always*)	MUCHAS VECES	A VECES	NUNCA (*never*)
6. Pongo mucho esfuerzo (*effort*) en aprender español.	☐	☐	☐	☐
7. Tengo que estudiar mucho.	☐	☐	☐	☐
8. Tengo ganas de asistir a clase.	☐	☐	☐	☐
9. Le digo a mi profesor(a): «No comprendo» o «Repita, por favor».	☐	☐	☐	☐

Paso 2 In groups of three or four, compare your answers. Do you all agree? Find at least two statements that you agree on and present them to the class. **¡OJO!** (*Watch out! Be careful!*) Be sure to use the **nosotros** form of the verb.

MODELO: Ponemos mucho esfuerzo en aprender español.

Actividad H ¿Qué haces?

Paso 1 Here is a list of activities. Use it to prepare at least five questions for another student to answer. Come up with at least one question about an activity that is not listed.

- hacer ejercicio (*to exercise*) en el gimnasio
- hacer la tarea en la biblioteca
- salir a los bares los fines de semana
- salir a las discotecas los fines de semana
- oír música mientras (*while*) estudias
- traer amigos a la habitación (*room*) (a casa, al apartamento)
- poner muy alto el volumen (*to turn up the volume a lot*) de la música
- tener fiestas en la habitación (la casa, el apartamento)
- decir secretos de otros amigos
- ¿ ?

Paso 2 Interview two different classmates using the questions you prepared. Be sure to note their answers.

Paso 3 How would you answer the questions you posed to your classmates, and how similar are you to the two classmates you interviewed? Write a short paragraph comparing the three of you. Here are some statements to help you.

MODELOS: (Nombre 1) y (Nombre 2) son muy parecidos/as (*similar*) en cuanto a (*regarding*) salir a los bares los fines de semana. Los/Las dos salen...

(Nombre 1), (Nombre 2) y yo somos muy parecidos/as en cuanto a... Los/Las tres (*The three of us*)...

Mis compañeros y yo somos (muy) diferentes en cuanto a...

Act. H,
Suggestion: As a follow-up, have students ask you 10 questions about what you do. Indicate whether to use the *tú* or *Ud.* form. After you answer their 10 questions, you may wish to give students a brief *cierto/falso* quiz to see if they were listening to your answers.

Vocabulario

Expressing Where
Things and Places
Are Located

¿Está lejos o cerca?

Prepositions of Location

Note: These
vocabulary items
can be heard in
this lesson's Textbook
Audio section of the Online
Learning Center Website.

1. El reloj está **en** la pared (*wall*).
2. Los estudiantes están **alrededor de** la profesora.
3. Los libros de la profesora están **encima del** escritorio.
4. Los libros del estudiante están **debajo de** la silla.
5. El escritorio está **entre** la profesora y la pizarra.
6. El lápiz está **al lado del** bolígrafo.
7. La profesora está **delante del** escritorio.

✳ MÁS VOCABULARIO

a la izquierda de	to the left of
a la derecha de	to the right of
cerca de	close to
detrás de	behind
enfrente de	across from; in front of
lejos de	far from
al norte de	to the north of
al sur de	to the south of
al este de	to the east of
al oeste de	to the west of

Here is a list of common places in a university, including ones that you have already seen in the **Lección preliminar**:

el bar	bar
la biblioteca	library
la cafetería	cafeteria
la capilla	chapel
el centro estudiantil	student center/union
el edificio de (ciencias, lenguas extranjeras)	(science, foreign languages) building
el estadio	stadium
el gimnasio	gym
la habitación	(dorm) room
la librería	bookstore
la residencia estudiantil	residence hall, dormitory
la torre	tower

Vistazo cultural

Las universidades en el mundo hispano

If you spend any time at a university in a Spanish-speaking country, you will notice a number of differences from universities in this country. First, many public universities in Spanish-speaking countries are not residential. In other words, the students do not live in university dormitories or housing, and there are no fraternities or sororities. If students attend universities close to home (usually less than an hour away), it is not uncommon for them to live at home and commute using public transportation. If the university is far from home, many students have to find housing on their own. Some may rent a room from a family; others may look for an apartment with other students. Because university students live "off campus," it is rare to have meal plans or to find a dining hall, as in many schools in North America.

Another difference is that students in most universities in Spanish-speaking countries take classes in their specialty only. Students apply to a particular **facultad** or *school* such as **derecho** (*law*), **bellas artes** (*fine arts*), **medicina, filosofía y letras** (*humanities*), or **ciencias naturales** or **sociales,** and take classes within that **facultad** only. There are usually no general education requirements, given that most students have already taken these in their final years of high school.

An additional difference is that there are no university-sponsored athletic teams on campus. Although sports are extremely popular (especially soccer), athletes belong to local club teams instead. If your college or university has study abroad programs with universities in Spanish-speaking countries, consider spending a summer, semester, or year abroad!

INPUT

Act. A, Statements: Remind students that they should answer from the perspective of the "X" on the map ("*Ud. está aquí*").
1. *La capilla está detrás de las oficinas de administración.* (*cierto*) 2. *La facultad de filosofía y letras está a la derecha de la biblioteca.* (*falso; está a la izquierda de la biblioteca*)
3. *La biblioteca está detrás del centro estudiantil.* (*falso; está enfrente del centro estudiantil*) 4. *La facultad de ciencias naturales está al lado de la facultad de filosofía y letras.* (*falso; está lejos de la facultad de filosofía y letras*) 5. *La librería está a la derecha de las oficinas de administración.* (*cierto*) 6. *La torre está entre*

Actividad A ¿Cierto o falso?

Listen as your instructor describes where places are on the following campus map. Indicate whether the description is true or not.

    1. ...   **2.** ...   **3.** ...   **4.** ...   **5.** ...   **6.** ...   **7.** ...

LA UNIVERSIDAD DE LAS AMÉRICAS

las facultades de filosofía y letras y ciencias sociales. (*falso; está entre la facultad de filosofía y letras y la biblioteca*)
7. *La facultad de medicina está a la izquierda de la capilla.* (*cierto*)

INPUT

Act. B, Suggestion: Use a variety of prepositions to describe places on campus or in your town/city using the vocabulary on pp. 88–89.

Actividad B ¿Dónde estás?

Your instructor will describe a location on your campus or in your town/city using prepositions of place but will not tell you what that place is. Based on your instructor's description, write down the name of the location.

    1. ...   **2.** ...   **3.** ...   **4.** ...   **5.** ...   **6.** ...   **7.** ...

OUTPUT

Act. C, *Paso 2,* **Suggestion:** Model a false statement for the students and have them come up with the correct location of the object.

Actividad C Una prueba (*quiz*)

Paso 1 Using the items on page 88 as a guide, write a five-item true/false quiz with the locations of five stationary objects in your classroom, using a preposition of location for each.

Paso 2 With a classmate, take turns reading your statements to each other. If you hear a statement and think it is false, provide the correct location of the classroom object.

OUTPUT
Actividad D

Actividad D ¡Te toca a ti!

Paso 1 Now it's your turn to describe the location of places in and around your campus. Write five questions that ask about a particular location, including the point of reference.

MODELO: Estás enfrente del gimnasio. ¿Qué edificio está a la derecha del gimnasio?

Paso 2 In groups of three, take turns reading your questions to each other. Each of you should write down the building that each question describes.

Paso 3 Now each group should read the statements again to check to see if everyone wrote down correct answers.

◀ La biblioteca de la Universidad Nacional Autónoma de México (UNAM) en México, D.F.

Enfoque cultural, **Optional:** Have students do a Web search for information on Chapultepec Park and Central Park (New York). Then have them bring information to class in order to compare and contrast these 2 parks.

SOL Y VIENTO: Enfoque cultural

City parks abound in Spanish-speaking countries, as they do in this country, but they are often used in different ways. In **Episodio 2** you will watch Jaime as he jogs through the Parque Forestal in Santiago. However, using a public park as a place to exercise is not the norm for most Spanish-speaking people. Instead, parks are often places to socialize, and on Sundays they may flourish with couples and families of all ages out for an old-fashioned Sunday afternoon stroll (**el paseo**). It is also typical to find vendors of all types in these parks selling everything from cotton candy to balloons, as well as entertainers working for donations, such as the organ-grinding fortune teller with his parrot that you will see in this episode. Some well-known parks in Spanish-speaking cities include the Retiro (Madrid), Lazema (Buenos Aires), and Chapultepec (Mexico City), among others.

▲ El parque Chapultepec (México, D.F.)

Gramática

Talking about
Location and What
People Are Doing

¿Dónde estás y qué estás haciendo?   **Two Uses of estar**

You have already seen one use of **estar,** which is to express the location of objects and people.

Jaime **está** en Santiago.	*Jaime is in Santiago.*
El auto de Mario **está** en frente del hotel.	*Mario's car is in front of the hotel.*

You have also previously seen how the simple present tense in Spanish can be used to convey the meaning of *-ing* in English, as in the following examples.

Mario **espera** a Jaime.	*Mario is waiting for Jaime.*
Jaime **corre** en el parque.	*Jaime is running in the park.*

These same meanings can be conveyed by **estar** when used with a special verb construction called the *present progressive.* The progressive is formed for most verbs by dropping the **-ar, -er,** and **-ir** of infinitive forms and adding **-ando** for **-ar** verbs and **-iendo** for **-er** and **-ir** verbs.

Mario **está esperando** a Jaime.	*Mario is waiting for Jaime.*
Jaime **está corriendo** en el parque.	*Jaime is running in the park.*

For **-er** and **-ir** verbs whose stems end in a vowel (e.g., **leer** → **le-, construir** [*to construct*] → **constru-**) the **i** of **-iendo** is changed to a **y** to keep from having three vowels together.*

María **está leyendo** un libro de antropología.

Están construyendo una nueva casa.

Depending on the dialect of Spanish, you may hear or read more simple present tense verbs to express the concept of *be* + *-ing* as opposed to **estar** + **-ndo.**

✳ **MÁS GRAMÁTICA**

Unlike English *-ing* verb forms, **-ndo** forms can never be the subjects of sentences. Instead, Spanish uses a corresponding noun or an infinitive.

Running is good for your health.	**Correr** es bueno para la salud.
Skiing is a good winter sport.	**El esquí** es un buen deporte para el invierno.

---

*You will learn other irregularities with progressive verb forms in future lessons.

TWO USES OF *estar*	
to express the location of people, objects, and places	
Juan **está** aquí.	*Juan is here.*
El perro **está** en la casa.	*The dog is in the house.*
México, D.F., **está** en el interior del país.	*Mexico City is in the interior of the country.*
to express an action in progress, similar *to be* + *-ing* in English	
Jaime **está** conversando con María.	*Jaime is conversing with María.*
Mario **está leyendo** el periódico.	*Mario is reading the newspaper.*

De *Sol y viento,* **Note:** You can access this film clip from a special menu section on Disc 5 of the Instructional Version on DVD.

DE SOL Y VIENTO

In **Episodio 2** of *Sol y viento,* you will watch a scene in which María asks Jaime about what he's doing in Santiago. Part of their exchange appears in the following dialogue.

JAIME
¡Qué coincidencia! Para allá voy... al Valle del Maipo, como turista, con mi conductor.[a]

MARÍA
¿Su conductor? ¿Está de vacaciones o tiene negocios[b] en Maipo?

JAIME
Bueno, la verdad es que _____ aquí por placer[c]... y un poco de negocio.

Keeping in mind what you just learned about expressing location, what verb do you think is missing from the dialogue?

(1.) estoy
2. soy

[a]*driver* [b]*business* [c]*por... for pleasure*

Actividad E ¿Dónde están?

Answer these questions with the names of one or more of the following characters.

María   Mario   Jaime

1. En este episodio, ¿quiénes están delante del Hotel Bonaparte?
2. Al principio (*At the beginning*) de este episodio, ¿quiénes están en el Parque Forestal?
3. ¿Quién está siempre cerca de su auto?
4. En el **Episodio 1,** ¿quiénes están en la recepción del Hotel Bonaparte?

Actividad F ¿Cierto o falso?

Paso 1 Listen as your instructor describes the location of various places on campus and around the city. Indicate whether each description is true or not.

1. ...   2. ...   3. ...   4. ...   5. ...   6. ...   7. ...

Paso 2 With a partner, make statements about where places are located in your city or on your campus. Use **estar** plus the prepositions of locations you have learned in this lesson. Can your partner determine whether your statements are true or false?

MODELO: E1: La biblioteca municipal está en la calle State, al lado de McDonald's.
           E2: Falso. Sí, está en la calle State, pero está al lado del Banco Chase.

Actividad G ¿Qué están haciendo?

Paso 1 Match each item in column A with the corresponding phrase from column B.

A	B
1. __d__ Cuando Jaime llega al aeropuerto de Santiago...	**a.** él está trabajando en su oficina en la viña.
2. __a__ Cuando Jaime llama a Carlos Sánchez...	**b.** muchas personas están caminando (*walking*) en las calles y paseando (*strolling*) en el parque.
3. __b__ Al ir del aeropuerto al hotel Jaime ve que...	**c.** Andy está escuchando y viendo toda la conversación.
4. __c__ Cuando Jaime está hablando con Rassner en la oficina en San Francisco...	**d.** Mario está esperando (*waiting*) a alguien que necesite (*may need*) su servicio de auto.

Paso 2 Imagine that the story of *Sol y viento* is unfolding at this minute. Take turns with a partner describing where you think each of the following characters is at this moment and what he or she is doing. Then share with the class. On what do you base your ideas? Be prepared to give an explanation.

MODELO: El Sr. Rassner está en la oficina en San Francisco. Está conversando con Andy, el colega de Jaime.

Jaime   Mario   Carlos   el recepcionista del hotel   ¿ ?

Actividad H Entrevista

Paso 1 Select someone you would like to work with and develop a series of statements about what he or she is doing at the following times:

9:00 de la mañana   4:00 de la tarde
10:00 de la noche   12:00 (**medianoche**)
12:00 (**mediodía**)

MODELO: A las 10:00 de la noche, Steve está estudiando.

Paso 2 Now interview that person, following the model. Jot down the responses.

MODELO: Son las 10:00 de la noche. ¿Qué estás haciendo?

Paso 3 Turn in your original statements to your instructor, along with your partner's responses in table form like the following. At the end, rate yourself on your guesses.

MIS IDEAS	LO QUE DICE MI COMPAÑERO/A
A las 9:00 de la mañana, …	
A mediodía, …	
A las 4:00 de la tarde, …	
A las 10:00 de la noche, …	
A medianoche, …	

Mi habilidad para adivinar (*to guess*) los hábitos de mi compañero/a:

excelente   muy buena   buena   mala   muy mala

Vocabulario

**Talking About
Where You
Do Things**

Note: These vocabulary items can be heard in this lesson's Textbook Audio section of the Online Learning Center Website.

Tengo que ir al banco.

Places in the City

En el centro^a

^a*downtown*

MÁS VOCABULARIO

las afueras	outskirts, suburbs
el barrio	neighborhood
el cajero automático	ATM machine
la catedral	cathedral
el centro comercial	shopping center, mall
la discoteca	dance club
la estación del tren	train station
el estanco	tobacco stand
el hospital	hospital
el lugar	place
la parada de autobuses	bus stop
el rascacielos	skyscraper
el supermercado	supermarket
la tienda	store, shop

Vistazo cultural,
Suggestion: Have students read the *Vistazo cultural* either for homework or silently to themselves in class. Find out if there are any local small shops like those described in the reading: *¿Hay una panadería cerca de donde vives? ¿Hay una carnicería?* You might also ask about farmers' markets in the area and if there are any what they contain: *¿Hay muchos puestos o pocos puestos en el mercado? ¿Qué productos venden? ¿Hay una carnicería? ¿Prefieren Uds. comprar en los mercados pequeños o en los supermercados?*

Vistazo cultural

Los mercados y supermercados

In this country, it's common to go to a large supermarket even if one only needs a loaf of bread or some milk. In many Spanish-speaking countries, large indoor **supermercados** have become popular only in the last twenty years or so, and they are normally found on the outskirts of cities and towns. In smaller towns and in the center of cities, shoppers usually go to smaller stores or shops (**tiendas**). For example, many people will buy their meat at a local **carnicería** (*butcher shop*), their bread at a **panadería** (*bakery*), and their fruit and vegetables at a **frutería**. In many cities, each neighborhood has a number of each of these smaller stores. This provides a community atmosphere within larger cities. In smaller towns, it's common to see an open-air market (**mercado**). Farmers, bakers, butchers, and artisans travel to different towns within a region and set up a stand (**puesto**) to sell their products one or two days a week. Similar to what has happened in this country, large supermarkets often offer a larger selection of items in one store. Consequently, many smaller, family-owned **tiendas** suffer financially, and some have had to close.

▲ Un mercado típico de Bolivia

INPUT

Act. B, Statements:
1. *A Rebeca le gusta ir de compras y visitar muchas tiendas diferentes. ¿Adónde va?* 2. *A Miguel le gusta mucho comer, pero no come en casa. ¿Dónde come?* 3. *A la familia Ruiz le gusta vivir cerca de la ciudad, pero no en la ciudad. ¿Dónde viven?* 4. *Marcos es muy religioso. ¿Adónde va cada domingo?* 5. *Los viernes, después del trabajo, a Elena le gusta tomar una cerveza y hablar con sus amigos. ¿Adónde va?* 6. *A Eduardo le gusta mucho ver películas. ¿Adónde va?* 7. *Ramón tiene un accidente de auto y está en muy malas condiciones. ¿Adónde necesita ir?* 8. *Isabel necesita 20 dólares para salir a comer con sus amigos. ¿Adónde va?*

Actividad A Lugares en la ciudad

INPUT
Actividad A

Match each city building or location with a name that represents it.

1. __c__ el hotel
2. __e__ el supermercado
3. __g__ el restaurante
4. __a__ la catedral
5. __h__ el almacén
6. __b__ la farmacia
7. __f__ el rascacielos
8. __d__ la tienda

a. St. Patrick's, Notre Dame
b. Walgreens, CVS
c. Holiday Inn, Hilton
d. Abercrombie & Fitch, Gap
e. Winn Dixie, IGA, Safeway
f. Empire State, la Torre de Sears
g. Olive Garden, Pizza Hut
h. Bloomingdale's, Macy's

Actividad B ¿Dónde?

Listen as your instructor describes the activities of different people. Then choose where the activity takes place or where the person needs to go.

1. **a.** al supermercado   **b.** al almacén   **(c.)** al centro comercial
2. **a.** en un hotel   **(b.)** en un restaurante   **c.** en una tienda
3. **a.** en el centro   **b.** en un barrio   **(c.)** en las afueras
4. **a.** a la escuela   **(b.)** a la iglesia   **c.** al cine
5. **(a.)** a un bar   **b.** a un estanco   **c.** a una farmacia
6. **a.** al teatro   **(b.)** al cine   **c.** al almacén
7. **a.** a la farmacia   **b.** a la tienda   **(c.)** al hospital
8. **(a.)** a un cajero automático   **b.** a un bar   **c.** a una tienda

¡Exprésate!

To say that your town or city does not have something, you can say the following:

No hay ningún (cine, centro comercial, hotel, etcétera).

There's not a single... (*masc. noun*).

No hay ninguna (tienda, escuela, etcétera).

There's not a single... (*fem. noun*).

Actividad C Alrededor de tu universidad

Paso 1 What do you know about the town or city in which your university is located? With a partner, review each question and then answer as best you can.

1. ¿Hay un supermercado cerca del campus? ¿Cómo se llama?
2. ¿Cuántos bares hay en el campus o alrededor del campus?
3. ¿Cuántas escuelas secundarias (*high schools*) hay en la ciudad? ¿Cómo se llaman?
4. ¿Dónde queda tu universidad? ¿En una ciudad? ¿en las afueras de una ciudad? ¿en un pueblo?
5. ¿Hay hoteles de lujo (*luxury*) cerca de la universidad? ¿Cómo se llaman?
6. ¿Cuántos cines hay?
7. ¿Cuántos centros comerciales importantes hay en tu ciudad o pueblo?

OUTPUT

Act. C, Suggestion: If your university is located within a large city, limit the scope of students' answers to the immediate neighborhood or "campus town."

Paso 2 Prepare a brief statement to share with the class about the city or town where your university is located.

MODELO: (Nombre de la ciudad o pueblo) es (muy) interesante porque hay...
(Nombre de la ciudad o pueblo) es (un poco) aburrido/a porque no hay...

Actividad D Nuestros lugares preferidos

Paso 1 Complete the following survey by writing down the names of the places that you go to for different things in the city or town where your university is located.

1. Cuando necesito una farmacia, voy a _____.
2. Si tengo que comprar ropa nueva (*buy new clothes*), voy a la tienda de _____.
3. Si deseo tomar unas cervezas, voy al bar de _____.
4. Si voy a la iglesia, voy a _____.
5. Si necesito comprar comida, voy al mercado/supermercado de _____.
6. Cuando deseo comer en un restaurante con mis amigos, normalmente vamos a _____.
7. Si deseo descansar o jugar (*to play*) en un parque voy a _____.
8. Si voy al cine, voy a _____.

Paso 2 With three or four classmates, compare your answers for **Paso 1** and take note of your classmates' answers. Be prepared to share with your instructor the most popular places in your town or city for each of the items in **Paso 1.**

▲ Santiago de Chile es una ciudad con edificios modernos y antiguos (*old*).

NAVEGANDO LA RED

Look for information about a Hispanic university and print out a map of its campus. Briefly describe where the buildings are in relation to others at the university. Is the layout of that campus similar to the layout of your campus?

Gramática

More on Talking
About Activities

Puedo caminar.   **e → ie, o → ue Stem-Changing Verbs**

STEM-CHANGING VERBS (e → ie)					
cerrar (*to close*)		**entender** (*to understand*)		**preferir** (*to prefer*)	
cierro	cerramos	entiendo	entendemos	prefiero	preferimos
cierras	cerráis	entiendes	entendéis	prefieres	preferís
cierra	cierran	entiende	entienden	prefiere	prefieren
cierra	cierran	entiende	entienden	prefiere	prefieren
poder (*to be able, can*)		(o → ue) **dormir** (*to sleep*)		**jugar*** (*to play*)	
puedo	podemos	duermo	dormimos	juego	jugamos
puedes	podéis	duermes	dormís	juegas	jugáis
puede	pueden	duerme	duermen	juega	juegan
puede	pueden	duerme	duermen	juega	juegan

You may recall that the vowel in the stem of the verbs **tener** and **venir** changes from **e** to **ie** in the forms for **tú, Ud./él/ella** and **Uds./ellos/ellas.** In addition to changes in these forms, the following verbs have the same stem change in the **yo** form as well.

Other **e → ie** verbs:

despertarse† (*to wake up*)   **perder** (*to lose*)
empezar (*to begin*)   **querer** (*to want; to love*)
pensar (*to think*)

A number of verbs also have a stem change from **o → ue** in the present tense. Like the **e → ie** stem-changing verbs, these verbs undergo a change in all forms except **nosotros/as** and **vosotros/as.**

Other **o → ue** verbs:

acostarse† (*to go to bed*)   **recordar** (*to remember*)
almorzar (*to eat lunch*)   **soler** + *infin.* (*to be in the habit of*
contar (*to tell; to count*)   [*doing something*])
costar (*to cost*)   **volver** (*to return* [*to a place*])

****Jugar** is the only verb in Spanish that has the **u → ue** stem change.
†**Despertarse** and **acostarse** are called *reflexive* verbs. Note the reflexive pronoun **se** at the end of each. This denotes that an action is being done by someone to him or herself: **me despierto** = *I wake* (*myself*) *up,* **me acuesto** = *I go* (*put myself*) *to bed.* You will learn more about reflexive verbs in **Lección 5A.** For now, just learn to recognize them when you see them.

✳ MÁS GRAMÁTICA

A number of stem-changing verbs take prepositions and/or infinitives to form a variety of useful expressions.

empezar a + *infin.*	to begin to (*do something*)	Manuel **empieza a trabajar** a las nueve.
pensar en	to think about	**Pienso** mucho **en** mi familia.
pensar de	to think of/about	¿Qué **piensas de** la película?
pensar que	to think (that)	**Pienso que** es una buena película.
pensar + *infin.*	to plan, intend to (*do something*)	Alicia **piensa trabajar** en el hospital.
querer + *infin.*	to want to (*do something*)	¿Dónde **quieres comer**?

De *Sol y viento,* Note: You can access this film clip from a special menu section on Disc 5 of the Instructional Version on DVD.

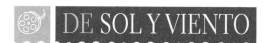 DE SOL Y VIENTO

In **Episodio 2** of *Sol y viento,* you will watch a scene in which Jaime and Mario talk about Jaime's encounter with María. Part of their exchange appears here in the dialogue.

MARIO
¡Bonita la muchacha, don Jaime!

JAIME
Sí, bonita e inteligente… Vayamos a lo nuestro.ª _____ en dos mínutos.

Selecting from the list below, what do you think is the verb that's missing from the dialogue?

1. Duermo
2. Pierdo
3. Vuelvo

ªVayamos… *Let's get back to business.*

INPUT/OUTPUT

Act. E, Suggestions:
Paso 1: Display the following paragraph on overhead or by other means so that all students can see it. Remove it after 1 minute (do not let students memorize the paragraph by giving them too much time).
Alternatively, read the paragraph twice, at slightly less than conversational speed, telling students to pay attention carefully: *Jaime duerme en el Hotel Bonaparte. Se despierta al día siguiente y quiere correr un poco en el parque. Está leyendo algo cuando choca con María. Luego, vuelve al hotel con María y ve a Mario.*
Paso 2: Allow approximately 5 minutes.
Follow-up: Call on one group to present its final version. Ask another group if it has the same wording. Finally, display the original so all groups can compare. Ask a few content questions to keep focus on meaning: *¿Duerme Jaime en el hotel o en la residencia estudiantil? ¿Adónde va con Maria?*, etc. Total time for dictogloss: 15–20 minutes. See the Instructor's Manual for information on dictogloss activities.

Actividad E ¿Qué leíste?

Paso 1 Quickly read the paragraph that your instructor displays to the class. Try to remember as much of the information as possible, but do not take notes.

Vocabulario útil

al día siguiente	the following day
chocar con	to run into
luego	then, next

Paso 2 In groups of three, recreate the paragraph as best as you can remember, writing out a final version to share with the class.

Actividad F ¿A quién describe?

Read the following descriptions and decide what kind of person best fits each description.

1. _____ pierde las cosas con mucha frecuencia y no recuerda dónde están.
   - **a.** Una persona irresponsable
   - **b.** Una persona responsable
   - **c.** Una persona organizada

2. _____ quiere ser muy puntual y hacer buen trabajo.
   - **a.** Una persona sociable
   - **b.** Una persona introvertida
   - **c.** Una persona dedicada

3. _____ prefiere estar a solas todo el tiempo.
   - **a.** Una persona responsable
   - **b.** Una persona introvertida
   - **c.** Una persona extrovertida

4. _____ no piensa nunca (*never*) en las necesidades de otras personas.
   - **a.** Una persona egoísta
   - **b.** Una persona generosa
   - **c.** Una persona sociable

5. _____ juega al basquetbol y al tenis.
   - **a.** Una persona atlética
   - **b.** Una persona artística
   - **c.** Una persona sedentaria

6. _____ suele tener muchos amigos y prefiere pasar mucho tiempo con ellos.
   - **a.** Una persona introvertida
   - **b.** Una persona egoísta
   - **c.** Una persona extrovertida

INPUT

Act. F, Suggestion: Have students choose statements that describe (or don't describe) themselves to share with the class. Have them support their descriptions.
MODELO: *No soy egoísta porque pienso en las necesidades de otras personas.*

Actividad G ¿Con qué frecuencia? INPUT/OUTPUT
Actividad G

Paso 1 When do you do the following activities? (Note: **durante** = *during*, **[casi] nunca** = [*almost*] *never*)

	DURANTE LA SEMANA	DURANTE EL FIN DE SEMANA	TODOS LOS DÍAS	(CASI) NUNCA
1. Vuelvo muy tarde a casa.	☐	☐	☐	☐
2. Duermo hasta mediodia.	☐	☐	☐	☐

	DURANTE LA SEMANA	DURANTE EL FIN DE SEMANA	TODOS LOS DÍAS	(CASI) NUNCA
3. Me despierto a las siete de la mañana o antes.	☐	☐	☐	☐
4. Empiezo las clases a las nueve.	☐	☐	☐	☐
5. Juego al* tenis por la mañana.	☐	☐	☐	☐
6. Me acuesto antes de (*before*) medianoche.	☐	☐	☐	☐
7. Suelo estudiar por la noche.	☐	☐	☐	☐
8. Pienso en mis notas (*grades*).	☐	☐	☐	☐

Paso 2 Compare your answers with those of a classmate. Based on your answers, decide when you are both most active. Use the following clues to help you, and share your answers with the class.

Nosotros/as preferimos... Por ejemplo,...

(Nombre) prefiere... , pero yo no. Por ejemplo,...

Prefiero... , pero (nombre) no. Por ejemplo,...

Actividad H Entrevista

Paso 1 You will be interviewing another classmate about his or her activities. First you need to come up with questions to ask. Use the list of question words and the list of activities to help you write ten questions. Create questions about at least four activities that are not in the list.

MODELO: ¿Dónde prefieres estudiar?

Palabras interrogativas	**Actividades**
¿adónde?	acostarse
¿a qué hora?	despertarse
¿con qué frecuencia?	empezar las clases
¿cuándo?	preferir estudiar
¿dónde?	soler...
	volver a casa (al apartamento, a la residencia)

Paso 2 Using the questions you have prepared, interview someone in the class with whom you have not worked before. Be sure to note his or her answers.

Paso 3 Write a paragraph describing your partner's activities. Include infor-mation about yourself as well so that you can decide how much you have in common.

¡Exprésate!

To ask a friend a question using a verb that ends in *-se*, place **te** directly before the conjugated verb.

¿A qué hora **te despiertas?**

¿A qué hora **te acuestas?**

To answer the question, place **me** directly before the conjugated verb.

Me despierto a las ocho.

Me acuesto a las doce.

To report the information about your partner, place **se** in front of the conjugated verb.

Ángela **se despierta** a las seis.

No **se acuesta** hasta medianoche.

---

*Note that **a** + *definite article* is used with **jugar** when talking about games and sports.

SOL Y VIENTO

A primera vista

Antes de ver el episodio

Actividad A ¿Qué recuerdas?

Indicate whether the following statements are **cierto** or **falso**, based on what you've seen so far in *Sol y viento*.

	CIERTO	FALSO
1. Jaime tiene ganas de ir a Santiago.	☐	☑
2. Jaime ya sabe (*already knows*) mucho de vinos.	☑	☐
3. Mario no puede llevar a Jaime al Valle de Maipo.	☐	☑
4. El hotel donde Jaime se aloja (*is staying*) se llama el Hotel Bonaparte.	☑	☐
5. Jaime necesita hablar con Andrés Sánchez de la viña «Sol y viento».	☐	☑

Act. B, Suggestion: Do not provide answers, as students verify their choices later.

Actividad B ¿Qué falta?

Here is part of the exchange between Jaime, María, and Mario in front of the hotel. Select from the choices to fill in each blank.

MARIO: Buenos días, don Jaime... ¡Lo esperaba!ª

JAIME: Fuiᵇ a _____¹ un poco. Bueno, hasta aquí llego yo. ¿_____² que la llevemosᶜ a algún sitio?

MARÍA: No, gracias. Mi trabajo _____³ cerca de aquí. Puedo _____.⁴

ªLo... *I was waiting for you!* ᵇ*I went* ᶜque... *us to take you*

1. **a.** charlar   **(b.)** correr   **c.** levantar pesas (*lift weights*)
2. **(a.)** Quiere   **b.** Tiene   **c.** Puede
3. **a.** es   **b.** no es   **(c.)** está
4. **(a.)** caminar (*walk*)   **b.** regresar   **c.** descansar

Act. C, Suggestion: Before students watch the episode, have them go over the **De** Sol y viento sections in this lesson to review some of the scenes they will see in the episode.

Actividad C El episodio

Now watch the episode. Don't worry if there are things you don't understand. You should be able to follow most of what happens without understanding every single word. You will watch the episode again in **Lección 2B,** and you will understand more then.

Después de ver el episodio

Actividad A ¿Qué recuerdas?

Answer each question according to what you remember from the episode.

1. ¿Qué ejercicio hace Jaime en el parque?
   - **a.** Juega al fútbol (*soccer*).
   - **(b.)** Corre.
   - **c.** Hace ejercicios aeróbicos.

2. ¿Cuánto cuesta el papelito de la suerte (*little fortune*)?
   - **a.** tres pesos
   - **b.** trece pesos
   - **(c.)** trescientos (300) pesos

3. ¿Cómo sabe (*knows*) Jaime el nombre de María? Lo sabe por (*because of*)...
   - **a.** el papelito de la suerte.
   - **b.** los libros de ella.
   - **(c.)** su tarjeta (*card*).

4. María trabaja en dos lugares: en la universidad y en...
   - **a.** el Hotel Bonaparte.
   - **(b.)** un sitio de excavación.
   - **c.** el Parque Forestal.

5. El papelito dice que _____ es un torbellino (*whirlwind*).
   - **(a.)** el amor
   - **b.** la antropóloga
   - **c.** el tiempo

6. Al final del episodio, ¿quién parece tener más interés en el papelito de la suerte?
   - **a.** Jaime
   - **(b.)** Mario

Actividad B ¿Lo captaste?

Go back to **Actividad B** of **Antes de ver el episodio** to verify your answers. If you need to, watch that particular section of the episode again.

Actividad C Utilizando el contexto

You have already begun to learn the skill of guessing the meaning of language in context. Did you deduce the meanings of the following phrases in italics? Watch this scene between Jaime, the kid (**el muchacho**), and María again if you think it will help.

> JAIME: ¡Le pido mil disculpas! *Andaba distraído.*
> MUCHACHO: El señor *estaba leyendo* el papelito de la suerte.
> MARÍA: Ah. Debe ser una suerte excepcional.

Detrás de la cámara

Although Jaime seems happy while talking with María, have you noticed in these beginning episodes that something seems to be gnawing at him? Is it professional? Or is it something in his personal life? Jaime has had to work hard to arrive where he is professionally, and his work has kept him from having much of a social life. Although he's had a few girlfriends in the past, Jaime has never had a serious relationship. When his friends bug him about settling down, his response is always "When I find someone, I'll know it."

RESUMEN DE VOCABULARIO

Verbos

acostarse (ue)	to go to bed
almorzar (ue)	to eat lunch
cerrar (ie)	to close
contar (ue)	to tell; to count
costar (ue)	to cost
decir (*irreg.*)	to say; to tell
despertarse (ie)	to wake up
dormir (ue)	to sleep
empezar (ie)	to begin
entender (ie)	to understand
hacer (hago)	to do; to make
jugar (ue)	to play (*a sport*)
oír (*irreg.*)	to hear
pensar (ie)	to think
perder (ie)	to lose
poder (ue)	to be able, can
poner (pongo)	to put, place
preferir (ie)	to prefer
querer (ie)	to want; to love
recordar (ue)	to remember
salir (salgo)	to leave; to go out
soler (ue) + *infin.*	to be in the habit of (*doing something*)
tener (*irreg.*)	to have
traer (traigo)	to bring
venir (*irreg.*)	to come
volver (ue)	to return (*to a place*)

Los números del 31 al 100

treinta y uno, treinta y dos…, cuarenta, cincuenta, sesenta, setenta, ochenta, noventa, cien

Lugares en la universidad

la capilla	chapel
el centro estudiantil	student center/union
el estadio	stadium
la habitación	(dorm) room
la torre	tower

Cognados: el bar, el gimnasio
Repaso: la biblioteca, la cafetería, el edificio, la facultad, la librería, la residencia estudiantil

Lugares en la ciudad

las afueras	outskirts, suburbs
el almacén	department store
el barrio	neighborhood
el cajero automático	ATM machine
el centro	downtown
el centro comercial	shopping center, mall
el cine	movie theater
el correo	post office
la escuela	school
el estanco	tobacco stand
la iglesia	church
el mercado	market
la parada de autobuses	bus stop
el rascacielos	skyscraper
la tienda	store, shop

Cognados: el banco, la catedral, la discoteca, la estación del tren, la farmacia, el hospital, el hotel, el parque, la plaza, el restaurante, el supermercado

Preposiciones de lugar

a la derecha de	to the right of
a la izquierda de	to the left of
al lado de	next to
alrededor de	around
cerca de	close to
debajo de	under
delante de	in front of
detrás de	behind
en	on; in
encima de	on top of
enfrente de	across from; in front of
lejos de	far from
al este de	to the east of
al norte de	to the north of
al oeste de	to the west of
al sur de	to the south of

Otras palabras y expresiones

la edad	age
el país	country
la tarea	homework
tener (*irreg.*)… **años**	to be . . . years old

LECCIÓN **2B**

¡Vamos de compras!ᵃ

OBJETIVOS

IN THIS LESSON, YOU WILL LEARN:

- how to talk about what people are wearing
- more about stem-changing verbs in the present tense to talk about what people do
- the numbers 100–1,000
- to use colors to describe clothing
- to describe places and things using demonstrative adjectives and pronouns
- to talk about shopping and making purchases
- more about the verbs **ser** and **estar** to talk about conditions and traits

In addition, you will watch **Episodio 2** of the film *Sol y viento* again.

¿Compras tú la ropa (*Do you buy clothing*) en una tienda elegante como esta (*this one*) en Barcelona, España?

ᵃ¡Vamos... *Let's go shopping!*

The following media resources are available for this lesson of *Sol y viento:*

Episodio 2 of *Sol y viento*

Online *Manual de actividades*

Online Learning Center Website

Note: These vocabulary items can be heard in this lesson's Textbook Audio section of the Online Learning Center Website.

Talking About What
People Wear

Vocabulario

La ropa

Clothing ✳

los pantalones

la gorra

la camisa

la camiseta

la chaqueta

el traje

la corbata

los vaqueros

los calcetines

las sandalias

los zapatos de tenis

✳ **MÁS VOCABULARIO**

llevar	to wear

la sudadera

el suéter

el traje de baño

la blusa

el vestido

el abrigo

la falda

la bolsa

las botas

los pantalones cortos

los zapatos

Vistazo cultural

Diseñadores[a] hispanos

For decades, a number of Hispanic designers have enjoyed international recognition for their elegant, high-end fashion designs. Cristóbal Balenciaga (Spain, 1895–1972) created a world-renowned fashion house in Paris, and his designs continue to enjoy success on both sides of the Atlantic. Venezuelan-born Carolina Herrera and the Dominican Óscar de la Renta have been at the forefront of the U.S. fashion industry for more than two decades. In addition to creating accessory and fragrance lines, both are well-known for creating designs described as both wearable and stylish. More recently, Cuban-American Narciso Rodríguez gained notoriety after designing the wedding gown for Carolyn Bessette Kennedy in 1996. His designs are often worn by famous actresses such as Salma Hayek and Sarah Jessica Parker.

In terms of popular fashion, perhaps the biggest success story is that of the Spanish-born entrepreneur Amancio Ortega. What started out as a small dress-making business in provincial Galicia in the early sixties has turned into an empire of more than one thousand stores worldwide and the third-largest clothing company in the world (after Gap and the Swedish HM). Ortega's flagship store is Zara, which can be found in many Spanish cities, as well as in major cities in Europe, the United States, and Asia.

[a]*Designers*

▲ Carolina Herrera

INPUT
Act. A, Statements:
1. *para ir a la playa*; 2. *para acostarse, para dormir*; 3. *para ir a clase*; 4. *cuando hace mucho frío*; 5. *para ir a una fiesta formal*; 6. *cuando hace mucho calor*; 7. *para ir al gimnasio*
Suggested follow-up: Have students provide other items that should not be worn in each situation named.

¡Exprésate!

You can use the preposition **para** plus an infinitive to express "in order to (*do something*)."

Para comprar ropa de última moda, necesitas mucho dinero.

In order to buy the latest fashions, you need lots of money.

INPUT/OUTPUT
Act. B, *Paso 2,*
Suggestion: Point out to students that they should use indefinite articles (*un, una, unos, unas*) when naming the items of clothing.

Actividad A ¡No lleves eso! (*Don't wear that!*)

Listen as your instructor names an action or a situation. Then choose the article of clothing that a person should *not* wear for that action or situation.

Vocabulario útil

   la playa   the beach

1. a. un traje de baño   b. un sombrero   (c.) unas botas
2. (a.) un traje   b. el pijama (*pajamas*)   c. una camiseta
3. a. una sudadera   b. unos vaqueros   (c.) un traje de baño
4. a. una gorra   (b.) pantalones cortos   c. un abrigo
5. (a.) una sudadera   b. un traje   c. un vestido
6. a. unas sandalias   b. una camiseta   (c.) un suéter
7. a. unos zapatos de tenis   (b.) una falda   c. unos calcetines

Actividad B ¿Qué llevas?

Paso 1 Write down the article(s) of clothing you would wear for each of the following situations.

1. para ir a un concierto de música rock
2. para ir a la playa
3. para ir a las montañas (*mountains*) en el invierno
4. para ir al gimnasio
5. para ir a clase
6. para ir a un restaurante formal
7. para ir a un partido (*game*) de fútbol americano en el otoño

Paso 2 With a partner, take turns saying only the articles of clothing that you would wear for various situations in **Paso 1.** Your partner will have to guess the situation.

MODELO: E1: un traje de baño, una camiseta y unas sandalias
         E2: para ir a la playa

▲ En cada episodio hasta el momento (*up until now*), Jaime lleva ropa diferente. ¿Puedes describir lo que lleva?

Actividad C ¿Qué llevan los compañeros?

Paso 1 Count the number of men and women in the class that are wearing each of the clothing items listed in the chart.

PRENDA DE ROPA (*ARTICLE OF CLOTHING*)	NÚMERO DE HOMBRES	NÚMERO DE MUJERES	TOTAL
vaqueros			
camisetas			
camisas			
zapatos de tenis			
zapatos			
sandalias			
sudaderas			
suéteres			
gorras			
calcetines			
chaquetas			
pantalones			
botas			
¿ ?			
Total			

Paso 2 With a partner, compare your numbers and answer the following questions.

1. ¿Hay un conjunto (*outfit*) típico de los estudiantes? ¿Cuál es?
2. ¿Hay diferencia entre lo que llevan las mujeres y lo que llevan los hombres en la clase? ¿Cuál es la diferencia?

☐ Los hombres llevan más (*more*)/menos (*less*) _____.

☐ Las mujeres llevan más/menos _____.

☐ Los hombres y las mujeres se visten (*dress*) más o menos (*more or less*) igual. Llevan...

NAVEGANDO LA RED

Search for a clothing store in a Spanish-speaking country, and decide what clothes you would buy for yourself with $200. Make sure you know what the exchange rate is between the dollar and the currency of the country in which the store is located.

Gramática

More on Talking About People's Activities

¿Qué dices?  **e → i Stem-Changing Verbs**

In **Lección 2A,** you learned about a number of verbs that undergo a stem change **(e → ie, o → ue)** in all forms except for **nosotros/as** and **vosotros/as.** Instead of changing from **e → ie,** some **-ir** verbs change from **e → i.** You may recall from **Lección 2A** that **decir** is one of these verbs.

PRESENT TENSE OF *e → i* STEM-CHANGING VERBS					
decir (*to say; to tell*)		**repetir** (*to repeat*)		**servir** (*to serve*)	
digo	decimos	repito	repetimos	sirvo	servimos
dices	decís	repites	repetís	sirves	servís
dice	dicen	repite	repiten	sirve	sirven
dice	dicen	repite	repiten	sirve	sirven
pedir (*to ask for; to order*)		**seguir*** (*to follow; to continue*)		**vestir** (*to dress*)	
pido	pedimos	sigo	seguimos	visto	vestimos
pides	pedís	sigues	seguís	vistes	vestís
pide	piden	sigue	siguen	viste	visten
pide	piden	sigue	siguen	viste	visten

COMUNICACIÓN ÚTIL

To say *to get dressed* or *to dress oneself,* use the verb **vestir** with reflexive pronouns, just like the verbs **despertarse** and **acostarse** that you learned in **Lección 2A.** You will learn more about reflexive pronouns and verbs in **Lección 5A.** For now, just learn these common expressions with **vestirse.**

Me visto rápidamente.	*I get dressed quickly.*
¡Vístete!	*Get dressed!*
¿Cómo **nos vestimos?**	*How do/should we dress?*

---

*The **u** in **seguir** is found in all forms except the **yo** form in order to maintain a hard **g** sound.

De *Sol y viento,* **Note:** You can access this film clip from a special menu section on Disc 5 of the Instructional Version on DVD.

DE SOL Y VIENTO

In **Episodio 2** of *Sol y viento,* you will again watch the scene in which Jaime bumps into María while he's reading a fortune. Part of their exchange appears in the dialogue.

JAIME
¡Le _____ mil disculpas!ᵃ Andaba distraído.

MUCHACHO
El señor estaba leyendoᵇ el papelito de la suerte.ᶜ

MARÍA
Ah. Debe ser una suerte excepcional.

Based on the context of the dialogue, select the verb that best completes Jaime's statement.

1. sirvo   2. me visto   3. repito   (4.) pido

ᵃLe... *I'm sorry!* (*lit.: A thousand pardons!*)   ᵇestaba... *was reading*   ᶜfortune

Enfoque lingüístico

Enfoque lingüístico, **Suggestion:** After students read, ask them to think about English and inflections on verbs. Give them the verb *talk* and see how many inflections they can add: *talk, talks, talking, talked.* Note: Some students might say something like *talker.* Tell them that *-er* is not an inflection on a verb but a way of converting a verb into a noun. Once they have thought about English inflections, ask them to make a statement of comparison about Spanish and English verb inflections (example: "Spanish has a much richer set of verb inflections / has many more verb inflections than English"). Then remind them that this is why they have to pay attention to word endings in Spanish.

Más sobre las inflexiones

You may recall that *inflections* are forms that are added to words that provide the listener with certain information. For example, you learned in **Lección 1A** that one way in which Spanish is an inflectionally rich language is that its verb inflections are unique for each person (e.g., *I, you, he/she, we,* and *they*). In the last few lessons, you've learned the present-tense inflections for Spanish **-ar, -er,** and **-ir** verbs. Later in *Sol y viento* you will learn other verb inflections to express various meanings and speaker perspectives. All of the Spanish verb inflections that you will learn are *suffixes;* that is, they are forms that are attached to the *end* of a word or stem. (Remember in **Lección 1A** you read that you will have to get used to listening to the ends of verbs to find out who is being talked about.)

However, not all languages use suffixes for verbal inflections. Some Native American languages like Navajo use *prefixes* (forms attached to the *beginning* of a word or stem). For example, to say *he is going* in Navajo, the prefix **naal** (roughly equivalent to *-ing* used with *is* in English) is added to the stem **nish** (*go*) to form **naalnish.** Instead of prefixes or suffixes, some languages use *infixes,* a form inserted in the *middle* of a word or stem. Tagalog, a language spoken in the Philippines, uses infixes to form commands (i.e., telling someone to do something). For example, to say to someone *Read!,* Tagalog inserts **-um-** after the first consonant of the verb *read,* **basa,** to form **Bumasa!** If you were learning a language like Tagalog, you would have to get used to listening to the middle of verbs to understand different meanings!

INPUT
Actividad D

Actividad D ¿Quién es?

You have already met a number of characters from *Sol y viento*. Can you identify them, based on the descriptions below? Pay close attention to the stem-changing verbs.

▲ Jaime   ▲ María   ▲ Mario   ▲ Carlos   ▲ la machi

1. _____Jaime_____ pide disculpas.
2. _____La machi_____ repite una historia (*tale, story*).
3. _____Jaime_____ se viste con pantalones cortos en el parque.
4. _____Mario_____ dice que es «el mejor (*best*) chofer de Chile».
5. _____Jaime_____ pide una reunion (*meeting*) con Carlos.
6. _____María_____ se viste con una blusa y una chaqueta.

INPUT

Act. E, *Paso 2*, Suggested
follow-up: Obtain point
totals from several
students and write them
on the board under the
headings **hombres** and
mujeres. Then ask the
students *En esta clase,
¿quiénes siguen la moda
más, los hombres o las
mujeres?*

Actividad E ¿Sigues la moda (*fashion*)?

Paso 1 Indicate whether the following statements are true for you (**Sí**), are sometimes true (**A veces**), or not true at all (**No**).

	SÍ	A VECES	NO
1. Leo revistas de moda.	☐	☐	☐
2. Sigo las modas de los diseñadores famosos.	☐	☐	☐
3. Me visto con ropa de marcas (*brand names*) famosas.	☐	☐	☐
4. Pido ropa de ciertas marcas para mi cumpleaños (*birthday*) y otros días festivos (*holidays*).	☐	☐	☐
5. Llevo zapatos de muy buena calidad (*quality*).	☐	☐	☐
6. Compro ropa sólo en ciertas tiendas.	☐	☐	☐
7. Tardo mucho en (*I take a long time to*) vestirme.	☐	☐	☐

Paso 2 Give yourself two points each time you answered **Sí,** one point for **A veces,** and zero for **No,** then add up your total number of points. Based on your total (between 0 and 14), check one of the following statements.

☐ (11–14 puntos) Sigo mucho la moda. No siempre puedo (*I can't always*) comprar ropa de moda, pero me gusta mucho.

☐ (5–10 puntos) A veces sigo la moda.

☐ (0–4 puntos) Casi nunca (*Almost never*) sigo la moda. No me importa para nada. (*It doesn't matter to me at all.*)

Actividad F Acciones típicas

Paso 1 Write five sentences, choosing from the verb phrases below to describe whether the actions are typical for students, professors, or both. Make at least two of your statements false.

MODELO: (*you see*) vestirse de manera formal (*formally*)
           (*you write*) Los estudiantes se visten de manera formal.

    decir que les gustan unas clases más que otras

    decir que van a tomar una clase fácil (*easy*)

    pedir ayuda con la tarea

    pedir ayuda (*help*) con las lecciones

    pedir respuestas (*answers*)

    repetir instrucciones

    seguir instrucciones

    vestirse de manera informal

Paso 2 Take turns reading your statements with a classmate, deciding whether the statements you hear are **cierto** or **falso**.

Actividad G ¿Cómo nos vestimos?

Paso 1 For each of the following situations, state how one should dress. Then, write what you think would be both appropriate and inappropriate for men and women to wear.

MODELO: (*you see*) la clase de español
           (*you write*) Uno se viste con ropa informal.
                         Los hombres pueden llevar... No deben (*They shouldn't*) llevar...
                         Las mujeres pueden llevar... No deben llevar...

1. una fiesta universitaria
2. una entrevista (*interview*) de trabajo
3. la boda (*wedding*) de un miembro de la familia
4. una primera cita (*date*) en _____
5. para ir de compras

Paso 2 Compare your list with three other classmates of the same sex. Do you agree with what they listed? Do you wish to modify or change your list?

Paso 3 Your instructor will ask a member from two men's groups and two women's groups to write their lists on the board. Does one sex dress more formally or informally than the other? Are there different expectations about what men and women expect each other to wear in certain circumstances?

¡Exprésate!

With reflexive verbs, use **uno** to mean *one* as in *one dresses*, as in the following expressions:

Uno se viste...
  con ropa
  (in)formal   (in)formal(ly)

  con ropa
  elegante   elegant(ly)

  con ropa   in comfortable
  cómoda   clothing

  de forma
  atrevida   daringly

SEGUNDA PARTE

Note: These vocabulary items can be heard in this lesson's Textbook Audio section of the Online Learning Center Website.

Vocabulario

More on Describing | **Hay doscientas blusas rojas.**   **Colors; Numbers 100–1,000**

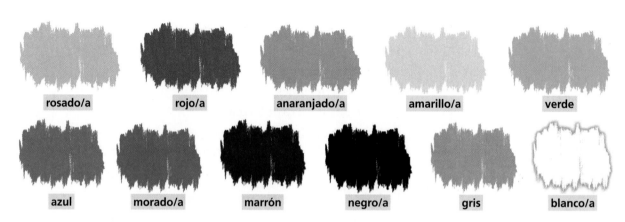

rosado/a   rojo/a   anaranjado/a   amarillo/a   verde

azul   morado/a   marrón   negro/a   gris   blanco/a

Like all adjectives, colors need to agree in gender and number with the noun they modify.

> los vaqueros azul**es**
> las camisas neg**ras**
> la blusa roj**a**

Los números del 100 al 1.000

100 cien	600 seiscientos/as
101 ciento uno/a	700 setecientos/as
200 doscientos/as	800 ochocientos/as
300 trescientos/as	900 novecientos/as
400 cuatrocientos/as	1.000* mil
500 quinientos/as	

When the numbers 200 through 900 modify a noun, they must agree in gender.

> doscient**as** tres personas
> quinient**os** veinte hombres

---

*In Spanish, a decimal point (**punto**) is often used where you would use a comma (**coma**) in English, and vice versa: **$1.000; 64,9%.**

Vistazo cultural

Vistazo cultural, **Point out:** Here are the cultural and historical references for the currencies of some countries: *colón (Cristóbal Colón); euro (la Unión Europea); quetzal (pájaro nacional de Guatemala que se encuentra en las selvas); guaraní (grupo indígena del Paraguay); sol (importante en la cultura incaica); bolívar (Simón Bolívar, libertador de Venezuela y otros países sudamericanos).*

La moneda[a] de los países hispanos

Below is a list of the different currencies of Spanish-speaking countries. You may notice that the currency names of some countries are linked to important historical and/or cultural references. Do you know what they are?

COUNTRY	CURRENCY	COUNTRY	CURRENCY
la Argentina	el peso	Honduras	el lempira
Bolivia	el peso boliviano	México	el nuevo peso
Chile	el peso	Nicaragua	el córdoba
Colombia	el peso	Panamá	el dólar estadounidense
Costa Rica	el colón	el Paraguay	el guaraní
Cuba	el peso	el Perú	el nuevo sol
el Ecuador	el dólar estadounidense	Puerto Rico	el dólar estadounidense
El Salvador	el dólar estadounidense	la República Dominicana	el peso
la Guinea Ecuatorial	el franco	el Uruguay	el peso
España	el euro	Venezuela	el bolívar
Guatemala	el quetzal		

You may have also noticed that a number of countries use the **peso;** however, the value of each country's **peso** is not the same. You may wish to do an Internet search to find out how much your country's unit of currency is worth in some of these countries.

[a]La... *Currency*

INPUT
Act. A, Suggestion:
Read the following
numbers once.
1. *quinientos treinta y
dos* 2. *ciento quince*
3. *setecientos ochenta y
seis* 4. *trescientos
veinticinco* 5. *novecientos
cuatro* 6. *seiscientos
cincuenta y nueve*
7. *cuatrocientos trece*

Actividad A ¿Qué número es?

In the spaces provided, write down each number your instructor reads aloud.

1. ___532___

2. ___115___

3. ___786___

4. ___659___

5. ___904___

6. ___325___

7. ___413___

INPUT/OUTPUT
Actividad B

Actividad B ¿Combinan bien?

Paso 1 Read the following clothing and color combinations. Then decide whether the combination is appropriate or if it depends on the situation.

	SÍ	NO	DEPENDE
1. una camiseta blanca con vaqueros azules	☐	☐	☐
2. un traje verde con una corbata morada	☐	☐	☐
3. unos pantalones negros con calcetines blancos	☐	☐	☐
4. una falda anaranjada sobre (*over*) unos vaqueros azules	☐	☐	☐
5. unas medias (*stockings*) rosadas con una falda negra de cuero (*leather*)	☐	☐	☐
6. unos zapatos negros con un traje negro	☐	☐	☐
7. una camisa de cuadros (*plaid*) con vaqueros azules	☐	☐	☐
8. unos pantalones de rayas (*striped*) con una blusa de lunares (*polka-dotted*)	☐	☐	☐
9. un vestido rojo con zapatos negros de tacón alto (*high-heeled*)	☐	☐	☐

Paso 2 In groups of four, compare your answers. If you all said certain combinations are not acceptable, indicate why. Also, if some of the outfits depend on the situation, for which situations are they acceptable? Use the following cues to help you.

> ¡El _____ (*color*) y el _____ (*color*) nunca combinan bien!
>
> Es una combinación horrible.
>
> Depende de la situación. En _____, está bien.

Paso 3 Report your discussion to the class.

> Creemos que _____ siempre combinan bien, pero _____ no.

OUTPUT
Act. C, Suggestion: You might have students first work out a chart of prices in *pesos* and dollar equivalents based on ten-dollar increments. They can then refer to this during both *pasos,* rather than having to mentally calculate the price of each item.

Actividad C ¿Cuánto cuesta?

Paso 1 First, choose three of the items below and come up with a price in Mexican **pesos** for each one (11 **pesos** equal about one U.S. dollar) to present to the class. You should provide prices that are too expensive (**demasiado caro**), about right (**buen precio**), or a real bargain (**una ganga**).

    una camiseta
    un diccionario
    un disco compacto
    una mochila
    un reloj
    un teléfono celular
    un televisor
    unos zapatos de tenis de marca (*brand*) _____

Paso 2 Listen to the prices that your classmates provide for various items. Be prepared to respond to the prices. If you think something is too expensive, what would be a reasonable price?

MODELO: (*you hear*) Una mochila cuesta cien pesos.
            (*you respond*) ¡Es una ganga!

OUTPUT
Actividad D

Actividad D Una prueba para tu compañero/a

Paso 1 Prepare a quiz consisting of at least five questions about what people are wearing in your class. Use the following model to help you.

MODELO: ¿Quién lleva sandalias marrones, pantalones cortos verdes y camiseta blanca?

Paso 2 With a partner, ask and answer the questions you prepared. A question should only be given once. If one of you needs to hear the question again, you must say **Repite, por favor.**

◀ ¿Qué llevan Mario, María y Jaime en esta (*this*) foto?

Gramática

Pointing
Things Out | **¿Qué es esto?**   **Demonstrative Adjectives and Pronouns**

DEMONSTRATIVE ADJECTIVES				
SINGULAR			PLURAL	
this	**este** suéter **esta** camiseta	*these*	**estos** pantalones	**estas** blusas
that	**ese** suéter **esa** camiseta	*those*	**esos** pantalones	**esas** blusas
that (*over there*)	**aquel** suéter **aquella** camiseta	*those* (*over there*)	**aquellos** pantalones	**aquellas** blusas

DEMONSTRATIVE PRONOUNS			
SINGULAR		PLURAL	
este suéter → **este** esta camiseta → **esta**	*this one*	estos pantalones → **estos** estas blusas → **estas**	*these* (*ones*)
ese suéter → **ese** esa camiseta → **esa**	*that one*	esos pantalones → **esos** esas blusas → **esas**	*these* (*ones*)
aquel suéter → **aquel** aquella camiseta → **aquella**	*that one*	aquellos pantalones → **aquellos** aquellas blusas → **aquellas**	*these* (*ones*)

Demonstrative adjectives are used to point out people and things. As you can see from the chart, they always precede the noun they modify and they agree in gender and number. Forms of **este** (*this/these*) are used to indicate that an object or person is close to the speaker. Unlike English, Spanish has two ways to indicate that something is not close to the speaker. Forms of **ese** (*that/those*) are used to indicate something that is not near the speaker but may be close to the listener. Forms of **aquel** (*that/those* [*over there*]) are used to communicate that something is far away from both the speaker and the listener.

All of the demonstrative adjectives can stand alone as pronouns, but as the chart shows, they must still agree in gender and number with the noun they are replacing. *Demonstrative pronouns* take the place of the person or thing being mentioned in order to avoid repetition.

| ¿Cuál de los dos abrigos quieres, **este** o **ese***? | *Which of the two coats do you want, this one or that one?* |

The neuter demonstrative pronouns (**esto, eso, aquello**) are used to refer to an unspecified object, an idea, or an entire situation:

¿Qué es **esto**?	*What is this (thing/situation)?*
Eso es increíble.	*That (situation) is unbelievable.*
Aquello fue horrible.	*That (situation) was awful.*

---

*Until 1994, demonstrative pronouns were usually written with accents (**éste, ése**) in order to distinguish them from demonstrative adjectives. However, context will generally determine meaning. You may still see accents on these pronouns from time to time, but the nonaccented pronouns will be used in *Sol y viento*.

De *Sol y viento,* **Note:** You can access this film clip from a special menu section on Disc 5 of the Instructional Version on DVD.

DE SOL Y VIENTO

Do you remember the scene from **Episodio 2** of *Sol y viento* in which Jaime returns a business card that María has dropped? Part of their exchange appears in the dialogue.

JAIME
¡Señorita Sánchez!

MARÍA
¿Viene a chocarse conmigo[a] otra vez?

JAIME
Eh, no. Creo que _____ es suyo.[b]

MARÍA
¡Ah! Por eso sabe[c] mi nombre. Si quiere, la guarda.[d]

Selecting from the following list, which demonstrative pronoun belongs in the space above?

1. esto   **2.** eso   **3.** aquello

[a]chocarse... *bump into me* [b]*yours* [c]Por... *That's how you know* [d]la... *you can keep it*

COMUNICACIÓN ÚTIL

In the exchange between Jaime and María, Jaime used the possessive **suyo.** In **Lección 1A** you learned the possessive adjectives **mi, tu, su,** and so forth. Just like demonstrative pronouns, *stressed possessives* (**los posesivos tónicos**) can also take the place of the noun, indicating to whom something belongs.

mío/a/os/as	*mine*	**nuestro/a/os/as**	*ours*
tuyo/a/os/as	*yours*	**vuestro/a/os/as**	*yours*
suyo/a/os/as	*yours (formal); his, hers*	**suyo/a/os/as**	*yours; theirs*
Son mis libros.	Son **míos.**	*They're mine.*	
¿Es tu cartera?	¿Es **tuya?**	*Is it yours?*	
Es nuestro auto.	Es **nuestro.**	*It's ours.*	
Es su casa.	Es **suya.**	*It's yours/his/hers/theirs.*	

INPUT
Actividad E

INPUT

Act. F, Suggestion: Stand at different places in the classroom. Using demonstrative adjectives, come up with about 7 true/false statements describing the clothing items of students. Examples: *Esta sudadera que lleva Sean es gris; Ese suéter que lleva Jennifer es rojo; Aquella camiseta que lleva Mark es de Abercrombie & Fitch;* and so on. Be sure to use all of the demonstrative forms.

INPUT

Act. G, Suggestion: Collect various objects from the students, including bags, caps, jackets, books, shoes, etc., and place them on a desk or table where everyone can see them. Make sure students know to whom the items belong. Also include some of your own items as well. Hold up or point to an item and then point to a person (or yourself) and say: *Este es mío / Estos son suyos* and so on. Be sure to use a variety of both demonstrative pronouns and possessives. Students will respond *sí* or *no* based on whether the object belongs to the indicated person.

OUTPUT

Act. H, Suggestion: Point out that €1 equals about $1.25.
Suggested follow-up: Ask different pairs of students which one of them spends more money and have them report the items they want to buy to the class.

Actividad E ¿Cerca o lejos?

Decide whether Mario, Jaime, or María would say the following statements. Then indicate whether the speaker is talking about something close (**cerca**), far (**lejos**), or even farther away (**muy lejos**).

	SPEAKER	CERCA	LEJOS	MUY LEJOS
1. Este auto es mío.	Mario	☑	☐	☐
2. Creo que esta tarjeta es suya.	Jaime	☑	☐	☐
3. Sí, esa tarjeta es mía.	María	☐	☑	☐
4. Me quedo (*I'm staying*) en aquel hotel.	Jaime	☐	☐	☑
5. Claro que conozco (*Of course I know*) ese lugar. Está cerca de mi trabajo.	María	☐	☑	☐

Actividad F ¿Cierto o falso?

Listen as your instructor points out and describes the clothing your classmates are wearing. Then decide whether the description is correct (**es correcto**) or not (**no es correcto**).

1. ...　　**2.** ...　　**3.** ...　　**4.** ...　　**5.** ...　　**6.** ...　　**7.** ...

Actividad G ¿Es suyo?

Listen as your instructor points out various items and indicates to whom they belong. Then indicate if the statement is true or not by responding **sí** o **no**.

1. ...　　**2.** ...　　**3.** ...　　**4.** ...　　**5.** ...　　**6.** ...　　**7.** ...

COMUNICACIÓN ÚTIL

You can use the words **aquí** (*here*) and **allí** (*there; over there*) to talk about spatial relationships between people, places, and things.

—¿Te gusta esta bolsa blanca que tengo **aquí**?

Do you like this white purse I have here?

—Sí, pero prefiero esa roja en la mesa **allí**.

Yes, but I prefer that red one on the table over there.

Actividad H En la tienda

Look at the items on the tables on the next page. Then, using the appropriate forms of **este** and **ese**, tell a partner three items you would like to buy. Your partner will tell you how much the items cost.

MODELO:　E1: Me gustaría comprar (*I would like to buy*) esta mochila, esa gorra y estos vaqueros. ¿Cuánto cuestan?
　　　　　E2: Ciento noventa euros.

OUTPUT
Actividad I

Actividad I Otra prueba para tu compañero/a

Paso 1 You are going to prepare a true/false quiz for a classmate. First, choose seven different clothing items from the following people: you, someone near you, and someone far from you. Then come up with a true or false statement about each item indicating its color, the brand name, or to whom it belongs. Your partner has to respond with **cierto** or **falso.**

MODELOS: (*for an item you're wearing*) Estos vaqueros son verdes.
(*for an item away from you*) Esos vaqueros son Levis.
(*for an item far away from you*) Aquellos vaqueros son del profesor.

Paso 2 Take turns reading your items to a classmate. When indicating an item, be sure to point to it so that the other person knows exactly what and where it is. Are you able to stump your classmate on any item?

◄
¿Sabes (*Do you know*) de qué material es esta chaqueta que lleva María? Es de pana (*corduroy*).

Vocabulario

Talking About
Buying Things

De compras

Shopping

Note: These
vocabulary items
can be heard in
this lesson's Text-
book Audio section of the
Online Learning Center
Website.

la cliente probarse (ue) el dinero

la tarjeta de crédito

el dependiente

la ganga

las rebajas

20% de descuento

100 pesos

el cliente pagar en efectivo la dependienta

✳ MÁS VOCABULARIO

buscar	to look for	de compras	shopping
comprar	to buy	la marca	brand name
encontrar (ue)	to find	el precio (fijo)	(fixed) price
gastar	to spend	la talla	size
quedar bien/mal	to fit well/poorly	grande	large
regatear	to bargain	mediano/a	medium
vender	to sell	pequeño/a	small
barato/a	inexpensive		
caro/a	expensive		

〰 Vistazo cultural

Los precios y el regateo[a]

Prices in department stores (**almacenes**) and most other shops (**tiendas**) in Spanish-speaking countries are **precios fijos**. However, you will also find **mercados** in Latin America or **rastros** in Spain where you can buy flowers, clothing, furniture, music, souvenirs (**recuerdos**), and even animals. In many of these markets, the prices are not fixed; rather, it is necessary and even expected to bargain (**regatear**) with the salesperson or vendor in

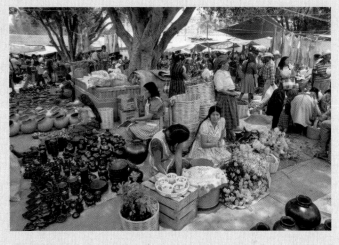

▲ ¿Crees que se puede regatear en este mercado en México?

order to get a good price. If you are unsure whether or not the prices are fixed, you can always ask **¿Son fijos los precios?** If they are not, be prepared to bargain! If you do bargain, a good strategy is to offer a price considerably lower than what you are willing to pay. The vendor will then offer a higher price, and you and the vendor can work out a compromise—you raise your original price a bit and the vendor lowers his or hers. Below is a sample exchange that might be heard in a typical Hispanic market:

CLIENTE
¿Cuánto cuesta esta bolsa?

VENDEDOR
Trescientos pesos.

CLIENTE
¡Ay, no! Es muy cara. Le doy[b] doscientos.

VENDEDOR
¿Cómo? Es muy poco; está hecha a mano.[c] Doscientos setenta y cinco, y es suya.

CLIENTE
Doscientos veinticinco y ya.[d]

VENDEDOR
Déme[e] doscientos cincuenta.

CLIENTE
Bueno. Aquí tiene.[f] Gracias.

Although some tourists find bargaining tiresome, most think it's fun and an excellent way to put their Spanish to use!

[a]el... *bargaining*   [b]Le... *I'll give you*   [c]está... *it's handmade*   [d]*that's it*   [e]*Give me*   [f]Aquí... *Here you are.*

INPUT
Act. A, Statements:
1. la ganga
2. el cliente
3. la marca
4. la tarjeta de crédito
5. el dependiente

Actividad A Descripciones

Listen as your instructor says the name of a person or thing related to shopping. Then write the number of the item mentioned next to the appropriate description.

a. __4__ en vez de (*instead of*) pagar en efectivo uno puede usar esto

b. __2__ la persona que compra algo (*something*)

c. __5__ la persona que trabaja en una tienda

d. __1__ un precio muy barato

e. __3__ muchas veces indica la calidad (¡o el precio!) de algo

INPUT
Actividad B

Actividad B En orden

Imagine that a friend is narrating her account of a trip to a store to buy a pair of jeans. Put her statements in order so that her story makes sense.

__4__ El dependiente tiene que buscar si hay más.

__7__ Me quedan muy bien.

__6__ Me pruebo los vaqueros en el probador.

__1__ Busco la talla que necesito.

__8__ Pago los vaqueros con tarjeta de crédito y me voy a casa.

__3__ Entonces le pregunto (*I ask*) al dependiente si tienen mi talla.

__10__ Tengo que regresar a la tienda para devolver los vaqueros.

__5__ Después de (*After*) unos minutos vuelve con unos vaqueros de mi talla.

__2__ Pero no encuentro mi talla.

__9__ En casa veo que están rotos (*torn*) los vaqueros.

¡Exprésate!

In addition to the expression **tener que** + *infinitive*, the following expressions also take infinitives:

Hay que...	*One must...*
Es buena idea...	*It's a good idea...*
Es necesario...	*It's necessary...*

INPUT
Actividad C

Actividad C ¿Qué hay que hacer? (*What must one do?*)

Match each verb with an appropriate situation.

1. __b__ Si uno quiere un precio más barato, hay que...

2. __d__ Antes de salir de la tienda con algo, es necesario...

3. __e__ Si uno compra algo pero luego le encuentra un defecto (*finds a defect in it*), hay que...

4. __a__ Si uno quiere ver si algo le queda bien o no, es buena idea...

5. __c__ Si una tienda quiere ganar (*earn*) dinero, tiene que... mucho.

a. probárselo*
b. regatear
c. vender
d. pagarlo
e. devolverlo (*return it*)

---

*The **lo** that you see attached to **probarse, pagar,** and **devolver** is a direct object pronoun, meaning *it* in this context. You will learn more about the uses of **lo** and other direct object pronouns in **Lección 3A.**

Actividad D Una historia

Paso 1 With a classmate, write five to eight sentences describing what takes place in the following pictures. Below are a few questions to consider when writing your description.

- ¿Cómo se llama la muchacha y qué quiere comprar?
- ¿Qué busca pero no encuentra?
- ¿Cómo ayuda el dependiente a la chica?
- ¿Qué hace antes de comprar algo?
- Al final, ¿cómo paga?

Paso 2 Share your group's description with the class. How similar or different is your description compared with those of other groups?

Actividad E Entrevista

Paso 1 Using the cues in columns A and B, write down five questions (in addition to the model) to use in an interview with a classmate to find out what kind of shopper he or she is. **¡OJO!** Many of the items in column A go with more than one expression in column B. Also, some questions can be formed without using an item from column A.

MODELO: ¿Cuáles son tus marcas preferidas de ropa?

A	B
¿Adónde... ?	ir de compras
¿Qué... ?	comprar
¿Te gusta... ?	pasar mucho tiempo de compras
¿Cuáles son... ?	gastar mucho dinero
¿Con qué frecuencia... ?	tus marcas preferidas de ropa
¿Dónde... ?	te gusta comprar

Paso 2 Take turns asking and answering the questions that you and a classmate have prepared. Be sure to jot down your classmate's responses.

Paso 3 Based on your classmate's answers, what adjectives from the following list would you choose to describe him or her as a shopper? Be prepared to provide information that would support your conclusions. Would he or she agree?

☐ pragmático/a   ☐ materialista   ☐ compulsivo/a
☐ decidido/a (*decisive*)   ☐ típico/a   ☐ fanático/a
☐ indeciso/a (*indecisive*) ☐ extraño/a (*strange*) ☐ obsesionado/a

Gramática

Está bien.

More on **ser** and **estar**

Up to this point you have been using the verb **ser** with adjectives to describe someone's physical characteristics or his or her personality.

Elena **es** elegante.	*Elena is elegant (by nature).*
Marcos **es** inteligente.	*Marcos is (has always been) intelligent.*

These examples communicate inherent or fundamental qualities of someone or something. To put it another way, they answer the question *What is he/she/it like?* (**¿Cómo es?**)

The verb **estar** can also be used with many adjectives to describe an unexpected change in someone's personality or physical appearance at a given point in time. Note that English often uses verbs other than *to be* to describe these changes.

Elena **está** muy elegante.	*Elena looks very elegant.*
Marcos **está** más delgado.	*Marcos looks (seems) thinner.*

When someone uses **estar** with **delgado/a** or **guapo/a,** the message normally conveyed is that a person looks particularly thin or good-looking at a particular time, not that the person is normally overweight or unattractive. In other words, these statements answer the question *How does she/he look or seem?* (**¿Cómo está?**)

Some adjectives that can be expressed with either **ser** or **estar** have different equivalents in English, depending on which verb is used. When used with **estar,** the meaning of **verde** is *green* as in *unripe.* The chart summarizes some of these common adjectives for you.

 MÁS GRAMÁTICA

Although **bien** is usually translated into English as *well,* when used with the verb **estar** it is usually translated as *to be OK/fine.*

Está bien.	*It's OK. / That's fine.*
Estoy bien, gracias.	*I'm fine, thanks.*
¿Necesitan algo más?	*Do you all need anything else?*
No, gracias. **Estamos bien.**	*No, thank you. We're fine.*

ser AND estar WITH ADJECTIVES	
¿Cómo es? (*What's he/she like?*)	**¿Cómo está?** (*How's he/she doing? / How does he/she look?*)
Es muy guapo. (*He's very good-looking.*)	**Está** muy guapo con ese traje. (*He looks very handsome in that suit.*)
Es seria. (*She's serious / a serious person.*)	**Está** seria hoy. (*She looks/seems serious today.*)
Es delgado. (*He's thin.*)	**Está** más delgado. (*He looks thinner.*)

DIFFERENCES IN MEANING WITH ser AND estar		
ADJECTIVE	WITH **ser**	WITH **estar**
aburrido/a	María **es** aburrida. (*María's boring. [She's a boring person.]*)	María **está** aburrida. (*María's bored.*)
listo/a	**Somos** listos. (*We're smart/clever.*)	**Estamos** listos. (*We're ready.*)
malo/a	**Son** muy malos. (*They're very bad/malicious.*)	**Están** malos. (*They're in bad shape, sick.*)
rico/a	La familia Ruiz **es** muy rica. (*The Ruiz family is very wealthy.*)	La comida **está** rica. (*The food tastes delicious.*)
verde	El suéter **es** verde. (*The sweater is green.*)	El plátano **está** verde. (*The banana is unripe, green.*)

De *Sol y viento,* **Note:** You can access this film clip from a special menu section on Disc 5 of the Instructional Version on DVD.

DE SOL Y VIENTO

In **Episodio 3** of *Sol y viento,* you will watch a scene in which Jaime and Mario arrive in the Valle del Maipo. Part of their exchange appears here.

MARIO
¿Se siente bien,[a] don Jaime? ¿Eh?

JAIME
Sí, Mario. Un recuerdo lejano.[b]

MARIO
Tan[c] serio que _____ ...

JAIME
Nah, no es nada. Vamos.

Selecting from the following list, which verb belongs in the space above?

1. eres   **2.** es   **3.** estás   **4.** está

[a]¿Se... *Do you feel OK*   [b]recuerdo... *distant memory*   [c]*So*

INPUT
Actividad F

Actividad F ¿*Ser* o *estar*?

Complete Jaime's statements with the correct form of **ser** or **estar**.

1. Creo que Santiago (es / está) muy interesante. Me gustaría (*I would like*) pasar más tiempo aquí.
2. Conocí a (*I met*) una mujer que (es / está) bonita e inteligente.
3. (Es / Está) bien, Carlos. Nos vemos (*We'll see each other*) mañana.
4. Mario, ya (soy / estoy) listo. Podemos salir ahora.

INPUT

Act. G, Suggestion:
Before beginning
activity, point out that
students will be listening
for cues that describe
inherent qualities
(*expected*) or temporary
(at a particular moment)
qualities (*unexpected*).
Statements:
1. *Estás muy guapo.*
(*inesperado*) 2. *Los
precios son muy altos.*
(*esperado*) 3. *Es delgado.*
(*esperado*) 4. *¡Qué cara
está la ropa!* (*inesperado*)
5. *Es un poco feo.*
(*esperado*) 6. *Es muy
seria.* (*esperado*)

Actividad G ¿Esperado o inesperado?

Listen as your instructor describes different people and things. Decide whether the description represents something *expected* (**esperado**) or *unexpected* (**inesperado**).

1. ...   2. ...   3. ...   4. ...   5. ...   6. ...

Actividad H ¿Cómo está?

INPUT
Actividad H

Choose the appropriate response to each description.

1. __f__ Esta mañana el profesor lleva un traje muy elegante.
2. __c__ Para Juan, hoy todo es malo.
3. __a__ Mi padre es una persona muy alegre, pero esta mañana no sonríe (*he isn't smiling*).
4. __e__ Marta piensa que va a tener una buena nota (*grade*) en el examen.
5. __b__ Hoy Elena no tiene interés en nada (*anything*).
6. __d__ A Marcos no le gusta estudiar, pero mañana tiene un examen y hoy pasa todo el día en la biblioteca.

a. Está serio.
b. Está indiferente.
c. Está pesimista.
d. Está muy estudioso.
e. Está optimista.
f. Está guapo.

INPUT

Act. I, Suggestion:
Read each
statement out loud and
then ask these questions.
1. *¿Es lista o está lista?*
(*Es lista.*) 2. *¿Es aburrido
o está aburrido?* (*Está
aburrido.*) 3. *¿Son listas o
están listas?* (*Están listas.*)
4. *¿Es rica o está rica?*
(*Es rica.*) 5. *¿Es malo o
está malo?* (*Está malo.*)
6. *¿Es verde o está
verde?* (*Es verde.*)

Actividad I ¿*Es* o *está*?

Listen as your instructor reads each of the following statements and then poses a question. Select the best option from his or her question.

1. Marta estudia mucho y siempre saca (*she always gets*) buenas notas en sus clases.
2. José no tiene interés en la clase hoy y no puede prestar atención (*pay attention*).
3. Las chicas quieren salir ahora.
4. Verónica tiene mucho dinero y cada año compra un coche nuevo.
5. Miguel tiene fiebre (*fever*).
6. Me gusta mucho el color de esa chaqueta.

OUTPUT
Actividad J

Actividad J ¿Es caro o está a buen precio?

Paso 1 Invent prices for the items in one of the lists below. A classmate will invent prices for the other list. Some of your prices should be inexpensive, others very expensive, and some at a good price.

A	B
unos zapatos de cuero (*leather*) elegantes	un traje Armani
	unos vaqueros Lucky
un disco compacto	un cinturón (*belt*) de cuero
un televisor grande	un traje de baño
una computadora portátil (*laptop*)	una falda
un suéter de lana (*wool*)	

Paso 2 Take turns sharing the prices for your items with your partner. Indicate your attitude toward each price your partner provides by reponding with **es barato/a (son baratos/as), está(n) a buen precio,** or **es caro/a (son caros/as)**. Does your partner agree with you?

MODELO: E1: Una camiseta cuesta cinco dólares.
E2: ¡Es barata!
E1: Sí, es barata. (No, está a buen precio.)

¡Exprésate!

The verb **ser** is often used with the adjectives **barato/a** and **caro/a**; however, to say that something is a good price, **está a buen precio** is used.

Es barato/a.	*It's cheap.*
Es caro/a.	*It's expensive.*
Está a buen precio.	*It's a good price.*

OUTPUT
Actividad K

Actividad K La ropa y la personalidad

Paso 1 How does what someone wears express his or her personality or mood? For each description of outfits listed, write a sentence that could describe that person's personality or mood today. You may use the following adjectives or others you have learned.

alegre	excéntrico/a	perezoso/a	soñador(a)
elegante	listo/a	perfeccionista	tonto/a
enérgico/a	optimista	profesional	

MODELO: Felipe siempre se viste de negro. → Es pesimista.

1. Para ir a clase hoy, Federico lleva sudadera, vaqueros, gorra y zapatos de tenis.
2. Para ir al trabajo, mi madre (*mother*) siempre lleva blusa, falda y chaqueta.
3. Para salir a la calle (*street*), un hombre de cincuenta años generalmente lleva un abrigo anaranjado y un gorra verde.
4. Para ir a un restaurante con su novio (*boyfriend*) esta noche, Ángela lleva un vestido negro y zapatos elegantes.
5. Para ir a correr esta tarde, Juan lleva una camisa de flores (*floral*) y unos pantalones cortos de cuadros.
6. Mi hermano (*brother*) siempre combina bien los colores de su ropa cuando se viste.

Paso 2 Compare your answers with a classmate's. Are there certain colors or clothes that project a particular personality or mood?

MODELO: El rojo da (*gives*) una imagen (*image*) enérgica.

SOL Y VIENTO

A segunda vista

Antes de ver el episodio

Actividad A ¿Qué recuerdas?

Based on what you remember from your previous viewing of **Episodio 2,** determine whether Jaime or María said each of the following lines. You will be asked to verify your answers when you watch the episode again.

1. «¡Le pido mil disculpas!» Jaime
2. «Por eso sabe mi nombre. Si quiere, la guarda.» María
3. «¿Viene a chocarse conmigo otra vez?» María
4. «Y ojalá que nos veamos de nuevo.» Jaime
5. «¿Está de vacaciones o tiene negocios en Maipo?» María

Actividad B ¡A escuchar!

**Act. B,
Suggestion:**
Have students
read the
exchange
before watch-
ing the
episode. They
do not need to
write anything
at this point.
Do not reveal
answers.
Alternative:
Have the class
brainstorm
possible
answers for
each blank but
do not have
them write
anything
down.

In a moment you will watch **Episodio 2** once again. Familiarize yourself with the following excerpt from the scene in which Jaime talks with a young boy in the park. You will be asked to listen closely and write the missing words in the blank. Do not look back at any previous excerpts from this episode!

JAIME: ¿__Tres__ pesos?
MUCHACHO: ¡Chis! ¡__Tres__ pesos no, señor! ¡Son __trescientos__ pesos!
JAIME: Ah, espere.
MUCHACHO: __Esa__, __esa__ y __esa__. Ya, __trescientos__.
JAIME: Ah, y __estos__ cien son para ti.
MUCHACHO: ¡Gracias, señor!

Actividad C El episodio

Now watch the episode again. Don't forget to verify your answers to **Actividad A** as you watch. Also remember to pay close attention to the scene in which Jaime talks with the young boy in the park and to write down the missing words for **Actividad B.**

Después de ver el episodio

Act. B, Suggestion: Replay the scene once for students. Replay a second time if needed. Then ask for volunteers to provide answers for each blank. Verify using the instructor notes from Act. B on the previous page.
Alternative: After students complete the conversation, have 2 students act it out.

Actividad A   Para pensar...

In this episode Jaime reads that love is a whirlwind (**El amor es un torbellino.**). With which of the following statements about love would you agree?

El amor es...
a. un túnel sin salida (*without an exit*).
b. ciego (*blind*).
c. un dolor (*ache, pain*) que no se puede curar.
d. como un accidente. No sabes (*You don't know*) cuándo va a ocurrir.

Actividad B   ¡A verificar!

Listen as your instructor replays the scene from **¡A escuchar!** on the previous page. Fill in the missing information based on what you hear.

Actividad C   ¿Cómo es María?

Paso 1   How would you describe María, based on what you've seen of her in this episode?

Creo que María es...
☐ aburrida   ☐ divertida   ☐ introvertida
☐ alegre   ☐ enérgica   ☐ reservada
☐ ambiciosa   ☐ ingenua   ☐ seria
☐ desconfiada   ☐ inteligente

Paso 2   Your instructor will survey the class to discover the most frequent adjectives used to describe María. Write the three most common adjectives in the blanks below.

Creemos que María es _____, _____ y _____.

Actividad D   ¡Te toca a ti!

Paso 1   Do you remember what Jaime, Mario, and María were wearing in

JAIME	MARIO	MARÍA

Episodio 2? Write down the clothes and the colors that each one had on.
Paso 2   In this lesson you talked about how clothing can reflect the personalities of the people who wear it. Do any of the clothes that Jaime, Mario, and María wear represent their personalities in any way? Write brief descriptions of each character's personality, based on his or her clothing. Compare your answers with those of three other classmates.

Detrás de la cámara

If you watch María carefully, you may have noticed that she has a determined walk. Even when she's in the park, she never strolls leisurely. What might that say about her personality? María is very goal-oriented, and she doesn't stop until she achieves her goals. Jaime seems to pick up on this, and perhaps that is why he is so persistent. Jaime realizes intuitively that María possesses much more than good looks. That's why when Mario says, "**¡Bonita la muchacha, don Jaime!**" Jaime emphasizes that she's also intelligent. Do you think Jaime and María would make a good match? Are they too much alike? Too dissimilar? Or is the combination just right?

133

RESUMEN DE VOCABULARIO

Verbos

combinar bien/mal	to go well/poorly with (*clothing*)
comprar	to buy
encontrar (ue)	to find
gastar	to spend
llevar	to wear
pedir (i)	to ask for; to order
probarse (ue)	to try on
quedar bien/mal	to fit well/poorly
regatear	to bargain
repetir (i)	to repeat
seguir (i)	to follow; to continue
servir (i)	to serve
vender	to sell
vestir(se)	to dress (get dressed)

Repaso: buscar, costar (ue), decir (*irreg.*)**, pagar**

Las prendas de ropa

el abrigo	coat
la blusa	blouse
la bolsa	purse
las botas	boots
los calcetines	socks
la camisa	shirt
la camiseta	T-shirt
la corbata	tie
la falda	skirt
la gorra	baseball cap
los pantalones	pants
los pantalones cortos	shorts
la sudadera	sweatshirt
el traje	suit
el traje de baño	bathing suit
los vaqueros	jeans
el vestido	dress
los zapatos	shoes
de tenis	tennis shoes, sneakers

Cognados: la chaqueta, las sandalias, el suéter

De compras

el/la cliente	customer
el/la dependiente/a	clerk
de compras	shopping
el dinero	money
el efectivo	cash
la ganga	bargain
la marca	brand name
el precio (fijo)	(fixed) price
las rebajas	sale(s)
la talla	size
mediano/a	medium
pequeño/a	small
la tarjeta de crédito	credit card
barato/a	inexpensive
caro/a	expensive

Repaso: grande

Los colores

amarillo/a	yellow
anaranjado/a	orange
azul	blue
blanco/a	white
gris	gray
marrón	brown
morado/a	purple
negro/a	black
rojo/a	red
rosado/a	pink
verde	green

Los números del 100 al 1.000

ciento uno/a, doscientos/as, trescientos/as, cuatrocientos/as, quinientos/as, seiscientos/as, setecientos/as, ochocientos/as, novecientos/as, mil

Repaso: cien

Los adjetivos y pronombres demostrativos

aquel, aquella	that; that one (over there)
aquellos/as	those; those (ones) (over there)
ese/a	that; that one
esos/as	those; those (ones)
este/a	this; this one
estos/as	these; these (ones)
eso	that (*neuter*)
esto	this (*neuter*)
aquello	that (over there) (*neuter*)

Los posesivos tónicos

mío/a/os/as	mine, of mine
tuyo/a/os/as	yours, of yours (*informal*)
suyo/a/os/as	yours, of yours (*formal*); his, hers, their

Repaso: nuestro/a, vuestro/a

Otras palabras y expresiones

la moda	fashion
aburrido/a	boring
listo/a	clever, smart
malo/a	bad; sick
rico/a	rich, wealthy; delicious
allí	there; over there
aquí	here
es buena idea + *infin.*	it's a good idea (*to do something*)
es necesario + *infin.*	it's necessary (*to do something*)
hay que + *infin.*	one must (*do something*)
para + *infin.*	in order to (*do something*)

Ciento treinta y seis

Entremés cultural
España: Diversidad geográfica, histórica y lingüística

VISTAZO

Situada en la península Ibérica, en el suroeste del continente europeo, España tiene una extensión total de 504.750 km^2 (quinientos cuatro mil setecientos cincuenta kilómetros cuadrados). El país es más grande que California pero no tan grande como[a] Texas. Dividida en diecisiete comunidades autónomas, España se caracteriza por su diversidad geográfica, climática, histórica y lingüística. En general existen cuatro climas diferentes que se corresponden con la geografía física de la península. La costa del norte del país (Galicia, Asturias, Cantabria y el País Vasco) tiene un clima húmedo. Llueve mucho y por eso es la zona más verde de España. El centro del país es mucho más árido y llueve poco. En el sur predomina un clima muy seco[b] con unas temperaturas máximas durante el verano que pueden llegar a 40 grados (104° Fahrenheit). En la costa del Mediterráneo el clima es más templado[c] y llueve poco.

[a]tan... *as big as* [b]*dry* [c]*moderate*

DATO INTERESANTE:
La variedad lingüística

Dentro del[a] estado español existen varias regiones geográficas que son oficialmente bilingües. En Cataluña son oficiales el español y el catalán. En el País Vasco, el español y el vasco (o el vascuence) son las dos lenguas oficiales. En Galicia, el español coexiste con el gallego, una lengua más parecida[b] al portugués que al español.

Idea: Busca información en el Internet sobre cómo se dicen los números del uno al cinco en catalán, gallego y vasco. Trae la información a clase.

Ejemplos de otras lenguas en España. ¿Son parecidas al español?

[a]Dentro... *Within* [b]*similar*

DATO INTERESANTE:
La influencia árabe

En el sur de España existe una gran influencia de la cultura árabe en la arquitectura y en las costumbres, debido a[a] la ocupación musulmana de la península Ibérica entre 711 d.C. (después de Cristo) y 1492 (mil cuatrocientos noventa y dos) d.C. Estas influencias se ven sobre todo en Andalucía, especialmente en las ciudades de Córdoba, Granada y Sevilla.

> **Idea:** Busca información sobre la contribución de los musulmanes a la cultura española actual,[b] concentrándote en uno o dos de los siguientes temas: la arquitectura, las ciencias, la lengua o cualquier otro tema. Trae por lo menos tres datos a la clase.

[a]debido... *due to*   [b]*current*

La mezquita (*mosque*) en Córdoba es un ejemplo de la influencia árabe en el sur de España.

DATO INTERESANTE:
El gobierno

Después de la dictadura[a] militar de Francisco Franco, que duró[b] casi cuarenta años (1939–1975 [de mil novecientos treinta y nueve a mil novecientos setenta y cinco]), se restauró[c] el sistema democrático en España en 1977 (mil novecientos setenta y siete). Desde entonces[d] España tiene una monarquía parlamentaria con un rey[e] que es el Jefe del Estado.[f] Sin embargo,[g] el gobierno es elegido[h] democráticamente cada cuatro años por el pueblo[i] español y dirige[j] la política interior y exterior del país.

> **Idea:** Haz una tabla comparando el gobierno español con el gobierno mexicano y con el gobierno de este país. Debes incluir por lo menos seis puntos de comparación.

[a]*dictatorship*   [b]*lasted*   [c]se... *was restored*   [d]Desde... *Since then*   [e]*king*   [f]Jefe... *Head of State*   [g]Sin... *Nevertheless*   [h]*elected*   [i]*people*   [j]*runs*

El Rey Juan Carlos I (primero) es el Jefe de Estado.

La Sagrada Familia en Barcelona es la obra más famosa de Gaudí.

DATO INTERESANTE:
El modernismo catalán

La ciudad de Barcelona tiene fama mundial[a] por un estilo de arquitectura que se llama el modernismo catalán. Este estilo se caracteriza por el uso de elementos decorativos inspirados en la naturaleza y en el pasado[b] medieval. Por ejemplo, en el exterior de los edificios se pueden encontrar hojas[c] de plantas, flores,[d] frutas y animales de piedra[e] o cerámica junto con[f] elementos arquitectónicos de la época medieval.

> **Idea:** Busca fotos de Barcelona que demuestran[g] el modernismo catalán, concentrándote en las obras[h] de Antoni Gaudí como la Sagrada Familia, el Parque Güell, Casa Batlló y La Pedrera.

[a]fama... *worldwide fame*   [b]*past*   [c]*leaves*   [d]*flowers*   [e]*stone*   [f]junto... *together with*   [g]*show*   [h]*works*

A la viña^a

En este episodio...

CARLOS

¿Quisiera hacer un breve recorrido?^b ¿Le gusta el vino chileno?

JAIME

Sí, me gusta mucho, pero prefiero esperar. Tenemos negocios^c importantes. ¿No es cierto?

CARLOS

Bueno, sí. Es cierto. ¿Por qué no vamos a mi oficina para tener así más privacidad?

¿Qué crees tú?

1. ¿Dónde están Jaime y Carlos?
2. ¿Cuáles son los «negocios importantes»?
3. Carlos está contento con la idea de hablar (*speaking*) con Jaime, ¿cierto o falso?

---

^aA... *To the Winery*   ^b¿Quisiera... *Would you like to take a quick tour?*   ^c*business*

La familia

LECCIÓN  3A

OBJETIVOS

IN THIS LESSON, YOU WILL LEARN:

- vocabulary to talk about members of your immediate and extended family

- to talk about knowing people, places, and factual information using the verbs **saber** and **conocer**

- how to use direct object pronouns to eliminate redundancy

- vocabulary to describe how people look

- to make comparisons to describe people and things

In addition, you will prepare for and watch **Episodio 3** of the film *Sol y viento*.

La mujer a la izquierda, ¿es la madre o la abuela (*grandmother*) de esta familia? (*Waiting for the Virgin,* por Nancie King-Mertz [estadounidense])

The following media resources are available with this lesson of *Sol y viento*:

Episodio 3 *of Sol y viento*

Online *Manual de actividades*

Online Learning Center Website

Note: These vocabulary items can be heard in this lesson's Textbook Audio section of the Online Learning Center Website.

Vocabulario

Describing Families | **Mi familia** **Members of the Immediate Family; Pets**

La familia de Antonio Trujillo

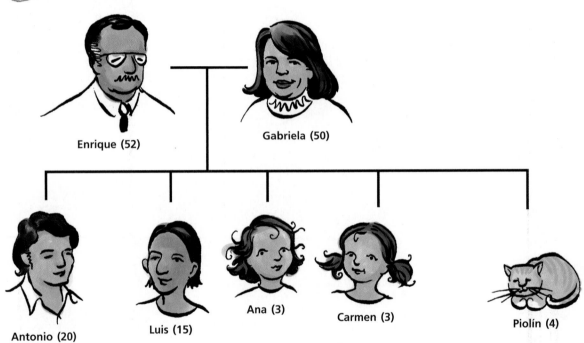

Enrique (52) Gabriela (50)

Antonio (20) Luis (15) Ana (3) Carmen (3) Piolín (4)

To talk about all the members of a family, English uses the plural form of the last name, as in *The Simpsons* or *The Osbournes*. Spanish uses the definite article **los** followed by the singular form of the last name, as in **los Trujillo** and **los Alexander.**

- Enrique es **el padre** de Antonio.
- Gabriela es **la madre** de Antonio.
- Enrique y Gabriela son **los padres.**
- Luis es **hermano** de Antonio.
- Ana es **una hermana** de Antonio.
- Carmen es otra **hermana** de Antonio.
- Piolín es **el gato** de la familia.
- Antonio tiene tres **hermanos** en total: un hermano (Luis) y dos hermanas (Ana y Carmen). Ana y Carmen son **gemelas.**
- Antonio, Luis, Ana y Carmen son **los hijos** de Enrique y Gabriela. Luis es **un hijo** y Carmen es **una hija.**

Las familias de Patricia Alexander

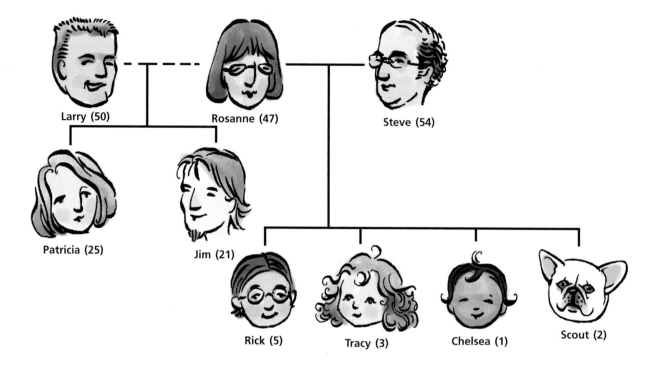

- Larry es **el padre** de Patricia. Es un **padre soltero.**
- Rosanne es **la madre** de Patricia.
- Larry y Rosanne son **los padres** de Patricia.
- Jim es el **hermano** de Patricia.
- Patricia no tiene **hermanas.**
- Patricia tiene **un hermano** y tres **medio hermanos:** Rick, Tracy y Chelsea. Chelsea es **la hija adoptiva** de Rosanne y Steve.
- Scout es **el perro** de la familia.
- Patricia tiene **un padrastro,** Steve.
- Patricia y Jim son **los hijos** de Larry y Rosanne.
- Rick, Tracy y Chelsea son **los hijos** de Rosanne y Steve.

✳ MÁS VOCABULARIO

la esposa / la mujer	wife
el esposo / el marido	husband
el hermanastro / la hermanastra	stepbrother, stepsister
el hijastro / la hijastra	stepson, stepdaughter
el hijo único / la hija única	only child
la madrastra	stepmother
la madre soltera	single mother
la mascota	pet
mayor	older
menor	younger

INPUT

Act. A, Note: From this point on in *Sol y viento*, the direction lines for most of the activities will be in Spanish. Be sure students know what's being asked of them before proceeding with in-class activities.
Suggestion: Allow 2 minutes to complete, then read each sentence out loud to the class. Ask for volunteers to answer. Students should correct the false statements by making them true.
Answers: 1. F (*Es el hermano menor de Antonio.*) 2. C 3. F (*Es el gato de Antonio.*) 4. F (*Hay dos hijos y dos hijas gemelas.*) 5. C 6. C

INPUT

Act. B, *Paso 1,* **Statements:** 1. *el padrastro de Patricia* (Steve) 2. *la hija adoptiva de Rosanne y Steve* (Chelsea) 3. *el medio hermano de Patricia* (Rick) 4. *el hijastro de Steve* (Jim) 5. *una hermana de Rick* (Tracy o Chelsea) 6. *el ex marido de Rosanne* (Larry) 7. *el perro de Rick, Tracy y Chelsea* (Scout)
Optional follow-up: Draw a tree of your immediate family (include names and ages!) on a transparency and bring it to class. Point out your place in the tree and then ask questions that require 1- or 2-word answers: *¿Cómo se llaman mis padres? ¿Quién es mayor, mi padre o mi madre? ¿Cuántos hermanos tengo en total? ¿Tengo hermanastros? ¿Cómo se llaman?* etc.

OUTPUT

Act. C, Note: Students will use this activity to build on one about Jaime's extended family in *Act. C* in the *Segunda parte.*

Actividad A ¿Cierto o falso?

Lee cada descripción sobre los Trujillo e indica si es cierta o falsa.

	CIERTO	FALSO
1. Luis es el hermano mayor de Antonio.	☐	☑
2. Los padres se llaman Enrique y Gabriela.	☑	☐
3. Piolín es el perro de Antonio.	☐	☑
4. En la familia Trujillo hay dos hijos gemelos y dos hijas, cuatro hijos en total.	☐	☑
5. Antonio no tiene hermanastros.	☑	☐
6. Ana y Carmen son las menores de la familia.	☑	☐

Actividad B ¿A quién se describe?

Paso 1 Escucha las descripciones que lee el profesor (la profesora) sobre las familias de Patricia Alexander y escribe el nombre de la persona que corresponde a cada descripción.

1. _____   5. _____
2. _____   6. _____
3. _____   7. _____
4. _____

Paso 2 Ahora compara tus respuestas (*answers*) con las de un compañero (una compañera) de clase.

Actividad C La familia de Jaime

Paso 1 ¿Cómo es la familia de Jaime Talavera? Con un compañero (una compañera), inventen por lo menos seis oraciones para describir a su familia. Deben incluir nombres y edades, dónde viven, etcétera.

MODELO: El padre de Jaime se llama Francisco. Tiene 60 años y...

Paso 2 Comparen su descripción con la descripción de otro grupo. ¿Tienen Uds. descripciones parecidas (*similar*)?

Suggestions:
Paso 1: Tell students that they are making up his family, not basing their work on facts they should already know. Allow students 2–3 minutes to formulate statements.
Paso 2: Call on several groups to present to the class. Pull out any common trends and illustrate them in a family tree. (You might say *Muchos de Uds. creen que Jaime tiene un hermano mayor y que sus padres están divorciados* as you draw the corresponding relationships on the board.) Try to work in vocabulary that students may not be using; for example, if everyone thinks he has a sibling say: *¿Todos creen que tiene hermanos? ¿No es hijo único?,* and so on.

▲ ¿Cómo es la familia de Jaime?

Actividad D Un árbol genealógico (*family tree*)

Paso 1   Entrevista (*Interview*) a un compañero (una compañera) de clase sobre su familia. Apunta (*Jot down*) los nombres y edades en los espacios en blanco, según (*according to*) el modelo.

	PADRES/PADRASTROS	HERMANOS/HERMANASTROS	MASCOTAS
MODELO:	Joseph (49)	Carolyn (17)	Wolfgang (3)
Nombre y edad	_____	_____	_____
	_____	_____	_____
	_____	_____	_____
	_____	_____	_____

Paso 2   Con la información que tienes, dibuja (*draw*) el árbol genealógico de la familia de tu compañero/a de clase.

La familia de _____

Paso 3   Entrégale (*Hand over*) a tu compañero/a el árbol genealógico. ¿Están correctas todas las relaciones?

〰 Vistazo cultural

Dos apellidos

En los países de habla inglesa los hijos suelen usar solamente el apellido de su padre, por ejemplo, Andrew *Knight* o Kelly *Croft*. En el mundo hispano los hijos toman el apellido del padre seguido por[a] el apellido de la madre, por ejemplo, Gabriel *García Márquez* o Ramón *del Valle Inclán*. En el primer ejemplo, el apellido paterno es García y el materno es Márquez. En el segundo ejemplo, del Valle es el apellido paterno e[*] Inclán es el apellido materno. En algunos países y en los Estados Unidos los hispanos tienden a[b] eliminar el apellido materno (por ejemplo: Evita Perón, Sammy Sosa, Salma Hayek), excepto en ocasiones oficiales o formales.

En los Estados Unidos es común ver nombres compuestos[c] como Cynthia Sánchez-Jones o Mary Higgins-Taylor. Los apellidos separados por guión[d] por lo general indican un matrimonio.[e] En el primer ejemplo, Sánchez es el nombre de soltera[f] y Jones es el nombre de casada.[g] En el otro ejemplo, el nombre de soltera es Higgins y el nombre de casada es Taylor.

María Teresa Sánchez Prieto

Cátedra de Antropología
Universidad del Sur

Teléfono: 555 39 63
Cel: 651 25 65

[a]seguido... *followed by* [b]tienden... *tend to* [c]*compound* [d]por... *by a hyphen* [e]*marriage*
[f]nombre... *maiden name* [g]nombre... *married name*

*The word **e** is used instead of **y** when the word immediately following it begins with **i** or **hi**.

Gramática

**Sí, conozco a la familia.
¿Sabes dónde están?**

**Saber and conocer;
Verbs That End in -zco**

USES OF *saber* AND *conocer*	
Saber expresses knowledge of facts or pieces of information.	**Conocer** expresses familiarity with a person, place, or thing; note the possible English equivalents.
¿Sabes la hora? *Do you know what time it is?*	No **conocemos** a la nueva profesora. *We don't know the new professor.*
No **sabemos** el número de teléfono del profesor. *We don't know the professor's phone number.*	**¿Conoces** el restaurante «Salpicón»? *Are you familiar with (Have you been to) the restaurant Salpicón?*
¿Sabes el origen de la palabra *chocolate* en español? *Do you know the origin of the word chocolate in Spanish?*	Juan **conoce** las obras de Shakespeare. *Juan knows (is familiar with, has read) the works of Shakespeare.*
saber + *infin.* = to know how to (*do something*) **Sé tocar** la guitarra. *I know how to play the guitar.*	**Conozco** bien la Ciudad de México. *I know Mexico City well.*

Unlike English, Spanish has two verbs that mean *to know:* **saber** and **conocer.***
Their uses are summarized in the chart. Both **saber** and **conocer** are irregular
in the **yo** form: **sé** and **conozco,** respectively.

✳ **MÁS GRAMÁTICA**

When **conocer** is used to talk about knowing a person, groups of people, or pets, it
may be difficult to distinguish who knows whom because objects can come before
verbs in Spanish. Compare the following sentences, both of which mean *Consuela
knows your best friend.*

> Consuela conoce a tu mejor amigo.
> A tu mejor amigo lo conoce Consuela.

Consuela is the subject of both sentences (she does the knowing) and **mejor amigo** is
the object (the one who is known), but in the second sentence the object precedes the
verb. Spanish uses **a** to mark the object in both sentences so that there is no confusion
as to who knows whom. This is called the **a personal,** and it has no English equivalent.
You will learn more about objects and the **a personal** in the **Segunda parte** of this lesson.

***Conocer** also means *to meet.*

Other Spanish verbs ending in **-cer** also show the same **-zco** irregularity in their first-person forms.

VERBS THAT END IN -*zco*		
VERB	MEANING	FIRST-PERSON SINGULAR (**yo**) FORM
agradecer	*to thank*	agrade**zco**
(des)obedecer	*to (dis)obey*	(des)obede**zco**
merecer	*to deserve*	mere**zco**
ofrecer	*to offer*	ofre**zco**
parecerse* (a)	*to resemble*	me pare**zco** (a)
reconocer	*to recognize*	recono**zco**

De *Sol y viento,* Note: You can access this film clip from a special menu section on Disc 5 of the Instructional Version on DVD.

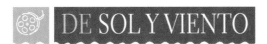
DE SOL Y VIENTO

In **Episodio 3** of *Sol y viento,* you will watch a scene in which Jaime and Mario are talking about the Sol y viento winery. Part of their exchange appears in the following dialogue.

MARIO
Bueno, don Jaime. Ya estamos en el Valle del Maipo. ¿Quiere visitar algún lugar en particular?

JAIME
Sí. Vamos a la viña «Sol y viento». ¿La **conoce**?

MARIO
¡Por supuesto! La «Sol y viento» es chiquita,ª pero produce buen vino. Y créameᵇ don Jaime: ¡_____ los vinos!

Selecting from the following options, what verb do you think Mario says in the sentence above?

(**1.**) conozco

2. sé

ªpequeña ᵇ*believe me*

---

*This is another example of a reflexive verb. You will learn more about these types of verbs in **Lección 5A.** For now, just learn to recognize their forms.

INPUT
Act. E, *Paso 2,*
Suggestion: Allow students 2–3 minutes to compare answers, then select 4 of the items and poll the class for their responses. Ask follow-up questions from time to time to generate brief discussion (*¿Qué instrumento sabe tocar María?,* etc.) Supply words in Spanish and write on board if students offer English.

Actividad E   ¿Qué sabe? ¿A quién conoce?

Paso 1   Basándote en (*Based on*) tus primeras impresiones, indica si las siguientes (*following*) oraciones describen a Jaime, a María o a los dos. Escribe el nombre apropiado en los espacios en blanco.

1. _____ no sabe(n) cocinar (*to cook*) muy bien.
2. _____ sabe(n) la lengua mapuche.
3. _____ sabe(n) mucho de la política.
4. _____ sabe(n) tocar un instrumento musical.
5. _____ conoce(n) los Estados Unidos.
6. _____ conoce(n) los mejores vinos de California.
7. _____ conoce(n) a muchos hombres ricos.
8. _____ conoce(n) México.

Paso 2   Comparte (*share*) tus respuestas con un compañero (una compañera) de clase. ¿Tienen las mismas (*same*) impresiones?

INPUT
Act. F, **Suggestions:**
Paso 1: Read each statement, pausing 5 seconds between statements for students to write. Then allow 2–3 minutes for students to think up famous people and write their names down.
1. *Sabe jugar al basquetbol.* 2. *Sabe escribir novelas.* 3. *Sabe mucho de la economía del país.* 4. *Sabe actuar en películas de acción.* 5. *Sabe cantar en inglés y español.* 6. *Sabe mucho de la moda.* You may want to write sentences on overhead so students can compare spelling before proceeding or have one student go to the board and write out.
Paso 2: Allow students 1–2 minutes to compare answers, then read each statement aloud as a question (*¿Quién sabe jugar al basquetbol?*). As students call out answers, ask follow-up questions to keep the focus on meaning (for example, *Sí, Shaquille O'Neal sabe jugar al basquetbol. ¿Para qué equipo juega?*).

Actividad F   ¿Qué saben hacer los famosos?

Paso 1   Tu profesor(a) va a leer una serie de oraciones. Escribe la oración que oyes. Después, escribe el nombre de una persona famosa que hace cada actividad.

MODELO: Profesor(a): Sabe tocar la guitarra.
          Tú: (*escribes*) Sabe tocar la guitarra.
          (*escribes*) Carlos Santana

   1. ...   **2.** ...   **3.** ...   **4.** ...   **5.** ...   **6.** ...

Paso 2   Compara tus respuestas con las de un compañero (una compañera) de clase. ¿Tienen las mismas personas famosas?

Actividad G   Asociaciones

INPUT
Actividad G

Empareja (*Match*) una frase de la columna A con una frase de la columna B para formar oraciones lógicas.

A	B
1. _d_ Merezco una «A» en mis clases porque...	**a.** me dan (*they give me*) dinero.
2. _f_ Me parezco...	**b.** invito a un amigo a tomar un café.
3. _b_ Ofrezco pagar la cuenta (*bill*) cuando...	**c.** no llevo los lentes (*glasses*).
4. _a_ Les agradezco a mis padres cuando...	**d.** estudio mucho.
5. _c_ No reconozco bien a las personas cuando...	**e.** para evitar (*avoid*) un accidente.
6. _e_ Obedezco las leyes de tráfico (*traffic laws*)...	**f.** a mi madre, pero no a mi padre.

Actividad H   La clase de español

Paso 1 Indica si cada oración es cierta o falsa para ti.

	CIERTO	FALSO
1. Conozco a todas las personas de mi clase de español.	☐	☐
2. Sé el número de ausencias (*absences*) que tengo en esta clase.	☐	☐
3. Conozco un país del mundo hispano.	☐	☐
4. Conozco bien al profesor (a la profesora).	☐	☐
5. Sé cuántos exámenes y composiciones tenemos que hacer.	☐	☐
6. Sé cuántas mujeres hay en mi clase.	☐	☐
7. Conozco bien a los personajes (*characters*) de *Sol y viento*.	☐	☐
8. Conozco la geografía de Chile.	☐	☐

Paso 2 Entrevista a dos compañeros/as de clase sobre las oraciones del **Paso 1**. Anota sus respuestas.

MODELO: E1: ¿Conoces un país del mundo hispano?
          E2: Sí. Conozco Costa Rica.

Paso 3 Prepara un breve resumen para presentárselo a la clase.

MODELO: Hablé (*I spoke*) con Ana y Miguel. Nosotros sabemos cuántas ausencias tenemos. Ana y Miguel conocen un país hispano, pero yo no...

⬤ Enfoque lingüístico

¿Dos verbos que significan lo mismo?

In the **Lección preliminar** you learned that Spanish has two verbs meaning *to be*. You now know that Spanish also uses **saber** and **conocer** to convey all of the meanings encompassed by the one English verb *to know*. This is not unique to Spanish. In fact, all Romance languages (French, Italian, Portuguese, and Romanian, among others) make this distinction, as do German and Russian.

   There are also cases in which English uses two verbs to express meanings conveyed by a single verb in other languages. For example, English distinguishes between doing something (*to do*) and making something (*to make*). We *do homework* but *make a bed.* In the Romance languages, Russian, and Hebrew, the same verb communicates the idea of making and doing. Spanish speakers say **hacer la tarea** and **hacer la cama.** Distinguishing between *doing* and *making* is very difficult for second-language learners of English whose first language uses just one verb for both meanings.

Note: These vocabulary items can be heard in this lesson's Textbook Audio section of the Online Learning Center Website.

More on Describing Families

Vocabulario, **Point out:** The meaning of Q.E.P.D. (*Que en paz descanse*) and its similarity to the English R.I.P. (Rest In Peace).

Vocabulario

Los otros parientes

Extended Family Members

La familia extendida de Antonio Trujillo

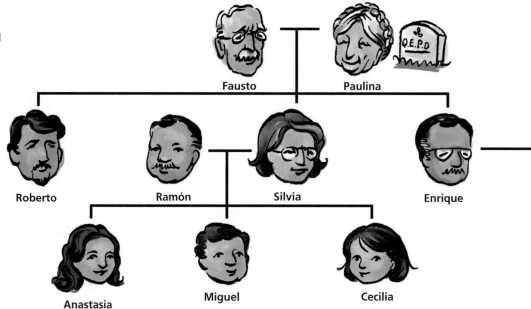

- Fausto, Paulina, Ignacio y Esperanza son **los abuelos** de Antonio.
- Fausto y Paulina son sus **abuelos paternos.**
- Ignacio y Esperanza son sus **abuelos maternos.**
- Paulina es su **abuela paterna** y Esperanza es su **abuela materna.**
- Paulina, su **abuela paterna, ya murió.**
- Ignacio, su **abuelo materno,** ya murió también.
- Antonio tiene seis **tíos** en total, cuatro **tíos** y dos **tías.**
- **Los tíos** de Antonio son: Roberto, Ramón, Freddie y Samuel. Silvia y Mónica son sus **tías.**
- Su tía Silvia y su tío Ramón tienen tres hijos: Anastasia, Miguel y Cecilia. Ellos son **los primos** de Antonio.

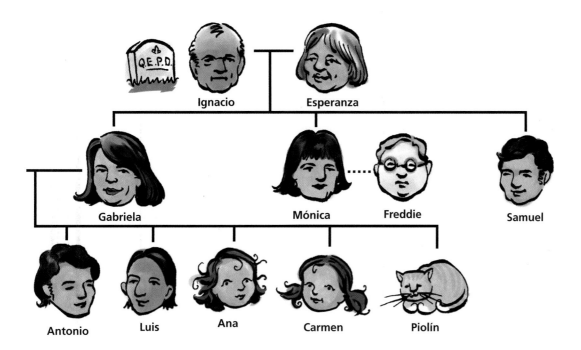

![*] **MÁS VOCABULARIO**

el cuñado / la cuñada	brother-in-law, sister-in-law
el nieto / la nieta	grandson, granddaughter
los parientes	relatives
el sobrino / la sobrina	nephew, niece
el suegro / la suegra	father-in-law, mother-in-law
casado/a	married
divorciado/a	divorced
separado/a	separated
soltero/a	single
viudo/a	widowed
vivo/a	alive
ya murió	he/she already died

INPUT

Act. A, State-ments: 1. *Ignacio es el abuelo materno de Antonio y está vivo.* (*F, Ya murió.*) 2. *Mónica es una tía de Antonio.* (*C*) 3. *Roberto es un tío de Antonio y no tiene esposa.* (*C*) 4. *Fausto es el abuelo paterno de Antonio y está vivo.* (*C*) 5. *Antonio tiene tres primos en total: dos primos y una prima.* (*F, Son dos primas y un primo.*) 6. *Una abuela de Antonio ya murió.* (*C*)

INPUT

Act. B, Suggestion: Allow students 1–2 minutes to review the *Más vocabulario* box on page 149. Then read each statement once. Do not repeat unless students ask for a repetition in Spanish. 1. *una persona que no tiene esposo o esposa* (a) 2. *padre o madre de tu esposo o esposa* (a) 3. *cuando el esposo o la esposa ya murió* (b) 4. *hijo de tu hermano/a* (b) 5. *cuando un esposo y una esposa se separan legalmente* (a) 6. *esposa de tu hermano* (b) 7. *hija de tus tíos* (a)

OUTPUT

Act. C, Suggestion: Allow students 5 minutes to write, then ask a few groups to volunteer their responses. Note any common trends and add them to the family tree you drew as a follow-up to Act. C in *Primera parte.*

Actividad A   La familia extendida

Estudia el dibujo (*drawing*) de la familia extendida de Antonio Trujillo. El profesor (La profesora) va a leer unas descripciones. Indica si son ciertas o falsas.

1. ...   2. ...   3. ...   4. ...   5. ...   6. ...

Actividad B   Relaciones familiares

Tu profesor(a) va a leer una definición. Selecciona la palabra que se define.

1. **(a.)** soltera   **b.** casada
2. **(a.)** suegro/a   **b.** abuelo/a
3. **a.** divorciado/a   **(b.)** viudo/a
4. **a.** cuñado   **(b.)** sobrino
5. **(a.)** divorciados   **b.** solteros
6. **a.** tía   **(b.)** cuñada
7. **(a.)** prima   **b.** hijastra

Actividad C   La familia extendida de Jaime

Con un compañero (una compañera), repasen (*review*) la descripción que escribieron (*you wrote*) sobre la familia de Jaime Talavera en **Primera parte, Actividad C.** Basándose en esa información, extiendan la descripción para incluir a su familia extendida. Usen las preguntas que acompañan a la foto de Jaime a continuación como punto de partida (*starting point*).

▲ ¿Qué sabes de Jaime? ¿Es numerosa su familia? ¿Tiene muchos tíos ¿Tiene sobrinos? ¿Están vivos sus abuelos?

Actividad D   Mi familia

Paso 1   En una hoja de papel (*sheet of paper*) dibuja el árbol genealógico de tu familia extendida. Incluye a tus tíos, primos y abuelos. Si quieres, ¡puedes inventar una familia!

Paso 2   En otra hoja aparte, escribe una lista de seis a ocho oraciones del tipo cierto/falso sobre tu familia. Sigue los ejemplos a continuación.

MODELOS: Mi abuela materna se llama Marisa.

Tengo una tía soltera.

Hay ocho nietos en mi familia.

Paso 3   Intercambia (*Exchange*) el dibujo de tu familia extendida con el dibujo de la familia de un compañero (una compañera) de clase. Luego (*Then*), léele a tu compañero/a las oraciones que escribiste (*you wrote*) sobre tu familia. Él/Ella va a indicar si las oraciones son ciertas o falsas. Cuando termines, cámbiense los papeles. (*When finished, switch roles.*)

MODELO: E1: Tengo una tía soltera.
          E2: Es cierto.
          E1: ¡Correcto!

Vistazo cultural

El habla[a] popular

Las palabras que suelen usarse para denotar relaciones familiares (**padre, madre, tío**) también tienen otros significados en el habla popular de varios países. En la Argentina y España, por ejemplo, las palabras **tío** y **tía**, además de[b] sus significados estrictos, se utilizan también como equivalentes de **hombre** y **mujer,** como se ve en los ejemplos a continuación.

Mariela es una **tía** bien simpática.   *Mariela is a really nice girl.*
No conozco a ese **tío.**   *I don't know that guy.*

En el español coloquial de México, la palabra **padre** se usa como adjetivo para expresar que algo parece muy bueno.

¡Qué **padre** coche!   *What a cool/awesome car!*

La palabra **madre** en el español coloquial mexicano se usa con el verbo **estar** para expresar algo parecido.

¡Está a toda **madre**!   *That's so cool/awesome!*

Estas expresiones son muy informales y sólo se usan entre personas que se tratan de[c] **tú.** Además, estas expresiones son particulares de su país de origen; es decir, no se usan en todos los países del mundo hispano.

[a]El... *Speech*   [b]además... *besides*   [c]se... *address each other as*

Gramática

Gramática, **Note:** Because pronouns can be a challenge, you may want to refer to the Instructor's Manual for information to help students with these concepts at the appropriate time. Alternatively, the same information is available on the Online Learning Center, available for digital download.

Eliminating Redundancy

¿La conoce?   Direct Object Pronouns

English avoids redundancy of nouns by using pronouns. For example, in the statements: *Where's John? Oh, he called. He's running late,* the answers to the question avoid the repetition of *John* by using the pronoun *he.* English also avoids redundancy with objects of verbs, as in *When did you see John? I saw him last night.* Here, John is the object of the verb *see* (object meaning that he is the person or thing seen), and English avoids redundancy in the answer by using the object pronoun *him.*

Spanish also uses object pronouns to avoid redundancy.

> ANA: ¿Llamas a tus padres con frecuencia?
> CECILIA: Pues, sí. **Los** llamo (*I call them*) todos los sábados.

Object pronouns in Spanish precede conjugated verbs or may be attached to infinitives.

¿Mi sobrina? **La** respeto mucho.	*My niece? I respect her a lot.*
¿Mi perro? **Lo** abrazo todos los días.	*My dog? I hug him every day.*
Mi tío quiere invitar**nos** a una fiesta.	*My uncle wants to invite us to a party.*

SUBJECT VERSUS OBJECT PRONOUNS	
yo: Conozco bien a mis padres.	**me**: Mis padres **me** conocen bien.
tú: ¿Conoces bien a tus padres?	**te**: ¿Tus padres **te** conocen bien?
Ud.: ¿Conoce Ud. bien a sus padres?	**lo/la**: ¿Sus padres **lo/la** conocen bien?
él/ella: Conoce bien a sus padres.	**lo/la**: Sus padres **lo/la** conocen bien.
nosotros/as: No conocemos a los abuelos.	**nos**: Nuestros abuelos no **nos** conocen.
vosotros/as: ¿Conocéis a los abuelos?	**os**: ¿Vuestros abuelos **os** conocen?
Uds.: ¿Conocen Uds. a sus abuelos?	**los/las**: ¿Sus abuelos **los/las** conocen?
ellos/ellas: No conocen a sus abuelos.	**los/las**: Sus abuelos no **los/las** conocen.

Remember that Spanish uses the **a personal** to mark full direct object nouns (but not pronouns). This is done to distinguish an object from a subject when both are capable of performing the action. This comes in handy when word order in Spanish is different from that in English. See the chart for examples.

OBJECT AND SUBJECT CAN PERFORM THE ACTION; *a personal* IS REQUIRED	OBJECT CANNOT PERFORM THE ACTION; *a personal* IS NOT REQUIRED
Juana conoce **a** mis primos. *Juana knows my cousins.*	Juana conoce las obras de Cervantes. *Juana knows Cervantes' works.*
El perro caza **al** gato. *The dog chases the cat.*	El perro caza su cola. *The dog chases his tail.*
Julia besa **al** perro. *Julia kisses the dog.*	Julia besa la foto. *Julia kisses the photo.*

De *Sol y viento,* **Note:** You can access this film clip from a special menu section on Disc 5 of the Instructional Version on DVD.

 DE SOL Y VIENTO

In **Episodio 3** of *Sol y viento,* you will watch a scene in which Traimaqueo, the foreman of the winery, informs Carlos of Jaime's arrival. Part of their exchange appears in the dialogue.

CARLOS
¡Traimaqueo! Ve qué quiere ese tipo.[a]

TRAIMAQUEO
El caballero[b] viene de los Estados Unidos, Carlos. Y dice que tú ＿＿＿ esperas.

Selecting from the following options, what pronoun do you think Traimaqueo says in the sentence above? Whom does this pronoun refer to?

1. lo (Jaime)

2. la

3. me

4. nos

[a]*guy* [b]*gentleman*

INPUT/OUTPUT
Act E., Suggestions:
Paso 1: Refer to information on dictogloss activities in the Instructor's Manual if you have not done one of these activities before. Paragraph: *Jaime conoce a María en el parque. La ayuda con sus papeles y libros.* *La acompaña Jaime hasta el Hotel Bonaparte, donde lo espera Mario. María se va y los dos hombres la miran caminando.*
Paso 2: Allow approximately 5 minutes. Students may still need to use some English to recreate the paragraph. Note: English speakers have a tendency to process the first noun or pronoun in a Spanish sentence as the subject, even when it is an object. For example, they interpret *la acompaña Jaime* as "she accompanies Jaime" and *lo espera Mario* as "he [Jaime] waits for Mario". Their knowledge of *Episodio 2* should help them arrive at the correct interpretation of these sentences.
Follow-up: Call on 1 or 2 groups to present their final versions, then display the original so all groups can compare. Be sure to ask a few content questions to keep the focus on meaning as well: *¿Qué le da María a Jaime en el parque? ¿Adónde va caminando María?*
INPUT/OUTPUT
Act. F, Suggestions:
Paso 1: Allow 2 minutes to complete.
Paso 2: Give students 3–4 minutes to conduct interviews, then ask the following question: *¿Cuántos de Uds. tienen parientes que los critican?* (Students raise hands.) Then ask

Actividad E ¿Qué leíste?

Paso 1 Lee rápidamente el párrafo que pone tu profesor(a) en la pizarra o el proyector. Trata de (*Try*) recordar la información, pero no tomes apuntes (*don't take notes*). Primero, estudia las siguientes palabras nuevas.

acompañar	to accompany
se va	he/she leaves
mirar a alguien caminando	to watch someone walking

Paso 2 En grupos de dos personas, escriban de nuevo (*rewrite*) el párrafo, incluyendo toda la información que recuerdan.

Actividad F Mi familia

Paso 1 Llena los espacios en blanco con información verdadera (*true*) sobre tu familia, según el modelo.

MODELO: Mi prima Ángela me llama frecuentemente.

1. Mi(s) _____ me abraza(n) (*hug*) cuando me ve(n).
2. Mi(s) _____ me molesta(n) (*annoy*).
3. Mi(s) _____ me visita(n) frecuentemente.
4. Mi(s) _____ me critica(n).
5. Mi(s) _____ me comprende(n) bien.
6. Mi(s) _____ me escucha(n).

Paso 2 Entrevista a un compañero (una compañera) de clase con las frases del **Paso 1.**

MODELO: ¿Te critican tus tías?

Actividad G Mi profesor(a)

INPUT
Actividad G

Indica la respuesta adecuada para cada situación a continuación.

1. Cuando tu profesor(a) llega a clase, ¿qué hace con sus cosas?
   Las pone _____.
2. ¿Con qué frecuencia da (*gives*) exámenes tu profesor(a)?
   Los da _____.
3. Cuando llega a clase, ¿qué hace tu profesor(a) con el libro de texto?
   Lo pone _____.
4. ¿Con qué frecuencia asigna las tareas tu profesor(a)?
   Las asigna _____.

individual students the following question: *¿Quién en tu familia te critica?* Tally the answers on the board. If time permits, repeat this procedure with another item from *Paso 1.*

INPUT

Act. H, Suggestion: After completing activity, ask students what other kinds of pets they have by saying: *¿Cuántos de Uds. tienen una mascota que no sea un perro o un gato?* Write the Spanish equivalent of a few pets they mention on the board and then poll the class to see if the same statements that apply to cats also apply to other pets.

Actividad H ¿Nos comprenden las mascotas?

Paso 1 Indica si los gatos nos hacen las siguientes cosas.

	SÍ, LO HACEN.	NO, NO LO HACEN.
1. Nos reciben con saltos (*jumping*).	☐	☐
2. Nos besan (*they kiss*).	☐	☐
3. Nos lamen (*they lick*).	☐	☐
4. Nos comprenden.	☐	☐
5. Nos obedecen.	☐	☐
6. Nos quieren.	☐	☐
7. Nos molestan.	☐	☐
8. Nos escuchan.	☐	☐

Paso 2 Ahora indica si los perros nos hacen las cosas del **Paso 1.** ¿Son diferentes las respuestas?

OUTPUT

Act. I, *Paso 2,* **Suggested follow-up:** Have students present their statements about one of the people they wrote about. Then ask the class: *¿Están de acuerdo con lo que dice* _____ (student's name) *de* _____ (famous person's name)? Then ask students to provide more opinions about that famous person by saying: *¿Qué más piensan de* _____ (famous person's name)?

Actividad I Personas famosas

Paso 1 Piensa en una mujer famosa (una actriz, mujer política, cantante [*singer*], etcétera) y escribe tres oraciones que indican tu opinión sobre ella. Los siguientes verbos pueden ser útiles.

admirar

adorar

apreciar (*to appreciate*)

detestar

estimar (*to think highly of*)

odiar (*to hate*)

querer (*to be fond of*)

respetar

MODELO: Nombre: Madonna

1. No la admiro.

2. La detesto.

Nombre: _____

1. _____

2. _____

3. _____

Ahora piensa en un hombre famoso y haz lo mismo (*do the same*).

Nombre: _____

1. _____

2. _____

3. _____

Paso 2 Léele a una persona de la clase el nombre de las personas y tus oraciones. ¿Está de acuerdo contigo?

Note: These vocabulary items can be heard in this lesson's Textbook Audio section of the Online Learning Center Website.

Vocabulario

Describing How People Look

No es muy alto.

Physical Traits

los ojos castaños

el pelo castaño

las orejas pequeñas

Es moreno.

Es de estatura mediana.

Miguel

el pelo canoso

la nariz larga

Es alto.

Thomas

el pelo rubio

el pelo lacio

los ojos verdes

la nariz pequeña

Es baja.

Abigail

Es pelirroja.

el pelo rizado

los ojos azules

las pecas

Kaitlin

* MÁS VOCABULARIO

las mejillas	cheeks
el mentón	chin
la piel	skin
los rasgos	traits
calvo/a	bald
corto/a	short (*except for height*)
delgado/a	thin
feo/a	ugly
gordito/a	chubby
guapo/a	handsome; good-looking
largo/a	long
¿Cómo es?	What does he/she look like? / What's it like? (e.g. hair, nose)

To describe physical characteristics related to parts of the body, Spanish uses the definite article (**el, la, los, las**), not a possessive, before a body part that is followed by an adjective. When an adjective is not used, the definite article is omitted.

> Ricardo tiene pelo.
> Ricardo tiene **el** pelo castaño.

Vistazo cultural,
Suggestion: Allow 2 minutes for students to read the text on their own. Then ask them the following questions: 1. *Un ejemplo del mestizaje es la mezcla de la herencia española con la indígena. ¿Cierto o falso?* (cierto) 2. *¿En qué países hay pocos mestizos de herencia africana o indígena* (el Uruguay, el Paraguay) 3. *¿Dónde hay muchos mestizos de herencia africana?* (la República Dominicana, Puerto Rico, Cuba, Venezuela, Colombia, Panamá). 4. *¿Dónde se encuentran mestizos de herencia indígena?* (answers include *México, Guatemala, El Salvador, Perú, Bolivia,* among others).
Follow-up: Use new vocabulary items to ask students questions about the photos (but do not require students to produce the new vocabulary until they have done activities on the next page): 1. *¿Quién tiene el pelo negro y largo?* (el mestizo peruano) 2. *¿Quién tiene el pelo rubio y corto* (el chico uruguayo) 3. *¿Quiénes tienen la piel morena* (el hispano del Caribe y el mestizo peruano), and so on.

Vistazo cultural

El mestizaje[a]

Entre las personas del mundo hispano hay mucha variedad de rasgos físicos. Esta variedad se debe[b] en parte a un fenómeno llamado **el mestizaje,** que se refiere a la mezcla[c] de razas[d] diferentes. En México, Centroamérica y Sudamérica el mestizaje se basa en la mezcla de la herencia[e] española con la indígena. Estas personas se llaman **mestizos.** Es cierto que muchos mestizos tienen la piel morena y los ojos oscuros,[f] pero no todos los hispanos son así. Por ejemplo, hay muchos mexicanos, peruanos y centroamericanos que tienen los ojos azules y el pelo rubio.

▲ Un mestizo peruano

En los países caribeños como Puerto Rico, Cuba y la República Dominicana, el mestizaje se refiere a la mezcla de la herencia española con la africana. Durante el período colonial, los españoles importaron[g] a muchos esclavos de África para trabajar en las minas y en los cañaverales de azúcar.[h] Por eso, muchas personas del Caribe, Venezuela, Colombia y Panamá tienen rasgos físicos que reflejan el mestizaje de estas dos culturas.

▲ Una mexicana de Guadalajara

Los uruguayos y paraguayos tienen características físicas europeas debido al[i] gran número de inmigrantes que llegaron[j] a sus países durante los siglos XIX y XX. Entre ellos había[k] muchos españoles, italianos y portugueses, así como japoneses y canadienses. En el Uruguay y el Paraguay hay pocos mestizos de herencia indígena o africana.

[a]El... *Mixing of races* [b]se... *is due* [c]*mixture* [d]*races* [e]*heritage* [f]*dark* [g]*imported* [h]cañaverales... *sugar cane fields* [i]debido... *due to the* [j]*arrived* [k]*there were*

▲ Un hispano del Caribe

▲ Un chico uruguayo

INPUT

Act. A, *Paso 2,*
Statements: 1. *¿Quién tiene la nariz larga?* (*Thomas*) 2. *¿Quién tiene los ojos azules?* (*Kaitlin*) 3. *¿Quién es un poco gordita?* (*Abigail*) 4. *¿Quién es de estatura mediana?* (*Miguel*) 5. *¿Quién tiene el pelo rizado?* (*Kaitlin*) 6. *¿Quién tiene la piel morena?* (*Miguel*)

Actividad A ¿A quién describe?

Paso 1 Estudia los dibujos en la página 156. En los espacios a continuación escribe el nombre de la persona que se describe.

1. _Miguel_ tiene las orejas pequeñas.
2. _Abigail_ tiene el pelo lacio.
3. _Thomas_ es alto.
4. _Miguel_ tiene los ojos castaños.
5. _Kaitlin_ es pelirroja.
6. _Abigail_ es baja.
7. _Kaitlin_ tiene pecas.
8. _Thomas_ tiene el pelo canoso.

Paso 2 Tu profesor(a) va a hacer una serie de preguntas. Contesta cada una con el nombre de la persona apropiada.

1. ...　　2. ...　　3. ...　　4. ...　　5. ...　　6. ...

INPUT

Act. B, Suggestion:
Read each statement once. Do not repeat unless students ask in Spanish for a repetition.
Statements: *Número 1. Esta persona tiene los ojos*

Actividad B Las estrellas de Hollywood

Tu profesor(a) va a leer una serie de descripciones. Selecciona la foto que corresponde a cada descripción y escribe el número de la descripción debajo de cada foto.

▲ Susan Sarandon __3__

azules. Tiene el pelo lacio y rubio. También es muy guapa. Número 2. Tiene las orejas pequeñas. Tiene el pelo rizado y negro. También es alto y guapo. Número 3. Es pelirroja y tiene los ojos castaños. Número 4. Tiene los ojos azules y el pelo canoso. También tiene el mentón grande. Número 5. Tiene el pelo lacio, largo y castaño. También tiene los ojos castaños. Número 6. Esta persona es baja y calva.

▲ Danny DeVito __6__

▲ Cameron Díaz __1__

▲ Salma Hayek __5__

▲ Will Smith __2__

▲ Jay Leno __4__

Act. B, Suggested follow-up: Bring additional magazine photos of other famous people and tape them on the chalkboard. Describe the photos and have the students guess which one you are describing.

INPUT/OUTPUT
Act. C, Suggestion:
Model the activity
with a student. Allow 3
minutes to complete the
activity. Make sure
students' descriptions are
polite.

Actividad C Veinte preguntas

Piensa en una persona de la clase sin mencionar su nombre. Un compañero (Una compañera) de clase va a hacerte preguntas del tipo sí/no para adivinar (*guess*) quién es esa persona. Luego, cambien de papeles.

MODELO: E1: ¿Tiene el pelo lacio?
  E2: Sí.
  E1: ¿Es alto?
  E2: No.
  E1: ¿Es mujer?
  E2: Sí.
  E1: Es baja... Es mujer... ¿Es Carolina?
  E2: ¡Sí!

OUTPUT
Actividad D

Actividad D ¿A quién se parece más?

Paso 1 Haz una lista de las características físicas de un compañero (una compañera) de la clase de español. Escribe sus características (los ojos azules, es alto, etcétera) en los espacios en blanco a continuación.

LOS RASGOS DE MI COMPAÑERO/A	PADRE	MADRE	LOS DOS	OTRO PARIENTE
1. _____	☐	☐	☐	☐
2. _____	☐	☐	☐	☐
3. _____	☐	☐	☐	☐
4. _____	☐	☐	☐	☐
5. _____	☐	☐	☐	☐
6. _____	☐	☐	☐	☐
7. _____	☐	☐	☐	☐
8. _____	☐	☐	☐	☐

Paso 2 Entrevista a esa persona para determinar si cada característica es heredada (*inherited*) de su padre, de su madre, de los dos o de otro pariente. Marca la caja (*box*) apropiada para cada característica física.

MODELO: E1: ¿Quién tiene los ojos azules?
  E2: Mi madre.
  E1: ¿Quién tiene pecas?
  E2: Mi padre.

Act. D, *Paso 3,* Point out:
Comparisons in Spanish
and their equivalents in
English. Comparisons are
presented in the next
Gramática section of this
lesson.

Paso 3 Con la información que tienes de los **Pasos 1** y **2,** indica cuál de las siguientes oraciones describe mejor a tu compañero/a de clase.

Mi compañero/a de clase se parece...

☐ más a su padre que a su madre.

☐ más a su madre que a su padre.

☐ tanto (*equally*) a su padre como a su madre.

☐ más a otro pariente.

NAVEGANDO LA RED 〰〰〰〰〰〰〰

Busca información en la red sobre la composición racial de cinco países latinoamericanos. Incluye dos países centroamericanos, dos sudamericanos y uno del Caribe. Indica el porcentaje (%) de la población que es mestizo, indígena y africano para cada país.

Gramática

| **Es más alto que yo.**

Comparisons of Equality and Inequality

COMPARISONS OF INEQUALITY		COMPARISONS OF EQUALITY	
Adjectives	Juanita es **más baja que** su madre. *Juanita is shorter than her mother.*	Adjectives	Claudia es **tan delgada como** María. *Claudia is as thin as María.*
	Marcos es **menos atlético que** su hermano. *Marcos is less athletic than his brother.*		Mis tíos son **tan cómicos como** mis padres. *My uncles are as funny as my parents.*
Adverbs	¿Hablas **más rápido que** el profesor? *Do you speak faster than the professor?*	Adverbs	Escriben **tan claramente como** nosotros. *They write as clearly as we do.*
	Salgo **con menos frecuencia que** ellos. *I go out less frequently than they do.*		No manejo **tan lento como** mis padres. *I don't drive as slowly as my parents do.*
Nouns	Tengo **más hermanos que** tú. *I have more siblings than you.*	Nouns	María tiene **tanto* trabajo como** Miguel. *María has as much work as Miguel.*
	Tengo **menos dinero que** otros estudiantes. *I have less money than other students.*		Pati compra **tanta ropa como** su hermana. *Pati buys as much clothing as her sister.*
			Tienes **tantos amigos como** yo. *You have as many friends as I do.*
			Tengo **tantas clases como** tú. *I have as many classes as you do.*

Comparisons of inequality compare differences involving adjectives, adverbs, and nouns using the expressions **más... que** and **menos... que.**

Comparisons of equality express similarities between things. Spanish uses **tan... como** with adjectives and adverbs and **tanto... como** with nouns, as indicated in the chart.

---

*Note that **tanto** must agree in gender and number with the noun that is being discussed.

When comparing similarities that do not involve an adjective, an adverb, or a noun, use **tanto como** (*as much as*).

Mis abuelos no trabajan **tanto como** mis padres.

My grandparents don't work as much as my parents.

De *Sol y viento,* **Note:** You can access this film clip from a special menu section on Disc 5 of the Instructional Version on DVD.

DE SOL Y VIENTO

In **Episodio 5** of *Sol y viento,* you will watch a scene in which Jaime tells María more about himself. Part of their exchange appears here.

JAIME
Oh, mi vida no es **tan fascinante como** la suya. Trabajo con una compañía de exportaciones, sigo la Bolsa[a] y corro para hacer un poco de ejercicio.

MARÍA
Tiene razón.[b] ¡Su vida no es **tan fascinante como** la mía!

Using **más... que** or **menos... que,** write one sentence in which you compare Jaime with María based on what you know about both of them.

[a]*stock market* [b]Tiene... *You're right.*

COMUNICACIÓN ÚTIL

To say that someone is *extremely* tall, happy, tired, and so forth, Spanish adds **-ísimo/a/os/as** to the end of adjectives. If the adjective ends in a consonant, simply add a form of **-ísimo** to the end of it.

La clase de literatura es **facilísima.**   *The literature class is extremely easy.*

If the adjective ends in a vowel, drop the final vowel, then add the correct form of **-ísimo.**

Roberto es **altísimo.**   *Roberto is extremely tall.*

If an adjective ends in **-c, -g,** or **-z,** a spelling change is necessary to maintain the original pronunciation of the adjective.

rico → ri**qu**ísimo

largo → lar**gu**ísimo

feliz (*happy*) → feli**c**ísimo

Actividad E Más sobre los personajes de *Sol y viento*

Paso 1 Llena los espacios en blanco con los nombres de personajes de *Sol y viento* para formar oraciones lógicas.

1. _____ es tan trabajador como _____.
2. _____ no cena en restaurantes tan frecuentemente como _____.
3. _____ no tiene tantas oportunidades para viajar (*to travel*) como _____.
4. _____ bebe tanto vino como _____.
5. _____ sufre (*suffers*) tanta presión en su trabajo como la sufre _____ en el suyo.

Paso 2 Ahora vuelve a las oraciones del **Paso 1** y cambia la comparación sin cambiar los nombres de las personas que indicaste (*you indicated*) para formular nuevas oraciones ciertas. Por ejemplo, si en el número 1 escribiste (*you wrote*) los nombres de Jaime y María, una nueva oración podría ser (*could be*) como las del modelo a continuación.

MODELO: Jaime es tan inteligente como María

o Jaime es tan guapo como María.

Actividad F Mi universidad

Paso 1 Indica si las siguientes oraciones son ciertas o falsas para ti.

En mi universidad... CIERTO FALSO

1. el equipo (*team*) de fútbol americano es mejor que el equipo de basquetbol. ☐ ☐
2. las residencias estudiantiles son tan feas como los apartamentos fuera del (*off*) campus. ☐ ☐
3. el rector (la rectora) (*president of the university*) es menor que mis padres. ☐ ☐
4. las humanidades son tan importantes como las ciencias naturales. ☐ ☐
5. el gimnasio es peor que un gimnasio privado. ☐ ☐
6. la vida social es tan importante como los estudios. ☐ ☐
7. las clases de español son tan grandes como las clases de psicología o sociología. ☐ ☐
8. la comida de la cafetería es mejor que comida rápida (*fast food*). ☐ ☐

Paso 2 Escribe de nuevo cada oración falsa para que sea verdadera (*so that it's true*) para ti.

MODELO: El equipo de fútbol americano es peor que el equipo de basquetbol.

¡Exprésate!

Just as in English, **bueno** and **malo** do not combine with **más** or **menos**. Instead, the following are used:

mejor que *better than*

peor que *worse than*

To indicate that something is *the best, the worst,* and so forth, use the definite article before these adjectives.

El equipo de basquetbol es **el peor** de todos.

INPUT/OUTPUT
Act. E., *Paso 1,* Suggestion: Allow students 2–3 minutes to complete, then poll the class for their answers to some of the items.
Paso 2, Suggestion: Explain to students that the idea is to keep the same person's name in the sentence but to change the comparison, forming a new comparison that is also true. Allow students 2–3 minutes to complete, then poll the class for their answers to some of the items.

INPUT/OUTPUT
Act. F, *Paso 1,* Suggestion: Allow 2 minutes to complete.
Paso 2, Suggestion: Allow 3 minutes to complete. Then put students in groups of 3 and have them compare answers. Afterward, call on a few groups to present their statements to the class.

Actividad G Los hermanos Alexander

Estudia los dibujos de Patricia y Jim Alexander a continuación. Luego, usa las expresiones **más... que** and **menos... que** para crear cuatro oraciones lógicas, según el modelo. Repasa la lista de adjetivos en las páginas 64–65 si es necesario. Luego, dos personas deben presentar sus oraciones a la clase. ¿Están todos de acuerdo?

MODELO: Patricia es más conservadora que Jim.

Actividad H Comparaciones

Paso 1 Entrevista a dos compañeros/as de clase para averiguar (*find out*) el tamaño (*size*) de su familia. Apunta el número de parientes de cada categoría a continuación.

MODELO: E1: ¿Cuántos hermanastros tienes?
E2: Dos. Un hermanastro y una hermanastra.

	E1	E2
1. hermanos	_____	_____
2. hermanastros	_____	_____
3. tíos solteros	_____	_____
4. primos	_____	_____
5. abuelos vivos	_____	_____
6. hijos	_____	_____
7. mascotas	_____	_____

Paso 2 Con la información del **Paso 1**, escribe tres afirmaciones con **tan/tanto... como** para hacer comparaciones sobre la familia de cada compañero/a de clase.

MODELO: Joe (no) tiene tantas hermanastras como hermanas.
La familia de Jen (no) es tan grande como la familia de Rob.

SOL Y VIENTO

A primera vista

Antes de ver el episodio

Actividad A ¿Qué recuerdas?

Indica si las siguientes oraciones son ciertas o falsas según lo que recuerdas del **Episodio 2** de *Sol y viento*.

	CIERTO	FALSO
1. Jaime juega al frisbee en un parque de Santiago.	☐	☑
2. Jaime se choca con (*bumps into*) María mientras lee un papelito de la suerte.	☑	☐
3. María trabaja en una excavación en el Valle del Maipo.	☑	☐
4. María permite que Jaime se quede con (*keep*) su tarjeta.	☑	☐
5. A Jaime no le importa (*Jaime doesn't care about*) la inteligencia de María.	☐	☑

Actividad B ¿Qué falta?

En el **Episodio 3** de *Sol y viento* vas a ver una escena en que Carlos y Jaime toman una copa de vino mientras hablan. A continuación hay unos fragmentos de su diálogo.

Act. B, Suggestion: Do not provide answers, as students verify their choices later.

CARLOS: ¡Salud![a]

JAIME: Hmmm... Delicioso... y un _____[1] color. Un merlot, si no me equivoco.[b]

CARLOS: Correcto. Una cosecha[c] muy especial, del 88. ¿Ud. _____[2] algo de vinos?

JAIME: Sí, algo. _____[3] pronto se dejará de producir.[d]

[a]*Cheers!* [b]*si... if I'm not mistaken* [c]*harvest* [d]*se... it won't be produced anymore*

Indica la respuesta más adecuada para cada espacio en blanco.

1. **a.** tan claro **b.** excelente **c.** monótono (*drab*)
2. **a.** dice **b.** lee **c.** sabe
3. **a.** Qué bueno que (*Good thing that*) **c.** Es cierto que (*It's certain that*)
   b. Lástima que (*Too bad that*)

Actividad C El episodio

Ahora mira el episodio. Si hay algo que no entiendes bien, puedes volver a ver la escena en cuestión.

Después de ver el episodio

Actividad A   ¿Qué recuerdas?

Contesta cada pregunta basándote en lo que recuerdas del **Episodio 3.**

1. ¿Quién es Traimaqueo?
   - **a.** un miembro de la familia Sánchez
   - **(b.)** un trabajador de la viña
2. Don Carlos está nervioso al reunirse con (*on meeting*) Jaime. ¿Cierto o falso?
   - **(a.)** cierto
   - **b.** falso
3. Carlos le dice a Jaime que su madre y su hermana están...
   - **(a.)** en Santiago.
   - **b.** en casa.
4. Según Carlos, su hermana no tiene interés en los asuntos (*matters*) de la viña. ¿Cierto o falso?
   - **(a.)** cierto
   - **b.** falso
5. Don Carlos y sus trabajadores están planeando...
   - **(a.)** una recepción para celebrar un vino nuevo.
   - **b.** una fiesta de cumpleaños (*birthday party*).
6. Jaime le dice a don Carlos que la venta (*sale*) tiene que suceder (*happen*) en los próximos días. ¿Cierto o falso?
   - **(a.)** cierto
   - **b.** falso

Actividad B   ¿Lo captaste?

Vuelve a la **Actividad B** en **Antes de ver el episodio** para verificar tus respuestas. Si es necesario, vuelve a ver el episodio.

Actividad C   Utilizando el contexto

Ya sabes que es difícil interpretar pronombres directos sin contexto. Al ver (*Upon watching*) más episodios de *Sol y viento*, trata de usar tus conocimientos (*knowledge*) del trama (*plot*) para ayudarte a identificar los pronombres. Considera el diálogo a continuación.

> JAIME: ¿Le molesta si primero doy[a] un tour por la viña?
> CARLOS: No, para nada. Pero yo necesito quedarme aquí en la oficina. Traimaqueo lo puede guiar. Yo lo voy a llamar a su celular. ¿Sabe llegar?

[a]*I take*

Basándote en el contexto, ¿a quién se refiere **lo** en **Traimaqueo lo puede guiar**? ¿Y en **Yo lo voy a llamar a su celular**?

Detrás de la cámara

After his father's death, Carlos assumed sole responsibility for managing the family winery, perhaps at an age when he was not yet ready or willing to do so. Lacking his father's good guidance, Carlos developed a stern and relentless demeanor that is immediately evident in the way he talks down to his workers. In short, Carlos orders people around because he can. The other members of the Sánchez family do not inquire into the runnings of the winery and as a result, his authority is unquestioned.

RESUMEN DE VOCABULARIO

Verbos

agradecer (zc)	to thank
conocer (zc)	to know, be familiar with
(des)obedecer (zc)	to (dis)obey
merecer (zc)	to deserve
ofrecer (zc)	to offer
parecerse (zc) (a)	to resemble
reconocer (zc)	to recognize
saber (*irreg.*)	to know (*facts, information*)
saber (*irreg.*) + *infin.*	to know how (*to do something*)

La familia

el/la abuelo/a	grandfather, grandmother
el/la cuñado/a	brother-in-law, sister-in-law
la esposa / la mujer	wife
el esposo / el marido	husband
el/la gemelo/a	twin
el/la hermanastro/a	stepbrother, stepsister
el/la hermano/a	brother, sister
el/la hijastro/a	stepson, stepdaughter
el/la hijo/a (único/a)	son, daughter; only child
la madrastra	stepmother
la madre (soltera)	(single) mother
el/la medio/a hermano/a	half brother, half sister
el/la nieto/a	grandson, granddaughter
el padrastro	stepfather
el padre (soltero)	(single) father
el/la primo/a	cousin
el/la sobrino/a	nephew, niece
el/la suegro/a	father-in-law, mother-in-law
el/la tío/a	uncle, aunt

el gato	cat
la mascota	pet
los parientes	relatives
el perro	dog

casado/a	married
soltero/a	single
viudo/a	widowed
vivo/a	alive

ya murió	he/she already died

Cognados: adoptivo/a, divorciado/a, extendido/a, materno/a, paterno/a, separado/a

¿Cómo es?

alto/a	tall
bajo/a	short
calvo/a	bald
castaño/a	brown (*hair, eyes*)
de estatura mediana	of medium height
delgado/a	thin
feo/a	ugly
gordito/a	chubby
guapo/a	handsome; good-looking
largo/a	long
moreno/a	dark-skinned
pelirrojo/a	redheaded

las pecas	freckles
los rasgos	traits

Algunas partes del cuerpo

las mejillas	cheeks
el mentón	chin
la nariz	nose
los ojos	eyes
las orejas	ears
el pelo	hair
canoso	gray
lacio	straight
rizado	curly
rubio	blond
la piel	skin

corto/a	short (*except for height*)

Las comparaciones

más... que	more . . . than
menos... que	less . . . than
tan... como	as . . . as
tanto/a/os/as... como	as much/many . . . as

mayor	older
mejor	better
menor	younger
peor	worse

¡A comer!

OBJETIVOS

IN THIS LESSON, YOU WILL LEARN:

- vocabulary to talk about what you eat for breakfast

- how to express negation

- vocabulary to talk about what you eat for lunch and for snacking

- more about the uses of **ser** and **estar**

- vocabulary to talk about what you eat for dinner

- to use indirect object pronouns

In addition, you will watch **Episodio 3** of the film *Sol y viento* again.

Las empanadas son una comida típica chilena.

The following media resources are available for this lesson of *Sol y viento*:

Episodio 3 of *Sol y viento*

Online *Manual de actividades*

Online Learning Center Website

PRIMERA PARTE

Note: These vocabulary items can be heard in this lesson's Textbook Audio section of the Online Learning Center Website.

Talking About What You Eat in the Morning

Vocabulario

El desayuno

Breakfast

Lo que **desayuna** Elsa Moreno, una estudiante de cine y televisión en la Universidad de California en Los Ángeles.

el café descafeinado

el jugo de naranja

una rosquilla con queso de crema (*a bagel with cream cheese*)

una media **toronja** (*half a grapefruit*)

el cereal con **leche** (*f.*)

una tostada de pan a la francesa

el pan tostado con **mermelada**

lunes

martes

miércoles

el yogur y una banana

el café con leche

unos panqueques

un huevo frito

jueves

viernes

los fines de semana

No desayuna. Tiene prisa. (*She's in a hurry.*)

No come **carne** (*f.*). Es **vegetariana.**

Lo que desayuna Franco Obregón, un estudiante de antropología en la Universidad Nacional Autónoma de México.

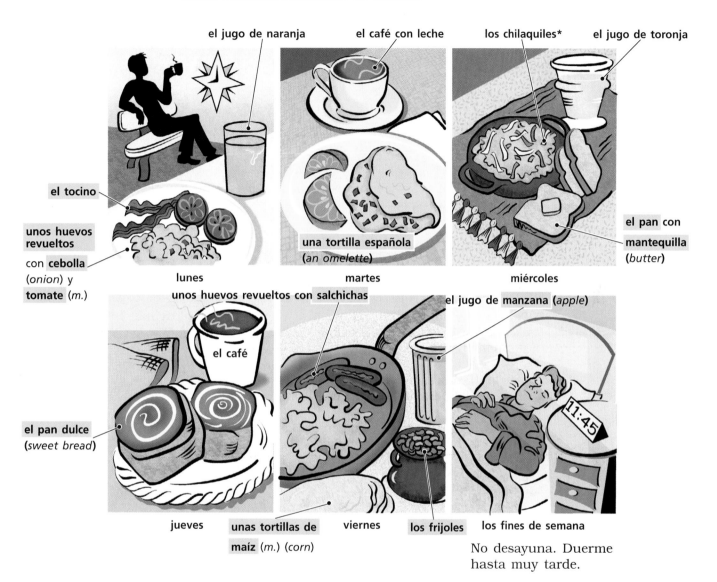

el jugo de naranja **el café con leche** **los chilaquiles*** **el jugo de toronja**

el tocino

unos huevos revueltos con **cebolla** (*onion*) y **tomate** (*m.*)

una tortilla española (*an omelette*)

el pan con **mantequilla** (*butter*)

lunes martes miércoles

unos huevos revueltos con salchichas

el jugo de manzana (*apple*)

el café

el pan dulce (*sweet bread*)

jueves **unas tortillas de maíz** (*m.*) (*corn*) viernes **los frijoles** los fines de semana

No desayuna. Duerme hasta muy tarde.

❋ MÁS VOCABULARIO

desayunar	to eat/have (for) breakfast
la barra de frutas/granola	fruit/granola bar
el cereal cocido	hot cereal
el té (caliente)	(hot) tea

*These are a Mexican specialty of strips of fried corn tortillas mixed with red or green salsa, onions, oregano, and crumbled cheese. They are sometimes mixed with scrambled eggs or shredded chicken.

Actividad A ¿Qué día es?

Tu profesor(a) va a mencionar unos alimentos (*food items*) que desayuna Elsa Moreno. Indica qué día de la semana corresponde a cada desayuno.

MODELO: PROFESOR(A): el jugo de naranja
ESTUDIANTE: Es martes.

1. ... **2.** ... **3.** ... **4.** ... **5.** ... **6.** ... **7.** ... **8.** ...

Actividad B ¿Cierto o falso?

Tu profesor(a) va a leer unas descripciones sobre los desayunos de Franco Obregón. Indica si cada oración es cierta o falsa.

1. ... **2.** ... **3.** ... **4.** ... **5.** ... **6.** ... **7.** ...

Actividad C ¿A quién describo?

Paso 1 Estudia los dibujos de Elsa y Franco en las páginas 168–169. Luego, escribe entre seis y ocho oraciones sobre lo que desayunan, pero no menciones sus nombres en las oraciones.

MODELO: Desayuna pan dulce los jueves.
Desayuna cereal con leche los miércoles.

Paso 2 Trabajando con un compañero (una compañera) de clase, primero dile «Cierra (*Close*) tu libro, por favor». Luego, léele tus oraciones. Él (Ella) tiene que adivinar (*guess*) a quién se refieren las oraciones. Después, cambien de papeles (*change roles*).

MODELO: E1: Desayuna pan dulce los jueves.
E2: Franco.
E1: ¡Correcto!

Actividad D ¿Qué desayunas tú?

Paso 1 Indica con qué frecuencia desayunas los siguientes alimentos.

	CON FRECUENCIA	DE VEZ EN CUANDO (*once in a while*)	RARAS VECES	NUNCA (*never*)
1. rosquillas	☐	☐	☐	☐
2. pan tostado	☐	☐	☐	☐
3. salchichas	☐	☐	☐	☐
4. jugo de naranja	☐	☐	☐	☐
5. yogur	☐	☐	☐	☐
6. huevos	☐	☐	☐	☐
7. cereal con leche	☐	☐	☐	☐

	CON FRECUENCIA	DE VEZ EN CUANDO (*once in a while*)	RARAS VECES	NUNCA (*never*)
8. café	☐	☐	☐	☐
9. tocino	☐	☐	☐	☐
10. barra de frutas	☐	☐	☐	☐
11. No desayuno.	☐	☐	☐	☐
12. ¿ ?	☐	☐	☐	☐

Paso 2 Entrevista a un compañero (una compañera) de clase para ver con qué frecuencia desayuna los alimentos del **Paso 1.**

MODELO: E1: ¿Con qué frecuencia desayunas pan tostado?
E2: De vez en cuando.

Paso 3 Escribe un breve resumen en el cual (*in which*) comparas tus preferencias con las de tu compañero/a de clase.

MODELO: Desayuno huevos y salchichas de vez en cuando, pero Miguel desayuna huevos y tocino con frecuencia. Nunca desayuno rosquillas, pero Miguel...

≋ Vistazo cultural

El horario de las comidas

El horario de las comidas varía de país a país. En los EE.UU.[a] y México, por ejemplo, la gente suele desayunar entre las 7:00 y las 9:00 de la mañana, pero en España desayunan a las 7:00. En los EE.UU., la gente almuerza a eso del[b] mediodía, pero en el mundo hispano suelen almorzar entre las 2:00 y las 4:00. La cena[c] típica norteamericana se come entre las 5:00 y las 7:00 de la tarde, pero en el mundo hispano tienden a cenar entre las 8:00 y las 11:00 de la noche, dependiendo del país y de otros factores.

▲ Los bolillos (*rolls*) con mantequilla y un café son un desayuno típico español.

Para los hispanos, el almuerzo tiende a ser la comida más fuerte[d] del día. Para el norteamericano, la cena es la comida más fuerte. Presta atención a[e] estas diferencias mientras estudias lo que comen Elsa y Franco en esta lección.

[a]Estados Unidos   [b]*a... around*   [c]*dinner*   [d]*más... heaviest*   [e]*Presta... Pay attention to*

	DESAYUNO	ALMUERZO	CENA
EE.UU.	7:00–9:00	11:00–1:00	5:00–7:00
España	7:00–8:00	2:00–4:00	10:00–11:00
México	7:00–9:00	2:00–4:00	8:00–10:00

Gramática

No lo sé tampoco.   Indefinite and Negative Words

In prior lessons of *Sol y viento* you have used indefinite words like **algo** and **alguien** and negative words like **nada** and **nunca**. The chart on the next page lists the indefinite and negative words commonly used in Spanish.

The simplest way to express negation in Spanish or English is to use the word **no.** Although English typically does not use double negation, Spanish must if **no** is used.

—¿Quieres desayunar **algo**?	*Do you want something for breakfast?*
—**No, no** quiero desayunar **nada.**	*No, I don't want anything for breakfast.*
—¿Tiene **algún** mensaje para la profesora?	*Do you have a message for the professor?*
—**No, no** tengo **ninguno.**	*No, I don't have any.*

Similar to subjects, negative words in Spanish can come before or after a verb. When a negative word comes after a verb, a **no** must precede the verb.

Nunca desayuno salchichas. **No** desayuno salchichas **nunca.**	*I never have sausage for breakfast.*
Tampoco voy a comer en ese restaurante. **No** voy a comer en ese restaurante **tampoco.**	*I'm not going to eat in that restaurant either.*

▲ **¿Siempre** tomas café en la mañana con el desayuno? ¿O **no** lo tomas **nunca**?

INDEFINITE AND NEGATIVE WORDS	
LAS PALABRAS INDEFINIDAS	LAS PALABRAS NEGATIVAS
algo (*something*) ¿Deseas **algo**?	**nada** (*nothing*) **No, no** quiero **nada**.
alguien (*someone, anyone*) **Alguien** viene.	**nadie** (*no one, not anyone*) **No** viene **nadie**. **Nadie** viene.
algún* (**alguno/a/os/as**) (*some, any*) Tengo **algunos** libros rusos.	**ningún*** (**ninguno/a**) (*none, not any*) **No** tengo **ningún** libro ruso.
siempre (*always*) **Siempre** veo a Juan en su oficina.	**nunca, jamás** (*never*) **Nunca** veo a Juan en su oficina. **No** veo a Juan **nunca** en su oficina. Juan **jamás** está en su oficina. Juan **no** está **jamás** en su oficina.
también (*also, too*) **También** conozco a Rudolfo.	**tampoco** (*neither, not either*) **Tampoco** conozco al chico nuevo. **No** conozco al chico nuevo **tampoco**.

De *Sol y viento,* **Note:** You can access this film clip from a special menu section on Disc 5 of the Instructional Version on DVD.

 DE SOL Y VIENTO

In **Episodio 3** of *Sol y viento*, Mario asks Jaime why he looks so reflective. Part of their exchange appears in the dialogue.

MARIO
¿Se siente bien,ᵃ don Jaime? ¿Eh?

JAIME
Sí, Mario. Un recuerdo lejanoᵇ...

MARIO
Tan serio que está.

JAIME
No es _____. Vamos.

Selecting from the following list, what word do you think Jaime says in this scene?

1. nadie
2. ninguno
3. nada *(circled)*

ᵃ¿Se... *Do you feel OK*   ᵇrecuerdo... *distant memory*

*The adjectives **alguno** and **ninguno** shorten to **algún** and **ningún** before masculine singular nouns. The plural forms **ningunos** and **ningunas** are not used.

Actividad E Los desayunos de Jaime Talavera

Basándote en lo que sabes de Jaime Talavera de *Sol y viento*, indica si las siguientes oraciones son ciertas o falsas.

	CIERTO	FALSO
1. No desayuna **nunca** en restaurantes de comida rápida.	☐	☐
2. Siempre toma un jugo de naranja por la mañana.	☐	☐
3. Jamás desayuna cereales para niños (*children*) como Trix o Lucky Charms.	☐	☐
4. Tampoco desayuna leche con chocolate.	☐	☐
5. En su refrigerador **no** hay **ningún** desayuno congelado (*frozen*).	☐	☐
6. Nadie le hace (*make him*) el desayuno. Él mismo lo prepara.	☐	☐

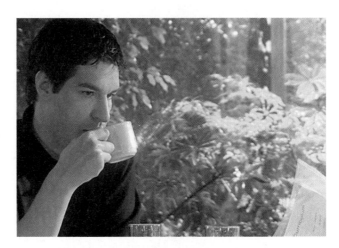

▲ ¿Crees que Jaime siempre toma café con azúcar (*sugar*) o nunca toma café con azúcar?

Actividad F El estudiante típico

Con otra persona, crea cinco oraciones utilizando las expresiones negativas para hablar del estudiante típico y cómo desayuna. Algunas oraciones deben ser lógicas y otras no. Luego, tú y tu compañero/a deben presentar sus oraciones a los demás miembros de la clase. ¿Cómo responden ellos?

MODELO: No desayuna nunca chilaquiles.
          Tampoco come panqueques en la mañana.

Actividad G   El profesor (La profesora) ideal

Paso 1   Usa expresiones indefinidas (**algo, siempre,** etcétera) y palabras negativas (**nada, nunca,** etcétera) para escribir cuatro oraciones sobre lo que el
profesor (la profesora) ideal hace o no hace.

MODELO: El profesor (La profesora) ideal siempre llega a clase a tiempo.

Paso 2   En grupos de tres personas comparen sus oraciones. ¿Están de
acuerdo con lo que dicen todos? Hagan una lista de las oraciones con las que
todos están de acuerdo para presentársela a la clase.

▲ ¿Siempre escucha a sus estudiantes María? ¿Crees
que ella es una profesora ideal?

◉ Enfoque lingüístico

Más sobre la negación

Although negation may seem like a simple concept, different languages make negative statements in different ways. English uses a form of the auxiliary verb *do* and the
adverb *not* before the verb, as in the following sentences: *I don't know you, James
does not speak Japanese,* and *Don't we need to go now?* French is somewhat different than English in that it uses a two-part adverb that surrounds the verb. To make a
sentence negative in French, you place *ne* in front of a conjugated verb and the adverb
pas after it. The French equivalent of *James does not speak Japanese* is *James **ne**
parle **pas** japonais.*

Negation in Spanish is interesting because it allows (and in some cases requires)
what English dislikes: double negation. Whenever a negative word is used after a verb
in Spanish, another negative word must precede the verb, as in **Juan no sabe nada.**
An English speaker can say *Juan doesn't know anything* or *Juan knows nothing* but
cannot combine both *doesn't* and *nothing.* This is not to say that double negatives
never happen in English. Few would fault the Rolling Stones for saying they "can't get
no satisfaction," nor would we be surprised to hear someone say "You ain't seen nothing yet." On the whole, however, most double negatives are seen as bad use of language by English speakers.

Note: These vocabulary items can be heard in this lesson's Textbook Audio section of the Online Learning Center Website.

Talking About
What You Eat
During the Day

Vocabulario

El almuerzo y la merienda

Lo que come Elsa durante el día

Lunch and Snacking

A las 10:00 A.M. Elsa **merienda...**

nueces (*f.*) (*nuts*)

o **una fruta.**

A mediodía almuerza...

**un sándwich de
atún** (*tuna*), una
manzana y **té** (*m.*)
helado

o **una porción** de **pizza** vegetariana
y **un refresco dietético**

o **una hamburguesa**
vegetariana con queso,
papas fritas y **agua** (*f.*).*

A las 2:00 P.M. merienda...

galletas

o algunos **dulces** (*m.*) (*candy*).

*The word **agua** is feminine, but the article **el** is used with it in its singular form: *el **agua** fría* but *las **aguas** frías.*

Lo que come Franco durante el día

A mediodía Franco merienda...

papitas (*potato chips*)

o unos dulces

o una manzana.

A las 2:00 P.M. almuerza...

sopa, bistec (*m.*) con frijoles, **ensalada mixta,** tortillas de maíz, **helado** (*ice cream*) de frutas, **una cerveza** o **vino tinto** (*red wine*)

o **arroz** (*m.*) con **zanahorias** (*carrots*), **chuleta de cerdo** (*pork chop*) con **puré** (*m.*) **de papas** (*mashed potatoes*), **verduras** mixtas, **flan** (*m.*) (*baked custard*) y agua

o sopa de **camarones** (*m.*) (*shrimp*), **pescado frito** (*fried fish*) con **limón** (*m.*) y **salsa,** ensalada de **aguacate** (*m.*) (*avocado*) y tomate y **vino blanco.**

A las 5:00 P.M. merienda...

pan dulce con café

o una fruta

o **galletas saladas** (*crackers*).

✱ MÁS VOCABULARIO

almorzar (ue)	to eat/have (for) lunch
merendar (ie)	to snack / have (for) a snack
la mantequilla de cacahuete	peanut butter
el sándwich de	
jamón (*m.*)	ham sandwich
pavo	turkey sandwich
pollo	chicken sandwich
rosbif (*m.*)	roast beef sandwich

INPUT
Act. A, Statements:
1. *bistec con verduras (almuerzo mexicano)* 2. *una porción de pizza (almuerzo norteamericano)* 3. *un sándwich de jamón y queso (almuerzo norteamericano)* 4. *un plato de pescado (almuerzo mexicano)* 5. *una cerveza (almuerzo mexicano)* 6. *una hamburguesa con papas fritas (almuerzo norteamericano)* 7. *un refresco (almuerzo norteamericano)*

INPUT/OUTPUT
Act. B, Statements: Note that there may be more than one correct answer in some instances.
1. *un refresco dietético (los dos)* 2. *una ensalada con pollo y jamón (almuerzo)* 3. *una hamburguesa con queso (almuerzo)* 4. *sopa de verduras (almuerzo)* 5. *nueces (merienda)* 6. *una naranja (los dos)* 7. *un sándwich de pavo con papitas (almuerzo)* 8. *dulces (merienda)* 9. *papas fritas (los dos)* 10. *galletas (merienda)*
Paso 2: This is a signature-search activity. Allow students 4–5 minutes to roam around the room to find people who eat the same snacks. To ensure that students interact with several classmates, tell them they cannot write the same name in any two blanks. You might wish to model for them before they begin by walking up to someone: *Hola. ¿Meriendas nueces? No, pues gracias.* or *¿Sí? Firma aquí, por favor,* then move on to someone else.

OUTPUT
Act. C, Suggestions
Paso 1: Review the 6 categories with your students and have them

Actividad A ¿Almuerzo norteamericano o almuerzo mexicano?

Escucha las comidas que menciona tu profesor(a) e indica si cada una se refiere al almuerzo norteamericano (lo que comería [*would eat*] Elsa) o al almuerzo mexicano (lo que comería Franco).

1. ... **2.** ... **3.** ... **4.** ... **5.** ... **6.** ... **7.** ...

Actividad B ¿Almuerzo o merienda?

Paso 1 Tu profesor(a) va a mencionar unos alimentos. Indica si cada alimento se come para **el almuerzo,** para **la merienda,** o para **los dos,** según los dibujos anteriores.

1. ... **2.** ... **3.** ... **4.** ... **5.** ... **6.** ... **7.** ... **8.** ... **9.** ... **10.** ...

Paso 2 En la primera columna de la tabla, menciona cuatro cosas que meriendas con frecuencia. Luego, trata de encontrar a dos compañeros de clase que meriendan cada alimento de tu lista y escribe sus nombres in la segunda columna.

MERIENDA   COMPAÑEROS DE CLASE

1. _____   _____   _____
2. _____   _____   _____
3. _____   _____   _____
4. _____   _____   _____

give additional examples of foods in each category.
Paso 2: Allow students 5 minutes to ask you questions.
Paso 3: Allow 2 minutes to complete. Poll class for answers to a few of the items. Ask students to recall which items you eat from each of the categories.
Paso 4: Allow 3 minutes to complete, then call on volunteers to offer their statements.

Actividad C ¿Qué almuerza mi profesor(a)?

Paso 1 Repasa la información en la pirámide de las comidas en la siguiente página.

Paso 2 La clase va a hacerle preguntas al profesor (a la profesora) para saber si come para el almuerzo y la merienda alimentos de todos los grupos básicos. ¿Cuánta información pueden Uds. obtener en sólo cinco minutos? Usen **tú** o **Ud.,** según la preferencia de tu profesor(a).

MODELO: ¿Almuerza Ud. manzanas? / ¿Almuerzas manzanas?

Paso 3 En grupos de dos personas, indiquen la cantidad de alimentos de cada categoría de la pirámide de las comidas que consume su profesor(a).

El grupo de...	MUCHOS ALIMENTOS	POCOS ALIMENTOS
1. grasas, aceites y dulces	☐	☐
2. leche, yogur y queso	☐	☐
3. carne, aves, pescado, frijoles, huevos y nueces	☐	☐
4. verduras	☐	☐
5. frutas	☐	☐
6. pan, cereales, tortillas, arroz y pasta	☐	☐

Paso 4 Usando las frases **más/menos... que** y **tanto... como,** escribe dos oraciones en las cuales comparas tu dieta con la de tu profesor(a).

MODELO: Yo como menos frutas que mi profesor(a).

Grasas,[a] aceite[b] y dulces

El grupo de la leche, el yogur y el queso

El grupo de la carne, las aves,[c] el pescado, los frijoles, los huevos y las nueces

El grupo de las verduras

El grupo de las frutas

El grupo del pan, los cereales, las tortillas, el arroz y la pasta

[a]*Fats* [b]*oil* [c]*poultry*

Vistazo cultural,
Suggestion: Have students read quickly. Then ask them the following questions: *Azúcar... ¿es palabra de origin náhuatl o árabe? ¿Qué es el origin de la palabra* chocolate? *¿Y la palabra* café?
Follow-up: Have students do an Internet search and come to class with a list of 10 Spanish words borrowed into English (one example is *patio*) and 10 English words borrowed into Spanish (one example is *los jeans*). Have students present their lists while you write the words on the board using semantic maps to group them into different categories such as foods, animals (example: alligator), clothing (example: poncho), battle terms (examples: armada, flotilla, conquistador), technology, ranch life (examples: ranch, rodeo, lasso), and colloquial usage (examples: siesta, nada, adiós). Compare the categories of words borrowed across the two languages and highlight any differences. For example, many English words borrowed into Spanish are related to technology, clothing, and pop culture while many Spanish words borrowed into English are related to foods, animals, etc.

Vistazo cultural

Las palabras préstamo[a]

Muchas palabras que se usan en español para nombrar las comidas tienen su origen en otros idiomas como el náhuatl y el árabe. El náhuatl es el idioma hablado por los aztecas de México. Muchas palabras del náhuatl se incorporaron[b] al español durante la conquista de México en el siglo XVI. ¿Puedes adivinar[c] el significado en español de estas palabras?

▲ Un mercado mexicano típico.

- ahuakatl
- chokolatl
- tomatl

Estás en lo correcto si dices que estas palabras quieren decir **aguacate, chocolate y tomate,** respectivamente. Hay también muchas palabras de origen árabe en el español moderno. Estas palabras se incorporaron a la lengua española entre 711 y 1492 (mil cuatrocientos noventa y dos), cuando los moros[d] dominaban[e] el territorio que hoy día es España y Portugal. Del árabe tenemos las siguientes palabras relacionadas con las comidas y bebidas.

aceite	alcohol	arroz	azúcar[g]	café	naranja
alcachofa[f]	alfalfa	atún	berenjena[h]	espinacas[i]	zanahoria

[a]*Las... Loan words* [b]*se... were incorporated* [c]*guess* [d]*Arabs* [e]*were in control of* [f]*artichoke* [g]*sugar* [h]*eggplant* [i]*spinach*

Gramática

Está muy serio. **Ser Versus estar with Adjectives**

You learned in the **Lección preliminar** and in **Lección 2B** that Spanish has two verbs for English *to be*—**ser** and **estar**—and you have been using these verbs in different contexts throughout *Sol y viento.* The chart on the next page shows a summary of how you have seen or used each verb so far.

Although the chart summarizes most of the uses of **ser** and **estar,** in this lesson you will use **ser** and **estar** with adjectives to talk primarily about food. Remember that **ser** is used to talk about inherent qualities and **estar** is used to talk about qualities that are not inherent in nature.

Los limones **son** agrios.	*Lemons are sour.*
Estas nueces **están** saladas.	*These nuts are salty.*

Here are some common adjectives you will use to describe food.

agrio/a	sour
amargo/a	bitter
cocido/a	cooked
crudo/a	raw
dulce	sweet
pasado/a	spoiled
picante / picoso/a	hot, spicy
salado/a	salty

Note that very often we use the verbs *taste, seem, look* where Spanish uses **estar.**

No **está** cocido.	*It doesn't seem cooked.*
Está bastante dulce.	*It tastes rather sweet.*

✳ **MÁS GRAMÁTICA**

In addition to being used with adjectives like **cansado, contento,** and **sucio, estar** is also used with past participles to describe people and things. Past participles are words derived from verbs. Most English past participles end in *-ed* or *-en* (*cooked, served, ordered, frozen, written, broken*). Spanish past participles are formed by adding **-ado** to the stem of **-ar** verbs and by adding **-ido** to the stem of **-er** and **-ir** verbs. When used with **estar,** past participles function as adjectives and must agree in gender and number with the nouns they modify.

lavar (*to wash*) → lav**ado**	Las papas **están lavadas.**
vender → vend**ido**	No **está vendido** el restaurante.
servir → serv**ido**	La sopa ya (*already*) **está servida.**

SUMMARY OF THE USES OF *ser* AND *estar*		
ser		
to express origin (with **de**)	**Soy de** Cuba. ¿**De** dónde **eres**?	*I'm from Cuba.* *Where are you from?*
to express time	¿Qué hora **es**? **Son** las dos y quince. Hoy **es** lunes.	*What time is it?* *It's 2:15.* *Today is Monday.*
to express possession (with possessive adjectives or with **de**)	**Es** mi libro. ¿**De** quién **es**? La mochila **es de** Juan.	*It's my book.* *Whose is this?* *The backpack is Juan's.*
to describe people and things	**Somos** inteligentes. **Es** una mujer seria. La clase **es** interesante.	*We're intelligent.* *She's a serious woman.* *The class is interesting.*
to identify people and things	¿**Sois** estudiantes? ¿Qué **es** esto? Tú y yo **somos** amigos.	*Are you students?* *What is this?* *You and I are friends.*
to talk about inherent qualities with adjectives	El suéter **es** verde. **Son** muy malos.	*The sweater is green.* *They're very bad (malicious)* *people.*
estar		
to express the location of objects and people	Mi tío **está** en México. ¿Dónde **están**?	*My uncle is in Mexico.* *Where are they?*
to express a condition or quality that is subject to change or that is not characteristic	La banana **está** verde. **Están** malos.	*The banana is green (unripe).* *They're in bad shape (sick).*

De *Sol y viento*, Note: You can access this film clip from a special menu section on Disc 5 of the Instructional Version on DVD.
Point out: Carlos uses the verb *está* in this context. Students may think the correct verb form is *es,* but point out the cue *ya* that indicates a change in inherent qualities, something they've learned earlier.

DE SOL Y VIENTO

In **Episodio 3** of *Sol y viento,* you will review the scene in which Carlos explains to Jaime why he wants to sell the winery. Part of their exchange appears in the dialogue.

CARLOS
Una viña siempre **es** mucho trabajo. Llevo muchos años entre toneles[a] y botellas.[b] Mi madre ya ___está___ muy vieja, y mi hermana no tiene ningún interés en estos asuntos. Prefiero hacer el negocio con Uds. y salirme de esto.[c]

JAIME
Por eso vine,[d] para finalizar el negocio.

What verb do you think Carlos uses in the preceding blank, es or está?

[a]*barrels*   [b]*bottles*   [c]*salirme... get out of all of this*   [d]*Por... That's why I came*

Actividad D ¿Cómo reacciona Jaime?

Empareja una frase de la primera columna con una de la segunda columna para formar oraciones lógicas sobre lo que probablemente hace Jaime Talavera en las siguientes situaciones.

Cuando...

1. __b__ está pasada la leche en el refrigerador
2. __c__ está malo el servicio en un restaurante
3. __e__ está bien vestida María
4. __d__ está muy ocupado (*busy*) con su trabajo
5. __a__ está fresco el aire

Jaime probablemente...

a. corre en el parque.
b. la tira en la basura (*he throws it in the garbage*).
c. no vuelve a almorzar allí.
d. trabaja toda la noche sin dormir.
e. le da un cumplido (*he gives her a compliment*).

Actividad E Correspondencias

Tu profesor(a) va a mencionar un alimento o una bebida. Indica la oración que mejor describe ese alimento o bebida.

1. **(a.)** Es agria.   **b.** Es dulce.
2. **(a.)** Son picosos. **b.** Son salados.
3. **a.** Es cara.   **(b.)** Es barata.
4. **(a.)** Es amargo.   **b.** Es agrio.
5. **a.** Son duras (*hard*). **(b.)** Son blandas (*tender*).
6. **a.** Es picante.   **(b.)** Es dulce.
7. **(a.)** Son saladas. **b.** Son crudas.

Actividad F ¿Te molesta? (*Does it bother you?*)

Paso 1 Indica si las siguientes cosas te molestan en un restaurante.

5 = Me molesta mucho.
3 = Me molesta un poco.
0 = No me molesta para nada.

1. ___ Los refrescos están aguados (*watered down*).
2. ___ Las papas fritas están muy saladas.
3. ___ Los cubiertos (*silverware*) no están bien lavados.
4. ___ La mantequilla no está fría.
5. ___ El jugo de naranja está agrio.
6. ___ La salsa está muy picosa.
7. ___ El bistec está quemado (*burned*).
8. ___ La ensalada está servida en un tazón (*bowl*) y no en un plato (*plate*).

Paso 2 Ahora entrevista a un compañero (una compañera) de clase, según el modelo.

MODELO: E1: ¿Te molesta si los refrescos están aguados?
         E2: Sí, me molesta mucho.

Paso 3 Ahora compara tus respuestas con las de tu compañero/a. ¿Quién se molesta más en cuanto al (*with regard to the*) servicio en los restaurantes?

Actividad G Una historia

Paso 1 Con un compañero (una compañera), inventen una historia sobre lo que pasa en los siguientes dibujos. A continuación hay algunas ideas para considerar.

- ¿Cómo se llaman el hombre y la mujer?
- ¿Qué celebran?
- ¿Qué cenan en el restaurante?
- ¿Les gusta la comida?
- ¿Cómo se sienten (*do they feel*) durante la cena?
- ¿Cómo termina (*end*) la noche?

Paso 2 Compartan su historia con el resto de la clase. ¿Quiénes inventaron la mejor historia?

NAVEGANDO LA RED

Busca un menú en español de un restaurante en *una* de las siguientes regiones: 1) la costa mediterránea de España; 2) el Caribe; 3) La Pampa (la Argentina). Menciona algunas comidas y bebidas interesantes del menú y sus ingredientes principales.

 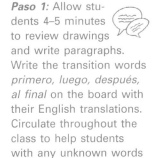

Vocabulario

Talking About What
You Eat at Night

Note: These vocabulary items can be heard in this lesson's Textbook Audio section of the Online Learning Center Website.

La cena

✳ **Dinner**

Unas cenas típicas de Elsa

A las 6:00 P.M. Elsa **cena**...

(1)

una hamburguesa de **soja** (*soy*), una papa **al horno** (*baked*), maíz (1), una cerveza y un helado (2)

(2)

(3)

o **mariscos** (*seafood*) como **la langosta** (3), los camarones y el pescado, **bróculi** (*m.*) y **coliflor** (*f.*) **al vapor** (*steamed*), arroz, una porción de **pastel** (*m.*) (4) y vino blanco

(4)

o **los espaguetis** con salsa roja y una ensalada mixta (5).

(5)

Como es vegetariana, Elsa no come ni bistec ni pollo para la cena.

Unas cenas típicas de Franco

A las 9.00 P.M. Franco cena...

(6)

un sándwich de carne (pavo, jamón o rosbif) y un refresco o unos tamales* con **chocolate** (*m.*) **caliente** (6)

o **las sobras** (*leftovers*) del almuerzo y una cerveza

o pan dulce o **pasteles** (7) con café.

(7)

✳ MÁS VOCABULARIO	
cenar	to eat/have (for) dinner
la carne de res	beef
los espárragos	asparagus
la lechuga	lettuce
los postres	desserts

◀ ¿Es esta una cena norteamericana o mexicana? ¿Cómo lo sabes?

---

*Tamales are cornmeal dough filled with seasoned meat or other ingredients that are then wrapped in corn husks and steamed.

INPUT
Actividad A

INPUT
Act. B, Statements:
1. *Voy a cenar pollo al horno y puré de papas. Quiero preparar también una ensalada mixta. Para postre, voy a comer una porción de pastel de chocolate.* (un norteamericano) 2. *Voy a cenar unas sobras del almuerzo... quizás un bistec con frijoles y una cerveza.* (un mexicano) 3. *Para la cena voy a comer pasteles de fruta y un café descafeinado.* (un mexicano) 4. *Esta noche quiero tomar un vino tinto. Después voy a preparar espaguetis con una salsa de carne de res y verduras al vapor.* (un norteamericano)

Actividad A Asociaciones

Empareja un alimento de la primera columna con el estado de los Estados Unidos con que se asocia en la segunda columna.

1. _d_ Las naranjas		**a.** California
2. _g_ Las papas		**b.** Maine
3. _i_ El maíz		**c.** Wisconsin
4. _f_ Las manzanas		**d.** Florida
5. _h_ El bistec	se asocia(n) con el estado de	**e.** Colorado
6. _b_ La langosta		**f.** Washington
7. _a_ Los vinos		**g.** Idaho
8. _e_ La cerveza Coors		**h.** Texas
9. _c_ El queso		**i.** Iowa

Actividad B ¿Quién habla?

Escucha lo que dicen las siguientes personas sobre lo que van a cenar esta noche. Luego, indica si lo dice un norteamericano o un mexicano.

1. ...

2. ...

3. ...

4. ...

INPUT/OUTPUT
Act. C, Statements:
1. *el pollo asado* (las proteínas)
2. *el pan* (los carbohidratos)
3. *el pastel* (los dulces)
4. *el aceite de oliva* (las grasas)
5. *el helado* (los productos lácteos, los dulces, las grasas)
6. *la langosta* (las proteínas)
7. *el arroz* (los carbohidratos)
8. *la mantequilla* (los productos lácteos, las grasas)
9. *la leche* (los productos lácteos, las proteínas)
10. *los espaguetis* (los carbohidratos)

Actividad C Categorías

Tu profesor(a) va a leer una lista de comidas. Escribe cada comida en la categoría apropiada. Es posible que algunas comidas pertenezcan a (*belong to*) más de una categoría.

LOS CARBOHIDRATOS	LAS PROTEÍNAS	LOS PRODUCTOS LÁCTEOS (*dairy products*)	LAS GRASAS	LOS DULCES

Suggestion: After completing activity say: *Ahora voy a mencionar una categoría de comidas y Uds. me van a decir unos ejemplos de alimentos que pertenecen a esa categoría.* Mention the categories from the table in this activity as well as others (*frutas, verduras, bebidas*).

¡Exprésate!

In Spanish, the concept of *(the)*
both of is usually rendered with
los dos with the verb form or
other structure indicating who
the two people are.

Los dos vamos.	*Both of us are going.*
Los dos van.	*The two of them are going.*

Remember that with **gustar**, you
will need to use an **a** before **los
dos** because **gustar** literally
means *to be pleasing to.*

A los dos nos gustan verduras.	*We both like vegetables. (lit.: Vegetables are pleasing to us both.)*

Actividad D ¿Qué cenas?

Paso 1 Entrevista a un compañero (una compañera) de clase para averiguar (*find out*) lo que le gusta cenar. Trata de obtener todos los detalles posibles.

MODELO: E1: ¿Qué te gusta cenar?
E2: Me gustan los espaguetis.
E1: ¿Cómo te gustan? ¿Con salsa de tomate? ¿Con carne?

Paso 2 A base de la información obtenida en el **Paso 1,** decide si tú y tu compañero/a serían (*would be*) buena compañía para salir a cenar. Explica por qué sí o por qué no con dos o tres ejemplos.

MODELO: Roberto sería buena compañía de cena. A los dos nos gusta...

Actividad E Un menú

Paso 1 Repasa brevemente lo que cenan Elsa, la estudiante de California, y Franco, el estudiante de México. ¿Crees que estas cenas son típicas de los estudiantes de tu universidad? En grupos de dos, hagan los cambios necesarios para crear un menú que refleje lo que los estudiantes de su universidad cenan.

Paso 2 Presenten su menú a la clase. ¿Están de acuerdo sus compañeros de clase con respecto a lo que cenan los estudiantes de esta universidad?

〰 Vistazo cultural

Las comidas regionales

En varias partes del mundo hispano se comen alimentos que para los norteamericanos son exóticos. En Santander, Colombia, por ejemplo, las hormigas[a] fritas son una de las meriendas populares. Según los residentes de esa región, saben a[b] nueces.

Una especialidad del estado de Oaxaca, México, son los chapulines[c] fritos. Se comen como merienda (**botana** en México) o como aperitivo.[d] La ciudad de Dolores Hidalgo en el estado de Guanajuato, México, es conocida por sus helados de sabores[e]

▲ ¿ A qué crees que sabe el cuy?

raros. Además de chocolate, vainilla, fresa[f] y otros sabores conocidos, también son populares los helados de aguacate, tequila, camarón, maíz, queso, chicharrón[g] y cerveza.

En el Perú y otros países andinos, la carne del cuy[h] es un alimento de los nativos desde la época precolonial. El cuy es alto en proteínas y muy bajo en grasas, y por eso es una carne ideal para muchos andinos. ¿A qué crees que sabe el cuy?

[a]*ants* [b]*saben... they taste like* [c]*grasshoppers* [d]*appetizer* [e]*flavors* [f]*strawberry*
[g]*fried pork skin* [h]*guinea pig*

Gramática

Talking About
To Whom and
For Whom

¿Le gusta el vino?   **Indirect Object Pronouns and gustar**

You may remember that the verb **gustar** means *to be pleasing to* even though in English the common equivalent is *to like.*

Me gustan las verduras al vapor.	*Steamed vegetables are pleasing to me. (I like steamed vegetables.)*

With **gustar,** Spanish and English have reverse word orders to express the same thing because the subjects of each sentence type are different.

Me gustan las verduras al vapor.	(**Las verduras** is the subject and typically comes after the verb.)
I like steamed vegetables.	(*I* is the subject and comes before the verb.)

Gramática, **Suggestion:** Because pronouns can be a challenge, you may refer to the Instructor's Manual for information to help students with these concepts. Alternatively, the same information can be found on the Online Learning Center, available for digital download.

The verb **gustar** requires what are called *indirect objects* or *indirect object pronouns.* An indirect object is a noun that expresses *to whom, for whom,* or *to what, for what* something happens. In the example *I spoke to John, John* is the indirect object of the verb *spoke,* and *I* is the subject. In the example *Mary bought the tie for her friend, her friend* is the indirect object of the verb, *Mary* is the subject, and *the tie* is the direct object.

Indirect object pronouns are those little words that aren't nouns like *Mary, the boy, the cats,* and so on. In English, the indirect object pronouns are: *me, you, him, her, us,* and *them.* Remember they are often preceded by *to/for.* In Spanish, the indirect object pronouns are **me, te, le, nos, os, les.**

Steamed vegetables are pleasing to me/you/them.

The above sentence in Spanish would be rendered as: **Me/Te/Les gustan las verduras al vapor.** When an indirect object noun is present, an **a** must be used before the noun to indicate *to/for* and the indirect object pronoun is used at the same time.

A Mary no le gustan las verduras al vapor.
A mis compañeros les gustan las verduras al vapor.

The preposition **a** can also be used with **mí, ti, él, ella, usted, nosotros/as, vosotros/as, ustedes** to add emphasis or clarification.

Pues, **a mí** no me gustan las verduras al vapor.
¿**A ti** te gustan?

The chart summarizes indirect objects and indirect object pronouns for you.

✳ MÁS GRAMÁTICA

Indirect objects don't occur just with *to be pleasing/***gustar.** They also occur with any verb to which you can add a *to whom, for whom, to what, for what,* and so forth.

I'm giving my vegetables to you.	**Te doy*** mis verduras.
Are you talking to me seriously?	¿**Me hablas** en serio?

Don't be fooled by verbs like *to give* (**dar**) and *to tell* (**decir**). English can reverse direct and indirect objects with these verbs, thus eliminating the *to,* but Spanish never can. In the following, **Juan** is the indirect object in all three sentences.

I'm giving my veggies to Juan.	
I'm giving Juan my veggies.	**Le doy** mis verduras **a Juan.**

*Note the irregular **yo** form of **dar: doy.** All other forms of the verb are regular in the present tense.

INDIRECT OBJECT PRONOUNS	
me	**nos**
Me gustan los postres. *Desserts are pleasing to me. (I like desserts.)* María **me da** consejos. *María gives advice to me (gives me advice).*	**Nos gustan** los postres. *Desserts are pleasing to us. (We like desserts.)* María **nos da** consejos. *María gives advice to us (gives us advice.)*
te	**os**
Te gustan los postres. *Desserts are pleasing to you. (You like desserts.)* María **te da** consejos. *María gives advice to you (gives you advice).*	**Os gustan** los postres. *Desserts are pleasing to you. (You like desserts.)* María **os da** consejos. *Marí a gives advice to you (gives you advice).*
le	**les**
Le gustan los postres. *Desserts are pleasing to you (form. s.). (You like desserts.)* María **le da** consejos. *María gives advice to you (form. s.) (gives you advice).*	**Les gustan** los postres. *Desserts are pleasing to you (form. pl.). (You like desserts.)* María **les da** consejos. *María gives advice to you (form. pl.) (gives you advice).*
le	**les**
Le gustan los postres. *Desserts are pleasing to him/her. (He/She likes desserts.)* María **le da** consejos. *María gives advice to him/her (gives him/her advice).*	**Les gustan** los postres. *Desserts are pleasing to them. (They like desserts.)* María **les da** consejos. *María gives advice to them (gives them advice).*

De *Sol y viento*, Note: You can access this film clip from a special menu section on Disc 5 of the Instructional Version on DVD.

 # DE SOL Y VIENTO

You are about to watch **Episodio 3** of *Sol y viento* again, in which Jaime emphasizes how important it is for the Sánchez family to close the deal soon. Part of their exchange appears below.

JAIME
La venta tiene que suceder[a] en los próximos días. ¿Y su familia? ¿Aceptan la venta?

CARLOS
Bueno, a mi madre ya casi la tengo convencida.

JAIME
¿Y su hermana?

CARLOS
Con ella no hay problema. Si firma[b] mi madre, firma mi hermana. Como ya __le__[1] dije,[c] a mi hermana no __le__[2] interesan los asuntos de la viña.

What indirect object pronouns do you think Carlos uses in the blanks above? Whom do these pronouns refer to? (1. Jaime 2. la hermana)

[a]*take place* [b]*signs* [c]*I told*

INPUT
Actividad F

Actividad F   ¿A quién se refiere?

Imagina que Jaime Talavera menciona las siguientes cosas sobre su viaje a Chile. Indica el personaje de *Sol y viento* que es el sujeto de cada oración.

MODELO: Me da mucho trabajo. (Rassner)

▲ Rassner   ▲ Carlos   ▲ María   ▲ Mario   ▲ el adivino (*fortune-teller*)

1. Me da su tarjeta. ____María____

2. Me hace un brindis (*makes a toast*). ____Carlos____

3. Me cobra (*charges*) precios justos (*fair*). ____Mario____

4. Me da un papelito que dice «El amor es un torbellino». ____el adivino____

5. No me ofrece la opción de no ir a Chile. ____Rassner____

INPUT
Act. G, Suggested follow-up: Read a few complete sentences to the class and ask students to add more examples. Instructor: *Si a una persona le gustan las bebidas alcohólicas, probablemente le gustan las cervezas importadas. ¿Qué más le gusta a esta persona?* Students say: *Le gusta el vino tinto (el vino blanco, el tequila, el vodka, etcétera).*

OUTPUT
Act. H, *Paso 1,*
Suggestion: Allow 1–2 minutes to complete.
Paso 3, **Follow-up:** Call on a few students to present their results to the class.

Actividad G   Asociaciones

Empareja una oración de la primera columna con una de la segunda columna para formar oraciones lógicas.

Si a una persona...

1. __b__ le gustan los mariscos,

2. __f__ no le gusta la carne,

3. __a__ no le gustan los huevos,

4. __e__ le gusta la comida rápida,

5. __d__ le gustan las bebidas alcohólicas,

6. __c__ le gustan los postres,

probablemente...

a. no le gusta la tortilla española.

b. le gusta la langosta.

c. le gusta el helado.

d. le gustan las cervezas importadas.

e. le gustan las comidas grasosas.

f. no le gusta el bistec.

Actividad H   ¿A quién le... ?

Paso 1   Llena los espacios en blanco con información que es verdadera para ti.

1. Le(s) doy consejos a _____ cuando/porque _____.

2. _____ me da consejos cuando/porque _____.

3. Le(s) cuento mis problemas a _____ cuando/porque _____.

4. _____ me cuenta sus problemas cuando/porque _____.

Paso 2   Usando las oraciones del **Paso 1,** entrevista a alguien de la clase.

MODELO: ¿A quién le das consejos? ¿Por qué?

Paso 3   Basándote en la información del **Paso 2,** escribe dos conclusiones de tu entrevista para presentárselas a la clase.

MODELO: Mark y yo somos semejantes porque tenemos un amigo especial. Por ejemplo, Mark le cuenta sus problemas a...

Actividad I ¿Qué te gusta merendar?

Paso 1 Escribe en los espacios en blanco a continuación seis comidas y/o bebidas que te gusta merendar.

De merienda me gusta(n)...	E1 SÍ	E1 NO	E2 SÍ	E2 NO
1. _____.	☐	☐	☐	☐
2. _____.	☐	☐	☐	☐
3. _____.	☐	☐	☐	☐
4. _____.	☐	☐	☐	☐
5. _____.	☐	☐	☐	☐
6. _____.	☐	☐	☐	☐

Paso 2 Entrevista a dos compañeros de clase para averiguar si les gustan las mismas comidas como merienda que a ti. Anota sus respuestas en las columnas apropiadas.

MODELO: ¿Te gustan las galletas saladas con queso como merienda?

Paso 3 Con la información de los **Pasos 1** y **2,** escribe dos oraciones con **nos** y dos con **les** para presentárselas a la clase.

MODELO: A Juan y a Ana les gusta la leche como merienda. A nosotros tres nos gustan las frutas frescas como merienda.

SOL Y VIENTO: Enfoque cultural

En el **Episodio 3,** Jaime y Mario llegan al Valle del Maipo, y Mario compra unas empanadas para Jaime y para él. En muchos países hispanos, sobre todo en Latinoamérica, son típicos estos puestos[a] pequeños donde se vende comida. En Puerto Rico, al lado de algunas carreteras[b] hay puestos con letreros hechos a mano[c] que anuncian «pollo asado y frutas». En México, es típico ver en la ciudad puestos pequeños en forma de «carritos»[d] donde se venden tacos y tortas (sándwiches). En las zonas rurales, son más comunes los lugares pequeños como el puesto en donde Mario compró[e] las empanadas. Este tipo de comida tiene mucha demanda: es barata y se encuentra por todas partes en los países latinos. Pero, lo principal[f] es que les ofrece a personas de pocos recursos[g] la oportunidad de ganar algún dinero.

▲ Unos puestos de comida en México.

[a]*stands* [b]*highways* [c]*letreros... hand-made signs* [d]*carts* [e]*bought* [f]*lo... the main thing* [g]*financial resources*

SOL Y VIENTO

A segunda vista

Antes de ver el episodio

Actividad A ¿Qué recuerdas?

Basándote en lo que recuerdas de la primera vista del **Episodio 3,** pon en orden cronológico (del 1 al 6) los eventos de la interacción entre Jaime y Carlos, desde el punto de vista de Jaime. Vas a verificar tus respuestas cuando veas (*you see*) el episodio de nuevo.

Carlos...

a. _2_ me ofrece un tour de la viña, pero no acepto.

b. _6_ me dice «Hasta luego».

c. _4_ me cuenta las dificultades de manejar (*running*) una viña.

d. _3_ me sirve una copa de vino en su oficina.

e. _1_ me da la bienvenida (*welcome*) a «Sol y viento».

f. _5_ me menciona la recepción que va a tener.

Actividad B ¡A escuchar!

Pronto vas a volver a ver el **Episodio 3.** Repasa brevemente el siguiente fragmento del diálogo entre Carlos y Jaime. Cuando veas el episodio, llena los espacios en blanco con las palabras correctas. ¡No vuelvas a ver otros fragmentos de este episodio!

JAIME: Bonita _bodega_.[1]
CARLOS: Y muy buen _vino_.[2]
   ¿Quisiera[a] hacer un breve recorrido[b]? ¿Le gusta el _vino chileno_[3]?
JAIME: Sí, me gusta mucho, pero _prefiero_[4] esperar. Tenemos negocios[c] _importantes_.[5] ¿No es cierto?
CARLOS: Bueno, sí. Es cierto. ¿Por qué no vamos a mi _oficina_[6] para tener así más privacidad?

[a]*Would you like* [b]*tour* [c]*business*

Actividad C El episodio

Ahora mira el episodio de nuevo. No te olvides de (*Don't forget*) verificar tus respuestas a la **Actividad A** mientras ves el episodio. Presta atención también a la escena en que Carlos y Jaime se conocen (*meet*) y apunta las palabras que faltan para la **Actividad B.**

Después de ver el episodio

Actividad A Para pensar...

Paso 1 Con un compañero (una compañera) de clase, comparen sus opiniones sobre las siguientes preguntas. Si es necesario, vuelve a ver la escena en cuestión.

1. ¿Cómo describirían Uds. (*would you describe*) la interacción entre Carlos y Traimaqueo cuando llega Jaime a la viña?

2. ¿Tienen una buena o mala relación? ¿Qué evidencia tienen para apoyar (*support*) su opinión?

Paso 2 Compartan sus opiniones con la clase. ¿Están todos de acuerdo con la descripción de la relación entre Carlos y Traimaqueo?

Actividad B ¡A verificar!

Vas a ver otra vez la escena de **¡A escuchar!** en la página anterior. Llena los espacios en blanco, según lo que oyes.

Actividad C ¡Te toca a ti!

Paso 1 Ahora sabes más sobre Jaime y Carlos. ¿Crees que tienen gustos similares o diferentes? Basándote en lo que aprendiste (*you learned*) en esta lección, describe los gustos de Jaime y Carlos con oraciones completas.

MODELO: A Jaime y a Carlos les gusta(n)... A Jaime también le gusta(n)... pero a Carlos (no) le gusta(n)...

Paso 2 Comparte tus oraciones con un compañero (una compañera) de clase y prepara una lista de las ideas que tienen en común para presentársela a la clase.

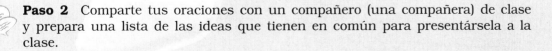

Detrás de la cámara

You probably noticed that Jaime looks quite young to be handling a $200 million deal, but don't be fooled by his appearance. Jaime quickly sizes up Carlos after seeing him yell at Traimaqueo and determines exactly how to handle him. Did you notice how Jaime leans in and stares down Carlos when he gives him the ultimatum to sign the contract? Jaime doesn't need to yell or put on airs to show he means business. Jaime also uses his knowledge of wines to show Carlos he won't have the rug pulled out from under him. This is what makes Jaime so good at what he does.

RESUMEN DE VOCABULARIO

Verbos

cenar	to eat/have (for) dinner
dar (*irreg.*)	to give
dar consejos	to give advice
desayunar	to eat/have (for) breakfast
gustar	to be pleasing to
merendar (ie)	to snack / have for a snack
regalar	to give (*as a gift*)

Repaso: almorzar (ue)

Las carnes y las aves

el bistec	steak
la carne de res	beef
la chuleta de cerdo	pork chop
los huevos (fritos, revueltos)	(fried, scrambled) eggs
el jamón	ham
el pavo	turkey
el pollo	chicken
la salchicha	sausage
el tocino	bacon
la tortilla española	omelette

Cognados: la hamburguesa, el rosbif

El pescado y los mariscos

el atún	tuna
los camarones	shrimp
la langosta	lobster

Las verduras

el aguacate	avocado
la cebolla	onion
la ensalada mixta	tossed salad
los frijoles	beans
la lechuga	lettuce
el maíz	corn
la papa	potato
las papas fritas	French fries
el puré de papas	mashed potatoes

la soja	soy(bean)
las zanahorias	carrots

Cognados: el bróculi, la coliflor, los espárragos, el tomate

Las frutas

la manzana	apple
la naranja	orange
la toronja	grapefruit

Cognados: la banana, el limón

Los productos lácteos

la leche	milk
la mantequilla	butter
el queso (de crema)	(cream) cheese
el yogur	yogurt

Los carbohidratos

el arroz	rice
el cereal (cocido)	(hot) cereal
el pan	bread
el pan dulce	sweet bread (*Mex.*)
el pan tostado	toast
la rosquilla	bagel
la tortilla (de maíz)	(corn) tortilla
la tostada de pan a la francesa	French toast

Cognados: los espaguetis, los panqueques

Los postres

el flan	flan (*baked custard*)
el helado	ice cream
el pastel	cake
los pasteles	pastries

Las meriendas

los dulces	candy
la galleta	cookie
la galleta salada	cracker
la nuez (*pl.* **las nueces**)	nut
las palomitas de maíz	popcorn
las papitas	potato chips

Las bebidas

el agua (*f.*)	water
el café (descafeinado)	(decaffeinated) coffee
el chocolate caliente	hot chocolate
el jugo	juice
el refresco (dietético)	(diet) soft drink
el té (caliente, helado)	(hot, iced) tea
el vino (blanco, tinto)	(white, red) wine

Repaso: la cerveza

Otros alimentos

la barra de frutas/ granola	fruit/granola bar
la mantequilla de cacahuete	peanut butter
la mermelada	jam
la sopa	soup

Cognados: la pizza, la salsa, el sándwich

Adjetivos

agrio/a	sour
amargo/a	bitter
blando/a	soft, tender
cocido/a	cooked

crudo/a	raw
dulce	sweet
duro/a	hard
pasado/a	spoiled
picante	hot, spicy
picoso/a	hot, spicy
salado/a	salty

Palabras indefinidas y negativas

algo	something
algún (alguno/a/os/as)	some, any
siempre	always
jamás	never
nada	nothing
nadie	no one, not anyone
ningún (ninguno/a)	none, not any
nunca	never
tampoco	neither, not either

Repaso: alguien, también

Otras palabras y expresiones

el almuerzo	lunch
la cena	dinner
el desayuno	breakfast
la comida rápida	fast food
la porción (de pastel, pizza)	slice (of cake, pizza)
las sobras	leftovers
el/la vegetariano/a	vegetarian
al horno	baked
al vapor	steamed
de vez en cuando	once in a while

Entremés cultural

Los hispanos: Una presencia creciente[a] en los Estados Unidos

Los Ángeles, California. Los hispanos forman el grupo étnico más grande de los Estados Unidos.

VISTAZO

En los Estados Unidos viven más de 42 millones de personas de ascendencia[b] hispana, según la información del censo publicada en 2005 (dos mil cinco). Esta cifra[c] indica que de cada siete personas en este país, una —o sea,[d] el 13% (por ciento) de la población entera del país— es de ascendencia hispana. La mayoría[e] son de ascendencia mexicana, seguida de[f] los de ascendencia puertorriqueña y los de ascendencia cubana. Las personas de origen centro- y sudamericano forman los porcentajes[g] más pequeños. Los hispanos se encuentran en todas partes de los Estados Unidos, aunque[h] hay concentraciones grandes en el suroeste del país, en Chicago, en Nueva York y en Miami. Sin embargo,[i] hasta[j] en ciudades como Charleston (la Carolina del Sur) y en pueblos como Eudora, Kansas, no es difícil encontrar a gente de raíces[k] hispanas.

[a]*growing* [b]*heritage* [c]*number* [d]*o… or rather* [e]*majority* [f]*seguida… followed by* [g]*percentages* [h]*although* [i]*Sin… Nevertheless* [j]*even* [k]*roots*

DATO INTERESANTE:
¿Es común el bilingüismo?

No hablan español todos los hispanos. Los datos revelan que sólo la mitad[a] de los hispanos en los Estados Unidos «dominan bien» el español. De hecho,[b] el famoso cantante[c] Ritchie Valens (nacido[d] Richard Valenzuela) no hablaba[e] español y tuvo que[f] memorizar las palabras para la canción[g] «La Bamba.»

IDEA: Busca información sobre las habilidades con el español que tienen los hispanos en este país y las preferencias en cuanto al[h] uso de lenguaje, revisando los informes[i] del Censo y/o del Centro Pew.

[a]*la… half* [b]*De… In fact* [c]*singer* [d]*born* [e]*no… didn't speak* [f]*tuvo… he had* [g]*song* [h]*en… regarding* [i]*reports*

Ritchie Valens

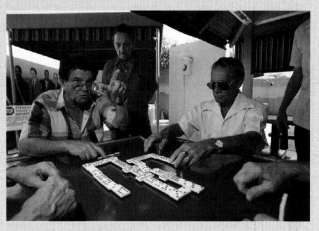

Miami, Florida. Los hispanos en los Estados Unidos tienen dialectos, comidas y costumbres variados.

DATO INTERESANTE:
Una población creciente

Los expertos calculan que para el año 2050 (dos mil cincuenta), la población de hispanos sobrepasará[a] 120 millones de personas, formando el 25% de la población total del país.

> **IDEA:** Con un compañero (una compañera), investiga las cifras sobre la población hispana en comparación con otros grupos étnicos desde 1960 (mil novecientos sesenta) hasta el presente. Preparen una figura gráfica para demostrar los cambios.[b]

[a]*will exceed* [b]*para... to show the changes*

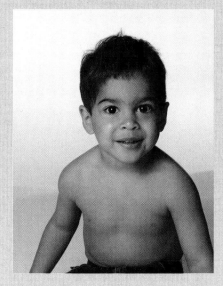

De adulto, este bebé será (*will be*) uno de 120 millones o más de hispanos en los Estados Unidos.

DATO INTERESANTE:
Los dialectos distintos

Como vienen de distintos orígenes nacionales, los hispanos en los Estados Unidos que hablan español no siempre hablan el mismo dialecto. Por ejemplo, un chico méxicoamericano diría[a] **el camión** o **el bus** para hablar de *bus*, mientras una chica cubanoamericana diría **la guagua**. También varían los sonidos[b] dependiendo del dialecto. En el español méxicoamericano no se pierden las consonantes fácilmente[c] mientras en el español cubanoamericano sí.

> **IDEA:** Busca ejemplos del español hablado en la radio, el Internet o en los programas de televisión y grábalos.[d] Tráelos a clase para hacer comparaciones con tus compañeros con la ayuda del profesor (de la profesora).

[a]*would say* [b]*sounds* [c]*no... consonants aren't readily dropped* [d]*record them*

DATO INTERESANTE:
La salsa

La salsa, comida muy típica de México, ahora sobrepasa[a] el *ketchup* como el condimento más vendido[b] en los Estados Unidos.

> **IDEA:** Hay salsas rojas y verdes. Busca una receta[c] para una salsa verde y prepárala para la clase. O trae la receta a clase para repartirla[d] entre tus compañeros. O, busca una salsa verde en el supermercado y tráela a la clase. Alternativa: Entre todos, hagan un concurso[e] para la mejor salsa de la clase. ¿Quién la prepara mejor?

[a]*surpasses* [b]*sold* [c]*recipe* [d]*distribute* [e]*hagan... hold a contest*

La salsa ahora es una comida tanto norteamericana como mexicana.

Otro encuentro

En este episodio...

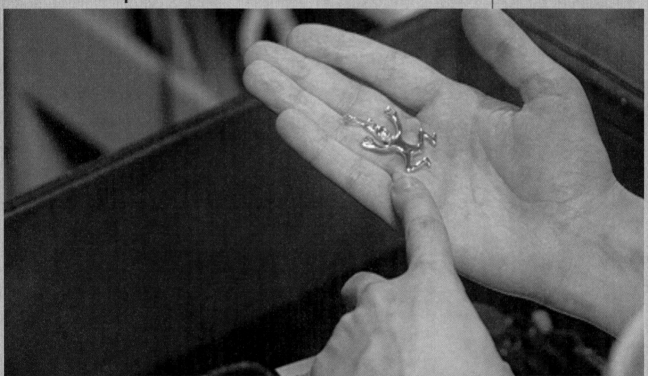

JAIME

¿Tiene algún significado esta figura?

TENDERA[a]

Sí, esta figura simboliza un espíritu protector de los mapuches.

JAIME

¿Los mapuches? Son una cultura indígena, ¿no?

¿Qué crees tú?

1. ¿Dónde está Jaime en este momento, probablemente?
2. ¿Por qué tiene interés en la figura Jaime?
3. ¿Crees que Jaime va a comprarla?

---

[a]*shopkeeper*

Cuando no trabajo...

OBJETIVOS

IN THIS LESSON, YOU WILL LEARN:

- how to talk about pastimes and leisure activities
- vocabulary related to sports and fitness activities
- how to talk about special occasions and holidays
- how to talk about activities in the past using the preterite tense

In addition, you will prepare for and watch **Episodio 4** of the film *Sol y viento.*

Esta es una celebración de la Noche Vieja (*New Year's Eve*) en la Puerta del Sol (Madrid, España).

The following media resources are available for this lesson of *Sol y viento:*

Episodio 4 of *Sol y viento*

Online *Manual de actividades*

Online Learning Center Website

PRIMERA PARTE

Vocabulario

Talking About What
You Do When You
Don't Study or Work

Note: These vocabulary items can be heard in this lesson's Textbook Audio section of the Online Learning Center Website.

El tiempo libre

Leisure Activities ✳

En las fiestas

Roberto

A Roberto no le gustan **las fiestas.** Es un poco tímido y no le gusta **rozarse con la gente.** No hace más que **tomar** y **picar.** ¿Eres tú como él?

bailar	to dance
dar (*irreg.*) **una fiesta**	to throw a party
picar	to nibble
rozarse con la gente	to mingle with people
tocar (el piano, la guitarra)	to play (the piano, the guitar)
tomar	to drink

 MÁS VOCABULARIO

divertir (ie)	to entertain	**el juego**	game (*as in chess*)
pasarlo bien/mal	to have a good/bad time	**los ratos libres**	free (spare) time
		divertido/a	fun
el aguafiestas	party pooper		
el equipo	equipment		

En casa

En sus ratos libres, Roberto y sus compañeros de casa hacen diferentes actividades. Roberto ve películas. A Tomás le gusta **pintar** (tiene aspiraciones artísticas). A Jaime le gusta **limpiar la casa** (dice que es relajante). Alicia **practica el yoga** y **medita.** ¿Cuál de los cuatro es más como tú?

cocinar	to cook
coleccionar (estampillas, monedas)	to collect (stamps, coins)
dibujar	to draw
jugar (ue) al* ajedrez	to play chess
limpiar la casa	to clean the house
pintar	to paint
sacar un vídeo/DVD	to rent a video/DVD

Fuera de casa^a   ^aFuera... *Outside*

En el parque, la gente hace varias actividades. Unos **patinan en línea.** Otros **dan un paseo.** A unos les gusta **andar en bicicleta.** En el lago, otros prefieren **navegar en barco.** ¿Dónde está Roberto? Ah, ¡claro! Probablemente está en casa.

andar en bicicleta	to ride a bicycle
dar (*irreg.*) **un paseo**	to take a walk; to stroll
navegar en barco	to sail
patinar (en línea)	to (inline) skate
visitar un museo	to visit a museum

---

*Remember that **a** + *definite article* is used with **jugar** when talking about games and sports.

¡Exprésate!

To make impersonal statements, ones in which the verb is singular and the subject is not specified, use the reflexive pronoun **se.** The rough equivalent in English is *one, you,* or *they.*

Se puede llamar a la profesora si hay preguntas.

One (You, They) can call the professor if there are questions.

Se necesita practicar el español todos los días.

One needs (You/They need) to practice Spanish every day.

INPUT
Act. A, Suggestions
Paso 1: Tell students *Voy a leer cada actividad una sola vez. Escriban Uds. la actividad en uno de los cuadros.* (If they don't understand, do the following example.) *Por ejemplo, si yo digo* ***tocar el piano,*** *Uds. escriban «tocar el piano» o en* ***se necesita equipo especial,*** *o en* ***se puede hacer a solas*** *o en* ***se necesita cierto talento*** *o en* ***se requiere mucho esfuerzo físico.*** Then read all items. Review at end, accepting any response that makes sense.
1. *cocinar* 2. *meditar* 3. *patinar en línea* 4. *dar un paseo* 5. *ir al cine* 6. *sacar un DVD y verlo en casa* 7. *navegar en barco* 8. *jugar al ajedrez*
Paso 2: Call on students to read an activity aloud and give their opinion. Does everyone agree? See which activities seem to be more group-oriented in the students' minds.
Suggested follow-up: Ask students to rate the activities on a scale from 5 (*muy divertida*) to 1 (*poco divertida*).

Actividad A ¿Cómo lo ves?

Paso 1 Escucha mientras tu profesor(a) menciona una actividad. ¿En qué categoría la pondrías (*would you put it*)?

Se necesita equipo especial	**Se puede hacer a solas**
Se necesita cierto talento	**Se requiere mucho esfuerzo** (*effort*) **físico**

Paso 2 Mirando (*Looking at*) las actividades que has escrito (*you have written*), indica para cuáles, en tu opinión, se necesitan (*are needed*) dos personas y para cuáles se necesita un grupo de personas.

MODELO: Para jugar al ajedrez se necesitan dos personas.

INPUT
Act. B, Suggestion: Do as a game. Students have 5 minutes to write as many names as possible for each activity. At the end, call time and then ask questions such as *¿Qué grupo tiene dos (tres, cuatro, etc.) nombres para la actividad de cocinar?* The group with the most names wins that activity.

Actividad B Las personas célebres

¿Qué personas célebres o personajes conocidos asocias con cada actividad?

1. cocinar
2. pintar
3. tocar el piano
4. ir a una discoteca
5. bailar
6. andar en bicicleta
7. dar fiestas
8. dibujar

INPUT/OUTPUT
Act. C, Suggestions
Paso 1: Read each statement out loud so students can hear it. Then allow 2 minutes for students to answer.
Paso 2: Allow 4 to 5 minutes. Then call on one person to report. You may model how to report.
Optional: Students convert statements into questions and ask you.

Actividad C En una fiesta

Paso 1 Indica cuáles de las siguientes oraciones se te aplican a ti (*apply to you*) en una fiesta.

	SE ME APLICA.	NO SE ME APLICA.
1. Me gusta mucho rozarme con la gente.	☐	☐
2. No me gusta bailar.	☐	☐
3. Me gusta picar la comida.	☐	☐
4. Me gusta divertir a los demás (*others*) (y ser el centro de la atención de todos).	☐	☐
5. Me gusta escuchar a otra persona tocar el piano o la guitarra. Y siempre canto con esa persona.	☐	☐
6. Me gusta dar fiestas tanto como ser invitado/a a una.	☐	☐
7. No me gustan las fiestas. Soy un aguafiestas.	☐	☐

Paso 2 Escoge las cuatro oraciones del **Paso 1** que mejor te caracterizan y conviértelas en preguntas para otra persona. ¿Son sus respuestas iguales a las tuyas?

MODELO: ¿Te gusta dar fiestas tanto como ser invitado/a a una?

OUTPUT
Actividad D

Actividad D   En busca de amigos

Imagina que se podría (*one could*) entrevistar a las personas al conocerlas para ver si son compatibles como amigos. Utilizando el nuevo vocabulario, escribe diez preguntas para entrevistar a dos personas. Luego, indica quién de las dos personas (o ninguna) podría ser buena compañía para ti.

Vistazo cultural,
Suggestion: Have students read quickly, then ask questions about the content: *¿Quiénes beben más en las fiestas, los estudiantes norteamericanos o los hispanos?* (*los norteamericanos*); *¿A quiénes les gusta más bailar en las fiestas, los norteamericanos o los hispanos?* (*los hispanos*).
Suggested follow-up: Ask the class as an open question: *¿Eres aguafiestas o no?* Then have them rate themselves on the following scale for each statement: (5) *sí, mucho* (4) *sí* (3) *algo* (2) *no* (1) *para nada.* Statements: 1. *Me gusta bailar en las fiestas.* 2. *Cuando tocan música, soy la primera persona en bailar.* 3. *No es difícil para mí invitar a otra persona a bailar.* 4. *Si doy una fiesta, bailo para darles motivación a mis invitados.* 5. *Si hay una fiesta, llevo música para bailar.* At the end, the person with the least points is the most *aguafiesta* of them all.

≈ Vistazo cultural

Las fiestas

Cuando un hispano viene a los Estados Unidos por primera vez y es invitado[a] a una fiesta, una de las cosas que suele notar es que para él las fiestas parecen un poco aburridas. Algunos hispanos han comentado[b] que a los estudiantes norteamericanos, sólo les interesa beber y emborracharse.[c] En el mundo hispano, la idea de «beber para emborracharse» no es parte de la mentalidad estudiantil. Claro, los estudiantes toman cerveza o vino, pero el concepto de un *keg party,* por ejemplo, es algo ajeno[d] a su experiencia. En contraste, salen a «tomar copas», lo cual quiere decir que unos amigos salen en la noche y disfrutan de[e] una o dos copas de vino (o cerveza) mientras charlan y pican comidas ligeras.[f]

En las fiestas, tanto de los jóvenes[g] como de los mayores, es muy común poner música y bailar o tocar la guitarra y cantar. Así que si vas a una fiesta hispana, no te sorprendas[h] si alguien te dice «Vamos a bailar» o si te llama «aguafiestas» si dices que no quieres bailar.

▲ En las fiestas hispanas, bailar es casi una obligación.

[a]*es... is invited* [b]*han... have mentioned* [c]*getting drunk* [d]*foreign* [e]*disfrutan... enjoy* [f]*light* [g]*young people* [h]*no... don't be surprised*

Gramática

Lo pasé muy bien.   **Preterite Tense of Regular -ar Verbs**

REGULAR -ar VERBS IN THE PRETERITE bailar			
yo	bail**é**	nosotros/as	bail**amos**
tú	bail**aste**	vosotros/as	bail**asteis**
Ud.	bail**ó**	Uds.	bail**aron**
él/ella	bail**ó**	ellos/ellas	bail**aron**

To talk about past events in Spanish, at a minimum you will need to know how to use two sets of verb forms: the *preterite* and the *imperfect.* This lesson will focus solely on the preterite. In this section of the lesson, you will learn the forms of the preterite for regular **-ar** verbs.

The preterite (**el pretérito**) has several equivalents in English to express a single event in the past. Look at the examples that follow.

Lo **pasé** muy bien.   *I had a good time.*

De veras, lo **pasé** muy bien.   *Honestly, I did have a good time.*

What you see is that the preterite is used to talk about finished or completed events in the past. If the action or event is viewed by the speaker as completed by a certain time point—no matter how long the action or event lasted—it will be expressed in the preterite.

Sólo **canté** una canción.   *I sang only one song.*

Los dinosaurios **reinaron**   *Dinosaurs reigned for millions*
por millones de años.   *of years.*

Note the following about **-ar** verb forms of the preterite.

1. The **nosotros** form is the same as that used in the present tense. Context usually lets you know whether past or present is intended.

   Ayer **visitamos** el Museo   *Yesterday we visited the Prado*
   del Prado.   *Museum.*

2. Verbs that end in **-car, -gar,** and **-zar** have spelling changes in the **yo** form to keep the *k,* hard *g,* and soft *c* sounds, respectively.

   tocar: -car → qu   to**qu**é, tocaste,...

   pagar: -gar → gu   pa**gu**é, pagaste,...

   empezar: -zar → c   empe**c**é, empezaste,...

3. Verbs with present-tense stem changes show no stem changes in the preterite.

   com**ie**nza *but* com**e**nzó

   alm**ue**rza *but* alm**o**rzó

4. Note the accent marks on the **yo, Ud.,** and **él/ella** forms. These are important to demonstrate the shift of stress from the stem of the verb to the verb ending.

De *Sol y viento,* Note: You can access this film clip from a special menu section on Disc 5 of the Instructional Version on DVD.

DE SOL Y VIENTO

In **Episodio 4,** Jaime runs into María again by chance. She asks him about his trip to the Maipo Valley, and he responds. Read part of their exchange below.

MARÍA
Ya volvió^a de su viaje. ¿Cómo le fue?^b

JAIME
—————————.

Which response do you think Jaime gave María?

(**1.**) Lo pasé muy bien, gracias.   2. ¡Huy! Lo pasé muy mal.

^a*you returned*   ^b¿Cómo... *How was it?*

Enfoque lingüístico, **Suggestion:** After students read, have them quickly tell you in their own words how English and Spanish differ in the way they mark past tense. Here are some ideas: 1. English uses one form, *-ed,* for all regular verbs; Spanish has particular past-tense endings for verbs. 2. English uses subject pronouns to mark the subject; Spanish has unique endings to mark the subject. 3. Spanish verb endings tell you which class of verbs the verb belongs to (*-ar,* *-er/-ir*); English doesn't have verb classes so this indication doesn't apply. Tell students that later on they will learn another past-tense form, and they will learn that preterite verb forms also mark an important function in the past tense that English verbs do not.

Enfoque lingüístico

Más sobre los tiempos verbales

Remember that *tense* (**el tiempo**) refers to the relative time frame in which an event or action occurs: past, present, and future. The word *tense* can be confusing because actions or states that are all part of the same time frame (past, present, future) are often called tenses as well. For example, in this lesson you are learning how to use the preterite tense. Why not just say "past tense"? This is because, as you will learn later, there is another very important verb form used to talk about the past, the *imperfect,* which you may hear referred to as the *imperfect tense.* These really aren't tenses but sets of forms that refer to past tense events.

Languages vary in how they indicate past tense on verbs. In English, for example, the past tense of *I talk* is *I talked.* So English adds a simple *-ed* to all forms (*I, you, he/she,* etc.) of regular verbs. However, some forms are irregular and don't add *-ed.* For example, *I swim* in the past is *I swam* and *I think* in the past is *I thought.* Spanish has irregular forms that you will learn later in this lesson. French and Italian, languages related to Spanish, form the equivalent of the past tense much differently. Instead of a singular verb they use a compound verb that resembles English *have eaten, have studied,* and so on. In French, the equivalent of *I studied* and **estudié** is *j'ai étudié;* in Italian it is *ho studiato.* Thus, **ayer estudié** would be, in French and Italian, literally *Yesterday I have studied.*

Chinese is a language without past tense forms. To speak in the past in Chinese one would use words like *yesterday, last week,* and so on. In contrast, Spanish has a verb inflection for all persons (*I, you, he/she, we,* etc.) and for the different types of verbs: *-ar, -er/-ir.* Again, this is an example of how Spanish is what we call an inflectionally rich language, one in which verb endings convey a lot of information.

Actividad E ¿Quién lo diría (*would say it*)?

Basándote en episodios previos de *Sol y viento*, ¿quién podría (*could*) decir las siguientes oraciones?

1. Trabajé con mis estudiantes. María
2. Llegué a Santiago el lunes. Jaime
3. Lo llevé al Hotel Bonaparte. Mario
4. Compré un papelito de la suerte. Jaime
5. Caminé y hablé con un hombre simpático. María
6. Grité (*I yelled*) a un empleado. Carlos
7. Busqué a la señorita para darle su tarjeta. Jaime
8. Después de llevar al señor a la viña, almorcé con algunos amigos en nuestro bar favorito. Mario

▲ ¿Qué hizo Jaime (*did Jaime do*) cuando llegó a chile?

Actividad F En el pasado

Da el nombre de dos o más personas que hicieron (*did*) cada actividad a continuación.

MODELO: Actuaron en muchas películas de horror. → Boris Karloff y Bela Lugosi actuaron en muchas películas de horror.

1. Inventaron aparatos o máquinas importantes.
2. Pintaron cuadros (*paintings*) famosos durante el Renacimiento (*Renaissance*).
3. Viajaron grandes distancias en un avión (*airplane*).
4. Actuaron en las películas de James Bond.
5. Buscaron su fortuna en el Nuevo Mundo (*New World*).
6. Tocaron la guitarra en bandas de música rock en los años 60 (*the sixties*).

¡Exprésate!

To express the concept of *ago*, Spanish uses **hace** plus the amount of time elapsed. For example, **hace unos días** means *a few days ago*, and **hace unas semanas** means *a few weeks ago*. How would you say *a month ago*? *several years ago*?

INPUT/OUTPUT
Act. G, Suggestions
Paso 1: Allow 2 minutes to complete.
Paso 2: Allow students about 3 minutes to write verb forms first. Then review: *Para el número 1, ¿todos tienen* **bailaste**? *Bien. Entonces la pregunta sería ¿Cuándo fue la última vez que bailaste en una fiesta? ¿Sí? OK. Número 2…* Allow students about 6 minutes to find people who answer the same as they do. Then ask a few students some follow-up questions: *Roberto, ¿cuándo fue la última vez que cocinaste algo? ¿Y quién respondió igual que tú?* (to Roberto) *¿Qué cocinaste?* (to other student) *Y tú, ¿qué cocinaste?*

OUTPUT
Actividad I

Actividad G ¿Cuándo?

Paso 1 Indica cuándo fue (*was*) la última vez que hiciste (*you did*) cada actividad.

	ANOCHE O AYER (*last night or yesterday*)	HACE UNOS DÍAS	HACE ____
1. Bailé en una fiesta.	☐	☐	☐
2. Bailé en una discoteca.	☐	☐	☐
3. Cociné.	☐	☐	☐
4. Limpié la casa.	☐	☐	☐
5. Saqué un DVD.	☐	☐	☐
6. Visité un museo.	☐	☐	☐
7. Estudié toda la noche para un examen.	☐	☐	☐
8. Lo pasé muy bien con mis amigos.	☐	☐	☐

Paso 2 Convierte las oraciones del **Paso 1** en preguntas para hacérselas a tus compañeros. Luego, busca a personas que dieron (*gave*) respuestas iguales a las tuyas en por lo menos cinco de las actividades.

MODELO: ¿Cuándo fue la última vez que estudiaste toda la noche?

Actividad H El estudiante y el profesor

INPUT/OUTPUT
Actividad H

Paso 1 Agrupa las siguientes actividades según lo que crees que hizo (*did*) anoche un estudiante o un profesor o los dos. Todas las oraciones se refieren a posibles actividades de anoche. Compara tus respuestas con las de un compañero (una compañera) para ver si son iguales.

1. Tomó una cerveza.
2. Habló con un amigo por teléfono.
3. Navegó la red para buscar información.
4. Charló con alguien por correo electrónico.
5. Regresó a casa después de las 5:00 de la tarde.
6. Preparó la cena.
7. Bailó en una fiesta.

Paso 2 Entrevisten al profesor (a la profesora) entre todos para ver si hizo las actividades anteriores anoche. Usen **tú** o **Ud.,** según la costumbre (*custom*) de la clase. ¿Creen Uds. que su profesor(a) es típico/a?

Actividad I Las personas famosas

Paso 1 ¿Qué sabes de los «célebres»? Escribe dos o tres preguntas sobre una persona famosa. **¡OJO!** Debes usar el pretérito en tus preguntas.

MODELO: ¿En qué película cantó John Travolta «Greased Lightning»?

Paso 2 Cada persona va a presentar sus preguntas a la clase. ¿Cuáles son las preguntas más difíciles?

SEGUNDA PARTE

Note: These vocabulary items can be heard in this lesson's Textbook Audio section of the Online Learning Center Website.

Talking More About
Leisure Activities

Vocabulario

El ejercicio y el gimnasio

Sports and Fitness

Raúl y Elena

Juan Ignacio

Antonia

Marisela

José

Susanita, Carol, Juan Pablo, Billy

Algunas actividades

caminar	to walk
competir (i)	to compete
correr	to run
esquiar (esquío)	to ski
ganar	to win
hacer (*irreg.*) **ciclismo estacionario**	to ride a stationary bike
hacer (*irreg.*) **ejercicio (aeróbico)**	to exercise (do aerobics)
hacer (*irreg.*) **gimnasia**	to work out
jugar (ue) (gu) al golf	to play golf
levantar pesas	to lift weights
nadar	to swim
perder (ie)	to lose
sudar	to sweat
trotar	to jog

Lugares y objetos

el campeonato	championship
la cancha (de tenis)	(tennis) court
el equipo	team
el estadio	stadium
el gimnasio	gymnasium
la natación	swimming
el partido	game, match
la piscina	swimming pool
la pista	track
la rueda de andar	treadmill

✳ MÁS VOCABULARIO

estar (*irreg.*) **en (buena) forma**	to be in (good) shape
fortalecer (zc)	to strengthen
quemar calorías	to burn calories
ser (*irreg.*) **aficionado/a (a)**	to be a fan (of)
el/la atleta	athlete
el kilómetro	kilometer
el metro	meter
la milla	mile
fuerte	strong

Cognados: el basquetbol, el béisbol, el fútbol,* el fútbol americano, el tenis, el vólibol

---

***El fútbol** is the term for *soccer*, whereas **el fútbol americano** is used for *football*.

INPUT
Act. A,
Suggestion: Direct students' attention to the drawing on page 208. Read each description once. Students provide the name of each person described.
1. *Esta persona nada. La piscina del gimnasio no es muy grande, así que la persona necesita hacer repeticiones para nadar un kilómetro.* (Antonia)
2. *Esta persona corre en la rueda de andar. No camina.* (José)
3. *Esta persona escucha música mientras hace ejercicio.* (Marisela)
4. *Estas personas son bastante fuertes. Levantan pesas. Los dos están en buena forma. ¿Quiénes son?* (Raúl y Elena)
5. *Esta persona hace ciclismo estacionario y suda mucho. Debe tomar mucha agua mientras hace ejercicio, ¿no creen?* (Juan Ignacio)
6. *Estos dos hombres participan en una clase de ejercicio aeróbico. Muchos hombres prefieren este tipo de ejercicio para quemar calorías en vez de correr o trotar.* (Juan Pablo y Billy)

INPUT/OUTPUT

Act. C., Suggestion: After students complete activity, do a quick survey asking which activities cause the most sweating and which the least. Follow up asking individuals whether or not they like to sweat: *Claro, a nadie le gusta sudar durante su trabajo o cuando están estudiando, pero algunos creen que si sudan mucho durante el ejercicio, es algo bueno. ¿Qué piensas*

Actividad A   ¿Quién es?

Escucha las descripciones que da tu profesor(a). Todas tienen que ver (*have to do*) con las actividades en la página 208. ¿Puedes indicar a quién se refiere cada descripción?

1. ...   **2.** ...   **3.** ...   **4.** ...   **5.** ...   **6.** ...

Actividad B   ¿Qué es?

Escucha lo que dice el profesor (la profesora). Luego indica lo que se describe.

1. a. el verano
   (b.) el Super Bowl
   c. la piscina
2. a. la cancha
   b. el partido
   (c.) la pista
3. (a.) trotar
   b. sudar
   c. esquiar
4. (a.) pierde
   b. juega
   c. es aficionado
5. a. levantar pesas
   b. correr
   (c.) el ciclismo
6. a. la piscina
   (b.) la rueda de andar
   c. el invierno

INPUT

Act. B, Statements:
1. *Es un campeonato.* (el Super Bowl)
2. *Es el lugar donde las personas corren 1,000 metros.* (la pista)
3. *Este ejercicio es una forma de correr, pero no tan rápido, y no tan lento como caminar.* (trotar)
4. *Al final de un partido, uno de los equipos gana y el otro hace esto.* (pierde)
5. *Lance Armstrong practicó este deporte.* (el ciclismo)
6. *Si llueve y no quieres correr afuera, puedes ir a un gimnasio para utilizar este aparato.* (la rueda de andar)
Suggested follow-up: Ask students if any go to the gym regularly. Then ask 1 or 2 students who do some questions that describe the gym, e.g., *¿Es grande o pequeño? ¿Qué equipo tiene? ¿Tiene, por ejemplo, máquinas para levantar pesas? ¿Cuántas ruedas de andar tiene?* The idea here is not to get students producing yet, but to get them to hear more target vocabulary in context.

Actividad C   ¿Cuándo sudas?

Paso 1 Mirando la lista de actividades en la página 209, determina durante cuáles una persona suele sudar mucho, suda algo, suda poco o no suda nada. (Imagina que es un día bonito, de unos 70 grados Fahrenheit.)

Paso 2 Compara lo que tienes con otra persona. ¿Son iguales sus ideas?

MODELO: E1: Uno suda poco cuando nada. ¿Qué dices tú?
          E2: Estoy de acuerdo.

Paso 3 ¿A quién le gusta sudar más, a ti o a tu compañero/a?

MODELO: A mí me gusta sudar mucho. ¿Y a ti? ¿También te gusta?

tú? ¿Te gusta sudar? ¿Crees que es bueno sudar? ¿Te gustan las saunas o prefieres sudar mientras practicas un deporte?, etc. What is the class consensus?

Actividad D ¿Son importantes los deportes?

Paso 1 Utilizando las preguntas a continuación como guía, entrevista a dos personas de la clase sobre la importancia del ejercicio y los deportes en su vida.

1. ¿Haces ejercicio regularmente? ¿Cuántas veces a la semana? ¿Qué haces?
2. ¿Practicas algún deporte? ¿Cuándo lo practicas?
3. ¿Cuál es tu deporte favorito? ¿Ves muchos partidos en la televisión? ¿Cuáles?
4. ¿Vas a ver muchos partidos?
5. ¿Eres aficionado/a a algún equipo o a algún (alguna) atleta en particular? ¿Cuál es el equipo o quién es el/la atleta? ¿Por qué te gusta?
6. ¿ ?

Paso 2 Basándote en la información que obtuviste (*you obtained*) en el **Paso 1**, contesta la siguiente pregunta en un párrafo de entre 25 y 50 palabras.

¿Son el ejercicio y los deportes importantes para las dos personas?

≋ Vistazo cultural

El fútbol y otros deportes

Ya sabes que en los Estados Unidos los deportes más populares son el fútbol americano, el basquetbol y el béisbol. Las universidades grandes y también muchas ciudades tienen equipos que compiten para ganar un campeonato al final de la temporada.[a] Pero en los países hispanos, el fútbol es el rey[b] de los deportes y la Copa Mundial[c] es tan importante como el Super Bowl lo es en los Estados Unidos. Los niños juegan al fútbol en la calle, en los parques y, claro, en las escuelas.

También uno puede ver que el tenis gana más importancia cada día, sobre todo en España, Chile y la Argentina. En los campeonatos del Grand Slam, es frecuente ver a un jugador de origen hispano. Y el béisbol todavía es importante en el Caribe, sobre todo en la República Dominicana. El gran beisbolista Sammy Sosa es dominicano.

[a](*sport*) *season*   [b]*king*
[c]*Copa... World Cup*

▲ La selección (*national team*) argentina juega en la Copa Mundial.

Gramática

| **Volví tarde.** **Preterite of Regular -er and -ir Verbs**

REGULAR -er AND -ir VERBS IN THE PRETERITE			
volver, escribir			
yo	volví escribí	**nosotros/as**	volvimos escribimos
tú	volviste escribiste	**vosotros/as**	volvisteis escribisteis
Ud.	volvió escribió	**Uds.**	volvieron escribieron
él/ella	volvió escribió	**ellos/ellas**	volvieron escribieron

As in the preterite forms of **-ar** verbs, the stress shifts from the stem of the verb to the vowel in the ending of **-er/-ir** verbs.

Note the following.

1. Unlike those for the present tense, the preterite forms for **-er** and **-ir** verbs are exactly the same, including the **nosotros** and **vosotros** forms.

2. As with stem-changing **-ar** verbs, **-er** verbs do not change in the preterite. However, some **-ir** verbs do show a stem change in the preterite, but only in the **Ud., él/ella, Uds.,** and **ellos/ellas** forms. This is true of two verbs you have learned in this lesson.

    competir (i, i):* yo competí, ella compitió, Uds. compitieron

    divertir (ie, i):* tú divertiste, Ud. divirtió, ellas divirtieron

    You will learn more about stem-changing **-ir** verbs in the preterite in **Lección 4B.** For now, just keep in mind the changes for these two verbs as you work through this lesson.

3. An unstressed **i** between vowels becomes **y** for spelling and pronunciation purposes.

    leí, leíste, le**y**ó, leímos, leísteis, le**y**eron

4. Note that the verb **conocer** in the preterite translates as *met.*

    Conocí al nuevo estudiante.   *I met the new student.*

---

*The first vowel or vowel pair in parentheses is the stem change for the present tense. The second shows the stem change in the preterite.

De *Sol y viento,* Note: You can access this film clip from a special menu section on Disc 5 of the Instructional Version on DVD.

DE SOL Y VIENTO

At the beginning of **Episodio 4,** Traimaqueo concludes the tour of the winery with Jaime. Read the following exchange. Use the following verbs to aid your comprehension of the exchange and to complete the activity.

Vocabulario útil

nacer	to be born
enterrar*	to bury

JAIME
Muy interesante, señor. Es evidente su pasión por la viña.

TRAIMAQUEO
¿Pasión? No sé. Pero nací en estos terrenos[a] y me enterrarán en estos terrenos, señor. ¿No es así como debe ser?

Examine Traimaqueo's statement beginning with **Pero nací...** . Knowing that the verb **enterrar** is in the future tense, what is the English equivalent of this sentence?

[a]*lands*

✳ MÁS GRAMÁTICA

Although you will learn irregular past tense forms later, here are two irregular verbs in the preterite that are useful at this point.

hacer: hice, hiciste, hizo,[†] hicimos, hicisteis, hicieron

ir/ser: fui, fuiste, fue, fuimos, fuisteis, fueron

Note that **ir** and **ser** share the same forms in the preterite. Context will determine meaning.

¿**Fue** Roberto al cine?	*Did Roberto go to the movies?*
Bill Clinton **fue** presidente de 1993 a 2001.	*Bill Clinton was president from 1993–2001.*

---

*This is an example of a cognate that you may not immediately recognize. Do you know another term for *to bury*? How about *to inter,* as in *She was interred at Hill Crest Cemetery in 1906?* Be on the lookout for such cognates of less frequent English words.
[†]Note that for **Ud., él,** and **ella, hizo** is spelled with a **z** to maintain the soft **c** sound of the other forms.

Actividad E Jaime

Paso 1 ¿Cuáles de las siguientes oraciones sobre las actividades de Jaime en los **Episodios 2** y **3** son ciertas?

			C	F
a.	_5_	Bebió vino en la viña.	☑	☐
b.	___	Comió un sándwich.	☐	☑
c.	_4_	Conoció a Carlos.	☑	☐
d.	_2_	Conoció a María.	☑	☐
e.	_1_	Corrió en el parque.	☑	☐
f.	___	Leyó su correo electrónico.	☐	☑
g.	___	Recibió un mensaje de los Estados Unidos.	☐	☑
h.	_3_	Salió para el Valle del Maipo.	☑	☐

Paso 2 De las que son ciertas, ¿puedes ponerlas en el orden en que ocurrieron?

▲ ¿Cuándo salió Jaime para la viña «Sol y viento», en el **Episodio 2** o en el **Episodio 3**?

Actividad F Lo que hice en el pasado

Paso 1 Completa las oraciones a continuación con información verdadera (*true*) para ti. No le reveles tus respuestas a nadie.

Una vez en el pasado, yo...

1. comí _____.
2. perdí _____.
3. conocí a _____.
4. leí _____.
5. salí con mis amigos y no volví a casa hasta _____.

Paso 2 Una persona servirá de (*will serve as a*) voluntaria. Los demás (*The rest*), utilizando lo que ya saben de esa persona, más sus impresiones de él/ella, tratarán de (*will try*) adivinar lo que hizo haciéndole preguntas del tipo **sí/no.** El profesor (La profesora) puede ayudar con el vocabulario.

MODELOS: ¿Comiste algo malo?

¿Comiste algo vivo?

¿Comiste algo y luego te llevaron al hospital?

Actividad G   Una historia

Paso 1   Con un compañero (una compañera), inventen una historia sobre lo que pasa en los siguientes dibujos. A continuación hay algunas ideas para considerar.

- ¿Cómo se llama el chico?
- ¿Adónde fue?
- ¿Qué hizo allí?
- ¿Cuánto tiempo pasó allí?
- ¿A qué hora volvió a casa?

Paso 2   Compartan su historia con el resto de la clase. ¿Quiénes inventaron la mejor historia? ¿Es parecida la historia a un día en la vida de alguien en la clase?

Actividad H   La semana pasada

Paso 1   Contesta las siguientes preguntas sobre la semana pasada con información verdadera.

1. ¿Hiciste ejercicio? ¿Qué ejercicio hiciste?
2. ¿Cuántas veces saliste con los amigos?

Paso 2   Utilizando las preguntas del **Paso 1,** entrevista a dos personas en la clase y apunta sus respuestas.

Paso 3   Haz una comparación de lo que hiciste tú la semana pasada con lo que hicieron las personas que entrevistaste, a base de la información que tienes de los **Pasos 1** y **2.** Usa las frases **fue activa** ([*it*] *was active*) y **fue solitaria** ([*it*] *was solitary, quiet*).

MODELO: Para mí, la semana pasada fue bastante activa. Hice mucho ejercicio cada día. También salí cuatro veces con mis amigos.
Para Anne, la semana fue menos activa y más solitaria...

NAVEGANDO LA RED

Busca información en la red sobre algún equipo de fútbol en un país hispano. En clase, indica cuántos partidos ganó el equipo la última temporada y un dato (*fact*) interesante más sobre el equipo. Aquí hay algunas sugerencias:

- Real Madrid (España)
- Cobreloa (Chile)
- Boca Juniors (la Argentina)
- Peñarol (el Uruguay)
- Guadalajara (México)

TERCERA PARTE

Vocabulario

¿Cuándo celebras tu cumpleaños?

**Special Occasions
and Holidays**

Note: These vocabulary items can be heard in this lesson's Textbook Audio section of the Online Learning Center Website.

Los días festivos

el **Día de San Valentín** (de los Enamorados)	St. Valentine's Day
el **Martes de Carnaval**	Mardi Gras
el **Día de San Patricio**	St. Patrick's Day
la **Pascua** (de los judíos)	Passover
la **Pascua** (Florida)	Easter
el **Día de Acción de Gracias**	Thanksgiving
la **Fiesta de las Luces**	Hanukkah
la **Nochebuena**	Christmas Eve
la **Navidad**	Christmas
la **Noche Vieja**	New Year's Eve

▲ Los brindis (*toasts*) son comunes en las fiestas hispanas, como esta en Chile.

Algunos brindis populares, **Point out:** Give the meaning of the three *brindis.* The third is done with gestures performed with each phrase. First, the glass is raised, then it is lowered, then it is moved to the center of the body, then, after the last line, a sip is taken.

Algunos brindis populares

«¡ Salud.ᵃ amor y dinero, y tiempo para disfrutarlosᵇ!»

«Por don Pablo: ¡ Que cumpla muchos más !»

«Para arriba, para abajo, para el centro, ¡ para adentro !»ᶜ

ᵃ*Health* ᵇ*enjoy them* ᶜ*Para... Up, down, to the center, inside!*

✱ MÁS VOCABULARIO

celebrar	to celebrate
cumplir... años	to be . . . old (*on a birthday*)
regalar	to give (*a gift*)
el brindis	toast
el cumpleaños	birthday
la fiesta (de sorpresa)	(surprise) party
el regalo	gift
la tarjeta	card
¿Cuándo es... ?	When is . . . ?
¿Cuántos (años) cumples?	How old are you (turning)?

〰 Vistazo cultural

Los días festivos en el mundo hispano

Es verdad que todos tenemos un día especial: el cumpleaños. Pero en el mundo hispano también existe el día del santo. En el calendario católico, cada día corresponde a un santo y si tú llevas un nombre igual al del[a] santo, ese día es el día de tu santo. Por ejemplo, una persona llamada Juan o Juanita tiene el mismo nombre que San Juan el Bautista. El día de San Juan es el 24 de junio. Entonces, el día del santo para los Juanes y las Juanitas es el 24 de junio. Así que en el mundo hispano se celebran tu cumpleaños y el día de tu santo.

▲ En San Francisco, como en otras partes de los Estados Unidos y el Canadá, el Cinco de Mayo es un día festivo importante para la comunidad mexicoamericana.

Muchos creen que el Cinco de Mayo es el día de la independencia de México. La verdad es que el día de la independencia de México es el 16 de septiembre, el día en que los mexicanos se declararon independientes del Imperio Español en 1810 (mil ochocientos diez). El Cinco de Mayo corresponde a otra fecha[b] importante. En 1862 (mil ochocientos sesenta y dos) los franceses invadieron México. El cinco de mayo de ese año, los mexicanos derrotaron[c] a las tropas francesas en la ciudad de Puebla, y todo el país celebró la victoria.

Aunque en el mundo hispano se celebra la Navidad tanto como en los Estados Unidos y el Canadá, en muchos países de habla española el día para intercambiar[d] regalos no es el 25 de diciembre. El día en que las personas se hacen regalos es el 6 de enero, el Día de los Reyes Magos.[e] ¿Por qué? Porque este día marca la llegada de los Reyes Magos con sus regalos para el Niño Jesús.

[a]al... *to that of the* [b]*date* [c]*defeated* [d]*exchanging* [e]Reyes... *Three Wise Men*

¡Exprésate!

Some holidays don't fall on a specific date but rather on the first, second, third, or fourth Monday, Tuesday, and so forth, of a particular month. To express this concept use **el primer, el segundo, el tercer, el cuarto,** or **el último.** For example, **el tercer lunes de febrero es el Día de los Presidentes.**

Actividad A   ¿En qué día cae... ?

INPUT
Act. A, Suggested follow-up: Survey students to find out which holiday is their favorite and why.

Indica en qué día cae (*what day is*) cada día festivo.

1. el Día de San Valentín el 14 de febrero
2. la Navidad el 25 de diciembre
3. la Noche Vieja el 31 de diciembre
4. el Día de San Patricio el 17 de marzo
5. el Día del Padre el tercer domingo de junio
6. el cumpleaños del Dr. Martin Luther King, Jr. el 15 de enero; celebrado el tercer lunes de enero
7. el Día de los Veteranos el 11 de noviembre
8. el Día del Trabajo (*Labor*) el primer lunes de septiembre
9. el Día de la Madre el segundo domingo de mayo
10. el Día de Acción de Gracias el cuarto jueves de noviembre (EE.UU.) / el segundo lunes de octubre (el Canadá)

INPUT
Actividad B

Actividad B   ¿Es importante?

Paso 1   Por orden de importancia (del 1 al 6), indica si cada día o evento es muy importante (1–2), algo importante (3–4) o poco importante (5–6) para ti.

_____ una ceremonia de graduación

_____ el nacimiento (*birth*) del hijo de un amigo/pariente

_____ la muerte (*death*) de una persona célebre

_____ el Día de San Valentín

_____ el Día de San Patricio

_____ el Martes de Carnaval

Paso 2   ¿Qué indican las respuestas sobre la personalidad de una persona?

☐ La persona piensa más en sí misma (*him/herself*) que en los otros.

☐ La persona piensa más en los otros que en sí misma.

INPUT/OUTPUT
Actividad C

Actividad C   Mi cumpleaños

¡Exprésate!

As you find out about people's birthdays in **Actividad C**, see if you can tell what zodiac sign that person is. Once again, here are the names in Spanish (in alphabetical, not chronological, order).

Acuario	**Leo**
Aries	**Libra**
Cáncer	**Piscis**
Capricornio	**Sagitario**
Escorpio	**Tauro**
Géminis	**Virgo**

Paso 1   Indica lo que pasa regularmente el día de tu cumpleaños.

1. ☐ Recibo muchos/algunos regalos.
2. ☐ Recibo muchas/algunas tarjetas.
3. ☐ Lo anuncio de antemano (*ahead of time*). Así las personas no se olvidan (*don't forget*).
4. ☐ Doy una fiesta.
5. ☐ Salgo con mis amigos.
6. ☐ Los miembros de mi familia me llaman para felicitarme (*congratulate me*).
7. ☐ Mis amigos me llaman para felicitarme.

¡Exprésate!, **Point out:** Zodiac dates. Dates are only approximate. The exact beginning or end of the different signs varies from year to year. *Capricornio* (Dec. 22–Jan. 19) // *Acuario* (Jan. 20–Feb. 18) // *Piscis* (Feb. 19–March 20) // *Aries* (March 21–April 19) // *Tauro* (April 20–May 20) // *Géminis* (May 21–June 20) // *Cáncer* (June 21–July 22) // *Leo* (July 23–Aug. 22) // *Virgo* (Aug. 23–Sept. 22) // *Libra* (Sept. 23–Oct. 22) // *Escorpio* (Oct. 23–Nov. 21) // *Sagitario* (Nov. 22–Dec. 21).

8. ☐ Lo considero como un día festivo. No voy a clases y no trabajo.

9. ☐ ¿ ?

Paso 2 Presenta a la clase las oraciones apropiadas del **Paso 1.** ¿Pasan todos el cumpleaños más o menos de igual forma?

Paso 3 Utilizando las expresiones apropiadas de **Más vocabulario** en la página 217, trata de encontrar a dos personas en la clase cuyo (*whose*) cumpleaños cae en el mismo mes que el tuyo.

MODELO: E1: ¿Cuándo es tu cumpleaños?
E2: Es el 22 de octubre.
E1: ¡Ah! Entonces, eres Libra, como yo.

Actividad D   Un perfil (*profile*) personal

Entrevista a un compañero (una compañera) de clase para hacer un breve perfil de él/ella. Utiliza el siguiente cuadro como guía. Luego, entrégale el perfil a tu profesor(a).

Nombre de la persona: _____

Día de su cumpleaños: _____

   Cómo le gusta celebrarlo: _____

_____

_____

_____

_____

Día festivo favorito: _____

   Cómo le gusta celebrarlo: _____

_____

_____

_____

Gramática

| **¿Qué hiciste?** | **Irregular Preterite Forms** ✳

IRREGULAR VERB FORMS IN THE PRETERITE		
VERB	STEM	FORMS (**yo, tú, Ud./él/ella, nosotros/as, vosotros/as, Uds./ellos/ellas**)
andar	**anduv-**	anduve, anduviste, anduvo, anduvimos, anduvisteis, anduvieron
decir	**dij-**	dije, dijiste, dijo, dijimos, dijisteis, dijeron
estar	**estuv-**	estuve, estuviste, estuvo, estuvimos, estuvisteis, estuvieron
poder	**pud-**	pude, pudiste, pudo, pudimos, pudisteis, pudieron
poner	**pus-**	puse, pusiste, puso, pusimos, pusisteis, pusieron
querer	**quis-**	quise, quisiste, quiso, quisimos, quisisteis, quisieron
saber	**sup-**	supe, supiste, supo, supimos, supisteis, supieron
tener	**tuv-**	tuve, tuviste, tuvo, tuvimos, tuvisteis, tuvieron
traer	**traj-**	traje, trajiste, trajo, trajimos, trajisteis, trajeron
venir	**vin-**	vine, viniste, vino, vinimos, vinisteis, vinieron

Gramática, **Point out:** Verbs whose stem consists of a compound built on one of the verbs in the chart carry the same irregularities.

contraer (to contract): *contraje, contrajiste,...*

obtener (to obtain, get): *obtuve, obtuviste,...*

Many common verbs have irregular preterite forms. You will notice that the forms in the chart are irregular in that (1) the stem is different from that of the present tense; (2) there is no stress shift in the **yo, Ud.,** and **él/ella** forms; and (3) all endings are the same regardless of whether the verb is **-ar, -er,** or **-ir.**

Note the following about some irregular preterites.

1. The verb **saber** in the preterite translates as *to find out* or *to come to know* in English.

    ¿Y cuándo **supiste** eso?   *And when did you find that out?*

2. Verbs whose irregular preterite stems end in **j** or a vowel drop the **i** in the **Uds./ellos/ellas** form: **dijeron, trajeron.**

Another irregular verb is the verb **dar.** It takes regular **-er/-ir** endings in the preterite. There are no accent marks on the **yo** and **Ud./él/ella** forms because they consist of one syllable.

dar: di, diste, dio, dimos, disteis, dieron

MÁS GRAMÁTICA

You learned earlier that **conocer** and **saber** in the preterite are translated as *to meet* and *to find out,* respectively. Here are some other verbs whose meanings change in the preterite.

querer: normally translates as *to want,* but in the preterite it means *to try*

> **Quise** hacerlo.   *I tried to do it.*

no querer: normally translates as *not to want,* but in the preterite it means *to refuse*

> **No quise** hacerlo.   *I refused to do it.*

poder: normally translates as *to be able, can,* but in the preterite it means *to succeed* or *to manage to* (*do something*)

> Por fin **pude** hacerlo.   *Finally I managed to do it.*

no poder: normally translates as *not to be able, can't,* but in the preterite means *to fail* (*in doing something*)

> **No pude** hacerlo.   *I failed to do it.*

De *Sol y viento,* Note: You can access this film clip from a special menu section on Disc 5 of the Instructional Version on DVD.
Point out: Remind students at the end that María and Jaime have maintained formalities so far and are using *Ud.* with each other. Later, students will see how they switch to addressing each other as *tú.*

 # DE SOL Y VIENTO

Jaime runs into María again in **Episodio 4.** Look over the exchange here, then select the verbs that you think fit best in each blank.

MARÍA
¡Don Jaime Talavera! ¿Qué hace aquí?
¿Me anda siguiendo?[a]

JAIME
¿Yo? No, es una feliz casualidad.[b] Bueno,
feliz para mí, por lo menos...
No sé si lo es para Ud....

MARÍA
A mí también me hace muy feliz verlo
de nuevo.

JAIME
¡Whoo! Me alegra[c] oír eso...

MARÍA
Ya _____[1] de su viaje. ¿Cómo
le _____[2]?

JAIME
Lo pasé muy bien, gracias.

1. **a.** volvió   **b.** volviste
2. **a.** estuvo   **b.** fue

[a]¿Me... *Are you following me?*   [b]feliz... *happy coincidence*   [c]Me... *I'm glad*

INPUT
Actividad E

Actividad E ¿A quién se refiere?

Basándote en los episodios anteriores de *Sol y viento*, ¿a qué personaje se refiere cada oración a continuación?

1. Hizo ejercicio. Jaime
2. Dijo: «Bonita la muchacha… » Mario
3. Le trajo a Jaime algo de comer. Mario
4. Fue a la universidad a pie (*on foot*). María
5. No tuvo éxito (*success*) con su primera visita con Carlos. Jaime
6. No vino a la conversación con el contrato firmado. Carlos

INPUT

Act. F, Suggestion: Follow up some matches with additional questions using the preterite tense, e.g., 1. (*Muchos inmigrantes mexicanos…*) *¿Cuántos años duró la Revolución, saben?* (*siete años, oficialmente*) *¿Saben cuántos inmigrantes vinieron durante la Revolución?* (*más de 800.000, legalmente*) 2. (*Los españoles…*) *¿Qué más trajeron?* (*la religión católica, la lengua española, muchas enfer-medades*) *¿Qué les dieron los indígenas a los españoles?* (*comidas nuevas: la papa, el tomate, el maíz y muchas más; el tabaco; palabras nuevas como* huracán, canoa *y muchas más…*) 3. (*Washington y Adams…*) *¿Saben quién fue el primer presidente de México?* (*Guadalupe Victoria, nacido José Miguel Ramón Adaucto Fernández y Félix*).

Actividad F ¿Qué sabes?

Haz las correspondencias correctas para formar oraciones verdaderas.

1. __f__ Muchos inmigrantes mexicanos…
2. __a__ Los españoles…
3. __d__ Washington y Adams…
4. __e__ Los mexicanos del siglo XIX…
5. __b__ Adán y Eva…
6. __c__ Neil Armstrong y Buzz Aldrin…

a. trajeron el caballo (*horse*) al Nuevo Mundo.
b. tuvieron dos hijos.
c. hicieron el primer viaje a la luna.
d. fueron los dos primeros presidentes de los Estados Unidos.
e. no pudieron impedir (*stop*) la ocupación francesa.
f. vinieron a los Estados Unidos durante la Revolución de 1910.

Actividad G La Noche Vieja pasada

INPUT/OUTPUT
Actividad G

Paso 1 ¿Qué hicieron tú y tu familia o tú y tus amigos la Noche Vieja pasada? Indica las oraciones que se te aplican.

1. ☐ Dimos una fiesta en casa.
2. ☐ Fuimos a una fiesta.
3. ☐ Fuimos a un bar.
4. ☐ Tuvimos que cancelar nuestros planes.
5. ☐ No hicimos nada en especial.

Paso 2 Comparte tus respuestas con la clase. ¿Cúantos dieron una fiesta? ¿Cuántos no hicieron nada en especial? ¿Qué indican las respuestas en cuanto a la actitud de la clase hacia este día festivo?

OUTPUT
Actividad H

Actividad H Historietas incompletas

Completa las siguientes «historietas» de manera lógica. Luego compáralas con las de otras dos personas. ¿Quién tiene la historieta más imaginativa?

Marta quiso _____,[1] pero no pudo. De repente[a] vino su mamá y _____,[2] arruinando sus planes.

Anoche Juan supo que _____.³ Pues, claro, en seguida^b fue a ver a _____⁴ para contárselo.^c ¡Ese Juan es un metiche^d!

Para mi cumpleaños, Elisa me trajo _____.⁵ Cuando la miré perplejo,^e ella me dijo «_____».⁶ En fin, no creí su excusa.

^aDe... *Suddenly*   ^ben... *right away*   ^c*tell him/her/them about it*   ^d*gossip*   ^e*perplexed*

OUTPUT
Act. I, Suggestions
Paso 1: Allow about 6–7 minutes for the interview.
Paso 2: Call on some people to answer the question by prompting, e.g., *¿A quién entrevistaste, Paul? ¿a Caroline? Muy bien. A ver, ¿quién pasó mejor su cumpleaños, tú o ella? ¿Por qué?*

Actividad I Entrevista

Paso 1 Utilizando las siguientes preguntas como guía, entrevista a otra persona y apunta sus respuestas.

1. ¿Cuándo es tu cumpleaños?
2. ¿Hiciste algo especial para tu último cumpleaños?
3. ¿Cuánto tiempo estuvieron Uds. allí?
4. ¿A qué hora terminó la fiesta / volviste a casa?

Paso 2 Ahora contesta la siguiente pregunta: «¿Quién lo pasó mejor en su cumpleaños, mi compañero/a de clase o yo?» ¿Por qué? Da algunos ejemplos.

Enfoque cultural, **Suggestion:** Ask students if they have noticed that Traimaqueo and Yolanda are descendents of indigenous people, whereas Isabel and Carlos are not.
Suggested follow-up: Have students do a Web search to compare the tribal and reservation system in the United States with the systems that exist in Chile, Peru, or another Latin American country. Students should include population statistics and bring the information to class.

SOL Y VIENTO: Enfoque cultural

En el **Episodio 4,** vas a ver a María colocar carteles^a para una reunión a favor de los mapuches. Como muchas personas en Latinoamérica, María lucha^b por los derechos^c de los grupos indígenas que no tienen voz^d ni mucha influencia en la política de su país. El activismo por los indígenas no se limita a Chile sino también se observa en México, el Paraguay, Guatemala, el Perú y otros países. Muchas veces estos indígenas no tienen suficiente conocimiento del idioma español, lo cual impide su participación activa en la sociedad. En tales^e casos necesitan de personas como María que los ayudan a obtener los beneficios que les corresponden según las leyes^f del país.

▲ Un indígena ecuatoriano

Además, luchan por un sistema de educación bilingüe o, por lo menos, cursos de español como segunda lengua.

^acolocar... *hanging up posters*   ^b*fights*   ^c*rights*   ^d*voice*   ^e*such*   ^f*laws*

SOL Y VIENTO

A primera vista

Antes de ver el episodio

Actividad A ¿Qué recuerdas?

¿Qué recuerdas hasta el momento? Escribe el nombre de los personajes apropiados en los espacios.

1. Después de correr, ___Jaime___ compró una fortuna.
2. Al leer (*Upon reading*) su fortuna, se chocó con (*he bumped into*) ___María___, una profesora de antropología.
3. ___Mario___ lo llevó a la viña «Sol y viento». Allí habló con ___Carlos___ sobre la venta de la viña.
4. No pudo ver a ___la madre de Carlos___. ___Carlos___ le dijo a Jaime que ella se fue a Santiago.

Actividad B Repaso

Revisa las escenas en las varias secciones **De *Sol y viento*** en esta lección para comprender mejor lo que vas a ver en el episodio.

Actividad C ¿Qué falta?

En este episodio, Jaime oye a Traimaqueo decir que doña Isabel lo espera en la casa. Lee el diálogo entre Jaime y Traimaqueo.

Act. C, Suggestion: Don't give students the answer, as they will verify their response later.

YOLANDA: Oye, viejo.* ¿Vas a llegar muy tarde?

TRAIMAQUEO: Un poquito. La señora Isabel me espera en la casa.

JAIME: Creía que la señora Isabel estaba† en Santiago.

TRAIMAQUEO: No, no, no. La señora Isabel no hace muchos viajes en estos días. _____.

¿Qué razón crees que va a ofrecer Traimaqueo para explicar por qué doña Isabel no hace muchos viajes?

    a. La señora está muy ocupada (*busy*) con la viña.

    b. La señora no está de muy buena salud (*health*).

Actividad D El episodio

Ahora mira el episodio. Si hay algo que no entiendes bien, puedes volver a ver la escena en cuestión.

*****Viejo/a** is a term of endearment often used among people who have known each other for a long time. It is used more typically among married people.
†**Estaba** is a past-tense verb form you will learn in the next lesson. In this context, it means (*she*) *was*.

Después de ver el episodio

Actividad A ¿Qué recuerdas?

Contesta cada pregunta sobre el **Episodio 4.**

1. ¿Quién le dio un tour de la viña a Jaime? ¿Los acompañó Mario? Traimaqueo; Mario no los acompañó.
2. Cuando Jaime oyó que la señora Isabela estaba en casa, decidió ir a verla en seguida. ¿Sí o no? no
3. ¿Le dijo Carlos la verdad a Jaime? ¿Sí o no? No, no le dijo la verdad.
4. ¿Para quién compró Jaime la figurita del espíritu mapuche? para María

Actividad B ¿Lo captaste?

Ahora verifica tu respuesta a la **Actividad C** de **Antes de ver el episodio.** Puedes ver esa escena de nuevo si quieres.

Actividad C Usando el contexto

¿Pudiste deducir el significado de las palabras y expresiones que aparecen *en letra cursiva,* según el contexto en que aparecen?

1. TRAIMAQUEO: Pasemos a la viña, *¿le parece?*
2. JAIME: ¿Tiene algún significado esta figurita? ... *¿A cuánto me sale?*
   TENDERA (*Shopkeeper*): Diecinueve mil quinientos pesos.
   JAIME: Perfecto. *Me la llevo.*

Actividad D En resumen

Completa la siguiente narración con las palabras y expresiones apropiadas de la lista a la derecha.

En este episodio, Jaime __conoce__[1] la viña «Sol y viento» gracias a un tour que le da Traimaqueo. Al final del tour, Traimaqueo recita parte de un __poema__[2] sobre el vino, demostrando[a] su __pasión__[3] por el vino. Jaime llega a saber que Carlos no es una persona honesta, pues le mintió[b] sobre su __madre__.[4] Más tarde, Jaime tiene un encuentro __agradable__[5] con María. Ella está en el mercado colocando[c] anuncios en apoyo[d] del __pueblo mapuche__.[6] Jaime le da una sorpresa: una figurita del __espíritu__[7] protector de los mapuches. ¿Cómo crees que van las relaciones entre Jaime y María?

agradable
conoce
espíritu (*m.*)
madre
pasión (*f.*)
poema (*m.*)
pueblo mapuche

[a]*showing* [b]*he lied* [c]*hanging* [d]*support*

Detrás de la cámara

Who is Traimaqueo? Having worked for the winery ever since he was young (as did his father), Traimaqueo is close to doña Isabel, but he is not considered a "member" of the family. He has little respect for Carlos but says nothing. Part Mapuche, he has learned to have patience and also that bad situations work themselves out. He is a simple man, but not stupid and certainly not ignorant of what goes on around him. In fact, he most likely has an idea about why Jaime is visiting.

RESUMEN DE VOCABULARIO

Verbos

andar (*irreg.*) **en bicicleta**	to ride a bicycle
caminar	to walk
cocinar	to cook
coleccionar (estampillas, monedas)	to collect (stamps, coins)
cumplir... años	to be . . . old (*on a birthday*)
dar (*irreg.*) **una fiesta**	to throw a party
dar (*irreg.*) **un paseo**	to take a walk; to stroll
dibujar	to draw
divertir (ie, i)	to entertain
esquiar (esquío)	to ski
estar (*irreg.*) **en (buena) forma**	to be in (good) shape
fortalecer (zc)	to strengthen
ganar	to win
hacer (*irreg.*) **ciclismo estacionario**	to ride a stationary bike
hacer (*irreg.*) **ejercicio (aeróbico)**	to exercise (do aerobics)
hacer (*irreg.*) **gimnasia**	to work out
levantar pesas	to lift weights
limpiar la casa	to clean the house
nadar	to swim
navegar (gu) en barco	to sail
pasarlo bien/mal	to have a good/bad time
patinar (en línea)	to (inline) skate
picar (qu)	to nibble
pintar	to paint
quemar calorías	to burn calories
rozarse (c) con la gente	to mingle with people
sacar (qu) un vídeo/DVD	to rent a video/DVD
ser (*irreg.*) **aficionado/a (a)**	to be a fan (of)
sudar	to sweat
trotar	to jog

Cognados: celebrar, competir (i, i), meditar; el golf, el museo, el yoga
Repaso: bailar, correr, leer, perder (ie), regalar, tocar (qu) (el piano, la guitarra), tomar

Sobre los deportes

el campeonato	championship
la cancha (de tenis)	(tennis) court
el equipo	equipment; team
la milla	mile
la natación	swimming
el partido	game, match
la piscina	swimming pool
la pista	track
la rueda de andar	treadmill

Cognados: el/la atleta, el basquetbol, el béisbol, el fútbol, el fútbol americano, el kilómetro, el metro, el tenis, el vólibol
Repaso: el estadio, el gimnasio

Los días festivos

el Día de Acción de Gracias	Thanksgiving
el Día de San Patricio	St. Patrick's Day
el Día de San Valentín (de los Enamorados)	St. Valentine's Day
la Fiesta de las Luces	Hanukkah
el Martes de Carnaval	Mardi Gras
la Navidad	Christmas
la Noche Vieja	New Year's Eve
la Nochebuena	Christmas Eve
la Pascua (de los judíos)	Passover
la Pascua (Florida)	Easter
¿Cuántos (años) cumples?	How old are you (turning)?

Otras palabras y expresiones

el aguafiestas	party pooper
el ajedrez	chess
el brindis	toast
el cumpleaños	birthday
los/las demás	others
la fiesta (de sorpresa)	(surprise) party
el juego	game (*as in chess*)
los ratos libres	free (spare) time
el regalo	gift
la tarjeta	card
anoche	last night
ayer	yesterday
fuerte	strong

Repaso: divertido/a

LECCIÓN 4B

En casa

OBJETIVOS

IN THIS LESSON, YOU WILL:

- learn how to talk about dwellings and buildings
- continue talking about activities in the past with stem-changing **-ir** verbs in the preterite
- learn how to talk about rooms, furniture, and other items found in a house
- learn the basic uses of reflexive verbs
- describe typical household chores
- learn some preliminary distinctions between **por** and **para**

In addition, you will watch **Episodio 4** of the film *Sol y viento* again.

Los pisos (*apartments*) y casas del Barrio de Santa Cruz en Sevilla, España, son muy impresionantes (*impressive*).

The following media resources are available for this lesson of *Sol y viento*:

Episodio 4 of *Sol y viento*

Online *Manual de actividades*

Online Learning Center Website

PRIMERA PARTE

Vocabulario

Talking About
Buildings and
Where People Live

Note: These vocabulary
items can be heard in
this lesson's Textbook
Audio section of the
Online Learning Center
Website.

¿Dónde vives?

Dwellings and Buildings

Lugares

el apartamento	apartment
el barrio / la vecindad	neighborhood
la casa	house; home
la casa particular/privada	private residence
el condominio	condo(minium)
el cuarto	room (*general*)
el edificio	building
el hogar	home (*as in "home, sweet home"*)
la oficina	office
la residencia	residence
la residencia estudiantil	dormitory
la torre	tower
la vivienda	housing

Las personas

el/la compañero/a de cuarto (casa)	roommate (housemate)
el/la dueño/a	owner; landlord, landlady
el/la inquilino/a	tenant
el/la portero/a	doorperson; building manager
el/la vecino/a	neighbor

▲ El centro de Bogotá, Colombia, tiene edificios altos y modernos.

▲ El centro de Guanajuato, México, está rodeado de (*surrounded by*) barrios pequeños y casas particulares.

✻ MÁS VOCABULARIO

el alquiler	rent
el balcón	balcony
la dirección	address
el piso (*Sp.*)	flat, apartment
el piso, la planta (*Sp.*)	floor (*of a building*)
la vista	view
alquilar	to rent
firmar (un contrato)	to sign (a lease)

Vistazo cultural,
Suggestion: After students read, have them describe what's on the *planta baja* in various buildings on campus (e.g., *¿Qué hay en la planta baja de Lincoln Hall?*).

≋ Vistazo cultural

¿Primer piso?

E n los Estados Unidos, *ground floor* y *first floor* tienden a ser lo mismo. Y en algunos edificios, entre el *ground floor* y el segundo piso, tienen el *mezzanine.* El sistema de nombrar los pisos es diferente en el mundo hispano. Examina los equivalentes a continuación.

En un país hispano	En edificios norteamericanos	En ciertos edificios norteamericanos
la planta baja	first floor, ground floor	first floor, ground floor
el primer piso	second floor	mezzanine
el segundo piso	third floor	second floor
el tercer piso	fourth floor	third floor
el cuarto piso	fifth floor	fourth floor

Así que cuando entras en un ascensor[a] en el mundo hispano, el botón marcado **B** o **PB** no quiere decir *basement* sino[b] **baja (planta baja)** y el botón marcado **1** no se refiere a *ground floor* sino al primer piso (*second floor*).

▲ ¿En qué piso está la recepción del Hotel Bonaparte? ¿Está en la planta baja o en el primer piso?

[a]*elevator* [b]*but rather*

INPUT

Act. A, Suggestion: Read each definition aloud once. Repeat if students ask for it.

Statements: 1. *la zona donde una persona vive* (*el barrio*) 2. *la persona que paga el alquiler* (*la inquilina*) 3. *un lugar en la universidad donde viven muchos estudiantes* (*la residencia estudiantil*) 4. *una persona que vive en la misma vecindad que tú* (*la vecina*) 5. *lo que ves desde una ventana o un balcón* (*la vista*) 6. *el número y la calle donde vive una persona* (*la dirección*) 7. *una vivienda separada de otras, que no tiene vecinos ni arriba ni abajo* (*la casa particular*) 8. *el dinero que uno paga por vivir en un apartamento* (*el alquiler*)

Suggested follow-up: Ask a few personal questions related to the vocabulary just reviewed. For example: *Charles, ¿vives en una residencia estudiantil o en un apartamento? ¿Tienes balcón? ¿Cómo es la vista que ves desde el balcón?* etc.

INPUT

Act. B, Note: Answers vary depending on your locale. Students may have conflicting, but correct, answers.

Actividad A ¿A qué se refiere?

El profesor (La profesora) va a leer algunas descripciones. ¿A cuál de las opciones se refiere cada descripción?

1. (a.) el barrio   b. el hogar
2. a. la dueña   (b.) la inquilina
3. a. el edificio   (b.) la residencia estudiantil
4. (a.) la vecina   b. la portera
5. a. el piso   (b.) la vista
6. (a.) la dirección   b. la torre
7. (a.) la casa particular b. el condominio
8. a. la vivienda   (b.) el alquiler

Actividad B ¿Cierto o falso?

Indica si cada oración es cierta o falsa para los edificios y viviendas en tu universidad y ciudad.

		CIERTO	FALSO
1.	Si no pagas el alquiler a tiempo, te pueden poner una multa (*fee*).	☐	☐
2.	Para alquilar un apartamento o una casa en esta ciudad, es necesario firmar un contrato de un año.	☐	☐
3.	La residencia estudiantil más alta de la universidad tiene sólo cuatro pisos.	☐	☐
4.	La universidad tiene una torre. Es un campanario (*bell tower*).	☐	☐
5.	Si vives en un apartamento, eres dueño y no inquilino.	☐	☐
6.	No hay barrios peligrosos (*dangerous*) en esta ciudad.	☐	☐
7.	En esta universidad, la Facultad de Psicología tiene su propio (*own*) edificio. No lo comparte (*share*) con otras facultades.	☐	☐
8.	En esta ciudad, $500 por el alquiler de un apartamento de un cuarto es mucho.	☐	☐

NAVEGANDO LA RED ∼∼∼∼∼∼∼∼∼∼∼∼∼∼∼∼∼

Busca información en la red sobre algún pueblo o ciudad en España que data de (*dates back to*) la Edad Media (*Middle Ages*) o algún pueblo o ciudad colonial en Latinoamérica. Describe la parte central del pueblo o de la ciudad.

Actividad C   Un anuncio (*advertisement*)

Paso 1   Con un compañero (una compañera), inventen un anuncio para un apartamento disponible (*available*). Incluyan toda la información necesaria: el número de cuartos, el alquiler, el piso en que está, el tipo de barrio, etcétera.

Paso 2   Los anuncios deben circular en la clase. ¿Ves uno interesante? ¿Qué tiene que te gusta?

Paso 3   En grupos de dos, alguien debe hacer el papel (*play the role*) de una persona interesada en el apartamento y la otra persona debe hacer el papel de Tim. La primera persona llama a Tim para conseguir más información.

APARTAMENTO PARA ALQUILAR
¡Puedes caminar a tus clases!

Se alquila apartamento
de dos cuartos en la zona
universitaria. Balcón amplio,
buena vista de la universidad.
$600 al mes más depósito igual.
Llama al 555-3456.
Pregunta por Tim.

Actividad D   Comparaciones

Paso 1   Mira las fotos en la página 228. ¿Puedes describir las dos ciudades utilizando el vocabulario nuevo? Escribe dos o tres oraciones.

Paso 2   Algunos estudiantes van a leer sus descripciones. ¿Hay otras oraciones que la clase pueda añadir (*could add*) a las descripciones de estos lugares? ¿Cómo se comparan los dos lugares?

Paso 3   Ahora imagina que una estudiante viene a los Estados Unidos a estudiar por un año. Ha sido aceptada (*She's been accepted*) en dos universidades. Una está en la Ciudad de Nueva York y la otra en Iowa. Entre todos, ¿qué le podrían decir (*could you tell her*) sobre los dos lugares?

Actividad E   Entrevista

Paso 1   Entrevista a otra persona utilizando las siguientes preguntas como guía. Puedes añadir otras preguntas si quieres.

1. Para ti, ¿es necesario vivir cerca de la universidad?
2. ¿Qué prefieres, un apartamento, una residencia estudiantil o una casa?
3. Para ti, ¿es importante el barrio donde vives? ¿Qué barrio o zona de esta ciudad prefieres?
4. ¿Te molestan las alturas (*heights*)? ¿Puedes vivir en un piso alto?
5. ¿Cuánto puedes pagar de alquiler?

Paso 2   Utilizando la información que obtuviste en el **Paso 1,** escribe un breve párrafo sobre las preferencias y necesidades de la persona a quien entrevistaste.

Gramática

More on Talking
About the Past

No durmió bien.   e → i, o → u Preterite Stem Changes

-ir STEM CHANGES IN THE PRETERITE e → i, o → u			
yo	pedí repetí seguí dormí morí	**nosotros/as**	pedimos repetimos seguimos dormimos morimos
tú	pediste repetiste seguiste dormiste moriste	**vosotros/as**	pedisteis repetisteis seguisteis dormisteis moristeis
Ud.	pidió repitió siguió durmió murió	**Uds.**	pidieron repitieron siguieron durmieron murieron
él/ella	pidió repitió siguió durmió murió	**ellos/ellas**	pidieron repitieron siguieron durmieron murieron

As you have learned, **-ar** and **-er** verbs with stem changes in the present do not have stem changes in the preterite.

| **perder (ie):** | ¿Perdiste algo? | *Did you lose something?* |
| **empezar (ie):** | Ya empezó la clase. | *Class already started.* |

As you saw briefly in the previous lesson, the **-ir** stem-changing verbs do have a stem change in the preterite but only in the **Ud., él/ella,** and the **Uds., ellos/ellas** forms. The -**ir** verbs whose stem changes from **e → ie** in the present change from **e → i** in the preterite in the forms just mentioned. Similarly, **-ir** verbs that in the present tense have **o → ue** stem changes have the following stem change in the **Ud., él/ella,** and **Uds., ellos/ellas** forms: **o → u.**

MÁS GRAMÁTICA

Here are some other verbs that undergo **e** → **i** stem changes. You will encounter others throughout *Sol y viento*.

conseguir (*to get, obtain*)*: consiguió, consiguieron
divertir: divirtió, divirtieron
mentir (*to lie, tell a lie*): mintió, mintieron
preferir: prefirió, prefirieron
sentir (*to feel*): sintió, sintieron
servir: sirvió, sirvieron
sugerir (*to suggest*): sugirió, sugirieron
vestirse: se vistió, se vistieron

De *Sol y viento,* **Note:** You can access this film clip from a special menu section on Disc 5 of the Instructional Version on DVD.

DE SOL Y VIENTO

In a future episode of *Sol y viento,* you will meet doña Isabel, Carlos' mother. As Carlos talks about running the winery, she reminds him of why he took on the duties he has. Read their exchange and then answer the questions that follow.

ISABEL
Cuando **murió** tu papá, te encargaste de los negocios.[a] Yo ya estaba vieja y tu hermana tenía[b] otros intereses.

CARLOS
Sí. Ella siempre ha tenido[c] otros intereses.

ISABEL
¡Carlos! ¡Estás grande para estar resentido!

1. ¿Se sabe cuándo murió el padre de Carlos?
2. ¿Crees que murió joven o que murió viejo?

[a]te... *you took over the business* [b]*had* [c]ha... *has had*

*****Conseguir** + *infinitive* means *to succeed in* (*doing something*).

INPUT

Act. F, Suggestion: Read each statement out loud once so students can hear it. Then allow students a few minutes to come up with their answers. Review each statement and ask a volunteer for an answer. Students may not be able to use Spanish at this point to explain why they think what they do. If they attempt to use English, recast what they say into Spanish. Otherwise, offer students logical alternatives, e.g., 1. *¿Por qué crees eso? ¿Porque el viaje es muy largo o porque estaba muy cansado?* 2. *¿Lo dices porque notaste algo en la cara* (point to your face) *de Jaime o porque él dijo algo?* etc.

INPUT/OUTPUT
Actividad G

Actividad F ¿Qué crees tú?

Para cada oración a continuación, indica si es **probable, improbable, posible** o **imposible** según lo que recuerdas de los personajes y la historia de *Sol y viento.*

1. Durante el viaje a Chile, Jaime no durmió. Leyó y trabajó un poco.
2. Cuando conoció a María, Jaime sintió una gran atracción por ella.
3. Carlos sirvió unas copas de vino antes de hablar con Jaime de los negocios porque quería distraerlo (*he wanted to distract him*).
4. Jaime no le pidió un contrato firmado a Carlos porque entendía (*he understood*) que Carlos no lo tenía (*didn't have it*).
5. Los padres de Jaime murieron hace unos años.

Actividad G ¿A quién(es) se refiere?

Paso 1 ¿Puedes identificar a quién(es) se refiere cada oración? Escoge entre las siguientes personas o personajes.

- María Antonieta y Luis XVI
- el Mad Hatter
- Rip Van Winkle
- Butch Cassidy y el Sundance Kid
- Marilyn Monroe
- los ángeles de Charlie
- Robin Hood
- Elvis Presley

1. Murió joven, a los 36 años, de un aparente suicidio. Marilyn Monroe
2. Murieron en la guillotina. María Antonieta y Luis XVI
3. Murió de un infarto cardíaco (*heart attack*). Elvis Presley
4. Consiguió robarles dinero a los ricos para luego dárselo a los pobres. Robin Hood
5. Murieron en la última escena de la película. Butch y Sundance
6. Durmió 20 años. Rip Van Winkle
7. Sirvió té en una fiesta muy conocida. el Mad Hatter
8. Divirtieron a muchos televidentes (*TV viewers*) de los años 70. los ángeles de Charlie

Paso 2 Inventa una o dos oraciones como las del **Paso 1** y léelas en voz alta. ¿Pueden adivinar los demás a quién(es) se refiere(n)?

¡Exprésate!

In case you aren't sure about something, you can say

Creo que... or

No estoy seguro/a, pero creo que...

If you are sure, you can say

Eso lo sé muy bien.

and then give your answer.

INPUT
Act. H, Answers:
1. It is not clear whether they served turkey or not. They served duck for sure.
2. They followed "a star to the East."
3. *su escoba*
4. Richard Nixon
5. Agassi won all four Grand Slam titles: U.S. Open, French Open, Australian Open, Wimbledon. Sampras never did win a title at the French Open.

OUTPUT
Act. I,
Suggestions:
Paso 1: Circulate to assist with vocabulary.
Paso 2: After students present to each other, ask for volunteers to offer descriptions to see if the rest of class can guess. Are any particularly difficult?

OUTPUT
Actividad J

Actividad H ¿Cuánto sabes?

¿Crees que sabes mucho de historia? ¿de eventos importantes en los deportes? ¿de hechos (*facts*) triviales relacionados con las películas y las novelas? Contesta cada pregunta a continuación para ver cuánto sabes sobre estos temas.

1. ¿Qué sirvieron los peregrinos (*pilgrims*) el primer Día de Acción de Gracias? ¿Pavo o pato (*duck*)?
2. ¿Qué estrella (*star*) siguieron los Reyes Magos para llegar a Belén (*Bethlehem*)? La del oeste, del norte, del sur o del este?
3. ¿Qué le pidió el Mago de Oz a Dorotea como prueba de la muerte de la bruja (*witch*)? ¿Sus zapatos, su escoba (*broom*) o su sombrero?
4. ¿Qué presidente mintió cuando anunció que no sabía (*he didn't know*) nada del robo (*break-in*) en el Hotel Watergate?
5. ¿Qué consiguió hacer Andre Agassi que no consiguió Pete Sampras? ¿Ganar el trofeo en cada uno de los campeonatos del Grand Slam? ¿O ser la primera persona en ganar dos trofeos seguidos (*back to back*) del Australian Open?

Actividad I Una prueba de la historia

Paso 1 Piensa en presidentes, políticos (*politicians*), actores y otras personas famosas que murieron repentinamente (*suddenly*). Escribe por lo menos cuatro descripciones breves, sin mencionar el nombre de la persona.

MODELO: Este político murió durante su campaña para ser presidente. Murió en el lobby de un hotel en Los Ángeles. Lo mató un hombre. (Bobby Kennedy)

Paso 2 Preséntale tus oraciones a un compañero (una compañera). ¿Puede deducir a quién se refiere?

Actividad J ¿Mienten los políticos (*politicians*)?

Paso 1 Muchas personas dicen que los políticos mienten. Con un compañero (una compañera) de clase, indiquen si las siguientes personas mintieron o no, sobre qué mintieron y si su mentira (*lie*) fue grande o no. Si quieren, pueden hablar de otro político también. El profesor (La profesora) les puede ayudar (*help*) con el vocabulario necesario.

1. Richard Nixon
2. Ronald Reagan
3. Bill Clinton
4. George W. Bush
5. ¿ ?

Paso 2 Cada grupo debe presentar sus ideas a la clase. ¿Están todos de acuerdo?

SEGUNDA PARTE

Talking About Things in the House

Vocabulario

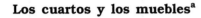

Es mi sillón favorito.

Furniture and Rooms

Los cuartos y los muebles^a

^a furniture

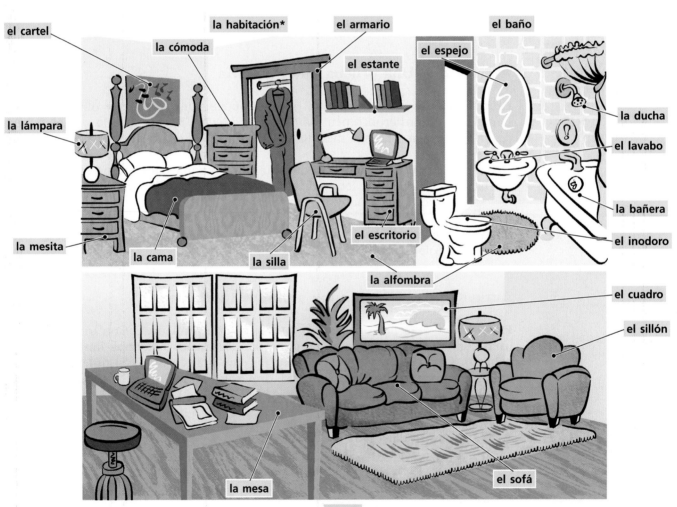

el cartel

la habitación*

el armario

el baño

la cómoda

el espejo

el estante

la ducha

la lámpara

el lavabo

la bañera

la mesita

el escritorio

el inodoro

la cama

la silla

la alfombra

el cuadro

el sillón

la mesa

el sofá

la sala

---

*Other terms for *bedroom* used in various parts of the Spanish-speaking world are **la alcoba, el dormitorio,** and **la recámara.**

❋ MÁS VOCABULARIO

la cama matrimonial*	queen bed
la cama sencilla	twin bed
la cocina	kitchen
el comedor	dining room
los pies (metros) cuadrados	square feet (meters)
el tamaño	size

Cognados: el garaje, el jardín, el patio

amueblado/a	furnished
¿De qué tamaño es... ?	What size is . . . ?
de venta	for sale
se alquila	for rent

▲ 1.

▲ 2.

▲ 3.

Aquí están tres fotos de la *suite* de Jaime en el Hotel Bonaparte en Santiago.
¿Cuántos muebles y objetos del vocabulario nuevo puedes identificar?

---

*In some parts of the Spanish-speaking world, the English words *queen* and *king* have been adopted as bed sizes: **una cama queen, una cama king.**

INPUT/OUTPUT

Act. A, *Paso 1,* **Note:**
1. *pies* would be wrong
because the whole apart-
ment would be about the
size of a living room.
Four hundred square
meters equals
approximately
1,200 square feet.

Actividad A   Busco piso amueblado

Paso 1   Mira el siguiente anuncio. Utiliza el vocabulario nuevo para llenar los espacios en blanco con palabras apropiadas.

```
┌─────────────────────────────────┐
│      PARA ALQUILAR/PISO          │
│           AMUEBLADO              │
│                                  │
│   Se alquila un piso de 400      │
│   ___metros___ ¹ cuadrados. Sala,│
│   ___comedor___,² cocina y dos   │
│   habitaciones,³ Garaje y patio/jardín ⁴ │
│   compartido.ª Muebles incluyen: │
│   sofá y dos sillones/mesitas;⁵ mesa │
│   y sillas, camas queen, cómodas,│
│   ___escritorio___ ⁶ para computadora y │
│   dos ___estantes___ ⁷ para libros. │
│       Llame al 55-64-99.         │
└─────────────────────────────────┘
```

ª*shared*

Vistazo cultural,
Suggestion (p. 239): After
students read, ask them
to write out 4–5
sentences in which
they compare the
concept of what's in the
reading with what they
know about the United
States. You might offer
them two alternatives to
begin: *Semejante a lo
que existe en el mundo
hispano, en los Estados
Unidos...* or *A diferencia
de lo que existe en el
mundo hispano, en los
Estados Unidos...* Have
them exchange and com-
pare before turning in to
you.

Paso 2   Di a la clase si este apartamento parece ser más grande, más pequeño o casi igual de tamaño comparado con tu propia vivienda. Describe las diferencias.

Actividad B   ¿Qué tienes?

INPUT/OUTPUT
Actividad B

Paso 1   Combina las frases de las dos columnas para formar oraciones lógicas.

En...

1. _b_ mi mesita
2. _d_ mi habitación
3. _a_ el comedor
4. _c_ la sala
5. _e_ mi armario

hay...

a. una mesa con cuatro sillas.
b. fotos, una lámpara y un reloj despertador.
c. sólo dos sillones. No tengo sofá.
d. una cama matrimonial y una cómoda.
e. ropa, cajas (*boxes*) y zapatos.

Paso 2   Indica si las oraciones que formaste en el **Paso 1** son verdaderas para ti o no.

Actividad C   ¿Te importa?

INPUT/OUTPUT

Act. C, *Paso 2,*
Suggestion: Tell students
to jot down names as
they go. They should not
ask more than 2 questions
in a row of any 1 person.
The idea here is to
circulate, not interview.

Paso 1   Indica si te importa o no que una casa tenga (*has*) cada una de estas cosas. Añade algo más en los números 9 y 10.

	ME IMPORTA.	NO ME IMPORTA.
1. un armario amplio (de tipo *walk-in*)	☐	☐
2. una cocina grande	☐	☐
3. una bañera sin ducha	☐	☐

	ME IMPORTA.	NO ME IMPORTA.
4. un espejo largo	☐	☐
5. una habitación privada	☐	☐
6. alfombra de pared a pared (*wall to wall*)	☐	☐
7. una sala aparte (*separate*) del comedor	☐	☐
8. inodoro aparte del resto del baño	☐	☐
9. ¿ ?	☐	☐
10. ¿ ?	☐	☐

Paso 2 Convierte las oraciones en preguntas y busca personas que tengan las mismas respuestas que tú.

MODELO: ¿Te importa tener un inodoro aparte del resto del baño?

Actividad D Busco compañero/a de casa

Paso 1 Imagina que necesitas mudarte (*to move*) de casa y vas a hablarle a un compañero (una compañera) para ver si Uds. son compatibles o no. Tu decisión no depende de la personalidad de la persona sino de la casa y lo que incluye el precio. Por ejemplo, ¿te importa tener tu propio baño? ¿Necesitas un cuarto amueblado? ¿Qué tienes que necesitas llevar a la nueva casa? ¿Qué tamaño de cuarto esperas tener? ¿Necesitas un armario amplio? Escribe por lo menos cinco preguntas pensando en estas ideas.

Paso 2 Entrevista a varias personas en la clase. ¿Encuentras a la persona y el lugar apropiados? Presenta la información a la clase.

≋ Vistazo cultural

Hogar, dulce hogar

No hay casas o apartamentos «típicos» del mundo hispano. Como en muchos otros países, el tipo de vivienda depende principalmente del lugar geográfico. En las ciudades grandes, predominan los apartamentos y edificios altos. En las zonas rurales y los suburbios, las casas particulares son más prevalentes. Algo que sí es común en el mundo hispano es el concepto del jardín, balcón o terraza. A los hispanos, en general, les gusta tener un lugar fuera de la casa para sentarse[a] y gozar del[b] tiempo. Es frecuente ver casas con patios interiores y balcones llenos[c] de plantas y flores, con sillas cómodas[d] donde la gente puede pasar una tarde con amigos o familiares tomando una bebida y charlando.

[a]*sit down* [b]*gozar... enjoy the* [c]*full*
[d]*comfortable*

▲ ¿Te gustaría (*Would you like*) tener una casa con patio y fuente (*fountain*), como esta en Ponce, Puerto Rico?

Gramática

Talking About What People Do to and for Themselves

Me conozco bien.   **True Reflexive Constructions**

In **Lecciones 3A** and **3B**, you learned about objects and object pronouns. Can you identify the subjects and direct objects in each sentence below?

> RAMÓN: No sé si Elena conoce bien a Juan.
> SILVIA: Pues sí. Elena lo conoce bien porque son vecinos.

In the preceding example, the subjects and objects are different people. **Elena** is the subject of **conoce** and **Juan/lo** are the direct objects. But what if the subject and object are the same? What happens when María is talking about knowing herself? What if you are looking at yourself? When the subject and object are the same, the sentence is called a *reflexive* sentence. In Spanish, you can use regular object pronouns for reflexive sentences except for **Ud./Uds.** and **él/ella/ellos/ellas,** all of which require **se.** That is, the reflexive pronouns are **me, te, se, nos,** and **os.** Look at the chart to see how this works.

Cuando el gato está ausente, los ratones **se divierten.**

Art, Point out: Students already know that the verb *divertir* means *to entertain.* Ask students: *¿Cuál es el sujeto del verbo* ***divertir*** *en el refrán?* (los ratones) *¿Y el objeto?* (los ratones) *¿Conocen un refrán parecido en inglés? ¿Cuál es?*

Gramática, **Note:** Because pronouns can be a challenge, you may refer to the Instructor's Manual for information to help students with these concepts. Alternatively, the same information is available on the Online Learning Center, available for digital download.

REFLEXIVE AND NONREFLEXIVE SENTENCES	
SUBJECT AND OBJECT ARE DIFFERENT	SUBJECT AND OBJECT ARE THE SAME
Juan **me conoce** bien. *Juan knows me well.*	**Me conozco** bien. Sé mis puntos fuertes y débiles. *I know myself well. I know my strong and weak points.*
¿**Te pone** restricciones tu trabajo? *Does your job put restrictions on you?*	¿**Te pones** restricciones? *Do you put restrictions on yourself?*
No **le hablo** a Roberto. *I don't speak to Roberto.*	Roberto **se habla** constantemente. *Robert speaks to himself constantly.*
No **sabemos** cómo expresar **eso.** *We don't know how to express that.*	**Nos expresamos** muy bien. *We express ourselves very well.*
Ramona no **os ve** mucho, ¿verdad? *Ramona doesn't see you (all) much, right?*	¿Cómo **os veis** en tres años? *How do you (all) see yourselves in three years?*
Elena **les prepara** el desayuno a los hijos. *Elena prepares breakfast for her kids.*	Los hijos **se preparan** el desayuno. *The kids prepare breakfast for themselves.*

Just as with direct and indirect object pronouns, reflexive pronouns precede the conjugated verb, but they may also be attached to the end of an infinitive.

Miguel no **se quiere mirar** en el espejo.

Miguel no **quiere mirarse** en el espejo.

MÁS VOCABULARIO

Here are some useful reflexive verbs that you may use to talk about things that people do to or for themselves, some of which you have already seen. Note that many of them have to do with daily routines.

acostarse (ue)	to go to bed
afeitarse	to shave
bañarse	to take a bath
despertarse (ie)	to wake up
dormirse (ue, u)	to fall asleep
ducharse	to take a shower
lavarse los dientes	to brush one's teeth
levantarse	to get up
sentirse (ie, i)	to feel
vestirse (i, i)	to get dressed

De *Sol y viento,* Note: You can access this film clip from a special menu section in the Instructional Version on DVD.
Optional follow-up: You may wish to ask students *¿Cómo es una profesora típica? ¿Cómo es un profesor típico?*

 DE SOL Y VIENTO

In **Episodio 5** of *Sol y viento* you will watch a scene in which Jaime tells María that she's not a typical professor. Part of their conversation appears in the dialogue.

JAIME
De verdad me parece muy interesante lo que hace Ud. No es una profesora... típica.

MARÍA
¿«Típica» cómo? ¿Porque no uso anteojos gruesosª y vestidos formales?

JAIME
¡Exactamente! ¡Nah! No, no es eso, precisamente. Es que Ud. no **se limita** a _____.

¿A qué no se limita María?

1. a su especialización

2. a su trabajo con la comunidad indígena

3. a la sala de clase y a sus libros

¿Estás de acuerdo con Jaime en que María no es una profesora típica? ¿Conoces a profesores como María? ¿Cómo son?

ªanteojos... *thick glasses*

INPUT

Act E, Suggestions:
Paso 1: Refer to information on dictogloss activities in the Instructor's Manual if you have not done one of these activities before. Paragraph: *Esta persona se dedica a su trabajo pero no se define por su trabajo. Tiene muchos intereses diferentes. Es confidente porque se conoce bien y no se engaña con las cosas triviales de la vida. También, cuando se encuentra en situaciones nuevas, generalmente las toma con una actitud positiva.*
Paso 2: Allow approximately 5 minutes. Students may still need to use some English to recreate the paragraph.
Follow-up: Call on 1 or 2 groups to present their final versions, then display the original so all groups can compare. Be sure to ask who the students think the paragraph refers to, with additional content questions to keep the focus on meaning as well (*¿A quién se refiere el párrafo? Si se refiere a María, ¿cuáles son otros intereses que tiene ella?*, etc.).

Actividad E ¿Qué leíste?

Paso 1 Lee rápidamente el párrafo que pone tu profesor(a) en la pizarra o el proyector. Trata de recordar la información, pero no tomes apuntes.

Paso 2 Con otras dos personas, escriban de nuevo el párrafo, incluyendo toda la información que recuerdan. Luego, los tres deben determinar si el párrafo describe a Jaime, a María, a Traimaqueo o a Carlos —o si se les aplica a varios personajes.

Actividad F ¿Una mañana típica?　INPUT/OUTPUT
Actividad F

Paso 1 Mira los dibujos y pon en orden lo que dice Ángela, una mujer profesional, de una mañana típica.

　　_5_　Me visto para ir al trabajo.

　　_3_　Me conecto con el Internet para leer las noticias y mi correo electrónico (*e-mail*).

　　_1_　Me levanto temprano, como a las cinco y media.

　　_8_　Salgo para el trabajo.

　　_2_　Me preparo un café para despertarme porque siempre estoy muy cansada por la mañana.

　　_7_　Me lavo los dientes.

　　_4_　Me ducho rápidamente.

　　_6_　Desayuno algo ligero (*light*), normalmente sólo pan tostado.

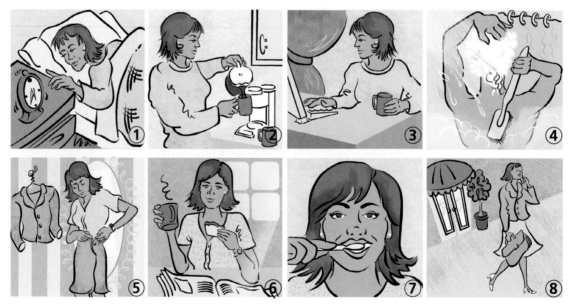

Paso 2 Mira otra vez lo que dice Ángela y prepara tres oraciones comparando su mañana con una mañana típica tuya.

MODELOS:　Como Ángela, me preparo un café para despertarme.

　　　　　Ángela se despierta a las cinco y media, pero yo no. Me despierto a las nueve.

Actividad G Más descripciones

Elige la frase más lógica para completar cada descripción.

1. Roberto pasa mucho tiempo solo, pero habla mucho. Entonces Roberto...
   - ☐ habla con otra persona.
   - ☑ se habla.

2. El cumpleaños de la madre de Sara es el próximo sábado. Entonces Sara...
   - ☑ le compra un regalo.
   - ☐ se compra un regalo.

3. El compañero de casa de Marcos nunca oye su despertador (*alarm clock*) y tiene una clase a las ocho. Entonces Marcos...
   - ☑ tiene que despertarlo.
   - ☐ tiene que despertarse.

4. Elisa sabe muy bien cuáles son sus virtudes y cuáles son sus defectos. Entonces Elisa...
   - ☐ la conoce bien.
   - ☑ se conoce bien.

5. El hijo de Ramón sólo tiene un año. Entonces, obviamente, este niño...
   - ☐ no puede vestirlo.
   - ☑ no puede vestirse.

6. A Juan le cae muy bien su profesor de filosofía. No sólo es famoso e inteligente, sino también (*but also*) es muy bueno. Entonces Juan...
   - ☑ lo respeta mucho.
   - ☐ se respeta mucho.

7. Diana rompió con (*broke up with*) su novio porque lo vio con otra mujer. Diana está furiosa con él y en este momento ella...
   - ☑ lo detesta.
   - ☐ se detesta.

Actividad H Ayer...

Paso 1 Hazle las siguientes preguntas a un compañero (una compañera) de clase y apunta sus respuestas. Todas las preguntas tienen que ver con lo que hizo ayer.

1. ¿A qué hora te levantaste?
2. ¿Te duchaste o te bañaste por la mañana?
3. ¿Te afeitaste?
4. ¿Te compraste algo? ¿Qué te compraste?
5. ¿Te acostaste muy tarde? ¿A qué hora? ¿Te dormiste en seguida (*right away*)?
6. ¿Cuántas veces te lavaste los dientes?

Paso 2 Usando la información del **Paso 1**, escribe tres oraciones comparando lo que hiciste tú y lo que hizo tu compañero/a.

MODELOS:　(Nombre) y yo nos acostamos tarde.

　　　　　　(Nombre) se compró un libro, pero yo no me compré nada.

TERCERA PARTE

Note: These vocabulary items can be heard in this lesson's Textbook Audio section of the Online Learning Center Website.

Talking About Domestic Tasks

Vocabulario

¿Te gusta lavar la ropa?

Los quehaceres domésticos[a]

Domestic Chores and Routines

[a]Los... *Household chores*

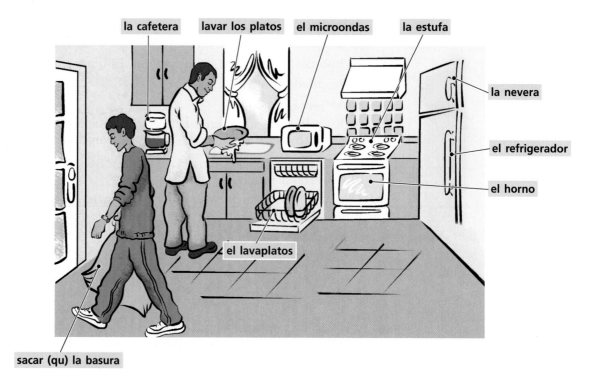

la cafetera   lavar los platos   el microondas   la estufa

la nevera

el refrigerador

el horno

el lavaplatos

sacar (qu) la basura

* MÁS VOCABULARIO

los aparatos domésticos	household appliances
los productos de limpieza	cleaning products
el detergente	detergent
el jabón	soap
la lejía	bleach
las toallas de papel	paper towels

la secadora

planchar la ropa

la lavadora

lavar la ropa

la plancha

quitar el polvo

lavar las ventanas

la aspiradora

pasar la aspiradora

barrer el piso

hacer (*irreg.*) **la cama**	to make the bed
limpiar la casa (entera)	to clean the (whole) house
poner (*irreg.*) **las cosas en orden**	to put things in order

INPUT/OUTPUT
Act. A, *Paso 3,*
Suggestion: Give
students 2 minutes to
write to the left of each
activity how often they
do it. Then conduct a survey. On what items don't
all students agree?

Actividad A ¿Lo quieres hacer?

Paso 1 Indica lo que piensas de cada actividad, poniendo un círculo alrededor del número apropiado de la escala a continuación. Nota: **odiar** = *to hate.*

	ODIO HACERLO.	NO ME IMPORTA HACERLO.	ME GUSTA HACERLO.
1. pasar la aspiradora	1	2	3
2. lavar los platos	1	2	3
3. lavar las ventanas	1	2	3
4. planchar la ropa	1	2	3
5. quitar el polvo	1	2	3
6. limpiar el inodoro	1	2	3
7. lavar la ropa	1	2	3
8. limpiar el horno	1	2	3
9. sacar la basura	1	2	3
10. barrer el piso	1	2	3

Paso 2 Busca a dos personas, una que odia una de las mismas actividades
que tú y otra a quien no le importa una de las mismas actividades que a ti no
te importa.

Paso 3 Entre todos, indiquen cuándo se debe hacer cada actividad del **Paso 1:**
cada día, cada semana, en semanas alternas o una vez al mes.

INPUT/OUTPUT
Actividad B

Actividad B El aparato más importante

Paso 1 Clasifica cada aparato según las categorías a continuación. **¡OJO!** Solamente pueden aparecer en la misma categoría tres aparatos.

la aspiradora	la nevera	la secadora
la cafetera	el refrigerador	la plancha eléctrica
el microondas	la lavadora	el lavaplatos

INDISPENSABLES (*essential*)	IMPORTANTES	NO SON NECESARIOS

Paso 2 Todos deben compartir sus ideas. ¿Hay consenso entre todos? ¿Qué
indican sus selecciones?

OUTPUT
Actividad C

Actividad C Los productos de limpieza

Con otra persona, describan tres productos de limpieza diferentes sin revelar sus nombres. ¿Puede deducir tu compañero/a qué producto es?

MODELO: E1: Este producto sirve para quitar el polvo. Se puede utilizar con muebles, aparatos, casi con todo.
E2: ¿Es Pledge?
E1: No, eso sólo sirve para los muebles.
E2: ¿Es Endust?
E1: ¡Sí!

OUTPUT
Actividad D

Actividad D ¿Quién hace qué?

Paso 1   Imagina que compartes un cuarto o una casa con una persona de la clase. ¿Quién hace qué en la casa? Vuelvan a la lista de quehaceres domésticos en las páginas 244–245 y hagan un plan indicando quién hace qué y cuándo.

MODELO: E1: ¿No te importa limpiar el baño? Porque a mí no me gusta.
E2: No. No me importa. ¿Lo hago una vez a la semana?

Paso 2   Una de las parejas (*pairs*) debe presentar su plan a la clase. ¿Les parece razonable a los demás? ¿Es justa la distribución del trabajo? ¿Es suficiente la frecuencia con que se hace cada actividad?

Vistazo cultural,
Suggestion: After students read, ask them to what extent the information also applies to households in this country. Does it matter whether families are urban or rural? Then survey students to find out if in their homes, their fathers and mothers share(d) housework, and if so, who does/did what?

 # Vistazo cultural

Ayudar a mamá

En muchos lugares del mundo hispano es típico que las niñas ayuden a su mamá con los quehaceres domésticos, mientras que los hombres y los niños se ocupan de otras cosas. Es poco frecuente, por ejemplo, ver a un niño lavar platos o limpiar el polvo. En fin, «cuidar la casa» es trabajo de la mujer mucho más que del hombre. Y en los hoteles, igual que en este y en otros países, los quehaceres domésticos son reservados casi exclusivamente para las mujeres.

Claro, con el tiempo y la modernización, las cosas cambian. Las jóvenes parejas[a] en las ciudades grandes hoy tienden a compartir[b] los quehaceres, sobre todo si la mujer tiene una ocupación profesional fuera de la casa. Y cada vez más,[c] los niños tanto como las niñas aprenden a utilizar muchos aparatos domésticos y, en algunos casos, hasta a cocinar.

▲ En México, los quehaceres domésticos suelen ser dominio de la mujer.

[a]*couples* [b]*share* [c]*cada... more and more*

Gramática

¿Para mí?   Introduction to **por** Versus **para**

In this lesson, you will learn three basic distinctions between the prepositions **por** and **para**.

The first distinction is their use with people. Generally, **para** + *person* indicates that the person will be the *recipient* of something. **Por** + *person* indicates that something is done *on behalf of* or *on account of* that person.

Lo hago **para mi familia.**	*I'm doing it for my family.* (I'm buying a car and am giving it to them.)
Lo hago **por mi familia.**	*I'm doing it for my family.* (As in: I'm surrendering myself to the police so that my family doesn't have to suffer any longer; I'm doing it on account of them.)

A second distinction is with things. Generally, the use of **para** + *thing* indicates *what something is used for* whereas **por** + *thing* indicates a *substitution, something in place of something else.*

Esta copa es **para vino tinto.**	*This glass is for red wine (is used for red wine).*
Cambiamos esta taza **por otra.**	*We're exchanging this cup for another.*

The third distinction is the use of **por** and **para** with space and time. **Para** + *location* indicates a *destination* and **para** + *time* indicates a *deadline.* **Por** + *location* indicates a *route* or the *space through which something travels.* **Por** + *time* indicates the *time during which something happens.*

Mañana salgo **para Bogotá.**	*Tomorrow I'm leaving for Bogota.*
Voy **por la Ruta 66.**	*I'm taking (going by way of) Route 66.*
¿Puedes llegar **para las 3:00?**	*Can you arrive by three o'clock?*
¿Puedes hacerlo **por la tarde?**	*Can you do it in the afternoon?*

✳ MÁS GRAMÁTICA

Subject pronouns can be used with most prepositions, as in **para él, para Ud., por ellos, por vosotros,** and so forth. The exceptions are **yo** and **tú.** After prepositions, the special pronouns **mí** and **ti** are required. With the preposition **con,** the endings **-migo** and **-tigo** are added.

—Esto es **para ti.**	—¿Quieres ir **conmigo?**
—¿**Para mí?** ¡Gracias!	—No, no puedo ir **contigo.**

Here is a summary of common prepositions. You already know most of them.

a	to; at	**para**	for; to
con	with	**por**	for; because of
de	of; from	**sin**	without
en	in; at; on	**sobre**	about; over

SOME CONTRASTS BETWEEN *por* AND *para*	
With People	
para = *recipient* Este regalo es **para** mi hermano.	**por** = *on behalf of, on account of* Lo hago **por** mi hermano.
With Things	
para = *use* Esta taza (*cup*) es **para** café.	**por** = *in lieu of, instead of* Sustituimos *Nutrasweet* **por** el azúcar.
In Space and Time	
para = destino (*destination; deadline*) Vamos **para** Chicago. Lo voy a hacer **para** las 2:00.	**por** = transición (*route; time*) Pasamos **por** Chicago. Lo puedes hacer **por** la mañana.

De *Sol y viento,* **Note:** You can access this film clip from a special menu section on Disc 5 of the Instructional Version on DVD.

 DE SOL Y VIENTO

Just before Jaime leaves the winery, Traimaqueo presents him and Mario with bottles of wine on behalf of Carlos. Read what Traimaqueo says and select whether **Ud.** or **ti** should be placed in the blanks.

TRAIMAQUEO
Don Carlos quiere hacerles un regalito. Sí.
(*a Jaime*) Un merlot **para** <u>Ud.</u>
... (*a Mario*) Y un cabernet sauvignon **para** <u>ti</u>.

You may also recall the exchange in which Jaime asks María about a poster she is hanging. How would you translate **por** in María's response?

MARÍA
Bueno, además de ser[a] profesora, trabajo **por** los derechos del pueblo mapuche.

[a]además... *besides being a*

INPUT

Act. E, Statements:
1. *Carlos quiere vender la viña por...* 2. *Jaime hace su visita a la viña por...*
3. *Para ir al Valle del Maipo, Jaime y Mario tuvieron que pasar por...*
4. *Traimaqueo le da a Jaime un tour por...*

Actividad E Por...

Escucha lo que dice tu profesor(a). Luego, escoge la respuesta que complete mejor cada oración. Después, explica el uso de **por.**

1. **a.** sus propios intereses.
   b. el bien de la familia.
2. **a.** la mañana.
   b. la tarde.
3. **a.** unas colinas (*hills*).
   b. un desierto.
4. **a.** la bodega (*wine cellar*) y las viñas.
   b. las viñas solamente.

INPUT

Act. F, Suggestion: As you review each item, go over the meaning.
1. What the soldier is saying is "On behalf of my country!"
2. This is intended for you now.
3. I want to substitute one for the other.
4. This is intended to help improve your health.
5. The person is still egotistical and unpleasant. He's not there because of your concerns and wants to be left alone.

Actividad F ¿*Por* o *para*?

Escoge la mejor opción en cada situación.

1. Un soldado (*soldier*) levanta la bandera (*flag*) de su país. ¿Qué dice el soldado?
   a. ¡Por mi patria! **b.** ¡Para mi patria!
2. Una persona acaba de comprar algo que su amigo admira. La persona le dice entonces:
   a. Toma (*Here*). Es por ti. **b.** Toma. Es para ti.
3. Llegas a casa con un detergente. Luego recuerdas que ese detergente es malo para el medio ambiente (*environment*). Vuelves a la tienda y le dices al empleado:
   a. Debo cambiar (*exchange*) este detergente por otro.
   b. Debo cambiar este detergente para otro.
4. Alguien llega a tu casa con una gran cantidad de ajos (*garlic*). Le preguntas para qué y te contesta:
   a. Es bueno por la salud (*health*). **b.** Es bueno para la salud.
5. Hay una reunión importante de estudiantes. Una persona bastante egoísta y desagradable está presente, pero no contribuye nada a la discusión. Entonces, tú le preguntas algo, y él te responde:
   a. Déjame en paz. (*Leave me alone.*) No estoy aquí por ti.
   b. Déjame en paz. No estoy aquí para ti.

INPUT/OUTPUT
Actividad G

Actividad G Rutas y destinos

Paso 1 Completa cada oración con información verdadera o falsa.

1. Para llegar a la biblioteca desde (*from*) aquí, es necesario pasar por _____.
2. Para llegar a la librería desde aquí, es necesario pasar por _____.
3. Yo vivo en _____. Para llegar a mi casa desde aquí es más fácil pasar por _____.

Paso 2 Presenta tus oraciones a la clase. ¿Pueden decir los demás si cada oración es cierta o falsa?

Paso 3 Completa otra vez cada oración con información real o imaginaria.

   1. Mañana salgo para _____. Necesito _____. Quiero _____.

   2. La próxima semana salgo para _____. Tengo boletos para ver _____.

Paso 4 Presenta tus oraciones a la clase. ¿Pueden decir los demás si lo que dice cada oración es real o imaginario?

OUTPUT
Actividad H

Actividad H Cambios

Paso 1 Imagina que estás en varias situaciones en que puedes cambiar una cosa por otra. Indica si lo haces o no.

   1. Mañana hay que entregar una composición importante. Un amigo necesita tu ayuda pero tú sabes que ese tipo de ayuda no es permitido. Tu amigo te dice «Te cambio un DVD por tu ayuda». ¿Lo aceptas?

   2. Te gusta mucho una camisa que tiene un amigo. ¿Qué ofreces cambiar por esa camisa?

   3. Necesitas pintar las paredes de tu casa. ¿Qué cambias con tu amigo por su ayuda? ¿Una cena? ¿Otra cosa?

Paso 2 Compara tus ideas con las de otra persona. ¿En qué coinciden?

Enfoque lingüístico,
Suggestion: After students read, see if they can name five prepositions in English and five in Spanish. Afterward, ask them about the preposition "at" in English. What is its translation into Spanish? Answer: It depends. It can be *a* as in *a la vez, al mediodía.* It can be *en* as in *en la oficina* (I'm at the office). It can be *por* as in *por fin* (at last). Sometimes it's not translated at all, as in the case of English verbs that require *at:* "He's looking at a picture." *Está mirando una foto.* Lesson to be learned: Prepositions can be the most difficult things to master, especially if we blindly rely on translation as a language learning tool.

⦿ Enfoque lingüístico

Las preposiciones

Prepositions are called that because they are "preposed" (i.e, placed in front of something). Prepositions are generally followed by nouns (think of nouns as representatives of some entity or thing in the real world) because prepositions show the relationship of a noun to verbs and other nouns. In Spanish, for example, the preposition **de** signals, among other things, ownership between one entity and something else (**el sillón favorito *de* mi papá**) or direction away from an entity (**salió *del* apartamento**).

Some languages don't have prepositions—or at least have fewer than languages like Spanish and English—and signal such relationships through inflections on nouns or what are called *postpositions.* Nahuatl, the language of the Aztecs and one that is still spoken in certain areas of Mexico, is a language of this type. Note the differences with Spanish.

Spanish	Nahuatl
la casa	cal-li
de la casa	cal-pa
en la casa	cal-co
sobre la casa	cal-pan
con la casa	cal-tica

Whereas in Spanish you are learning to pay attention to the ends of verbs for lots of information, in Nahuatl you would also have to pay attention to the ends of nouns.

SOL Y VIENTO
A segunda vista

Antes de ver el episodio

Actividad A ¿Qué recuerdas?

Contesta cada pregunta indicando lo que recuerdas hasta el momento.

1. En la bodega, Traimaqueo hace un comentario filosófico sobre la vida. ¿Sí o no? Sí

2. Al final del tour de la viña, Traimaqueo recita unas líneas de un poema. ¿Quién es el poeta? Pablo Neruda

3. Yolanda le trae a Traimaqueo un almuerzo; es un sándwich. ¿Sí o no? No, es una cazuelita.

4. ¿Cómo sabe Jaime que doña Isabel no está en Santiago?
   a. Porque Traimaqueo se lo dice.
   b. Porque Yolanda se lo dice.

5. ¿Qué representa la figurita mapuche que compra Jaime?
   a. el dios de la lluvia   **b.** un espíritu protector   **c.** el amor

6. Jaime y María van a verse (*see each other*) más tarde, a las siete. ¿Sí o no? No, van a verse a las cinco.

Actividad B ¡A escuchar!

Vas a ver el **Episodio 4** de nuevo. Primero, repasa la siguiente escena. Luego, mientras la veas, completa lo que dicen los personajes con las palabras y expresiones que oyes.

MARÍA: Bueno, además de ser ___profesora___, trabajo por los derechos del pueblo mapuche.

JAIME: ¡Ah! Entonces, a lo mejor le gusta esto. Es ___para___ Ud.

MARÍA: ¿Para míííí? ¡Oye! ¡Qué ___lindo___! ¿Cómo sabía... ?

JAIME: Su ___tarjeta___.

MARÍA: ¡Ah, por supuesto!ᵃ

ᵃpor... *of course*

Actividad C El episodio

Ahora mira el episodio de nuevo. No te olvides de hacer la **Actividad B** en **Antes de ver el episodio** mientras lo ves.

Después de ver el episodio

Actividad A Para pensar...

Ya sabes que Carlos le mintió a Jaime en cuanto a la ausencia de la señora Isabel. Como clase, comenten las siguientes preguntas.

1. ¿Por qué mintió Carlos? ¿Esconde algo?
2. ¿Hay algún problema en la viña? ¿Cuál es?
3. ¿Qué sabe doña Isabel de la venta de «Sol y viento»?

Actividad B ¡A verificar!

Vas a ver otra vez la escena de **¡A escuchar!** en la página anterior. Llena los espacios en blanco, según lo que oyes.

Act. B, Suggestion: Replay the scene once for students. Replay a second time if needed. Then ask for volunteers to provide answers for each blank. Verify using the instructor notes from *Act. B* on the previous page.
Alternative: After students complete the conversation, have 2 students act it out.

Actividad C Otro encuentro

Paso 1 Este episodio se titula «Otro encuentro». ¿A qué se refiere el título? ¿Un encuentro entre quiénes? En grupos de dos, contesten estas preguntas y luego propongan (*propose*) un título alternativo. Cada grupo debe presentar su título a la clase.

Paso 2 Como clase, hagan un perfil de Traimaqueo. Deben incluir aspectos de su personalidad y su apariencia física. También comenten sobre sus relaciones con Carlos y con Yolanda.

Detrás de la cámara

Jaime comments on Traimaqueo's evident passion about wine. Traimaqueo does indeed love the land and the winery. He also cares deeply about the family he works for, especially doña Isabel. Traimaqueo and his wife Yolanda have been with the family for a long, long time. Having been with the winery for so long, they both try to keep an eye out for doña Isabel. When doña Isabel's husband died, Traimaqueo felt the need to watch over things in his absence. Yolanda is less conspicuous than Traimaqueo, playing the classic rural female role of servant. She is indeed close to doña Isabel, but she also "knows her place" as a housekeeper. Like Traimaqueo, she is honest and simple. The two of them would do anything for doña Isabel and the winery.

Act. C, *Paso 2*, Suggestion: Lead as a discussion in which students offer ideas and you put words on board. Do as a semantic map. Then have students copy down notes, take home, and write up a description of Traimaqueo, about 50–100 words.

EPISODIO 4 ✱ OTRO ENCUENTRO

RESUMEN DE VOCABULARIO

Verbos

afeitarse	to shave
alquilar	to rent
bañarse	to take a bath
conseguir (i, i) (g)	to get, obtain
conseguir + *infin.*	to succeed in (*doing something*)
dormirse (ue, u)	to fall asleep
ducharse	to take a shower
firmar	to sign
lavarse los dientes	to brush one's teeth
levantarse	to get up
mentir (ie, i)	to lie, tell a lie
morir (u, ue)	to die
odiar	to hate
sentir(se) (ie, i)	to feel
sugerir (ie, i)	to suggest
vestirse (i, i)	to get dressed

Repaso: acostarse (ue), despertarse (ie), repetir (i, i)

Los cuartos, muebles y aparatos domésticos

el balcón	balcony
el baño	bathroom
la alfombra	rug; carpet
la bañera	bathtub
la ducha	shower
el espejo	mirror
el inodoro	toilet
el lavabo	(bathroom) sink
la cocina	kitchen
la cafetera	coffeemaker
la estufa	stove
el horno	oven
el lavaplatos	dishwasher
el microondas	microwave
la nevera	freezer
el refrigerador	refrigerator
el comedor	dining room
la habitación	bedroom
el armario	closet
la cama (matrimonial, sencilla)	(queen, twin) bed
el cartel	poster
la cómoda	dresser
el estante	bookshelf
la lámpara	lamp
la mesita	end table

la sala	living room
el cuadro	painting
el sillón	armchair
el sofá	sofa

Cognados: el garaje, el jardín, el patio
Repaso: el escritorio, la mesa, la silla

Los quehaceres domésticos

barrer el piso	to sweep the floor
hacer (*irreg.*) la cama	to make the bed
lavar (los platos)	to wash (the dishes)
limpiar la casa (entera)	to clean the (whole) house
pasar la aspiradora	to vacuum
planchar la ropa	to iron the clothing
poner (*irreg.*) las cosas en orden	to put things in order
quitar el polvo	to dust
sacar (qu) la basura	to take out the garbage

la aspiradora	vacuum cleaner
el jabón	soap
la lavadora	washing machine
la lejía	bleach
la plancha	iron
los productos de limpieza	cleaning products
la secadora	dryer
las toallas de papel	paper towels

Cognado: el detergente
Repaso: la ropa, la ventana

La vivienda

la casa	house; home
la casa particular/privada	private residence
el compañero/a de cuarto (casa)	roommate (housemate)
el contrato	lease
la dirección	address
el/la dueño/a	owner; landlord, landlady
el hogar	home (*as in "home, sweet home"*)
el/la inquilino/a	tenant
los pies (metros) cuadrados	square feet (meters)

el piso	flat, apartment (*Sp.*)
el piso / la planta (*Sp.*)	floor (*of a building*)
el/la portero/a	doorperson; building manager
el tamaño	size
la vecindad	neighborhood
el/la vecino/a	neighbor
la vista	view

Cognados: el apartamento, el condominio, la residencia
Repaso: el alquiler, el barrio, el edificio, la oficina, la residencia estudiantil, la torre

Otras palabras y expresiones

amueblado/a	furnished
mí	me (*obj. of prep.*)
por	for; because of
sin	without
sobre	about; over
ti	you (*obj. of prep.*)
¿De qué tamaño es… ?	What size is . . . ?
de venta	for sale
se alquila	for rent

Entremés cultural
El Caribe y la Guinea Ecuatorial

VISTAZO

Dos zonas que forman partes distintas del mundo hispano son el Caribe y la Guinea Ecuatorial. La zona caribeña hispana consiste en tres países: Cuba, la República Dominicana y Venezuela, más Puerto Rico, un territorio de los Estados Unidos. Estos países, menos Venezuela, son parte de una cadena[a] de islas[b] llamada las Indias Occidentales.[c] Aquí predomina un clima tropical, aunque en las tierras altas[d] de Venezuela se encuentra un clima más frío.

Miles de millas al este se sitúa el único país de habla española en

África: la Guinea Ecuatorial. El país más pequeño del mundo hispano, la Guinea Ecuatorial también es el país hispano que más recientemente se ganó[e] la independencia de España, en 1968. Su capital, Malabo, se ubica[f] en una isla llamada Bioko.

[a]*chain* [b]*islands* [c]*West* [d]*tierras... highlands* [e]*se... won* [f]*se... is located*

DATO INTERESANTE:
Una mezcla[a] de culturas

En las islas caribeñas se ve una mezcla de culturas: la española, la africana y, mucho menos, la indígena. (Muchas tribus[b] originales desaparecieron[c] por la muerte[d] causada por varias enfermedades[e] que trajeron los europeos). Esta mezcla se ve claramente en la santería cubana, un producto del sincretismo[f] que ocurrió cuando los esclavos[g] africanos se vieron forzados a adaptar su religión politeísta[h] a las enseñanzas del catolicismo.

> **IDEA:** Busca información sobre la santería, concentrándote en el origen africano de los esclavos, los nombres de unos dioses[i] y lo que representan y los elementos cristianos de la religión.

La santería refleja la fusión de las creencias del oeste de África con las de la religión católica.

[a]*mixture* [b]*tribes* [c]*disappeared* [d]*death* [e]*diseases* [f]*blending*
[g]*slaves* [h]*polytheist (believing in many gods)* [i]*gods*

DATO INTERESANTE:
El Salto Ángel

En Venezuela se encuentra la catarata[a] más alta del mundo, el Salto Ángel. Situada en el Parque Nacional Canaima (en el sureste del país), la catarata es de **979** metros de altura. Interesantemente, la catarata lleva el nombre de un norteamericano, James Crawford Angel, quien fue el primer descendiente europeo que la vio. En la lengua indígena, la catarata se llama «salto del lugar más profundo».[b]

IDEA: Busca información sobre el Salto Ángel y las cataratas de Niágara, haciendo una comparación de por lo menos cinco puntos de interés.

[a]*waterfall* [b]*salto… leap from the deepest place*

El Salto Ángel en Venezuela es el más alto del mundo.

Aunque el inglés también es una lengua oficial de Puerto Rico, el español se habla con más frecuencia.

DATO INTERESANTE:
¿Inglés o español?

Puerto Rico es el único territorio de los Estados Unidos donde el español es la lengua que más se habla. Un poco más del 97% de la población lo habla como lengua principal.[a] Aunque el inglés y el español son las dos lenguas oficiales, el inglés se limita más o menos a los documentos federales y también se usa en las zonas turísticas. Los puertorriqueños siguen participando en un debate político sobre el estatus de los dos idiomas. Algunos prefieren que el español sea[b] la única lengua oficial de la isla mientras otros prefieren mantener los dos idiomas como oficiales.

IDEA: Como clase, determinen si el español debería ser[c] la única lengua oficial de Puerto Rico. ¿Qué significaría[d] este cambio en términos prácticos? ¿Qué factores socio-políticos refleja el debate sobre el uso de lengua?

[a]*main* [b]*be* [c]*debería… should be* [d]*would mean*

DATO INTERESANTE:
Los nombres en la Guinea Ecuatorial

La gente de la Guinea Ecuatorial suele tener un nombre en español además de un nombre y un apellido africanos. En su forma escrita, el apellido paterno y el apellido materno siguen a los dos nombres (español y africano). Así que una persona puede tener hasta cuatro nombres como, por ejemplo, Teodoro Obiang Nguema Mbasogo, una figura importante en la historia del país.

IDEA: Busca información sobre Obiang Nguema. ¿Por qué es importante en la historia de la Guinea Ecuatorial? ¿Qué hizo?

Teodoro Obiang Nguema Mbasogo

Un día perfecto

En este episodio...

MARÍA

Tú eres gente de la tierra,ᵃ como los mapuches.

JAIME

¿Por qué como los mapuches?

MARÍA

Mapu significa «tierra». *Che* significa «gente». «Gente de la tierra», como tu familia.

¿Qué crees tú?

1. ¿A qué crees que se refiere el título de este episodio? ¿Para quién es un día «perfecto»?
2. ¿Por qué dice María que Jaime es «gente de la tierra»? ¿Qué sabes de la familia de Jaime?
3. ¿Qué piensa Jaime de María? ¿Le gusta? ¿Qué piensa María de él?

ᵃ*earth, land*

La tecnología y yo

OBJETIVOS

IN THIS LESSON, YOU WILL LEARN:

- words and expressions associated with computers and the Internet
- more verbs like **gustar** to talk about what interests you, bothers you, and so forth
- to talk about useful electronic devices
- how to avoid redundancy by using direct and indirect object pronouns together
- to talk about your pastimes and activities now and when you were younger
- about imperfect verb forms and how to use them to talk about what you used to do

In addition, you will prepare for and watch **Episodio 5** of the film *Sol y viento*.

¿Usas una agenda electrónica? ¿Cuáles son otros aparatos electrónicos que sueles usar?

The following media resources are available for this lesson of *Sol y viento*:

Episodio 5 of *Sol y viento*

Online *Manual de actividades*

Online Learning Center Website

PRIMERA PARTE

Note: These vocabulary items can be heard in this lesson's Textbook Audio section of the Online Learning Center Website.

Talking About Everyday Technology

Vocabulario

Mi computadora

Computers and Computer Use

La computadora*

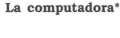

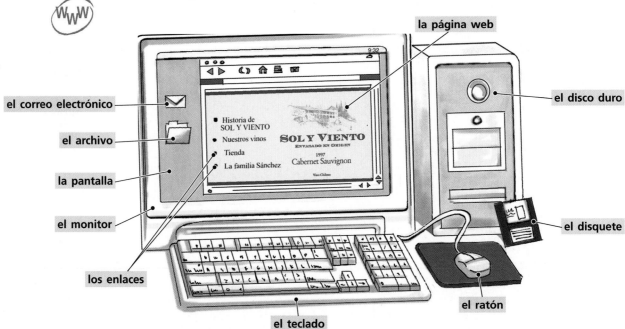

- la página web
- el correo electrónico
- el archivo
- la pantalla
- el monitor
- los enlaces
- el teclado
- el disco duro
- el disquete
- el ratón

On screen:
- Historia de SOL Y VIENTO
- Nuestros vinos
- Tienda
- La familia Sánchez

SOL Y VIENTO
ENVASADO EN ORIGEN
1997
Cabernet Sauvignon
Vino Chileno

✳ MÁS VOCABULARIO

la contraseña	password
el Internet / la red	Internet
el mensaje	message
el módem	modem
apagar (gu)	to turn off
conectar	to connect
congelarse	to freeze up (*screen*)
copiar	to copy
descargar (gu)	to download
encender (ie)	to turn on (*machines*)
enviar (envío) / mandar	to send
guardar (documentos)	to save (documents)
hacer (*irreg.*) clic	to click
hacer (*irreg.*) una búsqueda	to do a search
navegar (gu) la red	to surf the Web

*In Spain, **el ordenador** is used for *computer.*

Vistazo cultural

El uso del Internet en el mundo hispano

E n los últimos años, el uso del Internet ha experimentado[a] un crecimiento[b] considerable en casi todos los países del mundo. En los países hispanos, el crecimiento ha superado[c] el 200% entre 2000 (dos mil) y 2006 (dos mil seis). Dos de los factores que han contribuido[d] a este crecimiento son el acceso gratis[e] al Internet promocionado por[f] las compañías de telecomunicaciones y la bajada[g] de los precios de las computadoras.

El acceso fácil al Internet ha contribuido, obviamente, a su incorporación en la vida diaria de los hispanos. En este sentido, nos podemos preguntar: ¿cuáles son las actividades principales de los internautas[h]? Según el Instituto Nacional de Estadística[i] en España, la actividad más frecuente de los internautas españoles entre 15 y 34 años es usar un buscador[j] para obtener información sobre productos y servicios (79%). Otras actividades frecuentes son el correo electrónico (77%), acceder a los medios de comunicación —periódicos, revistas, programas de radio o de televisión— (61%) y descargar música, vídeos o juegos (48%). Una de las actividades menos frecuentes es comprar productos. De hecho, la mayoría de los españoles prefieren hacer sus compras en las tiendas. Sin embargo, cuando usan el Internet para las compras, los principales productos están relacionados con viajes[k] y las entradas[l] a espectáculos como, por ejemplo, conciertos.

Para muchos hispanos, el Internet es tan importante como la televisión y el teléfono.

[a]*ha... has experienced* [b]*growth* [c]*ha... has surpassed* [d]*han... have contributed* [e]*free*
[f]*promocionado... promoted by* [g]*lowering* [h]*Internet users* [i]*Statistics* [j]*search engine*
[k]*traveling* [l]*tickets*

Actividad A Asociaciones

Empareja cada sustantivo con el verbo apropiado. **¡OJO!** Algunos verbos van con más de un sustantivo.

1. __d__ el teclado
2. __d, f, h__ un mensaje
3. __a, g__ la red
4. __e, h__ un programa
5. __b__ el ratón
6. __d, f, h__ el documento
7. __c__ la pantalla
8. __g, i__ la computadora
9. __g__ el módem

a. navegar
b. hacer clic
c. congelarse
d. escribir
e. descargar
f. enviar
g. conectar
h. guardar
i. apagar

Actividad B Descripciones

Tu profesor(a) va a mencionar un objeto relacionado con la computadora. Pon (*Place*) el número del objeto mencionado al lado de su descripción.

a. __3__ Se hace clic aquí para ir de una página web a otra página interesante.

b. __6__ Se usa para guardar documentos relacionados.

c. __8__ Se usa para mover el cursor en la pantalla.

d. __4__ Se usa para escribir en la computadora.

e. __7__ Contiene todos los programas y documentos guardados en la computadora.

f. __1__ Se usa para conectar la computadora con el Internet.

g. __5__ Se ven todos los documentos y páginas web aquí.

h. __2__ Se usa para proteger (*protect*) el correo electrónico.

Actividad C ¿Qué debes hacer (*should you do*)?

Las situaciones a continuación ocurren cuando usamos la computadora. Algunas son muy frecuentes y otras menos frecuentes. Para cada situación, escribe una solución para compartir con la clase.

MODELOS: (*ves*)   La conexión va muy lenta (*slow*).

          (*escribes*) Debes intentar conectarte otra vez o esperar hasta más tarde.

1. Quieres buscar información sobre alguien.
2. Quieres tener una canción en el reproductor de MP3 (emepetrés) (*MP3 player*).
3. Tienes un virus en un documento.
4. Quieres guardar un documento para poder revisarlo en otra computadora.
5. La computadora se congela.

¡Exprésate!

To say *to spend time doing something,* Spanish uses **pasar tiempo** + *present participle.* The participle (or *gerund*) is formed by adding **-ando** to the stem of **-ar** verbs and **-iendo** to **-er** and **-ir** verbs and is translated as the *-ing* form of the verb in English. The verb **leer,** however, adds **-yendo** instead of **-iendo.** The examples below will help you with **Actividad D.**

¿Cuánto tiempo **pasas leyendo** y **contestando** el correo electrónico?
How much time do you spend reading and answering e-mail?

Paso mucho tiempo haciendo investigaciones por el Internet.
I spend a lot of time doing research on the Internet.

You will learn more about the present participle in **Lección 8A.**

Actividad D ¿Cuánto tiempo pasamos en la computadora?

Paso 1 A continuación hay una tabla con varias actividades relacionadas con la computadora. Llena la primera columna (**yo**) con las horas que tú pasaste haciendo cada actividad la semana pasada.

	YO	(NOMBRE)	(NOMBRE)	(NOMBRE)	PROMEDIO DE HORAS
1. leyendo y contestando el correo electrónico					
2. escribiendo tareas/trabajos					
3. haciendo investigaciones para las clases					
4. charlando en las salas de chat o con mensajero instantáneo					
5. descargando música o imágenes					
6. jugando (juegos / por dinero)					
7. haciendo compras					
8. leyendo las noticias					
Número de horas en total					

Paso 2 En grupo, comparte tus respuestas con otras tres personas. Apunta las respuestas de tus compañeros en las tres columnas correspondientes.

Paso 3 Ahora calcula el promedio (*average*) de las horas de cada actividad de tu grupo. Tu grupo va a compartir esta información con toda la clase. Además de presentar el promedio de las actividades, contesta las siguientes preguntas.

1. ¿En qué actividad pasan Uds. más tiempo?
2. ¿Hay diferencias entre las mujeres y los hombres? ¿Cuáles son?

Paso 4 (Optativo) Escribe un párrafo en que compares el uso que tú haces de la computadora con el de tus compañeros.

Gramática

More on Talking
About Likes
and Dislikes

¡Me fascina!

Verbs Like gustar

OTHER VERBS LIKE *gustar*		
agradar	*to please*	**Me agrada** mucho. *It pleases me a lot.*
apetecer (zc)	*to appeal, be pleasing*	**¿Os apetece?** *Does it appeal to you (all)?*
caerle (*irreg.*) **bien/mal** **a alguien**	*to (dis)like someone* (lit.: *to strike someone* *well or poorly*)	Julio **me cae bien.** *I like Julio.* (lit.: *Julio strikes me well.*)
darle (*irreg.*) **miedo a alguien**	*to scare someone* (lit.: *to give someone fright*)	La tecnología no **me da miedo.** *Technology doesn't scare me.*
encantar	*to love* (lit.: *to enchant*)	**Nos encanta** la música. *We love music.* (lit.: *Music enchants us.*)
fascinar	*to love, be fascinated by* (lit.: *to fascinate*)	A Jorge **le fascinan** las computadoras. *Jorge loves (is fascinated by)* *computers.* (lit.: *Computers fascinate Jorge.*)
importar	*to be important; to* *matter*	**¿Les importa?** *Does it matter to you (all) / them?*
interesar	*to interest, be* *interesting*	**¿Te interesan** las lenguas? *Do languages interest you? /* *Are languages interesting to you?*
molestar	*to annoy, bother*	A nosotros **nos molestan** las conexiones lentas. *Slow connections annoy us.*
parecer (zc)	*to seem (like)*	**¿Te parece** buena idea? *Does it seem like a good idea to you?*

You have already been talking about your likes and dislikes using the verb **gustar.** As you may remember, **gustar** literally means *to be pleasing.* In order to say *I like to surf the Internet,* you say **Me gusta navegar el Internet** (literally: *Surfing the Internet pleases me.*) You may also remember that **gustar** always takes an indirect object pronoun in order to indicate *to whom* something is pleasing. The new verbs in this section, many of which you've already seen, function the same way. And as with **gustar,** the preposition **a** must be used if the indirect object noun is mentioned.

A Juan le importa mucho su familia.	*Juan's family really matters* *to him.*
A mis amigos les encantó la fiesta.	*My friends loved the party.*

To respond in agreement or disagreement when someone uses a verb like **gustar,** the following expressions are used. Note the use of the preposition **a.**

—Me encantó la película.	I loved the movie.
—**A mí también.**	Me too.
—No me apetece ir.	I don't feel like going.
—**A mí tampoco.**	Me neither. / Neither do I.
—No me interesa nada.	It doesn't interest me at all.
—**A mí sí.**	It does (interest) me.
—Me fascina navegar la red.	I love surfing the Web.
—**A mí no.**	Not me. / I don't.

De *Sol y viento,* **Note:** You can access this film clip from a special menu section on Disc 5 of the Instructional Version on DVD.

Possible verb choices: 1. *gustan, encantan, fascinan.* Correct verb is *encantan;* 2. *pareció*

DE SOL Y VIENTO

In **Episodio 5** of *Sol y viento,* you will see a segment in which Jaime gives something to María. Part of their conversation appears here. Before watching the segment, decide which verbs like **gustar** could be placed in the blanks.

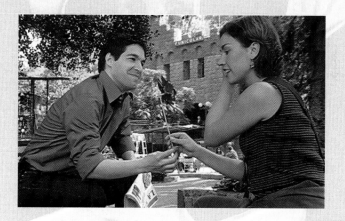

MARÍA
¡Un remolino! ¡Me __encantan__[1] los remolinos!

JAIME
Lo compré allí. Me __pareció__[2] bonito.

INPUT

Act. E, Suggested follow-up: Have students work in pairs to come up with 2 more statements about the characters from *Sol y viento* using verbs like *gustar*. They can present their sentences to the class, and the rest of the students can decide if they agree or not.

Actividad E ¿Estás de acuerdo?

Indica si estás de acuerdo o no con las oraciones a continuación.

	ESTOY DE ACUERDO.	NO ESTOY DE ACUERDO.
1. A Jaime le encanta Santiago.	☐	☐
2. A María no le agrada mucho su trabajo en la universidad.	☐	☐
3. A Mario le cae bien Jaime.	☐	☐
4. A María le interesa conocer mejor a Jaime.	☐	☐
5. A Jaime le importa más el aspecto físico de las mujeres que la inteligencia.	☐	☐
6. A Mario le molesta ser conductor de Jaime.	☐	☐
7. A Carlos le apetece vender «Sol y viento».	☐	☐

INPUT/OUTPUT
Actividad F

Actividad F Reacciones

Paso 1 Elige (*Select*) la oración que expresa tu reacción a cada situación.

1. comprar una computadora nueva
☐ Me apetece mucho.   ☐ Me apetece un poco.
☐ No me apetece para nada.

2. navegar el Internet por muchas horas
☐ Me fascina.   ☐ Me gusta de vez en cuando.
☐ No me gusta para nada.

3. descargar música del Internet
☐ Me encanta.   ☐ Me gusta un poco.
☐ No me interesa para nada.

4. recibir *spam*
☐ Me molesta mucho.   ☐ Me molesta un poco.
☐ No me molesta en absoluto (*at all*).

5. conocer a alguien en una sala de chat
☐ Me interesa mucho.   ☐ Me interesa un poco.
☐ Me da miedo.

6. las computadoras Dell
☐ Me parecen buenas.   ☐ Me parecen malas.
☐ No tengo opinión.

Paso 2 Compara tus respuestas con las de un compañero (una compañera) de clase, según los modelos.

MODELOS: E1: Me molestan mucho las computadoras.
          E2: A mí también. / ¿De veras? (*Really?*) A mí no. No me molestan nada.

o

          E1: No me molestan nada las computadoras.
          E2: A mí tampoco. / ¿De veras? A mí sí. Me molestan mucho.

INPUT/OUTPUT
Actividad G

Actividad G ¿Qué le molesta al profesor (a la profesora)?

Paso 1 A continuación hay una lista de los posibles gustos de tu profesor(a). En grupos de tres, elijan la oración que (en su opinión) describa mejor los sentimientos (*feelings*) de él o ella.

	SÍ	A VECES	NO
1. A mi profesor(a) le caen bien todos sus estudiantes.	☐	☐	☐
2. A mi profesor(a) le caen mal algunos colegas.	☐	☐	☐
3. A mi profesor(a) le encanta enseñar español.	☐	☐	☐
4. A mi profesor(a) le fascinan otras culturas.	☐	☐	☐
5. A mi profesor(a) le molestan las llamadas por teléfono de los vendedores (*telemarketing calls*).	☐	☐	☐
6. A mi profesor(a) le importa mucho la puntualidad (*punctuality*).	☐	☐	☐
7. A mi profesor(a) le fascina la película *Sol y viento*.	☐	☐	☐
8. A mi profesor(a) le apetece viajar a África.	☐	☐	☐
9. A mi profesor(a) le gustan las películas de ciencia ficción.	☐	☐	☐

Paso 2 Trabajando en los mismos grupos, piensen en por lo menos tres oraciones más sobre los gustos de su profesor(a). Usen las oraciones del **Paso 1** como modelo.

Paso 3 Compartan sus oraciones de los **Pasos 1** y **2** con su profesor(a). ¿Acertaron Uds. (*Were you right*) en sus opiniones?

M O D E L O: Creemos que a (nombre del profesor [de la profesora]) le...

OUTPUT

Act. H, Suggestions:
Paso 1: You may first wish to find out which courses students take either online or partially online and have them answer the questions specifically about those courses.
Paso 3: Survey the class to find out students' attitudes toward online courses. What do they see as the advantages and disadvantages of online coursework?

Actividad H Una entrevista

Paso 1 Contesta cada pregunta a continuación sobre los cursos por Internet.

1. ¿Te interesa tomar un curso por Internet? ¿Cuál(es)?
2. Si ya tomas un curso por Internet, ¿te gusta? ¿Por qué (no)?
3. ¿Te parece buena idea ofrecer cursos por Internet en tu universidad? ¿Por qué (no)?
4. ¿Te importa pasar menos tiempo en clase y más tiempo en el Internet para los cursos?
5. ¿Qué te molesta de los cursos por Internet? ¿Por qué (no)?

Paso 2 Hazle a tu compañero/a las preguntas del **Paso 1** y anota sus respuestas.

Paso 3 Escribe un párrafo con la información de tu compañero/a. Di (*Say*) también si estás de acuerdo o no con él (ella). En general, ¿tienen los/las dos una actitud positiva o negativa hacia los cursos por Internet?

Note: These vocabulary items can be heard in this lesson's Textbook Audio section of the Online Learning Center Website.

Talking About Reliance on Technology

Vocabulario

Mi celular

Electronic Devices

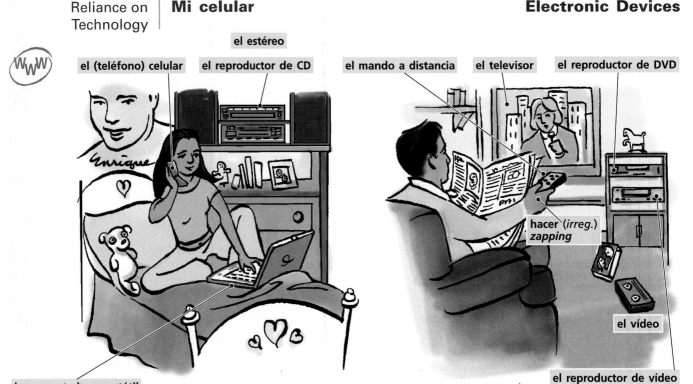

el estéreo

el (teléfono) celular

el reproductor de CD

el mando a distancia

el televisor

el reproductor de DVD

hacer (*irreg.*) zapping

el vídeo

la computadora portátil

el reproductor de vídeo

el contestador automático

la videocámara

la cámara digital

✱ MÁS VOCABULARIO

la agenda electrónica	electronic organizer (*PDA: personal digital assistant*)
la calculadora	calculator
la máquina fax	fax machine
el reproductor de MP3	MP3 player
cambiar de canal	to change channels
funcionar	to work, function (*machines*)
grabar	to record

≋ Vistazo cultural

El uso de los teléfonos celulares en Latinoamérica

Aunque el uso de los teléfonos celulares en este país ha aumentado[a] en los últimos años, en Latinoamérica ha aumentado aún[b] más. Son muchas las razones de este fenómeno. Primero, a diferencia de los teléfonos tradicionales, los celulares no requieren una infraestructura de cables, la cual[c] no existe en muchas zonas rurales. Por eso, es más fácil y menos caro instalar sistemas celulares que instalar cables en cada casa. Además, en las zonas rurales más aisladas,[d] es común tener que esperar meses hasta poder usar un teléfono de casa a causa de los gastos y el tiempo que se requieren para instalar los cables. Lo que más ha impactado[e] el uso de los celulares es el cambio en cuanto a[f] quién paga. Como sucede[g] con frecuencia en este país (y antes en Latinoamérica), tanto la persona que llama como la persona que recibe la llamada tienen que pagar por los minutos de uso. Ahora, en muchos países latinoamericanos, sólo la persona que llama paga la llamada.

[a]ha... *has increased* [b]*even* [c]la... *which* [d]*isolated* [e]ha... *has impacted*
[f]en... *regarding* [g]*happens*

¡Exprésate!

The expression **se usa** in this activity is what is called an *impersonal expression.* You have seen many of these throughout *Sol y viento.* English normally translates this as *one uses* or sometimes *you use,* but the *you* does not refer to any specific person. You will learn more about impersonal expressions in **Lección 9A.**
You will learn another use of **se** in the next **Gramática** section.

Actividad A ¿Para qué se usa?

INPUT
Actividad A

Empareja las descripciones con los aparatos correspondientes.

1. __e__ el celular
2. __d__ la máquina fax
3. __h__ la calculadora
4. __c__ la videocámara
5. __b__ el contestador automático
6. __g__ el reproductor de DVD
7. __a__ el mando a distancia
8. __f__ la cámara digital

a. Se usa para cambiar de canal en el televisor.

b. Se usa para dejar un mensaje cuando nadie contesta una llamada.

c. Se usa para grabar eventos personales y luego verlos en el televisor.

d. Se usa para recibir y mandar documentos.

e. Se usa para llamar a otras personas, especialmente cuando uno está fuera de la casa.

f. Se usa para sacar fotos y verlas en la computadora.

g. Se usa para ver películas.

h. Se usa para hacer cálculos.

INPUT
Act. B, Statements:
1. *organizarse*
2. *grabar*
3. *escuchar música*
4. *ver programas*
5. *hacer* zapping

Actividad B Asociaciones

Escucha las actividades que menciona tu profesor(a) y pon el número de la actividad al lado del aparato correspondiente.

a. __2__ el reproductor de vídeo

b. __5__ el mando a distancia

c. __1__ la agenda electrónica

d. __4__ el televisor

e. __3__ el reproductor de MP3

Navegando la red, **Suggestion:** You may want to direct students to a particular brand name (Sony, Toshiba, Apple, etc.) and have them look at the website of that brand in a particular Spanish-speaking country.

NAVEGANDO LA RED

Busca información sobre los precios de las computadoras y otros aparatos electrónicos en algún país hispanohablante. Teniendo en cuenta (*Keeping in mind*) el cambio de moneda, ¿qué te parecen los precios? ¿Son más caros o más baratos que en este país? Menciona los nombres de tres aparatos que no conocieras (*you didn't know*) antes.

¡Exprésate!

To say that one *needs* or *misses* something, Spanish uses the expression **hacerle falta (a alguien)**.

Me hace falta.	*I miss/need it.*
No me hace falta.	*I don't miss/need it.*

INPUT/OUTPUT
Act. C, Suggested follow-up: Have groups present their opinions to the class. For example, *No podemos vivir sin... porque...* Which electronic device are students most dependent on?

Actividad C ¿De qué dependes más?

Paso 1 Elige la oración que mejor representa tu opinión sobre cada aparato electrónico.

	NO PUEDO VIVIR SIN ESTO.	PUEDO VIVIR SIN ESTO; NO ME SERÍA (*it wouldn't be*) DIFÍCIL.	NO LO/LA USO Y NO ME HACE FALTA.
1. el celular	☐	☐	☐
2. la computadora	☐	☐	☐
3. la agenda electrónica	☐	☐	☐
4. el televisor	☐	☐	☐
5. la calculadora	☐	☐	☐
6. la cámara digital	☐	☐	☐
7. el mando a distancia	☐	☐	☐
8. el contestador automático	☐	☐	☐
9. el reproductor de DVD	☐	☐	☐
10. el reproductor de MP3	☐	☐	☐

Paso 2 Compara tus respuestas con las de tres compañeros/as y justifica cada opinión que elegiste en el **Paso 1.**

MODELOS: E1: ¿Puedes vivir sin calculadora?

E2: Sí, no la uso y no me hace falta porque no tengo clase de matemáticas.

OUTPUT
Act. D,
Suggestion: You may wish to organize the groups either by gender, underclassmen/upperclassmen, or rural/urban backgrounds to see how students differ in terms of what they think are necessary items.

Actividad D ¿Qué necesita un estudiante nuevo?

Paso 1 En grupos de tres o cuatro personas, hagan una lista de los aparatos electrónicos que va a necesitar un estudiante de primer año en la universidad.

Paso 2 Ahora indiquen si cada aparato mencionado en el **Paso 1** es **absolutamente necesario** o **no es necesario pero sería** (*it would be*) **bueno tenerlo.** Justifiquen el uso de cada aparato.

MODELO: Un reproductor de MP3 es absolutamente necesario. Hay mucho trabajo y estrés con las clases y un nuevo estudiante necesita relajarse (*to relax*).

Gramática

More on Avoiding
Redundancy

Ya te lo dije.

Double-Object Pronouns

DOUBLE-OBJECT PRONOUNS
The Indirect Object Precedes the Direct Object

me lo (la, los, las)	nos lo (la, los, las)
te lo (la, los, las)	os lo (la, los, las)
se lo (la, los, las)	se lo (la, los, las)

¿Los libros? **Te los** doy más tarde.	Sí, la computadora. ¿**Nos la** vendes?

le/les → se

¿<u>Le</u> diste <u>el televisor</u> a tu mamá?

Sí. <u>Se</u> <u>lo</u> di la semana pasada.

<u>Mis hermanos</u> quieren <u>los dos teléfonos</u> que tenemos.

¿Por qué no <u>se</u> <u>los</u> regalamos de sorpresa?

It is typical to use two object pronouns together to avoid redundancy.

> Do you have my book?
>
> Yes. I'll give it to you right now.

In the preceding exchange, the response includes a direct object pronoun, *it,* and an indirect object pronoun, *you.* In Spanish, when both direct and indirect object pronouns appear together, the indirect object pronoun always precedes the direct object pronoun.

> ¿Tienes mi libro?
>
> Sí. Ahora mismo **te lo** doy.

The order is always indirect object followed by direct object no matter whether the pronouns appear before the verb, as in the above example, or are attached to the end of an infinitive.

> ¿Tienes mi libro?
>
> Sí, pero no quiero dár**telo** ahora.

When both indirect and direct object pronouns begin with the letter **l** (i.e., **le/les** and **lo, la, los, las**), the indirect object pronoun changes to **se.** This is not a reflexive construction. Look at the chart to see how this works.

There are several other points to keep in mind about double-object pronouns.

■ Given that **se** can refer to both singular and plural indirect objects, it is often accompanied by a phrase with **a** that explains who the indirect object is if context does not make the meaning clear.

> Ya **se** lo di **a mi hermano.**
>
> **Se** la escribimos **a mis padres.**

■ With the verb **decir,** it is typical to use **lo** when a direct object is implied, that is, that something was said.

> ¿No te **lo dije**?   *Didn't I tell you? (lit.: Didn't I tell it to you?)*

■ Remember that these pronouns are not subjects of the verb, so **se** does not translate as *you/he/she/them* but rather as *to* or *for you/him/her/ them.*

COMUNICACIÓN ÚTIL

The use of two pronouns with **decir** is common in Spanish. Examine the following sentences.

> Ya **te lo dije.**   *I already told (it to) you.*
>
> ¿**Me lo** vas a **decir**?   *Are you going to tell me (it)?*

The **lo** represents the "thing" that was said or is to be said. Note that the pronoun is always masculine singular.

De *Sol y viento,* **Note:** You can access this film clip from a special menu section on Disc 5 of the Instructional Version on DVD.

DE SOL Y VIENTO

At the end of his tour of the winery in **Episodio 4,** Jaime notes the deep feelings Traimaqueo has about wine, wine making, and the Sol y viento vineyard. Read the following exchange and then answer the questions.

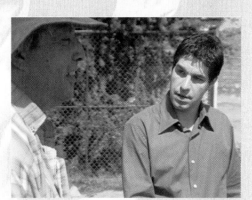

TRAIMAQUEO
¡El vino es un regalo de los dioses,[a] don Jaime! ¡Algo maravilloso! Como decía[b] el poeta, don Pablo Neruda:
  «Vino color de día,
  vino color de noche,
  vino con pies de púrpura
  o sangre de topacio,[c]
  vino... »

JAIME
Ya ____se____ lo dije, señor. Su pasión es evidente.

Which indirect object pronoun do you think Jaime uses here, **te** or **se?** What does this sentence mean literally?

[a]*gods* [b]*said* [c]*sangre... topaz-colored blood*

Actividad E ¿Qué pasó?

Escoge la respuesta correcta según lo que recuerdas de *Sol y viento*.

1. ¿Qué hizo María con la tarjeta que encontró Jaime en el parque?
   a. Se la dio.
   b. Se la quitó (*She took it away*).

2. Cuando Jaime habló con Carlos por teléfono, ¿le dio su número en el hotel?
   a. Sí, se lo dio.
   b. No, no se lo dio.

3. Al final del **Episodio 2**, ¿qué hizo Jaime con el papelito de la suerte que decía «El amor es un torbellino»?
   a. Se lo dio a María.
   b. Se lo dio a Mario.

4. ¿A quién le dijo Jaime «Lo veo mañana, como a las diez»?
   a. Se lo dijo a María.
   b. Se lo dijo a Mario.

Actividad F Preguntas

Paso 1 Escoge las respuestas que se te aplican a ti.

1. ¿Te dan dinero tus padres o amigos cuando lo necesitas?
   a. Sí. Me lo dan sin problema.
   b. Depende. Me lo dan sólo cuando es algo urgente.
   c. No. Nunca me lo dan.

2. ¿Te piden dinero tus hijos o amigos cuando lo necesitan?
   a. Sí. Me lo piden porque tenemos relaciones muy estrechas (*we're very close*).
   b. Depende. Me lo piden, pero les da vergüenza (*shame*).
   c. No. Nunca me lo piden.

Paso 2 Ahora escoge las respuestas para continuar las ideas del **Paso 1**.

1. ¿Se lo pides frecuentemente? (el dinero a tus padres o amigos)
   a. Sí. Se lo pido con frecuencia.
   b. Sólo se lo pido de vez en cuando.
   c. Nunca se lo pido.

2. ¿Se lo das? (el dinero a tus hijos o amigos)?
   a. Sí. Se lo doy sin problema.
   b. Sólo se lo doy si puedo.
   c. No. No se lo doy. Creo que causa problems.

 Paso 3 Comparte tus respuestas con otras personas. ¿Hay algunas tendencias comunes entre los miembros del grupo?

Actividad G ¿Se lo/la prestas (*loan, lend*)?

Indica a quién(es) le(s) prestas o das las cosas a continuación.

1. mi celular
   a. No se lo presto a nadie.
   b. Se lo presto a _____.
2. mi computadora portátil
   a. No se la presto a nadie.
   b. Se la presto a _____.
3. mi reproductor de MP3
   a. No se lo presto a nadie.
   b. Se lo presto a _____.
4. mi contraseña del correo electrónico
   a. No se la doy a nadie.
   b. Se la doy a _____.
5. información sobre un examen
   a. No se la doy a nadie.
   b. Se la doy a _____.

Actividad H ¿Dónde está?

Esta actividad consiste en un juego.

1. La clase va a dividirse en dos grupos, A y B. Una persona del grupo A y otra del grupo B deben ir al frente de la clase. Estas personas serán (*will be*) «los capitanes» de sus respectivos grupos.
2. A cada persona, menos a los capitanes, se le va a dar un papel con el nombre de algún aparato electrónico (por ejemplo, el reproductor de MP3, la cámara digital, etcétera). Esta información (nombre de la persona y el aparato) se verá (*will be displayed*) en la pizarra también.
3. Los capitanes deben cerrar los ojos o no mirar a los demás.
4. Mientras los capitanes no miran, los demás deben hablar con otras personas (o hacer algún tipo de ruido) y, si quieren, pueden intercambiar sus «objetos».
5. Luego los capitanes abrirán (*will open*) los ojos y por turnos van a escoger a personas de su grupo diciendo: «Barbara, el profesor (la profesora) te dio el televisor. Lo tienes todavía / Se lo diste a otra persona», dependiendo de lo que el capitán crea (*believes*).
6. El objetivo: el grupo del capitán que primero se equivoque (*is wrong*) tres veces, pierde.

¡BONO! Si el capitán adivina (*guesses*) que una persona le pasó el aparato a otra persona y también *adivina a quién*, a su grupo se le va a asignar un bono. Entonces, si hace un error después, el bono cancela ese error. No se toma como error si el capitán no adivina el nombre de la persona que recibió el aparato.

TERCERA PARTE

Vocabulario

Talking About When You Were Younger | **Mi niñez y juventud**

Typical Childhood and Adolescent Activities ✳

Algunas actividades típicas de los niños y los jóvenes

dibujar y colorear

jugar (ue) (gu) a los videojuegos

meterse en líos

sacar (qu) la licencia de conducir

subirse a los árboles

enamorarse (de)

✱ MÁS VOCABULARIO

hacer (*irreg.*) **novillos**	to skip/cut school
jugar (**ue**) (**gu**) **al escondite**	to play hide and seek
llevarse bien/mal con	to get along well/poorly with
pelearse	to fight
portarse bien/mal	to behave well/poorly
soñar (**ue**) **con**	to dream about
la cita	date (*social*)
la juventud	youth; adolescence
el/la mentiroso/a	liar
las muñecas	dolls
el/la niñero/a	baby-sitter
la niñez	childhood
el recreo	recess
las tiras cómicas	comics

Características de los niños y los adolescentes

adaptable	adaptable	**precavido/a**	cautious
cabezón (cabezona)	stubborn	**torpe**	clumsy
(im)paciente	(im)patient	**travieso/a**	mischievous
obediente	obedient		

Vistazo cultural,
Suggestion: Before having students read, ask the following questions: *Para sacar la licencia de conducir en este país, ¿cuántos años hay que tener?* (depends on the state/province). *¿Cuánto cuesta sacar la licencia? ¿Hay que tomar un examen sobre las reglas? ¿Hay que tomar un examen práctico?* Have students read quickly, then create a table comparing the process of getting a driver's license in this country, in Mexico, and in Spain.

〰 Vistazo cultural

Sacar la licencia de conducir en dos países hispanos

Sacar la licencia de conducir significa ganar más independencia tanto para los adolescentes norteamericanos como para los hispanos. Sin embargo, el proceso de sacar la licencia es distinto de país a país. En México, por ejemplo, los jóvenes de 16 años pueden conseguir un permiso de conducir limitado. Pero para sacar la licencia, hay que ser mayor de 18 años y tomar un examen sobre las señales de tráfico[a] y la mecánica general del coche. Además, es necesario tomar un examen médico, toxicológico y psicológico, pero no hay examen práctico.[b] Sacar una licencia de tres años cuesta 800 pesos ($80), pero si la licencia es de cinco años, cuesta 1.500 (mil quinientos) pesos ($150).

¿Cuántos años debería tener (*should have*) una persona para sacar una licencia de conducir?

En España, el proceso es mucho más caro y complicado. Además de tomar un examen escrito sobre las reglas[c] de conducir, una persona necesita tomar entre 15 a 20 horas de clases prácticas en una autoescuela como preparación para un examen del mismo tipo. El proceso entero puede costar hasta mil euros ($1.250: mil doscientos cincuenta). Sin embargo, el período de instrucción no termina al pasar el examen práctico. Al pasar el examen se recibe la licencia, pero también es obligatorio llevar un anuncio con una **L** ("*learner*") en el parabrisas posterior[d] del auto durante un año. Esta **L** implica ciertas restricciones para el conductor,[e] ya que no se puede conducir a más de 80 kilómetros (50 millas) por hora.

[a]señales... *traffic signals and signs* [b]examen... *physical driving exam* [c]*rules* [d]parabrisas... *rear window* [e]*driver*

INPUT
Act. A, Statements:
1. juego en que una persona busca a otra persona 2. imágenes de plástico de personas 3. una persona que recibe dinero por cuidar a los niños 4. no ir a una clase o a la escuela 5. hacer la cama, limpiar la habitación, lavar el auto 6. hora en que los niños salen a jugar afuera durante la escuela 7. una reunión romántica entre dos personas

Actividad A Definiciones

Pon el número de cada descripción que lee tu profesor(a) al lado de la palabra o expresión correspondiente.

- **a.** __7__ la cita
- **b.** __1__ el escondite
- **c.** __3__ el/la niñero/a
- **d.** __6__ el recreo
- **e.** __4__ hacer novillos
- **f.** __2__ las muñecas
- **g.** __5__ las tareas domésticas

INPUT
Act. B, Suggestion:
Survey the class to find out how many students were *traviesos, obedientes,* etc. *¿Cuántos de Uds. eran cabezones? ¿Entonces no obedecían a sus padres? ¿y a sus maestros* (teachers)*? ¿Todavía son cabezones?*

Actividad B Asociaciones

Un niño que...
1. no dice la verdad es __d__.
2. tiene muchos accidentes es __f__.
3. se mete en mucho líos es __b__.
4. hace lo que le dicen los padres es __i__.
5. se acostumbra fácilmente es __g__.
6. es muy creativo es __h__.
7. no quiere obedecer a nadie es __e__.
8. no sabe esperar es __c__.
9. no es impulsivo es __a__.

- **a.** precavido
- **b.** travieso
- **c.** impaciente
- **d.** mentiroso
- **e.** cabezón
- **f.** torpe
- **g.** adaptable
- **h.** imaginativo
- **i.** obediente

INPUT/OUTPUT
Act. C, *Paso 2,*
Suggestion: If students answer *depende de la situación,* provide various situations for them to respond to. For example, for *juega con las muñecas,* you may wish to provide *¿Si lo hace con los hijos?*

Actividad C ¿Es normal?

Paso 1 Determina si las actividades a continuación son normales o no para una persona de 30 años. Usa la siguiente escala: es normal ↔ depende de la situación ↔ es muy raro.

¿Cómo afecta la tecnología las actividades de los niños? ¿Son menos activos ahora que antes?

Una persona de 30 años...

1. juega con las muñecas.
2. lee tiras cómicas.
3. se lleva mal con los padres.
4. colorea para divertirse.
5. saca la licencia de conducir por primera vez.
6. tiene amigos imaginarios.
7. hace novillos.
8. juega al escondite.
9. se pelea con los hermanos.
10. se enamora por primera vez.

Paso 2 Comparte tus reacciones con la clase. Si piensas que una actividad es rara para una persona de 30 años, ¿hay una edad más apropiada?

OUTPUT
Actividad D

Actividad D Los pasatiempos favoritos

Paso 1 Completa la tabla con una lista de las actividades o pasatiempos favoritos de tu niñez y de ahora.

LAS ACTIVIDADES FAVORITAS DE MI NIÑEZ	MIS PASATIEMPOS FAVORITOS AHORA

Paso 2 Compara tus actividades con las de tres compañeros/as. ¿Qué actividades tienen en común para la niñez y para ahora?

Paso 3 ¿En cuál de las dos etapas son más comunes actividades o pasatiempos que tienen que ver con la tecnología? ¿Por qué?

Gramática

Talking About What You Used to Do

¿En qué trabajabas?   Introduction to the Imperfect Tense

Thus far you have been using the preterite to talk about what you did yesterday, last weekend, and so forth. But to talk about repeated, habitual, ongoing events and activities in the past (i.e., what you *used to do*), Spanish uses a different verb form: the *imperfect.** As the chart indicates, the imperfect is formed by adding **-aba** to the stem of **-ar** verbs and **-ía** to the stem of **-er** and **-ir** verbs. Verbs that have a stem change in the present tense do not change in the imperfect. Furthermore, the imperfect has only three irregular verbs: **ir, ser,** and **ver.**

Cuando **era** niño, **jugaba** mucho al escondite.	When I was a child, I used to play hide and seek a lot.
¿**Te metías** en muchos líos?	Did you used to / Would you get in a lot of trouble?
Me **gustaba** mucho leer las tiras cómicas.	I used to like to read comics.

Notice that this use of the imperfect is normally translated as *would . . .* or *used to . . .* and is used to communicate actions that used to be normal or habitual occurrences in the past.

The imperfect of **hay** is **había** (*there was / there were*).

THE IMPERFECT OF REGULAR VERBS					
jugar		**comer**		**vivir**	
jug**aba**	jug**ábamos**	com**ía**	com**íamos**	viv**ía**	viv**íamos**
jug**abas**	jug**abais**	com**ías**	com**íais**	viv**ías**	viv**íais**
jug**aba**	jug**aban**	com**ía**	com**ían**	viv**ía**	viv**ían**
jug**aba**	jug**aban**	com**ía**	com**ían**	viv**ía**	viv**ían**
IRREGULAR VERBS IN THE IMPERFECT					
ir		**ser**		**ver**	
iba	íbamos	era	éramos	veía	veíamos
ibas	ibais	eras	erais	veías	veíais
iba	iban	era	eran	veía	veían
iba	iban	era	eran	veía	veían

---

*Although there are a number of uses of the imperfect, in this section you will be using the imperfect to talk about activities that you *used to do.* You will learn more uses of the imperfect in **Lección 5B.**

MÁS GRAMÁTICA

There are two uses of the verb *would* in English: to express habitual actions in the past such as *When I was younger, I would always get into trouble,* and unreal conditions such as *I would go if I could.* For the first kind of *would,* Spanish uses the imperfect (**Cuando era más joven, siempre me metía en líos.**) For the second kind, Spanish uses a different verb form called the conditional (**Yo iría...**). You will learn more about this second kind of *would* and conditional forms in **Lección 8A.**

De *Sol y viento,* **Note:** You can access this film clip from a special menu section on Disc 5 of the Instructional Version on DVD.

DE SOL Y VIENTO

In **Episodio 5** of *Sol y viento* you will watch a scene in which Jaime explains to María why he knows so much about wine. Part of their conversation appears here.

MARÍA
Parece que sabes mucho de vino.

JAIME
Algo. He estado rodeadoª de uvas,ᵇ o jugo de uvas, toda mi vida.

MARÍA
¿Cómo?

JAIME
Mis padres ____eran____... campesinos.ᶜ En el Valle Central de California.

Which verb in the imperfect would you put in the blank above?

ªHe... *I've been surrounded* ᵇ*grapes* ᶜ*farm workers*

Actividad E ¿Cómo eran?

¿Cómo eran las vidas de Jaime y María hace quince o veinte años? Completa las oraciones sobre lo que piensas de las juventudes de Jaime y María.

1. Jaime vivía en _____ y era muy _____.
   Le gustaba _____.
2. María vivía en _____ y era muy _____.
   Le gustaba _____.

Actividad F Generaciones diferentes

A continuación hay una lista de oraciones que describen lo que dos estudiantes hacían con sus amigos durante sus años en la universidad. Con otra persona, indiquen si cada descripción se refiere a estudiantes que se graduaron en el año 1980 (mil novecientos ochenta) o treinta años más tarde, en 2010 (dos mil diez) o en los dos.

	1980	2010	LOS DOS
1. «Leíamos el correo electrónico tres veces al día.»	☐	☐	☐
2. «Usábamos un catálogo para buscar libros en la biblioteca.»	☐	☐	☐
3. «Escribíamos los trabajos a mano (*by hand*) o a máquina (*typewriter*).»	☐	☐	☐
4. «Descargábamos mucha música, vídeos y juegos.»	☐	☐	☐
5. «Escuchábamos música en cintas (*tapes*).»	☐	☐	☐
6. «Salíamos a tomar cerveza.»	☐	☐	☐
7. «Llamábamos a los amigos por teléfono celular.»	☐	☐	☐
8. «Les escribíamos cartas (*letters*) a amigos de otras universidades.»	☐	☐	☐
9. «Dejábamos (*We would leave*) las tareas hasta el último momento.»	☐	☐	☐
10. «Teníamos acceso al Internet en la residencia estudiantil.»	☐	☐	☐

Actividad G ¿Cómo era tu compañero/a?

Paso 1 Usando las expresiones a continuación, escribe ocho preguntas en el imperfecto para averiguar (*find out*) cómo era un compañero (una compañera) de clase cuando tenía 14 años.

obedecer a los padres	jugar a los videojuegos
estudiar mucho	meterse en líos
decirles mentiras (*lies*) a los padres	portarse bien en la escuela
llevarse bien con los hermanos	subirse a los árboles
hacer novillos	practicar algún deporte

Paso 2 Ahora hazle las preguntas a un compañero (una compañera) de clase y apunta sus respuestas. Además, contesta las preguntas que te hace a ti.

Paso 3 Tomando en cuenta (*Keeping in mind*) las respuestas de tu compañero/a en el **Paso 2,** ¿cómo crees que era tu compañero/a a los 14 años? Elige uno de los siguientes adjetivos y justifica tu selección.

☐ obediente

☐ tranquilo/a (*calm*)

☐ rebelde (*rebellious*)

☐ trabajador(a)

☐ travieso/a

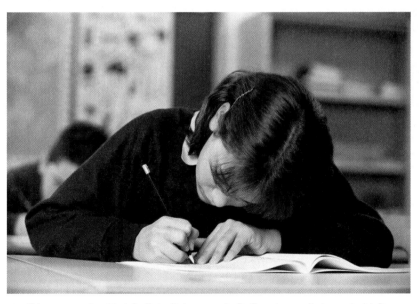

▲ ¿Cómo eras de niño/a? ¿Estudiabas mucho? ¿Eras tranquilo/a o rebelde?

Actividad H ¿Y tu profesor(a)?

Prepara tres oraciones para describir cómo era tu profesor(a) cuando era adolescente. Tu profesor(a) te va a decir si tienes razón o no.

SOL Y VIENTO

A primera vista

Antes de ver el episodio

Act. A, Answers: 1. *F, Jaime no conoció a doña Isabel. Carlos le dijo que estaba en Santiago, pero era mentira.* 2. *C* 3. *C* 4. *F, La figura simboliza un espíritu protector de los mapuches.* 5. *F, Quedaron en reunirse en el Cerro San Cristóbal, en la subida del funicular.*

Actividad A ¿Qué recuerdas?

¿Recuerdas lo que viste en el **Episodio 4**? Indica si las oraciones a continuación son ciertas o falsas. Si la oración es falsa, cámbiala.

		CIERTO	FALSO
1.	Jaime pudo conocer a doña Isabel.	☐	☑
2.	Carlos le regaló a Jaime una botella de vino.	☑	☐
3.	Diego no sabe si va a continuar con sus estudios por presiones familiares.	☑	☐
4.	La figura que compró Jaime simboliza un espíritu azteca.	☐	☑
5.	Jaime y María quedaron en reunirse en el bar del hotel de Jaime.	☐	☑

Actividad B ¿Qué falta?

A continuación hay parte de una conversación entre doña Isabel y Carlos que no has visto (*that you haven't seen*). Antes de ver el episodio, escoge la opción apropiada para llenar cada espacio en blanco.

Act. B, Suggestion: Don't reveal answers to students, as they will verify them later.

CARLOS: Mamá, ¿qué te parecería si vendiéramos[a] la viña?

ISABEL: ¿Vender «Sol y viento»? ¿Tú sabes cuánto _____[1] tu papá, cuánto _____[2] yo, para tener esta viña? ¡_____[3] este país sin nada!

[a]¿qué... *how would you feel if we sold*

1.	**a.** trabajaba	(**b.**) trabajó	**c.** trabaja
2.	**a.** trabajaba	(**b.**) trabajé	**c.** trabajo
3.	(**a.**) Vinimos a	**b.** Vivimos en	**c.** Salimos de

Actividad C El episodio

Ahora mira el episodio. Si hay algo que no entiendes bien, puedes volver a ver la escena en cuestión.

Después de ver el episodio

Actividad A ¿Qué recuerdas?

Contesta cada pregunta según lo que recuerdas del episodio.

1. ¿Qué hacía Jaime mientras esperaba a María?
   a. Hablaba por teléfono con Andy.
   b. Leía un artículo en el periódico.

2. Jaime piensa que María tiene una vida más interesante que la suya.
   a. cierto   b. falso

3. ¿Con quién habló doña Isabel después de la salida (*exit*) de Carlos? Habló con su esposo que ya murió.

4. ¿Qué significa la palabra «mapuche»? Significa «gente de la tierra».

5. ¿En qué trabajaba Jaime en su juventud?
   a. Trabajaba en la exportación de los vinos.
   b. Trabajaba en la fermentación de los vinos.

6. María tiene muchos amigos norteamericanos.
   a. cierto   **b.** falso

7. ¿Por qué colgó (*hung up*) el teléfono Jaime mientras hablaba con Andy?
   a. Porque había una mala conexión.
   b. Porque no quería seguir hablando con él.

Actividad B ¿Lo captaste?

Ahora verifica tus respuestas a la **Actividad C** en **Antes de ver el episodio.** Puedes ver esa escena de nuevo si quieres.

Actividad C En resumen

Completa la siguiente narración con las palabras y expresiones apropiadas de la lista a la derecha.

En este episodio, las cosas <u>no van bien</u>[1] con la viña. Carlos le dice a su madre que <u>quiere vender</u>[2] «Sol y viento», pero a doña Isabel <u>no le gusta nada</u>[3] la idea.

Mientras tanto,[a] Jaime y María <u>pasan</u>[4] la tarde juntos. Hablan de sus profesiones y a Jaime <u>le parece que</u>[5] el trabajo de María es más interesante que el suyo. Mientras toman una copa de vino, Jaime <u>le cuenta</u>[6] a María por qué sabe tanto de los vinos. Las cosas <u>van bien</u>[7] entre ellos hasta que María recibe una llamada de Diego y tiene que salir. Pero antes de despedirse[b] <u>le da</u>[8] un beso[c] a Jaime.

le cuenta
le da
le parece que
no le gusta nada
no van bien
pasan
quiere vender
van bien

[a]Mientras... *In the meantime* [b]*saying good-bye* [c]*kiss*

RESUMEN DE VOCABULARIO

Verbos

afeitarse	to shave
agradar	to please
apetecer (zc)	to appeal, be pleasing
bañarse	to take a bath
caerle (*irreg.*) **bien/mal a alguien**	to (dis)like someone
darle (*irreg.*) **miedo a alguien**	to scare someone
dormirse (ue, u)	to fall asleep
ducharse	to take a shower
encantar	to love
lavarse los dientes	to brush one's teeth
levantarse	to get up
parecer (zc)	to seem (like)
sentirse (ie, i)	to feel

Cognados: fascinar, importar, interesar
Repaso: acostarse (ue), despertarse (ie), gustar, molestar, vestirse (i, i)

Las computadoras y el Internet

apagar (gu)	to turn off
congelarse	to freeze up (*screen*)
descargar (gu)	to download
encender (ie)	to turn on (*machines*)
enviar (envío)	to send
guardar (documentos)	to save (documents)
hacer (*irreg.*) **clic**	to click
hacer (*irreg.*) **una búsqueda**	to do a search
mandar	to send
el archivo	file
la contraseña	password
el correo electrónico	e-mail
el disco duro	hard drive
el enlace	link
el mensaje	message
la página Web	Web page
el ratón	mouse
el teclado	keyboard

Cognados: conectar, copiar; la computadora portátil, el disquete, el módem, el monitor
Repaso: navegar (gu) la red; la computadora, la pantalla

Otros aparatos electrónicos

cambiar de canal	to change channels
funcionar	to work, function (*machines*)
grabar	to record
hacer (*irreg.*) ***zapping***	to channel surf
la agenda electrónica	electronic organizer (*PDA: personal digital assistant*)
el contestador automático	answering machine
el mando a distancia	remote control
el reproductor de CD (DVD, MP3, vídeo)	CD (DVD, MP3, video) player

Cognados: la calculadora, la cámara digital, el estéreo, la máquina fax, el (teléfono) celular, la videocámara
Repaso: el televisor, el vídeo

Los niños y jóvenes

dibujar	to draw
enamorarse (de)	to fall in love (with)
hacer (*irreg.*) **novillos**	to skip/cut school
jugar (gu) al escondite	to play hide and seek
jugar (gu) a los videojuegos	to play video games
llevarse bien/mal con	to get along well/poorly with
meterse en líos	to get into trouble
pelearse	to fight
portarse bien/mal	to behave well/poorly
sacar (qu) la licencia de conducir	to get a driver's license
soñar (ue) con	to dream about
subirse a los árboles	to climb trees
la cita	date (*social*)
la juventud	youth; adolescence
el/la mentiroso/a	liar
las muñecas	dolls
el/la niñero/a	baby-sitter
la niñez	childhood
el recreo	recess
las tiras cómicas	comics
cabezón (cabezona)	stubborn
precavido/a	cautious
torpe	clumsy
travieso/a	mischievous

Cognados: colorear; el/la adolescente; adaptable, impaciente, obediente, paciente

LECCIÓN

5B

Érase una vez...[a]

OBJETIVOS

IN THIS LESSON, YOU WILL LEARN:

- to express years, decades, and centuries
- to use the preterite and the imperfect together to narrate events
- to talk about important historical events
- to talk about important personal events

In addition, you will watch **Episodio 5** of the film *Sol y viento* again.

La llegada de Cristóbal Colón a América fue un evento histórico importante y controvertido (*controversial*).

[a]Érase... *Once upon a time . . .*

The following media resources are available for this lesson of *Sol y viento*:

Episodio 5 of *Sol y viento*

Online *Manual de actividades*

Online Learning Center Website

PRIMERA PARTE

Vocabulario

Expressing Years

En 1972...   ## Numbers 1,000 and Higher

1.000	mil	102.000	ciento dos mil
1.001	mil uno	200.000	doscientos mil
1.002	mil dos	300.000	trescientos mil
1.998	mil novecientos	400.000	cuatrocientos mil
	noventa y ocho	500.000	quinientos mil
2.000	dos mil	600.000	seiscientos mil
2.005	dos mil cinco	700.000	setecientos mil
3.000	tres mil	800.000	ochocientos mil
10.000	diez mil	900.000	novecientos mil
100.000	cien mil	1.000.000	un millón
101.000	ciento un mil	2.000.000	dos millones

Years are expressed in Spanish by saying the whole number.

1898	mil ochocientos noventa y ocho
1985	mil novecientos ochenta y cinco
2009	dos mil nueve

Remember that when numbers 200 through 900 modify a noun, they must agree in gender:

30.200 personas   treinta mil doscient**as** person**as**

Mil does not have a plural form when used in front of a noun, but **millón** does. Also, when used with a noun, **millón** must be followed by **de**.

5.000	cinco **mil** habitantes
5.000.000	cinco **millones de** habitantes

✳ MÁS VOCABULARIO

los años veinte (treinta)	the 20s, 30s (*decades*)
la década	decade
la fecha	date (*calendar*)
el siglo	century
el siglo XXI	the 21st century

Vistazo cultural

Fechas importantes en el mundo hispano

¿Cuánto sabes de la historia de los países hispanohablantes? A continuación hay una lista de algunas fechas históricas importantes de España y de Latinoamérica.

1492	Cristóbal Colón llegó a América
1519–1521	La conquista del Imperio azteca por Hernán Cortés
1531–1533	La conquista del Imperio inca por Francisco Pizarro
1808–1826	Guerras[a] de independencia; los países hispanoamericanos se independizaron de España
1898	Guerra Hispano-Americana; Puerto Rico se convirtió en territorio de los Estados Unidos
1910–1917	La Revolución mexicana
1914	Fin de la construcción del Canal de Panamá
1936–1939	Guerra Civil española; comienzo de 36 años de dictadura[b] bajo el General Francisco Franco
1952	Puerto Rico se hizo[c] Estado Libre Asociado de los Estados Unidos
1959	Fidel Castro subió al poder[d] en Cuba
1973	El presidente de Chile, Salvador Allende, fue asesinado; empezó la dictadura de Augusto Pinochet
1979–1988	Revolución sandinista en Nicaragua
1979–1991	Guerra civil en El Salvador
1985	Terremoto[e] en México; murieron más de ocho mil personas
1992	Rigoberta Menchú, activista indígena guatemalteca, ganó el Premio Nóbel de la Paz[f]
1994	Se firmó el Tratado de Libre Comercio de América del Norte (TLCAN)[g] entre México, los Estados Unidos y el Canadá
1999	El huracán[h] Mitch causó destrucción y muerte en Honduras, Nicaragua y Guatemala
2002	La Argentina pasó por una seria crisis económica con graves consecuencias en todos los sectores del país
2004	Ataques terroristas en los trenes de Madrid, España
2006	Hugo Chávez es elegido presidente de Venezuela de nuevo[i] y —junto con Evo Morales, presidente de Bolivia— muestra una creciente[j] tendencia anti-estadounidense en Latinoamérica.

Photos: Emiliano Zapata (la Revolución mexicana), Fidel Castro (la Revolución cubana), Rigoberta Menchú (el Premio Nóbel de la Paz)

[a]*Wars* [b]*dictatorship* [c]*se... became* [d]*subió... rose to power* [e]*Earthquake* [f]*Peace* [g]*Tratado... North American Free Trade Agreement (NAFTA)* [h]*hurricane* [i]*de... again* [j]*growing*

¿Quiénes son estas famosas personas históricas? ¿Con qué evento histórico se asocia cada una?

Vistazo cultural, **Suggestion:** Ask students questions about the dates. Example: *¿En qué año hubo un terremoto desastroso en México? ¿Cuándo ocurrió la Guerra Civil española?* etc. You may also wish to compare important events in the history of this country with those in Spanish-speaking countries. *¿Cuándo ocurrió la guerra de independencia de los Estados Unidos, antes de las guerras de independencia de Hispanoamérica o después?*

Actividad A ¿Qué año?

Paso 1 Escribe los años que lee tu profesor(a).

1. _1994_   3. _1519_   5. _1910_   7. _1959_
2. _1492_   4. _1898_   6. _1936_

Paso 2 ¿Sabes la importancia en el mundo hispano de los años del **Paso 1**? Empareja cada evento a continuación con el año correspondiente del **Paso 1.**

- **a.** el comienzo de la Guerra Civil española 1936
- **b.** la Revolución mexicana 1910
- **c.** la llegada de Colón a América 1492
- **d.** la llegada de Hernán Cortés a México 1519
- **e.** el Tratado de Libre Comercio de América del Norte 1994
- **f.** la Revolución cubana 1959
- **g.** la Guerra Hispano-Americana 1898

Actividad B ¿Cuántos habitantes?

Paso 1 Pensando en la geografía del mundo hispano, ¿sabes cuál de los siguientes países tiene más habitantes? ¿menos habitantes? Pon en orden los países según el número de habitantes que crees que es correcto (1 = más habitantes, 7 = menos habitantes).

- **a.** _2_ Colombia
  _46.621.000_
- **b.** _4_ Cuba
  _11.326.400_
- **c.** _7_ la Guinea Ecuatorial
  _1.102.750_
- **d.** _1_ México
  _105.150.000_
- **e.** _6_ Panamá
  _3.123.055_
- **f.** _3_ España
  _44.352.000_
- **g.** _5_ el Uruguay
  _3.261.570_

Paso 2 Tu profesor(a) va a leer el número de habitantes de los países del **Paso 1.** Escribe ese número debajo del nombre de cada país.

Paso 3 Compara el número que escribiste en el **Paso 1** con las poblaciones que leyó tu profesor(a). ¿Adivinaste (*Did you guess*) bien cuáles son los países con más y menos habitantes?

Actividad C Los precios

Paso 1 Con un compañero (una compañera) de clase, indiquen un precio razonable para las siguientes cosas.

MODELO: un libro de texto → cincuenta dólares

1. un auto nuevo   _____
2. un auto usado   _____
3. una nueva computadora portátil   _____
4. una casa de tres habitaciones   _____
5. el alquiler de un apartamento de dos habitaciones   _____
6. un televisor con pantalla amplia (*wide*)   _____
7. un reproductor de DVD   _____

Paso 2 Ahora conviertan esos precios en dólares a la moneda que les dé su profesor(a).

Paso 3 Cada grupo va a compartir cuánto costarían (*would cost*) algunas de las cosas del **Paso 1** en la moneda de un país hispano. ¿En qué país les sería (*would it be*) más difícil manejar la tasa de cambio (*to manage the exchange rate*)?

Actividad D ¿En qué año fue?

Paso 1 Antes de llegar a clase, elige algún año histórico. Luego, prepara una lista de tres eventos importantes que ocurrieron en ese año.

MODELO: mil novecientos ochenta y nueve →
Cayó (*Fell*) el muro (*wall*) de Berlín.
Hubo una invasión en Panamá.
Inició su presidencia George Bush (padre).

Paso 2 Lee tu lista de eventos a cinco compañeros. ¿Pueden adivinar (*guess*) el año que describes?

Paso 3 Ahora tu profesor(a) va a describir la época en que él/ella nació. ¿Puedes adivinar *el año* en que nació?

NAVEGANDO LA RED

Busca información sobre uno de los siguientes personajes importantes en la historia: José Martí (Cuba), Violeta Chamorro (Nicaragua), Pancho Villa (México), Ernesto «Che» Guevara (la Argentina) o Felipe II (España). ¿En qué año nació (*was he/she born*) y/o murió? ¿Con qué evento(s) histórico(s) se asocia este personaje? ¿Qué hizo para ganar tanta fama?

Gramática

More on Talking About the Past | ¿Qué hacías cuando te llamé? | **Contrasting the Preterite and Imperfect**

THE IMPERFECT: ONGOING ACTIONS	
Anoche a las diez yo **estudiaba** en la biblioteca.	*Last night at 10:00 I was studying in the library.*
Mientras María **trabajaba** en la excavación, Jaime **visitaba** la ciudad de Santiago.	*While María was working at the excavation site, Jaime was visiting Santiago.*
THE PRETERITE: COMPLETED ACTIONS	
La Guerra Civil española **duró** tres años.	*The Spanish Civil War lasted three years.*
«Vine, vi, vencí.» (Julio César)	*"I came, I saw, I conquered."*
Anoche **trabajé** hasta las nueve y luego **salí** con unos amigos.	*Last night I worked until nine, and then I went out with some friends.*

THE PRETERITE AND IMPERFECT TOGETHER: NARRATING A STORY OR DESCRIBING A SITUATION	
IMPERFECT (actions in progress, gives background information)	PRETERITE (specific events in the past, advances the story)
Mis amigos y yo **jugábamos** afuera... *My friends and I were playing outside . . .*	cuando **empezó** a llover. *when it began to rain.*
Lo **pasábamos** muy bien... *We were having a very good time . . .*	hasta que los vecinos **se quejaron.** *until the neighbors complained.*
Ya **existían** grandes civilizaciones en América... *Great civilizations already existed in America . . .*	cuando **llegaron** los españoles. *when the Spaniards arrived.*

You have already learned the two main Spanish verb forms used to talk about the past: the preterite and the imperfect. So far, you have used each tense separately, as in the following examples.

Preterite

El sábado **fui** al cine.   *On Saturday I went to the movies.*

Vimos una película muy buena.   *We saw a very good movie.*

Imperfect

Mi hermana y yo **jugábamos** al escondite.

My sister and I used to play hide and seek.

Mi familia **iba** a la playa todos los veranos.

My family used to (would) go to the beach every summer.

Besides expressing repeated and habitual actions in the past, the imperfect is also used to signal that an event or condition was in progress at a specific point in time or that two events were simultaneously in progress in the past. The words **mientras** (*while*) and **cuando** are often used with the imperfect. The English equivalent of this use of the imperfect is usually *was/were -ing* (e.g., *was studying, were playing, were living,* and so forth).

The preterite and imperfect may be used together in the same sentence. In fact, it is often difficult to tell a story in the past without using both. The imperfect describes an activity or condition in progress (i.e., provides background information), whereas the preterite communicates an interruption of that activity or condition. As such, it is the verb form that moves the narrative along in time. Note that the preterite is almost always used when a specific time frame or other information limits the event, as in *it rained **for three days**, I ran **six miles**, he lived **his whole life** in Mexico City.*

Note: Contrast the 3 example sentences in which the preterite is used with the following sentences, in which the imperfect would be used for background information: "*It was raining* when we arrived," "*I was running* when my cell phone rang," "*He was living* in Mexico when the earthquake struck."

De *Sol y viento,* Note: You can access this film clip from a special menu section on Disc 5 of the Instructional Version on DVD.

 ## DE SOL Y VIENTO

In **Episodio 5** of *Sol y viento* you will again watch the scene in which Carlos complains to his mother about the work that he has at the vineyard. Part of their conversation appears in the dialogue. Before watching the segment, think about which verb forms you think the characters will use.

CARLOS
Entonces sabrás[a] que tengo mucho trabajo con la viña, mamá.

ISABEL
Cuando _____[1] tu papá, _____[2] de los negocios. Yo ya _____[3] vieja y tu hermana _____[4] otros intereses.

1. **a.** murió   **b.** moría
2. **a.** te encargaste[b]   **b.** te encargabas
3. **a.** estuve   **b.** estaba
4. **a.** tuvo   **b.** tenía

[a]*you must know* [b]*encargarse = to take over*

Actividad E Cuando...

Escoge la mejor opción para completar cada oración.

1. Cuando llegó María a la entrada del funicular, Jaime...

   a. hablaba por   **b.** leía el periódico.   **c.** tomaba un
   teléfono.   vino.

2. Cuando recibió María una llamada por teléfono, ella y Jaime...

   a. tomaban un vino   **b.** cenaban.   **c.** se besaban
   y hablaban.   (*were
   kissing*).

3. Cuando María le preguntó a Jaime sobre la foto en el periódico, ellos...

   a. caminaban en   **b.** estaban en   **c.** subían en
   el parque.   un bar.   el funicular.

4. Hasta el momento en que María salió para ver a Diego, ella y Jaime...

   a. lo pasaban muy bien.   **b.** lo pasaban mal.   **c.** jugaban en
   el parque.

5. Jaime colgó (*hung up*) el teléfono mientras...

   a. hablaba con María.   **b.** hablaba con Andy.   **c.** hablaba
   con Mario.

Actividad F Un poco de historia

Paso 1 Empareja las condiciones en proceso de la columna A con los eventos de la columna B.

A	B
1. __f__ Ya existía una civilización muy avanzada en México cuando...	**a.** los conquistó Francisco Pizarro.
2. __c__ George W. Bush era presidente de los Estados Unidos cuando...	**b.** los Estados Unidos ganó una guerra contra México.
3. __a__ Los incas vivían en la región andina cuando...	**c.** un grupo terrorista atacó las torres gemelas en Nueva York.
4. __g__ La Argentina era un país muy próspero hasta que...	**d.** murió el General Franco.
5. __b__ Texas era territorio mexicano hasta que...	**e.** entró en la Segunda Guerra Mundial
6. __d__ España vivía bajo una dictadura militar hasta que...	**f.** llegó Hernán Cortés.
7. __e__ Los Estados Unidos sufría una depresión económica cuando...	**g.** sufrió una gran crisis económica.

Paso 2 ¿Hay algunos eventos del **Paso 1** que no sabías antes? ¿Cuáles son?

MODELO: No sabía que...

Actividad G   Una historia

Paso 1   Con un compañero (una compañera) escriban una historia de cuatro a seis oraciones que describen lo que ocurre en los dibujos a continuación. Deberías usar el pretérito y el imperfecto en tu narración.

Paso 2   Compartan su historia con la clase. ¿Tienen todos los grupos la misma información?

Actividad H   Un evento inolvidable (*unforgettable*)

Paso 1   Toda la clase va a identificar algún evento que todos recuerdan muy bien. Puede ser algo que tuvo impacto en la universidad, en la ciudad donde viven, en el país y/o el mundo.

Paso 2   Contesta las preguntas a continuación acerca del (*about the*) evento.

1. Cuando ocurrió, ¿dónde estabas?
2. ¿Qué hora era cuando te enteraste (*you found out*) del evento?
3. ¿Con quién(es) estabas?
4. ¿Cómo te sentías? (feliz, triste, enojado/a, confundido/a [*confused*], emocionado/a, asustado/a [*frightened*])
5. ¿Qué hiciste después de enterarte de lo que pasó?

Paso 3   Comparte tus respuestas con un compañero (una compañera) de clase y apunta lo que él/ella te dice. Luego, escribe un párrafo sobre el evento incluyendo la información que diste en el **Paso 2** y la de tu compañero/a.

SEGUNDA PARTE

Vocabulario

Talking About
Historical Events

Note: These vocabulary
items can be heard in
this lesson's Textbook
Audio section of the
Online Learning Center
Website.

Durante la guerra...   Important Events and Occurrences

Algunos eventos históricos importantes

▲ **El encuentro** de dos culturas:
Hernán Cortés con el emperador
azteca Moctezuma

▲ **La guerra** (*Los fusilamientos* [shootings]
del 3 de mayo por Francisco de Goya
[español, 1746–1828])

✴ MÁS VOCABULARIO

celebrar	to celebrate	**la invasión**	invasion
colonizar (c)	to colonize	**la llegada**	arrival
conquistar	to conquer	**la migración**	migration
descubrir	to discover	**la revolución**	revolution
establecer (zc)	to establish		
explorar	to explore	**difícil**	difficult
invadir	to invade	**emocionante**	exciting
		estable	stable
la conquista	conquest	**feliz**	happy
la depresión (económica)	(economic) depression	**oscuro/a**	dark; scary
		pacífico/a	peaceful
el descubrimiento	discovery	**tumultuoso/a**	tumultuous; unstable
el encuentro	encounter; meeting		
la exploración	exploration		
la fundación	founding		
la guerra	war		
la independencia	independence		
el/la inmigrante	immigrant		

Los desastres naturales

▲ Los efectos del **huracán** Mitch (Honduras)

▲ Los efectos de un **terremoto** en México

▲ Las **inundaciones,** el resultado de lluvias excesivas (Puerto Rico)

Vistazo cultural,
Suggestion: Have students read quickly. Then ask some follow-up questions: 1. *El descubrimiento de América representa el punto de vista indígena. ¿Cierto o falso?* (falso) 2. *Muchos latinoamericanos prefieren la palabra «encuentro» en vez de «descubrimiento». ¿Cierto o falso?* (cierto) 3. *¿Cuáles son los dos mundos que «se encontraron» en 1492?* (el mundo europeo y el mundo indígena)

≈ Vistazo cultural

¿Un descubrimiento?

Muchos aprenden desde una edad temprana que el año 1492 es la fecha del «descubrimiento de América», o que Cristóbal Cólon «descubrió» América en ese año. Pero hay que tener en cuenta[a] que este acontecimiento[b] es un descubrimiento sólo desde el punto de vista[c] europeo. A muchos indígenas y latinoamericanos no les agrada el término **descubrimiento.** Para ellos, la llegada de los europeos no representa ningún descubrimiento del continente americano, ya que[d] los indígenas vivían allí durante muchos siglos. Según la perspectiva de una persona americana, los europeos que vinieron *invadieron* y *conquistaron* los terrenos[e] nativos de los indígenas. Por eso, en vez de hablar del «descubrimiento de América en 1492», se habla del «encuentro» de los dos mundos: el mundo europeo y el indígena americano.

▲ ¿Descubrimento o encuentro?

[a]tener... *keep in mind* [b]*event* [c]punto... *point of view* [d]ya... *since* [e]*lands*

INPUT
Actividad A

Actividad A Definiciones

Empareja cada palabra con la definición apropiada.

1. __c__ el terremoto
2. __g__ la fundación
3. __e__ la independencia
4. __f__ la exploración
5. __a__ la migración
6. __d__ el descubrimiento
7. __b__ la guerra

a. el movimiento (*movement*) de personas de un lugar a otro
b. un conflicto violento entre dos países
c. un movimiento de la tierra
d. el encuentro de algo nuevo
e. cuando un país ya no está bajo el control de otro
f. el proceso de aventurarse en un territorio nuevo
g. el establecimiento de una ciudad o una organización

INPUT/OUTPUT
Actividad B

Actividad B Algunos ejemplos

Paso 1 Escribe el primer ejemplo que te venga a la mente (*comes to mind*) de cada evento a continuación. Incluye la fecha si la sabes.

MODELO: un encuentro → 1492, Cristóbal Colón en América

1. una lucha (*struggle*) por la independencia
2. una migración
3. una guerra
4. un terremoto
5. una invasión
6. un huracán
7. una exploración

Paso 2 Compara los ejemplos que escribiste en el **Paso 1** con los de tres compañeros/as. ¿Tienen los mismos ejemplos? Si todos tienen los mismos ejemplos para algunos eventos, ¿cuál puede ser la razón?

Paso 3 Comparte los ejemplos de tu grupo con la clase. Da una posible explicación en caso de que haya (*there are*) ejemplos comunes.

INPUT/OUTPUT
Actividad C

Actividad C ¿Cómo era durante esa época?

Paso 1 Con un compañero (una compañera) de clase, indiquen los adjetivos de la siguiente lista que describan mejor las siguientes épocas de la historia norteamericana.

MODELO: los años treinta del siglo XX → difíciles, oscuros, espantosos

difícil	espantoso/a (*scary*)	feliz	pacífico/a
emocionante	estable	oscuro/a	tumultuoso/a

1. la Revolución norteamericana
2. la Guerra Civil
3. los años veinte
4. la Guerra Fría
5. los años sesenta
6. los años noventa
7. los meses después del 11 de septiembre de 2001

Paso 2 Piensa en los adjetivos que escribiste en el **Paso 1.** ¿Cuáles son los eventos que influyeron en tu selección de adjetivos?

MODELO: los años treinta del siglo XX → la depresión económica, conflictos en Europa

OUTPUT
Actividad D

Actividad D Esperanzas y preocupaciones (*Hopes and worries*)

Paso 1 ¿Cuáles son las esperanzas y preocupaciones que tienes acerca del mundo de hoy? En grupos de tres o cuatro personas, llenen la tabla a continuación.

TENEMOS LA ESPERANZA DE...	NOS PREOCUPA(N)...
MODELO: encontrar vida en otros planetas.	MODELO: la posibilidad de un terremoto en California.

Paso 2 ¿Cómo ven Uds. el mundo de hoy? ¿Son Uds. optimistas o pesimistas?

Enfoque cultural, **Suggestion:** Have students research the established religions in this country and the percentage of people who practice each. Then ask students to discuss whether an abundance of religious beliefs in a country is a benefit or a detriment to society. What are the advantages and disadvantages of a large majority of people who practice a single religion, as seen in most Hispanic countries?

SOL Y VIENTO: Enfoque cultural

En el **Episodio 5** vas a ver un parque con una estatua enorme de la Virgen María. Los habitantes de Chile son, en su mayoría, católicos, como en la mayoría de los demás países hispanos. Por ejemplo, en España el 94% de la población es católica; en Chile, el 70%; en Venezuela, el 96%; y en Puerto Rico, el 85%.* Hasta en la Guinea Ecuatorial, donde hay una fuerte influencia de las culturas africanas, la mayoría de las personas se identifica con la Iglesia católica. Compara esas cifras[a] con el número de personas estadounidenses que se identifican como católicos: sólo llega al 24%. Claro, la manera en que se practica el catolicismo varía de país a país. Por ejemplo, en México la devoción a la Virgen de Guadalupe es casi más fuerte que la devoción a Jesucristo. Y en la zona andina (el Perú, Bolivia, el Ecuador) los indígenas han forjado[b] un catolicismo con restos[c] de la mitología y creencias de sus antepasados,[d] los incas.

[a]*figures* [b]*han... have created* [c]*remnants* [d]*ancestors*

▲ La estatua de la Virgen María en el Cerro San Cristóbal en Santiago

*C.I.A. World Fact Book, 2007.

Gramática

More on Talking About the Past

¡No lo sabía!

More on Using the Preterite and Imperfect Together

When using verbs that express states or conditions in the past, Spanish often uses the imperfect. This is because states and conditions are usually ongoing, and they provide background information in relation to a specific event or action in the past.

Tenía dieciséis años cuando...	**aprendí** a conducir.
I was sixteen years old when . . .	*I learned to drive.*
Eran las ocho cuando...	me **llamaron.**
It was eight o'clock when . . .	*they called me.*

You have already learned that when some verbs that express states or conditions are used in the preterite, the English equivalent may be different.

—¿**Sabías** que Julio y Marta eran novios?	*Did you know that Julio and Marta were boyfriend and girlfriend?*
—Lo **supe** ayer.	*I found out about it yesterday.*
Quería ir al concierto, pero no **pude.**	*I wanted to go to the concert, but I couldn't.*
No **quiso** oírme.	*He refused to hear me.*

You will learn more about the uses of verbs that describe states and conditions in **Lección 7A.**

VERBS WITH MEANING CHANGES IN THE IMPERFECT AND PRETERITE			
IMPERFECT		PRETERITE	
conocía	I knew (*a person*)	conocí	I met (*a person*)
podía	I was able, could	pude	I could (and did)
no podía	I wasn't able, couldn't	no pude	I couldn't (and didn't)
quería	I wanted	quise	I tried
no quería	I didn't want	no quise	I refused
sabía	I knew (*something*)	supe	I found out
no sabía	I didn't know	no supe	I never knew / found out

DE SOL Y VIENTO

In **Episodio 4** of *Sol y viento,* you watched a scene in which Jaime talked with Traimaqueo at the vineyard. Part of their conversation appears in the dialogue. Which form of the verb would you put in the blank?

TRAIMAQUEO
La señora Isabel me espera en la casa.

JAIME
Creía que la señora Isabel _____ en Santiago.

TRAIMAQUEO
No, no, no. La señora Isabel no hace muchos viajes en estos días. No está de muy buena salud.

1. estuvo
2. estaba

Enfoque lingüístico

El tiempo y el aspecto

Thus far in *Sol y viento* you have seen two different verb forms that communicate that something occurred in the past: the preterite and the imperfect. The difference between the two is not one of *tense* but rather of *aspect.* Tense is a grammatical expression of time (usually indicated by verb endings in Romance languages and in English). You will recall from **Lección 4A** that tense locates an event or situation in the present, past, or future. Aspect, on the other hand, is a grammatical expression that communicates a speaker's perspective of a situation or event. For example, consider the difference in perspective of these sentences:

John sang.   John was singing.   John used to sing.

All of these sentences are in the past tense (as opposed to the present or future) but represent different perspectives. In *John sang,* the perspective communicated is of completion. The event is viewed from the "outside." The singing is over. The speaker communicates that it ended in some moment in the past. But in *John was singing,* the perspective is different. The event is viewed from the "inside" as an event in progress and may leave us expecting more information about what happened while he was singing. In *John used to sing,* the event is viewed as habitual or recurring. Unlike *John sang,* this last sentence communicates that the singing occurred more than one time in the past. Languages vary as to whether they express aspectual distinctions or not and in what way. Keep in mind that in Spanish you need to distinguish between an event being "in progress" or "recurring" in the past and the event being completed.

Actividad E ¿Quién lo diría (*would say it*)?

Indica cuál de los personajes de *Sol y viento* diría cada oración a continuación. Presta atención al uso del pretérito y del imperfecto.

> **a.** Jaime   **b.** María   **c.** doña Isabel

1. __a__ Leía un papelito de la suerte cuando me choqué con (*I bumped into*) alguien en el parque.
2. __b__ Colgaba (*I was hanging*) unos carteles cuando vi al norteamericano otra vez.
3. __c__ Estaba en el jardín cuando Carlos vino a hablar conmigo.
4. __b__ Estaba en el café cuando me llamó Diego.
5. __a__ Hablaba con Traimaqueo cuando supe que doña Isabel estaba en casa.
6. __a__ Me dijo que mi vida no era tan interesante como la suya.

Actividad F ¿Cuántos años tenías?

Paso 1   Llena los espacios en blanco con la edad que tenías cuando cada evento ocurrió.

1. Tenía _____ años cuando supe que Papá Noel (*Santa Claus*) no existía.
2. Tenía _____ años cuando aprendí a conducir un auto.
3. Tenía _____ años cuando tuve mi primera cita romántica.
4. Tenía _____ años cuando hice mi primer viaje en avión.
5. Tenía _____ años cuando empecé a asistir a la universidad.
6. Tenía _____ años cuando empecé a afeitarme la cara / las piernas (*my face / my legs*).
7. Tenía _____ años cuando mis padres me permitieron usar el auto a solas.
8. Tenía _____ años cuando mis padres me dejaron solo/a (*alone*) en casa sin niñero/a.
9. Tenía _____ años cuando mis padres me permitieron salir con mis amigos hasta medianoche.

Paso 2   Compara tus respuestas con las de tres compañeros. ¿Tienen las mismas respuestas? ¿Hay una edad típica en que ocurren ciertos eventos?

MODELO: Nosotros teníamos dieciocho años cuando empezamos a asistir a la universidad. Nos parece una edad típica.

Actividad G ¿A quién conociste?

Paso 1 Piensa en el momento en que conociste a alguien que ha tenido (*has had*) gran influencia en tu vida. Puede ser una persona famosa, un novio (una novia), tu mejor amigo/a o cualquier persona importante en tu vida.

Nombre de la persona _____

Paso 2 Escribe cuatro o cinco oraciones que describen el momento en que lo/la conociste. Usa las preguntas a continuación para organizar lo que vas a decir.

1. ¿En qué año lo/la conociste?
2. ¿Dónde estabas cuando lo/la conociste?
3. ¿Con quién estabas?
4. ¿Cómo era esa persona? (simpático/a, guapo/a, bonito/a, etcétera)
5. ¿Quién habló primero, tú o la otra persona?
6. ¿Cómo te sentías? (nervioso/a, emocionado/a, contento/a, etcétera)

Paso 3 Cuéntales tu historia a tres compañeros/as.

MODELO: Conocí a <u>(nombre)</u> en el año... Estaba en...

Paso 4 ¿De quiénes hablaron tus compañeros? ¿Hablaron de personas famosas? ¿de profesores? ¿de novios/as?

Actividad H ¿Qué querías hacer?

Paso 1 Cuando estabas en el último año de la escuela secundaria, ¿qué planes tenías para ese año o para después de graduarte? ¿Qué querías hacer? Escribe cinco oraciones que describan tus planes.

MODELO: En el año 2008 quería asistir a la universidad de...

Paso 2 ¿Pudiste realizar (*achieve*) lo que querías hacer? Ahora añade más información a las oraciones del **Paso 1** para indicar lo que pasó.

MODELOS: En el año 2008 quería asistir a la universidad de _____ y lo hice. ¡Aquí estoy!

En el año 2008 quería asistir a la universidad de _____, pero no pude. No pude pagar la matrícula (*tuition*).

Paso 3 Compara la información que tienes en los **Pasos 1** y **2** con la de un compañero (una compañera). Luego prepara dos oraciones para compartir con la clase.

MODELOS: (Nombre) y yo queríamos asistir a la universidad de _____, y lo hicimos.

(Nombre) quería asistir a la universidad de _____ y yo quería asistir a la universidad de _____, pero no pudimos. A (nombre) no lo/la aceptaron y yo no pude pagar la matrícula.

TERCERA PARTE

Note: These vocabulary items can be heard in this lesson's Textbook Audio section of the Online Learning Center Website.

Vocabulario

Talking About Special Events | **Me gradué en 2000.**

Personal Events, Triumphs, and Failures

Algunos eventos importantes de la vida

la graduación

graduarse (me gradúo)

la boda

la novia

el novio casarse (con)

el nacimiento

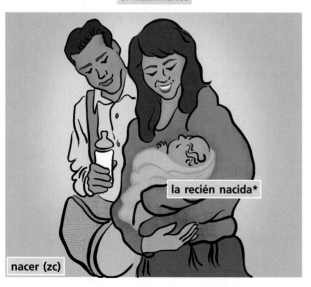

la recién nacida*

nacer (zc)

la mudanza

mudarse

---

*A newborn boy would be referred to as **el recién nacido.**

MÁS VOCABULARIO

divertirse (ie, i)	to have fun
divorciarse (de)	to get divorced (from)
fracasar	to fail
morir (ue, u)	to die
tener (*irreg.*) **éxito**	to succeed, be successful
el divorcio	divorce
el éxito	success
el fracaso	failure
el matrimonio	marriage
la muerte	death

Vistazo cultural,
Suggestion: Before having students read, ask them the following questions: 1. *¿A qué hora empiezan las bodas en este país, por lo general?* 2. *En general, ¿cuántos padrinos de boda y damas de honor hay?* 3. *¿Cuántas horas dura la fiesta después de una boda?* Then have students read the text and look for specific differences between weddings in Spanish-speaking countries and this country.

 # Vistazo cultural

Las bodas en los países hispanos

Como en muchos países del mundo, las bodas en los países hispanos son grandes celebraciones y es común invitar a más de doscientas personas para celebrarlas. Si tienes la oportunidad de asistir a una boda en un país hispano, puedes notar algunas diferencias con las bodas norteamericanas. Por ejemplo, muchas bodas hispanas empiezan a eso de las siete de la tarde, y el novio va al altar acompañado de su madre o madrina.[a] Muchas veces no hay ni padrinos de boda[b] ni damas de honor.[c] Durante la ceremonia, el sacerdote[d] pone un rosario largo alrededor de los hombros[e] y las manos[f] de la pareja para simbolizar la unión y la protección del matrimonio. En algunos países el novio le da a la novia trece monedas o **arras** para simbolizar la habilidad del novio de sostener[g] y cuidar a[h] su esposa. La ceremonia no suele durar más de una hora, pero la fiesta después de la boda puede durar hasta la madrugada[i] del día siguiente.

▲ Una boda española

[a]*godmother* [b]*padrinos... groomsmen* [c]*damas... bridesmaids* [d]*priest* [e]*shoulders* [f]*hands*
[g]*support* [h]*cuidar... care for* [i]*dawn*

INPUT
Act. A, Statements:
1. *Es una ceremonia religiosa o civil en la que se celebra la unión legal entre dos personas.*
2. *Es cuando uno se muda de una casa a otra.*
3. *Es la separación legal de dos personas casadas.*
4. *Es una ceremonia en la que se celebra el fin de los estudios en una escuela o universidad.*
5. *Es el comienzo de una vida.* 6. *Es el fin de una vida.* 7. *Es el resultado de no tener éxito al intentar hacer algo.*

¡Exprésate!

Important events often provoke certain emotions, which can be described using the verb **sentirse.**

Me siento...

ansioso/a	anxious
deprimido/a	depressed
enojado/a	angry
feliz, contento/a	happy
nervioso/a	nervous
orgulloso/a (de)	proud (of)
triste	sad

Also, **al** + *infinitive* in Spanish means *upon/while/when* (*doing something*). For example, **al cumplir veintiún años** means *upon turning* (*when turning*) *twenty-one.*

Actividad A ¿Qué evento se describe?

Tu profesor(a) va a leer descripciones de algunos eventos importantes. Escribe el número de la descripción al lado del evento correspondiente.

a. _2_ la mudanza
b. _6_ la muerte
c. _1_ la boda
d. _7_ el fracaso
e. _4_ la graduación
f. _5_ el nacimiento
g. _3_ el divorcio

Actividad B ¿Cómo te sentías? INPUT/OUTPUT
Actividad B

Paso 1 Empareja las emociones de la columna B con cada evento de la columna A. Hay más de una respuesta posible en muchos casos.

A	B
Uno se siente...	
1. ____ después de un divorcio.	**a.** feliz
2. ____ antes de casarse.	**b.** deprimido/a
3. ____ al conseguir un trabajo.	**c.** nervioso/a
4. ____ al graduarse.	**d.** enojado/a
5. ____ después de un nacimiento.	**e.** triste
6. ____ al cumplir veintiún años.	**f.** orgulloso/a
7. ____ al cumplir cuarenta años.	
8. ____ antes de mudarse a otra ciudad.	
9. ____ en la boda de unos amigos.	

Paso 2 Con un compañero (una compañera), comenten las respuestas posibles para los eventos del **Paso 1.** ¿Es posible sentir emociones opuestas (*opposite*) en algunas circunstancias? ¿Por qué?

Paso 3 Elige tres de los eventos del **Paso 1** que te han pasado (*that have happened to you*) y describe cómo te sentías. Comparte tus descripciones con tres compañeros.

MODELO: E1: Al cumplir veintiún años me sentía muy feliz.
E2: Yo también me sentía muy feliz.

o

¿Ah, sí? Yo no. Me sentía muy deprimida.

Actividad C

Actividad C Un éxito memorable

Paso 1 Piensa en algún éxito personal que has experimentado (*you've experienced*). Puede ser la graduación de la escuela secundaria, ganar una competición, conseguir un trabajo, una carta de aceptación para ir a la universidad, salir con el hombre / la mujer de tus sueños (*dreams*), etcétera. Escribe el evento en el siguiente espacio en blanco.

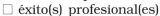

Paso 2 Escribe cuatro oraciones que describan el evento. Puedes usar las preguntas a continuación para organizar tus ideas.

¿En qué año ocurrió?

¿Cuántos años tenías?

¿Cómo te sentías?

¿Qué hiciste para celebrar el éxito?

Paso 3 Comparte tu experiencia con otras tres personas. Luego, escucha bien las experiencias de tus compañeros/as y apunta algunos momentos importantes.

Paso 4 ¿Cómo clasificas los éxitos de tus compañeros?

☐ éxito(s) académico(s)   ☐ éxito(s) en la vida personal
☐ éxito(s) deportivo(s)   ☐ ¿otro(s)?
☐ éxito(s) profesional(es)

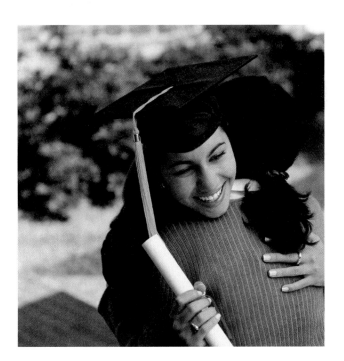

▲ Para algunos, graduarse de la universidad es uno de los éxitos más importantes de la vida.

Gramática

| **Tenía 30 años cuando nació mi primer hijo.** | **Summary of the Preterite and Imperfect**

The chart in this section summarizes the basic uses of the preterite and imperfect that you have learned.

USES OF THE PRETERITE
• to communicate that an event happened at a particular point in time Ramón **llegó** temprano.   *Ramón arrived early.* La fiesta no **terminó** hasta las 2:00 de   *The party didn't end until 2:00 in the morning.* la mañana.
• to communicate an event that was confined by time limits El partido **duró** tres horas.   *The game lasted three hours.* **Viví** allí desde 1995 hasta 2003.   *I lived there from 1995 to 2003.*
• to communicate a series of completed or consecutive events **Preparé** un café y **leí** el periódico.   *I made coffee and read the newspaper.*
• to express that one event occurred while another was in progress Mi madre **llamó** mientras comíamos.   *My mom called while we were eating.*
USES OF THE IMPERFECT
• to communicate that an event was in progress at a certain time A las 8:00 todavía **estudiaba.**   *I was still studying at 8:00.*
• to communicate that two events were taking place at the same time Mientras **comía, veía** la tele.   *While I ate (was eating), I watched (was watching) TV.*
• to communicate that an event occurred repeatedly in the past Mis amigos y yo **nos metíamos** en   *My friends and I used to get into a lot of* muchos líos.   *trouble.*
• to provide background information (time, weather, age, physical/mental characteristics, states) while narrating an event **Hacía** muy buen tiempo el día de la   *The weather was very good on the day of* fiesta. **Había** mucha gente allí que   *the party. There were lots of people there* **tenía** entre 25 y 40 años.   *who were between 25 and 40 years old.*

To ask about an event ("How was . . . ?"), Spanish uses the expression **qué tal** with the preterite of the verb **estar.**

¿Qué tal estuvo el partido (la película, la boda, la clase...)?
How was the game (the movie, the wedding, the class . . .)?
Estuvo bien (mal, interesante, aburrido/a, divertido/a...).
It was good (bad, interesting, boring, fun . . .).

Spanish can also use **fue,** but only with indirect objects.

¿Cómo te fue en la entrevista?
How did it go for you in the interview? / How was the interview?
Me fue muy bien, gracias.
It went really well for me, thanks. / It was great, thanks.

De *Sol y viento,* Note: You can access this film clip from a special menu section on Disc 5 of the Instructional Version on DVD.

DE SOL Y VIENTO

In **Episodio 5** of *Sol y viento,* you will again watch the scene in which María remembers that she had previously made plans with Diego and has to leave suddenly. Part of their conversation appears here. Before watching the segment, indicate which verb forms you think belong in the blanks.

MARÍA
Diego es un estudiante, es mi ayudante en la excavación. Lo _____¹ pasando tan bien contigo que no _____² en la hora.

JAIME
_____³ que... pues, que...

MARÍA
¿Que... que Diego _____⁴ mi novio?ª ¿Que _____⁵ contigo sólo para investigar quién _____⁶ este especimen norteamericano?

1. **a.** estaba **b.** estuve
2. **a.** me fijabaᵇ **b.** me fijé
3. **a.** Pensaba **b.** Pensé
4. **a.** era **b.** fue
5. **a.** venía **b.** vine
6. **a.** era **b.** fue

ªboyfriend ᵇfijarse = to notice

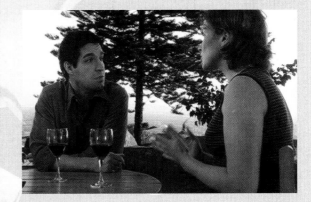

INPUT/OUTPUT

Act. D, Note: Formerly titled *¿Qué leíste?*, this recurring activity is now presented as an aural activity only, although you still have the option of displaying the paragraph with an overhead projector instead of reading it aloud. Total time for dictogloss: 15–20 minutes. Consult the Instructor's Manual for information on dictogloss activities.

Paso 1, **Suggestion:** Students listen but do not write down what they hear. Read the following paragraph twice, the first time at slower than normal speed: *Antes de llegar a Chile, mi trabajo era mi vida. No tenía mucha vida social y salía muy poco. Pero desde que conocí a María, lo veo todo diferente. Lo pasé muy bien hoy con ella en el parque, ¡y espero verla otra vez!*

Paso 2, **Suggestion:** Allow approximately 5 minutes.

Follow-up: Call on 1 group to present its final version. Ask another group if it has the same wording. Finally, display the original so all groups can compare, drawing attention to the preterite and imperfect verb forms. Ask a few content questions to keep focus on meaning (example: *¿Quién habla en este párrafo? ¿Por qué lo pasó bien?*)

Actividad D ¿Qué escuchaste?

Paso 1 Escucha el párrafo que lee tu profesor(a) a la clase. Vas a escuchar el párrafo dos veces. Trata de recordar la información, pero no tomes apuntes.

Paso 2 En grupos de tres, escriban una versión del párrafo para luego compartir con la clase.

Actividad E Mis primeras impresiones

INPUT/OUTPUT
Actividad E

Paso 1 Completa las oraciones a continuación sobre tus primeros días en la universidad.

1. Cuando llegué a la universidad por primera vez, el campus me parecía...
   ☐ grande.   ☐ pequeño.   ☐ confuso (*confusing*).
   ☐ emocionante.   ☐ _____

2. Cuando conocí a mi compañero/a de cuarto (una persona en una de mis clases) él/ella me parecía...
   ☐ simpático/a.   ☐ tímido/a.   ☐ distante.
   ☐ extrovertido/a.   ☐ _____

3. Mi primera clase en la universidad fue <u>(nombre)</u> y era a la(s) _____
   ☐ de la mañana.   ☐ de la tarde.   ☐ de la noche.

4. La clase era...
   ☐ interesante.   ☐ aburrida.   ☐ _____

5. Cuando salí de mi primera clase me sentía...
   ☐ ansioso/a.   ☐ contento/a.   ☐ preocupado/a (*worried*).
   ☐ deprimido/a.   ☐ aburrido/a.   ☐ entusiasmado/a.
   ☐ _____

Paso 2 Comparte tus respuestas con las de tres compañeros. ¿Tuvieron Uds. las mismas impresiones? Escribe dos oraciones sobre una experiencia que tú y otra persona tienen en común.

MODELO: Cuando <u>(nombre)</u> y yo llegamos a la universidad por primera vez, el campus nos parecía muy emocionante.

▲ ¿Cómo te sentías después de tu primer día en la universidad?

INPUT/OUTPUT

Act. F, *Paso 3,*
Suggestion: Either have
students read their own
versions or collect the
endings and randomly
select a few to read. You
may also want to point
out different uses of the
preterite and the imperfect
in the narrations.

Actividad F La primera cita

Paso 1 Pon en orden lógico las siguientes oraciones, que narran la primera cita entre dos personas. Presta atención a los verbos en el pretérito y en el imperfecto.

___4___ Entonces, el sábado, Arturo llegó a la casa de Raquel y salieron para el restaurante.

___7___ Mientras caminaban por el parque hablaban de sus gustos personales.

___1___ Un día Raquel trabajaba en casa cuando Arturo la llamó.

___8___ Todo iba muy bien hasta que...

___2___ Arturo le preguntó a Raquel si quería salir a cenar con él el sábado por la noche.

___6___ Después de cenar, Arturo la invitó a dar un paseo por el parque.

___5___ Como Raquel estaba nerviosa, no tenía mucha hambre y sólo pidió una ensalada.

___3___ Raquel le dijo que sí y que estaba muy contenta.

Paso 2 Compara el orden de las oraciones con el de un compañero (una compañera). Luego escribe tres oraciones para terminar la historia.

Paso 3 Tu profesor(a) va a pedir que varios grupos lean sus historias a la clase. ¿Qué grupo tiene el final de la historia más creativo?

OUTPUT

Act. G, *Paso 3,*
Suggestion: Have
students switch partners
every 4–5 minutes so that
they talk to a variety of
people. As a follow-up
students can write a
paragraph comparing
and contrasting their
important
events with
those of a
classmate.

Actividad G Eventos importantes en mi vida

Paso 1 Elige cinco eventos importantes en tu vida. Puedes incluir éxitos, tragedias, nacimientos, bodas, etcétera. Indica el año de cada evento en una línea como la de abajo, pero no escribas el evento.

MODELO:

1990   2008   Hoy

Paso 2 Prepara de tres a cinco oraciones para cada evento. Puedes usar las preguntas a continuación para organizar tus ideas.

¿Qué ocurrió?

¿Cuántos años tenías?

¿Cómo te sentías?

¿Dónde / Con quién estabas?

¿Qué pasó después?

Paso 3 Con un compañero (una compañera) compartan los eventos que describieron. Sigan el modelo a continuación para empezar su conversación. Además de la pregunta inicial, tienen que pensar en por lo menos una pregunta para hacerle a su compañero/a sobre cada evento.

MODELO: E1: ¿Qué ocurrió en dos mil ocho?
E2: Me gradué de la escuela secundaria. Tenía dieciocho años y estaba muy contento. Estaba con toda mi familia y mis amigos. Después de la ceremonia tuvimos una fiesta en mi casa.
E1: ¿De qué escuela te graduaste?

SOL Y VIENTO

A segunda vista

Antes de ver el episodio

Actividad A ¿Qué recuerdas?

Paso 1 Indica quién diría (*would say*) cada oración a continuación, Jaime o María.

1. _Jaime_ Decidió tutearme (*address me as* **tú**) por primera vez.
2. _María_ Quería saber si Diego era mi novio.
3. _María_ Desafortunadamente, tuve que salir.
4. _María_ Me dijo que mi vida parecía fascinante.
5. _Jaime_ Leí que trabajaba con los mapuches para protestar algo.
6. _Jaime_ ¡Me besó (*He/She kissed me*)! Pero tuvo que salir y me quedé solo.
7. _María_ Me compró un remolino.
8. _Jaime_ Recibió una llamada de Diego y yo estaba preocupado.

Paso 2 Ahora, pon las oraciones según el orden en que María o Jaime contaría (*would tell*) los hechos (*deeds*).

Jaime: _5_ _1_ _8_ _6_

María: _7_ _4_ _2_ _3_

Act. B, Suggestions: Have students read the exchange. They do not need to write anything at this point. Do not reveal answers. **Alternative:** Have the class brainstorm possible answers for each blank but do not have them write anything down.

Actividad B ¡A escuchar!

En un momento, vas a ver el **Episodio 5** de nuevo. Repasa la siguiente escena. Luego, mientras la ves, completa lo que dicen los personajes con las palabras que faltan.

ISABEL: ¡Hijo! Me ___quedé___[1] dormida. ¿Te ___pasa___[2] algo, hijo?
CARLOS: No, nada. ¿Por qué?
ISABEL: Sí, algo te ___pasa___.[3] Soy tu mamá y te ___conozco___[4] mejor que nadie.
CARLOS: Entonces sabrás que ___tengo___[5] mucho trabajo con la viña, mamá.
ISABEL: Cuando ___murió___[6] tu papá, te ___encargaste___[7] de los negocios. Yo ya ___estaba___[8] vieja y tu hermana ___tenía___[9] otros intereses.

Actividad C El episodio

Ahora mira el episodio. Presta (*Pay*) atención al diálogo en la **Actividad B** mientras lo ves.

Después de ver el episodio

Actividad A Para pensar...

Paso 1 En este episodio conociste a doña Isabel, la madre de Carlos. Piensa en lo siguiente y contesta las preguntas según tu propia opinión.

1. Doña Isabel le dijo a su hijo que había venido (*she had come*) a Chile sin nada. ¿De dónde vino, originalmente?
2. ¿Por qué no quiere vender la viña doña Isabel?
3. ¿Crees que doña Isabel debe hacer lo que quiere su hijo? ¿Por qué sí o por qué no?

Paso 2 Basándote en las respuestas del **Paso 1**, ¿qué adjetivos usarías (*would you use*) para describir a doña Isabel?

Actividad B ¡A verificar!

Vas a ver otra vez la escena de **¡A escuchar!** en la página anterior. Llena los espacios en blanco, según lo que oyes.

Act. B, Suggestion: Replay the scene once for students. Replay a second time if needed. Then ask for volunteers to provide the answers for each blank. Verify using the instructor notes from Act. B on the previous page.
Alternative: After students complete the conversation, have 2 students act it out.

Actividad C Un día perfecto

Paso 1 Este episodio se titula «Un día perfecto». Con un compañero (una compañera), contesten las siguientes preguntas.

1. ¿Para quién fue un día perfecto? ¿Fue perfecto para Jaime? ¿para María? ¿para los dos?
2. En su opinión, ¿por qué fue un día perfecto?
3. ¿Creen Uds. que van a experimentar (*experience*) más «días perfectos»? ¿Por qué sí o por qué no?

Paso 2 Con la misma persona, comparen el día perfecto de Jaime con el día de su llegada a Santiago. Utilicen algunos verbos de estado o condiciones como **querer, tener, estar,** etcétera.

MODELO: Cuando Jaime llegó a Santiago, no conocía a nadie, pero ahora tiene una amiga.

Detrás de la cámara

Did you notice who kissed whom first in this episode? As you have seen in previous episodes, Jaime is someone who likes to be in control of situations; however, his budding relationship with María is different. She seems to be the one in control. Although Jaime is not used to a woman taking the initiative in relationships, he doesn't complain!

RESUMEN DE VOCABULARIO

Eventos históricos e importantes	
colonizar (c)	to colonize
conquistar	to conquer
descubrir	to discover
establecer (zc)	to establish
explorar	to explore
invadir	to invade
los años veinte (treinta)	the 20s (30s) (*decades*)
la conquista	conquest
la década	decade
el desastre natural	natural disaster
el descubrimiento	discovery
el encuentro	encounter; meeting
la fecha	date (*calendar*)
la fundación	founding
la guerra	war
el huracán	hurricane
la inundación	flood
la llegada	arrival
el siglo (XXI)	(the 21st) century
el terremoto	earthquake

Cognados: la depresión (económica), la exploración, la independencia, el/la inmigrante, la invasión, la migración, la revolución

Eventos personales	
casarse (con)	to get married (to)
divertirse (ie, i)	to have fun
divorciarse (de)	to get divorced (from)
fracasar	to fail
graduarse (me gradúo)	to graduate
mudarse	to move (*to a new house*)
nacer (zc)	to be born
tener (*irreg.*) éxito	to succeed, be successful
la boda	wedding
el divorcio	divorce
el éxito	success
el fracaso	failure
la graduación	graduation
el matrimonio	marriage
la mudanza	move (*to a new house*)
la muerte	death
el nacimiento	birth
el/la novio/a	groom, bride
el/la recién nacido/a	newborn baby

Repaso: celebrar, morir (ue, u), pasarlo bien/mal, sentirse (ie, i)

Adjetivos

ansioso/a	anxious
contento/a	happy
deprimido/a	depressed
difícil	difficult
emocionante	exciting
enojado/a	angry
estable	stable
feliz (*pl.* **felices**)	happy
nervioso/a	nervous
orgulloso/a (de)	proud (of)
oscuro/a	dark; scary
pacífico/a	peaceful
tumultuoso/a	tumultuous; unstable

Repaso: triste

Los números del 1.000 al 2.000.000

dos (tres,...) mil, diez mil, cien mil, doscientos mil, trescientos mil, cuatrocientos mil, quinientos mil, seiscientos mil, setecientos mil, ochocientos mil, novecientos mil, un millón (de), dos millones (de)
Repaso: mil

Otras palabras y expresiones

al + *infin.*	upon/while/when (*doing something*)
mientras	while

Entremés cultural
Centroamérica: Riquezas[a] de hoy y de ayer

VISTAZO

Centroamérica es una larga zona geográfica que se extiende desde la frontera[b] sur de México hasta la frontera noroeste de Colombia en Sudamérica. Además de los países de Costa Rica, El Salvador, Guatemala, Honduras, Nicaragua y Panamá, en esta parte del continente americano se localiza Belice, un país de habla inglesa, antigua colonia de Gran Bretaña. La extensión territorial de Centroamérica es un poco más grande que la de California, pero tiene una gran diversidad geográfica: volcanes[c] activos (más de setenta), selvas[d] tropicales y playas[e] conocidas en todo el mundo. Centroamérica también posee mucha diversidad étnica. Guatemala tiene una población indígena de más de seis millones de habitantes, en la que todavía está muy presente la herencia cultural de la civilización maya. En cambio, en Costa Rica, se ve muy poca influencia indígena en la vida cotidiana.[f]

[a]*Riches* [b]*border* [c]*volcanoes* [d]*jungles* [e]*beaches* [f]vida... *daily life*

DATO INTERESANTE:
La civilización maya

La cultura maya forma parte de la tela[a] cultural del norte de Centroamérica desde hace más de tres mil años.[b] Durante el período clásico de los mayas (los años 320 a 987 d.C.) se construyeron[c] ciudades y centros ceremoniales como Tikal en Guatemala y Copán en Honduras. Hoy estos lugares constituyen algunas de las zonas arqueológicas más impresionantes[d] de las civilizaciones precolombinas. Se dice que la civilización maya desapareció[e] antes de la llegada de los españoles al continente americano. Sin embargo, esta información no es del todo correcta.[f] De hecho,[g] todavía existen millones de indígenas mayas en la zona y hablan 26 lenguas diferentes, pero de la misma familia lingüística. Para muchos hablantes de estas lenguas, el español es su segundo idioma.

El mercado famoso de Chichicastenango, Guatemala

[a]*fabric* [b]desde... *for more than 3,000 years* [c]*se... were constructed* [d]*impressive* [e]*disappeared* [f]*no... isn't completely correct* [g]*De... In fact* [h]*challenges*

Las ruinas de Tikal, en Guatemala

IDEA: Busca información sobre la situación de los grupos mayas hoy en Centroamérica y compárala con la situación de los indígenas en este país. ¿Qué problemas y/o desafíos[h] tienen los indígenas de las dos regiones?

DATO INTERESANTE:

Las riquezas naturales

Centroamérica se considera un paraíso[a] natural. Aunque el istmo[b] geográfico que une los segmentos norte y sur del continente está formado por menos del 0,5% de la tierra firme mundial, contiene entre el 7 y el 8% de toda la biodiversidad (plantas y animales) del mundo. Desafortunadamente, esta biodiversidad está en peligro[c] a causa de los incendios[d] forestales provocados por agricultores[e] que desean ganar más terrenos de cultivo.

> **IDEA:** Busca información sobre la protección de la biodiversidad en Centroamérica. ¿Qué hacen los gobiernos centroamericanos para proteger[f] las selvas tropicales?

[a]*paradise* [b]*isthmus (narrow strip of land)* [c]*danger* [d]*fires*
[e]*farmers* [f]*protect*

La biodiversidad es una gran atracción turística en Centroamérica.

La educación es muy importante en Costa Rica, un país con una alta tasa de alfabetización (*high literacy rate*).

DATO INTERESANTE:

La educación en Costa Rica

Costa Rica tiene una de las democracias más estables de toda América. Además, desde 1948 no tiene ejército[a] e invierte[b] mucho dinero en la educación. De hecho, la tasa de alfabetización en este país es del 95%, la tercera tasa más grande de Latinoamérica después de la Argentina y Cuba.

> **IDEA:** Busca información sobre la educación en Costa Rica, concentrándote en los siguientes temas: el costo de la educación, la enseñanza[c] de lenguas extranjeras, el sistema universitario y cualquier otro tema. Trae la información a la clase.

[a]*army* [b]*it invests* [c]*teaching*

DATO INTERESANTE:

El Canal de Panamá

El Canal de Panamá se encuentra en el punto más estrecho[a] que separa el mar Caribe y el océano Pacífico. La construcción del canal constituyó uno de los proyectos de ingeniería más ambiciosos de la historia. Aunque el canal se abrió oficialmente en 1914, la idea de construir un canal en el istmo centroamericano existía desde mucho antes. Ya en 1534, el Rey de España, el emperador[b] Carlos I, había sugerido[c] que la construcción de un canal en Panamá facilitaría[d] los viajes entre España y el Perú.

> **IDEA:** Busca información sobre el Canal de Panamá, concentrándose en los siguientes temas: problemas durante la construcción, los peajes[e] que se pagan para pasar por el canal y desafíos actuales.[f]

El Canal de Panamá une el mar Caribe con el océano Pacífico.

[a]*más... narrowest* [b]*emperor* [c]*había... had suggested* [d]*would make easier* [e]*tolls* [f]*desafíos... current challenges*

Confrontación

En este episodio...

JAIME

¡La verdad es que no tiene nada! ¡Mi compañía quiere estas tierras!

CARLOS

Por favor, espere un par de días más. Se las voy a conseguir.

JAIME

Tenemos que firmar el contrato esta semana... ¡y Ud. no tiene la influencia necesaria!

¿Qué crees tú?

1. Describe el estado de ánimo (*state of mind*) de Jaime. ¿Está contento? ¿furioso?

2. ¿Por qué vacila (*is hesitating*) Carlos? En realidad, ¿crees que tiene la autoridad de negociar las tierras de su familia?

3. ¿Qué va a pasar si Carlos no consigue las firmas de su madre y de su hermana?

Vamos al extranjero[a]

OBJETIVOS

IN THIS LESSON, YOU WILL LEARN:

- vocabulary related to taking trips and traveling

- how to give someone instructions using formal commands

- vocabulary related to giving and receiving directions

- vocabulary related to restaurants and ordering food

- to talk about what has happened using the present perfect

You will also prepare for and watch **Episodio 6** of the film *Sol y viento*.

El Aeropuerto Internacional de Maiquetía «Simón Bolívar» en Caracas, Venezuela

[a]al... *abroad*

The following media resources are available for this lesson of *Sol y viento*:

Episodio 6 of *Sol y viento*

Online *Manual de actividades*

Online Learning Center Website

PRIMERA PARTE

Vocabulario

Talking About
Taking Trips and
Traveling

Para hacer viajes

✳ **Travel Vocabulary**

Note: These vocabulary items can be heard in this lesson's Textbook Audio section of the Online Learning Center Website.

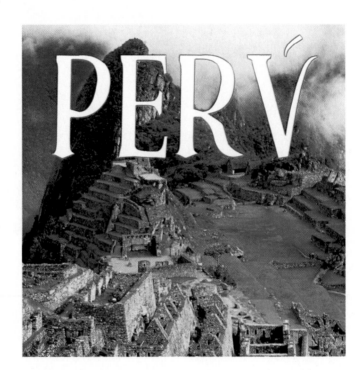

PERÚ

DESPIERTA · TUS · SEIS · SENTIDOS

El transporte

el autobús	bus
el avión	airplane
el barco	boat

En la agencia de viajes

el/la agente de viajes	travel agent
el boleto*	ticket
de ida	one-way
de ida y vuelta	round-trip
la clase turística	coach
el pasaporte	passport
la primera clase	first class
la reservación	reservation

En el aeropuerto

el asiento	seat
el/la asistente de vuelo	flight attendant
el equipaje	luggage
el maletero	skycap, porter
el/la pasajero/a	passenger
la sala de espera	waiting area
el/la viajero/a	traveler
el vuelo (directo)	(direct) flight

---

*El boleto** is used throughout Latin America, whereas **el billete** is used in Spain.

✳ MÁS VOCABULARIO

bajar (de)	to get off (of)
facturar el equipaje	to check luggage
hacer (*irreg.*) **cola**	to wait in line
hacer (*irreg.*) **escala**	to make a stopover
hacer (*irreg.*) **la maleta**	to pack a suitcase
hacer (*irreg.*) **un viaje**	to take a trip
ir (*irreg.*) **al extranjero**	to go abroad
marearse	to get nauseated, sick (*in a boat, car, plane*)
pasar por la aduana	to go through customs
pasar por seguridad	to go through security
subir (a)	to board, get on

◄
En el sur de España se nota la influencia árabe en la arquitectura, como en este hotel en Marbella.

El alojamiento^a

ᵃEl... *Lodging*

alojarse / quedarse	to stay (*in a place*)
el botones*	bellhop
la cama matrimonial	double bed
la cama sencilla	single bed
la habitación	room
con baño (privado)	with (private) bathroom
el hotel (de lujo)	(luxury) hotel
la pensión	boardinghouse
completa	room and all meals
la media pensión	room and one other meal (usually breakfast)
la propina	tip
el servicio de cuarto	room service

---

*__El mozo__ is also commonly used to mean *bellhop*.

INPUT
Act. A, Statements:
a. *ir al extranjero*
b. *el pasaporte*
c. *marearse*
d. *el maletero*
e. *la asistente de vuelo*
f. *la sala de espera*
g. *hacer escala*

Actividad A El transporte

Escucha lo que dice tu profesor(a) y luego indica la definición que corresponde a cada frase.

1. __e__ la persona que sirve las bebidas en el avión
2. __g__ cuando un vuelo no es directo
3. __c__ ponerse enfermo/a en un auto o avión
4. __b__ el documento que se presenta al pasar por la aduana de otro país
5. __f__ el lugar donde uno se queda antes de subir al avión
6. __a__ viajar a otro país
7. __d__ la persona que te ayuda con el equipaje

INPUT
Actividad B

Actividad B ¿En qué orden?

Indica en qué orden (del 1 al 12) sueles hacer los siguientes preparativos para un viaje en avión.

__5__ Hago cola para pasar por seguridad.
__9__ Le pido una almohada (*pillow*) al asistente de vuelo.
__1__ Hago la reservación.
__2__ Hago la maleta.
__10__ Me duermo durante el vuelo.
__3__ Llego al aeropuerto.
__8__ Busco mi asiento en el avión.
__4__ Facturo el equipaje con el maletero.
__11__ Llego a mi destino (*destination*).
__6__ Tomo asiento en la sala de espera.
__7__ Hago cola antes de subir al avión.
__12__ Bajo del avión.

OUTPUT
Act. C, *Paso 2,*
Suggestion: After students work in pairs, call on different pairs to present their sentences and write them in two columns on the chalkboard or on a transparency. Then poll the class on the statements in the student column to see if they reflect the tendency of your class. Examples: *¿Cuántos de Uds. hacen las reservaciones en Priceline o Expedia para ahorrar dinero? ¿Cuántos de Uds. toman vuelos con escala porque salen más baratos que los vuelos directos?*

Actividad C ¿Cómo viajan?

Paso 1 Haz una lista de cinco cosas que hace un hombre de negocios (*businessman*) cuando viaja y otra lista de cinco cosas que hace un estudiante típico cuando viaja.

MODELOS: Cuando hace escala, espera en el club de la línea áerea, no en la sala de espera.

Viaja en auto si sale más barato que viajar en avión.

Paso 2 Léele tus oraciones en orden mixta (*random order*) a un compañero (una compañera) de clase. ¿Puede decir a quién se refieren?

MODELO: E1: Viaja en auto si sale más barato que viajar en avión.
E2: Un estudiante.
E1: ¡Correcto!

Actividad D ¿Conoces bien al profesor (a la profesora)?

Paso 1 Indica si las siguientes oraciones sobre tu profesor(a) son ciertas (C) or falsas (F), según tu opinión.

Mi profesor(a) de español...	CIERTO	FALSO
1. viaja en primera clase con frecuencia.	☐	☐
2. se aloja en hoteles de lujo cuando viaja.	☐	☐
3. se marea cuando viaja en avión o auto.	☐	☐
4. pide servicio de cuarto en los hoteles.	☐	☐
5. ha hecho autostop (*has hitchhiked*).	☐	☐
6. ha perdido (*has lost*) un boleto del avión.	☐	☐
7. le pide una bebida alcohólica al asistente de vuelo.	☐	☐
8. se lleva las toallas (*towels*), el jabón o el champú de los hoteles.	☐	☐
9. ha hecho (*has taken*) un viaje en barco.	☐	☐
10. no viaja nunca en autobús.	☐	☐

Paso 2 La clase va a entrevistar al profesor (a la profesora) para saber si hace las actividades del **Paso 1**. Usen **tú** o **Ud.,** según la preferencia de su profesor(a). Anoten sus respuestas.

MODELO: ¿Viaja Ud. / Viajas en primera clase con frecuencia?

≋ Vistazo cultural

Las propinas

La costumbre[a] de dar propinas varía mucho de país a país. En los hoteles de este país se les dan propinas a los botones cuando ayudan al cliente con el equipaje o cuando le consiguen un taxi. Sin embargo, no es tan común dejarle propina al personal de limpieza.[b] En México, al contrario, es muy buena costumbre darle propina al personal de limpieza, sea[c] en un hotel barato o en un hotel de lujo. Esta costumbre también se practica en los países asiáticos como el Japón y la China, pero de manera muy discreta: el cliente pone la propina en un sobre[d] y lo deja en la habitación.

En cuanto al transporte, los taxistas hispanos por lo general no esperan[e] propina a menos que ayuden al[f] cliente con las maletas. Los taxistas norteamericanos suelen recibir propinas del 10 ó 15 por ciento. En el aeropuerto Changi de Singapur, sin embargo, es ilegal darles propinas a los maleteros, y en las islas Fiji y Salomón, darle una propina a alguien quiere decir que esa persona te debe[g] algo.

Como se puede ver, cuando se trata de propinas, tanto el dar como el no dar puede ser causa de gran ofensa. Si estás en un país hispano y tienes dudas[h] en cuanto a la manera apropiada de dar propinas, pregúntale a un nativo del país.

[a]*custom* [b]*personal... cleaning staff* [c]*whether it be* [d]*envelope* [e]*expect* [f]*a... unless they help the* [g]*owes* [h]*doubts*

Gramática

Giving
Instructions | **Vuelva Ud. mañana.**   **Affirmative Formal Commands**

—**Recuerde** Ud.: Como va al extranjero, **llegue** al aeropuerto con dos horas de anticipación (*two hours in advance*) antes de la salida de su vuelo.

Affirmative formal commands (**los mandatos formales**) directed at one person (**Ud.**) are formed by taking the **yo** form of the present-tense indicative, dropping the **-o** or **-oy** ending, and adding the "opposite" vowel. If the verb is an **-ar** verb, the opposite vowel is **-e.** If the verb is an **-er** or **-ir** verb, the opposite vowel is **-a,** as indicated in the chart. Commands directed at more than one person (**Uds.**) add **-en** to **-ar** verbs and **-an** to **-er** and **-ir** verbs.

Hable más despacio, por favor.	*Speak more slowly, please.*
Abra la puerta.	*Open the door.*
Vengan (Uds.) para las 2:00.	*Come at around 2:00.*

Verbs ending in **-car, -gar,** and **-zar** have a spelling change in order to maintain the original pronunciation of the **-c, -g,** and **-z** sounds.

Busque en el cajón.	*Look in the drawer.*
Paguen en la caja.	*Pay at the cashier.*
Empiecen ahora.	*Begin now.*

Ir and **ser** have irregular command forms.

Vaya para allá.	*Go over there.*
Sean pacientes.	*Be patient.*

The formal **Ud.** command for **dar** requires a written accent to distinguish it from the preposition **de.**

Dé un paseo por el parque.	*Take a walk through the park.*

Estar requires an accent on both **Ud.** and **Uds.** forms.

Esté aquí a mediodía.	*Be here at noon.*
Estén tranquilos.	*Be calm.*

Direct and indirect object pronouns, as well as reflexive pronouns, are attached to the end of affirmative formal commands. Remember that when both a direct and an indirect object pronoun are used, indirect objects come before direct objects. Note the written accents, which indicate where the stress would normally fall on the verb if there were no pronouns included.

¿La tarea? **Háganla.**	*The homework? Do it.*
Despiértense.	*Wake up.*
¿El libro? **Démelo.**	*The book? Give it to me.*

FORMAL COMMANDS				
INFINITIVE	**yo** FORM	STEM	ADD THE "OPPOSITE" VOWEL FOR **Ud.**	ADD THE "OPPOSITE" VOWEL AND **-n** FOR **Uds.**
hablar	hablo	habl-	+ e = **hable**	**hablen**
beber	bebo	beb-	+ a = **beba**	**beban**
abrir	abro	abr-	+ a = **abra**	**abran**
decir	digo	dig-	+ a = **diga**	**digan**
conducir	conduzco	conduzc-	+ a = **conduzca**	**conduzcan**
VERBS ENDING IN *-car*, *-gar*, AND *-zar*				
INFINITIVE	**yo** FORM	STEM	SPELLING CHANGES BEFORE ADDING THE "OPPOSITE" VOWEL FOR **Ud.**	ADD THE "OPPOSITE" VOWEL AND **-n** FOR **Uds.**
sacar	saco	sac-	c → qu + e = **saque**	**saquen**
pagar	pago	pag-	g → gu + e = **pague**	**paguen**
comenzar	comienzo	comienz-	z → c + e = **comience**	**comiencen**

De *Sol y viento*, Note: You can access this film clip from a special menu section on Disc 5 of the Instructional Version on DVD.

DE SOL Y VIENTO

In **Episodio 6** of *Sol y viento* you will watch a scene in which a new character, don Francisco (Paco) Aguilar, buys vegetables in a Mexico City street market. Part of his conversation with Lourdes, a vendor, is repeated in the dialogue.

PACO
¡Estos sí que son jitomates![a] ¡Firmes y de buen color! Así me gustan.

LOURDES
Como le dije: los mejores del mercado.

PACO
_____ dos kilos, por favor.

Selecting from the following list, what command do you think don Paco says in this scene?

1. Págueme
2. Cómpreme
3. Déme

[a]*red tomatoes (Mex.)*

Actividad E ¿A quién se lo diría Jaime (*would Jaime say it to*)?

Desde el principio (*beginning*) de la película hasta finales del **Episodio 5,** Jaime les habla de Ud. a los otros personajes. Basándote en lo que sabes de Jaime hasta ahora, indica a quién le diría cada mandato a continuación.

1. Tenga este regalo. Es para Ud.   Se lo diría a ___María___.
2. Lléveme al Valle del Maipo, por favor.   Se lo diría a ___Mario___.
3. Déme el contrato firmado.   Se lo diría a ___Carlos___.
4. Hábleme de su trabajo aquí en la viña.   Se lo diría a ___Traimaqueo___.

Actividad F Una receta (*recipe*)

A continuación hay una receta para preparar una ensalada de frutas. Ordena las instrucciones lógicamente, del 1 al 7.

Vocabulario útil

cortar	to cut
pelar	to peel
los pedacitos	small pieces
el tazón	large bowl

___6___ Ponga el tazón en el refrigerador por dos horas.
___3___ Pele las bananas y naranjas antes de cortarlas.
___2___ Lave las frutas con agua fría.
___7___ Sirva la ensalada bien fría.
___4___ Corte las manzanas, naranjas y bananas en pedacitos.
___1___ Compre manzanas, naranjas, bananas y uvas en el supermercado.
___5___ Ponga las frutas cortadas y las uvas en un tazón.

Actividad G En mi ciudad

Paso 1 Lee la lista de instrucciones e indica si cada una se dirige a (*is directed at*) un turista que visita Los Ángeles o a un turista que visita Nueva York.

	LOS ÁNGELES	NUEVA YORK
1. Visite la Estatua de la Libertad.	☐	☑
2. Dé un paseo por el Camino de la Fama en Hollywood.	☑	☐
3. Pase por las mansiones de Beverly Hills.	☑	☐
4. Vea un espectáculo (*show*) en Broadway.	☐	☑
5. Corra en el Parque Central.	☐	☑
6. Asista a un partido de los Lakers.	☑	☐

Paso 2 Usa mandatos afirmativos para hacer una lista de las seis cosas que un turista debe hacer si hace un viaje a tu ciudad u otra ciudad que conoces bien. Presenta tus resultados a la clase.

Nombre de la ciudad: _____

Paso 3 (Optativo) Usa los mandatos del **Paso 2** para crear un folleto (*brochure*) para viajeros a tu ciudad.

Actividad H Situaciones y recomendaciones

Tu professor(a) va a presentarles varias situaciones en que se encuentran muchos viajeros de avión. En grupos de tres, tienen dos minutos para escribir recomendaciones usando mandatos afirmativos. El grupo con más recomendaciones para cada situación gana.

MODELO: (*you see*): No nos gusta hacer cola en el aeropuerto.
(*you write*): Lleguen temprano.
Llévense pocas maletas.
Facturen el equipaje con el maletero.
Saquen los boletos y pasaportes antes de pasar por seguridad.

◀

¡Saque su identificación antes de pasar por seguridad!

Actividad I Consejos para los profesores

Paso 1 En grupos de tres, escriban cuatro consejos afirmativos sobre lo que los profesores deben hacer para llevarse bien con los estudiantes.

MODELO: Lleguen a clase a tiempo.

Paso 2 Presenten su lista a la clase. La clase va a decidir cuáles son las instrucciones más importantes.

Note: These vocabulary items can be heard in this lesson's Textbook Audio section of the Online Learning Center Website.

Vocabulario

Getting Around Town | **¿Cómo llego?**

Giving and Receiving Directions

Cruce la calle.	Cross the street.
Doble a la derecha.	Turn right.
Doble a la izquierda.	Turn left.
Siga derecho.	Go straight.
¿Cómo se llega a... ?	How do you get to . . . ?
¿Cuánto hay de aquí a... ?	How far is it to . . . ?

✳ MÁS VOCABULARIO

cruzar (c)	to cross
doblar	to turn
seguir (i, i) (g) derecho	to continue, go straight
la cuadra / la manzana	block
el mapa	map (*in general*)
el plano	city map

Repaso: el norte, el sur, el este, el oeste

 # Vistazo cultural

¿A cuántas curvas está?

Como en los países hispanos se usa el sistema métrico, las distancias se dan en kilómetros, no en millas. En las áreas montañosas de Chile, el Perú y otros países andinos, las carreteras[a] son muy sinuosas.[b] En estas regiones las distancias se dan en **curvas** y no en kilómetros. Si le preguntas a un andino: «Cuánto hay de aquí al pico[c] de la montaña?», es probable que te diga[d] algo como: «Está a 22 curvas.» Es decir, hay que dar la vuelta a 22 curvas para llegar al destino final.

Debido a[e] las carreteras sinuosas, es muy peligroso[f] conducir en los Andes y son frecuentes los accidentes. El Perú emplea un sistema de señales preventivas[g] para advertirles[h] de curvas peligrosas a los conductores.

Estas son sólo unas de las muchas señales que uno debe conocer para conducir con cautela[i] en las montañas de Sudamérica. ¿Crees que eres lo suficientemente aventurero/a para conducir en los Andes?

[a]*highways* [b]*winding* [c]*top* [d]*es... he will probably tell you* [e]*Debido... Due to* [f]*dangerous* [g]*señales... warning signs* [h]*warn (them)* [i]*caution*

INPUT
Act. A, Suggestion:
Choose five sites from
the map and create direc-
tions on how to get to
each one. Before you
read the directions, start
out by saying ¿Adónde
vamos? Then give direc-
tions. Make sure you
clearly indicate the starting point. After finishing
the directions, say
¿Dónde estamos? The
class will respond with
the site you have led
them to.
Optional follow-up: Put
students in groups of 2
and then write 3 pairs of
sites on the board that
you did not give
directions to earlier. Have
students write out direc-
tions on how to get to
these sites. Call on
groups to read their
instructions while the rest
of the class checks to see
if they are correct.

Actividad A ¿Adónde vamos?

Mira el siguiente plano de Alameda, un barrio conocido (*well-known*) de México, D.F. Tu profesor(a) va a leer una serie de direcciones. Sigue sus direcciones e indica cuál es el punto de llegada. Primero, estudia las siguientes abreviaturas (*abbreviations*).

Av.	Avenida
Fco.	Francisco
Pte.	Poniente (*West*)
Rep.	República

MODELO: PROFESOR(A): ¿Adónde vamos? Comiencen en el Hotel Ambassador. Sigan derecho hacia el norte en la calle Humboldt. Doblen a la derecha y sigan derecho dos cuadras. Doblen a la izquierda en la calle Doctor Mora. Sigan derecho una cuadra y media. El edificio queda a la izquierda. ¿Dónde estamos?

ESTUDIANTES: Estamos en la Pinacoteca Virreinal.

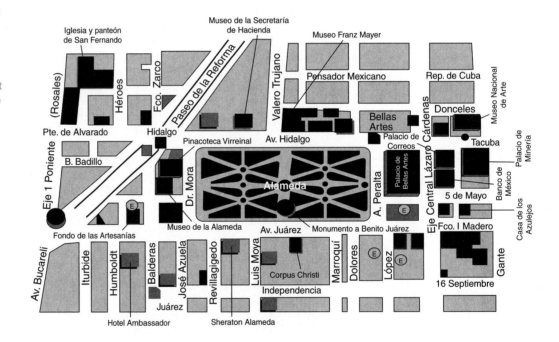

Actividad B ¿En qué sentido (*direction*)?

Escucha las descripciones que da tu profesor(a) e indica si son ciertas o falsas.

1. ... **2.** ... **3.** ... **4.** ... **5.** ... **6.** ... **7.** ... **8.** ...

INPUT
Act. B, Statements:
1. *San Francisco está al oeste de Chicago.* (*C*)
2. *Texas está al sur de México.* (*F, Está al norte de México.*)
3. *Atlanta está al este de Miami.* (*F, Está al oeste de Miami.*)
4. *El Canadá está al norte de los Estados Unidos.* (*C*)
5. *Chile está al oeste de la Argentina.* (*C*)
6. *España está al sur de Francia.* (*C*)

Desafíos:
7. *Puerto Rico está al este de Cuba.* (*C*)
8. *La República Dominicana está al este de Puerto Rico.* (*F, Está al oeste de Puerto Rico.*)

Actividad C ¿Cierto o falso?

Paso 1 Escribe seis oraciones sobre cómo ir de un lugar a otro en tu campus (o en la ciudad que rodea tu universidad). Tres oraciones deben ser verdaderas (*true*) y tres falsas.

MODELOS: Para ir de Jester Hall a la biblioteca Perry Castañeda, uno cruza la calle 21.
Para ir de Water Tower Place a Nordstrom, uno sigue derecho en la calle Michigan hacia el sur...

Paso 2 Léele sus oraciones a un compañero (una compañera) de clase. ¿Sabe cuáles son ciertas y cuáles son falsas?

MODELO: E1: Para ir de Jester Hall a la biblioteca Perry Castañeda, uno cruza la calle 21.
E2: Falso. Uno cruza la calle Speedway.

Actividad D ¿Conoce el campus mi profesor(a)?

Paso 1 En grupos de tres, piensen en un edificio o sitio muy conocido de su campus, pero no lo mencionen. Luego, escriban instrucciones sobre cómo llegar a ese edificio o sitio. Las instrucciones deben ser apropiadas para dárselas a una persona que visita el campus.

MODELO: Ud. está enfrente de la biblioteca. Siga derecho en la calle Speedway. Doble a la derecha en la calle Randolf. Doble a la izquierda en Riverside y cruce la calle.

Paso 2 Los grupos van a leerle las instrucciones al profesor (a la profesora) a ver si él/ella puede adivinar el punto de llegada. ¿Conoce muy bien el campus su profesor(a)?

▲ La Universidad de Cartagena (Cartagena, Colombia).

NAVEGANDO LA RED

Busca un mapa del viaje (de los viajes) que hizo un explorador español al Nuevo Mundo (por ejemplo: Álvar Núñez Cabeza de Vaca, Hernán Cortés, Francisco Pizarro, Ponce de León, Hernando de Soto) y describe una de las rutas de su expedición.

Gramática

¡No vuelvan tarde!

Negative Formal Commands

FORMAL COMMANDS USED WITH OBJECT AND REFLEXIVE PRONOUNS			
AFFIRMATIVE FORMAL COMMANDS **PRONOUNS ARE ATTACHED TO THE END**		**NEGATIVE FORMAL COMMANDS** **PRONOUNS COME BEFORE THE VERB**	
Háble**le**.	*Talk to him* (*her*).	No **le** hable.	*Don't talk to him* (*her*).
Cómpren**la**.	*Buy it.* (*it* = la comida)	No **la** compren.	*Don't buy it.*
Dé**melo**.	*Give me it.* (*it* = el libro)	No **me lo** dé.	*Don't give it to me.*
Siénten**se**.	*Sit down.*	No **se** sienten.	*Don't sit down.*

Negative formal commands are formed in the same way as affirmative commands. Drop the **-o** or **-oy** from the first-person form (**yo**) of the present-tense indicative and add the "opposite" vowel, plus an additional **-n** for plural (**Uds.**) forms. Remember: **ir** and **ser** have irregular formal command forms; the **Ud.** commands for **dar** and **estar** require written accent marks, as does the **Uds.** command for **estar.**

No lleguen tarde.	*Don't arrive late.*
No vaya sin mí.	*Don't go without me.*
No sean ridículos.	*Don't be ridiculous.*

The principal difference between affirmative and negative formal commands is the placement of object and reflexive pronouns. These pronouns come *before* negative command forms, not after them. When both a direct and an indirect object are used, the indirect object pronoun precedes the direct object pronoun, as indicated in the chart.

No me mire así.	*Don't look at me that way.*
No me lo dé ahora, por favor.	*Don't give it to me now, please.*
No se despierten tarde.	*Don't wake up late.*

COMUNICACIÓN ÚTIL

Formal commands can also be used to express what you want yourself and others to do (or not to do) together, as in *Let's make a toast* or *Let's not go out tonight*. These types of commands (often called **nosotros** commands) are formed by dropping the **-o** or **-oy** from the first-person form of the present-tense indicative and adding the "opposite" vowel plus **-mos**. The irregular forms for **ir** and **ser** can be used in this way too.

¡Comamos!	*Let's eat!*
Hablemos en serio.	*Let's talk seriously.*
No lo **molestemos**.	*Let's not bother him.*
No **seamos** pesimistas.	*Let's not be pessimistic.*
Vayamos a lo nuestro.	*Let's get back to our business.*

Cómo viajar en avión sin problemas

- Verifique el estatus de su vuelo antes de ir al aeropuerto.
- Llegue al aeropuerto con dos horas de anticipación.[a]
- Escriba su nombre y dirección en todas las maletas.
- Quítese las joyas[b] antes de pasar por seguridad.
- No ponga cosas frágiles en la maleta.
- No haga más maletas de las que pueda llevar.
- No se olvide de llevar su teléfono celular para emergencias.
- No descuide[c] su equipaje.

[a]con... *two hours in advance* [b]*jewelry* [c]*leave unattended*

De *Sol y viento,* **Note:** You can access this film clip from a special menu section on Disc 5 of the Instructional Version on DVD.

DE SOL Y VIENTO

In **Episodio 3** of *Sol y viento* you will recall a scene in which Carlos barks out some orders to his workers after inviting Jaime to his office to talk. Part of his dialogue appears here.

CARLOS
¿Por qué no vamos a mi oficina para tener así más privacidad? ¡Traimaqueo! _____ y sigan trabajando ¡Ya vuelvo!

Do you remember what Carlos says to his workers?

1. No presten atención (*Don't pay attention*)
2. No se distraigan (*Don't get distracted*)
3. No me molesten (*Don't bother me*)

Actividad E ¿A quién se lo diría?

Basándote en lo que sabes de los personajes de *Sol y viento*, indica a quién Jaime le diría cada mandato a continuación.

1. No me dé más pretextos (*excuses*).
   Necesito las firmas.

   Se lo diría a __Carlos__.

2. No se limite solamente a carteles.
   Haga una campaña (*campaign*) efectiva
   para ayudar a los mapuches.

   Se lo diría a __María__.

3. No me deje (*drop me off*) en el hotel.
   Déjeme en el parque.

   Se lo diría a __Mario__.

COMUNICACIÓN ÚTIL

Direct commands can sometimes sound rude in certain contexts. One way to soften the force of a command is to use the phrase **¿Me hace el favor de... ?** followed by an infinitive, instead of a direct command.

¿Me hace el favor de abrir la ventana? Can you do me the favor of opening the window?

Favor de + *infinitive* is commonly used for instructions on street signs aimed at the general public.

Favor de no fumar. *Please don't smoke.*

Actividad F ¿Niños o adolescentes?

Lee la siguiente lista de algunos consejos que los padres suelen darles a sus hijos. Luego, indica si cada consejo es para los niños, para los adolescentes o para los dos.

	NIÑOS	ADOLESCENTES	LOS DOS
1. No coman comida chatarra (*junk food*).	☐	☐	☐
2. No corran con tijeras (*scissors*) en la mano.	☐	☐	☐
3. No se sienten cerca del televisor.	☐	☐	☐
4. No conduzcan bajo la influencia del alcohol.	☐	☐	☐
5. No hablen con desconocidos (*strangers*).	☐	☐	☐
6. No salten (*jump*) en la cama.	☐	☐	☐
7. No crucen la calle sin mirar primero en ambos sentidos (*both directions*).	☐	☐	☐
8. No salgan de la casa con el pelo mojado (*wet*) o se van a enfermar.	☐	☐	☐

Actividad G La etiqueta del uso de los teléfonos celulares

Paso 1 Con un compañero (una compañera), hagan una lista de consejos diri-
gidos (*directed*) a un consumidor sobre la etiqueta apropiada en cuanto al uso
de los teléfonos celulares en lugares públicos. Usen por lo menos tres mandatos negativos y tres mandatos afirmativos, según el modelo.

Vocabulario útil

apagar	to turn off
contestar	to answer
el correo de voz	voicemail
hacer una llamada	to make a call
el mensaje de texto	text message
prender	to turn on
el tono de timbre	ringtone

MODELOS: No seleccione un tono de timbre irritante (*annoying*).
Apáguelo antes de entrar al cine.

Paso 2 Presenten su lista a la clase. ¿Están todos de acuerdo en cuanto a qué
constituye buena etiqueta?

Paso 3 Como clase, hagan una lista de reglas (*rules*) sobre el uso de los
teléfonos celulares en la clase de español.

MODELO: No lean mensajes de texto durante exámenes.

Actividad H En el extranjero

Paso 1 Con un compañero (una compañera), diseñen (*design*) un folleto
(*brochure*) en el cual indican lo que un turista norteamericano debe o no debe
hacer cuando viaja al extranjero. Mencionen cinco cosas que debe hacer (con
mandatos afirmativos) y cinco cosas que no debe hacer (con mandatos negativos).

Paso 2 Entreguen su folleto al profesor (a la profesora). Su profesor(a) va a
leer algunos mandatos a la clase. Entre todos, indiquen si cada consejo es válido
para **todos los países** que visita o sólo para **algunos países.**

MODELO: PROFESOR(A): Pídales direcciones a los nativos.
TODOS: Para todos los países.
PROFESOR(A): No beba agua del grifo (*tap water*).
TODOS: Para algunos países.

TERCERA PARTE

Note: These vocabulary items can be heard in this lesson's Textbook Audio section of the Online Learning Center Website.

Ordering Meals in a Restaurant

Vocabulario

En el restaurante

Dining Out

la mesera

el cocinero

el mesero

la taza

el menú*

la copa

el plato

la servilleta

el cuchillo   la cuchara

el vaso   el tenedor

Los vinos y licores se sirven en **copas,** pero el agua, los refrescos, la leche y otras bebidas frías se sirven en **vasos.** Las bebidas calientes se sirven en **tazas.** Por eso, cuando se habla de las bebidas, se dice **una copa** de vino, **un vaso** de agua y **una taza** de café.

---

*La carta** is also used for *menu.*

MÁS VOCABULARIO

los cubiertos	silverware
la cuenta	bill, check (*in a restaurant*)
el primer (segundo, tercer) plato	first (second, third) course
atender (ie)	to wait on
dejar (una) propina	to leave a tip
ordenar / pedir (i, i)	to order
traer (*irreg.*)	to bring
¿Me podría traer... ?	Could you bring me . . . ?
¿Qué trae... ?	What does . . . come with?

 # Vistazo cultural

En los restaurantes hispanos

Comer en un restaurante en el mundo hispano es una experiencia muy diferente de lo que es en este país. Una costumbre norteamericana que no es común en los países hispanos es la de servir la comida al estilo bufé, donde el cliente paga un solo precio por comer todo lo que quiera.[a]

En cuanto a las bebidas, en el mundo hispano no existe el concepto del relleno gratis.[b] En muchos restaurantes de este país el cliente puede consumir cuatro refrescos, pero sólo paga uno. En los restaurantes hispanos, si uno toma cuatro refrescos tiene que pagarlos todos. La costumbre del relleno gratis también influye en[c] la manera en que los meseros atienden a los clientes. En muchos restaurantes norteamericanos, los meseros se afanan[d] por rellenar[e] las bebidas (¡aun cuando no están vacías![f]) con la intención de recibir una buena propina. En los restaurantes hispanos, los meseros no rellenan las bebidas; no le traen al cliente una bebida nueva hasta que termina la primera, y aun así es frecuente tener que pedirla. En general, los meseros hispanos no apresuran[g] a los clientes. Y a diferencia de los restaurantes norteamericanos, los meseros hispanos no traen la cuenta a la mesa hasta que el cliente diga:[h] «La cuenta, por favor.»

[a]todo... *whatever he wants* [b]relleno... *free refill* [c]influye... *influences* [d]se... *hurry* [e]*refill* [f]*empty* [g]no... *don't rush* [h]*says*

INPUT

Act. A, Suggested follow-up: Continue with some aural items. 6. *El/la cliente puede leer el menú y pedir la comida desde el auto.* 7. *Las tazas son de papel.* (comida rápida); 8. *Las servilletas son de tela (cloth).* (alta cocina); 9. *No hay un cocinero sino un chef.* (alta cocina); 10. *Es necesario dejar una propina.* (alta cocina).

Actividad A ¿Alta cocina (*Gourmet cooking*) o comida rápida?

Lee las oraciones a continuación e indica si se refieren a un restaurante de alta cocina o a un restaurante de comida rápida.

	RESTAURANTE DE ALTA COCINA	RESTAURANTE DE COMIDA RÁPIDA
1. La cuenta incluye la propina si hay más de ocho personas en la mesa.	☑	☐
2. Los cubiertos son de plástico.	☐	☑
3. Es común pagar la comida al momento de pedirla.	☐	☑
4. Los meseros visten trajes elegantes.	☑	☐
5. La comida se sirve en bandeja (*tray*) de plástico.	☐	☑

INPUT

Actividad B

Actividad B ¿En qué orden?

A continuación hay una lista de frases que los meseros les dicen a los clientes. Pon las frases en el orden en que ocurren, del 1 al 7.

___5/6___ ¿Les retiro (*May I take away*) los platos?

___2___ ¿Están listos para pedir?

___7___ Les dejo la cuenta. Fue un placer (*pleasure*) servirles.

___1___ ¿Desean algo de tomar mientras leen el menú?

___6/5___ ¿Desean algún postre o una taza de café?

___3___ El bistec para el señor y el pescado para la señora. Buen provecho. (*Enjoy your meal.*)

___4___ ¿Está bien la comida?

OUTPUT

Act. C, Suggestions

• Have students change roles and repeat *Paso 1* with drawing B.

• Have pairs make up a list of the differences between the 2 drawings. Say: *Ahora, hagan una lista de las diferencias entre los dos dibujos. ¿Saben Uds. cuál de los dibujos representa la manera aceptada para poner la mesa?*

Actividad C ¿Cómo se pone (*does one set*) la mesa?

En grupos de dos, un(a) estudiante va a describir cómo está puesta (*is set*) la mesa en el dibujo A. Sin mirar el dibujo, su compañero/a va a escuchar la descripción y dibujar la mesa en una hoja de papel aparte (*another sheet of paper*). Las siguientes frases pueden ser útiles: **a la izquierda/derecha de, al lado de, arriba de** (*above*), **abajo de** (*below*).

MODELO: E1: El tenedor para la ensalada está a la derecha de la cuchara.

Actividad D Cuando el servicio es malo

Paso 1 Lee cada situación a continuación e indica cómo reaccionarías (*you would react*).

1. El mesero te trae la comida y al probarla (*tasting it*), te das cuenta de (*you realize*) que tiene un pelo encima.
   a. Lo saco (*I remove it*) y sigo comiendo.
   b. Le pido otro plato de comida al mesero.
   c. Me quejo (*I complain*) con el gerente (*manager*).
   d. ¿ ?

2. Al rellenarte (*refilling*) la taza, el mesero derrama (*spills*) el café sobre tu camisa.
   a. Lo perdono.
   b. Le doy menos propina.
   c. No le doy ninguna propina.
   d. ¿ ?

3. Recibes la cuenta de otra mesa y es mucho más pequeña que la tuya.
   a. Le digo al mesero que se equivocó (*he made a mistake*).
   b. Pago la cuenta como si fuera (*as if it were*) mía.
   c. Pago la cuenta como si fuera mía, pero le doy al mesero una buena propina.
   d. ¿ ?

4. El mesero te trae un plato de comida, y al probarla te das cuenta de que está bien fría.
   a. La como sin decirle nada al mesero.
   b. Pido otro plato de comida.
   c. Me quejo con el gerente.
   d. ¿ ?

5. Tienes más de 40 minutos de esperar y la comida no ha llegado (*has not arrived*) todavía. El mesero llega, te pide perdón (*he apologizes*) y te explica que sólo hay un cocinero y que las órdenes se han atrasado (*have backed up*).
   a. Lo perdono y espero un rato más.
   b. Le pido al mesero que me dé (*gives me*) la comida para llevar (*to go*).
   c. Me desahogo con (*I take it out on*) el mesero y no le doy propina.
   d. ¿ ?

Paso 2 Con un compañero (una compañera) de clase, compartan (*share*) sus reacciones ante (*when faced with*) estas situaciones.

MODELO: ¿Cómo reaccionas si el mesero te trae un plato de comida que tiene un pelo encima?

Paso 3 Escoge una situación del **Paso 1** y describe brevemente cómo tú y tu compañero/a de clase reaccionan ante esa situación.

Gramática

Talking About What
Has Happened

¡Lo he pasado muy bien!

**Introduction to the
Present Perfect**

«He cometido el peor
pecado que uno puede
cometer: no he sido
feliz.»*
—Jorge Luis Borges
(1899–1986), escritor
argentino

To talk about what has happened, Spanish uses a form of the verb **haber** (*to have*)† plus a past participle. Past participles are formed by removing the **-ar,** **-er,** and **-ir** verb endings and adding **-ado, -ido,** and **-ido,** respectively.

He tomado dos aspirinas hoy.	*I have taken two aspirins today.*
¿Has conocido a una persona famosa?	*Have you met a famous person?*
Hemos salido tres veces esta semana.	*We have gone out three times this week.*

Verbs whose stems end in a vowel require a written accent in the past participle.

leer → **leído**

oír → **oído**

traer → **traído**

Some common verbs have irregular past participles, as indicated in the chart.

PRESENT PERFECT OF REGULAR VERBS				
haber			+ PAST PARTICIPLE	
(yo)	he	(nosotros/as)	hemos	viajado
(tú)	has	(vosotros/as)	habéis	conocido
(Ud.)	ha	(Uds.)	han	vivido
(él/ella)	ha	(ellos/ellas)	han	

IRREGULAR PAST PARTICIPLES		
VERB	PAST PARTICIPLE	EXAMPLES
decir	**dicho**	Mi novio no me **ha dicho** la verdad.
escribir	**escrito**	**¿Has escrito** la carta?
hacer	**hecho**	**Hemos hecho** un viaje a Nueva York.
morir	**muerto**	Mis abuelos ya **han muerto.**
poner	**puesto**	**He puesto** dinero en el banco.
ver	**visto**	No **he visto** la nueva película de Brad Pitt.
volver	**vuelto**	Los niños no **han vuelto** del parque.

---

*"I have committed the worst sin there is: I have not been happy."

†**Haber** is an auxiliary verb that is *not* interchangeable with **tener.** It is also an irregular verb. You already know several of its forms: **hay** (*there is / there are*), **hubo** (*there was*), **había** (*there was / there were*).

De *Sol y viento*, Note: You can access this film clip from a special menu section on Disc 5 of the Instructional Version on DVD.

DE SOL Y VIENTO

In **Episodio 6** of *Sol y viento* you will watch a scene in which Jaime and doña Isabel talk about the sale of the winery. Part of their exchange appears here.

JAIME
Nuestra oferta es muy buena, señora. Su hijo quiere vender, y me **ha indicado** que Ud. tal vez estaría de acuerdo.ª Piénselo bien, por favor.

ISABEL
Ya se lo ____. «Sol y viento» no está a la venta. Hasta luego, señor Talavera.

What do you think doña Isabel says in the space above?

1. he dicho
2. he vendido
3. he pagado

ªtal… *perhaps you would agree*

Enfoque lingüístico

***Enfoque lingüístico*, Suggestion:** Emphasize the difference between French/Italian on the one hand and English/Spanish on the other, but tell students that in Spain, the present perfect has taken on more and more functions of the preterite. Tell students that as they continue to learn Spanish, they will see that while the present perfect in English and the present perfect in Spanish are similar, they are not exact matches. Provide them with these examples: I have lived in Jester Hall for two years = *Hace dos años que vivo en Jester Hall* (or *Llevo dos años en Jester Hall*); I have just finished eating = *Acabo de comer*).

Los verbos perfectos

Contrary to its meaning in everyday use, the word *perfect* does not mean *without flaw* when applied to languages. The term *perfect* connotes the meaning *completed*. When used in relationship to the present time, it is used to express that an event began sometime in the past but is either still ongoing in the present or is somehow closely related to the present time. Note, for example, the difference between *I once ran a marathon* and *I have recently run a marathon*. The former clearly situates a completed event sometime in the remote past; the latter situates the event closer to the present time. Note how certain adverbs of time cannot be used with the present perfect in English: *I once have run a marathon, A long time ago I have lived in Arizona, Three weeks ago I have run a marathon.*

Spanish and English are similar in their use of the present perfect, although not completely identical. For example, in Spain, the present perfect is often used as a substitute for the preterite. This reflects a tendency common to Latinate languages. For example, both French and Italian no longer have active simple past-tense forms in spoken language; instead, the present-perfect forms function both as preterites and present perfects. Thus, *j'ai fini* in French can mean either *I have finished* or *I finished*.

One of the things you will notice about Spanish, French, and Italian on the one hand and English on the other is that English can drop the past participle in structures with *and* or *but;* the other languages cannot. Thus, *I have eaten, but John hasn't* is a grammatically correct sentence in English. To drop **comido** in Spanish would render the sentence ungrammatical.

Actividad E ¿Quiénes lo podrían (*could*) decir?

Basándote en los episodios de *Sol y viento* que has visto hasta ahora, indica los personajes que podrían decir las siguientes oraciones.

1. Hemos subido el funicular juntos (*together*).
　　☑ Jaime y María　　　　□ Jaime y Mario
2. Hemos hablado de contratos y negocios.
　　☑ Jaime y Carlos　　　　□ María y Jaime
3. Hemos hecho varios viajes en auto.
　　□ Carlos y María　　　　☑ Jaime y Mario
4. No hemos conocido a doña Isabel.
　　□ Traimaqueo y Carlos　　☑ Jaime y Mario

Actividad F Los famosos

Escucha lo que dice tu profesor(a). ¿Cuántas personas famosas puedes nombrar que corresponden a lo que oyes? ¿Cuántos hispanos puedes nombrar?

1. ...　　**2.** ...　　**3.** ...　　**4.** ...　　**5.** ...　　**6.** ...　　**7.** ...

Actividad G ¿Quiénes lo han hecho?

Paso 1 Marca las actividades a continuación que se te aplican. Luego, entrevista a algunos compañeros de clase sobre las mismas actividades. Si alguien contesta **sí** a una pregunta, dile **Firma aquí, por favor**. ¿Puedes encontrar a dos personas que contesten **sí** a cada actividad?

MODELO: E1: ¿Has hecho un papel (*played a role)* en un drama?
　　　　　E2: Sí. He hecho el papel de Hamlet.
　　　　　E1: Firma aquí, por favor.

YO		ESTUDIANTE 1	ESTUDIANTE 2
□	**1.** He hecho un papel en un drama.	_____	_____
□	**2.** He recibido un premio en una competición.	_____	_____
□	**3.** He renunciado a (*quit*) un trabajo.	_____	_____
□	**4.** He cantado en público (y no fue karaoke).	_____	_____
□	**5.** He perdido algo importante que nunca he encontrado.	_____	_____

Paso 2 Basándote en los resultados del **Paso 1,** presenta un dato interesante a la clase.

MODELO: John y Margaret han hecho un papel en un drama, pero yo no. Mark y yo hemos cantado en público.

Actividad H La clase de español

Paso 1 Indica si las siguientes oraciones sobre la clase de español se te aplican o no.

	SÍ, SE ME APLICA.	NO, NO SE ME APLICA.
1. No he llegado tarde a clase más de tres veces.	☐	☐
2. He entregado (*turned in*) todas mis tareas.	☐	☐
3. He hecho los ejercicios del Manual.	☐	☐
4. No he hablado mucho en inglés con mis compañeros de clase.	☐	☐
5. He visto todos los episodios de *Sol y viento*.	☐	☐
6. No he faltado a (*missed*) clase más de tres veces.	☐	☐
7. He saludado (*greeted*) a mi profesor(a) en español todos los días.	☐	☐
8. He leído la lección antes de venir a clase.	☐	☐

Paso 2 Entrevista a un compañero (una compañera) de clase para averiguar si se le aplican las oraciones del **Paso 1** o no. Escribe sus respuestas en una hoja de papel aparte.

MODELO: E1: ¿Has visto todos los episodios de *Sol y viento*?
E2: Sí, los he visto.

Paso 3 Suma (*Add up*) el número de tus respuestas afirmativas en el **Paso 1**. Suma también el número de respuestas afirmativas que te dio tu compañero/a de clase. Luego, indica dónde quedan Uds. en la siguiente escala.

Muy dedicado/a   Dedicado/a   No muy dedicado/a
16————————————8————————————1

Paso 4 Escribe un breve párrafo en el cual resumes los datos de tu entrevista.

MODELO: Miguel y yo somos estudiantes dedicados. Miguel ha... yo también he...

COMUNICACIÓN ÚTIL

To express what *had* happened or what you *had* done at a particular point in time in the past, use the imperfect of **haber** plus a past participle. The imperfect forms of **haber** are **había, habías, había, habíamos, habíais, habían.**

Yo **había esperado** dos semestres antes de tomar una clase de español.	*I had waited for two semesters before taking a Spanish class.*
Clinton y Bush (hijo) **habían sido** gobernadores antes de ser presidentes.	*Clinton and Bush (the son) had been governors before becoming presidents.*

SOL Y VIENTO

A primera vista

Antes de ver el episodio

Actividad A ¿Qué recuerdas?

Indica si las siguientes oraciones sobre la trama (*plot*) de *Sol y viento* son ciertas o falsas.

		C	F
1.	María trabaja por los derechos de la comunidad mapuche.	☑	☐
2.	Los padres de Jaime también eran personas de negocios.	☐	☑
3.	Doña Isabel está de acuerdo con Carlos en vender la viña porque es demasiado (*too much*) trabajo mantenerla (*to maintain it*).	☐	☑
4.	Carlos cree que la familia lo obligó a encargarse de (*take over*) la viña.	☑	☐
5.	María y Jaime lo pasaron muy bien en la cita.	☑	☐

Actividad B ¿Qué falta? Act. B, Suggestion: Do not provide answers, as students will verify their choices later.

A continuación hay un fragmento de una conversación telefónica que tiene don Paco.

> PACO: ¿Bueno?ª... ¿Bueno?... ¡Si no lo oigo bien! ¡_____¹ más fuerte!... ¿Bueno?... ¿Bueno?... Sí, _____² tantitoᵇ... ¿Bueno?... ¿Con quién?... ¡Ah, Isabel! ¡Qué sorpresa!

ªHello? (Mex.) ᵇa second (coll.)

Escoge entre las palabras que siguen la más apropiada para cada espacio en blanco.

1. (a.) Hable
   b. Habla
2. a. espérame
   (b.) espéreme

Actividad C El episodio

Ahora mira el episodio. Si hay algo que no entiendes bien, puedes volver a ver la escena en cuestión.

Detrás de la cámara

In **Episodio 6** of *Sol y viento* you will meet don Francisco (Paco) Aguilar, an old friend of the Sánchez family and owner of a fine restaurant in Mexico City. In addition to being a restaurateur, don Paco is also a distributor of fine wines. His job is to make contacts with wineries throughout the world and import their products into Mexico. He established a relationship with the Sánchez family many years ago on a trip through the Maipo Valley. He was so impressed with the wine produced at Sol y viento that he made it the house wine at his establishment.

Después de ver el episodio

Actividad A ¿Qué recuerdas?

Contesta cada pregunta a continuación según lo que recuerdas del episodio.

1. ¿A quién llama por teléfono doña Isabel?
   a. a Jaime, en su hotel   **b.** a don Paco, en México
2. ¿Cuál es la relación entre don Paco y María?
   a. Son amigos.   b. Son parientes.
3. Jaime se da cuenta de que María y Carlos son _____.
   a. primos   **b.** hermanos   c. cuñados
4. Jaime está harto de (*fed up with*) los pretextos (*excuses*) de Carlos y demanda _____ de la familia.
   a. las bodegas   **b.** las firmas   c. las cosechas (*harvests*)
5. María comprende que Jaime no sabía quién era Carlos y lo perdona.
   a. cierto   **b.** falso

Actividad B El episodio

Vuelve a la **Actividad B** de **Antes de ver el episodio** para verificar tus respuestas. Si es necesario, vuelve a ver la escena en cuestión.

Actividad C Utilizando el contexto

Act. C, Point out
Paso 1: ¿Qué tal están? in this context means "how are" or "what are _____ like." (How are your tomatoes today? / What are your tomatoes like today?)

Paso 1 Ya sabes que la frase **¿Qué tal?** es un saludo que quiere decir algo como *How's it going?* Repasa lo que dice don Paco en el mercado a continuación. ¿Qué crees que significa **¿Qué tal están... ?** en este contexto?

> PACO: ¡Buenas, doña Lourdes! *¿Qué tal están* sus jitomates hoy?

Paso 2 A diferencia de otros hispanos, los mexicanos dicen **¿Bueno?** al contestar el teléfono. ¿Qué dice Jaime cuando contesta su teléfono celular? ¿Sabes lo que dicen los españoles? Si no, pregúntaselo a tu profesor(a).

Paso 2: Although most Spanish speakers like Jaime say ¿Aló?, there are some regional differences. Reiterate that Mexicans say ¿Bueno? and point out that most Spaniards use the command form ¡Diga!

Actividad D En resumen

Completa la siguiente narración con las palabras y expresiones apropiadas de la lista a la derecha.

En este episodio, doña Isabel <u>está preocupada</u>[1] por lo que pasa en la viña. Por eso le pide ayuda a don Francisco (Paco) Aguilar, un amigo de la familia que vive en México. Se nota que a María <u>le cae bien</u>[2] su «tío» Paco y que <u>lo respeta</u>[3] mucho. Entretanto,[a] Jaime va a la viña donde <u>conoce a</u>[4] doña Isabel, la madre de Carlos. Doña Isabel afirma que «Sol y viento» no <u>está a la venta</u>[5] y Jaime y Carlos entran en una conversación agitada. Luego, María llega del <u>aeropuerto</u>[6] con don Paco y presencia[b] la confrontación. Pensando que Jaime la está engañando,[c] María se enoja[d] y deja caer[e] <u>el amuleto</u>[7] que Jaime le regaló.

aeropuerto
el amuleto
conoce a
está a la venta
está preocupada (*worried*)
le cae bien
lo respeta

[a]*Meanwhile* [b]*(she) witnesses* [c]*deceiving* [d]*se... gets angry* [e]*deja... drops*

RESUMEN DE VOCABULARIO

El transporte y los viajes

bajar (de)	to get off (of)
facturar el equipaje	to check luggage
hacer (*irreg.*) **cola**	to wait in line
hacer (*irreg.*) **escala**	to make a stopover
hacer (*irreg.*) **la maleta**	to pack a suitcase
hacer (*irreg.*) **un viaje**	to take a trip
ir (*irreg.*) **al extranjero**	to go abroad
marearse	to get nauseated, sick (*in a boat, car, plane*)
pasar por la aduana	to go through customs
pasar por seguridad	to go through security
subir (a)	to board, get on

el aeropuerto	airport
la agencia de viajes	travel agency
el/la agente de viajes	travel agent
el asiento	seat
el/la asistente de vuelo	flight attendant
el avión	airplane
el boleto	ticket
de ida	one-way
de ida y vuelta	round-trip
la clase turística	coach
el equipaje	luggage
el maletero	skycap, porter
el/la pasajero/a	passenger
la primera clase	first class
la sala de espera	waiting area
el/la viajero/a	traveler
el vuelo (directo)	(direct) flight

Cognados: el autobús, el pasaporte, la reservación
Repaso: el barco

El alojamiento

alojarse	to stay (*in a place*)
quedarse	to stay (*in a place*)
el botones	bellhop
la pensión	boardinghouse
completa	room and all meals
la media pensión	room and one other meal (usually breakfast)
la propina	tip
el servicio de cuarto	room service

con baño (privado)	with a (private) bathroom
de lujo	luxury

Repaso: la cama (sencilla, matrimonial), la habitación, el hotel

¿Cómo se llega a... ?

cruzar (c)	to cross
doblar	to turn
seguir (i, i) (g) derecho	to continue, go straight
¿Cuánto hay de aquí a... ?	How far is it to . . . ?
la calle	street
la cuadra / la manzana	block
el plano	city map

Cognado: el mapa
Repaso: a la derecha/izquierda, el este, el norte, el oeste, el sur

En el restaurante

atender (ie)	to wait on
dejar (una) propina	to leave a tip
¿Me podría traer... ?	Could you bring me . . . ?
¿Qué trae... ?	What does . . . come with?
el/la cocinero/a	cook
la copa	glass (*wine, liquor*)
los cubiertos	silverware
la cuchara	spoon
el cuchillo	knife
la cuenta	bill, check (*in a restaurant*)
el/la mesero/a	waiter, waitress
el primer (segundo, tercer) plato	first (second, third) course
la servilleta	napkin
la taza	coffee cup
el tenedor	fork
el vaso	glass (*water*)

Cognados: ordenar; el menú, el plato
Repaso: pedir (i, i), traer (*irreg.*)

La naturaleza y el medio ambiente^a

OBJETIVOS

IN THIS LESSON, YOU WILL LEARN:

- vocabulary to talk about geography and geographical features
- to give instructions to someone you address as **tú,** using informal commands
- vocabulary related to ecology and the environment
- vocabulary for things to do on vacation
- to talk about extremes using superlative expressions

In addition, you will watch **Episodio 6** of the film *Sol y viento* again.

La Pampa es una provincia argentina con grandes llanuras (*plains*).

^aLa... *Nature and the Environment*

The following media resources are available for this lesson of *Sol y viento:*

Episodio 6 of
Sol y viento

Online *Manual de actividades*

Online Learning Center Website

Note: These vocabulary items can be heard in this lesson's Textbook Audio section of the Online Learning Center Website.

Talking About the Natural World

Vocabulario

¿Cómo es el paisaje?

✳ **Geography and Geographical Features**

Algunas características de la geografía de Sudamérica

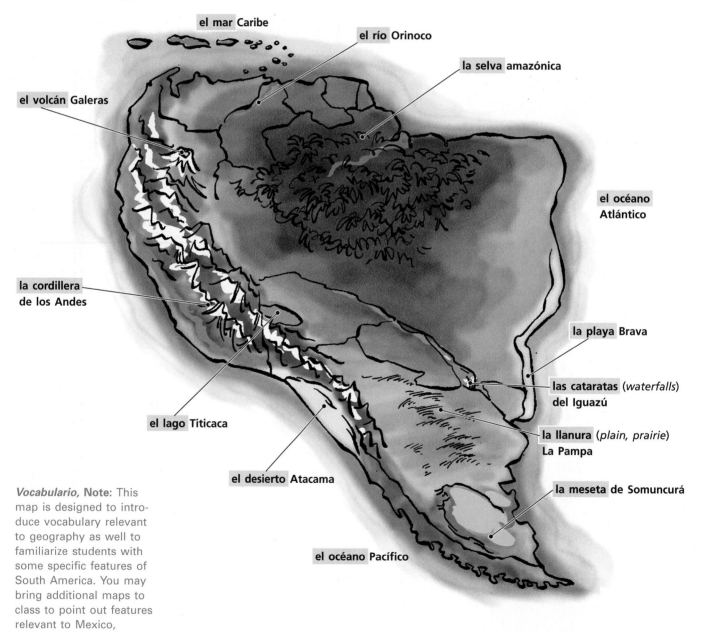

el mar Caribe

el río Orinoco

la selva amazónica

el volcán Galeras

el océano Atlántico

la cordillera de los Andes

la playa Brava

las cataratas (*waterfalls*) del Iguazú

el lago Titicaca

la llanura (*plain, prairie*) La Pampa

el desierto Atacama

la meseta de Somuncurá

el océano Pacífico

Vocabulario, **Note:** This map is designed to introduce vocabulary relevant to geography as well to familiarize students with some specific features of South America. You may bring additional maps to class to point out features relevant to Mexico, Central America, and Spain.

✳ MÁS VOCABULARIO

el bosque (lluvioso)	(rain)forest
la colina	hill
la costa	coast
el golfo	gulf
la isla	island
la montaña	mountain
el paisaje	landscape
el valle	valley

los continentes: África, Antártida, Asia, Australia, Europa, Norteamérica, Sudamérica

---

 ## Vistazo cultural

Los volcanes

Cuando se habla de volcanes, muchas personas piensan en las islas del Pacífico como Hawai, Japón, Indonesia y Nueva Zelanda. Sin embargo, en México, Centroamérica y Sudamérica también hay numerosos volcanes, muchos de ellos activos. En el norte de Chile, por ejemplo, está Ojos del Salado, el volcán activo más alto del mundo. Otro de los volcanes de la misma región, el Llullaillaco, también es uno de los volcanes activos más altos del mundo.

Otros países hispanos donde hay muchos volcanes son México, Guatemala, Costa Rica, El Salvador, Nicaragua y el Ecuador. El Popocatépetl, uno de los volcanes activos de México, se encuentra entre la Ciudad de México y Puebla. El Popo, como le dicen los mexicanos, ha estado activo desde la época de los aztecas, quienes le pusieron el nombre de[a] Popocatépetl, que significa «montaña humeante[b]» en náhuatl. Desde la llegada de los españoles en 1519, el Popo ha hecho erupción quince veces. Su actividad más reciente incluye una serie de frecuentes erupciones de gases y cenizas[c] volcánicos que comenzaron en 1994 y siguen hasta hoy día. Actualmente[d] hay un equipo de científicos que vigila[e] la actividad del Popocatépetl. Debido a su ubicación,[f] una erupción grande afectaría[g] a más de 20 millones de habitantes.

▲ El volcán Ojos del Salado, en la Puna* de Atacama, Chile

[a]le... *named it* [b]*smoking* [c]*ash* [d]*Currently* [e]*is monitoring* [f]*location* [g]*would affect*

*****Puna** is a word used in certain regions of South America to describe high, desolate regions. Due to the bleak cold of these regions, they're often not suitable for human populations.

Actividad A Asociaciones

Repasa el mapa y las expresiones en la lista de vocabulario en las páginas 348–349. Luego, empareja los nombres de la columna A con su definición en la columna B.

	A		B
1.	_d_ Titicaca		**a.** un volcán muy activo de Colombia
2.	_h_ Atacama		**b.** unas cataratas enormes entre la Argentina y el Brasil
3.	_a_ Galeras		**c.** una meseta de la Patagonia, en el sur de la Argentina
4.	_f_ la Pampa		**d.** un lago en la frontera (*border*) entre el Perú y Bolivia
5.	_b_ Iguazú		**e.** el nombre de un río y también de una selva
6.	_c_ Somuncurá		**f.** una llanura grande en la Argentina
7.	_g_ los Andes		**g.** una cordillera que extiende por muchos países sudamericanos
8.	_e_ el Amazonas		**h.** un desierto de Chile
9.	_i_ el Pacífico y el Atlántico		**i.** océanos grandes que rodean (*surround*) Sudamérica

Actividad B Los paisajes

Tu profesor(a) va a mencionar el nombre de algunos lugares conocidos. Indica la palabra que se asocia con cada lugar.

1. a. lago	**b.** mar	(**c.**) río
2. a. bosque	(**b.**) desierto	**c.** volcán
3. a. playa	**b.** meseta	(**c.**) montaña
4. (**a.**) mar	**b.** océano	**c.** río
5. a. colina	(**b.**) selva	**c.** llanura
6. a. valle	**b.** volcán	(**c.**) océano
7. (**a.**) cataratas	**b.** playa	**c.** isla
8. a. valle	(**b.**) isla	**c.** meseta

Actividad C Una prueba de geografía

Paso 1 Hazle a otro/a estudiante preguntas sobre la geografía, según el modelo. Cuando tu compañero/a falta (*misses*) una pregunta, cambien de papeles. La persona que contesta las más preguntas seguidas (*in a row*) gana la ronda (*round*).

MODELO: E1: ¿Qué es el Colorado?
E2: Es un río.
E1: ¡Correcto! ¿Qué son las Himalayas?
E2: Son unas playas.
E1: ¡Incorrecto! Son una cordillera.

Paso 2 Jueguen dos rondas más. ¡El/La que gana por lo menos dos de tres rondas es el campeón (la campeona)!

OUTPUT
Actividad D

Actividad D Un viaje al aire libre (*outdoors*)

Paso 1 Entrevista a un compañero (una compañera) de clase para ver si le gusta hacer las siguientes actividades o no. Si contesta que sí a alguna pregunta, pregúntale el nombre del lugar geográfico.

MODELO: E1: ¿Te gusta nadar en el mar?   E1: ¿Qué mar te gusta más?
         E2: Sí.   E2: El Atlántico.

1. nadar en el mar
2. tomar sol en la playa
3. escalar (*to climb*) montañas
4. hacer (*to go*) camping en un bosque
5. pescar (*to fish*) en un lago o río
6. caminar en (o conducir por) el desierto
7. visitar cataratas

Paso 2 Basándote en las respuestas del **Paso 2,** recomienda dos lugares que tu compañero/a de clase debe visitar.

MODELO: Como te gusta escalar montañas y hacer camping en el bosque, debes visitar Rocky Mountain National Park o las montañas Smoky de Tennessee.

Enfoque cultural,
Suggested follow-up:
Have students look up population figures and demographics for the following countries and create a graphic visualization (pie chart, bar graph, etc.) to share with others: Bolivia, Ecuador, Guatemala, Mexico, Peru, Paraguay. An optional follow-up would be to look up information on bilingualism and bilingual education in these countries and prepare a series of statements (e.g., what is the official policy, when was it implemented, etc.).

SOL Y VIENTO: Enfoque cultural

Has visto que en el **Episodio 6,** Jaime le dice a Carlos: «¡A que tampoco ha hecho nada con la comunidad mapuche!» Evidentemente, Carlos había prometido[a] conseguir las tierras de los mapuches que vivían en la zona. En cambio,[b] su hermana María lucha[c] por esa comunidad indígena para preservar su cultura.

El indigenismo y los derechos de los indígenas en Latinoamérica son temas muy importantes en muchos países como el Perú, Chile, México y otros. Por seis siglos los indígenas han sufrido discriminación que los ha mantenido en las capas[d] más bajas de la sociedad. Afortunadamente, en el siglo XX empezó a demostrarse interés[e] en el indigenismo a través del arte del mexicano Diego Rivera y el novelista ecuatoriano Jorge Icaza, entre otros. En el Perú empezaron a reconocer la importancia de ofrecer a los indígenas educación en su lengua nativa, el quechua, y establecieron programas de educación bilingüe en el año 1972. Es más,[f] en 1979 la constitución peruana reconoció el español como lengua oficial del país, pero a la vez que el quechua forma parte integral de la cultura del país, y los dos idiomas quedaron como lenguas oficiales, con restricciones. Aun con estos avances, la situación no está completamente resuelta.[g] Por ejemplo, en 1994 los indígenas del estado mexicano de Chiapas se sublevaron[h] contra el gobierno, reclamando más tierra y más inclusión en el sistema político. Seguramente, la situación de los grupos minoritarios indígenas seguirá siendo[i] un tema central en varios países hispanos por muchos años.

▲ El indigenismo sigue siendo un tema central en la vida de los indígenas, como estas en el Ecuador.

[a]*promised* [b]*En... On the other hand* [c]*fights* [d]*layers* [e]*empezó... interest began to appear*
[f]*Es... What's more* [g]*resolved* [h]*se... rose up* [i]*seguirá... will continue to be*

Gramática

More on Giving
Instructions

¡Ten paciencia!

Affirmative Informal Commands

AFFIRMATIVE INFORMAL COMMANDS
• use the third-person present-tense form as the command

tomar → toma →
Toma café si estás cansado.　　　*Drink some coffee if you're tired.*
escribir → escribe →
Escribe un párrafo de 50 palabras.　　*Write a 50-word paragraph.*

• attach object and reflexive pronouns to the end of the command
　　Dámelo, por favor.　　　　　　*Give it to me, please.*
　　Levántate ya. Es tarde.　　　　*Get up already. It's late.*

IRREGULAR INFORMAL COMMAND FORMS		
VERB	COMMAND FORM	EXAMPLE
decir	di	**Di** mi nombre. *Say my name.*
hacer	haz	**Haz** la cama. *Make the bed.*
ir	ve*	**Ve** al supermercado. *Go to the supermarket.*
poner	pon	**Pon** las flores allí. *Put the flowers there.*
salir	sal	**¡Sal** de mi casa! *Get out of my house!*
ser	sé	**Sé** bueno. *Be good.*
tener	ten	**Ten** paciencia. *Have patience. (Be patient.)*
venir	ven	**Ven** aquí. *Come here.*

COMUNICACIÓN ÚTIL

In addition to using third-person singular verbs to make informal commands, it is also common for Spanish speakers to give instructions in the form of a question using second-person singular verb forms. Instead of saying **Pásame la sal, por favor,** a Spanish speaker might say **¿Me pasas la sal, por favor?** This less direct way of giving instructions is commonly used to soften a request.

---

*The affirmative **tú** command form of the verb **ir** is identical to the regular **tú** command form for the verb **ver.** Context will determine meaning.

　Ve a la biblioteca para estudiar.　　*Go to the library to study.*
　Ve las estrellas.　　　　　　　　*Look at the stars.*

To give instructions to someone whom you address as **tú** (such as a friend, family member, or pet), Spanish uses third-person singular verb forms in the present tense. When used in this way, these forms are called affirmative **tú** commands or simply informal commands (**los mandatos informales**). You have already noticed the use of affirmative **tú** commands in the directions to many activities in this text.

Habla con un compañero de clase.	*Speak with a classmate.*
Escribe dos o tres oraciones.	*Write two or three sentences.*

All object and reflexive pronouns are attached to the end of affirmative **tú** commands, as they are to formal commands. Note the written accents to maintain the original stress.

Bébela.	*Drink it. (it = **la leche**)*
Háblale.	*Talk to him.*
¡Despiértate!	*Wake up!*

As with formal commands, when both a direct and an indirect object pronoun are used, the indirect object comes before the direct object.

Dímela ahora mismo.	*Tell it to me right now.* (it = **la verdad**)

Many commonly used affirmative **tú** commands have irregular forms, as indicated in the chart.

De *Sol y viento,* Note: You can access this film clip from a special menu section on Disc 5 of the Instructional Version on DVD.

DE SOL Y VIENTO

At the end of **Episodio 5,** you saw a scene in which María has to leave her date with Jaime to meet up with her student, Diego. Jaime gets up to follow María, but she stops him. Part of their conversation appears below.

MARÍA
No, no, no, _____.
Aprovecha la puesta del sol.[a]

JAIME
¿Solo?

MARÍA
¡Llámame!

Do you remember what María says to Jaime in the space above? Select the most logical response from the following choices, then check your answer by watching the scene again.

1. levántate
2. quédate
3. duérmete

[a]Aprovecha... *Enjoy the sunset.*

Actividad E ¿María o doña Isabel?

A finales del **Episodio 5,** Jaime tutea (*addresses as* **tú**) a María pero trata de Ud. a doña Isabel. Tu profesor(a) va a mencionar una serie de instrucciones que Jaime podría (*could*) dar. Indica si cada una se dirige a (*is directed to*) María (informal) o a doña Isabel (formal).

1. … **2.** … **3.** … **4.** … **5.** … **6.** … **7.** … **8.** …

▲ Jaime le trata de Ud. a doña Isabel.

Actividad F ¿Qué escuchaste?

Paso 1 Escucha el párrafo que lee tu profesor(a) a la clase. Vas a escuchar el párrafo dos veces. Trata de recordar la información, pero no tomes apuntes.

Paso 2 En grupos de tres, escriban una versión del párrafo para luego compartirla con la clase.

Actividad G Los anuncios (*advertisements*)

Paso 1 Los anuncios usan mandatos informales para comunicarse con los consumidores. Con un compañero (una compañera), inventen un anuncio para una compañía asociada con cada categoría de producto a continuación.

MODELOS: una comida preparada: Pasa más tiempo en la mesa que en la cocina. (Stouffers)
una automóvil: Sé la envidia (*envy*) de todos. (Mercedes-Benz)

- una comida preparada o congelada (*frozen*)
- un producto de limpieza
- una bebida
- un automóvil
- un producto de belleza (*beauty*)

Paso 2 Presenten sus anuncios a la clase. La clase va a votar por el anuncio más creativo de cada categoría.

Example: *¿Qué quiere decir «Ven a clase preparado»?* (You are not asking for a translation but for behaviors—that is, what it means to be prepared.)

Actividad H En este país

Paso 1 Con un compañero (una compañera), hagan una lista de seis de las cosas que debe hacer un estudiante de intercambio (*exchange*) de tu universi- dad para disfrutar (*enjoy*) de los paisajes de este país. Usen verbos diferentes.

MODELO: Maneja por el desierto de Arizona.

Paso 2 Intercambien su lista con la de otro grupo. Lean la lista de recomen- daciones de sus compañeros y ordénenlas por su proximidad geográfica. La primera actividad debe ser la que está más cerca de su campus.

◉ Enfoque lingüístico

La sociolingüística

Sociolinguistic competence refers to one's ability to use socially accepted forms of lan- guage in proper contexts. Many languages use different pronouns and verb forms to address people in different social contexts. Spanish, for example, distinguishes between **tú** and **Ud.** in all verb forms, including command forms. This distinction is also tied to notions of politeness. Simply put, it would not be polite to use informal commands to give instructions to someone you should address as **Ud.** If you think learning this distinction is difficult, try learning Japanese, which has four affirmative command forms that vary in degree of politeness!

Language that is socially appropriate in one region or country may not necessarily be so in another. Spaniards, for example, are often direct when making requests. A client in a restaurant might tell a waiter **Dame un tenedor** or may just catch the waiter's attention and say **¡Un tenedor!** This client would likely come across as brusque or rude in Latin America. In a similar circumstance a Mexican would likely say **¿Me podría traer un tenedor?** or even **¿Sería tan amable de traerme un tenedor?** (*Would you be so kind as to bring me a fork?*).

▲ ¿Qué significa «Abróchate el cinturón. Abróchate a la vida.»?

SEGUNDA PARTE

Note: These vocabulary items can be heard in this lesson's Textbook Audio section of the Online Learning Center Website.

Vocabulario

Talking About the Environment | **El medio ambiente**

Environmental and Ecological Matters ✳

los combustibles fósiles

la contaminación del aire

la fábrica

la contaminación del agua

la deforestación

los pesticidas

la basura

el basurero

las cajas de cartón

la botella de vidrio

la botella de plástico

el periódico

las latas de aluminio

✳ MÁS VOCABULARIO

conservar	to conserve
construir (y)	to build
contaminar	to pollute
descomponer (*like* poner)	to decompose
desperdiciar	to waste
echar / tirar	to throw out
proteger (j)*	to protect
reciclar	to recycle
salvar	to save (*from danger*)
la capa de ozono	ozone layer
los desperdicios	wastes

*Proteger** uses a **j** in the **yo** form to maintain the [h] sound: **protejo**.

≈ Vistazo cultural

Las islas Galápagos

El archipiélago Galápagos es una serie de islas de origen volcánico ubicadas[a] al oeste de la costa ecuatoriana en el océano Pacífico. La región consiste en un parque terrestre[b] y una reserva marina. Desde la época de los estudios de Darwin,* los cuales resaltaron[c] la flora y la fauna de la región, el factor humano ha llegado a ser una gran amenaza[d] a las islas. Por ejemplo, la intensa industria pesquera[e] (a veces ilegal) en la región ha reducido el número de muchas especies, entre ellas el pepino de mar[f] y la langosta. Además, la población de las islas ha aumentado mucho por la llegada de inmigrantes. Debido a una planificación inadecuada para acomodar a los habitantes nuevos, las comunidades han generado grandes cantidades de desechos[g] sólidos y líquidos que se echan al mar sin ser tratados[h] adecuadamente.

Debido a la situación peligrosa[i] de las islas, en 1998 el Ecuador aprobó[j] la Ley de Régimen Especial para la Conservación de las Islas Galápagos. La ley fomenta[k] tanto la conservación del medio ambiente como el desarrollo sustentable[l] de las Galápagos. Hoy día el Instituto Nacional Galápagos (INGALA) regula la inmigración a las islas y las actividades humanas dentro del archipiélago. Está también la Autoridad Interinstitucional (AI) que regula las actividades de la reserva marina. Como se puede ver, conservar el medio ambiente requiere un delicado balance entre los intereses humanos y los de la naturaleza.

▲ Una iguana en las islas Galápagos

[a]*located* [b]*terrestrial* [c]*highlighted* [d]*threat* [e]*fishing* [f]pepino... *sea cucumber* [g]*wastes* [h]*treated* [i]*dangerous* [j]*passed* [k]*encourages* [l]desarrollo... *sustainable development*

el efecto invernadero	greenhouse effect
la escasez (*pl.* **las escaseces**)	shortage
las especies en peligro de extinción	endangered species
la falta	lack
el medio ambiente	environment
la naturaleza	nature
el petróleo	petroleum
el producto biodegradable (desechable)	biodegradable (disposable) product
el reciclaje	recycling
los recursos naturales	natural resources

*Charles Darwin (1809–1882) fue un naturalista británico que escribió *El origen de las especies*, un estudio sobre sus investigaciones en las islas Galápagos.

INPUT
Actividad A

Actividad A   Definiciones

Empareja una definición de la primera columna con la palabra apropiada de la segunda columna.

1. _e_ describe un producto que descompone rápida y naturalmente
2. _j_ químicas que se usan para eliminar insectos
3. _a_ la falta de una cosa
4. _i_ describe algo que se usa una o dos veces y luego se tira
5. _g_ el agua, el aire, los árboles, los combustibles fósiles
6. _h_ se necesita hacer esto a favor de las especies en peligro de extinción
7. _f_ lo que tiramos porque ya no sirve
8. _d_ lugar donde se hacen productos como autos o televisores
9. _c_ la temperatura global aumenta (*is increasing*) a causa de esto
10. _b_ lo opuesto de conservar

a. la escasez
b. desperdiciar
c. el efecto invernadero
d. la fábrica
e. biodegradable
f. la basura
g. los recursos naturales
h. proteger
i. desechable
j. los pesticidas

INPUT

Act. B, Suggestion: Allow 2 minutes to complete. Tell students to compare their list with that of a classmate.
Optional follow-up: Have students work in pairs to add 2 problems to the list in *Paso 1.* Call on groups to present their suggestions and have the class vote on which problems are most important.

Actividad B   ¿Qué importancia tienen para ti?

A continuación hay una lista de problemas medioambientales que afectan a todo el planeta. Pon los problemas en orden de importancia para ti, del 1 (más importante) al 10 (menos importante).

____ la falta de basureros
____ la escasez de combustibles fósiles
____ la deforestación
____ las especies en peligro de extinción
____ el uso de pesticidas en los productos alimenticios
____ la contaminación del aire
____ la contaminación del agua
____ la destrucción de la capa de ozono
____ el efecto invernadero
____ la escasez de los recursos naturales

INPUT/OUTPUT
Actividad C

Actividad C   ¿Qué hacemos con la basura?

Paso 1 A continuación hay una lista de soluciones posibles para resolver el problema de los basureros repletos (*overflowing*) de basura. Indica si cada solución te parece buena idea o mala idea.

Para resolver el problema de los basureros repletos de basura debemos...	BUENA IDEA	MALA IDEA
1. enterrar (*bury*) la basura en el desierto.	☐	☐
2. contratar (*hire*) compañías para reciclar la basura.	☐	☐

	BUENA IDEA	MALA IDEA
3. quemar la basura, como lo hacen en otros países.	☐	☐
4. enviar la basura a otro planeta.	☐	☐
5. echar la basura al océano.	☐	☐
6. comprar más basureros en otros países.	☐	☐

Paso 2 En grupos de tres personas, expliquen sus opiniones acerca de las soluciones del **Paso 1**. Cada grupo debe decidir cuál es la mejor solución para resolver el problema de los basureros repletos de basura.

INPUT/OUTPUT
Act. D, Suggestions
Paso 1: Allow 2 minutes to complete.
Paso 2: Model with a student, then give students 4 minutes to interview each other.
Paso 3: Allow 1 minute to complete, then ask for volunteers to present the results of their interview.

Actividad D ¿Conservas o desperdicias?

Paso 1 Indica si las siguientes afirmaciones son ciertas o falsas para ti.

	CIERTO	FALSO
1. Voy en auto a lugares que están a una milla más o menos de mi casa.	☐	☐
2. Dejo que corra el agua (*I leave the water running*) mientras me lavo los dientes.	☐	☐
3. No uso los dos lados de una hoja de papel antes de tirarla.	☐	☐
4. Echo latas de aluminio y botellas de plástico y vidrio.	☐	☐
5. Subo el regulador del termostato en el invierno y lo bajo en el verano.	☐	☐
6. No apago el monitor de mi computadora.	☐	☐
7. Uso muchos productos desechables.	☐	☐
8. Dejo prendidas (*turned on*) las luces al salir de casa.	☐	☐

Paso 2 Entrevista a un compañero (una compañera) de clase para averiguar si las oraciones del **Paso 1** son ciertas o falsas para él/ella.

Paso 3 Date un punto para cada respuesta que marcaste «cierto». Suma el número de puntos que tú y tu compañero/a de clase sacaron e indica dónde quedan en la siguiente escala.

> 0–2 = EXCELENTE: Conservas muchos recursos naturales.
>
> 3–5 = BIEN: Conservas algunos recursos, pero desperdicias otros.
>
> 6–8 = MAL: Desperdicias muchos recursos naturales.

MODELO: Yo saqué tres puntos y Joe sacó cinco. Los dos conservamos algunos recursos, pero desperdiciamos otros.

NAVEGANDO LA RED ～～～～～～～～～～～～～～～

Busca un sitio hispano en la red de una organización dedicada a proteger el medio ambiente. Describe las regiones donde está trabajando y cuáles son las actividades que hace en protección del medio ambiente.

Gramática

| **¡No me hables!**   **Negative Informal Commands**

Si pierdes el cabello, no pierdas el tiempo

To tell someone whom you address as **tú** *not* to do something, Spanish uses negative informal commands. These are formed in the same way that formal negative commands are: by taking the present-tense **yo** form, dropping the **-o** or **-oy** ending, and adding the "opposite" vowel plus **-s.**

No me **vengas** con tus quejas.	*Don't come to me with your complaints.*
No hables de esas cosas.	*Don't talk about such things.*

Ir and **ser** have irregular forms.

No vayas a casa sin mí.	*Don't go home without me.*
No seas tan perezoso.	*Don't be so lazy.*

As with negative formal commands, all object and reflexive pronouns precede negative commands. Remember that when both a direct and an indirect object are present, the indirect object precedes the direct object. Examples are in the following chart.

NEGATIVE INFORMAL COMMANDS			
INFINITIVE	**yo** FORM	STEM	ADD THE "OPPOSITE" VOWEL AND **-s**
hablar	hablo	habl-	+ **es** = **hables**
beber	bebo	beb-	+ **as** = **bebas**
abrir	abro	abr-	+ **as** = **abras**
decir	digo	dig-	+ **as** = **digas**
estar	estoy	est-	+ **es** = **estés***
conducir	conduzco	conduzc-	+ **as** = **conduzcas**

USING PRONOUNS WITH INFORMAL COMMANDS	
PRONOUNS ARE PLACED AFTER AFFIRMATIVE COMMANDS	PRONOUNS ARE PLACED BEFORE NEGATIVE COMMANDS
Dile la verdad. *Tell him the truth.*	**No le digas** la verdad. *Don't tell him the truth.*
Cómprala. *Buy it. (it =* **la comida***)*	**No la compres.** *Don't buy it.*
Dámelo. *Give me it. (it =* **el libro***)*	**No me lo des.** *Don't give it to me.*
Acuéstate. *Go to bed.*	**No te acuestes.** *Don't go to bed.*

De *Sol y viento,* **Note:** You can access this film clip from a special menu section on Disc 5 of the Instructional Version on DVD.

DE SOL Y VIENTO

In **Episodio 6** of *Sol y viento,* you saw María talking with don Paco at the airport. Part of their exchange appears here.

MARÍA
Mamá me dijo que venías e insistí en venir a buscarte.

PACO
A ver.[a] Mis ojos no lo creen. Tan bella[b] como siempre.

MARÍA
Ay, tío. No _____.

From the following options, choose the one that best fits the blank in the conversation.

1. exageres
2. seas cruel
3. me ofendas

[a]*A... Let me see.* [b]*beautiful*

---

*Note that the command form **estés** carries a written accent.

INPUT
Act. E, Suggestion:
Use activity to stimulate discussion of the plot and characters. Have students provide evidence from the movie to support the options they choose.

Actividad E Consejos para María

Considerando las frustraciones de María en el **Episodio 6** de *Sol y viento*, indica si los siguientes consejos son buenos o malos para ella.

	BUEN CONSEJO	MAL CONSEJO
1. No llegues a conclusiones falsas; Jaime es un buen hombre.	☐	☐
2. No confíes en (*Don't trust*) tu hermano; tiene malas intenciones.	☐	☐
3. No seas cabezona; debes perdonar a Jaime.	☐	☐
4. No pierdas la confianza en Carlos; es tu hermano y necesita tu ayuda.	☐	☐
5. No le digas nada a tu madre; no debe preocuparse (*worry*) tanto.	☐	☐
6. No tengas confianza en Jaime; lo más importante para él es el trabajo.	☐	☐

Actividad F Mi mejor amigo/a   INPUT Actividad F

Empareja una situación de la primera columna con un mandato apropiado de la segunda columna.

Si mi mejor amigo/a...

1. __c__ quiere ponerse un suéter cuando hace calor afuera

2. __e__ no ha dormido bien y tiene un examen mañana

3. __d__ se pelea con su novio/a todos los días

4. __a__ me cuenta algo que no puedo creer

5. __f__ está deprimido/a y quiere llorar (*to cry*)

6. __b__ quiere darme un regalo que no quiero aceptar

yo le digo...

a. ¡no me digas!*

b. no me lo des, por favor.

c. no te lo pongas.

d. no le hables más.

e. no te acuestes tarde.

f. no estés tan triste.

OUTPUT
Act. G, Suggestions:
Paso 1: Allow students 4–5 minutes to review drawings and write paragraphs with dialogue. On the board, write some transition words (e.g., *primero, luego, después, al final*) with their English translations. Instruct students to write what father says in this way: *El papá le dice al niño: «No hables cuando comes»* (in order to avoid a clause with the subjunctive). Circulate throughout the class to help students with any unknown words they might want to add to their story description. You may wish to provide each group with an overhead transparency on which to write their description. *Paso 2*: Ask various groups to share their descriptions orally or using the overhead projector. Draw students' attention to details that differ across groups. Correct any misuses of affirmative or negative command forms. **Optional:** After groups share their descriptions, you may wish to have students write a final version of the description to turn in.

Actividad G Una historia

Paso 1 Con un compañero (una compañera), escriban una historia sobre lo que pasa en los dibujos en la siguiente página. Para esta historia, incluye lo que dice el padre. A continuación hay algunas ideas para considerar.

- ¿Cómo se llama el padre? ¿Dónde trabaja?
- ¿Cómo se llaman los hijos? ¿Qué edad tienen?
- ¿Cómo se portan los niños?
- ¿Qué les dice el padre a sus hijos para controlarlos?
- ¿Cómo termina la noche?

Paso 2 Comparten su historia con el resto de la clase. ¿Quiénes inventaron la mejor historia?

*In addition to its literal meaning of *Don't tell me*, **¡No me digas!** also has the colloquial meaning *You're kidding!* or *You don't say!* It is often said in response to something surprising or unexpected.

Actividad H ¿Es «verde» tu compañero/a de clase?

Paso 1 Entrevista a un compañero (una compañera) de clase e indica sus respuestas.

	SÍ	NO
1. ¿Tiras a la basura los productos reciclables como el papel, el plástico y el vidrio?	☐	☐
2. ¿Te duchas por más de diez minutos?	☐	☐
3. ¿Dejas prendidas las luces cuando sales de tu casa?	☐	☐
4. ¿Tomas el transporte público?	☐	☐
5. ¿Limpias la casa con productos en forma de aerosol?	☐	☐
6. ¿Usas toallas y servilletas de papel?	☐	☐
7. ¿Compras productos hechos de materiales reciclados?	☐	☐

Paso 2 Basándote en las respuestas del **Paso 1,** indica si tu compañero/a es «muy verde», «algo verde» o «poco verde». Luego, inventa mandatos para ayudarle a conservar más.

MODELO: No tires a la basura las botellas de plástico. Recíclalas.

Actividad I Un cartel

Paso 1 Con un compañero (una compañera), hagan una lista de diez consejos que le sirvan a un estudiante de tu universidad para conservar energía. Usen mandatos afirmativos en cinco de los consejos, y usen mandatos negativos en los otros cinco.

MODELOS: Dúchate rápidamente.

No dejes las luces prendidas cuando sales de casa.

Paso 2 En otra hoja de papel, diseñen (*design*) un cartel titulado «Cómo conservar energía». Incluyan los diez consejos que escribieron y unos dibujos creativos.

TERCERA PARTE

More on Talking About Trips

Vocabulario

De vacaciones

Activities to Do While on Vacation

Actividades al aire libreª

ªal... *outdoor*

escalar montañas

montar a caballo

pescar (qu)

practicar (qu) el alpinismo de rocas

acampar / hacer (*irreg.*) camping

ir (*irreg.*) de excursión

bucear

ir (*irreg.*) a un parque de diversiones

remar en canoa

Actividades interiores

ver (*irreg.*) **un espectáculo**

charlar en un café

comprar recuerdos

ir (*irreg.*) **a un concierto**

cenar en un restaurante elegante

degustar vinos

✳ **MÁS VOCABULARIO**

hacer (*irreg.*) **kayak**	to go kayaking
hacer (*irreg.*) **el salto bungee**	to bungee jump
hacer (*irreg.*) **rafting**	to go rafting
practicar (qu) el paracaidismo	to sky dive
surfear	to surf

INPUT

Act. A, *Paso 1,*
Suggestion: Read
the following items once:
*bucear, escalar montañas,
hacer camping, remar en
canoa, surfear, ir de
excursión, pescar, montar
a caballo.*
Paso 2, **Suggestion:** Tell
the class the following:
*Voy a leer una lista de
actividades. Uds. me
dicen si requieren mucha
energía o no.* Repeat
items from *Paso 1* plus
the following phrases:
*comprar recuerdos, prac-
ticar el alpinismo de
rocas, degustar vinos,
charlar en un café.*
Optional follow-up: Repeat
the items in *Paso 2* but
tell students to classify the
activities based on
whether or not they
require a lot of mental
concentration (*mucha o
poca concentración
mental*).

Actividad A Clasificaciones

Paso 1 Tu profesor(a) va a leer una lista de actividades. Escribe cada actividad en la caja apropiada.

ACTIVIDADES ACUÁTICAS	ACTIVIDADES TERRESTRES (*land*)

Paso 2 Tu profesor(a) va a leer otra lista de actividades. Escribe cada actividad en la caja apropiada.

REQUIERE MUCHA ENERGÍA	NO REQUIERE MUCHA ENERGÍA

INPUT

Act. B, Statements:
1. *pescar*
2. *ver un espectáculo*
3. *ir de excursión*
4. *practicar el alpinisimo
de rocas*
5. *remar en canoa*
6. *montar a caballo (a)*
7. *comprar recuerdos*
8. *ir a un concierto*
Optional follow-up: Ask
students to give examples
of other activities that are
done in these places. Say:
*¿Qué otras actividades se
hacen en el océano?*
(*surfear, bucear, navegar
en barco* [presented in an
earlier lesson]).

Actividad B ¿Dónde se hace?

Indica dónde se hace cada una de las actividades que menciona tu profesor(a).

1.	**a.** en la selva	**(b.)** en el océano
2.	**a.** en el museo	**(b.)** en el teatro
3.	**a.** en un lago	**(b.)** en un bosque
4.	**(a.)** en las montañas	**b.** en la playa
5.	**(a.)** en un río	**b.** en el desierto
6.	**(a.)** en la llanura	**b.** en un volcán
7.	**a.** en un café	**(b.)** en una tienda
8.	**(a.)** en un auditorio	**b.** en un restaurante

Actividad C Pistas (*Clues*)OUTPUT

Actividad C

Paso 1 Escribe una pista para cinco actividades en las páginas 364–365 sin
mencionar el nombre de la actividad.

MODELOS: Hay que tener 21 años para hacer esta actividad en los Estados
Unidos.
Uno necesita brazos (*arms*) y piernas (*legs*) fuertes para hacer
esta actividad.

Paso 2 Léele tus pistas a un compañero (una compañera) de clase. ¿Puede adivinar todas las actividades que describiste?

MODELO: E1: Uno necesita brazos y piernas fuertes para hacer esta actividad.
E2: Practicar el alpinismo de rocas.

INPUT/OUTPUT
Act. D, Suggestions
Paso 2: Model 1–2 examples with a student. Then allow 4 minutes to complete.
Paso 3: Poll the class to find out how many students consider themselves daring. Say: *¿Cuántos de Uds. son arriesgados? ¿Sí?* (to a student) *¿Por qué te consideras arriesgado/a?*, etc.

Actividad D ¿Eres arriesgado/a (*daring*)?

Paso 1 Indica si has hecho las siguientes actividades o no.

	SÍ	NO
1. He practicado el paracaidismo.	☐	☐
2. He practicado el alpinismo de rocas.	☐	☐
3. He buceado con tiburones (*sharks*).	☐	☐
4. He acampado donde había osos (*bears*) o coyotes.	☐	☐
5. He hecho el salto bungee.	☐	☐
6. He practicado el parapente (*hang gliding*).	☐	☐
7. He practicado la escalada (*rappeling*).	☐	☐
8. He montado un caballo indómito (*untamed*).	☐	☐

Paso 2 Entrevista a un compañero (una compañera) de clase para averiguar si ha hecho las actividades del **Paso 1.**

MODELO: ¿Has practicado el paracaidismo alguna vez?

Paso 3 Ahora, indica si las siguientes oraciones son ciertas o falsas.

1. Soy una persona arriesgada.
2. Mi compañero/a de clase es una persona arriesgada.

Vistazo cultural,
Suggestion: Have students read quickly. Then ask them to define *ecoturismo* in their own words and state its two primary goals.
Follow-up: Have the class vote on which ecotouristic activity they would prefer to do (see end of first paragraph). Are there any other activities they can think of?

〰 Vistazo cultural

El ecoturismo

En muchos países del mundo hispano, el ecoturismo se ha hecho[a] un gran negocio en los últimos años. El ecoturismo se refiere al desarrollo[b] de una industria turística con fines de lucro[c] que pone a los turistas en contacto con la naturaleza. La mayoría de los ecoturistas son personas urbanas que viajan con el deseo de ver paisajes, animales y flores que no pueden ver en su propio país. Algunas de las actividades ecoturísticas comunes son: bucear con peces tropicales, remar en canoa en un río que va por un bosque tropical, ir de excursión a una selva, montar a caballo e ir en un safari fotográfico.

El ecoturismo tiene dos metas:[d] una es estimular la economía de países que tienen muchas riquezas biológicas, y la otra es proteger esas riquezas, incluyendo especies que ahora están en peligro de extinción. La idea es que el ecoturismo crea trabajos nuevos y genera fondos[e] para crear programas cuyo[f] fin es proteger el medio ambiente. Los países que tienen programas establecidos de ecoturismo son México, Costa Rica, Panamá, Venezuela, Bolivia y el Ecuador, entre otros. El ecoturismo como se conoce en el mundo hispano no existe en los Estados Unidos, con excepción de Alaska, que ofrece muchos viajes para gozar de[g] la flora y la fauna y de sus paisajes. La próxima vez que te dé la gana[h] hacer un viaje, ¡piensa en un viaje ecológico en el mundo hispano!

[a]se... *has become* [b]*development* [c]con... *for profit* [d]*goals* [e]*funds* [f]*whose*
[g]gozar... *enjoying* [h]te... *you feel like*

Gramática

Expressing *the Most* and *the Least* | **Es el más guapo de todos.**   **Superlatives**

Superlative expressions are those used to denote the extreme state expressed by a particular adjective. Take the adjective *smart,* for example. You may think your brother is smart and you are smarter, but that your uncle Bob is the smartest person in the family. *The smartest* is called a superlative expression. English forms most superlatives by adding *-est* to the ends of adjectives and using the definite article *the* before the adjective. Some adjectives take a different form using *most*—for example, *popular, more popular, the most popular.*

Superlatives can also be used to talk about negative qualities. For example, maybe you think you are smart, that your cousin is less smart than you, and that of the three your brother is the *least smart.* In English, adjectives like *funny* and *popular* don't have a direct opposite adjective to which one could add *-est.* Adjectives like these use the word *least* before them: *John is the least funny person I know,* or *Mary is the least popular girl in school.*

Spanish forms superlatives by joining the following words: *definite article* + *noun* + **más/menos** + *adjective* + **de,** as indicated in the chart on the next page. The noun may be left out if the person or thing being talked about has already been established.

—¿Quién es **la persona más alta de** tu familia?   *Who is the tallest person in your family?*

—Sin duda mi hermana es **la más alta.**   *Without a doubt, my sister is the tallest (person).*

Mejor (*Best*) and **peor** (*worst*) can be used in superlative constructions, but without an adjective.

—**La mejor clase de** mi horario es la geografía.   *The best class in my schedule is geography.*

—**La peor actriz del** año fue Madonna.   *The worst actress of the year was Madonna.*

—Sí, fue **la peor.**   *Yes, she was the worst.*

In a previous lesson you learned another form of the superlative, one that consists of adding **-ísimo/a/os/as** to the end of an adjective, as in **La montaña es altísima.** Note that adjectives ending in **-ísimo/a/os/as** are already in a superlative form and therefore cannot be used with the structure you just learned.

◄

La escasez de agua potable[a] es uno de los problemas **más graves** que debe resolver la humanidad, pues su consumo crece[b] y los recursos hídricos[c] están altamente contaminados.

[a]*drinkable* [b]*is growing* [c]*water*

SUPERLATIVES					
ARTICLE +	NOUN +	**más/menos** +	ADJECTIVE +	**de**	
el	volcán	**más**	alto	de	México
los	ríos	**más**	grandes	de	Sudamérica
la	persona	**menos**	apreciada	de	mi familia
las	canciones	**menos**	populares	del	año
SUPERLATIVES WITH *mejor* AND *peor*					
el **mejor** amigo			del hombre		
la **peor** idea			de la reunión		

De *Sol y viento,* **Note:** You can access this film clip from a special menu section on Disc 5 of the Instructional Version on DVD.

 DE SOL Y VIENTO

In **Episodio 6** of *Sol y viento*, you saw a conversation between a waiter and some patrons in don Paco's restaurant in Mexico City. Their exchange appears here.

MESERO
El vino de la casa: «Sol y viento».

CLIENTE 1
Hmmm... ¿De dónde es?

MESERO
De Chile. Es _____ de todos los
vinos importados.

CLIENTE 2
Un vino chileno. ¡Qué interesante!

Which of the following expressions does the waiter use in the preceding blank?

1. el mejor
2. el peor

Actividad E Opiniones

Indica lo que opinas de las siguientes oraciones sobre los personajes de *Sol y viento.*

1. La característica más fascinante de María es su _____.

   a. belleza (*beauty*)　　**b.** dedicación　　**c.** inteligencia　　**d.** ¿ ?
   　　　　　　　　　　　　　　　　al trabajo

2. El momento más difícil (*awkward*) entre Jaime y María fue cuando _____.

   a. se chocaron　　**b.** Diego llamó　　**c.** María se　　**d.** ¿ ?
   　　(*they bumped*　　　durante su　　　enojó en la
   　　into each other)　　cita　　　　　viña
   　　en el parque

3. El personaje menos respetado de *Sol y viento* es _____.

   a. Mario　　**b.** Traimaqueo　　**c.** Carlos　　**d.** ¿ ?

4. El problema más serio que enfrenta (*faces*) Jaime es/son _____.

   a. su relación con　　**b.** las mentiras　　**c.** las demandas　　**d.** ¿ ?
   　　María　　　　　　　de Carlos　　　　de sus jefes

5. La mejor característica de Mario es _____.

   a. su sentido　　**b.** su lealtad　　**c.** su compasión　　**d.** ¿ ?
   　　(*sense*) del　　　(*loyalty*)
   　　humor

Actividad F Los famosos

Paso 1 Indica si estás de acuerdo o no con las afirmaciones sobre los siguientes personajes famosos.

	ESTOY DE ACUERDO.	NO ESTOY DE ACUERDO.
1. La mujer más dinámica de los Estados Unidos es Hillary Clinton.	☐	☐
2. Halle Berry es la mujer más guapa del mundo.	☐	☐
3. Steven Spielberg es el director más creativo de Hollywood.	☐	☐
4. El hombre más influyente de nuestro país es Bill Gates.	☐	☐
5. El atleta más conocido del mundo es Tiger Woods.	☐	☐
6. La persona famosa más fotografiada es Jennifer López.	☐	☐

Paso 2 Entrevista a un compañero (una compañera) de clase para ver si está de acuerdo o no con las oraciones del **Paso 1.**

MODELO:　E1: ¿Crees que Hillary Clinton es la mujer más dinámica de los Estados Unidos?

　　　　　E2: No. La mujer más dinámica de los Estados Unidos es Oprah Winfrey.

INPUT/OUTPUT
Actividad G

Actividad G Más sobre el medio ambiente

Paso 1 Completa las oraciones a continuación según tus opiniones sobre el medio ambiente.

MODELO: La peor manera de desperdiciar el agua es usar el lavaplatos todos los días.

1. El problema más serio para el medio ambiente es _____.
2. La mejor manera de protegernos contra los pesticidas es _____.
3. La actividad más dañina (*harmful*) para la capa de ozono es _____.
4. La peor manera de desperdiciar el papel es _____.
5. La solución menos eficaz (*effective*) para conservar energía es _____.
6. La peor manera de desperdiciar el agua es _____.

Paso 2 Compara tus respuestas con las de dos compañeros/as de clase. ¿En qué están de acuerdo y en qué no?

OUTPUT

Act. H, Suggestions
Paso 1: Give students
1–2 minutes to complete.
Paso 2: Allow students
4–5 minutes to interview
their classmates.

Actividad H Una entrevista

Paso 1 Lee las preguntas a continuación y escribe tus respuestas en la primera columna.

En tu opinión,...	YO	E1	E2
1. ¿cuál es la mejor película del año? ¿y la peor?	_____	_____	_____
2. ¿quién es el actor más guapo? ¿y la actriz más guapa?	_____	_____	_____
3. ¿quién es la cantante más talentosa? ¿y el cantante más talentoso?	_____	_____	_____
4. ¿cuál es el programa de televisión más cómico? ¿y el más serio?	_____	_____	_____
5. ¿cuál es la canción más irritante (*annoying*) en la radio en estos momentos? ¿y la más popular?	_____	_____	_____
6. ¿cuál es el videojuego más interesante en estos momentos? ¿y el más difícil de ganar?	_____	_____	_____

Paso 2 Luego, hazles las mismas preguntas a dos de tus compañeros/as de clase. Indica sus respuestas en las columnas dos y tres.

Paso 3 Escribe un breve resumen comparando tus opiniones con las de tus compañeros de clase.

MODELO: Mis compañeros de clase creen que los actores más guapos son Tom Cruise y Colin Farrell. En mi opinión, el más guapo es Matt Damon.

SOL Y VIENTO
A segunda vista

Antes de ver el episodio

Actividad A ¿Qué recuerdas?

Basándote en lo que recuerdas de la primera vista, determina quién dice las oraciones a continuación. Escoge entre doña Isabel, Carlos y María.

1. «La verdad es que mi madre no se siente bien hoy.» Carlos
2. «Ay, tío. No exageres.» María
3. «¡Carlos! Deja que pase el señor. (*Let the gentleman in.*)» doña Isabel
4. «Oh, es muy buena moza (*girl*). Es profesora en Santiago. Mírela. ¿No es bonita?» doña Isabel
5. «¡No diga nada más, señor! ¡Ahí tiene su regalito!» María
6. «Escuche, señor Talavera. "Sol y viento" no está a la venta.» doña Isabel

Actividad B ¡A escuchar!

Repasa brevemente el siguiente fragmento de un diálogo entre Jaime y Carlos. Luego, mientras ves el episodio, llena los espacios en blanco con las palabras correctas.

Act. B, Suggestion: Have students read the exchange. They do not need to write anything at this point. Do not reveal answers.
Alternative: Have the class brainstorm possible answers for each blank but do not have them write anything down.

JAIME: ¡Esta cosa no va a funcionar! __Nos__ [1] prometió[a] las firmas de su madre, de su hermana y de los vecinos. ¡A que __tampoco__ [2] ha hecho nada con la comunidad mapuche! Así es, ¿no? ¡La verdad es que no tiene nada! ¡Mi compañía quiere estas __tierras__ [3]!

CARLOS: Por favor, __espere__ [4] un par de días más. Se las voy a conseguir.

JAIME: Tenemos que firmar el contrato esta semana... ¡y Ud. no tiene la influencia __necesaria__ [5]!

CARLOS: Ya __le dije__ [6] yo voy a convencer a mi madre ¡y a mi __hermana__ [7] le da lo mismo![b]

JAIME: ¡Lo dudo![c] Según lo que __he visto__ [8] y oído, ¡pienso que a su hermana *sí* le __importa__ [9] el destino de estas tierras!

[a]*you promised* [b]*le... doesn't care* [c]*¡Lo... I doubt it!*

Actividad C El episodio

Ahora vas a ver el episodio de nuevo. No te olvides de verificar tus respuestas a la **Actividad A** mientras ves el episodio.

Después de ver el episodio

Actividad A Para pensar...

Ya sabes que Jaime y María tuvieron una confrontación horrible. Entre todos, comenten las siguientes preguntas.

1. ¿Qué creen Uds. que piensa María de la relación entre su hermano y Jaime? ¿De quién sospecha (*is she suspicious*) más, de Carlos o de Jaime?

2. ¿Cuál creen que es la causa principal de su enojo (*anger*), la venta de las tierras familiares? ¿las consecuencias de la venta para los mapuches? ¿la decepción que siente con respecto a Jaime?

Actividad B ¡A verificar!

Vas a ver otra vez la escena de **¡A escuchar!** en la página anterior. Llena los espacios en blanco, según lo que oyes.

Act. B, Suggestion: Replay the scene once for students. Replay a second time if needed. Then ask for volunteers to provide answers for each blank. Verify using the instructor notes from Act. B on the previous page.
Alternative: After students complete the conversation, have 2 students act it out.

Actividad C ¡Te toca a ti!

Paso 1 Sabes que María está muy enojada con Jaime. ¿Qué crees que quiere decirle María? Con todo lo que has aprendido sobre los mandatos, escribe dos mandatos afirmativos y dos mandatos negativos para expresar lo que tú le dirías (*would say*) a Jaime si fueras (*you were*) María. ¿Vas a usar **tú** or **Ud.**? ¿Por qué?

Paso 2 Ahora ponte en el lugar de Jaime. ¿Qué le dirías a María para que te perdonara (*to get her to forgive you*)? Escribe dos mandatos afirmativos y dos mandatos negativos. ¿Vas a usar **tú** o **Ud.**? ¿Por qué?

Actividad D Utilizando el contexto

El verbo **deber** significa *must, should, ought to*. Repasa la siguiente parte del diálogo entre don Paco y Lourdes en el mercado. ¿Puedes deducir el significado de la frase en letra itálica?

> PACO: ¡Buenas, doña Lourdes! ¿Qué tal están sus jitomates hoy?
> LOURDES: ¡Pruébelos! *Ud. debería de saber.* ¡Son los mejores del mercado!
> PACO: ¡Estos sí que son jitomates! ¡Firmes y de muy buen color! Así me gustan.
> LOURDES: Como le dije: los mejores del mercado.

Act. C, Suggestions
Paso 1: Before students begin writing the commands, ask them whether they think María would address Jaime with formal or informal commands. Remind them that María has lost trust in Jaime and would likely address him as *señor Talavera* until he earns back her respect, if at all.
Paso 2: Repeat the suggestion in *Paso 1*, pointing out that Jaime, being the type of person that he is, will realize he has to deal on María's terms to win her back. This includes using formal commands until they reestablish the comfort of addressing each other informally.

RESUMEN DE VOCABULARIO

La geografía

el bosque (lluvioso)	(rain)forest
las cataratas	waterfalls
la colina	hill
la cordillera	mountain range
el lago	lake
la llanura	plain, prairie
el mar	sea
el paisaje	landscape
la playa	beach
el río	river
la selva (tropical)	(tropical) jungle
el valle	valley

los continentes: África, Antártida, Asia, Australia, Europa, Norteamérica, Sudamérica
Cognados: la costa, el desierto, el golfo, la isla, la meseta, la montaña, el océano, el volcán

El medio ambiente

construir (y)	to build
contaminar	to pollute
descomponer (*like* **poner**)	to decompose
desperdiciar	to waste
echar	to throw out
proteger (j)	to protect

salvar	to save (*from danger*)
tirar	to throw out
el basurero	landfill
la botella (de plástico/ vidrio)	(plastic/glass) bottle
la caja de cartón	cardboard box
la capa de ozono	ozone layer
los combustibles fósiles	fossil fuels
la contaminación (del agua/aire)	(water/air) pollution
los desperdicios	wastes
el efecto invernadero	greenhouse effect
la escasez (*pl.* **las escaseces**)	shortage
las especies en peligro de extinción	endangered species
la fábrica	factory
la falta	lack
la lata de aluminio	aluminum can
la naturaleza	nature
el producto desechable	disposable product
el reciclaje	recycling
los recursos naturales	natural resources

Cognados: conservar, reciclar; la deforestación, los pesticidas, el petróleo, el producto biodegradable
Repaso: la basura, el periódico

Actividades turísticas

acampar	to camp, go camping
bucear	to snorkel
cenar en un restaurante elegante	to eat in a fancy restaurant
charlar en un café	to chat in a café
comprar recuerdos	to buy souvenirs
degustar vinos	to go wine tasting
escalar montañas	to mountain climb
hacer (*irreg.*) **el salto bungee**	to bungee jump
ir (*irreg.*) **a un concierto**	to go to a concert
ir (*irreg.*) **a un parque de diversiones**	to go to an amusement park
ir (*irreg.*) **de excursión**	to go on a hike, go hiking
montar a caballo	to ride a horse, go horseback riding
pescar (qu)	to fish
practicar (qu) el alpinismo de rocas	to rock climb
practicar (qu) el paracaidismo	to sky dive
remar en canoa	to go canoeing
ver (*irreg.*) **un espectáculo**	to see a show

Cognados: hacer (*irreg.*) **camping, hacer** (*irreg.*) **kayak, hacer** (*irreg.*) **rafting, surfear**

Otras palabras y expresiones

al aire libre	outdoor(s)
interior (*adj.*)	indoor

Repaso: mejor, peor

Entremés cultural
La región andina: Colombia, el Ecuador, el Perú, Bolivia

VISTAZO

La región andina recibe su nombre de los Andes, una cordillera que recorre toda Sudamérica y que caracteriza el paisaje de Colombia, el Ecuador, el Perú y Bolivia. Aunque los cuatro países comparten los Andes y grandes extensiones de la selva amazónica, la geografía y el clima varían mucho dentro de cada país y de un país a otro. Colombia cuenta con[a] llanuras extensas y regiones tropicales mientras que el sur del Perú y Bolivia incluyen partes del Atacama, el desierto más árido del planeta. La mayoría de la población andina es rural. Sin embargo, el 75% de la población colombiana vive en centros urbanos como Bogotá, la capital. Con unos 44 millones de habitantes, Colombia es el tercer país más grande de Latinoamérica, tras[b] el Brasil y México.

[a]cuenta... *has*   [b]*after*

DATO INTERESANTE:
Los asiáticos[a] en el Perú

Aunque la gran mayoría de la gente andina es mestiza (de herencia europea e indígena) o indígena, el Perú cuenta con la población más grande de personas de ascendencia china en Latinoamérica y la segunda población más grande de personas de ascendencia japonesa, el Brasil siendo la primera.

Idea: Busca información sobre la composición étnica de los países andinos y organízala en gráficos que representan cada país. Incluye por lo menos cuatro puntos de comparación.

Alberto Fujimori, peruano de ascendencia japonesa, fue presidente del Perú de 1990 hasta 2000.

[a]Los... *Asians*

DATO INTERESANTE:

El bilingüismo en los Andes

Aunque el español es la lengua oficial en todos los países andinos, algunos son bilingües. En el Perú y Bolivia, el quechua (la lengua de los incas) es una lengua oficial y el aimará (otra lengua indígena de los Andes) es una lengua oficial de Bolivia. En el Perú se ofrecen programas de educación bilingüe para niños que hablan español y quechua.

Idea: Haz una búsqueda por el Internet de por lo menos cinco palabras del español sudamericano que tienen su origen en el quechua. ¿Por qué crees que estas palabras se incorporaron al español de esa región?

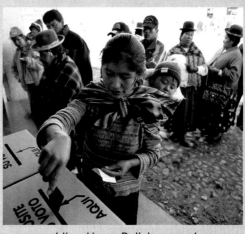

El votar es una obligación en Bolivia, como lo es en varios países sudamericanos.

DATO INTERESANTE:

¿Obligatorio o no?

En este país, el votar es un derecho[a] que se puede ejercer[b] o no, pero es una obligación en el Perú, el Ecuador y Bolivia. Como en este país, el servicio militar es voluntario. Sin embargo, en Bolivia se permite reclutar[c] a jóvenes de 14 años si el número de voluntarios es bajo. El 40% del ejército[d] boliviano tiene menos de 18 años y la mitad[e] de estos tienen menos de 16 años.

Idea: Como clase, comenten las ventajas y desventajas de tener el voto obligatorio. ¿Cómo afectaría[f] el voto obligatorio las elecciones de este país?

[a]*right* [b]*se... one can exercise* [c]*to recruit* [d]*army* [e]*la... half* [f]*would affect*

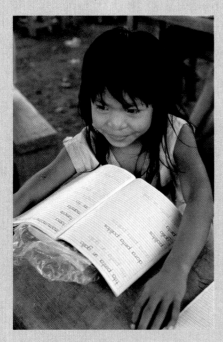

Esta niña peruana recibe instrucción en español y quechua, su lengua nativa.

DATO INTERESANTE:

La economía andina

Las economías de los países andinos se basan principalmente en la exportación de productos agrícolas, textiles, minerales y metales preciosos y combustibles fósiles. El Ecuador exporta muchos productos agrícolas a los Estados Unidos y es uno de tres países hispanos (junto con[a] El Salvador y Panamá) que usan el dólar estadounidense como moneda[b] nacional.

Idea: Busca información sobre una de las siguientes alianzas económicas de Sudamérica: MERCOSUR, ALCA, ALADI, CAN. Prepara una breve presentación para la clase que incluye el significado de la sigla,[c] las metas[d] de la alianza y los países que son miembros de la alianza.

El café es uno de los productos agrícolas más importantes de Colombia.

[a]*junto... along with* [b]*currency* [c]*acronym* [d]*goals*

Bajo el sol

En este episodio...

JAIME

Ud. me recuerda a^a mi mamá. Ella siempre me hablaba de la tierra. Era campesina.

ISABEL

¿Entonces no aprendió nada de su mamá? ¿Por qué está trabajando con esa gente que quiere cambiar nuestras vidas?

PACO

He averiguado que su compañía quiere construir una represa ^b en esta zona. ¿Comprende Ud. el daño^c que eso causaría^d por estas tierras?

---

^ame... *remind me of* ^b*dam* ^c*harm* ^d*would cause*

¿Qué crees tú?

1. ¿Por qué crees que doña Isabel le recuerda a Jaime a su mamá? ¿Qué tienen en común las dos mujeres?

2. ¿Qué efecto tendría (*would have*) una represa en la comunidad del valle?

3. ¿Qué crees que va a hacer Jaime de aquí en adelante (*from here on out*)?

¿Cómo te sientes?

OBJETIVOS

IN THIS LESSON, YOU WILL LEARN:

- to talk about feelings and mental conditions
- to use certain verbs to describe changes in emotion or mood
- vocabulary for describing parts of the body and health-related issues
- more about using the imperfect to talk about conditions in the past
- vocabulary for talking about a visit to the doctor's office
- to use the verb **hacer** to express *ago* in a variety of contexts

In addition, you will prepare for and watch **Episodio 7** of the film *Sol y viento.*

El bienestar (*well-being*) emocional contribuye mucho a la buena salud (*health*) física.

The following media resources are available for this lesson of *Sol y viento:*

Episodio 7 of *Sol y viento*

Online *Manual de actividades*

Online Learning Center Website

PRIMERA PARTE

Note: These vocabulary items can be heard in this lesson's Textbook Audio section of the Online Learning Center Website.
Talking About Feelings and Mental Conditions

Vocabulario

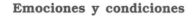

Estoy tenso.

Describing Emotions

Emociones y condiciones

alegre, contento/a   avergonzado/a   cansado/a   confundido/a   enamorado/a (de)

enojado/a   frustrado/a   furioso/a   irritado/a   nervioso/a

perplejo/a   preocupado/a   relajado/a   triste

afectar	to affect
alegrar	to make happy
cansar	to tire
confundir	to confuse
enojar	to anger
frustrar	to frustrate
irritar	to irritate
molestar	to bother
ofender	to offend
preocupar	to worry
reaccionar	to react

✱ MÁS VOCABULARIO

estar (*irreg.*) **celoso/a**	to be jealous
llorar	to cry
reírse (i, i) (me río)	to laugh
tener(le) (*irreg.*) **envidia* (a alguien)**	to be envious (of someone)
tener(le) (*irreg.*) **miedo* (a alguien)**	to be afraid (of someone)
tener (*irreg.*) **sueño***	to be sleepy
tomarse algo muy a pecho	to take something to heart; to feel something intensely

≋ Vistazo cultural

Las telenovelas

Las telenovelas son programas televisivos muy populares en Latinoamérica. Son melodramas parecidos a las *soap operas* de este país. Ambos tipos de programas presentan los mismos conflictos sentimentales: emociones exageradas, pasiones tormentosas,[a] amores celosos, envidia, homicidios...

Una de las diferencias entre las novelas (como suelen llamarse) y las *soap operas* es que las novelas tienen mucha más aceptación entre el público. De hecho,[b] estos programas se transmiten en la tarde y en la noche, horas que en este país equivalen a la hora estelar.[c] Las estrellas de las novelas son muy populares en el mundo hispano. Muchos de estos actores aceptan papeles en novelas y películas alternativamente, mientras que en este país, el ideal de muchos actores es salir de la pantalla pequeña para lanzarse a[d] la pantalla grande.

Otra diferencia importante es que las novelas corren por un tiempo limitado. La idea de una telenovela de la misma longitud[e] de, por ejemplo, *All My Children,* es ajena[f] en el mundo hispano. La telenovela es una historia que tiene un principio,[g] un medio y un fin.

▲ La cadena (*network*) hispana Univisión tiene varias páginas en la red dedicadas a las telenovelas.

[a]*stormy*   [b]*De... In fact*   [c]*hora... prime time*   [d]*lanzarse... break into*   [e]*length*   [f]*foreign*   [g]*beginning*

---

*The words used in these **tener** expressions are not adjectives but nouns. The literal meaning of the phrases is *to have envy, to have fear,* and *to have sleepiness,* respectively. To qualify these expressions, use **mucho/a/os/as** or **un poco de** and not **muy** or **poco: Tengo mucho sueño.**

INPUT

Act. A, *Paso 1,*
Statements:
1. *Marcos se siente frustrado porque...*
2. *Elena está cansada porque...*
3. *Paco y Gonzalo están preocupados porque...*
4. *Juanita está confundida porque...*
5. *Jorge está avergonzado porque...*

INPUT

Act. B, Suggestions
Paso 1: Give students 2 minutes to complete.
Paso 2: Give students 3–4 minutes to interview a partner, then have students reverse roles.
Optional follow-up: Ask students to present their findings to the class. They should compare how they responded to a few items with how their partner responded. Model exchanges for students. Say: *Alfredo, ¿te frustran las matemáticas? (Alfredo) Sí, me frustran mucho. (you) A Alfredo le frustran las matemáticas, pero a mí no. Me gustan mucho las matemáticas,* etc.

Actividad A Oraciones lógicas

Paso 1 Escucha lo que dice el profesor (la profesora). Luego indica la frase que completa cada oración lógicamente.

1. a. ...tiene un auto nuevo.
   b. ...estudia mucho, pero no entiende la lección.

2. **a.** ...no durmió bien anoche.
   b. ...sacó una A en su examen.

3. **a.** ...necesitan pagar el alquiler y no tienen suficiente dinero.
   b. ...mañana van a comenzar las vacaciones de verano.

4. **a.** ...lo que le dijo el profesor es diferente de lo que dice el libro.
   b. ...necesita planear una fiesta de sorpresa y tiene mucho que hacer.

5. a. ...trabaja demasiado y no tiene suficiente tiempo libre.
   b. ...lo van a expulsar de la universidad.

Paso 2 Ahora indica si cada oración es lógica o no.

	SÍ	NO
1. Si uno está enojado, normalmente se ríe de la situación.	☐	☑
2. Si uno está muy triste, típicamente llora.	☑	☐
3. Si uno está enamorado de alguien, piensa mucho en esa persona.	☑	☐
4. Si uno está perplejo, está seguro de sus acciones.	☐	☑
5. Si uno está relajado, se come las uñas (*fingernails*).	☐	☑

Actividad B ¿Se te aplica o no?

Paso 1 Indica si se te aplica cada oración o no.

	SE ME APLICA.	NO SE ME APLICA.
1. Me enoja cuando otras personas hablan durante una película.	☐	☐
2. Me preocupa la economía del país.	☐	☐
3. Me confunden los planos.	☐	☐
4. Me frustran las matemáticas.	☐	☐
5. Me molesta cuando otros me piden ayuda con su tarea académica.	☐	☐
6. Me irrita el humo (*smoke*) de los cigarrillos en los lugares públicos.	☐	☐
7. Me enoja el uso flagrante de teléfonos celulares en lugares públicos.	☐	☐
8. Me ofenden las palabras verdes (*swearwords*) y temas sexuales que se presentan en muchos programas televisivos.	☐	☐

¡Exprésate!

Verbs such as **preocupar** and **molestar,** among others in this section's vocabulary list, require an indirect object pronoun.

Eso **me preocupa.**

¿**Te molestan** las personas tensas?

 Paso 2 Ahora entrevista a un compañero (una compañera) de clase para saber si se le aplican las oraciones del **Paso 1** o no. ¿Coinciden sus respuestas con las tuyas?

Actividad C Situaciones y consejos

Paso 1 Empareja el consejo más apropiado para responder a cada problema o situación a continuación.

¡Exprésate!

To say that someone is *too* frustrated, sad, angry, and so forth, use the adverb **demasiado.**

| Elena está **demasiado tensa** estos días. | *Elena is too tense these days.* |

PROBLEMA/SITUACIÓN

1. __d__ Siempre tengo sueño en clase.
2. __a__ Estoy celoso/a de los amigos de mi pareja (*partner*).
3. __e__ Me tomo todo a pecho.
4. __c__ Le tengo envidia a mi compañero de cuarto. Es muy inteligente y para él todo es fácil.
5. __b__ No le tengo miedo a nada.

CONSEJO

a. Eso está mal. Habla con él o ella sobre tus sentimientos de inseguridad. Si la situación no mejora (*improves*), busca ayuda profesional.

b. Puede ser bueno, pero puede ser problemático si crees que eres invencible y que nada te puede pasar.

c. Eso es natural. Pero no debe llegar a tal punto que sientes un odio porque él tiene más éxito que tú.

d. Debes consultar con un médico (*doctor*) para ver qué lo está causando. Si no tienes ninguna enfermedad (*disease*), quizás (*perhaps*) no duermes lo suficiente.

e. Eres demasiado sensible (*sensitive*). Necesitas distinguir entre lo que es importante y lo que no es importante.

Paso 2 Con un compañero (una compañera) de clase, indiquen cuál es el problema o la situación más grave (*serious*) y cuál es el/la menos grave. Luego determinen si los consejos son buenos o no. Compartan lo que piensan con los demás miembros de la clase.

Actividad D ¿Cómo te sientes?

Paso 1 Completa cada oración con algo verdadero para ti.

1. Una de las cosas que más me molesta o me irrita es cuando...
2. Me frustra(n)...
3. Me ofende cuando alguien...
4. A veces estoy nervioso/a cuando...
5. Me preocupa(n)...

Paso 2 Basándote en las oraciones del **Paso 1,** entrevista a otra persona.

MODELO: ¿Cuál es una de las cosas que más te molesta o irrita?

Paso 3 Escribe un párrafo de unas 100 palabras en el que compares tus respuestas con las de la persona que entrevistaste.

MODELO: Una de las cosas que más me irrita es cuando las personas no llegan a tiempo a una cita. En cambio (*On the other hand*), a Robert le molesta más cuando su compañero de cuarto le cambia el canal cuando está viendo la televisión...

Gramática

¿Cómo se siente?   Pseudo-Reflexive Verbs

There is a class of verbs in Spanish called pseudo-reflexives that are used to express a change in emotion. The equivalent in English is *to get* or *to become* + a state or condition. The English equivalent does not normally contain *-self/-selves*, which would be a true reflexive. Compare the following.

Juan **se vio.**	*John saw himself.* (true reflexive)
Juan **se enojó.**	*John got angry.* (pseudo-reflexive)
Me hablo constantemente.	*I talk to myself constantly.* (true reflexive)
Me ofendo fácilmente.	*I get offended easily.* (pseudo-reflexive)

Regular reflexive pronouns (**me, te, se, nos,** and **os**) are still required. Many of the verbs you learned earlier in this lesson, as well as others, can be used in pseudo-reflexive constructions.

aburrirse	to get bored
alegrarse	to become happy
cansarse	to get tired
confundirse	to become confused
deprimirse	to get depressed
frustrarse	to get frustrated
irritarse	to get irritated
ofenderse	to get offended
preocuparse	to become worried
sentirse (ie, i)	to feel

FORMS OF PSEUDO-REFLEXIVE VERBS	
enojarse (*to get angry*) **sentirse (ie, i)** (*to feel*)	
me enojo **me** siento	**nos** enojamos **nos** sentimos
te enojas **te** sientes	**os** enojáis **os** sentís
se enoja **se** siente	**se** enojan **se** sienten
se enoja **se** siente	**se** enojan **se** sienten

COMUNICACIÓN ÚTIL

In Spanish, several verbal phrases also express the equivalent of *to get* or *to become* + a state or condition. One of these is **ponerse,** which can be used with a number of adjectives to express the same meanings as certain pseudo-reflexive verbs.

Me puse muy enojado.	*I got (became) very angry.*
Marta **se puso** bien frustrada.	*Marta got (became) really frustrated.*

In addition, **volverse** can be used with adjectives like **loco/a** (*crazy*) to express a more permanent type of change, one that is often but not always sudden. Such expressions don't usually mean *crazy* in the temporary sense of *he went nuts.* This would be rendered by **ponerse** or **actuar,** often with another adjective.

El señor **se volvió loco.**	*The man went crazy (insane).*
Se puso furioso.	*He went nuts.*
Actuó de una manera loca.	*He was (acting) crazy.*

Finally, **hacerse** is used to express changes such as *getting rich, becoming famous,* and so forth. In such cases, the subject tends to cause the action directly, which is why **hacer** is used.

Se hizo millonario.	*He became a millionaire.*

De *Sol y viento*, **Note:** You can access this film clip from a special menu section on Disc 5 of the Instructional Version on DVD.

DE SOL Y VIENTO

In **Episodio 7,** you will see a scene in which Mario asks an upset Jaime about María. Part of their exchange is presented here.

MARIO
Don Jaime, no entiendo. Esa señorita que _____ con Ud., María, es la misma que yo vi con Ud. el otro día, ¿no es cierto?

JAIME
Sí, es cierto…

MARIO
¿Y? ¿Por qué _____ con Ud.? ¿Lo vio con otra mujer?

JAIME
Mario, calla y maneja.[a]

Based on what you remember from the previous episode, which of the following makes the most sense to fill in both blanks?

a. se enojó　　**b.** se volvió　　**c.** se ofendió

[a]calla… *shut up and drive*

INPUT
Actividad E

Actividad E ¿Quién es?

Indica el nombre del personaje de *Sol y viento* que contesta cada pregunta a continuación. **¡OJO!** Hay más de una respuesta posible en algunos casos.

¿Qué personaje...

1. se enojó con Jaime? María

2. se siente mal por lo que piensa María? Jaime

3. se cansa de las excusas de Carlos? Jaime

4. se confunde por la discusión (*argument*) entre María y Jaime? don Paco, Mario, Carlos

5. se preocupa por Carlos? doña Isabel

INPUT

Act. F, *Paso 2,*
Suggestion:
Tell the class: *Cada
oración del Paso 1 tiene
un valor. Para el número
1, dense un punto si con-
testan que no. Para el
número 2, un punto si
contestan que sí.
Número 3: un punto si la
respuesta es no. Número
4: un punto para sí.
Número 5: un punto para
sí. Número 6: un punto
para sí. Ahora, calculen el
total de puntos. ¿Cuántos
tienen un 6? ¿un 5?, etc.
Then reveal the fol-
lowing.
4 a 6 puntos =
Eres muy equilibrado/a.
3 puntos = Eres normal.
2 puntos = Tienes la ten-
dencia a tomarte las
cosas a pecho.
0 a 1 punto = ¡Requieres
atención médica!*

Actividad F ¿Eres equilibrado/a (*well-balanced*) o no?

Paso 1 Indica si las siguientes afirmaciones se te aplican o no.

	SÍ	NO
1. Cuando me enojo, suelo explotar (*explode*).	☐	☐
2. Cuando me ofendo, siempre se lo digo a la persona ofensiva.	☐	☐
3. Cuando me aburro, veo la televisión.	☐	☐
4. Cuando me frustro, suelo dejar (*stop*) lo que hago para concentrarme en otra cosa.	☐	☐
5. Si me confundo, siempre pido aclaración (*clarification*), especialmente en clase.	☐	☐
6. Si me irrito, busco algo para cambiar de humor (*mood*).	☐	☐

Paso 2 Ahora escucha las instrucciones y comentarios del profesor (de la profesora).

Actividad G ¿Cómo te sientes? ¿Cómo te pones? INPUT/OUTPUT
Actividad G

Paso 1 Utilizando adjetivos como **aburrido/a, nervioso/a,** etcétera, o las palabras **bien** o **mal,** indica cómo te sientes o cómo te pones en cada circunstancia.

MODELO: cuando sales bien en un examen →
Me siento bien. / Me pongo alegre.

1. antes de la primera cita con alguien que te gusta mucho

2. cuando tienes que hablar en público o enfrente de la clase

3. después de hacer ejercicio

4. cuando un profesor (una profesora) no contesta bien tu pregunta

5. cuando caminas a solas por la noche en tu barrio

6. cuando caminas a solas por la universidad por la noche

Paso 2 Ahora entrevista a un compañero (una compañera) de clase para ver cómo reacciona ante las situaciones del **Paso 1,** según el modelo. ¿Se sienten Uds. iguales o hay mucha diferencia entre sus reacciones a las situaciones?

MODELO: ¿Cómo te sientes cuando sales bien en un examen?

Actividad H ¿Reacciones apropiadas?

Paso 1 En grupos de tres, contesten cada pregunta a continuación.

¿Cuándo es apropiado...

1. ofenderse y confrontar a la persona ofensiva?
2. ofenderse y no decirle nada a la persona ofensiva?
3. preocuparse por el comportamiento (*behavior*) de un amigo (una amiga)?
4. no preocuparse por el comportamiento de un amigo (una amiga)?
5. sentirse mal por algo que uno dice?
6. no sentirse mal por algo que uno dice?

Paso 2 Los grupos deben reportar sus ideas a la clase. Luego voten para determinar cuáles de las ideas representan reacciones más apropiadas y cuáles no, según el caso.

SOL Y VIENTO: Enfoque cultural

En el **Episodio 7** don Paco va a mencionar el Internet. La imagen que muchas personas tienen de los países hispanos es una de países pobres, del «tercer mundo» y con poca modernización. En general, los países hispanos no gozan de[a] los excesos tecnológicos de una cultura como la de este país, pero no son tan atrasados[b] como algunos creen. España es tan moderna como cualquier otro país de Europa y las ciudades de Santiago, Buenos Aires, Caracas, México, D.F. y San Juan, entre otras, ofrecen casi todo lo que se podría[c] encontrar en las grandes ciudades norteamericanas. Por ejemplo, hay «cibercafés» donde la gente va para tomar un café y leer su correo electrónico. También, los negocios y bancos están tan bien equipados de tecnología como cualquier negocio en este país. Además, la viña donde se filmó *Sol y viento* poseía de[d] todo lo moderno como cualquier viña en Napa o Sonoma, California, por ejemplo. Finalmente, varios Premios Nóbel de Ciencia se han ortogado[e] a científicos de países hispanos. Claro, en las zonas rurales es un poco diferente, pero ¿no es así en casi cualquier país del mundo?

▲ Los cibercafés, como este en México, D.F., son muy populares en todas partes del mundo.

[a]no... *don't enjoy* [b]*backward* [c]se... *one could* [d]poseía... *possessed* [e]*awarded*

SEGUNDA PARTE

Note: These vocabulary items can be heard in this lesson's Textbook Audio section of the Online Learning Center Website.

Talking About Health

Vocabulario

Estoy un poco enfermo.

Las partes del cuerpo^a

Parts of the Body and Physical Health

La cabeza y la cara^b*

^a*body*
^b*face*

la cabeza

el cuello

el brazo

el pecho

el codo

la mano†

los dedos

el hombro

la espalda

la pierna

el pie

la rodilla

los dedos del pie

los ojos

la oreja

la mejilla

la nariz

los dientes

la boca

el mentón

la garganta

---

*Many of the vocabulary items presented here are review, but they will be useful to talk about physical health.
†Note that **mano** is actually a feminine noun, despite the fact that it ends in **-o: la mano derecha.**

La salud[a] y el estado físico

[a]*health*

cortar(se)	to cut (oneself)
enfermarse	to get sick
estar (*irreg.*) **enfermo/a**	to be sick
hacer (*irreg.*) **gárgaras**	to gargle
lastimar(se)	to hurt (oneself)
romper(se)	to break
tener (*irreg.*) **fiebre** (*f.*)	to have a fever
tener (*irreg.*) **(la) gripe**	to have the flu
tener (*irreg.*) **la nariz tapada**	to have a stuffed-up nose
tener (*irreg.*) **un resfriado**	to have a cold
tener (*irreg.*) **tos**	to have a cough
la aspirina	aspirin
el hueso	bone
la medicina	medicine

COMUNICACIÓN ÚTIL

When talking about parts of the body, native speakers of Spanish typically use the definite article where an English speaker would use a possessive adjective. Compare the following examples.

Tengo **la** nariz tapada.	*My nose is stuffed up.*
Rebeca se lastimó **la** pierna.	*Rebeca hurt her leg.*
¿Cuándo te rompiste **el** brazo?	*When did you break your arm?*

≋ Vistazo cultural

Los hospitales y las clínicas

La imagen que muchas personas tienen de Latinoamérica es de países en vías de desarrollo[a] con problemas de salud, agua no potable[b] y limitados recursos médicos. En realidad, esto se puede decir de casi cualquier zona rural del mundo, pero no es apropiada en cuanto a[c] los centros urbanos de Latinoamérica. En las grandes ciudades como Santiago de Chile, Buenos Aires y México, D.F., hay hospitales y clínicas modernos, bien equipados, adonde uno puede recurrir[d] si sufre de algo que requiere atención médica. En Costa Rica y México, entre otros países, hay escuelas de medicina que preparan a médicos excelentes. Costa Rica, en particular, es un lugar conocido para la cirugía cosmética.

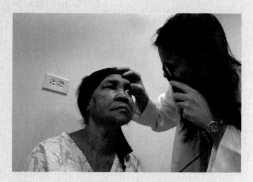
▲ San José, Costa Rica

[a]*en... developing*   [b]*drinkable*   [c]*en... in regard to*   [d]*go*

INPUT

Act. A, Suggestion: Do *Paso 1* as a whole-class activity. Conduct *Paso 2* as pair work, then bring the whole class together to review responses.

Actividad A Asociaciones

Paso 1 ¿Qué parte del cuerpo asocias con cada enfermedad o condición?

1. la poliomielitis (*polio*)   **a.** la cabeza   **(b.)** las piernas
2. el resfriado   **(a.)** el pecho y la nariz   **b.** los brazos y las manos
3. el mal aliento (*breath*)   **a.** los ojos   **(b.)** la boca
4. la escoliosis   **a.** las orejas   **(b.)** la espalda
5. las caries (*cavities*)   **(a.)** los dientes   **b.** la garganta
6. necesitar muletas (*crutches*)   **(a.)** las piernas   **b.** el codo
7. llevar yeso (*a cast*)   **a.** la cara   **(b.)** el brazo
8. cortarse   **(a.)** los dedos   **b.** los dientes

Paso 2 ¿Qué prenda(s) de ropa o complemento(s) (*accessory[ies]*) asocias con cada parte del cuerpo a continuación?

1. Con la cabeza asocio...
2. Con los pies asocio...
3. Con el cuello asocio...
4. Con las piernas asocio...
5. Con los hombros, la espalda y el pecho asocio...

¡Exprésate!

The verb **romper** can be used in two ways when talking about the breaking of a bone. It can be used reflexively to imply that someone caused or was involved in the breaking of his or her own bone.

Roberto **se rompió** una pierna.   *Roberto broke his leg.*

You can also use a construction with **se** and an indirect object to imply that the break happened to Roberto without any cause or involvement (that is, that it was completely accidental and he can't be blamed for it).

A Roberto **se le rompió** una pierna.   *Roberto broke his leg. (lit.: Roberto's leg was broken to him.)*

The same is also true for the verb **cortar**, among others.

Me corté un dedo.   }   *I cut my finger.*
Se me cortó un dedo.

INPUT/OUTPUT
Actividad B

Actividad B ¿Es inconveniente o no?

Con un compañero (una compañera) de clase, indiquen en qué categoría pondrían (*you would place*) cada una de las siguientes situaciones: **muy inconveniente, inconveniente** o **un poco inconveniente.** Luego, presenten sus ideas a la clase. ¿Están todos de acuerdo? ¿Pueden explicar sus razones?

MODELO: Si a uno se le rompe el dedo pequeño del pie, es un poco inconveniente. Uno puede caminar todavía y no necesita equipo especial.

Vocabulario útil

la muleta	crutch
la vendaje	bandage
el yeso	cast

1. si a uno se le rompe la nariz
2. si a uno se le rompe un brazo
3. si a uno se le rompe una mano
4. si a uno se le rompe una pierna
5. si a uno se le rompe un pie
6. si a uno se le rompe un diente
7. si a uno se le corta un dedo
8. si a uno se le corta la mejilla / la pierna (mientras se afeita)

INPUT/OUTPUT
Act. C, *Paso 2,*
Suggestion: Poll
the class on the products
and medicines they use
for the ailments listed in
Paso 1. Are any products
favored by the majority
of the class?

Actividad C ¿Qué producto o medicina?

Paso 1 Indica qué producto usas o qué medicina tomas en cada situación.

1. Tienes resfriado. También tienes la nariz tapada.
2. Tienes dolor de cabeza (*headache*).
3. Tienes dolor de garganta.
4. Estás mareado/a (*nauseated*). No te sientes bien del estómago (*stomach*).
5. Tienes fiebre.
6. Te cortas un dedo.
7. Se te lastima la espalda.
8. Tienes tos.

Paso 2 Compara tus respuestas con las de un compañero (una compañera) de clase. ¿Usan los mismos productos y medicinas?

Paso 3 Con tu pareja, vuelvan a las situaciones del **Paso 1**. ¿Hay remedios caseros (*home remedies*) o naturales que conocen para cada una? ¿Cuáles son? También indiquen si hacen algo más para aliviar la situación y sentirse mejor.

MODELO: Dicen que si tienes dolor de garganta, debes hacer gárgaras de (*gargle with*) agua tibia (*warm*) con un poco de sal.

OUTPUT
Act. D, Suggestions
Paso 1: The idea here is to
get students to
circulate around
the room and not
ask all the questions of 1
or 2 people.
Paso 2: Use follow-up
questions to probe results.
For example, John
answers for item 2. *A
David se le rompió una
pierna una vez.* You say to
David: *¿Sí? ¿Cómo pasó?
¿Estabas de vacaciones o
practicabas un deporte?,*
etc. This will serve as a
reminder and warm-up
for use of the imperfect
in the next section.

Actividad D ¡Firma aquí, por favor!

Paso 1 Busca personas que contesten **sí** a las siguientes preguntas. Pide sus firmas **(¡Firma aquí, por favor!).** No puedes hacerle dos preguntas seguidas (*in a row*) a la misma persona.

1. ¿Se te rompió un brazo alguna vez? _____
2. ¿Se te rompió una pierna alguna vez? _____
3. ¿Has estado enfermo/a por más de dos semanas alguna vez? _____
4. ¿Te cortaste un dedo alguna vez? _____
5. ¿Te lastimaste la espalda alguna vez? _____

Paso 2 Reporta a la clase lo que aprendiste en el **Paso 1.**

MODELO: A Juan se le rompió una pierna una vez.

Gramática

More on Talking About States of Being in the Past

Estaban contentos, ¿no?   **Review of the Imperfect**

As you know, the imperfect is used to talk about repeated actions in the past. It is also used to express any action, state of being, or condition that was in progress at a particular point in the past. Examine the following.

> No me presenté al examen porque **estaba** enferma. **Tenía** un poco de fiebre y **tenía** la nariz tapada.
> *I didn't show up for the test because I was sick. I had a bit of a fever and my nose was stuffed up.*

In the previous example, the reference point is the test—or rather the time that the person should have shown up for the test. At that point in time, there were three existent states described: being sick, having a fever, and having nasal congestion.

States and conditions in Spanish are typically described with **ser** and **estar.** However, many other verbs that you already know also represent states of being, such as those in the following list.

conocer	to know, be familiar with (*someone or something*)
hacer buen/mal tiempo	to be good/bad weather
parecer	to seem, resemble
poder	to be able to, can
quedar	to stay, remain
saber	to know (*facts, information*)
tener	to have
verse	to appear to be, look

> Al llegar al consultorio, me **parecía** que los síntomas disminuían.
> *When I arrived at the doctor's office, it seemed like the symptoms were going away.*

> Vi a Miguel ayer. No **se veía** muy bien.
> *I saw Miguel yesterday. He didn't look very well.*

> No hablé con el médico porque no lo **conocía.**
> *I didn't speak with the doctor because I didn't know him.*

As is the case with many other verbs, the use of the preterite with states of being implies one of two things: (1) the state is viewed as completed at a particular point in time; or (2) the state is viewed as just beginning at that point in time.

> No me **pareció** tan grave.
> *It didn't seem that serious to me.*
> (At that particular moment, it didn't seem that serious.)

> **Estuve** enferma por una semana entera.
> *I was sick for a whole week.*
> (The preterite is used because the state is confined to a particular time frame, for one week.)

> Por fin **conocí** al médico.
> *I finally met the doctor.*
> (The state of knowing the doctor began at a particular moment.)

George Washington **fue** el primer presidente de los Estados Unidos.
George Washington was the first president of the United States.
(He was president for a specific period of time, then it ended.)

Tuvo un hijo.
She had a boy.
(The use of the preterite indicates that she gave birth to the boy.)

For the most part, you will continue to use the imperfect to describe states of being and conditions in the past. Used in this way, the imperfect describes background information, not the events that cause a narrative to move forward (which are described by the preterite). In the following chart, you can see how time almost stands still as the imperfect is used to describe a number of states and conditions that were all happening at the same time.

USING THE IMPERFECT TO DESCRIBE STATES AND CONDITIONS

Eran las dos de la tarde y no **me sentía** muy bien. **Tenía** un poco de fiebre y **tenía** la garganta seca.[a] Tampoco **podía** ver muy bien. **Me parecía** que todo el mundo **se oscurecía**.[b] **Necesitaba** tomar medicina rápidamente antes de que me pusiera peor aún.[c]

[a]*dry* [b]*se... was getting dark* [c]*antes... before I got any worse*

De *Sol y viento*, Note: You can access this film clip from a special menu section on Disc 5 of the Instructional Version on DVD.

 DE SOL Y VIENTO

Here is the complete exchange between Mario and Jaime as Mario inquires about María's being upset. Note the use of the imperfect in their dialogue.

MARIO
Don Jaime, no entiendo. Esa señorita que se enojó con Ud., María, es la misma que yo vi con Ud. el otro día, ¿no es cierto?

JAIME
Sí, es cierto.

MARIO
Y Uds. **se veían** muy contentos.

JAIME
Así **creía** yo.

MARIO
¿Y? ¿Por qué se enojó con Ud.? ¿Lo vio con otra mujer?

JAIME
Mario, calla y maneja.

In the dialogue, Mario remarks that **"Y Uds. se veían muy contentos."** What must he have noticed beforehand to make this comment? Complete the following sentence with forms of **sonreír** (*to smile*) and **llevarse**.

Antes, Mario notó que María y Jaime <u>sonreían</u> [1] y <u>se llevaban</u>[2] muy bien.

INPUT

Act. E, Suggestion: Put students into pairs and allow 4 minutes to complete sentences. Then have a particular pair present their responses to the class. The rest of the class agrees, adds on, offers changes, etc.

INPUT/OUTPUT

Act F, Note: Formerly titled *¿Qué leíste?*, this recurring activity is now presented as an aural activity only, although you still have the option of displaying the paragraph on an overhead transparency instead of reading it aloud. Consult the Instructor's Manual for information on dictogloss activities.

Paso 1, **Suggestion:** Read the following paragraph twice, the first time at slower than normal speed: Students listen but do not write down what they hear: *El primer día de la clase de español, yo estaba un poco nerviosa. No quería estudiar español y no sabía ni una palabra. No conocía a nadie en la clase. Me parecía que el español era difícil porque no podía entender mucho. ¿Y ahora?*

Paso 2, **Suggestion:** Allow approximately 5 minutes.

Follow-up: Call on 1 or 2 groups to present their final versions, then display the original on an overhead transparency so all groups can see the text and compare. To keep meaning in focus, poll the class on statements from the dictogloss: *¿Cuántos de*

Actividad E ¿Qué pasaba?

Completa cada oración para describir la escena enfrente de la casa al final del **Episodio 6** de *Sol y viento*.

1. Cuando María se enojó con Jaime y le devolvió (*returned*) la figurita, estaban presentes ___Mario, don Paco y Carlos. (Doña Isabel estaba en la casa.)___

2. Al recoger la figurita, seguramente Jaime se sentía ___mal, triste___.

3. Don Paco y Carlos estaban perplejos porque no sabían nada de ___la relación entre Jaime y María___.

Actividad F ¿Qué escuchaste?

Paso 1 Escucha el párrafo que lee tu profesor(a) a la clase. Vas a escuchar el párrafo dos veces. Trata de recordar la información, pero no tomes apuntes.

Paso 2 En grupos de tres, escriban una versión del párrafo para luego compartir con la clase.

Uds. estaban nerviosos el primer día de esta clase? ¿Cuántos no conocían a nadie en la clase? ¿Y ahora?, etc.

▲ ¿Cómo se sentía María cuando vio a Jaime discutiendo (*arguing*) con Carlos?

Actividad G ¡Sean creativos!

OUTPUT
Actividad G

Escoge una de las siguientes historias breves y escribe la forma correcta de los verbos alistados en los espacios en blanco. Luego, agrega una oración más para continuar la historia y pásasela a otra persona. Esa persona debe agregar una oración más y pasársela a otra persona. Esto se debe repetir con dos personas más. La última persona debe devolverte la historia. ¿Cómo es la historia? ¿Es tal como la imaginabas? Por último, lee la versión final a la clase.

Vocabulario útil

creer, estar, hacer, sentir

Versión A

Para Manuel, el día era perfecto. ___Hacía___¹ buen tiempo. Brillabaᵃ el sol de manera que la Madre Naturaleza parecía estar contenta con todo. Manuel se ___sentía___² bien. Ya no ___estaba___³ nervioso ante la situación que le esperaba.ᵇ De hecho, ___creía___⁴ que estaba listo para enfrentarᶜ cualquier problema. Entonces sonóᵈ el teléfono. Era Miguel —y quería darle una noticia.ᵉ

ᵃ*Was shining* ᵇ*le... awaited him* ᶜ*face* ᵈ*rang* ᵉ*piece of news*

Versión B

Para Susana, el día era un catástrofe desde el comienzo. ___Hacía___[1] mal tiempo. Llovía sin parar[a] y el cielo[b] estaba poblado de nubes[c] oscuras, dando la sensación de que la Madre Naturaleza estaba irritada. Susana no se ___sentía___[2] bien. ___Estaba___[3] nerviosa ante la situación que le esperaba.[d] ___Creía___[4] que su futuro estaba en manos de otras personas, lo cual no le gustaba para nada. Pero su suerte estaba por cambiar.[e] Sonó[f] el teléfono. Era Miguel—y quería darle una noticia.[g]

[a]sin... *without stopping* [b]*sky* [c]*clouds* [d]le... *awaited her* [e]su... *her luck was about to change* [f]*Rang* [g]*piece of news*

OUTPUT
Actividad H

Actividad H La última vez

Paso 1 Describe la última vez que no fuiste a clases o al trabajo porque estabas enfermo/a o porque te lastimaste en alguna parte del cuerpo. Usa las siguientes preguntas como guía.

1. ¿Cuántos años tenías? ¿Estudiabas en la escuela secundaria o en la universidad?
2. ¿Qué síntomas tenías o qué te pasó? ¿Cómo te sentías?
3. ¿Cuánto tiempo duró la enfermedad (*sickness*) o la herida (*injury*)? ¿Cuándo pudiste regresar a las clases o al trabajo?

Paso 2 Algunos voluntarios deben leer sus descripciones en voz alta (*aloud*). ¿Quién estaba más enfermo o tenía la herida más grave?

Enfoque lingüístico, **Suggestion:** Remind students that states and conditions are not just a matter of a single verb but a verb phrase. For example, *tener*, as exemplified by *tener un resfriado* and *tener 20 años*, falls into the class of states and conditions. But what about *tener un bebé/niño* when the meaning is to give birth (i.e., She had a baby last night)? In this case, the entire verb phrase is no longer a state but a punctual-like event (like closing the door, dialing the phone) with a clear-cut ending. Ask students whether the preterite or the imperfect would be used to describe a recent birth. The preterite: *Tuvo un bebé/niño ayer.* Thus, students must focus not on just the verb alone but on what the entire verb phrase means.

⦿ Enfoque lingüístico

La adquisición del aspecto

In **Lección 5B** you learned that the difference between the preterite and the imperfect is not one of *tense*, but rather one of *aspect*. Investigations in second-language acquisition have shown that it takes learners a long time to control aspectual distinctions in Romance languages, and it has been hypothesized that learners tend to go through particular stages in acquiring these distinctions, regardless of whether they learn a second language in a structured environment (such as a classroom) or naturalistically (i.e., living and working in a different language community).

One hypothesis claims that preterite endings emerge in learners' speech first, but not with all types of verbs. Learners are more likely to start using preterite endings with certain "punctual" events such as *break, arrive, begin, end,* then gradually use these endings with verbs expressing activities (*run, play, work*), and then finally with states or conditions (*be, have, know, want*). This hypothesis also claims that imperfect endings appear later and, like the preterite, they tend to appear on certain types of verbs before others.

The imperfect tends to emerge first on verbs representing states or conditions, then on verbs expressing activities, and finally to "punctual" verbs—the opposite order of how preterite endings emerge.

If you encounter problems knowing when to use the preterite and the imperfect in spontaneous speech in Spanish, be patient! By working carefully through the activities in these sections and by paying attention to how the forms are used in *Sol y viento* and in other communicative contexts, you will be well on your way to a better (and faster!) understanding of aspectual distinctions in Spanish.

TERCERA PARTE

Vocabulario

Telling the Doctor
How You Feel

Note: These vocabulary items can be heard in this lesson's Textbook Audio section of the Online Learning Center Website.

Me duele la garganta.

In the Doctor's Office

Algunos órganos internos importantes

el cerebro	brain
el corazón	heart
el estómago	stomach
el hígado	liver
el pulmón	lung

En el consultorio del médico

examinar	to examine; to test
poner(le) (*irreg.*) una inyección (a alguien)	to give (someone) a shot
respirar	to breathe
sacar (qu) la lengua	to stick out one's tongue
sacar(le) (qu) sangre (a alguien)	to draw (someone's) blood
tomar(le) la temperatura (a alguien)	to take a (someone's) temperature
la alergia	allergy
el/la enfermero/a	nurse
el examen médico	checkup; medical examination
el/la médico/a	doctor
el/la paciente	patient
la pastilla	pill
la presión arterial	blood pressure
los rayos X	X-rays
la receta	prescription

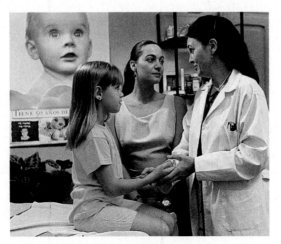

◄

A muchos niños no les gustan **los exámenes médicos**. ¡Tienen miedo de **las inyecciones**!

✱ MÁS VOCABULARIO

doler (ue)	to hurt, ache
Me duele la cabeza.	My head hurts.
padecer (zc) de	to suffer from
el/la farmacéutico/a	pharmacist
la farmacia	pharmacy

COMUNICACIÓN ÚTIL

When using verbs such as **examinar, poner,** and so forth to talk about medical exam-
inations, an indirect object pronoun is often used. Note that the definite article is also
used instead of a possessive adjective. Compare the following.

Me examinaron los ojos.	*They examined my eyes.*
¿Te pusieron una inyección?	*Did they give you an injection?*
Le sacaron sangre.	*They drew blood from him.*

Vistazo cultural

Las recetas

Algo que les sorprende[a] a muchos norteamericanos cuando viajan por o viven en un país extranjero es la facilidad con que se puede obtener medicinas en algunos lugares. En los Estados Unidos las medicinas y drogas son reguladas por la Administración Federal de Drogas y es necesario tener una receta firmada por un médico para obtener muchas de ellas. En cambio, en varios países hispanos no es necesario tener la receta de un médico para comprar muchas de las medicinas. Uno puede entrar a la farmacia y decirle a un farmacéu-tico lo que necesita (o los síntomas que tiene). El farmacéutico, que tiene entrenamiento especial, le

▲ El farmacéutico le recomienda a este estudiante una medicación. (Lima, el Perú)

recomienda una medicina a la persona. De hecho, a veces ni siquiera[b] es necesario consultar con un médico de antemano[c] —la farmacia puede servir tanto de consulto-rio como de distribuidor de medicinas.

[a]*surprises* [b]*ni... neither* [c]*de... beforehand*

INPUT
Act. A, Statements:
1. *Respiramos con estos órganos.* 2. *Es un órgano muy importante en el sistema digestivo.* 3. *Es un tipo de medicina que se toma oralmente.* 4. *Este órgano controla la circulación de la sangre.* 5. *Es lo que el médico le da al paciente para poder obtener una medicina específica.* 6. *Es una manera de tomar fotografías de las partes internas del cuerpo.* 7. *Esta persona ayuda al médico en el consultorio.* 8. *Este órgano regula el sistema nervioso.*

Actividad A Definiciones

Escucha las definiciones que da tu profesor(a) y escribe su número al lado de la palabra o frase que describe.

a. __6__ los rayos X
b. __4__ el corazón
c. __8__ el cerebro
d. __1__ los pulmones
e. __2__ el estómago
f. __3__ la pastilla
g. __5__ la receta
h. __7__ la enfermera

Actividad B En el consultorio del médico

INPUT
Actividad B

Indica si cada oración se refiere a algo que dice un paciente o un médico en el consultorio.

	PACIENTE	MÉDICO
1. Vamos a sacarle sangre para chequear el nivel (*level*) del colesterol.	☐	☑
2. No, no tengo alergias a ninguna medicina.	☑	☐
3. ¿Me van a poner una inyección?	☑	☐
4. Veo que su presión arterial está bien.	☐	☑
5. Me duele el estómago.	☑	☐
6. Le doy una receta.	☐	☑
7. ¿Le duele aquí?	☐	☑
8. ¿Padece su familia de la diabetes?	☐	☑

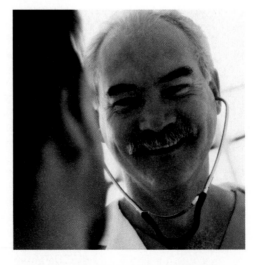

▲ ¿Cuáles son las preguntas que te hace el médico (la médica) en su consultorio?

¡Exprésate!

Spanish uses the verb **dar** to express the notion of *getting* or *catching* as it pertains to pains and illnesses.

Me **dio** la gripe.	I got/caught the flu.
¿Te **dio** dolor de cabeza?	Did you get a headache?

In these expressions, **dar** functions like **gustar** because it requires indirect object pronouns, the subject comes after the verb, and **a** must be used in combination with the indirect object pronoun when a noun is present.

A Miguel le dan dolores de cabeza todos los días.	Miguel gets headaches every day.

Actividad C Tu historia médica

Paso 1 Contesta cada pregunta a continuación sobre tu historia médica.

1. ¿Padeces de la alta presión arterial?
2. ¿Tienes alto el nivel de colesterol en la sangre?
3. ¿Con qué frecuencia te da un resfriado? ¿Y la gripe?
4. ¿Con qué frecuencia te dan dolores de cabeza?
5. ¿Te duele alguna parte del cuerpo con frecuencia?
6. ¿Tienes alergias a alguna medicina o comida?
7. ¿Te han tomado rayos X? ¿Cuándo y por qué?
8. ¿Tomas pastillas, vitaminas, suplementos o medicinas diariamente?

Paso 2 Hazle a un compañero (una compañera) de clase las preguntas del **Paso 1** y anota sus respuestas.

Paso 3 Escribe un breve párrafo en el cual comparas tu historia médica con la de tu compañero/a de clase. ¿Tienen experiencias parecidas?

Actividad D Un juego de charadas (*charades*)

Paso 1 La clase debe dividirse en dos grupos, el grupo A y el grupo B. El profesor (La profesora) repartirá (*will hand out*) palabras o expresiones de la lista de vocabulario de las páginas 396–397. Cada persona tiene que describir su palabra o expresión (¡sin hablar!) con gestos (*gestures*) para que los demás de su grupo puedan (*can*) adivinar esa palabra o expresión. ¿Quiénes son los mejores actores de la clase?

Paso 2 En grupos de dos, indiquen si una visita del perro al veterinario es diferente de o similar a una visita de su dueño/a al consultorio del médico. Luego, presenten sus ideas a la clase.

MODELOS: Una manera en que las dos visitas son similares es que...

Una manera en que las dos visitas son diferentes es que...

NAVEGANDO LA RED

Busca un sitio de una compañía de seguros (*insurance*) médicos. Imprime (*Print out*) una lista de servicios médicos que cubre (*covers*) la compañía y comparte la información con tus compañeros de clase.

Gramática

Hace dos años que se me rompió el brazo.

Hacer in Expressions of Time

hacer IN EXPRESSIONS OF TIME		
PRESENT	PRETERITE	IMPERFECT
Hace mucho tiempo **que vivo** en Chicago. *I've lived in Chicago for a long time.*	**Me enfermé hace** unos días. / **Hace** unos días **que me enfermé.** *I got sick a few days ago.*	**Hacía** varios meses **que trabajaba** en la novela. *I'd been working on the novel for several months.*
Hace más de un año **que no veo** al médico. *It's been over a year since I've seen the doctor.*		**Hacía** unos meses **que no veía** a Ramón. *It had been several months since I saw Ramón.*

You may recall from **Lección 4A** that **hacer** can be used with the preterite to express the concept of *ago.* However, **hacer** can also be used with other tenses and verb forms to express various temporal relationships. Examine the chart.

Note the following based on the examples in the chart.

1. With the present and the imperfect, **hace** and **hacía** are used to express *for* if the sentence is affirmative and *since* if the sentence is negative. When used with the preterite, only **hace** is used, and the meaning expressed is *ago.*

2. When used with the present and the imperfect, **que** is typically used. **Que** can be optional with the preterite. If it is used, the **hace** phrase appears before the verb. If it is omitted, the **hace** phrase comes after the verb.*

3. When used with the present and the imperfect, both verbs are in the same tense. That is, **hace** is used with the present tense to express *since* in a present time context, and **hacía** is used with the imperfect to express *since* in a past time context.

4. With the present and imperfect constructions, the English equivalent requires a helping verb (e.g., *have, has, had*). No helping verb is needed in Spanish in these constructions.

*****Que** is also sometimes omitted in the present and imperfect, but more rarely than with the preterite. Rules of placement of **hacer** apply as with the preterite.

COMUNICACIÓN ÚTIL

To ask *for how long* or *since when,* use a version of **¿Cuánto tiempo hace/hacía que… ?**

¿Cuánto tiempo hace que estudias español?

¿Cuánto tiempo hace que no hablas con Julio?

¿Cuánto tiempo hacía que tenían problemas cuando se divorciaron?

De *Sol y viento,* Note: You can access this film clip from a special menu section on Disc 5 of the Instructional Version on DVD.

🎞 DE SOL Y VIENTO

In **Episodio 7,** you will see don Paco and doña Isabel confront Jaime about his company's plans to build a dam. Read the following exchange and insert either **hace** or **hacía** in the blank. Do you understand what don Paco is saying?

PACO
He averiguado que su compañía quiere construir una represa en esta zona. ¿Comprende Ud. el daño que eso causaría por estas tierras?

ISABEL
Mi amigo Paco ha estado haciendo averiguaciones.ᵃ Hemos sabido muchas cosas interesantes con respecto a su compañía.

PACO
La magia del Internet y unas llamadas por teléfono. Pero obviamente a su compañía no le importa mucho el daño a la ecología… ni a la comunidad humana que habita estas tierras. ¡Lo que hicieron en Bolivia _____hace_____ dos años no tiene perdón!

ᵃ*investigations*

Actividad E ¿Qué sabes? ¿Qué crees?

Completa las siguientes oraciones según lo que sabes o crees sobre *Sol y viento* hasta el momento.

1. Hace _____ que Jaime llegó a Chile.

    (a.) unos días   **b.** unas semanas   **c.** un mes

2. Hace _____ que doña Isabel y su esposo se establecieron en Chile.

    a. diez años   **b.** veinte años   (c.) más de treinta años

3. Hace _____ que Carlos intenta (*has been trying*) vender la viña.

    a. unas horas   (b.) varios meses   **c.** varios días

4. Hacía _____ que la familia Sánchez planeaba la recepción para la nueva cosecha.

    (a.) unos meses   **b.** unos años   **c.** unos días

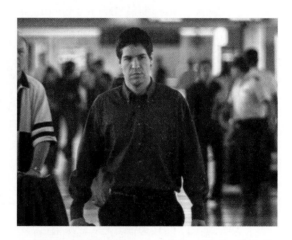

▲ ¿Cuánto tiempo hace que Jaime llegó a Chile? ¿Unos días? ¿una semana? ¿más?

Actividad F ¿Cuánto tiempo hace que... ?

Paso 1 Completa cada oración con información verdadera para ti.

1. Hace _____ que vivo en _____.
2. Hace _____ que estoy interesado/a en _____.
3. Hace _____ que visité al dentista.
4. Hace _____ que no _____.

Paso 2 Convierte las oraciones del **Paso 1** en preguntas y busca personas que contesten igual que tú. Luego presenta la información a la clase.

MODELO: E1: ¿Cuánto tiempo hace que vives en Ann Arbor?
         E2: Hace dos años.
         E1: (más tarde) Hace sólo un año que vivo en Ann Arbor, pero hace dos años que Tracy vive aquí.

Actividad G   ¿Cuánto tiempo hacía que... ?

¿Cuánto sabes de eventos históricos? Contesta cada pregunta con información verdadera.

1. ¿Cuánto tiempo hacía que George W. Bush era presidente cuando ocurrieron los atentados terroristas del 11 de septiembre?
2. ¿Cuánto tiempo hacía que Abraham Lincoln era presidente cuando lo asesinaron?
3. ¿Cuánto tiempo hacía que los Estados Unidos no participaban en una guerra cuando entraron en la Primera Guerra Mundial en 1917?
4. ¿Cuánto tiempo hacía que la Primera Guerra Mundial consumía al continente europeo cuando por fin entraron los Estados Unidos en el conflicto?
5. ¿Cuánto tiempo hacía que Julio César era «dictador vitalicio (*for life*)» cuando lo asesinaron?

Actividad H   Los exámenes médicos

Paso 1   Contesta las siguientes preguntas.

1. ¿Cuánto tiempo hace que tuviste un examen médico?
2. Cuando fuiste, ¿cuánto tiempo hacía que no tenías un examen médico?
3. ¿Te tomaron la presión arterial? Si no, ¿cuánto tiempo hace que no te examinan la presión?
4. ¿Te hicieron un examen completo? Si no, ¿cuánto tiempo hace que tuviste un examen completo?
5. ¿Te examinaron el nivel de colesterol en la sangre? Si no, ¿cuánto tiempo hace que te examinaron el colesterol?

Paso 2   Algunos voluntarios deben leer sus respuestas a la clase. ¿Son las respuestas de otras personas más o menos iguales? Como clase, determinen a qué edad es importante tener un examen médico completo regular (por ejemplo, cada año).

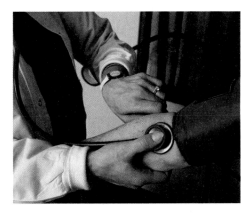

▲ ¿Cuánto tiempo hace que te tomaron la presión arterial?

SOL Y VIENTO

A primera vista

Antes de ver el episodio

Actividad A ¿Qué recuerdas?

Indica si las siguientes oraciones son ciertas o falsas, según lo que sabes de la trama (*plot*) de *Sol y viento*.

	CIERTO	FALSO
1. Don Paco es dueño de un restaurante en Chile.	☐	☑
2. El esposo de doña Isabel ya ha muerto.	☑	☐
3. Doña Isabel se preocupa por la viña.	☑	☐
4. Jaime sabe que Carlos y María son hermanos.	☑	☐
5. María sigue respetando a Jaime.	☐	☑

Actividad B Repaso

Antes de ver el **Episodio 7**, repasa las escenas que estudiaste en las actividades **De Sol y viento** en cada sección gramatical. Esas actividades te pueden ayudar con la comprensión.

Actividad C ¿Qué falta?

Act. C, Suggestion: Do not provide answers, as students will verify their choices later.

En el **Episodio 7** Jaime y Mario van a hablar del tiempo que falta para llegar a «Sol y viento». Llena los espacios en blanco con las opciones a continuación. Puedes verificar tus respuestas después de ver el episodio.

JAIME: ¿Estamos lejos?
MARIO: En automóvil, a siete minutos. A pie, cuarenta y cinco minutos, más o menos. Menos si se toma _____[1] por ahí...
JAIME: Me voy a pie. Nos vemos en la viña.
MARIO: ¡Don Jaime! ¡El sol está picando fuerte![a] ¡Que no le dé _____[2]!

1. **a.** la autopista (*highway*)
   b. un atajo (*shortcut*)
2. **a.** un infarto (*heart attack*)
   b. una insolación (*heatstroke*)

[a]picando... *really beating down*

Actividad D El episodio

Ahora mira el episodio. Si hay algo que no entiendes bien, vuelve a ver la escena.

Después de ver el episodio

Actividad A ¿Qué recuerdas?

Contesta las preguntas a continuación según lo que recuerdas del **Episodio 7.**

1. Mario no pudo arreglar (*fix*) la rueda pinchada (*flat tire*) porque no tenía...

   a. herramientas (*tools*)   **b.** gato (*tire jack*)   **c.** repuesto (*spare*)

2. Jaime sufrió una insolación antes de llegar a la casa de los Sánchez. ¿Cierto o falso?

   a. cierto   **b.** falso

3. Según don Paco, Bartel Aquapower hizo mucho daño a la ecología de este país.

   a. el Brasil   **b.** Bulgaria   **c.** Bolivia

4. Jaime renuncia a (*quits*) su trabajo con Bartel Aquapower. ¿Cierto o falso?

   a. cierto   **b.** falso

5. Doña Isabel le dijo a Jaime que María no _____ fácilmente.

   a. se enamora   **b.** perdona   **c.** se divierte

Actividad B ¿Lo captaste?

Vuelve a la **Actividad C** de **Antes de ver el episodio** para verificar tus respuestas. Si es necesario, vuelve a ver la escena en cuestión.

Actividad C En resumen

Completa la siguiente narración con las palabras y expresiones apropiadas de la lista a la derecha.

En este episodio, a Mario y Jaime <u>se les pinchó</u>[1] una rueda camino a la viña. Como Mario no tenía <u>repuesto</u>,[2] Jaime decidió seguir a pie. En ruta a la viña, Jaime sufrió una <u>insolación</u>[3] y se desmayó.[a] Mientras Jaime se recuperaba en casa de doña Isabel, don Paco <u>le informó</u>[4] que Bartel Aquapower quería construir una represa en el valle, lo cual le haría[b] mucho daño tanto al medio ambiente como a <u>la comunidad</u>[5] mapuche. Jaime comprendió el error de <u>sus acciones</u>[6] y en una conversación con Andy, renunció a su trabajo con Bartel Aquapower.

la comunidad
insolación
le informó
repuesto
se les pinchó
sus acciones

[a]se... *passed out*   [b]*would cause*

Detrás de la cámara

Have you noticed that while María and Jaime switched to the use of **tú** in a previous episode, Mario has continued to use **usted** with Jaime? Even though Mario feels the need to comment on María and Jaime's relationship, he and Jaime are not friends and are not of the same age group. Mario is, in effect, an employee of Jaime's. However, Jaime does use **tú** when addressing Mario. You may also have noticed that Traimaqueo uses **tú** with Carlos, although he is technically employed by the family. What is different here is that Traimaqueo has known Carlos since the latter was a little boy. The use of **tú** was natural in that adult–child relationship. That Traimaqueo now works for Carlos has not changed that fundamental and earlier pattern of interaction. María, of course, when finding out what Jaime has been up to, immediately drops the **tú** and reverts to **usted.** Did you catch this in the previous episode?

RESUMEN DE VOCABULARIO

Las emociones y condiciones

aburrir(se)	to bore (get bored)
alegrar(se)	to make happy (become happy)
cansar(se)	to tire (get tired)
confundir(se)	to confuse (become confused)
deprimirse	to get depressed
enojar(se)	to anger (get angry)
estar (*irreg.*) **celoso/a**	to be jealous
llorar	to cry
preocupar(se)	to worry (become worried)
reírse (i, i) (me río)	to laugh
tener(le) (*irreg.*) **envidia (a alguien)**	to be envious (of someone)
tener(le) (*irreg.*) **miedo (a alguien)**	to be afraid (of someone)
tener (*irreg.*) **sueño**	to be sleepy
tomarse algo muy a pecho	to take something to heart; to feel something intensely
avergonzado/a	embarrassed
cansado/a	tired
confundido/a	confused
enamorado/a (de)	in love (with)
perplejo/a	perplexed
preocupado/a	worried

Cognados: afectar, frustrar(se), irritar(se), ofender(se), reaccionar; frustrado/a, furioso/a, irritado/a, relajado/a, tenso/a
Repaso: molestar, sentirse (ie, i); alegre, contento/a, enojado/a, nervioso/a, triste

Las partes del cuerpo

la boca	mouth
el brazo	arm
la cabeza	head
la cara	face
el cerebro	brain
el codo	elbow
el corazón	heart
el cuello	neck
los dedos (del pie)	fingers (toes)
la espalda	back
el estómago	stomach
la garganta	throat
el hígado	liver
el hombro	shoulder
el hueso	bone

la mano	hand
el órgano interno	internal organ
el pecho	chest
el pie	foot
la pierna	leg
el pulmón	lung
la rodilla	knee

Repaso: los dientes, la mejilla, el mentón, la nariz, los ojos, las orejas

La salud y el estado físico

cortar(se)	to cut (oneself)
doler (ue)	to hurt, ache
enfermarse	to get sick
estar (*irreg.*) **enfermo/a**	to be sick
lastimar(se)	to hurt (oneself)
padecer (zc) de	to suffer from
poner(le) (*irreg.*) **una inyección (a alguien)**	to give (someone) a shot
respirar	to breathe
romper(se)	to break
sacar (qu) la lengua	to stick out one's tongue
sacar(le) (qu) sangre (a alguien)	to draw (someone's) blood
tener (*irreg.*) **fiebre**	to have a fever
tener (*irreg.*) **(la) gripe**	to have the flu
tener (*irreg.*) **la nariz tapada**	to have a stuffed-up nose
tener (*irreg.*) **un resfriado**	to have a cold
tener (*irreg.*) **tos**	to have a cough
tomar(le) la temperatura (a alguien)	to take a (someone's) temperature
el consultorio (del médico)	doctor's office
el/la enfermero/a	nurse
el/la médico/a	doctor
la pastilla	pill
la presión arterial	blood pressure
la receta	prescription

Cognados: examinar; la alergia, la aspirina, el examen médico, el/la farmacéutico/a, la medicina, el/la paciente, los rayos X
Repaso: la farmacia

Otras palabras y expresiones

hace + *time*	*time* ago

Los demás y yo

OBJETIVOS

IN THIS LESSON, YOU WILL LEARN:

- vocabulary to express your feelings toward others

- to talk about what people do to and for each other using **nos** and **se**

- vocabulary to talk about how people act in relationships

- to talk about your wishes and desires using the subjunctive mood

- vocabulary related to positive and negative aspects of relationships

- to talk about contingencies and conditions using the subjunctive with conjunctions

In addition, you will watch **Episodio 7** of the film *Sol y viento* again.

Dos personas se abrazan (*are hugging each other*). ¿Crees que este abrazo es romántico o es solamente la manera en que se saludan (*greet each other*) estas personas?

The following media resources are available for this lesson of *Sol y viento:*

Episodio 7 of *Sol y viento*

Online *Manual de actividades*

Online Learning Center Website

PRIMERA PARTE

Vocabulario

Talking About How
You Feel About
Someone

Note: These vocabulary items can be heard in this lesson's Textbook Audio section of the Online Learning Center Website.

Te tengo mucho cariño.

Feelings

▲ Esta mujer **le tiene mucho cariño** a su novio. Y él la **adora.**

Los sentimientos[a] positivos

ᵃLos... *Feelings*

adorar	to adore
amar	to love
caerle (*irreg.*) **bien a alguien**	to make a good impression on someone
estimar	to think highly of
extrañar	to miss (*someone*)
gustar	to be pleasing to
querer (*irreg.*)	to love
respetar	to respect
tenerle (*irreg.*) **cariño a alguien**	to be fond of someone

Los sentimientos negativos

caerle (*irreg.*) **mal a alguien**	to make a bad impression on someone
despreciar	to despise
detestar	to detest
no aguantar	not to be able to stand, put up with
odiar	to hate
tenerle (*irreg.*) **envidia a alguien**	to be envious of someone

As you know, the verb **gustar** and the phrase **caerle bien** can be used in Spanish to talk about liking someone. However, these expressions do not mean the same thing. **Gustar** means *to like* in the general sense that someone is agreeable to you, but it can also express romantic or physical attraction. Spanish speakers will often use their tone of voice for emphasis when saying **gustar** with the meaning of physical attraction.

Miguel, ¿**te gusta** Cecilia o
te gusta Cecilia?

*Miguel, do you like Cecilia
or do you <u>like</u> Cecilia?*

Caerle bien means *to like* in the sense of making a good impression on. Its opposite, **caerle mal,** means *to make a bad impression on.*

Nos caen bien los padres de Eduardo.

*We like Eduardo's parents.
(They make a good impression on us.)*

Me cae mal Jorge.

*I don't like Jorge.
(I have a bad impression of him.)*

Spanish also uses two verbs to talk about loving someone: **querer** and **amar.** Use **querer** to express love for anyone you care a lot about, including friends, pets, family members, boyfriends, and so forth. **Amar** is much stronger and is used to express a deep, intense love between people, usually in a romantic relationship.

Quieren mucho a sus abuelos.

They love their grandparents a lot.

Amas mucho a Ricardo, ¿no?

You love Ricardo a lot, don't you?

✳ MÁS VOCABULARIO

abrazar (c)	to hug
acariciar	to caress
besar	to kiss
darle (*irreg.*) escalofríos a alguien	to give someone chills
ponérsele (*irreg.*) la piel de gallina a alguien	to get goosebumps*
sonrojarse	to blush
trabársele la lengua a alguien	to get tongue-tied

COMUNICACIÓN ÚTIL

As you know, **tener** is used with **cariño,** a noun meaning *affection.* **Tener** can also be used with other nouns like **respeto** (*respect*), **envidia** (*envy*), and **celos** (*jealousy*). Some of these expressions are used with indirect object pronouns.

Le tengo respeto a Paul.

I respect Paul.

Les tiene envidia a sus primos.

She envies her cousins.

Los Trujillo **tienen celos** de nosotros.

The Trujillos are jealous of us.

*This Spanish phrase can be translated literally as *to get chicken skin.*

INPUT
Actividad A

Actividad A ¿Cómo reaccionabas?

Paso 1 Indica cómo reaccionabas de (*as an*) adolescente cuando veías a una persona que te gustaba mucho.

Cuando veía a alguien que me gustaba mucho,...	SIEMPRE	A VECES	NUNCA
1. me sonrojaba.	☐	☐	☐
2. se me trababa la lengua cuando le hablaba.	☐	☐	☐
3. me sudaban (*sweat*) las manos.	☐	☐	☐
4. me sentía muy inseguro/a (*insecure*).	☐	☐	☐
5. se me ponía la piel de gallina.	☐	☐	☐

Paso 2 Explica con dos o tres oraciones cómo reaccionas ahora cuando ves a una persona que te gusta mucho.

MODELO: Cuando veo a alguien que me gusta mucho, todavía estoy nerviosa, pero no me pongo insegura como antes...

INPUT/OUTPUT
**Act. B, *Paso 1*,
Statements:** 1. *María le tiene mucho cariño a doña Isabel.* (*cierto*) 2. *A Jaime le cae mal Mario.* (*falso*) 3. *Carlos le tiene envidia a María.* (*cierto*) 4. *Doña Isabel extraña a su esposo.* (*cierto*) 5. *Carlos respeta a Traimaqueo.* (*falso*) 6. *María estima a su tío Paco.* (*cierto*)
***Paso 3*, Follow-up:** Call on a few students to present their sentences to the class.

Actividad B ¿Cómo se sienten?

Paso 1 Escucha las oraciones que lee tu profesor(a) sobre los personajes de *Sol y viento* e indica si son ciertas o falsas.

1. ... **2.** ... **3.** ... **4.** ... **5.** ... **6.** ...

Paso 2 Forma tres oraciones más sobre los personajes de *Sol y viento* usando el vocabulario de las páginas 408–409.

MODELO: A Jaime no se le traba la lengua cuando habla con María.

Paso 3 Comparte las oraciones del **Paso 2** con un compañero (una compañera) de clase. ¿Estás de acuerdo con las afirmaciones de tu compañero/a?

INPUT/OUTPUT
Act. C, Suggestions
Paso 1: Give students 2–3 minutes to complete.
Paso 2: Model the activity with a student, then allow 3–4 minutes to complete.
Paso 3: Call on volunteers to present their information. Try to look for a trend in the class. If a student says *Admiro a mi abuelo,* then find out how many other students in the class admire their grandfathers. Personalize the dialogue by expanding on why students admire a relative. If students have trouble expressing their thoughts, try giving them either/or or yes/no questions.

Actividad C Mi familia

Paso 1 Llena los espacios en blanco a continuación con información verdadera sobre los miembros de tu familia (o de la familia de un amigo).

1. Le tengo mucho cariño a _____.
2. Quiero mucho a _____.
3. Le tengo mucho respeto a _____.
4. Le tengo envidia a _____.
5. No me cae bien _____.
6. Estimo a _____.
7. Adoro a _____.
8. No aguanto a _____.

Paso 2 Entrevista a un compañero (una compañera) de clase, usando las frases del **Paso 1.**

MODELO: ¿A quién de tu familia le tienes mucho cariño?

Paso 3 Presenta a la clase uno o dos datos (*pieces of information*) interesantes de tu entrevista.

MODELO: Jennifer le tiene mucho cariño a su abuelo Stephenson.

Vistazo cultural,
Suggestion: Allow students 2 minutes to read. Then ask the following comprehension questions: 1. *¿Cómo se llama la tercera esposa de Neruda?* (*Matilde*)
2. *¿Cómo se llama el poemario que Neruda dedicó a Matilde?* (*Cien sonetos de amor*).
Follow-up: Have students write a 4-line poem for a significant other, a friend, or a loved one, using references to nature. Provide a list of useful vocabulary on a transparency (e.g., *agua, sol, viento, lluvia, cielo, tierra, rosa, flor*). The class will vote for the most creative (or romantic or sentimental) poem.

 # Vistazo cultural

Pablo Neruda y los sonetos de amor

El poeta chileno Pablo Neruda (1904–1973), ganador del Premio Nóbel de Literatura, es uno de los poetas más reconocidos[a] de la literatura hispanoamericana moderna. Como la película *Sol y viento*, la poesía[b] de Neruda entrelaza[c] el tema del amor con elementos de la naturaleza. Uno de sus poemarios[d] más románticos es *Cien sonetos de amor* (1960), una colección de sonetos dedicados a su tercera esposa, Matilde Urrutia. En esta obra Neruda hace referencias a la naturaleza para expresar su profundo[e] amor por Matilde. En sus versos figuran[f] las hierbas,[g] las semillas,[h] la espuma[i] y las flores,

▲ Pablo Neruda

para mencionar algunas. A continuación está el primer verso del soneto XXXIV, en el que Neruda compara a Matilde con unos elementos básicos de la naturaleza.

Eres hija del mar y prima del orégano,

nadadora,[j] tu cuerpo es de agua pura,

cocinera, tu sangre es tierra viva

y tus costumbres son floridas[k] y terrestres.[l]

¿Qué opinas de la poesía de Neruda? ¿Crees que es profunda o superficial? ¿apasionada o indiferente?

[a]*renowned* [b]*poetry* [c]*intertwines* [d]*collections of poetry* [e]*profound, deep* [f]*appear* [g]*herbs* [h]*seeds* [i]*sea foam* [j]*swimmer* [k]*flowery, ornate* [l]*earthly*

NAVEGANDO LA RED

Busca información en español sobre los boleros, que tradicionalmente tratan (*deal with*) temas del amor. Describe el origen de este género (*genre*) musical y los temas específicos que tratan en su letra (*lyrics*). Menciona también algunos cantantes importantes y sus países de origen.

Gramática

Se conocen bien.

Reciprocal Reflexives

▲ Estas personas **se miran** cariñosamente (*lovingly*).

In **Lección 5A** you learned that the pronouns **nos** and **se** are used with reflexive verbs to express *ourselves* and *themselves*, respectively. **Nos** and **se** are also used to describe what people do or have done to or for each other, actions known as *reciprocal reflexives* (**los reflexivos recíprocos**).

You will notice that a sentence like **Ed y yo nos cantamos mientras trabajamos** can also be interpreted as *Ed and I sing to each other while we work.* Context will usually determine if the **se** means *themselves* or *each other* or if **nos** means *ourselves* or *each other*.

To emphasize a reciprocal action, Spanish can add the phrase **el uno al otro / los unos a los otros** (or **la una a la otra / las unas a las otras** if all of the people are female), phrases that literally mean *the one to the other*.

Nos saludamos **el uno al otro.***   *We greet each other (the one to the other).*

Se admiran **la una a la otra.**   *They admire each other (the one to the other).*

---

*This construction is used for a group of males or a mixed group of males and females.

REFLEXIVE AND RECIPROCAL EXPRESSIONS	
REFLEXIVE **se** = *THEMSELVES*	RECIPROCAL **se** = *EACH OTHER*
Mis amigos **se miran** mucho en el espejo. *My friends look at themselves a lot in the mirror.*	Mis amigos **se hablan** mucho por teléfono. *My friends talk to each other a lot on the phone.*
Los profesores **se escriben** notas. *The professors write notes to themselves.*	Juan y Laura **se escriben** cada semana. *Juan and Laura write each other every week.*
REFLEXIVE **nos** = *OURSELVES*	RECIPROCAL **nos** = *EACH OTHER*
Ed y yo **nos cantamos** mientras trabajamos. *Ed and I sing to ourselves while we work.*	Mis hermanos y yo **nos abrazamos.** *My siblings and I hug each other.*
No **nos tomamos** demasiado en serio. *We don't take ourselves too seriously.*	**Nos vemos** todos los días. *We see each other every day.*

De *Sol y viento,* **Note:** You can access this film clip from a special menu section on Disc 5 of the Instructional Version on DVD.

DE SOL Y VIENTO

In **Episodio 7** of *Sol y viento,* you saw the scene in which Jaime asks Mario how far it is to the winery. Part of their conversation appears here.

JAIME
¿Estamos lejos?

MARIO
En automóvil, a siete minutos. A pie, cuarenta y cinco minutos, más o menos. Menos si se toma un atajo[a] por ahí.

JAIME
¿Un atajo, eh?

MARIO
Si uno atraviesa[b] el campo,[c] se llega en media hora.

JAIME
Me voy a pie. _____ en la viña.

What do you think best fits in the preceding blank?

1. Nos extrañamos
2. Nos ayudamos
3. Nos vemos

[a]*shortcut* [b]*goes through* [c]*countryside*

Actividad D ¿Qué se hacen?

Indica si cada una de las siguientes oraciones describe o no la relación entre Jaime y María, según lo que crees.

Jaime y María...	SÍ	NO
1. se hablan por teléfono.	☐	☐
2. se saludan con un beso.	☐	☐
3. se gritan (*shout at each other*).	☐	☐
4. se quieren.	☐	☐
5. se guardan (*keep*) secretos.	☐	☐

Actividad E ¿Se respetan?

Paso 1 Escribe lo que dice tu profesor(a). Después, añade los nombres de personas famosas que corresponden a cada acción.

MODELO   PROFESOR(A): Se ayudan mucho en sus carreras (*careers*).
             TÚ: (escribes) Se ayudan mucho en sus carreras.
                 (escribes) Bill y Hillary Clinton

1. ... 2. ... 3. ... 4. ... 5. ... 6. ... 7. ... 8. ...

Paso 2 Compara tus respuestas con las de un compañero (una compañera) de clase. ¿Tienen una lista de las mismas personas famosas?

Actividad F Una historia

Paso 1 Con un compañero (una compañera), escriban una historia de cuatro a seis oraciones que describe lo que ocurre en los siguientes dibujos. A continuación hay algunas ideas para considerar.

■ ¿Cómo se llama el muchacho? ¿Qué edad tiene? ¿De dónde viene?
■ ¿Quién es la mujer que lo espera?
■ ¿Cómo se llevan el muchacho y la mujer?
■ ¿Cómo se sienten los dos cuando llega el muchacho? ¿Y cuándo se va?
■ ¿Cuándo se van a ver otra vez?

Paso 2 Compartan su historia con el resto de la clase. ¿Quiénes inventaron la mejor historia?

Actividad G   Una entrevista

Paso 1 Llena los espacios en blanco con el nombre de una persona (o una mascota), según el caso. Usa información verdadera para ti.

MODELO: Mi jefe (*boss*) Roberto y yo nos hablamos todos los días.

1. _____ y yo nos vemos todos los días.
2. _____ y yo nos damos la mano cuando nos saludamos.
3. _____ y yo nos enojamos mucho.
4. _____ y yo nos odiamos.
5. _____ y yo nos queremos mucho.
6. _____ y yo nos extrañamos cuando no estamos juntos.

Paso 2 Usa las oraciones del **Paso 1** para entrevistar a un compañero (una compañera) de clase y averiguar si sus experiencias son como las tuyas.

MODELO: E1: ¿Se ven todos los días tú y tu jefe?
           E2: No. Mi jefe y yo no nos vemos los fines de semana.

Paso 3 Escribe un breve párrafo en el cual mencionas uno o dos datos interesantes de tu entrevista.

◉ Enfoque lingüístico

Las acciones recíprocas

Have you noticed that ambiguity seems to be inherent in languages and that the interpretation of meaning may often rely on context? For example, the sentence **Se respetan** can mean either *they respect themselves* or *they respect each other*. English doesn't have this ambiguity in this case because it relies on distinct pronouns or phrases: *themselves* versus *each other*. Of course, the reverse is also true: There are ambiguous structures in English that are rendered in Spanish in different ways. And there are equivalent structures in both languages that are ambiguous in meaning.

     Why do languages allow such ambiguity? Wouldn't it be easier if languages obeyed the simple rule "one structure = one meaning/interpretation"? Of course this would be easier. But languages are evolving entities. They change over time in bits and pieces. As long as communication is a fluid and contextually-based enterprise among two or more people, language is likely to contain structures that result in ambiguity. What is more, the human mind also computes frequencies of structures, or what is more "typical." Thus, in addition to knowing that **Se respetan** means two things, the Spanish speaker's mind identifies *They respect each other* as the more frequent interpretation and thus it is the first one to come to mind.

     Here's an example in English to try on your friends. Ask them to complete the following sentence: *The lawyer examined . . .* What do your friends say? The typical way to complete the sentence is with an object such as *the witness* or *the evidence: The lawyer examined the witness.* But note that the incomplete phrase is structurally ambiguous without an object. It can just as easily be completed in the following way: *The lawyer examined by the Bar Association was found to be innocent of fraud.* As you can deduce, this last structure is less frequent and less typical than the other sentences. In short, your friends' minds are "predisposed" to one structure as opposed to the other.

SEGUNDA PARTE

Note: These vocabulary items can be heard in this lesson's Textbook Audio section of the Online Learning Center Website.

Vocabulario

More on Describing People's Traits

Eres muy romántico.

Describing People

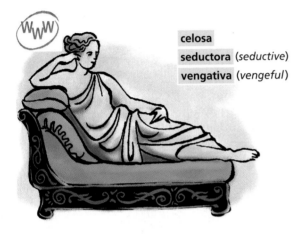

celosa
seductora (*seductive*)
vengativa (*vengeful*)

▲ Afrodita

coqueto (*flirtatious*)
cruel
engañador (*deceitful*)

▲ don Juan Tenorio

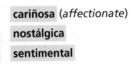

cariñosa (*affectionate*)
nostálgica
sentimental

▲ Julieta

fiel (*faithful*)
porfiado (*persistent*)
romántico

▲ Romeo

cabezona
emocional
resuelta (*determined*)

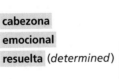

▲ Scarlett O'Hara

apasionado
divertido
encantador (*charming*)

▲ Casanova

MÁS VOCABULARIO

atento/a	considerate
comprensivo/a	understanding
detallista	detail-oriented
entrometido/a	nosy; meddlesome
mandón (mandona)	bossy
orgulloso/a	proud
sensible	sensitive
tacaño/a	stingy

Cognados: espontáneo/a, generoso/a, íntimo/a, posesivo/a

Vistazo cultural

Don Juan

El mito de don Juan tiene su origen en España a principios del siglo XVII. Aunque existen muchas versiones de esta leyenda,[a] todas relatan la historia de un hombre mujeriego,[b] seductor, engañador y libertino[c] llamado don Juan, quien seduce a las mujeres. En una ocasión don Juan seduce a la hija de un comandante militar. En un acto mórbido, don Juan mata[d] al comandante y luego invita a la estatua del comandante muerto a cenar con él. Durante la cena, la estatua se anima[e] y se lleva a don Juan al infierno[f] en donde paga por sus pecados.[g]

Don Juan es uno de los mitos de la literatura que de España se difundió[h] a otras partes del mundo. Don Juan apareció en la literatura española por primera vez en el drama *El Burlador de Sevilla* (1630) por Tirso de Molina, y más tarde en el drama *Don Juan Tenorio* (1844) de José Zorilla. El francés Molière escribió *Dom Juan, ou le Festin de Pierre*[i] (1665) y el italiano Lorenzo da Ponte escribió el libreto[j] para una ópera de Mozart, *Don Giovanni* (1787). Lord Byron y George Bernard Shaw escribieron sus versiones de don Juan en lengua inglesa. Una de las interpretaciones más recientes es la del actor Johnny Depp en la película *Don Juan De Marco* (1995). Como puedes ver, el mito de don Juan es una parte importante de la literatura universal que sigue evolucionando hasta hoy en día.

▲ Una presentación de *Don Giovanni,* ópera de Mozart

[a] *legend* [b] *womanizer* [c] *libertine (morally or sexually unrestrained)* [d] *kills* [e] *se... comes to life* [f] *hell* [g] *sins* [h] *se... spread* [i] *ou... or the Stone Guest* [j] *libretto, text of an opera*

Actividad A   Acciones

Tu profesor(a) va a mencionar algunas acciones. Indica el adjetivo que se asocia con cada acción.

1. **(a.)** engañador   **b.** fiel
2. **a.** posesivo   **(b.)** nostálgico
3. **a.** atento   **(b.)** cariñoso
4. **a.** resuelto   **(b.)** cabezón
5. **(a.)** detallista   **b.** entrometido
6. **(a.)** espontáneo   **b.** mandón
7. **a.** tacaño   **(b.)** porfiado
8. **(a.)** coqueto   **b.** vengativo

Actividad B   ¿Cómo es?

Paso 1   Indica cuáles de los siguientes adjetivos se le aplican a cada personaje de *Sol y viento.* A veces hay más de una respuesta posible.

1. Jaime: a. posesivo   b. tacaño   **(c.)** encantador
2. María: **(a.)** cabezona   **(b.)** porfiada   **(c.)** espontánea
3. Carlos: a. divertido   **(b.)** engañador   c. fiel
4. Mario: **(a.)** atento   b. cruel   c. vengativo
5. doña Isabel: **(a.)** orgullosa   b. celosa   **(c.)** resuelta
6. don Paco: a. mandón   **(b.)** generoso   **(c.)** comprensivo

Paso 2   Ahora indica dos adjetivos más para describir a los personajes del **Paso 1.**

MODELO: Carlos también es _____ y _____.

Paso 3   Comparte tus oraciones del **Paso 2** con un compañero (una compañera) de clase. ¿Tienen las mismas impresiones de los personajes de *Sol y viento*?

▲ ¿Qué tipo de persona engaña a su familia?

Actividad C Parejas famosas

Paso 1 Escribe los nombres de parejas (*couples*) famosas de la vida real o de programas de televisión que corresponden a cada oración a continuación.

MODELO: Son vengativos. → Carlos y Gabrielle Solís de *Desperate Housewives*

1. Son divertidos.
2. Son vengativos.
3. Son atentos y comprensivos.
4. Son apasionados.
5. Son resueltos y porfiados.
6. Son engañadores.

Paso 2 Con un compañero (una compañera), piensen en una pareja conocida cuya (*whose*) relación terminó por conflictos de personalidad. Mencionen por qué las dos personas hacían mala pareja.

MODELO: Carrie y Aidan de *Sex and the City* hacían mala pareja. Carrie era engañadora pero Aidan era muy fiel. Carrie también era divertida, coqueta y espontánea y le gustaba salir con sus amigas. Aidan era reservado y prefería quedarse en casa.

Actividad D ¿Con quién haces una buena pareja?

Paso 1 Piensa en una persona famosa con la cual haces una buena pareja. Describe en un párrafo de cinco o seis oraciones por qué crees que eres el novio (la novia) ideal para esa persona y viceversa. (O si quieres, menciona a una persona famosa con la cual *no* haces una buena pareja y explica por qué.) Puedes comenzar tu párrafo de la siguiente manera:

_____ y yo (no) hacemos una buena pareja por varias razones.

Puedes usar las siguientes palabras para pasar de una idea a otra.

primero   **luego** (*next*)   **por último / por fin** (*finally*)

Paso 2 Presenta tu párrafo a la clase. Tus compañeros van a indicar si están de acuerdo o no con tu análisis.

▲ ¿Crees que Jaime y María hacían una buena pareja? ¿Quieres que Jaime haga las paces con (*to make up with*) María?

Gramática

Espero que sea divertido.

**Introduction to the
Subjunctive**

So far you have been working with verb forms that are part of what is called the *indicative mood,* whose function is to report events, ask questions, and so forth. The present, preterite, and imperfect that you've already learned are all part of the indicative. Spanish also uses the *subjunctive mood,* which expresses things such as wants, desires, doubt, uncertainty, and other events that cannot be confirmed or verified. The subjunctive almost always appears in what is called a *dependent clause.* In the sentence *I hope that Mark can come, I hope* is the main or independent clause (because it can stand alone as a complete thought) and *that Mark can come* is the dependent clause (because it cannot stand alone as a complete thought).

In this lesson, you will learn to use the subjunctive mood in the present tense to talk about hopes and desires. The "trigger" for the subjunctive will be expressed in the main clause. The dependent clause in Spanish will begin with the Spanish conjunction **que** (*that*) and employ a subjunctive verb form. Note that the Spanish word **ojalá** is an invariable verb form meaning *I hope, wish.**

Espero que **vengas** a la fiesta.	*I hope (that) you come to the party.*
Ojalá que **saque** una A en el examen.	*I hope (that) I get an A on the test.*
Ojalá que **podamos** ir a Las Vegas.	*I hope (that) we can go to Las Vegas.*

The forms of the subjunctive are derived in the same manner as those used for formal commands, which you already know.

- Some irregular verbs in the subjunctive include the following.

  haber: haya, hayas, haya, hayamos, hayáis, hayan

  ir: vaya, vayas, vaya, vayamos, vayáis, vayan

  saber: sepa, sepas, sepa, sepamos, sepáis, sepan

  ser: sea, seas, sea, seamos, seáis, sean
- Some forms of the verbs **dar** and **estar** have accent marks.

  dar: dé, des, **dé,** demos, deis, den

  estar: esté, estés, esté, estemos, **estéis, estén**
- Stem-changing **-ir** verbs like **dormir, servir,** and **preferir** have an altered stem in the **nosotros** and **vosotros** forms.

  dormir: duerma, duermas, duerma, durmamos, durmáis, duerman

  servir: sirva, sirvas, sirva, sirvamos, sirváis, sirvan

  preferir: prefiera, prefieras, prefiera, prefiramos, prefiráis, prefieran

*Spanish also allows **ojalá** without **que,** but **que** will be used with **ojalá** throughout this textbook, except in some cases when characters in the film don't use it.

FORMATION OF THE PRESENT SUBJUNCTIVE				
INFINITIVE	**yo** FORM	STEM	ADD THE "OPPOSITE" VOWEL	ADD THE APPROPRIATE ENDINGS
hablar	hablo	habl-	+ e = **hable**	hable* hablemos hables habléis hable* hablen hable* hablen
beber	bebo	beb-	+ a = **beba**	beba bebamos bebas bebáis beba beban beba beban
abrir	abro	abr-	+ a = **abra**	abra abramos abras abráis abra abran abra abran
decir	digo	dig-	+ a = **diga**	diga digamos digas digáis diga digan diga digan
conducir	conduzco	conduzc-	+ a = **conduzca**	conduzca conduzcamos conduzcas conduzcáis conduzca conduzcan conduzca conduzcan

De *Sol y viento,* Note: You can access this film clip from a special menu section on Disc 5 of the Instructional Version on DVD.

DE SOL Y VIENTO

In **Episodio 7** of *Sol y viento,* doña Isabel and don Paco inform Jaime about the harm his company could do to the Maipo Valley. Part of their exchange appears in the dialogue.

PACO
Pero obviamente a su compañía no le importa mucho el daño a la ecología... ni a la comunidad humana que habita estas tierras...

JAIME
He cometido un grave error. Ojalá no _____ tarde para ayudarles a Uds....

What verb best fits in the preceding space?

1. haya   2. esté   sea

---

*Note that the **yo** and **Ud., él/ella** forms are the same in the subjunctive.

INPUT
Actividad E

Actividad E   Ojalá que...

Indica el nombre del personaje de *Sol y viento* de la lista que probablemente piensa lo siguiente. En algunos casos, es posible indicar más de un nombre.

Andy   Carlos   doña Isabel   Jaime   María   don Paco   Rassner

1. Ojalá que María me perdone pronto. Jaime
2. Espero que Carlos no haya hecho nada grave (*serious*). María
3. Espero que María no sepa nada del contrato con Bartel Aquapower. Carlos
4. Ojalá que Jaime no me vuelva a hablar (*doesn't speak to me again*). María, Carlos
5. Ojalá que salga bien la recepción para degustar el vino nuevo. Carlos, doña Isabel, don Paco
6. Espero que Jaime finalice el negocio pronto. Andy, Rassner

INPUT

Act. F, Suggestion: Give students 1 minute to complete, then read each statement out loud for the class to answer. You may wish to enunciate the subjunctive forms clearly and slowly so that students will begin to recognize subtle differences between words like *lleguen* and *llegan*.

Actividad F   ¿Dónde se dice?

Indica dónde se dice lo siguiente.

1. Ojalá que no llueva.
   a. en una reunión (*meeting*)   **b.** en un picnic
2. Esperamos que haya suficiente comida para todos.
   a. en una recepción   **b.** en una oficina
3. Espero que ganemos el partido.
   a. en el estadio   **b.** en el cine
4. Ojalá que los invitados (*guests*) lleguen a tiempo.
   a. en un concierto   **b.** en una fiesta
5. Espero que Ud. me pueda dar un reembolso (*refund*).
   a. en una biblioteca   **b.** en una tienda

INPUT
Actividad G

Actividad G   La política (*Politics*)

Indica si estás de acuerdo o no con las siguientes afirmaciones.

Espero que los políticos (*politicians*)...	ESTOY DE ACUERDO.	NO ESTOY DE ACUERDO.
1. nombren a una mujer como candidata para la presidencia.	☐	☐
2. prohíban fumar en los lugares públicos.	☐	☐
3. tomen más medidas (*measures*) para combatir el terrorismo.	☐	☐
4. aprueben leyes (*pass laws*) que limiten el uso de teléfonos celulares en autos y ciertos lugares públicos.	☐	☐
5. suban a 80 millas por hora el límite de la velocidad (*speed*) máxima en las carreteras (*highways*).	☐	☐
6. permitan el consumo legal de bebidas alcohólicas al llegar a los 18 años de edad.	☐	☐

INPUT/OUTPUT
Act. H, Suggestions
Paso 1: Allow 1–2
minutes to complete.
Paso 2: Allow 3–4
minutes for students to
complete the interviews.

Actividad H Mi trabajo

Paso 1 Indica si las siguientes oraciones son ciertas o falsas para ti.

Espero que mi trabajo futuro...	CIERTO	FALSO
1. requiera el uso del español.	☐	☐
2. esté cerca de mi familia.	☐	☐
3. me permita viajar por todo el mundo.	☐	☐
4. me dé muchas oportunidades para avanzar (*move up*).	☐	☐
5. esté relacionado con la carrera que hago en la universidad.	☐	☐
6. contribuya de alguna manera a la sociedad.	☐	☐

Paso 2 Entrevista a un compañero (una compañera) de clase para averiguar si las oraciones del **Paso 1** son ciertas o falsas para él/ella.

Paso 3 Escribe dos datos interesantes de la entrevista para presentárselos a la clase.

MODELO: Miguel espera que su trabajo esté cerca de su familia, pero yo no.

OUTPUT
Actividad I

Actividad I Las personas famosas

Paso 1 Piensa en alguna persona famosa sin mencionar su nombre. Escribe cinco oraciones sobre esa persona usando **ojalá que** y **espero que.**

MODELOS: Espero que no haga otra película como *The Break-Up.*

Ojalá que encuentre amor duradero (*long-lasting*).

Paso 2 Ahora léele tus oraciones a un compañero (una compañera). ¿Puede adivinar a quién describes? Si tu compañero/a no sabe, dale unas opciones: ¿Es Jennifer Garner o Jennifer Aniston?

COMUNICACIÓN ÚTIL

With **esperar** (and other verbs), if there is no change of subject between the main and dependent clauses, the subjunctive is not used. Instead, **esperar** is followed by an infinitive.

Espero ver a Claudia mañana. *I hope to see Claudia tomorrow.*

TERCERA PARTE

Vocabulario

Talking About
Good and Bad
Relationships

Note: These vocabulary
items can be heard in this
lesson's Textbook Audio
section of the Online
Learning Center Website.

¡Me engañó!

More on Relationships

Cuando las relaciones van bien

comprometerse (con)	to get engaged (to)
confiar (confío) (en)	to trust (in)
hacer (*irreg.*) **las paces con**	to make up with
perdonar	to forgive
salir (*irreg.*) **con**	to go out with

Cuando las relaciones van mal

discutir	to argue
engañar	to deceive; to cheat on
guardar(le) rencor (a alguien)	to hold a grudge (against someone)
ocultar(le) secretos (a alguien)	to hide secrets (from someone)
romper con	to break up with
terminar	to end (*a relationship*)
traicionar	to betray

✳ MÁS VOCABULARIO

arrepentirse (ie, i) (de)	to be sorry (about); to regret
castigar (gu)	to punish
conquistar	to succeed in seducing someone
seducir (zc)	to seduce
la amistad	friendship
el noviazgo	engagement

Repaso: casarse (con), divorciarse de, enamorarse de, estar enamorado/a de, lastimar, llevarse bien/mal con, mentir (ie, i), merecer (zc), pelearse; la boda, el divorcio

▲ Cuando las relaciones entre dos personas van bien, confían la una en la otra.

  # Vistazo cultural

El Día del Amor y la Amistad

E n los Estados Unidos y en muchos países del mundo, los amigos y enamorados[a] celebran sus relaciones el 14 de febrero, es decir, el Día de San Valentín. La costumbre existe también en los países hispanos, pero con algunas diferencias. En México y Colombia se le llama **el Día del Amor y la Amistad** y en otros países lleva el nombre de **Día de los Enamorados**. En México este día se celebra el 14 de febrero, pero en Colombia se celebra el tercer viernes y sábado de septiembre, por razones comerciales. En Colombia también es muy popular **el amigo secreto**, una tradición parecida al «Santa secreto» en los Estados Unidos, en la cual las personas se dan regalos anónimos.

[a]*lovers*

INPUT
Actividad A

Actividad A Descripciones

Indica el adjetivo más apropiado para cada descripción a continuación.

Una persona que...

1. se deja seducir fácilmente es ____.
   a. porfiada **b.** entrometida **(c.)** ingenua

2. miente a sus amigos no es ____.
   (a.) honesta **b.** desconfiada **c.** indiferente

3. castiga a otros sin motivo es ____.
   (a.) cruel **b.** humilde **c.** gregaria

4. no guarda un secreto es ____.
   a. introvertida **b.** reservada **(c.)** chismosa

5. se lleva bien con todos es ____.
   a. detallista **(b.)** encantadora **c.** celosa

6. guarda rencor por algo trivial es ____.
   a. generosa **(b.)** cabezona **c.** atenta

7. hace las paces con otra es ____.
   (a.) comprensiva **b.** vengativa **c.** divertida

Actividad B ¿Perdonas o guardas rencor?

INPUT/OUTPUT
Act. B, Suggested follow-up: Read each situation out loud to the class, then have the groups give you their advice.

Paso 1 ¿Cuánto tiempo tardas en (*do you take*) perdonar a alguien que...

	UN DÍA	2–3 DÍAS	UNA SEMANA	NUNCA LO PERDONO.
1. se pelea contigo cuando está estresado (*stressed out*)?	☐	☐	☐	☐
2. te oculta un secreto importante?	☐	☐	☐	☐
3. discute contigo en un lugar público?	☐	☐	☐	☐
4. se olvida de (*forgets*) darte un mensaje importante?	☐	☐	☐	☐
5. te miente sobre tu novio/a o tu familia?	☐	☐	☐	☐
6. te pone los cuernos?	☐	☐	☐	☐
7. rompe contigo?	☐	☐	☐	☐
8. se olvida de llamarte el día de tu cumpleaños?	☐	☐	☐	☐

Paso 2 Entrevista a un compañero (una compañera) de clase para saber cómo respondió a las preguntas del **Paso 1**.

Paso 3 Prepara un breve resumen explicando si tú y tu compañero/a de clase perdonan fácilmente o guardan rencor. Básate en lo que dijo en la entrevista.

INPUT/OUTPUT
Actividad C

Actividad C Consejos

En parejas, lean las situaciones a continuación y escriban dos o tres oraciones como respuesta a lo que debe hacer cada persona para resolver su problema.

MODELO: A mi novio le gusta discutir sobre pequeñeces (*little things*). Me castiga verbalmente, me guarda rencor y no me habla por varios días. ¿Qué debo hacer? →
¡No mereces sufrir tanto! Debes decirle que no te gusta pelear. Si no se arrepienta de sus acciones y no quiere hacer las paces, debes romper con él.

1. Mi novio es demasiado posesivo. Siempre quiere saber dónde y con quién estoy. Si salgo con mis amigas, me busca y se pelea conmigo en público. ¿Qué debo hacer?

2. Mi novia es muy desconfiada. Cree que le oculto secretos y que le miento. La verdad es que la quiero mucho y no tengo ninguna intención de lastimarla. ¿Qué debo hacer?

3. Mi novio de hace cinco años me dice que quiere casarse conmigo y tener hijos. No puedo imaginar mi vida sin él, pero tampoco quiero casarme ahora. ¿Qué debo hacer?

OUTPUT
Act. D,
Suggestions
Paso 1: Give students 3–4 minutes to brainstorm and make their list. You may opt to call on a few groups to present their lists before continuing with *Paso 2.*
Paso 2: Allow groups 3–4 minutes to complete. Then call on groups to present one of their situations followed by the proposed method for breaking up. The class will decide if the method is appropriate, given the reason for breaking up.

Actividad D ¿Cómo termina la relación?

Paso 1 En parejas, hagan una lista de por lo menos seis de las razones por las cuales dos personas terminan una relación amorosa.

MODELO: Una de las personas se enamora de otra persona.

Paso 2 Indiquen cuál de las siguientes formas de terminar es más apropiada para cada situación del **Paso 1.**

1. romper con él/ella inmediatamente
2. no contestar las llamadas de la otra persona hasta que deje de (*until he/she stops*) llamar
3. mandarle un correo electrónico explicándole por qué ya no quieres salir con él/ella
4. hablarle francamente de tus razones para terminar, aunque la otra persona se lastime
5. pedirle a un amigo (una amiga) que termine la relación por ti
6. ¿ ?

MODELO: Si una de las personas se enamora de otra persona, es mejor romper con él/ella inmediatamente.

Gramática

Talking About
Contingencies and
Conditions

✳

A menos que no quieras... Obligatory Subjunctive

In addition to being used with expressions of wishing and hoping, the subjunctive is also used with conjunctions of contingency* such as *in order that, so that, provided that,* and *without,* among others. See the chart for a list of expressions of contingency in Spanish and examples of their use with the subjunctive.

If there is no change in subject in the dependent clause, **antes de que** and **para que** shorten to **antes de** and **para** and are followed by an infinitive instead of the subjunctive. Compare the sentences below.

Voy a preparar café **antes de que vengan** los invitados.	*I'm going to make coffee before the guests come.*
Voy a preparar café **antes de estudiar.**	*I'm going to make coffee before studying.*
Lo escribo **para que entiendas** mejor.	*I'll write it down so (that) you understand better.*
Lo escribo **para recordarlo** más tarde.	*I'll write it down to remember it later.*

THE SUBJUNCTIVE WITH CONJUNCTIONS OF CONTINGENCY		
a menos que	*unless*	Vamos a la fiesta **a menos que** Marta no **quiera**. *We're going to the party unless Marta doesn't want to.*
antes (de) que	*before*	Tengo que llamar al banco **antes de que cierre**. *I have to call the bank before it closes.*
con tal (de) que	*provided (that)*	Voy a salir esta noche **con tal de que** me **paguen**. *I'm going out tonight provided that they pay me.*
en caso de que	*in case*	Llévate una chaqueta **en caso de que haga** frío. *Take a jacket in case it's cold.*
para que	*so (that)*	Te llevo en auto **para que** no **tengas** que caminar. *I'll drive you so you don't have to walk.*
sin que	*without*	No compro la casa **sin que** me **ofrezcan** el trabajo. *I won't buy the house without their offering me the job.*

*A *contingency* is an action or event that is dependent on something else.

De *Sol y viento,* Note:
You can access this film
clip from a special menu
section on Disc 5 of the
Instructional Version on
DVD.

 DE SOL Y VIENTO

In **Episodio 7,** you will again see the scene in which Jaime offers to help the Sánchez family. Part of this conversation follows.

JAIME
He cometido un grave error.
Ojalá no sea tarde para ayudarles a Uds. y para que su hija
me _____.[1]

ISABEL
¿María Teresa perdonar? ¡Huy!
¡Es durísima![a] Va a ser muy
difícil... A menos que Ud.,
don Jaime, _____[2] su
perdón.

Selecting from the following options, which verb do you think best fits in each space above?

1. a. mienta   **b.** lastime   **c.** perdone

2. a. compre   **b.** merezca   **c.** necesite

[a]*very tough*

INPUT
Actividad E

Actividad E ¿Cierto o falso?

Indica si las siguientes oraciones sobre los personajes de *Sol y viento* son ciertas o falsas.

		CIERTO	FALSO
1.	Carlos puede vender la viña con tal de que doña Isabel y María firmen el contrato.	☑	☐
2.	María conoce a Jaime antes de que Jaime conozca a Carlos.	☑	☐
3.	Jaime no puede renunciar a su trabajo sin que Rassner se enoje.	☑	☐
4.	Jaime no tiene que hacer mucho para que María lo perdone.	☐	☑
5.	Doña Isabel no puede resolver su problema con Carlos a menos que don Paco la ayude.	☑	☐

▲ María no va a perdonar a Jaime a menos que él merezca su perdón.

OUTPUT

Act. F, Suggestion: Allow students 30 seconds to look over the list of phrases to see if there are any questions.
Statements: 1. *Vamos a cenar en casa con tal de que...* (*haya comida en el refrigerador*) 2. *Los estudiantes trabajan para...* (*pagar los estudios,* Note: Not subjunctive in order to keep them on their toes!) 3. *Llevo dinero en efectivo en caso de que los taxis...* (*no acepten tarjetas de crédito*) 4. *Ramón, cierra la ventana para que...* (*no entren las moscas*) 5. *No puedo hablar de política con Cecilia sin que...* (*se enoje conmigo*) 6. *Los niños se bañan y se cepillan los dientes antes de...* (*dormirse,* Keep them on their toes!) 7. *Llamamos a mi abuela por la noche a menos que...* (*esté demasiado tarde*)

Actividad F ¿Es lógico?

Tu profesor(a) va a leer la primera parte de una oración. En una hoja de papel aparte, completa cada oración con una frase lógica de la lista a continuación, según el modelo.

MODELO: (*oyes*)   Los padres trabajan para que sus hijos...
(*escribes*) Los padres trabajan para que sus hijos tengan comida y ropa.

a. enojarse conmigo

b. entrar las moscas (*flies*)

c. haber comida en el refrigerador

d. dormirse

e. no aceptar tarjetas de crédito

f. estar demasiado tarde

g. pagar los estudios

Actividad G   Este fin de semana

Paso 1   Usa las expresiones de la página 428 para inventar cinco oraciones sobre lo que intentas (*you plan on*) hacer este fin de semana.

MODELOS: Voy a limpiar mi apartamento antes de que vengan mis padres.
Voy a ver una película a menos que mi amiga haga una fiesta.

Paso 2   Comparte tus oraciones con un compañero (una compañera) de clase. ¿Quién tiene más probabilidad de realizar sus planes?

Actividad H   En la universidad

Paso 1   Lee las oraciones a continuación y llena los espacios en blanco con información verdadera para ti.

MODELO: Le presto (*I loan*) _____ a un amigo para que _____. →
Le presto mi libro de química a un amigo para que pueda hacer la tarea.

1. Le presto _____ a un amigo para que pueda _____.
2. Trato de tomar _____ créditos cada semestre (trimestre) con tal de que _____.
3. Hago ejercicio _____ veces a la semana a menos que _____.
4. Limpio mi apartamento cada _____ días (semanas) para que _____.
5. Todas las noches, antes de acostarme yo _____.
6. Llevo dinero extra cuando voy a _____ en caso de que _____.

Paso 2   Entrevista a un compañero (una compañera) de clase con las oraciones que escribiste en el **Paso 1** para saber si hace lo mismo que tú.

MODELO: ¿Tratas de tomar doce créditos cada semestre con tal de que la universidad ofrezca los cursos que necesitas?

Paso 3   Prepara un resumen sobre los resultados de tu entrevista.

MODELO: Yo trato de tomar doce créditos cada semestre con tal de que la universidad ofrezca los cursos que necesito. En cambio, Jonah trata de tomar quince créditos con tal de que no tenga que trabajar.

SOL Y VIENTO

A segunda vista

Antes de ver el episodio

Actividad A ¿Qué recuerdas?

1. Según Mario, se tarda unos _____ en llegar a la viña caminando.

   a. siete minutos   **b.** quince minutos   **c.** treinta minutos   **(d.)** cuarenta y cinco minutos

2. Jaime dice que doña Isabel le recuerda a su abuela. ¿Cierto o falso?

   a. cierto   **(b.)** falso

3. Según doña Isabel, Jaime puede conseguir el perdón de María con _____.

   a. palabras   **b.** regalos   **(c.)** hechos (*deeds*)

4. Don Paco descubre información sobre Bartel Aquapower en el periódico. ¿Cierto o falso?

   a. cierto   **(b.)** falso

5. Según Jaime, pueden parar (*stop*) la venta de la viña si esperan unos _____ días más.

   a. dos   **b.** tres   **(c.)** cinco   **d.** siete

Actividad B ¡A escuchar!

Repasa el siguiente fragmento de la conversación entre doña Isabel, Jaime y don Paco. En unos momentos vas a escuchar la conversación y llenar los espacios en blanco con las palabras correctas. ¡No vuelvas a leer otros fragmentos de este episodio!

Act. B, Suggestion:
Have students read the exchange. They do not need to write anything at this point. Do not reveal answers.
Alternative: Have the class brainstorm possible answers for each blank but do not have them write anything down.

ISABEL: ¿María Teresa _perdonar_? ¡Huy! ¡Es durísima! Va a ser muy difícil...
A menos que [1] Ud., don Jaime, merezca su perdón.

JAIME: Entiendo que será[a] difícil y quizás[b] no me _merezca_ [2] su perdón, pero...

[a]*it will be* [b]*perhaps*

Actividad C El episodio

Ahora vas a ver el episodio de nuevo. No te olvides de verificar tus respuestas a la **Actividad A** mientras ves el episodio.

Después de ver el episodio

Actividad A Para pensar...

La familia Sánchez ya sabe que Carlos quiere vender la viña. ¿Por qué crees que quiere venderla si la viña ha tenido tanto éxito? (Recuerda que hace muchos años que Carlos es administrador y que la producción ha sido de muy buena calidad.) ¿Crees que Carlos va a revelar sus intenciones o que va a seguir engañando a la familia? Con un compañero (una compañera) de clase, apunta algunas ideas sobre los posibles motivos de Carlos y lo que crees que va a pasar con él.

Act. B, Suggestion: Replay the scene once for students. Replay a second time if needed. Then ask for volunteers to provide answers for each blank. Verify using the instructor notes from Act. B on the previous page.
Alternative: After students complete the conversation, have 2 students act it out.

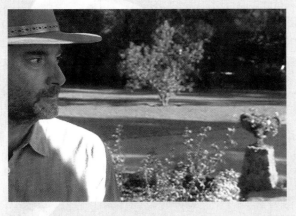

Actividad B ¡A verificar!

Vas a ver otra vez la escena de **¡A escuchar!** en la página anterior. Llena los espacios en blanco, según lo que oyes.

Actividad C ¡Te toca a ti!

Paso 1 Escribe cinco oraciones sobre lo que esperas que pase en los últimos episodios de *Sol y viento*, usando **ojalá que** y **espero que**.

MODELO: Espero que la familia Sánchez no venda la viña.

Paso 2 Comparte tus oraciones con un compañero (una compañera) de clase. Hagan una lista de las cosas con las que están de acuerdo para presentársela a la clase.

Act. C, Suggestions
Paso 1: Give students 3 minutes to complete.
Paso 2: Call on volunteers to present their statements and poll the class for their reactions to them. You may want to make a list of some of these items on an overhead transparency that you can pull out again after *Episodio 9* to see how many of them came true in the movie.

▲ Ojalá que María no le guarde rencor a Jaime.

Detrás de la cámara

You have seen doña Isabel in a few scenes, and you probably have some idea about the type of person she is. Doña Isabel is compassionate but also strong-willed and cares deeply about her family, the community, and, of course, the winery. After she immigrated with her husband from Spain to Chile, they built a prosperous winery from the ground up. Now an aging widow, doña Isabel is not in very good health. Despite her frailty, she is not afraid to speak her mind nor is she easily persuaded to do anything against her wishes. In a sense, she is typical of the "strong women" often portrayed by Katherine Hepburn, Bette Davis, and others in the glamour era of the silver screen. Can you think of any other movie characters who are like her?

RESUMEN DE VOCABULARIO

Para expresar los sentimientos

abrazar (c)	to hug
acariciar	to caress
amar	to love
besar	to kiss
darle (*irreg.*) **escalofríos a alguien**	to give someone chills
despreciar	to despise
estimar	to think highly of
extrañar	to miss (*someone*)
no aguantar	not to be able to stand, put up with
ponérsele (*irreg.*) **la piel de gallina a alguien**	to get goosebumps
querer (*irreg.*)	to love
sonrojarse	to blush
tenerle (*irreg.*) **cariño a alguien**	to be fond of someone
trabársele la lengua a alguien	to get tongue-tied

Cognados: adorar, detestar, respetar
Repaso: caerle (*irreg.*) **bien/mal a alguien, gustar, odiar, tenerle** (*irreg.*) **envidia a alguien**

Para describir la personalidad

atento/a	considerate
cariñoso/a	affectionate
comprensivo/a	understanding
coqueto/a	flirtatious
detallista	detail-oriented
encantador(a)	charming
engañador(a)	deceitful
entrometido/a	nosy; meddlesome
fiel	faithful
mandón (mandona)	bossy
porfiado/a	persistent
resuelto/a	determined
seductor(a)	seductive
sensible	sensitive
tacaño/a	stingy
vengativo/a	vengeful

Cognados: cruel, emocional, espontáneo/a, generoso/a, íntimo/a, nostálgico/a, posesivo/a, romántico/a, sentimental
Repaso: apasionado/a, cabezón (cabezona), celoso/a, divertido/a, orgulloso/a

Las relaciones personales

arrepentirse (ie, i) (de)	to be sorry (about); to regret
castigar (gu)	to punish
comprometerse (con)	to get engaged (to)
confiar (confío) (en)	to trust (in)
conquistar	to succeed in seducing someone
discutir	to argue
engañar	to deceive; to cheat on
guardar(le) rencor (a alguien)	to hold a grudge (against someone)
hacer (*irreg.*) **las paces con**	to make up with
ocultar(le) secretos (a alguien)	to hide secrets (from someone)
perdonar	to forgive
romper con	to break up with
salir (*irreg.*) **con**	to go out with
seducir (zc)	to seduce
terminar	to end (*a relationship*)
traicionar	to betray
la amistad	friendship
el noviazgo	engagement

Repaso: casarse (con), divorciarse de, enamorarse de, estar enamorado/a de, gritar, lastimar, llevarse bien/mal con, mentir (ie, i), merecer (zc), pelearse; la boda, el divorcio

Otras palabras y expresiones

darse (*irreg.*) **la mano**	to shake hands
esperar	to hope
saludar	to greet
ojalá que	I hope, wish that
los celos	jealousy
la pareja	couple
el respeto	respect
a menos que	unless
antes (de) que	before
con tal (de) que	provided (that)
en caso de que	in case
para que	so (that)
sin que	without

Entremés cultural
Chile: País en marcha^a

VISTAZO

Chile es un país largo y estrecho^b que se linda con^c la cordillera de los Andes al este y con el océano Pacífico al oeste. Chile cuenta con paisajes muy diversos. En el norte del país está el desierto Atacama. El valle central ocupa el centro del país e incluye áreas viticulturales^d como el Valle del Maipo. El sur del país cuenta con bosques, volcanes y lagos. El clima varía mucho de una región a otra. El desierto Atacama en el norte es una de las áreas más áridas del mundo. El valle central, que incluye las ciudades de Santiago y Valparaíso, tiene un clima mediterráneo y el sur suele estar fresco y húmedo. El estrecho de Magallanes^e en el sur del país conecta el océano Pacífico y el Atlántico. El territorio chileno incluye también la isla de la Pascua, entre otras islas pequeñas, y Chile suele incluir entre su territorio vastas partes de la Antártida.

^aen... *on the move* ^b*narrow* ^cse... *borders* ^d*wine-producing* ^eestrecho... *Strait of Magellan*

DATO INTERESANTE:
Santiago

Más del 40 por ciento de la población chilena vive en Santiago, la capital. Con unos 5,5 millones de habitantes, Santiago es una ciudad grande y moderna. Cuenta con rascacielos elegantes, almacenes grandes y un sistema de carreteras^a muy sofisticado.

Idea: Busca información sobre Santiago, concentrándote en los siguientes temas: el transporte, la economía, las universidades, las atracciones turísticas y cualquier otro tema. Trae la información a clase.

^a*highways*

Santiago es el centro financiero de Chile.

DATO INTERESANTE:
Michelle Bachelet

Políticamente, Chile es una democracia. La presidenta actual durante el período de 2006 hasta 2010 es Michelle Bachelet, la primera mujer en ocupar este puesto en la historia de Chile. Antes de asumir la presidencia, Bachelet, pediatra[a] y cirujana[b] de profesión, sirvió de ministra de Salud y de ministra de Defensa.

> **Idea:** Como clase, comenten si los Estados Unidos está listo para elegir a una mujer como presidenta. Mencionen quiénes son o serían[c] las mejores candidatas y por qué.

[a]*pediatrician* [b]*surgeon* [c]*would be*

La tierra y el clima de Chile son ideales para la cultivación de uvas (*grapes*).

Michelle Bachelet fue la primera mujer en Latinoamérica en ocupar el puesto de ministra de Defensa.

DATO INTERESANTE:
El vino chileno

Chile se conoce mundialmente[a] por sus vinos finos, sobre todo sus vinos tintos como el cabernet sauvignon y el merlot. En competiciones mundiales los vinos chilenos les han ganado a[b] los vinos de rivales tradicionales como Francia e Italia. En cuanto a la producción del vino, Chile figura entre los diez países más importantes del mundo.

> **Idea:** Visita la sección de vinos de un supermercado grande de tu ciudad y haz una lista de las marcas y clases de vinos chilenos que hay (por ejemplo: Concha y Toro, cabernet). Apunta también la región donde se produce.

[a]*worldwide* [b]*les… have beaten*

DATO INTERESANTE:
El «país de poetas»

Los chilenos suelen decir que viven en un «país de poetas», debido a[a] la fuerte tradición literaria de su país. Dos poetas chilenos, Gabriela Mistral y Pablo Neruda, han ganado el Premio Nóbel de Literatura. Isabel Allende, la sobrina del ex presidente Salvador Allende, es una novelista conocida mundialmente por su obra[b] *La casa de los espíritus,* entre otras novelas, ensayos[c] y colecciones de cuentos.

> **Idea:** ¿Cuáles son otros países hispanos que han producido ganadores del Premio Nóbel de Literatura? Busca la información y tráela a la clase.

[a]*debido… due to* [b]*work* [c]*essays*

Gabriela Mistral fue la primera mujer latinoamericana en ganar el Premio Nóbel de Literatura.

Sin alternativa

En este episodio...

MARÍA

...después que murió papá, te dejé sola con Carlos y no he cumplido con lo mío[a] para mantener la viña.

ISABEL

Hija, cada uno tiene su destino en la vida. Carlos ha tenido el suyo y tú tienes otro.

MARÍA

Hablando de Carlos, tengo que mostrarte[b] algo...

[a]no... *I haven't done my share* [b]*show you*

¿Qué crees tú?

1. ¿Cómo se siente María en este momento? ¿Se siente confidente? ¿preocupada? ¿triste?

2. Doña Isabel está irritada porque María no ayuda mucho con la viña. ¿Cierto o falso?

3. ¿Qué crees que María va a mostrarle a su madre? ¿Tiene algo que ver con (*Does it have anything to do with*) la compañía de Jaime?

El dinero y las finanzas

OBJETIVOS

IN THIS LESSON, YOU WILL LEARN:

- to talk about money and your personal finances
- more on the present progressive, as well as using infinitives as nouns
- to talk about debts you have and how to pay them off
- the conditional to talk about what you would do in certain situations
- to talk about the economy
- the imperfect subjunctive to talk about hypothetical events and how you would respond to them

In addition, you will prepare for and watch **Episodio 8** of the film *Sol y viento.*

Los cajeros automáticos son una parte importante de la vida moderna.

The following media resources are available for this lesson of *Sol y viento:*

Episodio 8 of
Sol y viento

Online *Manual
de actividades*

Online Learning
Center Website

PRIMERA PARTE

Vocabulario

Talking About Money | **¿Cómo manejas el dinero?** **Your Personal Finances**

Note: These vocabulary items can be heard in this lesson's Textbook Audio section of the Online Learning Center Website.

En el banco

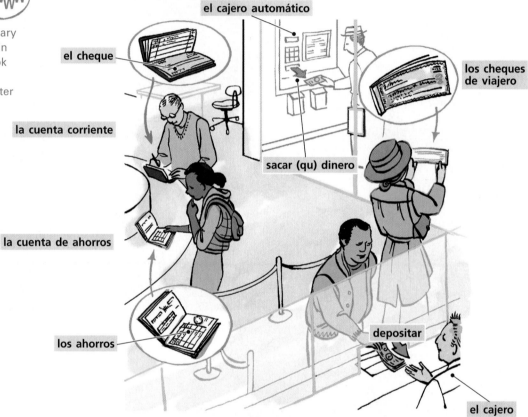

el cajero automático

el cheque

los cheques de viajero

la cuenta corriente

sacar (qu) dinero

la cuenta de ahorros

los ahorros

depositar

el cajero

✳ MÁS VOCABULARIO

ahorrar	to save	**el presupuesto**	(monthly)
cobrar	to charge (*a fee*)	**(mensual)**	budget
ganar	to earn	**el recibo**	receipt
manejar	to manage	**el sueldo**	salary
(bien/mal)	(well/poorly)		
pagar (gu) a	to pay in	**derrochador(a)**	wasteful
plazos	installments	**irresponsable**	irresponsible
		responsable	responsible
los gastos	expenses		
los ingresos	income		

Repaso: cargar (gu), gastar; la cuenta, el efectivo, la tarjeta de crédito

COMUNICACIÓN ÚTIL

Notice that Spanish has a number of ways to say *to save* and *to spend*. Be sure not to confuse these verbs and their meanings.

ahorrar	to save (*money*)	Necesitamos **ahorrar** más.
guardar	to save, keep (*things*)	¿Me **guardas** este recibo, por favor?
gastar	to spend (*money*)	**Gasté** demasiado en el centro comercial hoy.
pasar	to spend (*time*)	Elisa y Marcos **pasan** mucho tiempo juntos.

Vistazo cultural,
Suggestion: Have students read quickly, then ask the following questions: *¿Cuál es una desventaja de cambiar dinero en efectivo o cheques viajeros en otra moneda?* (*hay que pagar las altas comisiones*) *¿Por qué es muy importante llevar una tarjeta de repuesto cuando uno viaja?* (*si una tarjeta no funciona o si el cajero automático traga la tarjeta*).

Vistazo cultural

Los cajeros automáticos

Hace pocos años, era necesario llevar una gran cantidad de cheques de viajero o de dinero en efectivo para viajar al extranjero. Para cambiar dólares norteamericanos en la moneda[a] del país de destino, el turista tenía que pagar las altas comisiones que cobraban algunos bancos y casas de cambio.[b] Afortunadamente todo eso ha cambiado gracias a los cajeros automáticos, esas máquinas maravillosas que te dan el dinero que necesitas, dónde y cuándo lo necesitas. Con sólo introducir en el cajero una tarjeta de crédito o bancaria y un código personal, se obtiene en efectivo la moneda del país donde uno se encuentre.[c] Tanto en España como en Latinoamérica los cajeros automáticos aceptan la mayoría de las tarjetas de crédito e incluso algunas tarjetas bancarias. Además, las transacciones son, por lo general, mucho más baratas que en los bancos o casas de cambio. Sin embargo, puede ocurrir que un cajero automático en el extranjero se tragué[d] la tarjeta si no la reconoce. Por eso, siempre es conveniente apuntar los datos de la tarjeta en un lugar seguro,[e] para poder anularla[f] sin dificultad. Y claro, ¡siempre es buena idea llevar otra tarjeta de repuesto![g]

▲ Los cajeros automáticos, como este en México, han facilitado las oportunidades de sacar dinero en el extranjero.

[a]*currency* [b]*casas... currency exchange offices* [c]*donde... wherever one may be* [d]*se... swallows* [e]*safe* [f]*to cancel it* [g]*de... spare*

INPUT
Actividad A

Actividad A Definiciones

Empareja cada palabra o frase con la definición apropiada.

1. __d__ el cajero automático
2. __f__ las cuentas
3. __h__ el efectivo
4. __a__ el presupuesto
5. __g__ el recibo
6. __c__ el cheque
7. __e__ el sueldo
8. __b__ los gastos
9. __j__ la cuenta corriente
10. __i__ la tarjeta de crédito

a. lo que uno prepara para manejar bien el dinero cada mes y no gastar demasiado
b. el conjunto (*entirety*) de lo que una persona gasta
c. cosa que uno escribe y firma para pagar las cuentas o el alquiler
d. máquina que se usa para sacar dinero
e. lo que uno gana cada semana, mes o año
f. lo que nos mandan cada mes las compañías por servicios de crédito, electricidad, gas, etcétera
g. prueba (*proof*) de una compra
h. lo que uno saca del cajero automático
i. lo que uno utiliza en vez de pagar en efectivo
j. uno deposita el dinero aquí para luego poder escribir cheques

INPUT
Act. B, Questions:
1. *¿Me da el recibo, por favor?*
2. *¿Cómo prefiere pagar?* 3. *¿Dónde prefiere depositar este cheque?*
4. *¿Lo va a cargar en su tarjeta de crédito?*
5. *¿Cuánto desea sacar?*
6. *¿Se puede pagar con cheque?*

Actividad B Preguntas y respuestas

Escoge la respuesta apropiada para cada pregunta que escuchas.

1. (**a.**) Claro que sí. Aquí lo tiene.
   b. Prefiero pagar con tarjeta de crédito.

2. **a.** Mil pesos, por favor.
   (**b.**) Si es posible, con un cheque de viajero.

3. **a.** Prefiero sacarlo del cajero.
   (**b.**) En mi cuenta de ahorros, por favor.

4. (**a.**) No, lo voy a pagar en efectivo.
   b. Sí, en mi cuenta corriente.

5. (**a.**) Mil pesos, por favor.
   b. Prefiero pagarlo en efectivo.

6. **a.** Sí, se puede pagarlo a plazos.
   (**b.**) No, sólo en efectivo o con tarjeta de crédito.

OUTPUT
Act. C, *Paso 1,*
Suggestion: You may wish to provide an example of a description for *una persona generosa* prior to having them write their descriptions individually.
Paso 3, **Follow-up:** Survey the class to find out their overall attitude towards money.

Actividad C ¿Cómo manejan el dinero?

Paso 1 Escribe dos oraciones para describir la actitud hacia el dinero que tiene cada persona a continuación.

una persona derrochadora   una persona irresponsable
una persona responsable   una persona tacaña

Paso 2 En grupos de tres personas, cada persona va a leer dos de sus descripciones y los otros miembros del grupo van a adivinar el tipo de persona correcto.

Paso 3 ¿Te pareces a alguien del **Paso 1**? ¿De qué manera? Prepara una oración para luego compartirla con la clase.

MODELO: Soy (un poco/bastante/muy) ____(adjetivo)____ porque...

Actividad D Entrevista

Paso 1 Hazle a un compañero (a una compañera) las preguntas a continuación y apunta sus respuestas.

1. ¿Tienes muchos gastos cada mes?
2. ¿Puedes ahorrar un poco de dinero cada mes?
3. Por lo general, ¿cómo prefieres pagar tus compras?
4. ¿Tienes un presupuesto mensual?
5. ¿Sabes cuánto dinero tienes en tu cuenta corriente?
6. Si quieres comprar algo pero no tienes suficiente dinero, ¿lo compras? ¿Cómo pagas?
7. Antes de salir con tus amigos, ¿te pones un límite en lo que puedes gastar?
8. ¿Guardas los recibos después de ir de compras?
9. ¿Sueles gastar más de lo que ganas o ganas más de lo que gastas?

Paso 2 Contesta las siguientes preguntas utilizando la información que te dio tu compañero/a en el **Paso 1.**

1. ¿Qué adjetivo describe mejor la habilidad de manejar el dinero que tiene tu compañero/a?

   ☐ responsable   ☐ irresponsable

2. ¿Tienes alguna sugerencia que hacerle a él/ella?

   Creo que (no) debe...

3. En tu opinión, ¿quién maneja mejor el dinero, tú o tu compañero/a? ¿Por qué?

Paso 3 Comparte tus respuestas del **Paso 2** con la clase. ¿Está de acuerdo el compañero (la compañera) a quien entrevistaste?

▲ ¿Sueles hacer muchas compras con tarjeta de crédito?

Gramática

Using Verbs As Nouns | **Ver es creer.**   **Progressive Versus Infinitives**

You have learned that the Spanish ending **-ndo** is roughly equivalent to English *-ing* when used with a form of *be.*

    ¿Qué **estás haciendo**?   *What are you doing?*

You can also use **-ndo** with the verbs **seguir** and **continuar** to describe what someone continues doing. Infinitives are never used with these verbs as they are in English.

    Ramón **sigue gastando**   *Ramón continues spending /*
        dinero.   *to spend money.*

Another verb commonly used with **-ndo** is **andar.** However, the meaning suggests a sort of running around or repeated attempts to do something.

    Anda buscando un   *He's running around looking*
        cajero automático.   *for an ATM.*
    Anda diciendo mentiras.   *He's going around telling lies.*

There is one important context in which **-ndo** and *-ing* are not equivalent: when they are used as nouns. English regularly uses *-ing* as a noun but Spanish never can. Instead, in Spanish the infinitive form of the verb is used.

    Gastar dinero es fácil.   *Spending money is easy.*
    Ganarlo es difícil.   *Earning it is tough.*

When the noun is based on a reflexive verb, it appears with **se,** except when the statement is specific to a person.

    Despertarse temprano   *Getting up early is good.*
        es bueno.   *(nonspecific)*
    Despertarme temprano   *Getting up early is difficult*
        es difícil.   *(for me).*

▲ Parece que Carlos **anda diciendo** mentiras.

USES OF -*ndo*	
• with **estar** to mean *doing something*	¿Qué **estás haciendo**? **Estoy escuchando** música.
• with **seguir** to mean *to continue doing / to do something*	Carlos **sigue inventando** excusas.
• with **andar** to mean *running around* or *going around doing something*	Mi hermana **andaba gastando** dinero la semana pasada.
INFINITIVE AS NOUN	
Only infinitives in Spanish can be used as nouns; **-ndo** forms cannot function as nouns.	**Ahorrar** dinero no es fácil.

De *Sol y viento,* Note: You can access this film clip from a special menu section on Disc 5 of the Instructional Version on DVD.

DE SOL Y VIENTO

In **Episodio 8** of *Sol y viento,* you will watch a scene in which María confronts her brother Carlos. Part of their exchange follows.

CARLOS
¿Qué **estás intruseando**?ª

MARÍA
¡Si no lo hago, vas a seguir _____ a todos!

CARLOS
Me puedes preguntar y te respondo... lo que no me gusta es que te metas aᵇ mi oficina sin mi permiso.

Selecting from the following options, what is it that María thinks Carlos will continue doing?

1. engañándonos   **2.** ayudándonos   **3.** molestándonos

ªintruding upon   ᵇque... your going into

Actividad E ¿Quién lo está haciendo?

Escoge al personaje de la lista que corresponda a las oraciones a continuación.

1. ___Diego___ Está trabajando en la excavación con su profesora.
2. ___Jaime___ Obtener un contrato no es fácil para esta persona.
3. ___María___ Anda enterándose (*finding out*) de lo que ha hecho Carlos.
4. ___Jaime___ Está enamorándose de María.
5. ___Carlos___ Mentir es fácil para esta persona.
6. __don Paco__ Está visitando a unos amigos en Chile.
7. _doña Isabel_ Sigue pensando mucho en su esposo.
8. ___Jaime___ Está intentando comprar los terrenos de «Sol y viento».

Actividad F Si anda buscando un banco...

Escucha la acción que lee tu profesor(a). Luego indica la causa de la acción.

a. __2__ ...va a dar una fiesta.
b. __1__ ...necesita dinero ahora mismo.
c. __5__ ...quiere ejercer control sobre otras personas.
d. __3__ ...ha hecho algo que quiere ocultar (*to cover up*).
e. __4__ ...no le gusta malgastar (*to waste*) su dinero.

Actividad G ¿Fácil o difícil?

Paso 1 Escribe tres oraciones con un infinitivo que representan acciones difíciles para ti. Luego escribe tres que son fáciles.

MODELO: Decir mentiras es difícil para mí.
Hablar en público es fácil para mí.

Paso 2 Presenta sólo las acciones a un compañero (una compañera). ¿Puede adivinar si te son fáciles o difíciles?

MODELO: E1: Decir mentiras.
E2: Es fácil para ti.
E1: ¡No! Decir mentiras es difícil para mí.

Paso 3 (Optativo) Escoge una de las acciones que causó problemas para tu compañero/a en el **Paso 2** y preséntasela a la clase. ¿Pueden los demás decir si le es fácil o difícil?

Actividad H ¿Qué hacías? ¿Qué sigues haciendo?

Paso 1 En una hoja de papel aparte haz una lista de cinco de las actividades que hacías cuando asistías a la escuela secundaria. Incluye por lo menos dos actividades relacionadas con el dinero.

MODELO: Trabajaba en un restaurante para ganar dinero.

Paso 2 Intercambia tu lista con la de otra persona. Hazle preguntas a tu compañero/a para averiguar si sigue haciendo cada actividad de la lista o no.

MODELO: ¿Sigues trabajando en un restaurante para ganar dinero?

Paso 3 ¿Cuáles son las actividades que tu compañero/a sigue haciendo hoy en día? ¿Son las mismas actividades, más o menos, que sigues haciendo tú?

⦿ Enfoque lingüístico

Verb Invention

As you have seen, English and Spanish differ in how they use verbs as nouns: English uses *-ing* and Spanish exclusively uses the infinitive.

Gastar dinero es fácil.	*Spending money is easy.*
Ganarlo, no.	*Earning it, not so.*

Languages in general vary as to how they derive nouns from verbs—or even verbs from nouns. English has great flexibility in this regard. For example, from the proper nouns FedEx and Google, come the commonly phrased, *Just FedEx it to me* or *I Googled it and found lots of sites*. In Spanish, such inventing of verbs is rare. Spanish, however, like some other languages, can easily incorporate English verbs if they are derived from English nouns. Thus, *to fax* something (derived from *fax*, the shortened form of *facsimile*) has entered some Spanish dialects as **faxear**. More common and standard, however, is **enviar un fax**. The same goes with *e-mail*. While in English we can say *Send me an e-mail* or *E-mail me*, Spanish cannot derive a verb from **correo electrónico**. It can, however, "borrow" the verb *to e-mail,* and thus you might hear in some dialects **imeilear**. Again, **enviar un mensaje por correo electrónico** is the more standard and widespread form.

SOL Y VIENTO: Enfoque cultural

En el **Episodio 8,** mientras todos se preparan para la recepción, María va a ayudar a Traimaqueo con algo bastante pesado.[a] Él le dice «¡Cuidado![b] ¡Cuidado! Ay, gracias, m'hija.[c]» Claro, ya sabes que María no es hija de Traimaqueo. Es muy común entre los hispanohablantes emplear de forma afectuosa los términos **hijo** o **hija** al dirigirse[d] a una persona más joven. **Tío** y **tía** son utilizados para demostrar cariño a una persona mayor, como lo hace María con don Paco. Paco es amigo de la familia —no es pariente— pero María lo quiere mucho, y por eso le dice **tío Paco.**

En el **Episodio 4** ya viste a Yolanda llamar a Traimaqueo **viejo.** Entre parejas, es frecuente que se llamen **viejo** o **vieja** como muestra de la intimidad y cariño entre ellos. Compara esto con el inglés, en que *my old lady* y *the old man* no son términos tan cariñosos. **Viejo** y **vieja** también se usan entre amigos íntimos y, a veces, entre otros miembros de la familia.

▲ ¿Crees que usa términos de cariño esta pareja tejana (de Texas)?

[a]*heavy*   [b]*Careful!*   [c]*mi hija*   [d]*addressing*

SEGUNDA PARTE

Vocabulario

Talking About
Payments, Loans,
and Debts

Note: These vocabulary items can be heard in this lesson's Textbook Audio section of the Online Learning Center Website.

Las deudas

More on Personal Finances

Alicia González tiene muchas **deudas** (*debts*).

Sacó **un préstamo** (*loan*) para poder pagar los estudios...

...y también para comprar un auto nuevo.

Ahora, va a comprar una casa y necesita pagar **una hipoteca** (*mortgage*).

Además de sus deudas, tiene otros gastos, como...

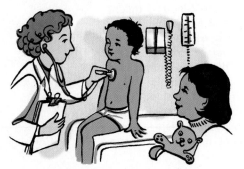

...**el seguro** (*insurance*) **médico** para ella y su familia

y **el seguro de automóvil** en caso de un accidente.

MÁS VOCABULARIO

amortizar (c) una deuda (una hipoteca)	to pay off a debt (a mortgage)
deber	to owe
pagar (gu) de una vez	to pay off all at once
pedir (i, i) prestado/a	to borrow
prestar	to lend
la comisión	commission
los intereses	interest
el seguro	insurance
antirrobo	antitheft
contra incendios	fire
de vida	life
de vivienda	homeowner's

Vistazo cultural, **Suggestion:** Ask students which system they would prefer. *¿Cuál de los dos sistemas prefieren Uds., un sistema de seguro como en Cuba o España o un sistema de seguro privado? ¿Pueden pensar en los beneficios de cada sistema?*

 # Vistazo cultural

El seguro médico

El seguro médico es uno de los gastos que les preocupa a muchos norteamericanos. El seguro médico en los Estados Unidos está en manos de compañías privadas y en la mayoría de los casos es bastante caro. Por eso sólo las personas con un empleo fijo o con suficiente dinero tienen acceso a una protección médica asegurada. Desafortunadamente, el resto de la población queda sin protección. Este no es el caso en algunos países hispanos, como Cuba y España, entre otros. En Cuba los gastos médicos de todos los ciudadanos[a] corren a cargo del estado.[b] Es decir que todos tienen acceso al seguro médico y no tienen que pagar nada cuando consultan con un médico o van a un hospital. En España, un porcentaje del sueldo de los españoles va directamente a la Seguridad Social (un organismo oficial del estado) que se dedica a cubrir[c] los gastos médicos de los ciudadanos. En muchos otros países hispanos, existen los dos tipos de seguros: seguro público y privado. Por ejemplo, en la Argentina, los ciudadanos que tienen empleo fijo o suficiente dinero pueden acceder a una buena protección médica en clínicas y hospitales privados. Los que no pueden tener acceso a ese tipo de seguro automáticamente tienen un seguro público que les ofrece protección, aunque no es necesariamente muy buena. En todo el mundo el seguro médico es un tema fundamental de la sociedad. La diferencia se encuentra en la forma de solucionar el problema. Mientras que en algunos países hispanos el estado parece tener un papel[d] más activo en la solución del problema, en los Estados Unidos es la responsabilidad del ciudadano solucionar sus propios problemas médicos.

[a]*citizens*   [b]*corren... are covered by the state*   [c]*covering*   [d]*role*

Actividad A Definiciones

Empareja cada palabra o frase con la definición apropiada.

1. _b_ los intereses
2. _d_ una deuda
3. _e_ el seguro
4. _a_ un préstamo
5. _c_ una hipoteca
6. _f_ la comisión

a. lo que uno saca para poder comprar un coche

b. los pagos que hay que hacer si uno no puede pagar la cuenta de una vez

c. lo que se necesita para comprar una casa

d. obligación que uno tiene de pagarle algo a alguien

e. contrato para proteger una casa, un coche, etcétera

f. lo que recibe el agente de bienes raíces (*real estate agent*) por vender una casa

Actividad B ¿Tienes seguro?

Paso 1 Escoge la opción más apropiada, según tu caso, para cada tipo de seguro.

	LO TENGO.	NO LO TENGO, PERO DEBO TENERLO.	NO LO TENGO Y NO LO NECESITO AHORA.
1. seguro de automóvil	☐	☐	☐
2. seguro de vida	☐	☐	☐
3. seguro de vivienda	☐	☐	☐
4. seguro antirrobo	☐	☐	☐
5. seguro contra incendios	☐	☐	☐
6. seguro médico	☐	☐	☐

Paso 2 Si no tienes algunos de los seguros mencionados en el **Paso 1,** explica por qué.

MODELO: No tengo seguro de vida porque no tengo esposo/a ni hijos.

Paso 3 En tu opinión, ¿cuál de los seguros es más importante para ti tener ahora? ¿Por qué?

Paso 4 Compara tus respuestas de los **Pasos 1** a **3** con las de tres compañeros. ¿Coinciden algunas de sus respuestas con las tuyas? ¿Están todos de acuerdo en cuanto a cuál es el seguro más importante?

Actividad C Las deudas que tenemos

Paso 1 Llena la tabla a continuación con información sobre las deudas que tienes ahora. Si no tienes ninguna deuda ahora, pon la información sobre las deudas que esperas (*you expect*) tener dentro de cinco años.

	DEUDA	AÑO EN QUE EMPEZÓ	LA ESTOY AMORTIZANDO AHORA.	LA PIENSO AMORTIZAR EN...
MODELO:	los estudios	dos mil ocho (2008)	no	dos mil dieciocho (2018)
1.				
2.				
3.				

Paso 2 Haz una encuesta entre otros estudiantes para averiguar cuáles son las deudas que tienen. ¿Cuál es la deuda más común entre todos? ¿Cuáles son las deudas que esperan tener en el futuro?

Actividad D Cómo salir de las deudas

Paso 1 Mucha gente tiene tantas deudas que no saben cómo van a amortizarlas todas. En grupos de tres o cuatro estudiantes, hagan una lista de siete sugerencias para ayudar a un amigo (una amiga) a limitar sus gastos y mejorar su crédito.

MODELO: No comas tanto en restaurantes.

Paso 2 Ahora pongan las sugerencias en orden de importancia. (1 = más importante)

Paso 3 Cada grupo va a presentar su lista a la clase. ¿Estás de acuerdo con las sugerencias de los otros grupos? ¿Qué grupo tiene el mejor plan para salir de deudas?

Gramática

¿Qué harías?   **Introduction to the Conditional**

You have already seen the expression **me gustaría** used to talk about what you *would* like (lit.: what *would please* you). Unlike English, which forms the conditional using *would* plus a main verb, Spanish marks the conditional by adding a set of endings to the infinitive. As the chart indicates, **-ar, -er,** and **-ir** verbs all have the same conditional endings, a form of **-ía-.** Some verbs have irregular stems but all use the regular endings.

Conditional verb forms allow you to express what you *would* do, given a particular situation or circumstance.

No sé qué **haría** en tu situación.	*I don't know what I would do in your situation.*
Sería buena idea mantener un presupuesto.	*It would be a good idea to maintain a budget.*
Te dije que te **ayudaría.**	*I told you that I would help you.*

CONDITIONAL FORMS (REGULAR VERBS)					
hablar		**comer**		**vivir**	
hablar**ía**	hablar**íamos**	comer**ía**	comer**íamos**	vivir**ía**	vivir**íamos**
hablar**ías**	hablar**íais**	comer**ías**	comer**íais**	vivir**ías**	vivir**íais**
hablar**ía**	hablar**ían**	comer**ía**	comer**ían**	vivir**ía**	vivir**ían**
hablar**ía**	hablar**ían**	comer**ía**	comer**ían**	vivir**ía**	vivir**ían**
IRREGULAR CONDITIONAL FORMS					

decir: **dir-**
haber:* **habr-**
hacer: **har-**
poder: **podr-**
poner: **pondr-**   +   -ía   -íamos
querer: **querr-**   -ías   -íais
saber: **sabr-**   -ía   -ían
salir: **saldr-**   -ía   -ían
tener: **tendr-**
venir: **vendr-**

---

*Note that since the verb **hay** is a form of **haber,** the conditional of **hay** is **habría.**

Remember that when *would* implies something that you *used to do* in the past as a habitual action, the imperfect is used, not the conditional.

Siempre **comíamos** en restaurantes mexicanos.
We always would (used to) eat in Mexican restaurants.

De *Sol y viento*, Note: You can access this film clip from a special menu section on Disc 5 of the Instructional Version on DVD.

Follow-up: Ask students if they think selling the winery would be the only option. *¿Están Uds. de acuerdo con Carlos? ¿Sería mejor vender «Sol y viento»? ¿Qué más podrían hacer?*

DE SOL Y VIENTO

In **Episodio 8** of *Sol y viento,* you will watch a scene in which doña Isabel confronts her son Carlos about how he's been managing the winery. Part of their conversation follows.

ISABEL
Quizá eso te lo hubiera podido perdonar.[a]
Pero, ¿engañarnos a nosotras? ¿Engañar a los vecinos, a la comunidad del valle? Nos has puesto en una posición muy difícil, Carlos.

CARLOS
¡Tuve que hacerlo, mamá! ¡Las inversiones[b] estaban a mi nombre! ¡No tenía nada! ¡Sólo la venta de la viña _____ las deudas!

Which verb in the conditional do you think best fits in the blank?

1. cobraría
2. debería
(3.) pagaría

[a]Quizá... *I might have been able to forgive you for that.* [b]*investments*

Actividad E

INPUT
Actividad E

Actividad E ¿Quién lo dijo?

Indica el personaje de la lista que se relaciona con cada afirmación a continuación.

1. ___Carlos___ dijo que conseguiría las firmas de doña Isabel, María y los vecinos.
2. ___María/doña Isabel___ dijo que jamás aprobaría la venta de «Sol y viento».
3. ___Don Paco___ dijo que iría a Chile para ayudar a doña Isabel.
4. ___María___ dijo que averiguaría (*he/she would find out*) lo que Carlos había hecho.
5. ___Jaime___ dijo que haría todo lo posible para conseguir el perdón de María.

INPUT
Act. F, Suggestion: Tell students to think about close friends, acquaintances, family, and instructors. Do their answers change depending on who they might lend their belongings to? **Follow-up:** Have 1 or 2 students provide responses from *Paso 1* in which they would lend something to one particular person but not to another. Does everyone agree? Can people offer reasons why?

Actividad F ¿Qué cosas prestarías?

Paso 1 Indica si prestarías las siguientes cosas y a quiénes se las prestarías.

¿Le prestarías a alguien...
1. tu coche?
2. cinco dólares?
3. cien dólares?
4. el libro de español?
5. tu camiseta favorita?
6. tus apuntes de una clase?
7. tu computadora?

Paso 2 Ahora indica si pedirías prestadas las siguientes cosas y a quiénes.

¿Le pedirías prestado a alguien...
1. su coche?
2. cinco dólares?
3. cien dólares?
4. el libro de español?
5. su camiseta favorita?
6. sus apuntes de una clase?
7. su computadora?

Paso 3 Compara tus respuestas del **Paso 1** y del **Paso 2**. ¿Eres una persona que se siente más cómoda (*comfortable*) prestando o pidiendo prestado? ¿Por qué?

Actividad G ¿Eres arriesgado/a (*daring*)?

Paso 1 A continuación hay una lista de preguntas para determinar si alguien es arriesgado/a o aventurero/a. Primero, lee las primeras seis preguntas. Luego, escribe dos preguntas más, utilizando el condicional.

	NO, NO LO HARÍA.	SÍ, LO HARÍA.	DEPENDE DE LA SITUACIÓN.
1. ¿Viajarías solo/a a otro país?	☐	☐	☐
2. ¿Comerías carne de serpiente (*snake*)?	☐	☐	☐
3. ¿Invertirías (*Would you invest*) tu dinero en una empresa desconocida?	☐	☐	☐
4. ¿Vivirías en un lugar muy lejos de tu familia?	☐	☐	☐
5. ¿Te casarías con alguien de otra religión, cultura o idioma?	☐	☐	☐
6. ¿Irías a una playa nudista?	☐	☐	☐
7. ¿Saldrías con alguien que conociste en el Internet?	☐	☐	☐
8. ¿ ?	☐	☐	☐

Paso 2 Ahora entrevista a un compañero (una compañera) utilizando las preguntas del **Paso 1.** Incluye las dos preguntas que escribiste. Apunta sus respuestas.

Paso 3 Indica si tu compañero/a es arriesgado/a o no. Prepara dos oraciones que justifiquen tu opinión, pero no las compartas (*share*) con tu compañero/a.

MODELO: _____(Nombre)_____ es bastante arriesgado/a porque comería carne de serpiente.

Paso 4 Comparte tus oraciones con la clase. ¿Está tu compañero/a de acuerdo con tu evaluación?

Actividad H ¿Qué harías?

Paso 1 Escribe cinco oraciones que describan, en orden de importancia para ti, lo que harías con un millón de dólares. Puedes usar los verbos de la lista, si quieres.

ahorrar	dar	regalar
comprar	invertir	viajar

Paso 2 Compara lo que tú harías con lo que harían tres compañeros. Apunta lo que te dicen.

Paso 3 Tomando en cuenta lo que tus compañeros indicaron en el **Paso 2,** ¿hay algún adjetivo (algunos adjetivos) que describa(n) mejor a tu grupo?

altruista	generoso	pragmático
derrochador	materialista	responsable

Note: These vocabulary items can be heard in this lesson's Textbook Audio section of the Online Learning Center Website.

Vocabulario

Talking About the Economy | **La economía**   **Local and World Markets** ✳

 ¿Cómo va la economía? Como muchas otras cosas, la economía también pasa por ciclos...

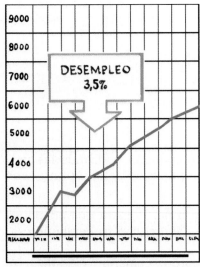

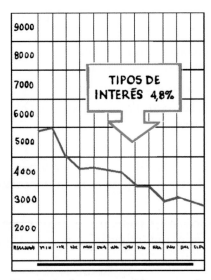

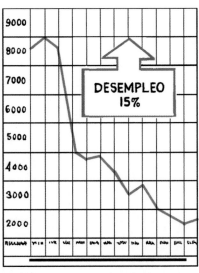

Hay épocas de **prosperidad** en las que hay **una alza** (*rise*) en **la Bolsa de valores** (*stock market*) durante varios meses, y hay una baja **tasa de desempleo** (*unemployment rate*).

También hay **recesión** cuando **los tipos de interés** (*interest rates*) son muy bajos y la Bolsa de valores va **bajando.**

También hay **depresión, una baja** drástica en la Bolsa de valores y, a la vez, **una subida** drástica de la tasa de desempleo.

✳ MÁS VOCABULARIO

invertir (ie, i)	to invest	**los países en vías de desarrollo**	developing countries
subir	to go up	**la pobreza**	poverty
las acciones	stocks	**la recuperación**	recovery
los bienes fabricados	manufactured goods	**la riqueza**	wealth
los bienes raíces	real estate		
la informática	information technology	**Cognados: exportar, importar; los automóviles, la**	
las inversiones	investments	**electrónica, la inflación, los metales preciosos, los**	
el mundo de los espectáculos	entertainment industry	**productos farmacéuticos, los textiles**	
los países desarrollados	developed countries		

La economía de todos los países depende mucho de la venta a buen precio de los productos de exportación.

Los productos agrícolas y comestibles

el azúcar

el cacao

el café

el tabaco

Los recursos naturales

el acero

la energía

la madera

el petróleo

Vistazo cultural, **Suggestion**: Ask students the following questions based on the information in the table provided: *¿Qué país tiene el PNB más alto?* (*España*) *¿Qué países tienen el PNB más bajo?* (*Bolivia y Honduras*) You may also wish to find out (or have students find out) the most recent GNP for this country as a comparison.

 # Vistazo cultural

El producto nacional bruto[a]

Uno de los indicadores de la riqueza de un país es el producto nacional bruto (PNB),[b] es decir, la riqueza o los ingresos que genera cada habitante de un país. A continuación se puede ver el PNB por habitante (en dólares estadounidenses) de algunos países hispanohablantes.

la Argentina	$15.200	España	$27.400
Bolivia	$3.100	Guatemala	$5.000
Chile	$12.700	Honduras	$3.100
Colombia	$8.600	México	$10.700
Costa Rica	$12.500	el Paraguay	$4.800
Cuba	$4.000	el Perú	$6.600
el Ecuador	$4.500	el Uruguay	$10.900
El Salvador	$4.900	Venezuela	$7.200

▲ El PNB de algunos países hispanohablantes (2006)

[a]producto... *Gross National Product* [b]*GNP*

Actividad A Las acciones

Empareja la categoría de acciones con una compañía correspondiente.

1. <u>d</u> los textiles
2. <u>f</u> el mundo de los espectáculos
3. <u>e</u> los automóviles
4. <u>b</u> la informática
5. <u>g</u> los productos farmacéuticos
6. <u>a</u> la electrónica
7. <u>c</u> los metales preciosos

a. Sony
b. Microsoft
c. Tiffany
d. Gap
e. Volkswagen
f. Time-Warner
g. GlaxoSmithKline

Actividad B ¿Qué exportan?

Paso 1 Según el mapa, ¿qué países exportan los siguientes productos?

1. café Costa Rica, Guatemala, Colombia, la República Dominicana, Honduras
2. pescado el Perú, Chile, el Ecuador, Cuba
3. petróleo México, Venezuela, el Perú
4. tabaco Cuba
5. azúcar Cuba, la República Dominicana, Guatemala
6. automóviles la Argentina
7. bananas Costa Rica, Colombia, el Ecuador, Honduras
8. cacao el Ecuador, Colombia

Paso 2 Mira otra vez el **Vistazo cultural** de la página 457. ¿Ves alguna relación entre los países que tienen un alto o bajo PNB y los productos que exportan?

Los países que exportan <u>automóviles, petróleo</u> por lo general tienen un PNB más alto que los países que exportan <u>café, azúcar, bananas</u>.

Actividad C ¿Desarrollado o en vías de desarrollo?

Usando los sustantivos y adjetivos a continuación, escribe seis oraciones sobre las condiciones económicas, políticas y sociales que se refieren, en términos generales, a los países desarrollados y a los países en vías de desarrollo. Luego, presenta tus oraciones a la clase.

Sustantivos	**Adjetivos**
el PNB	(in)estable
la economía	alto/a
la inflación	(in)controlable
la (in)seguridad	distribuido/a entre muchas/pocas
las tasas de desempleo	personas
la riqueza	político/a

MODELO: En general, los países en vías de desarrollo tienen una economía inestable.

Actividad D ¿Cómo va la economía?

Paso 1 Indica si, en tu opinión, estas condiciones económicas caracterizan la economía en una época de prosperidad, de recesión o de depresión.

	PROSPERIDAD	RECESIÓN	DEPRESIÓN
1. bajos tipos de interés	☐	☑	☐
2. una baja drástica de precios	☐	☐	☑
3. baja tasa de desempleo	☑	☐	☐
4. sigue el alza de la Bolsa de valores	☑	☐	☐
5. una baja moderada del PNB	☐	☑	☐
6. una subida drástica de la tasa de desempleo	☐	☐	☑
7. la Bolsa de valores sigue bajando	☐	☑	☐
8. una subida de confianza (*confidence*) de los consumidores	☑	☐	☐
9. una expansión rápida de la economía	☑	☐	☐

Paso 2 En grupos de tres estudiantes, contesten las siguientes preguntas.

1. ¿Cómo caracterizarían Uds. la economía de este país hoy en día? ¿Estamos en una época de prosperidad, de recesión o de depresión?
2. ¿Cuánto tiempo hace que estamos en esta situación?

NAVEGANDO LA RED ～～～～～～～

Busca información sobre la economía actual (*current*) de algún país hispanohablante. ¿Va subiendo o bajando la Bolsa de valores? ¿Cuál es la tasa de desempleo? Según la información que obtengas (*that you obtain*), ¿está el país en una época de prosperidad, de recesión o de depresión?

Gramática

Expressing
Hypothetical Events

Si tuviera más dinero...

Hypothetical Statements; Introduction to the Imperfect Subjunctive

In both English and Spanish, clauses with the words *if/***si** are used to speculate about possible situations. These situations or conditions can be real or they can be hypothetical. For example, the English sentence *If I have money, I spend it right away* represents a real condition. The speaker does *x* under the condition *y*. But in the sentence *If I had money, I would spend it right away*, the speaker implies that he or she has no money, and the statement therefore represents an *unreal* or *hypothetical* situation. Notice that English uses different verb forms to convey an unreal situation: present tense (real) versus past tense (unreal). Spanish also uses different verb forms in hypothetical *if* or **si** clauses, but they're different than those used in English.

In Spanish, if the **si** clause represents a real situation, the verb in the **si** clause is in the present tense and the verb in the main clause can either be in the present or the future. For an unreal or hypothetical condition, the verb in the **si** clause is in the *imperfect subjunctive,* and the verb in the main clause is in the conditional. The imperfect subjunctive is formed by taking the third-person plural of the preterite, minus the **-on** ending, and adding the endings **-a, -as, -a, -amos, -ais, -an,** as indicated in the chart on the next page.

Si **tuviéramos** tiempo,...	...lo **podríamos** hacer.
If we had time (but we don't), . . .	*. . . we could do it.*
Si me **sintiera** mejor,...	...**haría** ejercicio.
If I felt better (but I don't), . . .	*. . . I would exercise.*

■ Note that stem-changing **-ir** verbs in the preterite also have the same vowel change in all forms of the imperfect subjunctive:

   dormir: d**u**rmiera, d**u**rmieras, d**u**rmiera, d**u**rmiéramos, d**u**rmierais, d**u**rmieran

   pedir: p**i**diera, p**i**dieras, p**i**diera, p**i**diéramos, p**i**dierais, p**i**dieran

■ Verbs that undergo a change from **i** → **y** in the third-person preterite also keep the **y** in all forms of the imperfect subjunctive:

   creer: cre**y**era, cre**y**eras, cre**y**era, cre**y**éramos, cre**y**erais, cre**y**eran

   oír: o**y**era, o**y**eras, o**y**era, o**y**éramos, o**y**erais, o**y**eran

FORMING THE IMPERFECT SUBJUNCTIVE					
hablar → hablar~~on~~		comer → comier~~on~~		vivir → vivier~~on~~	
hablar**a**	hablár**amos**	comier**a**	comiér**amos**	vivier**a**	viviér**amos**
hablar**as**	hablar**ais**	comier**as**	comier**ais**	vivier**as**	vivier**ais**
hablar**a**	hablar**an**	comier**a**	comier**an**	vivier**a**	vivier**an**
hablar**a**	hablar**an**	comier**a**	comier**an**	vivier**a**	vivier**an**

IRREGULAR VERBS IN BOTH THE PRETERITE AND IMPERFECT SUBJUNCTIVE					
VERB	THIRD-PERSON PLURAL PRETERITE	IMPERFECT SUBJUNCTIVE	VERB	THIRD-PERSON PLURAL PRETERITE	IMPERFECT SUBJUNCTIVE
decir:	dijer~~on~~	**dijera**	poner:	pusier~~on~~	**pusiera**
estar:	estuvier~~on~~	**estuviera**	querer:	quisier~~on~~	**quisiera**
haber:	hubier~~on~~	**hubiera**	saber:	supier~~on~~	**supiera**
hacer:	hicier~~on~~	**hiciera**	ser:	fuer~~on~~	**fuera**
ir:	fuer~~on~~	**fuera**	tener:	tuvier~~on~~	**tuviera**
poder:	pudier~~on~~	**pudiera**	venir:	vinier~~on~~	**viniera**

EXAMPLES OF HYPOTHETICAL STATEMENTS	
Si **pudiera,** Manolo **se mudaría** a Chicago.	*If he could, Manolo would move to Chicago.*
Si **hiciéramos** eso, **ahorraríamos** mucho dinero.	*If we did that, we'd save a lot of money.*

De *Sol y viento,* **Note:** You can access this film clip from a special menu section on Disc 5 of the Instructional Version on DVD.
Follow-up: Ask students what they would do if they were Diego. (To a student) *¿Dejarías tus estudios si tu familia te necesitara en su negocio familiar? ¿Bajo qué circunstancias dejarías la universidad?*

 DE SOL Y VIENTO

In **Episodio 4** of *Sol y viento,* you watched a conversation between María and Diego about Diego's future. Part of their conversation follows.

MARÍA
Diego, sólo tú puedes escoger tu futuro. Pero te digo que _____¹ una penaª si _____² tus estudios. Tienes mucho talento.

DIEGO
Gracias, profesora. Es que... bueno... mi familia. Mi papá sobre todo. Quiere que trabaje con él, en los negocios de la familia.

Which verb forms do you think belong in the blanks?

1. a. es   **b.** fuera   (**c.**) sería

2. (**a.**) dejaras   **b.** dejas   **c.** dejarías

ªshame

Actividad E ¿Qué escuchaste?

Paso 1 Escucha el párrafo que lee tu profesor(a) a la clase. Vas a escuchar el párrafo dos veces. Trata de recordar la información, pero no tomes apuntes.

Paso 2 En grupos de tres, escriban una versión del párrafo para luego compartir con la clase.

Actividad F ¿Cómo reaccionarías? INPUT/OUTPUT
Actividad F

Paso 1 Indica cómo reaccionarías en cada situación.

1. Si un mendigo (*beggar*) me pidiera dinero en la calle, yo...
   a. seguiría caminando.
   b. le daría un poco de dinero.
   c. le diría que no tengo nada.
2. Si supiera que la novia de un amigo había ligado con (*had gotten together with*) otro hombre, yo...
   a. no haría nada.
   b. hablaría con ella.
   c. hablaría con mi amigo.
3. Si me quedara atrapado/a en un ascensor (*elevator*), yo...
   a. estaría tranquilo/a porque lo arreglarían pronto.
   b. me pondría a pensar en (*about*) cómo salir de allí.
   c. me pondría muy nervioso/a.
4. Si recibiera un regalo de alguien que no me gustara, yo...
   a. se lo devolvería.
   b. le daría las gracias y me quedaría con el regalo.
   c. no le daría las gracias, pero me quedaría con el regalo.
5. Si supiera que mi novio/a salió con otra persona, yo...
   a. rompería inmediatamente con él/ella.
   b. saldría con otra persona también.
   c. lo/la perdonaría si se arrepintiera de sus acciones.

Paso 2 Comparte tus respuestas con otras tres personas. ¿En qué situaciones reaccionarían Uds. de la misma manera?

Actividad G   Una encuesta

Paso 1   Contesta las siguientes preguntas. Inventa una situación hipotética para el número siete y luego contéstala.

1. Si tuvieras la oportunidad de viajar a un país hispanohablante, ¿adónde irías?
2. Si no asistieras a esta universidad, ¿qué harías?
3. Si pudieras conocer a cualquier persona, viva o muerta, ¿a quién te gustaría conocer?
4. Si compraras un auto nuevo, ¿qué modelo comprarías?
5. Si pudieras estar en otro lugar ahora mismo (*right now*), ¿dónde estarías?
6. Si cambiaras de especialización, ¿qué especialización escogerías?
7. Si _____, ¿_____?

Paso 2   Ahora, hazles las mismas preguntas a tres compañeros y apunta sus respuestas.

Paso 3   ¿Tienen Uds. algunas respuestas en común? Compártanlas con la clase.

Actividad H   ¿Bajo qué circunstancias?

Indica bajo qué circunstancias harías las siguientes cosas, utilizando el imperfecto de subjuntivo.

1. Estudiaría en otra universidad si...
2. Viviría en otro país si...
3. Me divorciaría si...
4. Compraría un coche nuevo si...
5. Me sentiría muy feliz si...
6. Estaría muy avergonzado/a si...
7. Le ocultaría un secreto a un amigo si...
8. Dejaría de hablarle a alguien si...
9. Me casaría si...
10. Tendría celos de mi mejor amigo/a si...

Actividad I   ¿Y su profesor(a)?

Paso 1   Con un compañero (una compañera), escriban respuestas que crees que daría su profesor(a) a cinco de las situaciones de la **Actividad G.**

MODELO: Si nuestra profesora tuviera la oportunidad de viajar a un país hispanohablante, iría a Cuba.

Paso 2   Lean sus oraciones a la clase. ¿Qué piensa su profesor(a)? ¿Está de acuerdo con lo que Uds. dicen?

SOL Y VIENTO

A primera vista

Antes de ver el episodio

Actividad A ¿Qué recuerdas?

A continuación hay unas paráfrasis (*paraphrases*) de lo que han dicho ciertos personajes en el episodio previo. De los personajes a continuación, ¿puedes indicar quién lo dijo y a quién se lo dijo?

1. «¡El sol está picando fuerte!» ___Mario___ se lo dijo a ___Jaime___.
2. «Ya le dije que esta tierra no se vende.» ___Doña___ se lo dijo a ___Jaime___.
3. «¿Comprende el daño de una represa en la zona?» ___Don Paco___ se lo dijo a ___Jaime___.
4. «Quizás no me merezca que me perdone.» ___Jaime___ se lo dijo a ___doña Isabel___.
5. «Si pasan cinco días más, no va el negocio.» ___Jaime___ se lo dijo a ___don Paco y a doña Isabel___.

Actividad B ¿Qué falta?

Act. B, Suggestion: Don't reveal answer to students, as they will verify their choices later.

En este episodio, doña Isabel se enfrenta con (*confronts*) Carlos. Lee el diálogo.

ISABEL: ¡Aquí hay más deudas que en todo el tiempo de la administración de tu papá! ¿Qué has hecho con el dinero de «Sol y viento»?

CARLOS: Mamá, estos son tiempos diferentes. El negocio es mucho más difícil.

ISABEL: ¿Me crees tonta? ¿Qué hiciste con el dinero de «Sol y viento»?

CARLOS: _____

¿Qué crees que dice Carlos en el espacio en blanco?

a. Invertí las ganancias (*earnings*) de la viña en varias compañías de tecnología.

b. Me enteré (*I found out*) de que papá había muerto sin pagar muchas de sus deudas y las tuve que pagar yo.

Actividad C El episodio

Ahora mira el episodio. Si hay algo que no entiendes bien, puedes volver a ver la escena en cuestión.

Después de ver el episodio

Actividad A ¿Qué recuerdas?

Contesta las siguientes preguntas sobre el **Episodio 8.**

1. Por fin Carlos le convence a María de que firme los papeles para vender «Sol y viento».

    a. cierto   **(b.)** falso

2. ¿Cuál fue la especialización de Jaime?

    a. economía   **b.** ecología   **(c.)** administración de empresas

3. ¿Quién invita a Jaime a la recepción de «Sol y viento»?

    (a.) Paco   **b.** Isabel

4. ¿Qué hizo Carlos con el dinero de «Sol y viento»?

    a. Lo depositó en una cuenta de ahorros en el extranjero.

    b. Lo usó para pagar las deudas de su padre.

    (c.) Lo invirtió en compañías de tecnología.

Actividad B ¿Lo captaste?

Verifica tu respuesta de la **Actividad B** en **Antes de ver el episodio.** Si es necesario, puedes ver el episodio de nuevo.

Actividad C Utilizando el contexto

¿Pudiste deducir el significado de las palabras y expresiones que aparecen en letra cursiva a continuación?

> YOLANDA: ¿Así vas a estar vestida para la recepción?
> MARÍA: No. Me voy a poner un vestido más tarde porque...
> YOLANDA: *¡Deja!* Yo me encargo de las flores. *Mejor anda a cambiarte* ahora mismo. ¡Ya van a llegar los invitados!

Actividad D En resumen

Completa la siguiente narración con las palabras y expresiones apropiadas de la lista a la derecha.

En este episodio, María __descubrió__[1] que Carlos __engañaba__[2] al resto de la familia y a los vecinos. María __le pidió__[3] explicaciones a su hermano, pero Carlos __respondió__[4] que sólo él __tenía__[5] el derecho de manejar los negocios de la viña. Luego, María __se lo contó todo__[6] a su madre. Entonces doña Isabel __le preguntó__[7] a su hijo qué __había hecho__[8] con el dinero de la viña. Parece que Carlos __lo había perdido__[9] en malas inversiones. A causa de este engaño, Isabel __le dio__[10] a su hijo dos opciones.

descubrió
engañaba
había hecho
le dio
le pidió
le preguntó
lo había perdido
respondió
se lo contó todo
tenía

Act. C, Suggestion: Ask students the meaning of italicized phrases. Students know the meaning of *dejar* as in *dejar una propina,* so they may deduce that it means something similar to "Leave it!" as in "Leave it (them) alone!" Based on context, its meaning could also be "Give me that!" since Yolanda takes the flowers from María as she says it. The second phrase should be more accessible to students. Its meaning is "You'd better go change."

Detrás de la cámara

You may recall that Carlos said his sister is not interested in helping to run the winery and that she has other interests. You may have also noticed Carlos' resentment when he says this. Although his pride would keep him from admitting it, Carlos has always been jealous of his younger sister. María is smart and independent, and she has enjoyed much success in her career apart from the family business. Carlos, on the other hand, continuously tries to prove himself and is filled with envy and self-doubt because of his sister's success. As a result, his insecurity has led him to make some unwise decisions in the family business as well as in his personal life.

RESUMEN DE VOCABULARIO

En el banco

ahorrar	to save
cobrar	to charge (*a fee*)
ganar	to earn
manejar (bien/mal)	to manage (well/poorly)
pagar (gu) a plazos	to pay in installments
sacar (qu) dinero	to withdraw money

los ahorros	savings
el/la cajero/a	teller
el cheque de viajero	traveler's check
la cuenta corriente	checking account
la cuenta de ahorros	savings account

Cognados: depositar; el cheque
Repaso: cargar (gu), gastar; el cajero automático, la cuenta, el efectivo, la tarjeta de crédito

Las finanzas personales

amortizar (c) una deuda (una hipoteca)	to pay off a debt (a mortgage)
deber	to owe
pagar (gu) de una vez	to pay off all at once
pedir (i, i) prestado/a	to borrow
prestar	to lend

la deuda	debt
los gastos	expenses
la hipoteca	mortgage
los ingresos	income
el préstamo	loan
el presupuesto (mensual)	(monthly) budget
el recibo	receipt
el seguro	insurance
antirrobo	antitheft
contra incendios	fire
de automóvil	car
de vida	life
de vivienda	homeowner's
médico	medical
el sueldo	salary

derrochador(a)	wasteful
irresponsable	irresponsible
responsable	responsible

Cognados: la comisión, los intereses

La economía

bajar	to go down
invertir (ie, i)	to invest
subir	to go up

las acciones	stocks
la alza	rise (*stock market*)
la baja	fall
los bienes fabricados	manufactured goods
los bienes raíces	real estate
la Bolsa de valores	stock market
la informática	information technology
las inversiones	investments
el mundo de los espectáculos	entertainment industry
los países desarrollados	developed countries
los países en vías de desarrollo	developing countries
la pobreza	poverty
la recuperación	recovery
la riqueza	wealth
la subida	rise
la tasa de desempleo	unemployment rate
los tipos de interés	interest rates

Cognados: exportar; la inflación, la prosperidad, la recesión
Repaso: importar; la depresión

Los productos de exportación

el acero	steel
el azúcar	sugar
el cacao	cocoa
el comestible	food item
la madera	wood
el producto agrícola	agricultural product

Cognados: el automóvil, la electrónica, la energía, los metales preciosos, los productos farmacéuticos, el tabaco, los textiles
Repaso: la banana, el café, el pescado, el petróleo, los recursos naturales

Los medios de comunicación[a]

OBJETIVOS

IN THIS LESSON, YOU WILL LEARN:

- to talk about the media, keeping up with current events, and types of TV programs

- more on **por** and **para** and a summary of their uses

- to talk about how the media presents information and how we react to it

- to use the subjunctive to express doubt and disbelief

- to talk about societal concerns

- to use the subjunctive to talk about what you want to happen

In addition, you will watch **Episodio 8** of the film *Sol y viento* again.

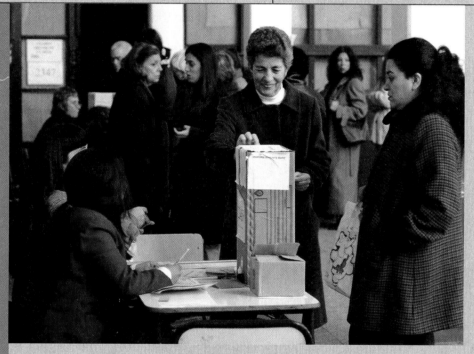

El derecho (*right*) al voto es una necesidad en toda sociedad libre. ¿Con cuánta frecuencia votas tú? (Mendoza, la Argentina)

[a]Los... *Media*

The following media resources are available for this lesson of *Sol y viento*:

Episodio 8 of *Sol y viento*

Online *Manual de actividades*

Online Learning Center Website

Note: These vocabulary items can be heard in this lesson's Textbook Audio section of the Online Learning Center Website.

Talking About Current Events

Vocabulario

¿Cómo te informas?

Getting Information

La prensa y las noticias

el periódico   el titular   el noticiero   el accidente

la presentadora

EL DIARIO
El presidente propone su plan de paz

La bolsa sufre otra caída

Manifestaciones contra la guerra

El pronóstico del tiempo **29°**

el pronóstico del tiempo   el artículo

la noticia   noticias 24   la cadena

el reportero   la testigo

✳ MÁS VOCABULARIO

estar (*irreg.*) **al corriente**	to be caught up (*with current events*)
informarse	to be informed; to inform oneself
el **acontecimiento**	happening, event
la **noticia**	piece of news
las **noticias (internacionales, locales, nacionales)**	(international, local, national) news
la **prensa**	press
el **reportaje**	report
la **revista**	magazine

A ver

Documental
23.00 (A&E Mundo). Moulin Rouge. Una cámara se interna tras bambalinas en el célebre club parisino, para mostrar que no todo es glamour y felicidad en vísperas de una premiere.

Biografía
21.00 (Film & Arts). Perfiles: Michael Douglas. Un resumen de la vida y carrera de este famoso actor de Hollywood. Con entrevistas a su padre Kirk Douglas y Oliver Stone.

Reportaje
22.00 (National Geographic). Tabú: curanderos. Conozca las técnicas de un chamán boliviano, un sanador indígena norteamericano y una hechicera etíope para curar enfermedades.

Misceláneo
13.00 (HBO). We stand alone together: The men of Easy Company. Conozca a los sobrevivientes de la Easy Company en que se inspiró la miniserie "The band of brothers".

Estreno
23.00 (MTV). Soda Stereo: La leyenda. Un novedoso documental que hace un recorrido por los 15 años de carrera de la banda pop más reconocida de latinoamérica. Con entrevistas exclusivas, fotos e imágenes de backstage. Artistas como Shakira, Marcelo Moura y Daniel Melero dan su testimonio sobre la importancia de Soda Stereo en el rock latino.

¿Qué hay de ver en la televisión?

el anuncio publicitario	commercial
la comedia	sitcom
el concurso	game show; contest
el documental	documentary
el drama	drama
el programa de entrevistas	talk show
el programa deportivo	sports program
el reality	reality show
la telenovela	soap opera

 # Vistazo cultural

La programación en español en los Estados Unidos

En 1961 se creó el primer canal en español en los Estados Unidos en San Antonio, Texas. Hoy, más de cuarenta años después, este canal local de San Antonio forma parte de la cadena *Univisión,* que ocupa el quinto[a] lugar entre las cadenas más vistas del país y la más vista por los hispanos en los Estados Unidos. Además de *Univisión* en los Estados Unidos hay otras cadenas en español, entre ellas *Telemundo, Galavisión* y *TeleFutura.* Desde el principio de los años noventa la audiencia de las cadenas en español en los Estados Unidos ha seguido creciendo un 14% cada año, más que cualquier otra cadena de televisión. Además, *Univisión* es la cadena más vista entre los habitantes de algunas ciudades norteamericanas como Los Ángeles, Miami y San Antonio. Aunque la programación de estas cadenas incluye programas de entrevistas, documentales, programas de música y telenovelas de México y Sudamérica, el noticiero de *Univisión* se ha destacado[b] por presentar noticias internacionales, sobre todo de Latinoamérica, que no se pueden recibir en otros noticieros norteamericanos. Según algunos críticos de la prensa norteamericana, las cadenas en español son las únicas cadenas de la televisión norteamericana en que realmente se puede recibir noticias internacionales. Es decir, los noticieros de las cadenas principales normalmente sólo presentan noticias relacionadas con los asuntos[c] norteamericanos. Si presentan algún acontecimiento que ocurre fuera del país, casi siempre está relacionado con algún interés político o económico de los Estados Unidos.

▲ Jorge Ramos y María Elena Salinas, presentadores del noticiero de Univisión

[a]*fifth* [b]*stood out* [c]*issues*

INPUT

Act. A, Suggestion:
Read the following
statements once.
1. *Lo que uno lee en un
periódico o una revista
sobre algún tema.*
2. *Indica si va a llover,
hacer sol o nevar.*
3. *Es una persona que
está presente cuando
ocurre algún
acontecimiento.*
4. *Es la persona que presenta las noticias en la
televisión.*
5. *Uno generalmente lee
esto primero para
determinar si un
artículo le interesa
o no.*

Actividad A   Definiciones

Tu profesor(a) va a leer descripciones de las palabras a continuación. Pon el número de la descripción al lado de la palabra que corresponde.

a. _2_ el pronóstico del tiempo
b. _4_ el presentador (la presentadora)
c. _1_ el artículo
d. _5_ el titular
e. _3_ el/la testigo

Actividad B   Asociaciones

INPUT
Actividad B

Empareja cada palabra con un ejemplo de la televisión.

1. _g_ el noticiero
2. _c_ la telenovela
3. _h_ el concurso
4. _b_ la cadena
5. _a_ el documental
6. _f_ el drama
7. _d_ el programa de entrevistas
8. _e_ el reality

a. *Biography on A&E*
b. *ABC, CBS, NBC, FOX*
c. *All My Children, Days of Our Lives*
d. *Oprah*
e. *Survivor*
f. *24, Lost*
g. *ABC World News Tonight*
h. *Deal or No Deal?*

INPUT/OUTPUT
Actividad C

Actividad C   ¿Estás al corriente?

Paso 1   Indica cuántas veces por semana te informas de lo que pasa en el mundo por los medios de comunicación mencionados a continuación.

	CADA DÍA	DE 3 A 5 VECES POR SEMANA	CASI NUNCA
1. Leo el periódico de la universidad.	☐	☐	☐
2. Leo un periódico nacional o local.	☐	☐	☐
3. Leo las noticias en el Internet.	☐	☐	☐
4. Leo una revista semanal (*weekly*).	☐	☐	☐
5. Miro el noticiero de una cadena principal (ABC, CBS, NBC, Univisión).	☐	☐	☐
6. Miro las noticias de una cadena de noticias (CNN, FOX News, MSNBC).	☐	☐	☐
7. Escucho la radio.	☐	☐	☐

Paso 2   Compara tus respuestas con las de tres compañeros de clase. Luego, prepara algunas oraciones para indicar a la clase las preferencias de tu grupo.

MODELO: En nuestro grupo nos informamos por el periódico de la universidad. Lo leemos casi todos los días. Casi nunca miramos el noticiero de una cadena principal.

Paso 3 Escucha las preferencias de los otros grupos. ¿Cuál es el medio de comunicación preferido por la clase para estar al corriente? ¿Refleja el estilo de vida de un estudiante universitario típico?

INPUT/OUTPUT
Actividad D

Actividad D ¿Qué miramos en la tele (*TV*)?

Paso 1 A continuación hay una tabla con varios tipos de programas televisivos. Llena la primera columna (**yo**) con el promedio (*average*) de horas que pasas por semana mirando ese tipo de programa.

TIPO DE PROGRAMA	YO	E1	E2	E3
1. las noticias				
2. las telenovelas				
3. los documentales				
4. los concursos				
5. los dramas				
6. los programas deportivos				
7. los programas de entrevistas				
8. los realities				
Total de horas				

Paso 2 De los tipos de programas que ves con mucha frecuencia, ¿cuál es el que nunca te pierdes (*miss*)?

MODELO: Veo muchos concursos. Nunca me pierdo *Jeopardy.*

Paso 3 Comparte tus respuestas con las de tres compañeros. Apunta sus respuestas en la tabla.

Paso 4 Ahora calcula el promedio de las horas de cada tipo de programa que ve tu grupo. Luego Uds. van a compartir esa información con toda la clase.

NAVEGANDO LA RED

Busca en la red un periódico de un país hispanohablante e imprime la página principal. ¿Cuál es el titular principal del periódico? En dos oraciones, indica de qué se trata el artículo. ¿Es una noticia sobre un evento político, económico, nacional o internacional? ¿Ya sabías algo de la noticia?

Gramática

Talking About How
You Do Something

Te llamó por teléfono.

Por and **para**: A Summary

Por una miradaᵃ

Por una mirada, un mundo;
por una sonrisa,ᵇ un cielo;ᶜ
por un beso... yo no sé
qué te diera por un beso.

—Gustavo Adolfo Bécquer, español (1836–1870)

ᵃ*glance* ᵇ*smile* ᶜ*heaven*

¿Cuál es el uso de **por** que se exhibe en este poema?

You have already learned a number of uses of the prepositions **por** and **para**. The charts summarize their most common uses.

USES OF *por*	
USE	EXAMPLES
• indicar movimiento por el espacio o tiempo (*along, through, during, in*)	Vamos a caminar **por** la playa. *Let's walk along the beach.* Jaime corrió **por** el Parque Forestal. *Jaime ran through Forestal Park.* Estuvo enfermo **por** toda su vida. *He was sick during his whole life.* Tengo dos clases **por** la mañana. *I have two classes in the morning.*
• expresar un medio (*by, by means of*)	Mándame el documento **por** fax. *Send me the document by fax.* Podemos hablar **por** teléfono más tarde. *We can talk by (on the) phone later.*
• expresar una causa (*because of, due to, on behalf of*)	No podemos ir **por** el mal tiempo. *We can't go due to bad weather.* Perdimos el partido **por** él. *We lost the game because of him.* Lo hago **por** mi familia. *I do it for (on behalf of) my family*
• indicar un cambio, sustitución (*in exchange for*)	¿Cuánto te debo **por** el libro? *How much do I owe you for the book?* Gracias **por** ayudarme. *Thanks for helping me.*
• otros usos (*in favor of, for the sake of*)	Votan **por** el candidato independiente. *They're voting for the independent candidate.*

USES OF *para*	
USE	EXAMPLES
• indicar el recipiente de una acción (*intended for, destined for*)	Compré flores **para** mi madre. *I bought flowers for my mother.*
• indicar un destino en el espacio o el tiempo (*to, in the direction of, by*)	Salen mañana **para** México. *They're leaving tomorrow for Mexico.* Tenemos que hacerlo **para** mañana. *We have to do it by tomorrow.*
• con un infinitivo: indicar un propósito (*purpose*) o meta (*goal*) (*in order to*)	**Para llegar** a tiempo, tenemos que salir ahora. *In order to arrive on time, we have to leave now.*
• indicar una comparación (*considering*)	**Para** ser tan joven, es muy sabio. *For being so young, he's very wise.*
• indicar el uso de algo (*to be used for*)	El vino es **para** la cena. *The wine is for dinner.*

De *Sol y viento,* **Note:** You can access this film clip from a special menu section on Disc 5 of the Instructional Version on DVD.

 DE SOL Y VIENTO

In **Episodio 8** of *Sol y viento,* you will watch a scene in which don Paco provides some advice to María. Part of their conversation follows.

PACO

Tú siempre te has guiado[a] _____ tu cerebro, María. Pero a veces tenemos que escuchar al corazón. ¿Qué dice el tuyo?

Do you think **por** or **para** belongs in the blank? Which of the uses of **por** or **para** justifies your answer?

a. por   **b.** para

[a]*guided*

474 cuatrocientos setenta y cuatro ❋ **Lección 8B** Los medios de comunicación

INPUT
Actividad E

Actividad E ¿*Por* o *para*?

Llena los espacios con **por** or **para,** según el contexto.

1. Jaime Talavera salió _para_ Chile _para_ conseguir las firmas de los dueños de «Sol y viento».
2. _Por_ el momento, Jaime no puede conseguir las firmas necesarias.
3. Mientras Jaime corría _por_ el Parque Forestal, conoció a María Sánchez.
4. El negocio de «Sol y viento» va mal _por_ culpa (*fault*) de Carlos.
5. _Para_ ser profesora, María no es muy típica.
6. Diego está pensando en dejar sus estudios _por_ presiones familiares.
7. Andy habla con Jaime _por_ teléfono _para_ saber si Jaime ha conseguido las firmas.

INPUT
Actividad F

Actividad F Situaciones

Escoge la expresión correcta, según el contexto.

1. Alguien te da un regalo que no esperas. Le dices:
   a. Gracias por pensar en mí.   **b.** Gracias para pensar en mí.
2. Un compañero de clase te pregunta cuándo hay que entregar la tarea. Le respondes:
   a. Es por el lunes.   **b.** Es para el lunes.
3. Un amigo quiere saber cómo te mantienes tan tranquilo/a. Le dices:
   a. Por no preocuparme por tonterías (*silly little things*).   **b.** Para no preocuparme por tonterías.
4. Alguien te ve con un ramo (*bouquet*) de flores y te pregunta:
   a. ¿Por quién son las flores?   **b.** ¿Para quién son las flores?
5. Alguien te pregunta cómo encontraste boletos tan baratos para viajar a México. Le contestas:
   a. Por Internet.   **b.** Para Internet.

INPUT
Act. G, *Paso 2,*
Suggestion: Provide a
model for the students,
such as: *Los padres
deben preocuparse por la
violencia en la tele
porque hay muchos pro-
gramas violentos.* Ask
several students their reasons for agreeing or dis-
agreeing with the
statements. *¿Por qué (no)
estás de acuerdo?*

Actividad G ¿Qué piensas?

Paso 1 Llena los espacios con **por** o **para** e indica si estás de acuerdo o no con cada oración.

	ESTOY DE ACUERDO.	NO ESTOY DE ACUERDO.
1. Los padres deben preocuparse _por_ la violencia en la televisión.	☐	☐
2. Hay algunos programas que no son apropiados _para_ los niños.	☐	☐
3. La televisión puede ser muy útil _para_ educar a los niños.	☐	☐
4. Se puede aprender mucho español _por_ mirar programas en español.	☐	☐
5. Me gustaría tomar clases _por_ Internet.	☐	☐

Paso 2 Comparte tus respuestas con las de un compañero (una compañera). ¿Pueden Uds. justificar cada una de las opiniones que indicaron en el **Paso 1**?

INPUT/OUTPUT

Act. H, Alternative: You may turn this into a "mixer" activity in which each person is assigned 1 of the items from *Paso 1* and forms a question to ask 10 different people in the class. For example: *¿Qué programa ves para reírte?* Each can then prepare a statement to share with the class: *Para reírse, la mayoría de mis compañeros prefiere ver...*

Actividad H ¿Para qué ves la televisión?

Paso 1 Escoge la opción que te describa mejor en cada situación.

Veo la televisión...	CASI SIEMPRE	ALGUNAS VECES	RARAS VECES	(CASI) NUNCA
1. ...para reírme.	☐	☐	☐	☐
2. ...para informarme de los últimos chismes (*gossip*) de los famosos.	☐	☐	☐	☐
3. ...para informarme de la política.	☐	☐	☐	☐
4. ...para entretenerme (*be entertained*).	☐	☐	☐	☐
5. ...para escaparme de la realidad.	☐	☐	☐	☐
6. ...para estar al corriente de los acontecimientos internacionales.	☐	☐	☐	☐

Paso 2 Ahora entrevista a un compañero (una compañera) de clase, basándote en las frases del **Paso 1**. Apunta sus respuestas.

MODELO: para reírme →
E1: ¿Qué programas ves para reírte?
E2: Veo *Saturday Night Live.*

Paso 3 Comparte los resultados de la entrevista con la clase. Entre todos, ¿cuál es la razón más popular de ver la televisión?

OUTPUT

Act. I, *Paso 2,*
Suggestion: After pairs share their responses, ask the class what it thinks is the most common idea (probably that people have died for love). Then, ask them if anyone has any unusual or less-than-typical responses.
Probe with questions (e.g., *¿Conoces a alguien que _____ por un amor? ¿Qué pasó?* etc.)
Suggested follow-up: Lead class into discussion about what literary characters and characters in movies have done for love (e.g., *¿Qué han hecho los personajes literarios y los del cine por un amor? Por ejemplo, ¿qué hizo Cleopatra? (se mató) ¿Cómo? (con una serpiente).*

Actividad I «Por un amor»

Paso 1 «Por un amor» es el título de una canción ranchera popular de México. Según el refrán (*chorus*), la persona que canta expresa las cosas que le pasan por un amor: «Por un amor, me desvelo y vivo apasionado» (*Because of love, I can't sleep and I live with passion*). En la vida, ¿qué hacen las personas (o qué les pasa) por un amor? Escribe por lo menos tres oraciones.

MODELO: Por un amor, muchos se desvelan.

Paso 2 Comparte tus oraciones con un compañero (una compañera). Explica la situación y/o las circunstancias si es posible. ¿Qué ideas tienen en común?

SEGUNDA PARTE

Vocabulario

No me convence.

Functions of the Media

Pepita y Gonzalo están casados, pero tienen opiniones muy distintas en cuanto a la parcialidad de los presentadores de los noticieros.

GONZALO: ¿Puedes creer lo que está diciendo? ¡Este presentador es totalmente **parcial**!

PEPITA: No **exageres.** Yo creo que es muy **objetivo.**

También, los dos prefieren diferentes tipos de programas.

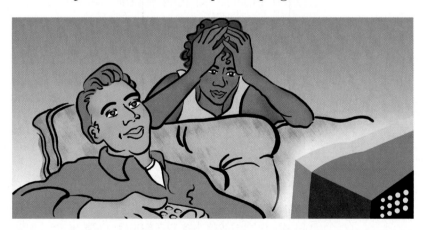

GONZALO: ¡Tienes que ver esto, amor! **Se trata de** un hombre que tiene que elegir a una esposa entre quince mujeres guapísimas.[a]

PEPITA: Me parece **una pérdida de tiempo.** Además de ser **cursi,** presenta **una imagen distorsionada** de la mujer.

GONZALO: ¡Qué va![b] Me **entretiene** y es muy **gracioso.**

[a]*gorgeous* [b]¡Qué... *No way!*

✳ MÁS VOCABULARIO

Me parece...	It seems . . .
aburrido/a	boring
atrevido/a	daring
chocante	shocking
controvertido/a	controversial
cursi	tacky
entretenido/a	entertaining
gracioso/a	funny
una pérdida de tiempo	a waste of time

Cognados: apropiado/a, distorsionado/a, escandaloso/a, exagerado/a, inapropiado/a, informativo/a, interesante, objetivo/a, ridículo/a, sensacionalista, violento/a

dañar	to harm
distraer (*like* **traer**)	to distract
entretener (*like* **tener**)	to entertain
ser (*irreg.*) **parcial (a favor de / en contra de)**	to be biased (in favor of / against)
tratarse de	to be about

Cognados: controlar, criticar (qu), educar (qu), escapar, exagerar, manipular

las imágenes	images

Vistazo cultural, **Point out**: During the filming of *Sol y viento,* the Chilean reality show *Conquistadores del fin del mundo* made its debut. The show pitted contestants against each other in extreme sporting contests in Patagonia. One of the hosts of the show was Javiera Contador, the actress who plays María Sánchez in *Sol y viento*!
Suggestion: After students read, ask them the following question: *¿Cuál es una diferencia cultural entre los realities norteamericanos y los hispanoamericanos?*
Follow-up: Ask students if they watch reality shows. Which ones? Have the class vote on their favorite and least favorite.

≋ Vistazo cultural

Los realities

A principios de los años setenta, salió una serie en la televisión pública (PBS) en los Estados Unidos en la que las cámaras de televisión seguían a una familia norteamericana de clase media. El objetivo del programa era mostrarle[a] al público norteamericano «la realidad» de una familia de esa época. Casi cuarenta años más tarde, el fenómeno de los realities se extiende por todo el mundo, incluyendo los países hispanos. De hecho, versiones de algunos programas como *Big Brother* y *American Idol* se estrenaron[b] en España antes que en los Estados Unidos con los nombres de *Gran hermano* y *Operación triunfo*, respectivamente. Aunque existen muchas semejanzas en los realities entre países diferentes, muchas veces los productores crean o adaptan programas según las normas

▲ Una escena de *Gran hermano* (*Big Brother*), un programa reality de España

culturales de cada país. Por ejemplo, un programa que ha tenido mucho éxito en Sudamérica es el programa *Camino a la gloria.* Debido a la importancia del fútbol en la cultura hispanoamericana, en este programa se trata de futbolistas jóvenes que sueñan con jugar profesionalmente algún día. Los futbolistas pasan por unos entrenamientos[c] duros y a lo largo del programa un jurado[d] va eliminando, uno por uno, a los futbolistas. El ganador del concurso no sólo gana mucha fama sino también recibe un contrato para jugar con un club profesional de fútbol.

[a]*to show*　[b]*se... made their debuts*　[c]*tryouts*　[d]*panel of judges*

Actividad A Definiciones

Empareja cada palabra o frase con la definición apropiada.

1. __c__ manipular
2. __e__ criticar
3. __a__ entretener
4. __b__ ser parcial
5. __d__ dañar

a. divertir, distraer
b. favorecer una perspectiva y no otra
c. distorsionar
d. causar mal
e. censurar (*to judge*) las acciones de otro

Actividad B Los programas televisivos

Indica si estás de acuerdo o no con las siguientes afirmaciones.

	ESTOY DE ACUERDO.	NO ESTOY DE ACUERDO.
1. La telenovela es ahora el tipo de programa más popular en los Estados Unidos.	☐	☐
2. La violencia en los medios de comunicación sólo refleja lo que pasa en la sociedad, no la influye.	☐	☐
3. Los medios de comunicación contribuyen a la violencia en la sociedad.	☐	☐
4. Los presentadores de los noticieros nos informan de las noticias sin ofrecer sus opiniones personales.	☐	☐
5. La objetividad en la prensa no existe.	☐	☐
6. Por lo general, la televisión tiene más influencia que los padres en la formación de los valores sociales de los niños norteamericanos.	☐	☐
7. «El sexo vende» en los anuncios publicitarios.	☐	☐
8. Los medios de comunicación perpetúan muchos estereotipos negativos sobre ciertos grupos minoritarios.	☐	☐

Actividad C ¿Es apropiado para los niños o no?

Paso 1 Piensa en tres de los programas de televisión que, en tu opinión, no son apropiados para los niños.

En mi opinión, _____, _____ y _____ no son programas apropiados para los niños.

Paso 2 Ahora piensa en las razones por las que esos tres programas no son apropiados para los niños. Puedes utilizar algunas palabras de la lista a continuación. Luego vas a leer tus oraciones a la clase.

Vocabulario útil

el contenido denso (*heavy*) el lenguaje fuerte (*strong language*)
el contenido sexual la violencia

A causa de... , creo que _____ no es un programa apropiado para los niños.

Paso 3 Escucha las oraciones de tus compañeros. ¿Mencionan algunos de los mismos programas y razones?

INPUT/OUTPUT
Actividad D

Actividad D ¿Qué te parece ese programa?

Paso 1 En tu opinión, ¿a qué programa de televisión se puede aplicar cada adjetivo?

1. gracioso
2. cursi
3. controvertido
4. sensacionalista
5. chocante

Paso 2 Compara tus respuestas con las de un compañero (una compañera). Sigue el modelo.

MODELO: E1: Me parece que *The Simpsons* es un programa muy gracioso.
E2: A mí también me parece gracioso.

o

A mí no. Me parece más gracioso *The Office*.

OUTPUT
Actividad E

Actividad E ¿Qué imágenes se presentan en los programas televisivos?

Paso 1 Vas a trabajar con un compañero (una compañera) de clase. A cada pareja su profesor(a) le va a asignar uno de los grupos sociales a continuación. Pensando en algunos programas televisivos específicos, tú y tu compañero/a deben escoger varios adjetivos que describan la imagen que se presentan de esas personas.

1. las mujeres
2. los afroamericanos
3. los hispanos
4. los homosexuales
5. las agrupaciones religiosas (cristianos, judíos, musulmanes [*Muslims*])

Adjetivos posibles:

atractivos/as	inteligentes	ricos/as
delgados/as	locos/as	sofisticados/as
fanáticos/as	perezosos/as	tontos/as
fuertes	pobres	trabajadores/as
graciosos/as	promiscuos/as (*promiscuous*)	violentos/as

Paso 2 Comparen los adjetivos que escogieron con los de otras parejas que describieron el mismo grupo social. ¿Escogieron los grupos los mismos adjetivos? ¿Creen que los programas televisivos presentan una imagen positiva o negativa de ese grupo? ¿Es una imagen realista o es exagerada?

Paso 3 Ahora compartan sus respuestas con toda la clase. ¿Qué grupo social tiene la imagen más positiva? ¿la más negativa?

Gramática

Expressing
Disbelief | **Dudo que lo sepa.**

Subjunctive of Doubt, Denial, and Uncertainty

In addition to using the subjunctive after expressions such as **ojalá, esperar que,** and certain adverbial expressions, the subjunctive is also used after expressions of doubt, denial, and uncertainty. Compare the two sentences below:

Creo que nos **dicen** la verdad.	*I think they're telling us the truth.*
No creo que nos **digan** la verdad.	*I don't think they're telling us the truth.*

In the first sentence, the statement *they're telling us the truth* is true in the mind of the speaker. However, in the second sentence, the speaker doubts the truth of the proposition. Because of this lack of affirmation, the subjunctive is used in the dependent clause. As the chart on the next page indicates, the subjunctive is "triggered" anytime an expression is used to express doubt, denial, or render uncertain the truth of a statement.

Note that when **no** precedes expressions of doubt or denial, the indicative is used. This is because the negation of doubt or denial is, in actuality, an affirmation.

No dudo que vienen.	*I don't doubt they're coming. = I believe they are.*
No niego que es verdad.	*I don't deny it's true. = I believe it is.*

Some expressions, upon first glance, may not seem to express doubt or denial. However, they do express uncertainty (the speaker isn't sure whether something is true or not) and require the subjunctive.

Es posible que **diga** la verdad.	*It's possible he's telling the truth. (The speaker doesn't know if he really is or not.)*
Es probable que **vayan** pronto.	*It's likely they'll leave soon. (The speaker doesn't know whether they will or not.)*

COMUNICACIÓN ÚTIL

Although in this section you will be using the present subjunctive only after expressions of doubt and denial, the imperfect subjunctive can also be used when the verb expressing doubt is in a past-tense form.

No pensaba que **fuera** verdad.	*I didn't think it was true.*
No podíamos creer que **ocurriera**.	*We couldn't believe it happened.*

Furthermore, a form called the present perfect subjunctive is used to express that someone presently disbelieves or denies that something *has happened.*

Dudo que lo **hayas hecho**.	*I doubt (that) you've done it.*
No es posible que **hayan roto**.	*It's not possible that they've split up.*

The present perfect subjunctive is formed by using the present subjunctive form of the verb **haber** (**haya, hayas, haya,** and so forth) and the past participle.

THE SUBJUNCTIVE WITH EXPRESSIONS OF DOUBT, DENIAL, AND UNCERTAINTY	
no (poder) creer/pensar	**No puedo creer** que te **guste** ese programa. *I can't believe you like that show.* **No pienso** que **sea** verdad. *I don't think it's true.*
dudar	**Dudamos** que **vengan.** *We doubt they're coming.*
no estar (*irreg.*) seguro/a de	**No está segura de** que **se casen.** *She's not sure they're getting married.*
negar (ie) (gu)	¿**Niegas** que lo **sepa**? *Do you deny that she knows?*
no es cierto/seguro/verdad	**No es cierto** que **haya** un examen hoy. *It's not true that there's a test today.*
(no) es posible / es imposible	**No es posible** que **sea** tan tarde ya. *It's not possible that it's so late already.* **Es posible** que **vayan** a otro lugar. *It's possible they'll go somewhere else.*
(no) es probable	**No es probable** que ese programa **continúe.** *It's not likely that program will continue.* **Es probable** que mis hijas **estudien** en la misma universidad. *It's likely that my daughters will study in the same university.*

De *Sol y viento,* Note: You can access this film clip from a special menu section on Disc 5 of the Instructional Version on DVD.

Point out: Other possible expressions that would still require subjunctive: *es imposible, no es posible.*

 DE SOL Y VIENTO

In **Episodio 8** of *Sol y viento,* you will again watch the scene in which doña Isabel confronts Carlos about his business dealings. Part of their exchange follows.

ISABEL
No puedo creer que _____ mi hijo. También tengo aquí unos documentos falsificados. ¡Falsificados! ¡Con mi nombre y el de tu hermana!

Which verb form do you think belongs in the blank?

1. eres **3.** seas

2. es **4.** sea

Besides **no puedo creer,** what other expressions could doña Isabel have used? Would these expressions change the verb in the blank?

INPUT

Act. F, Suggested follow-up: Have students work in pairs to come up with 2 more predictions using *Es posible que.*

Actividad F Predicciones

Paso 1 Completa las predicciones sobre lo que crees que va a pasar con los personajes de *Sol y viento*, utilizando las siguientes expresiones.

Es probable que   Es posible que   Dudo que

1. _____ María perdone a Jaime.
2. _____ Jaime vuelva a trabajar con Bartel Aquapower.
3. _____ Jaime trabaje para «Sol y viento».
4. _____ Carlos se quede como administrador de «Sol y viento».
5. _____ Diego deje sus estudios para trabajar con su familia.
6. _____ Jaime y María se casen algún día.

Paso 2 Comparte tus predicciones con la clase. ¿Están todos de acuerdo?

INPUT
Actividad G

Actividad G ¿Estás de acuerdo?

Indica si estás de acuerdo o no con las siguientes afirmaciones sobre los concursos en la televisión.

	ESTOY DE ACUERDO.	NO ESTOY DE ACUERDO.
1. Es probable que los concursos sean aún (*even*) más atrevidos en los próximos años.	☐	☐
2. Es posible que duren mucho tiempo los matrimonios entre personas que se casan en un concurso.	☐	☐
3. Es dudoso que los ganadores de los programas sean famosos por más de un mes.	☐	☐
4. No es cierto que los resultados de los programas sean predeterminados.	☐	☐
5. Es posible que los concursantes (*contestants*) se olviden de (*forget about*) las cámaras durante la filmación del programa.	☐	☐

INPUT/OUTPUT

Act. H, Suggested follow-up: Call on a variety of students to find out their opinions. After hearing a number of responses, ask if the students' opinions reflect a favorable or unfavorable view of the press. *En general, ¿tenemos una impresión favorable de la prensa?*

Actividad H La prensa norteamericana

Paso 1 Indica si se usa el indicativo (I) o el subjuntivo (S) con las expresiones a continuación.

creo que + _I_   no creo que + _S_
es dudoso que + _S_   no es dudoso que + _I_
es verdad que + _I_   no es verdad que + _S_
es probable que + _S_   es improbable que + _S_

Paso 2 Usando las expresiones del **Paso 1,** expresa tus opiniones sobre las siguientes afirmaciones.

MODELO: Los norteamericanos están bien informados de las noticias
          internacionales. →
          No es verdad que los norteamericanos estén bien informados de
          las noticias internacionales.

La prensa norteamericana...

1. ...es independiente de las ideas de los partidos políticos (*political
   parties*) principales.
2. ...es parcial a favor de una agenda conservadora.
3. ...se preocupa demasiado por la vida privada de los políticos.
4. ...normalmente favorece al gobierno.
5. ...presenta muchas noticias internacionales.
6. ...es sensacionalista.

INPUT/OUTPUT
Act. I, *Paso 1,*
Suggestion: Name
3 current films and
3 TV programs that
easily reflect some aspect
of the choices in *Paso 2:*
cultural diversity,
violence, technology, etc.

Actividad I   ¿Qué imagen tendrían?

Paso 1   Para muchas personas en el mundo, la única imagen que tienen de
los Estados Unidos es lo que les presentan los medios de comunicación. Tu pro-
fesor(a) va a mencionar algunos programas de televisión y películas norteamericanos. Apúntalos en los espacios en blanco.

	PELÍCULAS		PROGRAMAS DE TELEVISIÓN
1.	_____	1.	_____
2.	_____	2.	_____
3.	_____	3.	_____

Paso 2   Con un compañero (una compañera), escriban por lo menos tres oraciones que describan la imagen que alguien de otro país tendría de los Estados Unidos si sólo viera los programas y películas mencionados en el **Paso 1.**
Usa los temas a continuación como guía.

la diversidad cultural
el nivel económico
el racismo
la religión
la tecnología
la violencia

MODELO: Es probable que piense que somos un país muy violento.
          Es posible que piense que somos muy violentos.

Paso 3   Compartan con la clase las oraciones que Uds. escribieron. Según las
descripciones de sus compañeros, escojan una de las siguientes afirmaciones.
¿Tendría alguien de otro país una imagen positiva o negativa de los Estados
Unidos? ¿Sería una imagen realista o exagerada?

☐ Dudo que esa persona tenga una imagen muy positiva.

☐ Es posible que su imagen sea realista.

TERCERA PARTE

Vocabulario

La responsabilidad cívica

Civic Duty and Citizenship

Sonia es muy activa en su comunidad.

Vota en todas **las elecciones.**

Participa en **las reuniones cívicas.**

Trabaja de **voluntaria** en una organización que ayuda a los niños.

De vez en cuando, participa en **manifestaciones.**

El gobierno[a] y la responsabilidad cívica
[a]*government*

apoyar	to support
ayudar	to help
eliminar	to eliminate
protestar	to protest
el/la ciudadano/a	citizen
el deber	duty
el derecho	right
la ley	law
la libertad	liberty, freedom
la política	politics; policy
la preocupación	worry
la sociedad	society

MÁS VOCABULARIO

el analfabetismo	illiteracy
los derechos humanos	human rights
el desempleo	unemployment
el hambre (*f.*)	hunger
la pérdida de los valores tradicionales	loss of traditional values
la protección del medio ambiente	environmental protection
el SIDA (síndrome de inmunodeficiencia adquirida)	AIDS

Cognados: la corrupción, el crimen violento, la discriminación, la drogadicción, la inmigración ilegal, el terrorismo, la violencia doméstica

Vistazo cultural,
Suggestion: Before having students read, ask them the following question: *¿Cuántos de Uds. votan en las elecciones?* Survey the class to see what percentage of students actually vote. Then have them read quickly. Afterward, ask students to work in pairs to name at least one advantage and one disadvantage of obligatory voting. In the end, do they think obligatory voting is a good thing?

 # Vistazo cultural

El voto obligatorio

Se ha notado en los últimos años la apatía[a] de los votantes norteamericanos en las elecciones. De hecho, apenas[b] el 50% de los votantes ejerce su derecho en las elecciones presidenciales. En algunos países, votar no es un derecho sino una obligación. Entre los países hispanohablantes, hay varios que tienen leyes que obligan a los ciudadanos a votar: la Argentina, Bolivia, Chile, Costa Rica, Guatemala, el Ecuador, México, el Perú y el Uruguay. Aunque en algunos países no tiene consecuencias por no cumplir con la ley, en otros las consecuencias de la abstención pueden ser mínimas, como una multa[c] de $20, o pueden ser más severas. En el Perú, durante los tres meses después de las elecciones, los ciudadanos tienen que llevar una tarjeta con un sello[d] que confirme que han votado. Si no tienen la tarjeta, no pueden recibir ciertos beneficios del gobierno. En Bolivia, también hay que llevar una tarjeta como prueba de haber votado para poder recibir el sueldo en el banco.

▲ En Guatemala, como en otros países hispanos, el voto es obligatorio.

La idea del voto obligatorio tiene sus defensores y sus críticos. Los que defienden esta política afirman que las elecciones democráticas son más legítimas si la mayor parte de la población participa. Además, si la democracia es el gobierno del pueblo, es la responsabilidad de todo el pueblo participar en las elecciones. Por otro lado, los que critican la política del voto obligatorio afirman que infringe sobre el derecho de elección,[e] fundamental en una sociedad democrática. ¿Qué crees tú? ¿Sería buena idea tener una ley del voto obligatorio en este país?

[a]*apathy* [b]*hardly* [c]*fine* [d]*seal, stamp* [e]*choice*

Actividad A   Definiciones

Empareja las definiciones con la palabra o frase correspondiente.

1. __d__ el terrorismo
2. __f__ el desempleo
3. __a__ la inmigración
4. __c__ el analfabetismo
5. __h__ la drogadicción
6. __b__ el SIDA
7. __e__ la discriminación
8. __g__ la violencia doméstica

a. el movimiento de personas de un país a otro

b. una enfermedad (*disease*) que causa que el cuerpo humano no pueda protegerse de otras enfermedades

c. la condición de no saber leer ni escribir

d. actos de violencia para causar miedo entre la gente

e. tratar peor a un grupo de personas que a otro

f. la condición de no tener trabajo

g. actos de violencia que un miembro de una familia comete contra otros de la misma familia

h. la condición de depender físicamente de alguna sustancia química

Actividad B   La responsabilidad cívica

Paso 1   Indica si las actividades a continuación son sólo buenas ideas o si son deberes de los ciudadanos.

	ES BUENA IDEA, PERO NO ES UN DEBER.	ES UN DEBER DE TODO CIUDADANO.
1. votar en las elecciones nacionales y locales	☐	☐
2. participar en una manifestación cuando uno no está de acuerdo con una ley o disposición (*regulation*)	☐	☐
3. pagar los impuestos (*taxes*) a tiempo	☐	☐
4. participar en las reuniones cívicas	☐	☐
5. informarse de la política del país	☐	☐
6. apoyar a las fuerzas armadas (*armed forces*)	☐	☐
7. avisar a la policía si uno presencia (*witnesses*) algún crimen	☐	☐
8. trabajar de voluntario/a para una causa u organización	☐	☐

Paso 2   ¿Cuántas de las actividades del **Paso 1** has hecho o haces ahora? Da un ejemplo.

MODELO: Trabajo de voluntario con la organización *Habitat for Humanity.*

Paso 3 Comparte tus respuestas de los **Pasos 1** y **2** con la clase. Según las respuestas de tus compañeros, ¿cuál de las siguientes afirmaciones describe mejor a tu clase?

☐ Somos una clase que participa muy activamente en la sociedad.

☐ Somos una clase que participa de forma más o menos activa en la sociedad.

☐ Somos una clase apática (*apathetic*).

OUTPUT
Actividad C

Actividad C ¿Qué opinas?

Paso 1 Indica tu opinión sobre las ideas a continuación, utilizando una de las siguientes expresiones. **¡OJO!** Hay que usar el subjuntivo con **No creo que...**

Creo que...   No creo que...

1. es necesario perder algunas libertades para proteger el país contra el terrorismo.
2. los inmigrantes ilegales deben tener los mismos derechos que los ciudadanos.
3. el matrimonio es un derecho para todos, no sólo para los heterosexuales.
4. existe menos discriminación ahora que desde hace cinco años.
5. la edad para tomar bebidas alcohólicas debe ser la misma que la edad para votar.
6. votar en las elecciones debe ser obligatorio para todos los ciudadanos.
7. es buena idea aprobar (*to pass*) leyes más estrictas para la compra y posesión de armas.

Paso 2 Entrevista a un compañero (una compañera) para saber qué opina de las ideas del **Paso 1.**

Paso 3 ¿Estás de acuerdo con tu compañero/a? Prepara unas oraciones para compartir con la clase.

MODELOS: (No) Creemos que...

(Nombre) cree que... , pero yo no.

OUTPUT
Act. D,
Suggestions
Paso 1: Assign
each group 1
of the *preocupaciones
sociales* from page 485.
Paso 2: After a group
presents its answers, ask
the other students follow-
up questions such as
*¿Están de acuerdo con
las causas (las
consecuencias)? ¿Creen
que el problema sólo
afecta a... ?,* etc.

Actividad D Preocupaciones sociales

Paso 1 Tu profesor(a) va a asignarles a grupos de tres personas una preocupación social. En tu grupo, contesta las siguientes preguntas sobre esa preocupación.

1. ¿A quiénes afecta este problema?
2. ¿Cuáles son las causas del problema?
3. ¿Cuáles son las consecuencias?
4. ¿Sería fácil o difícil resolver el problema?
5. ¿Se puede aprobar leyes para combatir (*combat*) el problema?
6. ¿Qué pueden hacer los estudiantes universitarios para ayudar a resolver el problema?
7. ¿Cuál es el mayor obstáculo para resolver el problema?

Paso 2 Cada grupo va a presentar sus ideas a la clase. ¿Cuál de las preocupaciones tiene una solución más realista que las otras?

Gramática

Talking About
What You Want
to Happen

¿Qué quieres que haga?

Subjunctive of Volition and Desire

In addition to the uses of the subjunctive that you have already learned, Spanish also uses the subjunctive after certain verbs of volition or desire. Note that, unlike with the subjunctive with expressions of doubt, making a statement negative does not change the need to use the subjunctive. That is, whether the expression is **quiere** or **no quiere,** for example, the subjunctive will appear in the dependent clause.

THE SUBJUNCTIVE WITH EXPRESSIONS OF VOLITION AND DESIRE		
decir (*irreg.*)	*to tell* (*someone to do something*)	Juan me **dice** que **vaya** a verlo. *Juan tells me to go see him.*
desear	*to want, desire*	**Deseamos** que el gobierno **haga** algo más efectivo para combatir el terrorismo. *We want the government to do something more effective to combat terrorism.*
es necesario / **es preciso**	*it's necessary*	**Es necesario** que todos **hagamos** algo de nuestra parte para eliminar la discriminación. *It's necessary that we all do our fair share to eliminate discrimination.* **Es preciso** que los políticos nos **escuchen.** *It's necessary that the politicians listen to us.*
insistir en	*to insist*	Mi padre **insiste en** que yo **piense** bien en el asunto. *My father insists that I think hard about the matter.*
(no) permitir	*to permit, allow*	**No puedo permitir** que **manejes.** *I can't allow you to drive.*
prohibir (**prohíbo**)	*to prohibit, forbid*	Te **prohíbo** que se lo **digas.** *I'm forbidding you to tell her.*
querer (*irreg.*)	*to want*	**Quiero** que me **escuches** un momento. *I want you to listen to me for a moment.*
recomendar (ie)	*to recommend*	El médico me **recomienda** que **haga** más ejercicio. *The doctor recommends that I exercise more.*
sugerir (ie)	*to suggest*	El profesor nos **sugiere** que **estudiemos** mucho para el examen. *The professor suggests that we study a lot for the test.*

De *Sol y viento,* Note: You can access this film clip from a special menu section on Disc 5 of the Instructional Version on DVD.

DE SOL Y VIENTO

In **Episodio 8** of *Sol y viento,* you will again watch the scene in which doña Isabel asks Yolanda where Carlos is. Part of their exchange follows.

ISABEL
¿Has visto a Carlos?

YOLANDA
No, señora. ¿Quiere que _____¹?

ISABEL
Sí, por favor. Dile que _____² hablarle y que me _____³ en el jardín.

Which verb forms do you think belong in the parts of the dialogue that are missing?

1. **a.** lo busco   (**b.**) lo busque   **c.** lo busqué
2. (**a.**) necesito   **b.** necesite   **c.** necesité
3. **a.** busca   (**b.**) busque   **c.** busqué

Enfoque lingüístico, **Suggestion:** Ask the students to continue listing as many different uses and meanings of *run* as they can. Then have them look up all the different meanings in a Spanish-English dictionary. What have they come up with?

◉ Enfoque lingüístico

La ambigüedad de ciertos verbos

It may seem that a word means what a word means, regardless of the circumstance. But consider that a verb out of context may not capture its usual meaning in another context. For example, if you heard *to run* you might think of the action of moving very quickly with your legs. However, this is not the meaning in *she's running for office* or *my nose is running.*

The two verbs *tell* and *insist* are also ambiguous. On the one hand, they can be used in such contexts as *I'm telling you, John lies* and *I insist that John doesn't lie (isn't lying).* On the other hand, the words *tell* and *insist* can be used in contexts such as *I tell John not to lie* and *I insist that John not lie.* In the latter two cases, you could substitute verbs such as *command, demand,* or *order,* and the sense is retained: *I insist/demand that John not lie.* Note that you cannot do this in the first two examples, that is, *I'm telling you, John lies* cannot be *I'm demanding of you that John lies*!

Why is this important? In learning a language, you have to think about the meaning of a verb in context. The first two example sentences above require the indicative when they are expressed in Spanish.

I'm telling you, John lies.	**Te digo que John miente.**
I insist that John doesn't lie (isn't lying).	**Insisto en que John no miente.**

For the other two example sentences, the subjunctive is required in Spanish.

I tell John not to lie.	**Le digo a John que no mienta.**
I insist that John not lie.	**Insisto en que John no mienta.**

All languages have such ambiguities or multiple meanings, and this should not be a novel concept for you at this point. However, it is good to keep such things in mind because you wouldn't want to commit the *faux pas* of saying to someone **Insisto en que John mienta,** thereby implying that you are the source of John's lying habits!

Actividad E ¿Qué le dice que haga?

Completa cada oración con la frase más apropiada, según lo que ya sabes de *Sol y viento*.

1. _c_ Doña Isabel le dice a Yolanda que...
2. _f_ María y doña Isabel no permiten que «Sol y viento»...
3. _b_ María le sugiere a Diego que...
4. _d_ Carlos no desea que María...
5. _a_ Doña Isabel no insiste en que María...
6. _e_ Doña Isabel le dice a Carlos que...

a. trabaje más en la viña.
b. continúe con sus estudios.
c. busque a Carlos.
d. se meta en (*enter*) su oficina sin su permiso.
e. se vaya o va a llamar a las autoridades.
f. se venda.

Actividad F ¿Qué quieren?

Indica si, por lo general, quieren las siguientes cosas los conservadores o los liberales.

Quieren que el gobierno...	LOS CONSERVADORES	LOS LIBERALES
1. ...apruebe más leyes para controlar la compra y la posesión de armas de fuego.	☐	☑
2. ...apruebe más leyes contra el aborto (*abortion*).	☑	☐
3. ...baje los impuestos.	☑	☐
4. ...reduzca el presupuesto del ejército.	☐	☑
5. ...elimine la pena de muerte (*death penalty*).	☐	☑
6. ...permita el matrimonio entre los homosexuales.	☐	☑
7. ...proteja los valores tradicionales.	☑	☐
8. ...haga algo más efectivo para proteger el medio ambiente.	☐	☑
9. ...sea más pequeño.	☑	☐

Actividad G Una historia

Paso 1 Con un compañero (una compañera) escriban una historia de cuatro a seis oraciones que describen lo que ocurre en los dibujos en la siguiente página. Inventen nombres y detalles. Deben usar verbos como **querer, insistir, decir** y el subjuntivo.

Paso 2 Compartan su historia con la clase. ¿Tienen todos los grupos la misma información?

Actividad H ¿Qué le recomiendas?

Paso 1 Con un compañero (una compañera), termina las siguientes recomendaciones para un(a) estudiante nuevo/a en tu universidad.

1. Le recomiendo que viva en...
2. (No) Le recomiendo que tome clases de...
3. Le recomiendo que se aproveche de (*take advantage of*)...
4. Le recomiendo que no vaya a...
5. Le recomiendo que (no) coma en...
6. Le recomiendo que compre...

Paso 2 Ahora escriban dos recomendaciones más para el mismo (la misma) estudiante.

Paso 3 Compartan sus recomendaciones con la clase. ¿Están todos de acuerdo con las recomendaciones?

Actividad I Soluciones a los problemas

Paso 1 Escoge una de las preocupaciones sociales de la página 485. Trabajando con un compañero (una compañera), escribe cuatro oraciones que ofrezcan soluciones posibles al problema. Pueden utilizar las siguientes expresiones. **¡OJO!** No se olviden de usar el subjuntivo.

Es necesario que...	Queremos que...
Es recomendable que...	Se debe prohibir que...

Paso 2 Ahora compartan sus oraciones con otro grupo. ¿Qué piensan Uds. de las recomendaciones del otro grupo? ¿Están de acuerdo con ellas? ¿Son prácticas las recomendaciones? Respondan a cada recomendación, utilizando las siguientes expresiones.

¡Es una buena idea!	No creo que sea práctica.
(No) Estoy de acuerdo.	Me parece bien/mal porque...

SOL Y VIENTO

A segunda vista

Antes de ver el episodio

Actividad A ¿Qué recuerdas?

¿Cuál de los personajes de *Sol y viento* diría cada oración a continuación, según lo que sabes de la película?

1. __don Paco__ Si se construyera una represa en esta zona, causaría mucho daño a estas tierras.
2. __doña Isabel__ Si mi esposo estuviera aquí, el negocio de «Sol y viento» no iría tan mal.
3. __Carlos__ Si pudiera conseguir las firmas de algunas personas, podríamos vender «Sol y viento».
4. __Jaime__ Si no trabajara para Bartel Aquapower, María no estaría enojada conmigo.
5. __María__ Si no quisiera comprar nuestras tierras, lo vería otra vez.
6. __Carlos__ Si mi hermana me ayudara, no tendría tanto trabajo.
7. __Jaime__ Si no fuera por María, seguiría tratando de comprar «Sol y viento».

Actividad B ¡A escuchar!

Repasa la siguiente escena. Luego, mientras ves el episodio, completa lo que dicen los personajes con las palabras y expresiones que oyes.

Act. B, Suggestion: Have students read the exchange. They do not need to write anything at this point. Do not reveal answers.
Alternative: Have the class brainstorm possible answers for each blank but do not have them write anything down.

MARÍA: ¿En serio? ¿Me __ibas__ [1] a hablar? ¿Cuándo? Yo creo que ibas a tratar de engañarme... ¡como __engañaste__ [2] al señor Ayala para sacarle sus terrenos! ¿O acaso no es para eso que está aquí el señor Talavera, para __seducirme__ [3] y sacarme una firma?

CARLOS: ¿Ese inoportuno?[a] Ni siquiera[b] __sabía__ [4] que __se conocían__.[5] ¿Y desde cuándo te interesan los negocios de la viña «Sol y viento»? Nunca __has hecho__ [6] nada. Ni siquiera sabes cómo funciona. ¿Tú crees que esto __se maneja__ [7] solo?

[a]¿Ese... *That guy?* [b]*even*

Actividad C El episodio

Ahora mira el episodio.

492

Después de ver el episodio

Actividad A Para pensar...

¿Qué piensas de las opciones que le dio doña Isabel a Carlos? ¿Son justas (*fair*) o piensas que hay otra alternativa? ¿Piensas que Carlos va a aceptar las condiciones de su madre o va a rogarle (*beg her*) que él se quede en «Sol y viento»? Con un compañero (una compañera), comenten estas preguntas. Luego, compartan sus ideas con la clase.

Act. B, Suggestion: Replay the scene once for students. Replay a second time if needed. Then ask for volunteers to provide answers for each blank. Verify using the instructor notes from Act. B on the previous page.
Alternative: After students complete the conversation, have 2 students act out.

Actividad B ¡A verificar!

Vas a ver otra vez la escena de **¡A escuchar!** en la página anterior. Llena los espacios en blanco, según lo que oyes.

Actividad C ¿Qué quieres que ocurra?

Paso 1 Sólo queda un episodio más de *Sol y viento.* ¿Qué crees que va a pasar? ¿Qué quieres que ocurra? Da tu opinión sobre las afirmaciones a continuación y luego escribe dos oraciones más utilizando las siguientes expresiones. **¡OJO!** Recuerda que con estas expresiones es necesario usar el subjuntivo.

> Quiero que...
>
> Es posible que...
>
> (No) Es probable que...

1. María perdona a Jaime.
2. Doña Isabel llama a las autoridades.
3. Jaime decide quedarse a vivir y trabajar en Chile.
4. Carlos se queda como administrador de «Sol y viento».
5. Carlos se va.
6. ¿ ?
7. ¿ ?

Paso 2 Comparte tus oraciones con la clase. ¿Están todos de acuerdo en cuanto a lo que puede ocurrir o lo que quieren que ocurra?

Detrás de la cámara

María sometimes feels guilty because she has moved away from home and is not regularly involved in the family business. Yet, when María asks her mother if she wishes that María had stayed at home to work in the vineyard, doña Isabel promptly says "no." Doña Isabel also says that she is proud that her daughter is a university professor. In spite of having moved away, María and her mother maintain a very close relationship, and doña Isabel does not worry at all about María. Although María can be stubborn at times, doña Isabel trusts her daughter, and she knows that María's intelligence and self-confidence serve her well.

RESUMEN DE VOCABULARIO

Verbos

dudar	to doubt
estar (*irreg.*) **seguro/a de**	to be sure
insistir en	to insist
negar (ie) (gu)	to deny
permitir	to permit, allow
prohibir (prohíbo)	to prohibit, forbid
recomendar (ie)	to recommend
es imposible	it's impossible
es preciso	it's necessary
(no) es cierto	it's (not) certain
(no) es posible	it's (not) possible
(no) es probable	it's (not) likely
(no) es seguro/a	it's (not) certain
(no) es verdad	it's (not) true

Repaso: **es necesario, decir** (*irreg.*), **desear, querer** (*irreg.*), **sugerir (ie, i)**

La prensa y las noticias

estar (*irreg.*) **al corriente**	to be caught up (*with current events*)
informarse	to be informed; to inform oneself
el acontecimiento	happening, event
la cadena	network
los medios de comunicación	media
la noticia	piece of news
las noticias	news
internacionales	international
locales	local
nacionales	national
el noticiero	newscast
el/la presentador(a)	anchorman, anchorwoman

el pronóstico del tiempo	weather report
el reportaje	report
el/la testigo	witness
el titular	headline

Cognados: **el accidente, el artículo, el/la reportero/a**
Repaso: **el periódico, la revista**

Los programas televisivos

dañar	to harm
distraer (*like* **traer**)	to distract
entretener (*like* **tener**)	to entertain
ser (*irreg.*) **parcial**	to be biased
a favor de	in favor of
en contra de	against
tratarse de	to be about
el anuncio publicitario	commercial
el concurso	game show; contest
el programa de entrevistas	talk show
el programa deportivo	sports program
la telenovela	soap opera
atrevido/a	daring
chocante	shocking
controvertido/a	controversial
cursi	tacky
entretenido/a	entertaining
gracioso/a	funny
parcial	biased

Cognados: **controlar, criticar (qu), educar (qu), escapar, exagerar, manipular; la comedia, el documental, el drama, la imagen, el reality; apropiado/a, distorsionado/a, escandaloso/a, exagerado/a, inapropiado/a, informativo/a, objetivo/a, ridículo/a, sensacionalista, violento/a**
Repaso: **aburrido/a, interesante**

El gobierno y la responsabilidad cívica

apoyar	to support
aprobar (ue)	to pass (*a law*)
ayudar	to help
el/la ciudadano/a	citizen
el deber	duty
el derecho	right
la ley	law
la libertad	liberty, freedom
la manifestación	demonstration
la política	politics; policy
la reunión cívica	town meeting
el/la voluntario/a	volunteer

Cognados: eliminar, participar, protestar, votar; la elección

Preocupaciones de la sociedad

el analfabetismo	illiteracy
los derechos humanos	human rights

el hambre (*f.*)	hunger
la pérdida de los valores tradicionales	loss of traditional values
el SIDA (síndrome de inmunodeficiencia adquirida)	AIDS

Cognados: la corrupción, el crimen violento, la discriminación, la drogadicción, la inmigración ilegal, el terrorismo, la violencia doméstica
Repaso: el desempleo, la protección del medio ambiente

Otras palabras y expresiones

el impuesto	tax
la pérdida de tiempo	waste of time

Entremés cultural
La Argentina, el Paraguay y el Uruguay: Semejanzas y diferencias

VISTAZO

La Argentina, el Uruguay y el Paraguay tienen algunos rasgos comunes: el español como lengua oficial, la existencia de civilizaciones precolombinas, la dominación colonial, la lucha por la independencia y los turbulentos procesos políticos del último siglo. Sin embargo, existe mucha diversidad entre estos tres países. Por ejemplo, en la Argentina y el Uruguay, los descendientes de la población indígena original ya casi no existen, pero sí ha habido mucha inmigración de Europa. En cambio, en el Paraguay todavía existe una importante población indígena, cuya lengua, el guaraní, también es lengua oficial del país, ya que un 90 por ciento de la población la entiende.

DATO INTERESANTE:
El MERCOSUR

La Argentina, el Uruguay y el Paraguay (juntos con Brasil y Venezuela) forman parte del Mercado Común del Sur o MERCOSUR. Desde su creación en 1985, este bloque económico tiene el propósito de promover[a] el libre comercio[b] y también de desarrollar una colaboración política y cultural entre sus países miembros.

Idea: Busca información sobre algunos tratados[c] del MERCOSUR. ¿En qué se parecen a los tratados del Tratado de Libre Comercio (TLC)?[d]

[a]*promote* [b]*libre... free trade* [c]*treaties* [d]Tratado... *North American Free Trade Agreement (NAFTA)*

Una cumbre (*summit*) del MERCOSUR

DATO INTERESANTE:
La inmigración europea

Estos tres países han sido el destino[a] de muchos emigrantes europeos durante los siglos XIX y XX. En Buenos Aires, por ejemplo, hay mucha gente de ascendencia italiana, alemana y británica. En el oeste del Paraguay en la región del Chaco, hay diecisiete colonias de menonitas[b] alemanes que forman la mayoría de la población en esta zona del país y todavía preservan su lengua y su cultura.

Idea: Busca información sobre las comunidades menonitas alemanas en el Paraguay y los que están en México también. ¿Cómo y por qué decidieron instalar sus colonias en Latinoamérica?

[a]*destination*   [b]*Mennonites (Christian group influenced by the teachings of Dutch priest Menno Simons [1496–1561])*

Los uruguayos gozan de (*enjoy*) altos niveles de bienestar.

Dos mujeres menonitas en el Paraguay

DATO INTERESANTE:
«La Suiza[a] de América»

Desde los principios del siglo XX se ha considerado el Uruguay «la Suiza de América» por los altos niveles de bienestar de la población. Además, el Uruguay es uno de los primeros países del mundo de otorgarles[b] a las mujeres ciertos derechos como el derecho al divorcio (1907) y a votar en las elecciones nacionales (1938).

Idea: Busca información sobre el voto femenino en Latinoamérica. ¿Cuáles son los primeros y los últimos países en otorgarles el derecho de votar a las mujeres?

[a]*Switzerland*   [b]*grant*

DATO INTERESANTE:
El cine en la Argentina

El cine argentino tiene una larga y exitosa historia. De hecho, en la Argentina se produjo las primeras películas de dibujos animados[a] en 1917. En las últimas décadas el cine argentino ha ganado fama internacional con películas como *La historia oficial*, que ganó un premio Óscar en 1986 como la mejor película extranjera.

Idea: Busca información sobre una película argentina reciente. ¿De qué trata la película? Trae la información a clase. Entre todos, compartan su información sobre una película y escojan la película que quieren ver.

[a]*dibujos... cartoons*

Una escena de *La historia oficial*

Un brindis por el futuro

En este episodio...

MARÍA

Mi mamá y my tío Paco piensan que tú podrás[a] ayudarnos a organizar el negocio[b] de la viña. Por un tiempo, por lo menos hasta que yo aprenda un poco.

JAIME

Y tú, ¿qué piensas?

---

[a]*could* [b]*business*

¿Qué crees tú?

1. Es evidente que María ya no le guarda rencor a Jaime. ¿Qué crees que hizo Jaime para que María volviera a hablarle?

2. ¿Crees que María está contenta con la idea de que Jaime se quede a trabajar en la viña?

3. ¿Qué crees que va a pasar con las relaciones entre Jaime y María?

Obligaciones, responsabilidades y expectativas[a]

LECCIÓN

9A

OBJETIVOS

IN THIS LESSON, YOU WILL LEARN:

- vocabulary related to our relationships with animals

- to talk about what you are looking for in someone or something by using the subjunctive with indefinite and nonexistent antecedents

- vocabulary related to talking about work behaviors and responsibilities

- to use the impersonal and the passive **se**

In addition, you will prepare for and watch **Episodio 9,** the final episode of the film *Sol y viento.*

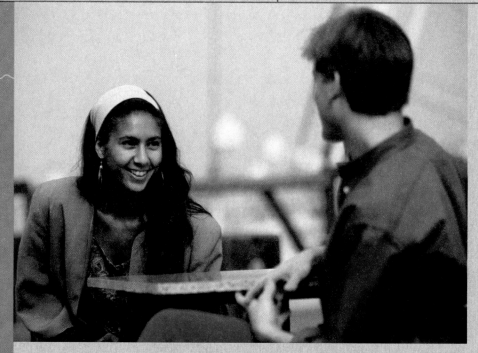

¿Qué nos hacen los buenos amigos? ¿Nos escuchan? ¿Nos consuelan (*do they comfort*) en momentos difíciles?

[a]*expectations*

The following media resources are available for this lesson of *Sol y viento:*

Episodio 9 of
Sol y viento

Online *Manual
de actividades*

Online Learning
Center Website

Note: These vocabulary items can be heard in this lesson's Textbook Audio section of the Online Learning Center Website.

Talking About Our Relationships with Animals

Vocabulario

Los animales   **Pets and Other Animals**

Las mascotas y otros animales

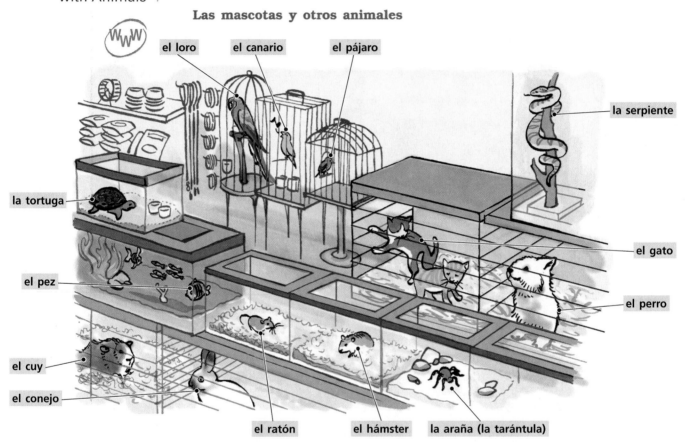

el loro   el canario   el pájaro

la serpiente

la tortuga

el gato

el pez

el perro

el cuy

el conejo

el ratón   el hámster   la araña (la tarántula)

Las acciones de las mascotas

aprender	to learn
morder (ue)	to bite (*animals*)
obedecer (zc)	to obey
picar (qu)	to bite (*insects*)
proteger (j)	to protect
ser (*irreg.*) **leal**	to be loyal
ser (*irreg.*) **obediente**	to be obedient
servir (i, i) de compañía	to give, keep company
volar (ue)	to fly
el comportamiento	behavior

Las acciones de los dueños

bañar	to bathe
cuidar	to take care of, care for
dar (*irreg.*) **de comer**	to feed
entrenar	to train
llevar al veterinario (a la veterinaria)	to take to the veterinarian
sacar (qu) a pasear	to take for a walk

 # Vistazo cultural

La llama

Además de las mascotas comunes como los perros, gatos, pájaros y peces, se usa la llama también como mascota en la región andina. La llama fue domesticada por los incas cerca del lago Titicaca alrededor de 4.000 a.C. En esa época la llama se usaba como medio de transporte y como ofrenda[a] de sacrificio en ceremonias religiosas. Además, la llama les proporcionaba a los incas lana, carne y fertilizantes. Se prohibía matar o dar caza[b] a la llama, y un grupo de pastores[c] empleados por el gobierno incáico controlaba su crianza.[d]

En el Perú, Bolivia y Chile la llama se sigue criando para la producción de lana y como medio de transporte, pero también se cría como mascota doméstica. Como mascota la llama es sociable y amistosa, pero puede ser muy cabezona. Si se le pone demasiada carga,[e] se detiene[f] completamente o se echa[g] en el camino.

▲ Unas llamas andinas

[a]*offering* [b]*dar... hunting* [c]*shepherds* [d]*breeding* [e]*weight* [f]*se... it stops* [g]*se... it lies down*

INPUT
Actividad A

Actividad A   Acciones

Indica el animal que se asocia mejor con cada acción.

1. volar   **a.** el ratón   **b.** el caballo   (**c.**) el loro
2. nadar   **a.** el cuy   (**b.**) el pez   **c.** el gato
3. picar   **a.** el hámster   **b.** el conejo   (**c.**) la tarántula
4. cantar   (**a.**) el canario   **b.** la serpiente   **c.** el pez
5. morder   **a.** la tortuga   (**b.**) el perro   **c.** la araña

INPUT/OUTPUT
Actividad B

¡Exprésate!

To talk about something being easy to care for, hard to train, and so forth, use the formula **ser** + *adjective* + **de** + *verb,* as in the following examples.

Las tortugas **son fáciles de cuidar.**

Los gatos **son difíciles de entrenar.**

Sin embargo, los perros **son fáciles de entrenar.**

Actividad B   ¿Qué animal?

Indica a qué animales se aplica cada acción a continuación. Puede haber más de una respuesta posible.

MODELO: Se llevan a la escuela de obediencia. → Los perros se llevan a la escuela de obediencia.

1. Son fáciles de cuidar.
2. Requieren visitas al veterinario (a la veterinaria).
3. Viven en jaulas (*cages*) o tanques.
4. Es costoso (*costly*) su mantenimiento (*maintenance*).
5. Es necesario bañarlos/las.
6. No sirven de buena compañía.
7. No es necesario darles de comer todos los días.
8. Hay que sacarlos/las a pasear.

INPUT/OUTPUT
Act. C,
Suggestion: Have groups present their suggestions and see if the class agrees.
Suggested follow-up: Ask the class to mention pets that would *not* be ideal for each person.

Actividad C   La mascota ideal

Con un compañero (una compañera), lean las descripciones a continuación e indiquen cuál es la mascota ideal para cada persona. ¿Puedes explicar por qué?

1. Trabajo todo el día y tengo que viajar los fines de semana. No tengo mucho tiempo para cuidar a una mascota.
2. Vivo en una zona peligrosa (*dangerous*) de la ciudad. Los ladrones (*thieves*) me han robado el auto y cosas de la casa. Necesito una mascota para protegerme.
3. Mi esposo murió hace un par (*a couple*) de años y ahora vivo sola. Pienso comprar una mascota para servirme de compañía.
4. Busco una mascota pero soy alérgico/a al pelo de los animales.
5. Tengo dificultad en dormir bien. Prefiero los animales que no hacen mucho ruido (*noise*).

Actividad D ¿Es miembro de la familia?

Paso 1 Indica si las siguientes oraciones sobre las mascotas son ciertas o falsas, según tu situación. (Si no tienes mascota, indica qué harías si tuvieras una.)

Mi mascota es como un miembro de la familia porque...	CIERTO	FALSO
1. me la llevo cuando hago un viaje.	☐	☐
2. le doy comida de la mesa.	☐	☐
3. la dejo dormir en la cama conmigo.	☐	☐
4. le doy un regalo en Navidad.	☐	☐
5. le hago una fiesta de cumpleaños.	☐	☐
6. me la llevo para hacer mandados (*run errands*).	☐	☐
7. le cuento mis problemas.	☐	☐
8. la incluyo en los retratos (*portraits*) de familia.	☐	☐

Paso 2 Entrevista a una persona de la clase usando las oraciones del **Paso 1** y apunta sus respuestas.

MODELO: me la llevo cuando hago un viaje →
¿Te llevas la mascota cuando haces un viaje?

Paso 3 Prepara un breve resumen en el cual indiques si tú y tu compañero/a de clase consideran a las mascotas como miembros de la familia.

MODELO: Yo considero a mi mascota como miembro de la familia porque... En cambio, Jason no considera a su mascota como miembro de su familia porque...

◀
¿Tienes mascota? ¿La consideras como miembro de tu familia?

Gramática

Quiero un perro que sea obediente.

Subjunctive with Indefinite and Nonexistent Antecedents

In Spanish, as in English, you can use simple adjectives to describe people and things, as in **Tengo un amigo sincero.** You can also use *adjective clauses* to describe the same people or things. In **Tengo un amigo que me escucha,** the clause **que me escucha** is called an adjective clause because, like the adjective **sincero,** it describes what kind of friend one has.

Notice that the sentence **Tengo un amigo que me escucha** has two clauses: a main clause **(Tengo un amigo)** and a dependent clause **(que me escucha).** The noun **amigo** in the main clause is called the *antecedent* because it precedes (*comes before*) the dependent clause, and the information in the dependent clause refers back to it.

Antecedents are either definite or indefinite. *Definite antecedents* refer to persons or things you know, have contact with, have seen before, and so forth. An *indefinite antecedent* is someone or something you are searching for, need, or want, and may or may not find (because you don't know if it exists or not). When the antecedent is definite, Spanish uses the indicative in the dependent clause. If the antecedent is indefinite, the verb in the dependent clause must be in the subjunctive, as indicated in the chart on the next page.

The subjunctive is also used in dependent clauses that are preceded by nonexistent or negated antecedents. A *nonexistent antecedent* is someone or something that does not exist or that is believed by the speaker not to exist.

> **No hay nadie** que **aprenda** un idioma en dos semanas.
>
> *There's no one that can learn a language in two weeks.*
>
> **No tenemos mascotas** que **hagan** trucos.
>
> *We don't have pets who can do tricks.*
>
> **No existen familias** que no **tengan** problemas.
>
> *No families exist that don't have problems.*

COMUNICACIÓN ÚTIL

In **Lección 6A** you learned the use of **haber** with present participles to form the present perfect indicative. The present perfect subjunctive is used in dependent clauses that require it. To form the present perfect subjunctive, use a subjunctive form of **haber** (**haya, hayas, haya, hayamos, hayáis,** or **hayan**) followed by a past participle.

Quiero conocer a una persona que **haya estudiado** en Panamá.

No conocemos a nadie que **haya probado** la carne de serpiente.

THE SUBJUNCTIVE WITH INDEFINITE ANTECEDENTS	
DEFINITE ANTECEDENT: INDICATIVE	INDEFINITE OR NEGATIVE ANTECEDENTS: SUBJUNCTIVE
Tengo una mascota que **cuesta** poco dinero mantener. *I have a pet that costs little money to maintain.*	Busco/Necesito una mascota que **cueste** poco dinero mantener. *I'm looking for / I need a pet that costs little money to maintain.*
Tengo un perro que **es** obediente. *I have a dog that's obedient.*	Prefiero tener un perro que **sea** obediente. *I prefer to have a dog that's obedient.*
Mi tía tiene un canario que **canta** bonito. *My aunt has a canary that sings beautifully.*	Quiero comprar un canario que **cante** bonito. *I want to buy a canary that sings beautifully.*
Hay mascotas que **son** fáciles de entrenar. *There are pets that are easy to train.*	¿Hay mascotas que **sean** fáciles de entrenar? *Are there pets that are easy to train?*
Tenemos un gato que no **necesita** mucho cuido. *We have a cat that doesn't need lots of care.*	No hay gatos que no **necesiten** mucho cuido. *There aren't any cats that don't need lots of care.*

De *Sol y viento,* Note: You can access this film clip from a special menu section on Disc 5 of the Instructional Version on DVD.

 **DE SOL Y VIENTO**

In **Episodio 9** of *Sol y viento,* you will hear a conversation in which don Paco asks María how she feels about taking a larger role in the operations of the winery. Part of their exchange follows.

PACO
Y tú, María, tendrás que estar más comprometida[a] con la viña e incluso hacerte cargo del[b] negocio. ¿Crees que podrás[c] hacerlo?

MARÍA
Oh, eh... No sé... Yo, de negocios... sé muy poco.

From the following options, indicate the type of person doña Isabel and don Paco need to run the winery. More than one answer may apply.

Necesitan una persona que...

1. sea honesta.
2. hable varios idiomas.
3. tenga un título en administración de empresas.
4. sepa mucho de finanzas.
5. ¿ ?

[a]tendrás... *you'll have to be more involved*   [b]hacerte... *running the*   [c]*you'll be able*

¡Exprésate!

In **Lección 3A** you learned that when the direct object of a verb is a person or pet, the personal **a** is required before the direct object, as in **Quiero mucho *a* mi abuelo.** However, the personal **a** is not used when the direct object is indefinite or hypothetical (nonexistent). Compare the following.

Busco **un** mecánico que **sepa** reparar autos importados.
Busco **al** mecánico que **sabe** reparar autos importados.

In the first example, the mechanic is an unknown person whom the speaker hopes exists. No personal **a** is necessary. In the second example, the speaker knows the mechanic exists and is looking for him. The personal **a** is required. Keep this in mind as you complete **Paso 2** of **Actividad F.**

Actividad E Es falso porque...

Paso 1 Cada una de estas oraciones sobre los personajes de *Sol y viento* es falsa. Explica por qué.

No hay ningún personaje que...
1. hable dos idiomas.
2. llore en una escena.
3. sepa lo que ha hecho Carlos.
4. se haya enamorado.
5. tenga interés en salvar la viña «Sol y viento».

Paso 2 Ahora inventa una oración parecida a las del **Paso 1** y léela a la clase. ¿Pueden decir los demás por qué tu oración es falsa?

Actividad F Mi compañero/a de casa

Paso 1 Escoge entre cada par de oraciones la que exprese mejor tu situación. Si no tienes compañero/a de casa, describe a alguien con quien has vivido en el pasado.

TENGO UN COMPAÑERO (UNA COMPAÑERA) DE CASA...	NO TENGO UN COMPAÑERO (UNA COMPAÑERA) DE CASA...
1. ☐ que se levanta temprano.	☐ que se levante temprano.
2. ☐ que fuma en el dormitorio.	☐ que fume en el dormitorio.
3. ☐ que se desvela (*stays up late*).	☐ que se desvele.
4. ☐ que habla por teléfono hasta muy tarde.	☐ que hable por teléfono hasta muy tarde.
5. ☐ que invita a su novio/a a pasar la noche.	☐ que invite a su novio/a a pasar la noche.
6. ☐ que limpia el baño y la cocina.	☐ que limpie el baño y la cocina.
7. ☐ que deja su ropa por todos lados.	☐ que deje su ropa por todos lados.
8. ☐ que pone la radio a todo volumen.	☐ que ponga la radio a todo volumen.

Paso 2 Con un compañero (una compañera) de clase, escriban cuatro oraciones usando el verbo **buscar** sobre el tipo de compañero/a de casa que buscan. Luego, presenten sus oraciones a la clase.

Actividad G   ¿Dónde quieres vivir?

Paso 1   Completa las siguientes oraciones con información verdadera para ti.

1. Tengo que vivir en una ciudad que tenga _____.
2. Espero vivir en una ciudad que esté cerca de _____.
3. Quiero vivir en una ciudad que ofrezca oportunidades para _____.
4. Busco una ciudad donde pueda _____.
5. Para mí, es importante vivir en una ciudad que no tenga _____.
6. Prefiero vivir en una ciudad que me permita _____.

Paso 2   Léele tu lista de oraciones a un compañero (una compañera) de clase. Basándose en tus respuestas, tu compañero/a va a recomendarte la ciudad ideal para ti.

MODELO: E1: Espero vivir en una ciudad que esté cerca de la playa.
E2: Debes vivir en San Diego o Miami.

Actividad H   La mascota ideal

Paso 1   Hazle las siguientes preguntas a un compañero (una compañera) de clase y apunta sus respuestas.

¿Prefieres una mascota que...

1. ...se quede en la jaula o que ande suelta (*runs loose*) en la casa?
2. ...cueste mucho o poco dinero mantener?
3. ...tengas que entrenar?
4. ...juegue contigo o que juegue solita (*by itself*)?
5. ...necesites bañar frecuentemente?
6. ...puedas abrazar y besar?
7. ...tengas que sacar a pasear todos los días?
8. ...te sirva de protección o compañía?
9. ...puedas dejar sola por un par de días?

Paso 2   Escribe un breve párrafo de cuatro o cinco oraciones en el cual indiques cuál es la mascota ideal para tu compañero/a de clase. Apoya tu opinión con evidencia de la entrevista.

Paso 3   Léele el párrafo a tu compañero/a. ¿Está de acuerdo con lo que dices? Si no, pídele que te explique por qué.

SEGUNDA PARTE

Note: These vocabulary items can be heard in this lesson's Textbook Audio section of the Online Learning Center Website.

Talking About Work
Responsibilities

Vocabulario

En el trabajo

Work Behaviors

Artemisa es **una empleada** modelo porque...

...llega a tiempo.

...**colabora** con los demás.

...felicita a sus **colegas**.

...**resuelve conflictos.**

...**respeta el espacio personal** de los demás.

...**comparte** (*she shares*) sus ideas.

...es **flexible.**

...**trabaja** bien **en equipo.**

Artemisa también es **cortés** (*courteous*), **justa** (*fair*), trabajadora, responsable, puntual, **tolerante,** paciente y **sociable.**

Arturo no es un buen empleado porque...

...cuenta chismes
(*he spreads gossip*).

...es **perezoso.**

...es pelotero (*a kiss-up*).

...les echa la culpa
(*blames*) a los demás.

...se mete (*he picks fights*)
con otros.

...se atribuye todo el mérito
(*he takes all the credit*).

Arturo también es muy **competidor** (*competitive*).

✱ MÁS VOCABULARIO

animar	to encourage
aprovecharse de	to take advantage of
cumplir las promesas	to keep one's word
gritar	to scream; to shout

Repaso: ayudar, competir (i, i), criticar (qu)

INPUT
Act. A, Statements:
1. *Respeta el espacio personal de los demás.* (Artemisa) 2. *Es tolerante y paciente.* (Artemisa) 3. *Se atribuye todo el mérito cuando hace un trabajo en equipo.* (Arturo)
4. *Felicita a sus compañeros cuando hacen un buen trabajo.* (Artemisa)
5. *Esta persona es pelotera.* (Arturo) 6. *Les echa la culpa de sus errores a los demás.* (Arturo) 7. *Sabe resolver conflictos.* (Artemisa)
8. *Se mete fácilmente con sus colegas.* (Arturo)

INPUT
Act. B, Statements:
1. *trabajar bien en equipo* 2. *aprovecharse de los demás* 3. *respetar el espacio personal de los demás* 4. *contar chismes* 5. *llegar a tiempo* 6. *echarles la culpa a otros*

OUTPUT
Act. D, Suggestions
Paso 1: Circulate to help with vocabulary and grammar. Allow about 5 minutes.
Paso 2: Allow about 5 minutes.
Follow-up: Ask students to present a description, then ask them if they know of any characters in film, literature, or TV who fit the profile. For example, ask them to name and describe the attributes of popular film or TV characters who work together.

Actividad A ¿Artemisa o Arturo?

Tu profesor(a) va a leer varias descripciones. Indica si cada una se refiere a Artemisa o a Arturo.

1. ... 2. ... 3. ... 4. ... 5. ... 6. ... 7. ... 8. ...

Actividad B ¿Qué adjetivo?

Tu profesor(a) va a mencionar algunas acciones. Indica el adjetivo que mejor califica (*illustrates*) cada acción. (Algunos de los adjetivos se presentaron en lecciones anteriores.)

1. **a.** tímido **(b.)** sociable **c.** introvertido
2. **(a.)** egoísta **b.** justo **c.** pelotero
3. **(a.)** cortés **b.** trabajador **c.** responsable
4. **a.** competidor **(b.)** indiscreto **c.** sensible
5. **a.** detallista **b.** tacaño **(c.)** puntual
6. **a.** resuelto **b.** porfiado **(c.)** engañador

Actividad C Antónimos

INPUT
Actividad C

Indica lo opuesto (*opposite*) de cada palabra o frase a la izquierda.

1. meterse con alguien **a.** gritar **(b.)** resolver conflictos
2. criticar **a.** ser pelotero **(b.)** animar
3. echar la culpa **a.** competir **(b.)** felicitar
4. competir **(a.)** trabajar en equipo **b.** respetar el espacio personal
5. ser puntual **(a.)** llegar tarde **b.** contar chismes
6. cumplir las promesas **a.** ayudar **(b.)** mentir
7. atribuirse todo el mérito **(a.)** colaborar **b.** ser perezoso

Actividad D ¿Qué atributo?

Paso 1 Escoge tres atributos de las páginas 508 a 509 y prepara una breve descripción para cada uno.

MODELO: trabaja bien en equipo → Si uno posee este atributo, la persona se lleva bien con otras personas. No intenta decirles qué hacer ni cómo hacerlo. Piensa que debe contribuir y no dirigir. Respeta a los demás.

Paso 2 Preséntale tus descripciones a un compañero (una compañera). ¿Puede deducir qué atributo describes?

OUTPUT
Actividad E

Actividad E ¿Es dedicado/a?

Paso 1 Haz una lista de seis a ocho preguntas para averiguar si una persona de la clase es dedicada al trabajo o no.

MODELOS: ¿Es importante para ti llegar al trabajo a tiempo?

¿Podrías trabajar horas extras gratis (*for free*)?

Paso 2 Entrevista a alguien de la clase con las preguntas que escribiste en el **Paso 1.**

Paso 3 Prepara un breve resumen en el cual indiques si tu compañero/a de clase es una persona dedicada en su trabajo. Apoya tu opinión con datos concretos de la entrevista.

MODELO: Jane es una persona bastante dedicada en su trabajo. Primero,...

Vistazo cultural,
Suggestion: Point out that the descriptions here are generalizations, but that there are general differences that some Hispanics note upon moving to this country. After students read, have them work in pairs to come up with a short list of differences between physical contact in this country and physical contact in the Hispanic world. Then, have them draw a conclusion: What does this suggest about values of or differences between the cultures?

≋ Vistazo cultural

El contacto físico

En general, los hispanos tienden a ser más expresivos en sus relaciones personales, y para ellos es natural el contacto físico con los otros. Seguramente has notado en los episodios de *Sol y viento* que los personajes se abrazan, se besan o se tocan de alguna manera en varias situaciones. De hecho, los hispanos expresan físicamente sus emociones y sentimientos en situaciones en que los norteamericanos no lo harían. En España, por ejemplo, las relaciones entre los profesores y los estudiantes tienden a ser menos formales, sobre todo en las clases pe-

▲ El contacto físico es más natural en las culturas hispanas.

queñas. Es común que un profesor le dé una palmada en la espalda[a] a un estudiante al saludarlo o que le tome el brazo al felicitarlo[b] por un trabajo bien hecho. ¿Te fijaste en el **Episodio 4** de *Sol y viento* cómo María le toca el hombro a su estudiante Diego mientras hablan? Tampoco se considera ofensa que un profesor haga bromas de[c] sus estudiantes. Debido a las cuestiones legales en cuanto al tema delicado del acoso[d] sexual, los profesores en este país deben evitar por completo el contacto físico con los estudiantes.

[a]dé... *gives a pat on the back* [b]*congratulating him* [c]haga... *makes jokes about* [d]*harassment*

Gramática

Talking About What
One Does

Se trabaja tarde cuando...

Impersonal and Passive se

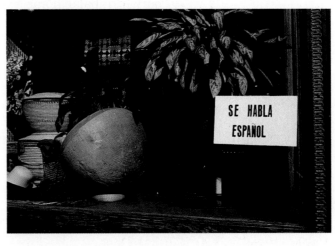

▲ ¿Has visto letreros (*signs*) como este? (Nueva York)

By now you have seen the pronoun **se** used in several constructions, including the use of **se** in impersonal sentences. In such sentences the verb is in the third-person singular, and the subject is not specified. In English, impersonal sentences include the nonspecific subject pronouns *one, you,* or *they.*

Se vive bien aquí.	*One lives well here.*
Se habla portugués en Brasil.	*They speak Portuguese in Brazil.*

It is important not to confuse this use of **se** with the reflexive or reciprocal reflexive constructions. Remember that those constructions are equivalent to *-self/-selves* or *each other.*

Se levanta a las seis todos los días.	*She gets up (gets herself up) at six every day.* (Reflexive **se**)
Se miran con admiración.	*They look at each other with admiration.* (Reciprocal **se**)

Se can also be used with third-person singular and plural verbs to make passive sentences. Passive sentences in English are formed with *is/are* + past participle, as in *My boss is paid well* or *Our employees are rigorously trained.*

Se aprende español con el tiempo.	*Spanish is learned over time.*
Se aprenden lenguas con práctica.	*Languages are learned with practice.*

In **Lección 7A** you learned the use of the passive **se** with indirect object pronouns to express unplanned or unexpected events that happen to someone.

Se me perdieron los lentes.	(lit.: *My glasses were lost to me* or *I lost my glasses.*)
Se me pinchó una rueda.	(lit.: *The tire went flat on me* or *I got a flat tire.*)

MORE USES OF *se* IN SPANISH	
IMPERSONAL **se** (SINGULAR)	PASSIVE **se** (SINGULAR OR PLURAL)
Se paga bien si **se trabaja** duro. *One gets paid well if one works hard.* *(You get paid well if you work hard).*	**Se firma** el contrato en la oficina. *The contract is signed in the office.*
Se entrena por un mes en esa compañía. *They train for one month in that company.*	**Se producen** buenos vinos en Chile. *Good wines are produced in Chile.*
PASSIVE *se* WITH INDIRECT OBJECT PRONOUNS	
Se me rompió un diente.	*I broke a tooth. (A tooth broke on me.)*
Se me cayeron los libros.	*I dropped my books. (My books fell on me.)*

De *Sol y viento,* Note: You can access this film clip from a special menu section on Disc 5 of the Instructional Version on DVD.

DE SOL Y VIENTO

In **Episodio 7** of *Sol y viento,* you saw Jaime in doña Isabel's parlor after he suffers a heat stroke. Part of their exchange follows.

PACO
¿Y por qué se vino caminando?

JAIME
Se nos ponchó* una rueda y... yo tenía
urgencia de hablar con la señora.

Now rewrite the dialogue between don Paco and Jaime, replacing the phrase **ponchar una rueda** with **acabar la gasolina** (*to run out of gas*). Which version of the event seems more credible?

---

*You may recall in this episode that Mario uses the verb **pinchar** when talking about the flat tire, whereas here Jaime uses the verb **ponchar.** This is yet another example of dialectal variance in the Spanish-speaking world, as both verbs mean the same thing.

Actividad F Se me...

Indica qué personaje de *Sol y viento* podría decir cada oración a continuación.

   1. Se me hizo tarde para la cita con Diego. María
   2. Se me arruinó el negocio de la viña. Carlos
   3. Se me cayeron los libros en el parque. María
   4. Se me presenta un problema, y tengo que hablar con mi hijo. doña Isabel
   5. Se me ha picado el corazón: creo que estoy enamorado. Jaime

Actividad G ¿Qué escuchaste?

Paso 1 Escucha el párrafo que lee tu profesor(a) a la clase. Vas a escuchar el párrafo dos veces. Trata de recordar la información, pero no tomes apuntes.

Paso 2 En grupos de tres, escriban una versión del párrafo para luego compartir con la clase.

Actividad H ¿Cómo se celebra?

Indica cuáles de las siguientes cosas se hacen para celebrar el cumpleaños de...

   a. ...alguien que conoces bien en el trabajo.
   b. ...alguien que no conoces bien en el trabajo.

   1. ___ Se le hace una fiesta en la oficina.
   2. ___ Se le da una tarjeta (*card*) firmada por todos, nada más.
   3. ___ Se le compra un pastel en el supermercado.
   4. ___ Se le hace un regalo barato.
   5. ___ Se le hace un regalo caro.
   6. ___ Se le canta «Feliz cumpleaños».
   7. ___ Se le paga un almuerzo en un restaurante.
   8. ___ Se le compra una cerveza después del trabajo.

▲ ¿Cómo se celebran los cumpleaños en la oficina típica?

INPUT/OUTPUT
Actividad I

¡Exprésate!

To make an impersonal statement with a reflexive verb or any other verb that already requires **se**, use the word **uno**.

Uno se levanta tarde los fines de semana.	*One gets up late on weekends.*
Uno se alegra cuando saca buenas notas.	*You get happy when you get good grades.*

Actividad I ¿Sabes qué hacer en el trabajo?

Con un compañero (una compañera) de clase, inventa dos situaciones para terminar cada oración. Luego comparen sus respuestas con las de otro grupo.

1. Se le puede gritar a un empleado si/cuando...
2. Se felicita a un colega de trabajo si/cuando...
3. Se despide a (*One fires*) un empleado si/cuando...
4. Se le ofrece ayuda a alguien en el trabajo si/cuando...

▲ ¿Cuándo se le puede gritar a un empleado?

Enfoque lingüístico,
Suggestion: After students read, tell them that they may have fewer problems interpreting reflexives compared to children because they already have an intuitive concept of reflexive. What will challenge them in Spanish is to interpret the correct functions and meanings of pronouns in context. This will take time.

⬤ Enfoque lingüístico

Cómo interpretan los pronombres reflexivos los niños

If it takes you a while to understand the function of all the pronouns in Spanish, don't be discouraged! Researchers have found that children may begin to utter multiword combinations between the ages of two and three while acquiring their native language, but they still have problems interpreting reflexive pronouns until around the age of five. In one study, children between the ages of two and a half to six and a half were given sentences such as "Barney points to himself" and were instructed to choose between two pictures: one of Barney pointing to himself while standing next to a friend and another of Barney pointing to his friend. Studies like these report that children make the correct interpretations around the age of five, but children who are four and under perform at about chance (50 percent correct). Why do younger children often misinterpret these reflexive pronouns? One possible explanation is that younger children initially interpret *himself* as a possessive construction, such as *his body* (i.e., someone else's body). It isn't until around the age of five that they understand that *himself* is really referring to the subject. If you know young children around this age, you may want to try this experiment!

NAVEGANDO LA RED

Busca un sitio en la red que tenga anuncios clasificados en español para trabajos profesionales. Escoge un anuncio y describe cómo debe ser (qué cualidades debe tener) la persona que lleva a cabo (*carries out*) el trabajo anunciado.

SOL Y VIENTO

A primera vista

Antes de ver el episodio

Actividad A ¿Qué recuerdas?

Contesta cada pregunta con información verdadera, según lo que sabes de *Sol y viento* hasta el momento.

1. ¿Qué palabra describe mejor la actitud de Carlos ante su hermana, María? ¿Está resentido, celoso o enojado Carlos?
2. ¿Cómo supo doña Isabel de los documentos falsificados por Carlos?
3. Jaime dijo que no lo invitaron a la recepción para degustar el vino. ¿Por qué fue, entonces?
4. Cuando doña Isabel confrontó a Carlos en el jardín, le dijo que le quedaban dos opciones. ¿Cuáles eran?
5. Al final del **Episodio 8,** don Paco dijo que María debía escuchar algo. ¿Qué debía escuchar?

Actividad B ¿Qué falta?

Lee la siguiente presentación (*introduction*) y brindis que da doña Isabel al principio del **Episodio 9.** ¿Puedes deducir las palabras y expresiones que faltan?

ISABEL: Señoras y señores: primero que nada, en nombre de mi __familia__,[1] quiero agradecer vuestra presencia en esta importante ocasión. Para la viña «Sol y viento», es un orgullo que Uds. la visiten. ¡Y espero que el vino que vamos a degustar esta noche __sea__[2] uno de los mejores que hayan probado en su vida! También les __quiero__[3] presentar a don Francisco Aguilar, gran amigo de nuestra familia y apreciado socio[a] de la viña «Sol y viento». Él ha venido desde México a probar nuestro vino. Bueno, sin más, les quiero __presentar__[4] nuestra nueva cosecha. ¡Salud!

[a]*partner*

Actividad C El episodio

Ahora mira el episodio. Si hay algo que no entiendes bien, puedes volver a ver la escena en cuestión.

Después de ver el episodio

Actividad A ¿Qué recuerdas?

Act. A, Answers:
1. *Quieren saber si es verdad que se vende la viña.*
2. *Paco anuncia que hay un nuevo contrato (acuerdo) para exportar el vino de «Sol y viento» y distribuirlo por toda Norteamérica.*

Contesta cada pregunta según lo que recuerdas del episodio.

1. ¿Qué preguntas hacen los vecinos e invitados? ¿Qué rumores han oído?

2. Don Paco hace un anuncio en público que para la familia implica la salvación de la viña. ¿Qué anuncia él?

Actividad B ¿Lo captaste?

Verifica tus respuestas para la **Actividad B** en **Antes de ver el episodio.** Puedes volver a ver la escena si es necesario.

Actividad C Usando el contexto

Act. C, Suggestion: Ask students the meaning of the italicized phrases. Students may or may not pick up on the forms they don't recognize (future tense), but they may get the general meaning. Contextual translations are as follow: 1. What's going on? (What's the truth?) 2. As long as I have a breath left in this body, nothing will happen to this winery nor to these lands! 3. Nothing is for sale here!

Utiliza el contexto y la situación para deducir el significado de las expresiones en letra cursiva. Puedes volver a ver esa parte del episodio si quieres.

> INVITADA: Isabel, ¿qué hay de los rumores de que van a vender «Sol y viento»?
> INVITADO: Yo también escuché algo así. *¿Qué hay de cierto?*[1]
> ISABEL: *Mientras me quede un soplo de vida, ¡no le pasará nada a esta viña ni a estas tierras!*[2] *¡Aquí no se venderá nada!*[3]

1. ...   2. ...   3. ...

Actividad D En resumen

Completa la siguiente narración con las palabras y expresiones apropiadas de la lista a la derecha.

Ya sabes que, antes de comenzar la recepción para degustar el vino de la nueva cosecha de «Sol y viento», don Paco le habla a María. Le __dice__[1] que escuche a su corazón y que no se guíe solamente __por__[2] su cerebro.

La degustación del vino empieza con una presentación de doña Isabel. __Les__[3] da a los invitados la bienvenida[a] y luego hace un brindis por la nueva cosecha. Después de probar el vino, algunos vecinos le preguntan sobre algunos rumores que circulan de que __se vende__[4] la viña. Doña Isabel, con aire de mujer decidida, dice: «__Mientras__[5] me quede un soplo de vida, no se venderá nada.»

dice
les
mientras
por
se vende

[a]da... *she welcomes the guests*

Detrás de la cámara

You probably noticed in **Episodio 8** of *Sol y viento* that María is not in total control of her destiny with Jaime. By inviting Jaime to the reception, don Paco and doña Isabel are conspiring to bring him and María together. They know that Jaime is right for María, even if she does not. As you approach the end of the movie, remember that *Sol y viento* is a story about harmony between the land and the peoples who inhabit it. In this story, individuals do not wholly control their destinies, and Jaime's and María's lives are part of a chain of inevitable events.

RESUMEN DE VOCABULARIO

Las mascotas y otros animales

la araña	spider
el conejo	rabbit
el cuy	guinea pig
el loro	parrot
el pájaro	bird
el pez (*pl.* **los peces**)	fish
el ratón	mouse
la serpiente	snake
la tortuga	turtle

Cognados: el canario, el hámster, la tarántula
Repaso: el/la dueño/a, el gato, el perro

Las acciones y las mascotas

cuidar	to take care of, care for
dar (*irreg.*) **de comer**	to feed
entrenar	to train
llevar al veterinario (**a la veterinaria**)	to take to the veterinarian
morder (**ue**)	to bite (*animals*)
picar (**qu**)	to bite (*insects*)
sacar (**qu**) **a pasear**	to take for a walk
servir (**i, i**) **de compañía**	to give, keep company
volar (**ue**)	to fly
el comportamiento	behavior

Repaso: aprender, bañar, obedecer (zc), proteger (j); leal, obediente

En el trabajo

animar	to encourage
aprovecharse de	to take advantage of
atribuirse (y) todo el mérito	to take all the credit
compartir	to share
contar (**ue**) **chismes**	to spread gossip
cumplir las promesas	to keep one's word
echar(le) la culpa (**a alguien**)	to blame (someone)
gritar	to scream; to shout
meterse	to pick a fight
renunciar a	to quit (*a job*)
ser (*irreg.*) **pelotero/a**	to be a kiss-up
trabajar en equipo	to work as a team
el/la empleado/a	employee
competidor(a)	competitive
cortés	courteous
justo/a	fair
perezoso/a	lazy

Cognados: colaborar, resolver (ue) conflictos, respetar el espacio personal; el/la colega; flexible, sociable, tolerante
Repaso: ayudar, competir (i, i), criticar (qu), felicitar, llegar (gu) a tiempo/tarde; paciente, puntual, responsable, trabajador(a)

LECCIÓN

9B

Lo que nos espera

OBJETIVOS

IN THIS LESSON, YOU WILL LEARN:

- vocabulary related to professions
- how to talk about future events with the future tense
- to talk about traits useful or necessary for particular jobs
- to discuss what your own future aspirations are

In addition, you will watch the final episode of the film *Sol y viento* again.

¿Qué piensas hacer después de graduarte? ¿Quieres ser hombre o mujer de negocios (*a businessman or businesswoman*)? ¿O piensas hacer estudios posgrados?

The following media resources are available for this lesson of *Sol y viento*:

Episodio 9 of *Sol y viento*

Online *Manual de actividades*

Online Learning Center Website

PRIMERA PARTE

Vocabulario

✳

Talking About Jobs
and Professions

Note: These vocabulary items can be heard in this lesson's Textbook Audio section of the Online Learning Center Website.

Las profesiones

Professions

Las profesiones y los oficios[a]	
la arquitectura	el/la arquitecto/a
el arte	el/la escultor(a) (*sculptor*), el/la pintor(a)
las ciencias	el/la astrónomo/a, el/la biólogo/a, el/la científico/a, el/la físico/a (*physicist*), el químico (la mujer química)
la computación (*computer programming*)	el/la diseñador(a) de sitios (*Web designer*), el/la programador(a), el/la técnico/a
el derecho (*law*)	el/la abogado/a (*lawyer*), el/la juez(a) (*judge*)
la enseñanza (*education*)	el/la bibliotecario/a (*librarian*), el/la maestro/a (*teacher*) (de primaria/secundaria), el/la profesor(a)
el gobierno	el político (la mujer político), el/la representante, el/la senador(a), el soldado (la mujer soldado) (*soldier*)
la ingeniería	el/la ingeniero/a (civil, eléctrico/a, mecánico/a)
los medios de comunicación	el actor (la actriz), el/la director(a), el/la fotógrafo/a, el/la periodista (*journalist*), el/la productor(a)
los negocios, la contabilidad y el mercadeo (*marketing*)	el/la analista de sistemas, el/la contador(a) (*accountant*), el hombre (la mujer) de negocios (*businessman, businesswoman*)
los servicios médicos	el/la dentista, el/la enfermero/a, el/la farmacéutico/a, el/la médico/a, el/la psicólogo/a, el/la psiquiatra, el/la terapeuta, el/la veterinario/a
los servicios sociales	el/la trabajador(a) social

[a]*trades*

MÁS VOCABULARIO

el/la asesor(a)	consultant
el/la ayudante	assistant
el/la especialista	specialist
dirigir (j) a los demás	to direct others
pensar (ie) de manera directa	to think in a direct (linear) manner
ser (*irreg.*) **hábil para (las matemáticas, las ciencias)**	to be good at (math, science)
tener (*irreg.*) **don de gentes**	to have a way with people

Vistazo cultural

Las mujeres y las profesiones

Con la entrada de la mujer en el mundo profesional durante el siglo pasado, los hispanohablantes se enfrentaron[a] con un problema lingüístico: el sistema relacionado con el género. Como ya sabes, el español distingue el género de muchas palabras por su terminación, por ejemplo, **un chico** y **una chica**, **un profesor** y **una profesora**. En cuanto a los términos nuevamente incorporados en el diccionario para referirse a las profesiones y oficios de mujeres, este sistema no es tan transparente. Por ejemplo, las palabras que terminan en **-ista** no tienen ningún cambio: **el dentista** y **la dentista**. Pero en cuanto al uso de otros términos hay cierta incertidumbre[b] entre muchos hablantes nativos. En el caso de **médico,** se oye **la médica** pero también **la médico.** Lo mismo pasa con **piloto: la pilota** y **la piloto.** En los casos en que pueda haber confusión, se le agrega[c] la palabra **mujer** al término: **la mujer soldado.** En fin, el hecho de que la distinción genérica sea una característica del español puede ocasionar dudas cuando la sociedad experimenta[d] cambios. Claro, en inglés esto no ocurre porque el inglés no representa el género gramaticalmente y se puede crear nuevas palabras para evitarlo: *steward, stewardess → flight attendant; waiter, waitress → server.*

▲ Una científica española en su laboratorio

[a]*se... were faced* [b]*uncertainty* [c]*se... is added* [d]*experiences*

INPUT

Act. A, Statements

Paso 1: 1. *el periodista* 2. *la abogada* 3. *el psicólogo* 4. *la escultora*

Paso 2: 1. *los negocios* 2. *la enseñanza* 3. *la computación* 4. *los servicios sociales*

Actividad A Asociaciones

Paso 1 Indica el campo (*field*) al que pertenece la profesión que menciona tu profesor(a).

1. **a.** el arte **b.** los servicios sociales **c.** los medios de comunicación
2. **a.** el derecho **b.** las ciencias **c.** el gobierno
3. **a.** la computación **b.** los servicios médicos **c.** la ingeniería
4. **a.** el arte **b.** la enseñanza **c.** el mercadeo

Paso 2 Ahora indica la profesión a la que pertenece el campo que menciona tu profesor(a).

1. **a.** el senador **b.** el contador **c.** la actriz
2. **a.** la maestra **b.** el pintor **c.** el enfermero
3. **a.** el físico **b.** el fotógrafo **c.** la diseñadora de sitios
4. **a.** la trabajadora social **b.** el periodista **c.** el bibliotecario

Actividad B ¿Qué actor? ¿Qué película?

Escucha la profesión que menciona tu profesor(a). ¿Puedes nombrar un actor (una actriz) que haya hecho ese papel en una película? ¿Qué película?

MODELO: (oyes) psiquiatra
(dices) Billy Crystal hizo el papel de un psiquiatra en *Analyze This*.

1. ... **2.** ... **3.** ... **4.** ... **5.** ... **6.** ... **7.** ... **8.** ... **9.** ... **10.** ...

INPUT

Act. B., Note: Tell students to listen carefully for gender! If they offer an actor for something like *profesora*, tell them: *No. Dije «profesora», no dije «profesor»*. For ambiguous gender, accept either, then probe to get examples for the other gender.

Statements:
1. *abogada* 2. *astrónoma* 3. *soldado* 4. *pintora* 5. *maestra de secundaria* 6. *enfermero* 7. *periodista* 8. *actriz* 9. *hombre de negocios* 10. *dentista*

Follow-up: Select a well-known actor or actress who has a long history and see how many professions students can name that the person has played on the screen (e.g., Meryl Streep, Jodie Foster, Julia Roberts, Russell Crowe).

Actividad C En la televisión

En la **Actividad B,** exploraste las profesiones en el cine. Esta vez, vas a concentrarte en la televisión. En grupos de dos, uno debe mencionar un programa televisivo, actual (*current*) o del pasado. La otra persona debe indicar qué profesión era prominente en ese programa. Deben hacerse turnos y cada persona debe mencionar por lo menos cuatro programas.

MODELO: E1: *Bewitched*
E2: El mercadeo y los anuncios. Darren trabajaba para una compañía de mercadeo.

OUTPUT

Act. C, Suggestion: Circulate to help with vocabulary. After students finish, call upon them to present some of the more difficult ones for the class.

Follow-up: If none of the following are mentioned, ask the class yourself or make up your own:
1. *M*A*S*H* (Hawkeye y B.J. eran soldados en Corea) 2. *The Golden Girls* (Dorothy era una maestra de secundaria) 3. *The West Wing* (todos trabajaban en el gobierno, eran políticos o ayudantes de políticos) 4. *The Brady Bunch* (el señor Brady era arquitecto) 5. *Bob Newhart* (Bob era psicólogo; su buen amigo Jerry era dentista)

OUTPUT
Actividad D

Actividad D ¿Qué piensas hacer?

Paso 1 Indica si cada afirmación te describe o no.

	ME DESCRIBE.	NO ME DESCRIBE.
1. Tengo don de gentes.	☐	☐
2. Pienso de manera directa.	☐	☐
3. Soy comprensivo/a.	☐	☐
4. Soy paciente.	☐	☐
5. Soy hábil para las matemáticas.	☐	☐
6. Sé dirigir a los demás.	☐	☐
7. Sé expresarme bien.	☐	☐

Paso 2 Ahora busca a personas que contestaron **Me describe** a por lo menos cuatro de las siete oraciones del **Paso 1.**

MODELO: ¿Piensas de manera directa?

Paso 3 Con un compañero (una compañera), compartan las ideas que tienen para una profesión futura. ¿Tienen algo en común? ¿Hay correspondencia entre las profesiones elegidas y la personalidad de cada uno/a de Uds.?

Enfoque cultural,
Suggested follow-up: Ask students how they think a Spanish speaker of their age would address the following: *un perro, un policía, una mesera, un taxista, un tío de otro país que conoces por primera vez.* Have students survey some Spanish speakers using those items and any others they think of. What do they find out?

SOL Y VIENTO: Enfoque cultural

En el **Episodio 9** Jaime tiene un problema con el uso de **tú** y **usted.** Acostumbrado a tratar de **tú** (tratamiento de confianza) a María, le cuesta[a] tratarla de **usted** (tratamiento de distancia) después de que ella puso distancia entre ellos, y él quiere decirle que siente mucho lo que ha pasado. Poco después, tiene que preguntarle a María si pueden volver a tutearse.

El uso de **tú** y **usted** en el mundo hispano no es igual de un país a otro. Claro, hay usos que son casi universales, como ocurre cuando un joven se dirige a una mujer mayor de edad, en cuyo[b] caso es indispensable el uso de **usted.** Lo mismo ocurre al dirigirse a una persona de más respetabilidad que la persona que habla, por ejemplo entre estudiantes y profesores: se da el trato de **usted** al profesor, aunque este llame de **tú** al estudiante.

Al hablar de las variaciones en el uso de **tú** frente a **usted,** es de mencionar que en España, por ejemplo, se utiliza **tú** en casos en los que en México y el Perú predomina el uso de **usted.** En algunos países, los miembros de una familia, incluyendo a los abuelos, se tratan de **usted,** mientras que en otras todos los familiares se tutean. Cuando lees algo en español que se dirige al lector, ya sea un artículo o un anuncio, algunas veces verás[c] que se usa **tú,** y en otras, **usted.**

[a]le... *it's hard for him* [b]*whose* [c]*you'll see*

Gramática

¿Qué pasará?　　　　　Introduction to the Future Tense

You have learned to express future events in several ways in Spanish.

simple present:	Mañana me **voy** para España.
	Tomorrow I'm going to Spain.
ir + **a** + *infinitive:*	**Voy a trabajar** esta noche.
	I'm going to work tonight.
pensar + *infinitive:*	**Pienso estudiar** un año más.
	I think I'll study another year.
subjunctive:	**No creo que llegue** Juan esta tarde.
	I don't think Juan will arrive this afternoon.

In addition to the aforementioned constructions, Spanish also uses the simple *future tense.* Unlike the English future, which requires the auxiliary verb *will,* no auxiliary is needed in Spanish. The simple future is formed by using the infinitive as the stem and adding future-tense endings. The endings are the same for **-ar** and **-er/-ir** verbs.

estudiar + **é** = estudiar**é**	*I will study*
comer + **é** = comer**é**	*I will eat*
dirigir + **é** = dirigir**é**	*I will direct*

Verbs that have irregular stems in the conditional have the same irregular stems in the future tense. As happens with the conditional, these verbs are irregular in their stems only; all endings are the same as those for regular verbs.

COMUNICACIÓN ÚTIL

The simple future tense can also be used to express conjecture about what is going on at the present time.

¿Dónde **estará** César?	*Where can César be? (I wonder where César is.)*
Estará para llegar.	*He must be about to arrive.*
¿En qué **trabajará**?	*I wonder what his job is.*

FUTURE FORMS (REGULAR VERBS)					
trabajar		**ser**		**ir**	
trabajar**é**	trabajar**emos**	ser**é**	ser**emos**	ir**é**	ir**emos**
trabajar**ás**	trabajar**éis**	ser**ás**	ser**éis**	ir**ás**	ir**éis**
trabajar**á**	trabajar**án**	ser**á**	ser**án**	ir**á**	ir**án**
trabajar**á**	trabajar**án**	ser**á**	ser**án**	ir**á**	ir**án**
IRREGULAR FUTURE FORMS					

decir: **dir-**
haber: **habr-**
hacer: **har-**
poder: **podr-**
poner: **pondr-**   +   -é   -emos
querer: **querr-**   -ás   -éis
saber: **sabr-**   -á   -án
salir: **saldr-**   -á   -án
tener: **tendr-**
venir: **vendr-**

De *Sol y viento,* **Note:** You can access this film clip from a special menu section on Disc 5 of the Instructional Version on DVD.

DE SOL Y VIENTO

In the final episode of *Sol y viento,* don Paco proposes something important to María and doña Isabel, but he also talks to María about her future involvement with the winery. Read the following exchange and insert the verbs **tendrás** and **podrás** into the correct blanks.

PACO
Y tú, María, __tendrás__[1] que estar más comprometida[a] con la viña e incluso hacerte cargo del[b] negocio. ¿Crees que __podrás__[2] hacerlo?

MARÍA
Oh, eh... No sé... Yo, de negocios... sé muy poco.

[a]*involved* [b]hacerte... *taking charge of the*

Actividad E ¿Probable o no?

Indica si crees que cada oración es probable o no.

	ES PROBABLE.	NO ES PROBABLE.
1. Jaime se quedará en Chile por el resto de su vida.	☐	☐
2. Carlos volverá a la viña algún día.	☐	☐
3. Doña Isabel perdonará a Carlos.	☐	☐
4. María y Jaime se casarán.	☐	☐
5. Traimaqueo asumirá más responsabilidades en la viña.	☐	☐
6. Don Paco invertirá dinero en la viña.	☐	☐
7. María dejará de ser profesora.	☐	☐

¡Exprésate!

You can use the future tense in *if/then* statements to tell under what conditions something might happen or to offer advice. This will be useful in some of the activities in this section.

Si dejas de fumar, **gozarás** de mejor salud.	*If you quit smoking, you'll enjoy better health.*
Si quieres ser médico, no **tendrás** vida social mientras estudias.	*If you want to be a doctor, you won't have a social life during your studies.*

Actividad F En el futuro

Indica en qué tipo de profesión una persona tendrá las siguientes experiencias en el futuro. Puede haber más de una posibilidad para cada oración.

Si una persona desea ser _____,...

1. ...ayudará a muchas personas.

2. ...pasará mucho tiempo en un laboratorio.

3. ...tendrá que practicar la habilidad de escuchar.

4. ...nunca ganará mucho dinero.

5. ...le será difícil tener vida social al principio.

6. ...necesitará un compañero (una compañera) de vida comprensivo/a.

7. ...pasará mucho tiempo sentada (*seated*).

◄

¿Qué pasará entre Jaime y María?
¿Se quedará Jaime en Chile?

Actividad G   Una historia

Paso 1   Con un compañero (una compañera), escriban una historia de seis a ocho oraciones que describe lo que pasa en los siguientes dibujos. A continuación hay algunas ideas para considerar.

■   ¿Cómo se llama el muchacho? ¿Qué edad tiene? ¿Con quién habla?

■   ¿Qué son las cosas que le pasarán en el futuro?

Paso 2   Compartan su historia con el resto de la clase. ¿Quiénes inventaron la mejor historia?

Actividad H   Si dejas de (*you quit*)...   OUTPUT

Actividad H

Paso 1   Escribe tres oraciones sobre algo que haces con frecuencia.

M O D E L O :   Compro mucha ropa. Me gusta mucho estar de moda (*in style*).

Paso 2   Pásale tus oraciones a otra persona, quien escribirá algo que te podrá pasar si dejas de hacer esa actividad. Luego, esa persona le pasará tus oraciones a una tercera persona, quien añadirá algo más sobre lo que has escrito.

M O D E L O :   Si dejas de preocuparte tanto por la moda, tendrás dinero para otras cosas...

Paso 3   Al final, alguien debe devolverte las oraciones con las ideas escritas por las otras personas. ¿Estás de acuerdo con lo que te dicen tus compañeros? ¿Vas a seguir sus consejos?

Note: These vocabulary items can be heard in this lesson's Textbook Audio section of the Online Learning Center Website.

Talking About Goals and Aspirations

Vocabulario

Mis metas personales

Future Aspirations

Las metas[a] **y aspiraciones**		ᵃLas... *Goals*
el deseo	desire	
el doctorado	doctorate	
los estudios de posgrado	graduate studies	
la maestría	master's (degree)	
el triunfo	triumph	
de corto/largo plazo	short/long term	

alcanzar (c) (una meta)	to reach, achieve (a goal)
instalarse en	to settle into (*a house*)
jubilarse	to retire
jurar	to vow; to swear
lograr + *infin.*	to succeed (*in doing something*)
prometer	to promise
realizar (c)	to accomplish

Repaso: cambiar, casarse, graduarse (me gradúo), mudarse, tener (*irreg.*) **éxito**

Vistazo cultural,
Suggestion: After students read, have them give the order from highest to lowest for graduation rates. They should do so without looking, e.g., *Pongan los grupos en orden, del grupo con la tasa más alta de graduación al grupo con la menos alta tasa de graduación.* Order is: *asiático-americanos* (79%), *blancos* (76%), *nativo-americanos* (57%), *afro-americanos* (55%), *hispanos* (53%).
Follow-up: Have them search the Internet to find graduation rates for the following countries: Spain, Mexico, Peru, Costa Rica. What do they find? How do the figures compare with those of Hispanics in the U.S.?

 # Vistazo cultural

Los hispanos y la tasa de graduación

S egún un estudio realizado por el Instituto Manhattan, las tasas de graduación de la escuela secundaria revelan ciertas tendencias. La tasa de graduación para los jóvenes norteamericanos en general es del 69%. Es decir, aproximadamente el 30% de personas no se gradúa de la escuela secundaria. ¿Cómo es la tasa entre la población hispana de los Estados Unidos? Los resultados del estudio revelan que, en comparación con el promedio[a] nacional, sólo un 53% de las personas identificadas como *hispanas* se gradúa. Esta cifra[b] debe compararse con otros grupos étnicos: la población blanca, 76%; la población asiático-americana, 79%, la población afroamericana, 55% y la población nativo-americana, 57%. Claro, la gran pregunta es: «¿Por qué se gradúan menos latinos?» Esta pregunta merece ser estudiada.

▲ Esta estudiante hispana ha tenido éxito en sus estudios y se gradúa con honores.

[a]*average* [b]*number*

Actividad A El estudiante típico

Paso 1 Indica si las siguientes afirmaciones son metas personales para el estudiante universitario típico.

1. ☐ Desea graduarse en cuatro años.
2. ☐ Quiere hacerse rico y famoso.
3. ☐ No quiere casarse hasta tener un buen trabajo y un sueldo estable.
4. ☐ Piensa hacer estudios de posgrado.
5. ☐ Después de graduarse, se mudará fuera de su ciudad de origen.
6. ☐ Piensa jubilarse a los 55 años.
7. ☐ Tendrá una familia numerosa con muchos hijos.

Paso 2 Comparte tus respuestas con las de los demás miembros de la clase. ¿Cuáles son las metas más seleccionadas? La clase debe determinar cuál de las siguientes oraciones representa mejor las metas del estudiante universitario típico.

☐ Tiene metas de corto plazo solamente.
☐ Tiene metas de corto y largo plazo.

Actividad B Metas personales

Entrevista a otra persona de la clase, utilizando las preguntas a continuación como guía. Apunta lo que dice y luego escribe un párrafo de 50 a 100 palabras en el que describas sus metas.

1. ¿Cuáles son tus metas de corto plazo, por ejemplo, para los próximos dos o tres años?
2. ¿Cuáles son tus metas de largo plazo? Por ejemplo, ¿cómo ves tu vida en diez años?

◄ ¿Cuáles son las metas de corto plazo que tienen don Paco y la familia Sánchez?

◄ ¿Y Jaime y María? ¿Tienen metas personales de largo plazo? ¿Cuáles son?

Enfoque lingüístico

El futuro del español

Spanish is the most studied foreign language in the United States. According to the most recent information from the American Council on the Teaching of Foreign Languages (ACTFL), 69% of the high school students who study a language in the U.S. select Spanish. The next most popular language is French, at 18%. The statistics are similar for the college and university level. Figures are unavailable for elementary school, adult evening school, private language institutes, and institutes funded by Spanish-speaking governments (such as the *Instituto Cervantes,* a worldwide program run by the Spanish government for teaching language and culture). Spanish is also one of the most studied languages in other countries, such as Japan and China. Why is the study of Spanish so popular?

As a student who has chosen to study Spanish, you can probably answer this best, but here is a statistic you may not know. In the last U.S. census, over 35 million people identified themselves as being of Hispanic heritage. Of that population, approximately 28 million claimed Spanish as a first or bilingual language. Given that the majority of these speakers are concentrated in California and the Southwest, Chicago, Florida, and the Eastern Metropolitan area from Boston to Washington D.C., the impression one gets is that Spanish is rapidly becoming a second language in *this* country. However, given the current population of the U.S., the figures suggest that only about 10% of the U.S. population speaks Spanish as a heritage language. Spanish is strong in this country, but it is far from invading and taking over as a dominant language, as some might claim. Nonetheless, its importance as a world language continues to grow as people recognize the economic and political power of the collection of 21 countries that claim Spanish as an official language.

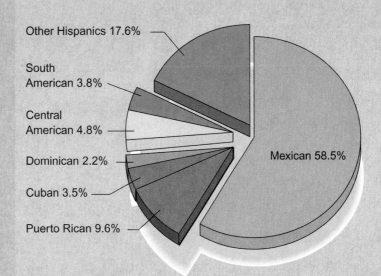

Comparing origins of U.S. Hispanic populations
Total population based on U.S. census, 2000 estimate* 35.3 million

Other Hispanics 17.6%

South American 3.8%

Central American 4.8%

Dominican 2.2%

Cuban 3.5%

Puerto Rican 9.6%

Mexican 58.5%

* Source: Census Bureau. The Hispanic Population:
Information from the 2000 Census.

Gramática

More on Talking
About the Future

No estaré contento hasta que...

**Subjunctive with
Future Time Events**

The subjunctive is generally used in what are called *adverbial clauses* when the event expressed is projected in the future. An adverbial clause is any clause that begins with an adverb of time such as those in the **Más vocabulario** box. Examine the chart on the following page, in which sentences with the indicative and subjunctive are contrasted.

Note that when the present indicative is used, the meaning is one of habituality; that is, how things tend to be. These are repeated events.* When the preterite is used, the situation is one of completed actions in the past; hence, no future meaning is intended. The use of the subjunctive, however, expresses a one-time action that has yet to occur.

Contrast the examples below.

Necesitas llamar al jefe **tan pronto como recibe** un mensaje.

You need to call the boss as soon as he gets a message. (Meaning: This is something you do every day; it is part of a job description)

Necesitas llamar al jefe **tan pronto como reciba** el mensaje del presidente.

You need to call the boss as soon as he gets the message from the president. (Meaning: This one time, if the boss gets a message from the president, you need to let him know)

See if you can explain the difference between the following two examples and offer contexts in which they might be said.

Debo depositar el dinero tan pronto como lo **recibo.**

Debo depositar el dinero tan pronto como lo **reciba.**

✳ **MÁS VOCABULARIO**

cuando	when
después (de) que	after
en cuanto	as soon as
hasta que	until
mientras	while, as long as
tan pronto como	as soon as

---

*The same is true for repeated events in the past expressed by the imperfect: **Lo hacía cuando podía.**
(*I always did it when I could.*)

THE SUBJUNCTIVE WITH ADVERBIAL CLAUSES	
INDICATIVE	SUBJUNCTIVE
Siempre lo **hago** cuando **puedo.** *I always do it when I can.*	Lo **haré** cuando **pueda.** *I will do it when I can (get to it).*
Carmen **tiene que trabajar** hasta que **llega** otra persona. *Carmen has to work until someone else comes in.*	Carmen **tendrá que trabajar** hasta que **llegue** otra persona. *Carmen will have to work until someone else comes in.*
Llamé a Rodolfo después de que **volvió** Victoria. *I called Rodolfo when Victoria returned.*	**Voy a llamar** a Rodolfo en cuanto **vuelva** Victoria. *I'm going to call Rodolfo as soon as Victoria returns.*

De *Sol y viento,* Note: You can access this film clip from a special menu section on Disc 5 of the Instructional Version on DVD.

DE SOL Y VIENTO

In the final episode of *Sol y viento,* the Sánchez family hosts a party to taste a special wine. Some guests ask doña Isabel about rumors they've heard. Read the exchange and then answer the question that follows.

INVITADA
Isabel, ¿qué hay de los rumores de que van a vender «Sol y viento»?

INVITADO
Yo también escuché algo así. ¿Qué hay de cierto?

ISABEL
_____ me quede un soplo de vida, ¡no le pasará nada a esta viña ni a estas tierras! ¡Aquí no se venderá nada!

Which word best completes doña Isabel's statement?

1. Hasta   **2.** Mientras   **3.** En cuanto

Actividad C   ¿Sí o no?

Indica cuál de las afirmaciones crees que es más probable.

1. Mientras María aprenda a manejar los negocios, Jaime ayudará a la familia.

2. Don Paco se quedará en Chile hasta que encuentren a una persona que ayude con los negocios de «Sol y viento».

Actividad D   ¿Quién lo diría?

Indica quién de la lista a continuación diría cada oración.

    a. una mujer de negocios   **c.** un estudiante de 21 años
    b. un perro   **d.** el dueño del perro

1. _a_ Podré jubilarme cuando tenga 55 años.
2. _c_ No podré comprar un auto hasta que termine de pagar mis deudas de la universidad.
3. _b_ Cuando lleguen los invitados, me voy a comportar como un ángel.
4. _d_ Cuando lleguen los invitados, no quiero que hagas mucho ruido.
5. _b, d_ Después de que comamos, saldremos a dar un paseo.
6. _b_ Me levantaré en cuanto oiga el auto de mi dueño.
7. _c_ No pienso tener hijos hasta que tenga una situación económica estable.
8. _d_ Tan pronto como volvamos del parque, te daré de comer.
9. _a_ Firmarán el contrato sólo cuando estén convencidos de los beneficios de trabajar con nosotros.

Actividad E Lo normal y lo que pienso hacer

Paso 1 Indica si las acciones a continuación son cosas que haces normalmente.

1. ☐ Pago una cuenta tan pronto como la recibo.
2. ☐ Reviso (*I look over*) un examen bien cuando me lo devuelven (*they return*).
3. ☐ Estudio para un examen hasta que tengo sueño y necesito dormir.
4. ☐ Salgo con mis amigos sólo después de que he terminado mis tareas.

Paso 2 Ahora indica si las acciones a continuación son cosas que piensas hacer.

1. ☐ Pagaré los préstamos y cuentas de la universidad tan pronto como me gradúe.
2. ☐ Revisaré muy bien el próximo examen cuando me lo devuelvan.
3. ☐ Para el próximo examen, estudiaré hasta que tenga sueño y necesite dormir.
4. ☐ Esta noche saldré con mis amigos sólo después de que haya terminado mis tareas.

Actividad F ¿Bajo qué condiciones?

Paso 1 Completa la siguiente oración con algo verdadero para ti.

No voy a estar contento/a con mi vida hasta que _____.

Paso 2 Comparte con la clase lo que escribiste. ¿Cuántos ponen una condición a base de...

1. ____ lo económico?
2. ____ la vida familiar?
3. ____ las relaciones con otra persona?
4. ____ alguna contribución a la sociedad?
5. ____ ¿otra cosa?

¿Qué revelan las respuestas de las metas de los miembros de la clase?

NAVEGANDO LA RED

Busca un sitio en español que describa algún programa de estudios de posgrado que te gustaría completar. Imprime la página con la descripción de los requisitos del programa. Luego, escribe cinco oraciones en las que describes qué necesitas hacer para o cómo lograrías entrar en el programa.

MODELO: se requieren por lo menos tres años de estudios avanzados en y buen conocimiento de la lengua española →
En cuanto haya estudiado dos años o más del español, podré entrar en el programa.

SOL Y VIENTO

A segunda vista

Antes de ver el episodio

Actividad A ¿Qué recuerdas?

Empareja cada oración con el personaje que la dice.

A

1. __d__ «Les quiero presentar nuestra nueva cosecha. ¡Salud!»
2. __b__ «Isabel, ¿qué hay de los rumores de que van a vender "Sol y viento"?»
3. __a__ «No dejemos que rumores infundados nublen (*darken*) nuestros espíritus.»
4. __e__ «Comenzando con esta cosecha, ¡vamos a expandir las exportaciones del vino "Sol y viento" a toda Norteamérica!»
5. __c__ «Y brindemos por la salud de doña Isabel, ¡por su integridad y su gracia! ¡Salud!»

B

a. María
b. una invitada
c. un invitado
d. doña Isabel
e. don Paco

Actividad B ¡A escuchar!

Repasa la siguiente escena. Luego, mientras ves el episodio, completa lo que dicen los personajes con las palabras y expresiones que oyes.

Act. B, Suggestion:
Have students read the exchange. They do not need to write anything at this point. Do not reveal answers.
Alternative: Have the class brainstorm possible answers for each blank but do not have them write anything down.

MARÍA: ¿Piensa que __debo darle__ [1] las gracias por ayudar a mi familia?

JAIME: ¡No! En realidad yo __quería hablar__ [2] de otras cosas. Y en todo caso, soy yo el que tiene que __pedir__ [3] disculpas por haber causado tantos problemas. Pero la verdad es que yo no __sabía que__ [4] tú... que Ud.... estaba en medio de todo esto.

MARÍA: ¡Aaah! O sea, si yo no hubiera estado en medio, ¿Ud. habría seguido siendo parte de __ese negocio__ [5] con mi hermano?

Actividad C El episodio

Ahora mira el episodio de nuevo. No te olvides de prestar atención especial a la escena de la **Actividad B**.

536

Después de ver el episodio

Actividad A   Para pensar...

Ya sabes que hace sólo un día, María no quiso hablar con Jaime. Le dijo a su mamá: «Ese es un nombre que jamás quiero oír de nuevo.» Pero ahora parece que ella perdona a Jaime. ¿A qué crees que se debe este cambio de actitud?

Act. B, Suggestion: Replay the scene once for students. Replay a second time if needed. Then ask for volunteers to provide answers for each blank. Verify using the instructor notes from Act. B on the previous page.
Alternative: After students complete the conversation, have 2 students act out.

Actividad B   ¡A verificar!

Vas a ver otra vez la escena de **¡A escuchar!** en la página anterior. Llena los espacios en blanco, según lo que oyes.

Actividad C   Las pruebas de Jaime

Paso 1   Al final de la escena con Jaime, María le dice: «No, en serio. No eres tan malo. Pero tienes mucho que probar todavía... » En grupos de tres, indiquen qué cosas debería hacer Jaime para pasar la prueba. Luego presenten sus ideas a los demás.

Paso 2   La clase entera debe determinar si las relaciones entre María y Jaime tienen futuro o no. ¿De qué dependen estas relaciones entre ellos? Hagan una lista en la pizarra con todas las ideas posibles.

RESUMEN DE VOCABULARIO

Los campos

la computación	computer programming
el derecho	law
la enseñanza	education
el mercadeo	marketing
los negocios	business

Cognados: la arquitectura, los servicios médicos, los servicios sociales
Repaso: el arte, las ciencias, la contabilidad, el gobierno, la ingeniería, los medios de comunicación

Las profesiones y los oficios

el/la abogado/a	lawyer
el/la asesor(a)	consultant
el/la ayudante	assistant
el/la bibliotecario/a	librarian
el/la contador(a)	accountant
el/la diseñador(a) de sitios	Web designer
el/la escultor(a)	sculptor
el/la físico/a	physicist
el hombre (la mujer) de negocios	businessman, businesswoman
el/la juez(a)	judge
el/la maestro/a (de primaria/secundaria)	(elementary, high school) teacher
el/la periodista	journalist
el soldado (la mujer soldado)	soldier

Cognados: el actor / la actriz, el/la analista de sistemas, el/la arquitecto/a, el/la astrónomo/a, el/la

biólogo/a, el/la científico/a, el/la dentista, el/la director(a), el/la especialista, el/la fotógrafo/a, el/la ingeniero/a (civil, eléctrico/a, mecánico/a), el/la pintor(a), el político (la mujer político), el/la productor(a), el/la programador(a), el/la psicólogo/a, el/la psiquiatra, el químico (la mujer química), el/la representante, el/la senador(a), el/la técnico/a, el/la terapeuta, el/la trabajador(a) social
Repaso: el/la enfermero/a, el/la farmacéutico/a, el/la médico/a, el/la profesor(a), el/la veterinario/a

Las metas y aspiraciones

alcanzar (c) (una meta)	to reach, achieve (a goal)
instalarse en	to settle into (a house)
jubilarse	to retire
jurar	to vow; to swear
lograr + infin.	to succeed (in doing something)
prometer	to promise
realizar (c)	to accomplish
el deseo	desire
el doctorado	doctorate
los estudios de posgrado	graduate studies
la maestría	master's (degree)
el triunfo	triumph
de corto/largo plazo	short/long-term

Repaso: cambiar, casarse, graduarse (me gradúo), mudarse, tener (irreg.) éxito

Otras palabras y expresiones

dirigir (j) a los demás	to direct others
pensar (ie) de manera directa	to think in a direct (linear) manner
ser (*irreg.*) **hábil para (las matemáticas, las ciencias)**	to be good at (math, science)
tener (*irreg.*) **don de gentes**	to have a way with people

después (de) que	after
en cuanto	as soon as
hasta que	until
tan pronto como	as soon as

Repaso: cuando, mientras

Entremés cultural
¿Quiénes son los hispanos?

VISTAZO

Como has visto a través de los **Entremeses culturales** en este libro, el mundo de habla española es vasta y diversa. Incluidos son veintiún países en cuatro continentes. Es natural, entonces, hacerse uno la pregunta «¿Qué es un hispano?» Es decir, aunque se puede utilizar una palabra para referirse a toda la gente de habla española en el mundo, ¿qué realidad lleva el término **hispano**? Podría hacerse la comparación con el término *anglo* en inglés. ¿Qué es un *anglo*? Claro, es una persona de habla inglesa, pero además de este concepto unificador, ¿hay algo más que identifique y que haga distintos a los anglos?

DATO INTERESANTE:
¿Hispano o latino?

No es raro oír los términos **hispano** y **latino** utilizados como sinónimos, pero en realidad no son iguales. **Hispano** se deriva del viejo nombre de España (Hispania) y se refiere a cualquier persona de habla española. Así que un mexicano, un cubanoamericano, un maya-mexicano, un polaco-argentino y un catalán-español son todos hispanos. **Latino** se refiere al lugar de origen del imperio romano y a la lengua de la gente de ese lugar (derivada del latín). Este concepto, técnicamente, incluye cualquier persona de un país que se liga con[a] el imperio romano y que habla una lengua derivada del latín. Así que, cualquier persona hispana es también un latino, pero no todos los latinos son hispanos. Por ejemplo, un brasileño, un portugués, un francés y un rumano (de Rumania) son todos latinos, pero no lo es un greco. La Grecia fue parte del imperio romano, pero en ese país no se habla una lengua latina.

Idea: ¿Puedes explicar la diferencia técnica e histórica entre **hispano** y **latino**? Con un compañero (una compañera), intenta hacerlo, utilizando sus propias palabras.

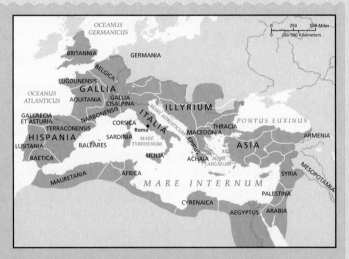

El imperio romano en 150 d.C.[b] El latín era la lengua oficial del imperio romano, pero sólo unas cuantas naciones subsecuentes lo adoptaron como lengua oficial. ¿Sabes cuáles son?

[a]se... *is tied to*   [b]después de Cristo (*A.D.*)

DATO INTERESANTE:
¿Cómo se identifican?

Aunque el término **hispano** se le puede aplicar a cualquier persona de un país de habla española (incluso los Estados Unidos), por lo general la gente de los diferentes países se identifica con su país de origen («Soy chileno», «Soy cubana», etcétera). Hasta algunos hispanos y latinos en los Estados Unidos prefieren términos parecidos, como «Soy mexicano», aun si nacieron en este país. Bill VanPatten, uno de los autores de este libro, se identifica como una persona de ascendencia mexicana, pues sus abuelos eran mexicanos que inmigraron a este país en 1912.

¿Cómo se identifica esta persona? ¿Como hispano o como mexicano?

Estos niños son de ascendencia incaica. Son hispanos porque son de un país de habla española.

> **Idea:** Si hay gente hispana donde vives, haz un cuestionario entre diez de ellos para averiguar cómo se identifican. Diles que enumeren[a] en orden de preferencia (el número uno indica la preferencia más alta) los siguientes términos para identificarse a sí mismos: americano, norteamericano, latino, hispano, mexicano, méxicoamericano (cubano, cubanoamericano, etcétera). Trae la información a la clase.

[a]Diles... *Tell them to number*

DATO INTERESANTE:
Las raíces étnicas

Si el término **hispano** puede aplicarse a cualquier persona de un país de habla española, no se refiere a las raíces étnicas de una persona. Tomemos los casos de la gente de las ciudades capitales de Buenos Aires (la Argentina), Cuzco (el Perú) y Malabo (la Guinea Ecuatorial). La gente de estas ciudades tiende a ser blanca, mestiza (de herencia española e incaica) y negra, respectivamente. A la vez, las personas de estos lugares suelen tener costumbres locales muy diferentes, incluyendo la práctica de religiones diferentes y perspectivas distintas sobre la familia, la vida social y el gobierno, entre otros asuntos.

> **Idea:** Busca información sobre los grupos étnicos de dos o tres países de habla española como, por ejemplo, Chile, Guatemala y Puerto Rico. ¿Cómo se comparan?

DATO INTERESANTE:
¿Hispano o no?

El uso del término **hispano** en este país se hizo oficial durante los años 80 del siglo pasado. El gobierno estadounidense empezó a utilizarlo en el censo oficial para designar a cualquier persona de ascendencia hispana. Muchas personas se opusieron al uso[a] del término, como la muy conocida autora Sandra Cisneros, mientras otros lo aceptaron sin problema. La pregunta básica, según el debate sobre el término, es: ¿Se acepta un término impuesto por personas fuera del grupo al cual se lo asigna o tiene el grupo mismo el derecho de decidir cómo llamarse? ¿Qué implica el uso de **hispano** ante los otros términos utilizados en el censo: *White, African-American, Asian-American, Native-American*, etcétera? Todos estos términos implican grupos étnicos pero, ¿son todos los hispanos iguales en cuanto a su ascendencia étnica?*

> **Idea:** Busca información en el Internet sobre Sandra Cisneros y el uso del término **hispano**. ¿Qué dice ella sobre el asunto?

La escritora Sandra Cisneros (*The House on Mango Street, Woman Hollering Creek, Caramelo*) rechaza (*rejects*) el término **hispano**.

*También se puede debatir los términos *Asian-American* y *Native-American*. ¿Es una persona de ascendencia china igual a una persona de ascendencia coreana? ¿Es una persona de la nación Lakota igual a una de la nación Hopi?

[a]se... *opposed the usage*

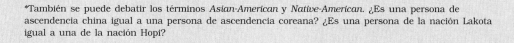

APPENDIX Verbs

A. Regular Verbs: Simple Tenses

INFINITIVE PRESENT PARTICIPLE PAST PARTICIPLE	INDICATIVE					SUBJUNCTIVE		IMPERATIVE
	PRESENT	IMPERFECT	PRETERITE	FUTURE	CONDITIONAL	PRESENT	IMPERFECT	
hablar hablando hablado	hablo hablas habla hablamos habláis hablan	hablaba hablabas hablaba hablábamos hablabais hablaban	hablé hablaste habló hablamos hablasteis hablaron	hablaré hablarás hablará hablaremos hablaréis hablarán	hablaría hablarías hablaría hablaríamos hablaríais hablarían	hable hables hable hablemos habléis hablen	hablara hablaras hablara habláramos hablarais hablaran	habla / no hables hable hablemos hablad / no habléis hablen
comer comiendo comido	como comes come comemos coméis comen	comía comías comía comíamos comíais comían	comí comiste comió comimos comisteis comieron	comeré comerás comerá comeremos comeréis comerán	comería comerías comería comeríamos comeríais comerían	coma comas coma comamos comáis coman	comiera comieras comiera comiéramos comierais comieran	come / no comas coma comamos comed / no comáis coman
vivir viviendo vivido	vivo vives vive vivimos vivís viven	vivía vivías vivía vivíamos vivíais vivían	viví viviste vivió vivimos vivisteis vivieron	viviré vivirás vivirá viviremos viviréis vivirán	viviría vivirías viviría viviríamos viviríais vivirían	viva vivas viva vivamos viváis vivan	viviera vivieras viviera viviéramos vivierais vivieran	vive / no vivas viva vivamos vivid / no viváis vivan

B. Regular Verbs: Perfect Tenses

INDICATIVE										SUBJUNCTIVE			
PRESENT PERFECT		PAST PERFECT		PRETERITE PERFECT		FUTURE PERFECT		CONDITIONAL PERFECT		PRESENT PERFECT		PAST PERFECT	
he has ha hemos habéis han	hablado comido vivido	había habías había habíamos habíais habían	hablado comido vivido	hube hubiste hubo hubimos hubisteis hubieron	hablado comido vivido	habré habrás habrá habremos habréis habrán	hablado comido vivido	habría habrías habría habríamos habríais habrían	hablado comido vivido	haya hayas haya hayamos hayáis hayan	hablado comido vivido	hubiera hubieras hubiera hubiéramos hubierais hubieran	hablado comido vivido

C. Irregular Verbs

INFINITIVE PRESENT PARTICIPLE PAST PARTICIPLE	INDICATIVE						SUBJUNCTIVE		IMPERATIVE
	PRESENT	IMPERFECT	PRETERITE	FUTURE	CONDITIONAL		PRESENT	IMPERFECT	
andar andando andado	ando andas anda andamos andáis andan	andaba andabas andaba andábamos andabais andaban	anduve anduviste anduvo anduvimos anduvisteis anduvieron	andaré andarás andará andaremos andaréis andarán	andaría andarías andaría andaríamos andaríais andarían		ande andes ande andemos andéis anden	anduviera anduvieras anduviera anduviéramos anduvierais anduvieran	anda / no andes ande andemos andad / no andéis anden
caer cayendo caído	caigo caes cae caemos caéis caen	caía caías caía caíamos caíais caían	caí caíste cayó caímos caísteis cayeron	caeré caerás caerá caeremos caeréis caerán	caería caerías caería caeríamos caeríais caerían		caiga caigas caiga caigamos caigáis caigan	cayera cayeras cayera cayéramos cayerais cayeran	cae / no caigas caiga caigamos caed / no caigáis caigan
dar dando dado	doy das da damos dais dan	daba dabas daba dábamos dabais daban	di diste dio dimos disteis dieron	daré darás dará daremos daréis darán	daría darías daría daríamos daríais darían		dé des dé demos deis den	diera dieras diera diéramos dierais dieran	da / no des dé demos dad / no deis den
decir diciendo dicho	digo dices dice decimos decís dicen	decía decías decía decíamos decíais decían	dije dijiste dijo dijimos dijisteis dijeron	diré dirás dirá diremos diréis dirán	diría dirías diría diríamos diríais dirían		diga digas diga digamos digáis digan	dijera dijeras dijera dijéramos dijerais dijeran	di / no digas diga digamos decid / no digáis digan
estar estando estado	estoy estás está estamos estáis están	estaba estabas estaba estábamos estabais estaban	estuve estuviste estuvo estuvimos estuvisteis estuvieron	estaré estarás estará estaremos estaréis estarán	estaría estarías estaría estaríamos estaríais estarían		esté estés esté estemos estéis estén	estuviera estuvieras estuviera estuviéramos estuvierais estuviera	está / no estés esté estemos estad / no estéis estén
haber habiendo habido	he has ha hemos habéis han	había habías había habíamos habíais habían	hube hubiste hubo hubimos hubisteis hubieron	habré habrás habrá habremos habréis habrán	habría habrías habría habríamos habríais habrían		haya hayas haya hayamos hayáis hayan	hubiera hubieras hubiera hubiéramos hubierais hubieran	
hacer haciendo hecho	hago haces hace hacemos hacéis hacen	hacía hacías hacía hacíamos hacíais hacían	hice hiciste hizo hicimos hicisteis hicieron	haré harás hará haremos haréis harán	haría harías haría haríamos haríais harían		haga hagas haga hagamos hagáis hagan	hiciera hicieras hiciera hiciéramos hicierais hicieran	haz / no hagas haga hagamos haced / no hagáis hagan

C. Irregular Verbs (*continued*)

INFINITIVE PRESENT PARTICIPLE PAST PARTICIPLE	INDICATIVE					SUBJUNCTIVE		IMPERATIVE
	PRESENT	IMPERFECT	PRETERITE	FUTURE	CONDITIONAL	PRESENT	IMPERFECT	
ir yendo ido	voy vas va vamos vais van	iba ibas iba íbamos ibais iban	fui fuiste fue fuimos fuisteis fueron	iré irás irá iremos iréis irán	iría irías iría iríamos iríais irían	vaya vayas vaya vayamos vayáis vayan	fuera fueras fuera fuéramos fuerais fueran	ve / no vayas vaya vamos / no vayamos id / no vayáis vayan
oír oyendo oído	oigo oyes oye oímos oís oyen	oía oías oía oíamos oíais oían	oí oíste oyó oímos oísteis oyeron	oiré oirás oirá oiremos oiréis oirán	oiría oirías oiría oiríamos oiríais oirían	oiga oigas oiga oigamos oigáis oigan	oyera oyeras oyera oyéramos oyerais oyeran	oye / no oigas oiga oigamos oíd / no oigáis oigan
poder pudiendo podido	puedo puedes puede podemos podéis pueden	podía podías podía podíamos podíais podían	pude pudiste pudo pudimos pudisteis pudieron	podré podrás podrá podremos podréis podrán	podría podrías podría podríamos podríais podrían	pueda puedas pueda podamos podáis puedan	pudiera pudieras pudiera pudiéramos pudierais pudieran	
poner poniendo puesto	pongo pones pone ponemos ponéis ponen	ponía ponías ponía poníamos poníais ponían	puse pusiste puso pusimos pusisteis pusieron	pondré pondrás pondrá pondremos pondréis pondrán	pondría pondrías pondría pondríamos pondríais pondrían	ponga pongas ponga pongamos pongáis pongan	pusiera pusieras pusiera pusiéramos pusierais pusieran	pon / no pongas ponga pongamos poned / no pongáis pongan
querer queriendo querido	quiero quieres quiere queremos queréis quieren	quería querías quería queríamos queríais querían	quise quisiste quiso quisimos quisisteis quisieron	querré querrás querrá querremos querréis querrán	querría querrías querría querríamos querríais querrían	quiera quieras quiera queramos queráis quieran	quisiera quisieras quisiera quisiéramos quisierais quisieran	quiere / no quieras quiera queramos quered / no queráis quieran
saber sabiendo sabido	sé sabes sabe sabemos sabéis saben	sabía sabías sabía sabíamos sabíais sabían	supe supiste supo supimos supisteis supieron	sabré sabrás sabrá sabremos sabréis sabrán	sabría sabrías sabría sabríamos sabríais sabrían	sepa sepas sepa sepamos sepáis sepan	supiera supieras supiera supiéramos supierais supieran	sabe / no sepas sepa sepamos sabed / no sepáis sepan
salir saliendo salido	salgo sales sale salimos salís salen	salía salías salía salíamos salíais salían	salí saliste salió salimos salisteis salieron	saldré saldrás saldrá saldremos saldréis saldrán	saldría saldrías saldría saldríamos saldríais saldrían	salga salgas salga salgamos salgáis salgan	saliera salieras saliera saliéramos salierais salieran	sal / no salgas salga salgamos salid / no salgáis salgan

C. Irregular Verbs (*continued*)

INFINITIVE PRESENT PARTICIPLE PAST PARTICIPLE	INDICATIVE					SUBJUNCTIVE		IMPERATIVE
	PRESENT	IMPERFECT	PRETERITE	FUTURE	CONDITIONAL	PRESENT	IMPERFECT	
ser siendo sido	soy eres es somos sois son	era eras era éramos erais eran	fui fuiste fue fuimos fuisteis fueron	seré serás será seremos seréis serán	sería serías sería seríamos seríais serían	sea seas sea seamos seáis sean	fuera fueras fuera fuéramos fuerais fueran	sé / no seas sea seamos sed / no seáis sean
tener teniendo tenido	tengo tienes tiene tenemos tenéis tienen	tenía tenías tenía teníamos teníais tenían	tuve tuviste tuvo tuvimos tuvisteis tuvieron	tendré tendrás tendrá tendremos tendréis tendrán	tendría tendrías tendría tendríamos tendríais tendrían	tenga tengas tenga tengamos tengáis tengan	tuviera tuvieras tuviera tuviéramos tuvierais tuvieran	ten / no tengas tenga tengamos tened / no tengáis tengan
traer trayendo traído	traigo traes trae traemos traéis traen	traía traías traía traíamos traíais traían	traje trajiste trajo trajimos trajisteis trajeron	traeré traerás traerá traeremos traeréis traerán	traería traerías traería traeríamos traeríais traerían	traiga traigas traiga traigamos traigáis traigan	trajera trajeras trajera trajéramos trajerais trajeran	trae / no traigas traiga traigamos traed / no traigáis traigan
venir viniendo venido	vengo vienes viene venimos venís vienen	venía venías venía veníamos veníais venían	vine viniste vino vinimos vinisteis vinieron	vendré vendrás vendrá vendremos vendréis vendrán	vendría vendrías vendría vendríamos vendríais vendrían	venga vengas venga vengamos vengáis vengan	viniera vinieras viniera viniéramos vinierais vinieran	ven / no vengas venga vengamos venid / no vengáis vengan
ver viendo visto	veo ves ve vemos veis ven	veía veías veía veíamos veíais veían	vi viste vio vimos visteis vieron	veré verás verá veremos veréis verán	vería verías vería veríamos veríais verían	vea veas vea veamos veáis vean	viera vieras viera viéramos vierais vieran	ve / no veas vea veamos ved / no veáis vean

D. Stem-Changing and Spelling Change Verbs

INFINITIVE PRESENT PARTICIPLE PAST PARTICIPLE	INDICATIVE					SUBJUNCTIVE		IMPERATIVE
	PRESENT	IMPERFECT	PRETERITE	FUTURE	CONDITIONAL	PRESENT	IMPERFECT	
construir (y) construyendo construido	construyo construyes construye construimos construís construyen	construía construías construía construíamos construíais construían	construí construiste construyó construimos construisteis construyeron	construiré construirás construirá construiremos construiréis construirán	construiría construirías construiría construiríamos construiríais construirían	construya construyas construya construyamos construyáis construyan	construyera construyeras construyera construyéramos construyerais construyeran	construye / no construyas construya construyamos construid / no construyáis construyan
dormir (ue, u) durmiendo dormido	duermo duermes duerme dormimos dormís duermen	dormía dormías dormía dormíamos dormíais dormían	dormí dormiste durmió dormimos dormisteis durmieron	dormiré dormirás dormirá dormiremos dormiréis dormirán	dormiría dormirías dormiría dormiríamos dormiríais dormirían	duerma duermas duerma durmamos durmáis duerman	durmiera durmieras durmiera durmiéramos durmierais durmieran	duerme / no duermas duerma durmamos dormid / no durmáis duerman

D. Stem-Changing and Spelling Change Verbs (*continued*)

INFINITIVE PRESENT PARTICIPLE PAST PARTICIPLE	INDICATIVE					SUBJUNCTIVE		IMPERATIVE
	PRESENT	IMPERFECT	PRETERITE	FUTURE	CONDITIONAL	PRESENT	IMPERFECT	
pedir (i, i) pidiendo pedido	pido pides pide pedimos pedís piden	pedía pedías pedía pedíamos pedíais pedían	pedí pediste pidió pedimos pedisteis pidieron	pediré pedirás pedirá pediremos pediréis pedirán	pediría pedirías pediría pediríamos pediríais pedirían	pida pidas pida pidamos pidáis pidan	pidiera pidieras pidiera pidiéramos pidierais pidieran	pide / no pidas pida pidamos pedid / no pidáis pidan
pensar (ie) pensando pensado	pienso piensas piensa pensamos pensáis piensan	pensaba pensabas pensaba pensábamos pensabais pensaban	pensé pensaste pensó pensamos pensasteis pensaron	pensaré pensarás pensará pensaremos pensaréis pensarán	pensaría pensarías pensaría pensaríamos pensaríais pensarían	piense pienses piense pensemos penséis piensen	pensara pensaras pensara pensáramos pensarais pensaran	piensa / no pienses piense pensemos pensad / no penséis piensen
producir (zc) produciendo producido	produzco produces produce producimos producís producen	producía producías producía producíamos producíais producían	produje produjiste produjo produjimos produjisteis produjeron	produciré producirás producirá produciremos produciréis producirán	produciría producirías produciría produciríamos produciríais producirían	produzca produzcas produzca produzcamos produzcáis produzcan	produjera produjeras produjera produjéramos produjerais produjeran	produce / no produzcas produzca produzcamos producid / no produzcáis produzcan
reír (i, i) riendo reído	río ríes ríe reímos reís ríen	reía reías reía reíamos reíais reían	reí reíste rió reímos reísteis rieron	reiré reirás reirá reiremos reiréis reirán	reiría reirías reiría reiríamos reiríais reirían	ría rías ría riamos riáis rían	riera rieras riera riéramos rierais rieran	ríe / no rías ría riamos reíd / no riáis rían
seguir (i, i) (g) siguiendo seguido	sigo sigues sigue seguimos seguís siguen	seguía seguías seguía seguíamos seguíais seguían	seguí seguiste siguió seguimos seguisteis siguieron	seguiré seguirás seguirá seguiremos seguiréis seguirán	seguiría seguirías seguiría seguiríamos seguiríais seguirían	siga sigas siga sigamos sigáis sigan	siguiera siguieras siguiera siguiéramos siguierais siguieran	sigue / no sigas siga sigamos seguid / no sigáis sigan
sentir (ie, i) sintiendo sentido	siento sientes siente sentimos sentís sienten	sentía sentías sentía sentíamos sentíais sentían	sentí sentiste sintió sentimos sentisteis sintieron	sentiré sentirás sentirá sentiremos sentiréis sentirán	sentiría sentirías sentiría sentiríamos sentiríais sentirían	sienta sientas sienta sintamos sintáis sientan	sintiera sintieras sintiera sintiéramos sintierais sintieran	siente / no sientas sienta sintamos sentid / no sintáis sientan
volver (ue) volviendo vuelto	vuelvo vuelves vuelve volvemos volvéis vuelven	volvía volvías volvía volvíamos volvíais volvían	volví volviste volvió volvimos volvisteis volvieron	volveré volverás volverá volveremos volveréis volverán	volvería volverías volvería volveríamos volveríais volverían	vuelva vuelvas vuelva volvamos volváis vuelvan	volviera volvieras volviera volviéramos volvierais volvieran	vuelve / no vuelvas vuelva volvamos volved / no volváis vuelvan

SPANISH-ENGLISH VOCABULARY

This Spanish-English Vocabulary contains all the words that appear in the text, with the following exceptions: (1) most identical cognates that do not appear in the chapter vocabulary lists; (2) verb forms; (3) diminutives in **-ito/a;** (4) absolute superlatives in **-ísimo/a;** and (5) most adverbs in **-mente.** Active vocabulary is indicated by the number of the lesson in which a word or given meaning is first listed (P = **Lección preliminar**). Vocabulary that is glossed in the text is not considered to be active vocabulary, and no lesson number is indicated for it. Only meanings that are used in this text are given.

Gender is indicated except for masculine nouns ending in **-o,** feminine nouns ending in **-a,** and invariable adjectives. Stem changes and spelling changes are indicated for verbs: **dormir (ue, u); llegar (gu).**

Because **ch** and **ll** are no longer considered separate letters, words with **ch** and **ll** are alphabetized as they would be in English. The letter **ñ** follows the letter **n: añadir** follows **anuncio,** for example.

The following abbreviations are used:

adj.	adjective	*m.*	masculine
adv.	adverb	*Mex.*	Mexico
Arg.	Argentina	*n.*	noun
aux.	auxiliary	*neut.*	neuter
conj.	conjunction	*obj.*	object
def. art.	definite article	*p.p.*	past participle
d.o.	direct object	*pl.*	plural
f.	feminine	*poss.*	possessive
fam.	familiar	*prep.*	preposition
form.	formal	*pron.*	pronoun
gram.	grammatical term	*refl.*	reflexive
indef. art.	indefinite article	*s.*	singular
inf.	infinitive	*Sp.*	Spain
inv.	invariable	*sub. pron.*	subject pronoun
i.o.	indirect object	*v.*	verb
irreg.	irregular		

A

a to, at (1B); **a continuación** following; **a la derecha de** to the right of (2A); **a la izquierda de** to the left of (2A); **a la misma hora** at the same time (1A); **a la(s)...** at ... o'clock (1A); **a menos que** unless (7B); **a menudo** often; **a pesar de** *prep.* in spite of, despite; **¿a qué hora?** at what time? (1A); **a solas** alone (1B); **llegar (gu) a tiempo** to arrive on time (1A)
abajo (de) below, underneath
abierto/a (*p.p. of* **abrir**) open
abogado/a lawyer (9B)
abogar (gu) por to advocate
abordar to board

aborto abortion
abrazar (c) to embrace (7B)
abreviatura abbreviation
abrigo overcoat (2B)
abril *m.* April (1B)
abrir (*p.p.* **abierto/a**) to open (1B)
abrochar(se) (el cinturón) to fasten (one's seatbelt)
absoluto/a absolute; complete
abstención *f.* abstention
abstracto/a abstract
abuelo/a grandfather, grandmother (3A); *pl.* grandparents
aburrido/a bored (1B); boring (2B)
aburrir(se) to bore (oneself) (7A)
abusar de to abuse (*someone*)

acá here
acabar to finish; **acabar de** + *inf.* to have just (*done something*)
academia academy
académico/a academic
acampar to camp (6B)
acaparado/a monopolized
acariciar to caress (7B)
acaso: por si acaso just in case
acceder to access; **acceder a** to consent to
acceso access
accesorio accessory
accidente *m.* accident (8B)
acción *f.* action; **Día** (*m.*) **de Acción de Gracias** Thanksgiving (4A); *pl.* stocks (8A)

aceite *m.* oil; **aceite de oliva** olive oil
aceptable acceptable
aceptación *f.* acceptance
aceptar to accept
acerca de about
acero steel (8A)
acertar (ie) to guess right
ácido acid
aclaración *f.* clarification
acomodar to settle; to make comfortable
acompañar to accompany; to go with
acondicionado: aire (*m.*) **acondicionado** air conditioning
aconsejar to advise
acontecimiento event, happening (8B)
acostarse (ue) to go to bed (2A)
acostumbrarse a to get used to, to become accustomed to
actitud *f.* attitude
actividad *f.* activity
activista *m., f.* activist
activo/a active
acto act
actor *m.* actor (9B)
actriz *f.* (*pl.* **actrices**) actress (9B)
actual current; contemporary
actualidad *f.*: **en la actualidad** currently
actuar (actúo) to act
acuario Aquarius
acuático/a aquatic
acuerdo agreement; **estar** (*irreg.*) **de acuerdo** to agree; **ponerse** (*irreg.*) **de acuerdo** to come to an agreement
adaptable adaptable (5A)
adaptar(se) to adapt
adecuado/a appropriate
adelante *adv.* ahead; **de aquí en adelante** from here on out
además moreover; **además de** besides
adentro *adv.* inside
adicional additional
adiós good-bye
adivinar to guess
adjetivo adjective
administración *f.* administration; **administración de empresas** business administration (P)
administrador(a) administrator
admirador(a) fan, admirer
admirar to admire
adolescencia adolescence
adolescente *m., f.* adolescent, teenager (5A)
¿adónde? where (to)? (1B)
adoptar to adopt
adoptivo/a adopted (3A)
adorar to adore, worship (7B)
adquirido/a acquired; **síndrome** (*m.*) **de inmunodeficiencia adquirida (SIDA)** Acquired Immune Deficiency Syndrome (AIDS) (8B)

adquisición *f.* acquisition
aduana *s.* customs; **pasar por la aduana** to go through customs (6A)
adulto/a adult; **edad** (*f.*) **adulta** adulthood
adverbio adverb
advertir (ie, i) (de) to warn (about)
aéreo/a: línea aérea airline
aeróbico aerobic; **hacer** (*irreg.*) **ejercicio aeróbico** to do aerobics (4A)
aeropuerto airport (6A)
afán *m.* desire
afectar to affect (7A)
afectuoso/a affectionate
afeitarse to shave (4B)
aficionado/a fan; **ser** (*irreg.*) **aficionado/a (a)** to be a fan (of) (4A)
afirmación *f.* statement
afirmar to affirm
afirmativo/a *adj.* affirmative
afluencia throng, horde
afortunadamente fortunately, luckily
África Africa (6B)
africano/a *n., adj.* African
afroamericano/a *n., adj.* African-American
afuera *adv.* outside; *n. pl.* suburbs, outskirts (2A)
agencia agency; **agencia de viajes** travel agency (6A)
agenda electrónica electronic organizer, PDA (personal digital assistant) (5A)
agente *m., f.* agent; **agente de inmobilaria** real estate agent; **agente de viajes** travel agent (6A)
agitado/a agitated, shaken
agosto August (1B)
agradable pleasant, nice (1B)
agradar to please (5A)
agradecer (zc) to thank (3A)
agradecido/a thankful
agregar (gu) to add
agrícola *adj. m., f.* agricultural (8A)
agricultor(a) farmer
agrio/a sour (3B)
agrupación *f.* group
agrupar to group
agua *f.* (*but* **el agua**) water (3B); **agua corriente** running water; **agua del grifo** tap water; **agua potable** drinking water; **contaminación** (*f.*) **del agua** water pollution (6B); **esquiar (esquío) en el agua** to water ski (4A)
aguacate *m.* avocado (3B)
aguado/a watered down
aguafiestas *m., f. s.* party-pooper (4A)
aguantar to endure; **no aguantar** not to be able to stand, put up with (7B)
ahí there
ahora now (1A)
ahorrar to save (8A)

ahorros *pl.* savings (8A); **cuenta de ahorros** savings account (8A)
aimará *m.* Aimara (language)
aire *m.* air; **aire acondicionado** air conditioning; **al aire libre** outdoor(s) (6B); **contaminación** (*f.*) **del aire** air pollution (6B)
aislado/a isolated
ajedrez *m.* chess (4A)
ajeno/a foreign
ajo garlic
al (*contraction of* **a** + **el**) to the; **al aire libre** outdoors (6B); **al este de** to the east of (2A); **al horno** baked (3B); **al igual que** just like; **al lado de** beside (2A); **al norte de** to the north of (2A); **al oeste de** to the west of (2A); **al sur de** to the south of (2A); **al vapor** steamed (3B)
alarma *m.* alarm
alarmante alarming
alberca (*Mex.*) swimming pool
alcachofa artichoke
alcanzar (c) (una meta) to reach, achieve (a goal) (9B)
alcoba bedroom
alcohol *m.* alcohol
alcohólico/a *adj.* alcoholic; **bebida alcohólica** alcoholic drink
alegrarse to get, become happy (7A)
alegre happy (1B)
alegría happiness
alemán *m.* German (*language*) (P)
alemán, alemana *n., adj.* German
alergia allergy (7A)
alérgico/a allergic
alfabetización: tasa de alfabetización literacy rate
alfombra rug; carpet (4B)
algo something, some (3B)
algodón *m.* cotton
alguien someone (1B)
algún, alguno/a some, any (3B)
alianza alliance
aliento breath; **mal aliento** bad breath
alimenticio/a nutritional
alimento food item (3B)
aliviar to alleviate
allá (way) over there
allí there (2B); over there (2B)
almacén *m.* department store (2A)
almendrado/a almond-shaped
almohada pillow
almorzar (ue) (c) to eat lunch (2A)
almuerzo lunch (3B)
alojamiento lodging (6A)
alojarse to stay (*in a place*) (6A)
alpinismo rock climbing; **practicar (qu) el alpinismo de rocas** to rock climb (6B)
alquilar to rent (4B); **se alquila** for rent (4B)
alquiler *m.* rent (1A)

alrededor de *prep.* around (2A)
alternativa *n.* alternative, choice
alterno/a alternating
alto/a tall (3A); high; **en voz alta** aloud; **tierras altas** highlands; **zapatos de tacón alto** high-heeled shoes
altruista *adj. m., f.* altruistic
altura height
alubia bean
aluminio aluminum; **lata de aluminio** aluminum can (6B)
alza *f.* (*but* **el alza**) rise (8A)
amable friendly
amante *m., f.* lover
amar to love (7B)
amargo/a bitter (3B)
amarillo/a yellow (2B)
Amazonas: río Amazonas Amazon River
amazónico/a *adj.* Amazon
ambicioso/a ambitious (1B)
ambiente *m.* atmosphere; **medio ambiente** environment (6B)
ambigüedad *f.* ambiguity
ambos/as *pl.* both
amenaza threat
americano/a *n., adj.* American; **fútbol** (*m.*) **americano** football (4A)
amerindio/a *adj.* indigenous to the Americas
amigo/a friend
amistad *f.* friendship (7B)
amor *m.* love
amoroso/a affectionate, loving
amortizar (c) una deuda to pay off a debt (8A); **amortizar una hipoteca** to pay off a mortgage (8A)
amplio/a ample, broad
amueblado/a furnished (4B)
amuleto amulet
analfabetismo illiteracy (8B)
análisis *m. inv.* analysis
analista *m., f.* analyst; **analista de sistemas** systems analyst (9B)
analítico/a analytical
anaranjado/a orange (*color*) (2B)
andar *irreg.* to walk; **andar en bicicleta** to ride a bicycle (4A); **rueda de andar** treadmill (4A)
andino/a Andean
anfitrión, anfitriona host, hostess
ángel *m.* angel
anglohablante *m., f.* English speaker; *adj.* English-speaking
angloparlante *m., f.* English speaker
animado/a: dibujo animado cartoon
animal *m.* animal
animar to encourage (9A); to animate; to energize
ánimo: estado de ánimo state of mind
aniversario anniversary
anoche *adv.* last night

anónimo/a anonymous
anotar to note, take note of
ansioso/a worried, anxious (5B)
Antártida Antarctica (6B)
ante *prep.* before; faced with; in the presence of
antemano: de antemano ahead of time
anteojos *pl.* glasses (*vision*)
antepasado/a ancestor
antes *adv.* before; **antes de** (*prep.*) + *inf.* before (*doing something*); **antes (de) que** *conj.* before (7B)
anticipación *f.*: **con dos horas de anticipación** two hours ahead of time
anticipar to anticipate, foresee
antiguo/a old
antioxidante antioxidizing
antirrobo/a antitheft; **seguro antirrobo** antitheft insurance (8A)
antropología anthropology (P)
antropólogo/a anthropologist
anuncio advertisement; announcement; **anuncio publicitario** commercial (8B)
añadir to add
año year (1B); **cada año** each year; **¿cuántos años cumples?** how many years old are you (*turning*) (*fam. s.*)? (4A); **cumplir... años** to be ... old (*on a birthday*) (4A); **hace... años** ... years ago; **tener** (*irreg.*)**... años** to be ... years old (2A)
apagar (gu) to turn off (*light*) (5A)
aparato appliance; **aparato doméstico** household appliance (4B); **aparato electrónico** electronic device (5A)
aparecer (zc) to appear
aparente apparent
apariencia appearance
apartamento apartment (4B)
aparte *adv.* apart; besides; **hoja de papel aparte** separate piece of paper
apasionado/a passionate (1B)
apatía apathy
apático/a apathetic
apellido last name; **¿cuál es su apellido?** what's his/her last name? (P); **¿cuál es tu apellido?** what's your (*fam. s.*) last name? (P); **mi apellido es...** my last is ... (P)
apenas *adv.* hardly; barely
aperitivo appetizer
apetecer (zc) to appeal, be pleasing (5A)
aplicarse (qu) to apply oneself
apodarse to be nicknamed
apoyar to support (8B)
apoyo support
apreciar to appreciate
aprender to learn (1B)
apresurar to rush
aprobar (ue) to approve, pass (8B)
apropiado/a appropriate (8B)

aprovecharse (de) to take advantage (of) (9A)
aproximadamente approximately
apuntar to note, jot down
apunte *m.* note; **tomar apuntes** to take notes (1A)
apurado/a hurried, rushed
aquel, aquella *adj.* that (over there) (2B); *pron.* that one (over there) (2B)
aquello *neut. pron.* that (2B); that thing (2B)
aquí here (2B); **de aquí en adelante** from here on out
árabe *n., adj. m., f.* Arab
araña spider (9A)
árbol *m.* tree; **árbol genealógico** family tree; **subirse a los árboles** to climb trees (5A)
archipiélago archipelago, group of islands
archivo archive, file (5A)
área *f.* (*but* **el área**) area
arena sand
argentino/a *n., adj.* Argentine
árido/a arid, dry
arma *f.* (*but* **el arma**) **de fuego** firearm
armado/a armed; **fuerzas armadas** armed forces
armario closet (4B)
armonía harmony, agreement
arquitecto/a architect (9B)
arquitectónico/a architectural
arquitectura architecture (9B); **arquitectura paisajista** landscape architecture
arreglar to fix
arrepentirse (ie, i) (de) to be sorry (about); to regret (7B)
arriba (de) *prep.* up; above
arriesgado/a daring
arrogante arrogant (1B)
arroz *m.* rice (3B)
arruinar to ruin
arte *m.* (*but* **las artes**) art (9B); *pl.* arts (P)
arterial: presión (*f.*) **arterial** blood pressure (7A)
artesanía *s.* arts and crafts
artículo article (8B)
artista *m., f.* artist
artístico/a artistic
ascendencia heritage
ascensor *m.* elevator
asegurado/a insured
asesinar to murder
asesor(a) consultant (9B)
así thus, so; **así así** so-so, fair; **así que** so (that), therefore
Asia Asia (6B)
asiático/a *n., adj.* Asian
asiáticoamericano *n., adj.* Asian-American

asiento chair (6A)
asignar to assign
asistente (*m., f.*) **de vuelo** flight attendant (6A)
asistir (a) to attend (1B)
asociación *f.* association
asociado/a associated; **Estado Libre Associado** Free Associated State, Commonwealth
asociar to associate; to combine
aspecto aspect; appearance
aspiración *f.* aspiration, hope (9B)
aspiradora vacuum (4B); **pasar la aspiradora** to vacuum (4B)
aspirina aspirin (7A)
astronomía astronomy (P)
astrónomo/a astronomer (9B)
astuto/a astute, clever (1B)
asumir to assume
asunto subject, topic, issue
atacar (qu) to attack
atajo shortcut
atención *f.* attention
atender (ie) to wait on (6A)
atentado *n.* attack
atento/a attentive (7B)
atlántico/a: océano Atlántico Atlantic Ocean
atleta *m., f.* athlete (4A)
atlético/a athletic
atracción *f.* attraction; *pl.* amusements
atractivo/a attractive
atrapado/a trapped
atrasado/a backward
atravesar (ie) to cross; to run through (*river*)
atrevido/a daring (8B)
atribuirse (y) todo el mérito to take all the credit (9A)
atún *m.* tuna (3B)
audiencia audience
auditorio/a auditorium (P)
aumentar to augment, increase
aumento *n.* increase
aun *adv.* even
aún *adv.* still, yet
aunque although
ausencia absence
Australia Australia (6B)
auto car
autobús *m.* bus (6A); **parada de autobuses** bus stop (2A)
autoconsciente *m., f.* self-conscious
autoescuela driving school
automático/a automatic; **cajero automático** ATM (2A); **contestador** (*m.*) **automático** answering machine (5A)
automóvil *m.* automobile (8A); **seguro de automóvil** automobile insurance (8A)
autonomía *individual political entity or region* (*Sp.*)

autónomo/a autonomous
autoridad *f.* authority
autorizar (c) to authorize
autostop *m.:* **hacer** (*irreg.*) **autostop** to hitchhike
avance *m.* advance
avanzar (c) to advance
ave *f.* (*but* **el ave**) bird; *pl.* poultry (3B)
avenida avenue
aventurarse to risk
aventurero/a adventurous
avergonzado/a embarrassed (7A)
averiguar (averigüo) to find out
avión *m.* airplane (6A)
ayer yesterday (4A)
ayuda *n.* help; **pedir (i, i) ayuda** to ask for help
ayudante *m., f.* helper; assistant (9B)
ayudar to help (8B)
ayuntamiento city (town) hall
azteca *n. m., f.; adj.* Aztec
azúcar *m.* sugar (8A); **cañaveral** (*m.*) **de azúcar** sugar cane field
azul blue (2B)

B

bailar to dance (1A); **salir** (*irreg.*) **a bailar** to go dancing
baile *m.* dance
baja *n.* fall (*stocks*) (8A)
bajada *n.* lowering
bajar to go down (8A); **bajar de** to get off (6A); **bajar de peso** to lose weight
bajo *prep.* under
bajo/a *adj.* short (*height*); low (3A); **los Países Bajos** The Netherlands
balcón *m.* balcony (4B)
bambalina: tras bambalinas behind the scenes
banana banana (3B)
bancario/a *adj.* banking, financial
banco bank (2A)
banda band
bandeja tray
bandera flag
bañar to bathe (9A); **bañarse** to take a bath (4B)
bañera bathtub (4B)
baño bathroom (4B); **con baño (privado)** with a (private) bathroom (6A); **traje** (*m.*) **de baño** bathing suit (2B)
bar *m.* bar (2A)
barato/a inexpensive, cheap (2B)
barbacoa *n.* barbecue
barco ship, boat; **navegar (gu) en barco** to sail (4A)
barra bar; **barra de frutas** fruit bar (3B); **barra de granola** granola bar (3B)
barrer (el piso) to sweep (the floor) (4B)
barrio neighborhood (2A)

basar to base, support
base *f.* base, foundation; **a base de** based on
básico/a basic
basquetbol *m.* basketball (4A); **jugar (ue) (gu) al basquetbol** to play basketball
bastante *adv.* somewhat, rather (1B)
basura garbage; **sacar (qu) la basura** to take out the trash (4B)
basurero landfill (6B)
bata robe
bebé *m., f.* baby
beber to drink (1B)
bebida *n.* drink; **bebida alcohólica** alcoholic drink
béisbol *m.* baseball (4A)
beisbolista *m., f.* baseball player
belleza beauty
bello/a beautiful
beneficios *pl.* benefits
berenjena eggplant
besar to kiss (7B)
beso *n.* kiss
biblioteca library (P)
bibliotecario/a librarian (9B)
bicicleta bicycle; **andar** (*irreg.*) **en bicicleta** to ride a bicycle (4A)
bien *adv.* well; **caerle** (*irreg.*) **bien a alguien** to like someone (5A); **combinar bien** to go well with (*clothing*) (2B); **llevarse bien con** to get along well with (5A); **manejar bien** to manage well (8A); **pasarlo bien** to have a good time (4A); **portarse bien** to behave well (5A); **quedarle bien** to fit well (2B)
bienes *m. pl.:* **bienes fabricados** manufactured goods (8A); **bienes raíces** real estate (8A)
bienestar *m.* well-being
bilingüe bilingual
bilingüismo bilingualism
billar *m. s.* pool, billiards
billete *m.* ticket (*Sp.*)
biodegradable: producto biodegradable biodegradable product (6B)
biodiversidad *f.* biodiversity
biografía biography
biología biology (P)
biólogo/a biologist (9B)
bistec *m.* steak (3B)
blanco/a white (2B); **vino blanco** white wine (3B)
blando/a soft (3B)
blindar to shield
bloque *m.* block
blusa blouse (2B)
boca mouth (7A)
bocacalle *f.* intersection
boda wedding (5B); **padrino de boda** groomsman

bodega wine cellar
bolero love song
boleto ticket (6A)
bolígrafo pen (P)
boliviano/a *n., adj.* Bolivian
bolsa purse (2B); **Bolsa de valores** stock market (8A)
bolso pocketbook; handbag
bonito/a pretty
bono voucher
borrador *m.* eraser (P)
bosque *m.* **(lluvioso)** (rain)forest (6B)
botana (*Mex.*) appetizer
botas *pl.* boots (2B)
botella bottle; **botella de plástico** plastic bottle (6B); **botella de vidrio** glass bottle (6B)
botón *m.* button
botones *m. inv.* bellhop (6A)
Brasil *m.* Brazil
brasileño/a *n., adj.* Brazilian
bravo/a wild
brazo arm (7A)
brécol *m.* broccoli
bretaña: Gran Bretaña Great Britain
breve *adj.* brief
brillar to shine
brindar to toast
brindis *m.* toast (4A)
británico/a *n., adj.* British
bróculi *m.* broccoli (3B)
bruto/a: producto nacional bruto gross national product
bucear to snorkel (6B)
buen, bueno/a good (1B); **buen provecho** enjoy your meal; **buenas noches** good night (P); **buenas tardes** good afternoon/evening (P); **buenos días** good morning (P); **es buena idea** it's a good idea (2B); **estar** (*irreg.*) **a buen precio** it's a good price; **estar** (*irreg.*) **en buena forma** to be in good shape (4A); **hace buen tiempo** it's good weather (1B)
bufanda scarf
burlador(a) *adj.* seducer
burlarse de otros to make fun of others
buscador *m.* search engine
buscar (qu) to look for (1A)
búsqueda *n.* search; **hacer** (*irreg.*) **una búsqueda** to do a search (5A)

C

caballero gentleman
caballo horse; **montar a caballo** to go horseback riding (6B)
cabello hair
cabeza head (7A); **dolor** (*m.*) **de cabeza** headache
cabezón(a) headstrong (5A)

cacahuete *m.* peanut; **mantequilla de cacahuete** peanut butter (3B)
cacao cocoa (8A)
cacique *m.* chief (*of a tribe*)
cada *inv.* each (1A); **cada año** each year; **cada día** every day; **cada mes** each month; **cada uno** each one; **cada vez** each time; **cada vez más** more and more
cadena (TV) network (8B); chain
caer(se) *irreg.* to fall; **caerle bien/mal a alguien** to (dis)like someone (5A); **¿en qué día (mes) cae... ?** what day (month) is ... ?
café *m.* **(descafeinado)** (decaffeinated) coffee (3B); **café con leche** coffee with milk; **charlar en un café** to chat in a cafe (6B); **tomar café** to drink coffee (1A)
cafetera coffeepot (4B)
cafetería cafeteria (P)
caída *n.* drop
caja box; cashier's station, checkout counter; **caja de cartón** cardboard box (6B)
cajero/a teller (8A); **cajero automático** ATM (2A)
cajón *m.* large box
calcetines *m. pl.* socks (2B)
calculadora calculator (5A)
calcular to calculate
cálculo calculus
calendario calendar
calidad *f.* quality
caliente hot; **chocolate** (*m.*) **caliente** hot chocolate (3B); **té** (*m.*) **caliente** hot tea (3B)
callar to silence someone; *refl.* to shut up
calle *f.* street (6A)
calmado/a calm
calmante *m.* tranquilizer
calor *m.* heat; **hace (mucho) calor** it's (very) hot (1B)
caloría calorie; **quemar calorías** to burn calories (4A)
calvo/a bald (3A)
cama bed (4B); **cama matrimonial** queen bed (4B); **cama sencilla** twin bed (4B); **hacer** (*irreg.*) **la cama** to make the bed (4B)
cámara digital digital camera (5A)
camarero/a waiter, waitress
camarones *m. pl.* shrimp (3B)
cambiar (por) to change, exchange (for); **cambiar de canal** to change channels (5A)
cambio change; **en cambio** on the other hand
caminar to walk (4A)
camino road; **camino a** on the way to

camión *m.* truck; bus (*Mex.*)
camisa shirt (2B)
camiseta T-shirt (2B)
campanario bell tower
campaña campaign
campeonato championship (4A)
campesino/a peasant
camping: hacer (*irreg.*) **camping** to go camping (6B)
campo country(side); field (*of work*) (9B); **¿cuál es tu campo?** what's your major? (P)
campus *m.* campus
canadiense *n., adj.* Canadian
canal *m.* canal; **cambiar de canal** to change channels (5A); **canal de televisión** television channel
canario canary (9A)
cancelar to cancel
cancha (de tenis) (tennis) court (4A)
canción *f.* song
candidato/a candidate
canoa canoe; **remar en canoa** to go canoeing (6B)
canoso/a: pelo canoso gray hair (3A)
cansado/a tired (7A)
cansarse to tire (7A)
cantante *m., f.* singer
cantar to sing (1A)
cantidad *f.* quantity
cañaveral (*m.*) **de azúcar** sugar cane field
caótico/a chaotic (1B)
capa de ozono ozone layer (6B)
capilla chapel (2A)
cápita: renta per cápita per capita income
capital *f.* capital (*city*)
capitán *m.* captain
captar to grasp
cara *n.* face (7A)
característica characteristic
caracterizar (c) to characterize
carbohidrato carbohydrate (3B)
cardíaco/a: infarto cardíaco heart attack
cardiopatía cardiopathy
cargar (gu) to charge
cargo: hacerse (*irreg.*) **cargo de** to take charge of (*something*)
Caribe *m.* Caribbean (Sea)
caribeño/a *n., adj. of or from the Caribbean*
caries *f. inv.* cavity
cariño affection; **tenerle** (*irreg.*) **cariño a alguien** to be fond of someone (7B)
cariñoso/a affectionate (7B)
carnaval *m.* carnival; **Martes** (*m.*) **de Carnaval** Mardi Gras (4A)
carne *f.* meat (3B); **carne de res** beef (3B)
carnero *n.* ram
carnicería butcher's shop

caro/a expensive (2B)
carrera major; career; **¿qué carrera haces?** what's your (*fam. s.*) major? (P)
carretera highway
carro *m.* car
carta letter
cartel *m.* poster (4B)
cartelera billboard
cartera wallet
cartón *m.* cardboard; **caja de cartón** cardboard box (6B)
casa house (4B); **casa particular** private residence (4B); **casa privada** private residence (4B); **compañero/a de casa** housemate (4B); **limpiar la casa (entera)** to clean the (whole) house (4B); **regresar a casa** to go home (1A)
casado/a married (3A)
casamentero/a matchmaker
casarse (con) to marry, get married (5B)
casero/a *adj.* home
casi almost; **casi nunca** almost never; **casi siempre** almost always
caso case; **en caso de que** *conj.* in case (7B)
castaño/a brown (3A)
castellano *n.* Spanish (*language*)
castellano/a *adj.* Castilian
castigar (gu) to punish (7B)
castillo castle
casualidad *f.* chance; coincidence
catalán/catalana *n., adj.* Catalonian
catálogo *n.* catalog
cataratas *pl.* waterfall (6B)
catástrofe *f.* catastrophe
catedral *f.* cathedral (2A)
categoría category; class
catolicismo Catholicism
católico/a *n., adj.* Catholic
catorce fourteen (1A)
causa cause; **a causa de** because of
causar to cause
cautela caution
cazuela casserole
CD: reproductor (*m.*) **de CD** CD player (5A)
cebolla onion (3B)
ceder to hand over
celebración *f.* celebration
celebrar to celebrate (4A)
célebre famous
celos *pl.* jealousy (7B); **tener** (*irreg.*) **celos** to be jealous
celoso/a jealous; **estar** (*irreg.*) **celoso/a** to be jealous (7A)
celular: (teléfono) celular cell phone (5A)
cena dinner (3B)
cenar to eat/have (for) dinner (3B); **cenar en un restaurante elegante** to eat in a fancy restaurant (6B)

cenizas *pl.* ashes
censo census
censurar to judge
centígrado/a centigrade
centro downtown (2A); **centro comercial** shopping center, mall (2A); **centro estudiantil** student center/union (2A)
Centroamérica Central America
centroamericano/a *n., adj. of or from Central America*
cepas *pl.* vine stocks
cepillo brush
cerámica *s.* ceramics
cerca de *prep.* close to (2A)
cerdo: chuleta de cerdo pork chop (3B)
cereal (cocido) (cooked) cereal (3B)
cerebral cerebral (1B)
cerebro brain (8A)
ceremonia ceremony
cero zero (1A)
cerrar (ie) to close (2A)
cerveza beer; **tomar cerveza** to drink beer (1A)
chamán *m.* shaman
champiñones *m. pl.* mushrooms
champú *m.* shampoo
chapulín *m.* grasshopper
chaqueta jacket (2B)
charadas: juego de charadas charades
charlar to chat (1A); **charlar en un café** to chat in a cafe (6B)
chatarro/a: comida chatarra junk food
chau ciao
cheque *m.* check (8A); **cheque de viajero** traveler's check (8A)
chequear to check
chícharo pea
chico/a *n. m., f.* boy, girl (P); *adj.* small
chileno/a *n., adj.* Chilean
chimpancé *m.* chimpanzee
chino/a *n., adj.* Chinese
chisme *m.* gossip; **contar (ue) chismes** to gossip (9A)
chismear to gossip
chismoso/a gossipy (1B)
chiste *m.* joke
chocante shocking (8B)
chocar (qu) to run into
chocolate *m.* chocolate; **chocolate caliente** hot chocolate (3B)
chubasco rainstorm
chuleta de cerdo pork chop (3B)
cibercafé *m.* cybercafe
ciclismo cycling; **hacer** (*irreg.*) **ciclismo estacionario** to ride a stationary bike (4A)
cielo sky; heaven
cien, ciento one hundred (2A); **ciento uno/a** (2B); **por ciento** percent
cien mil one hundred thousand (5B)
ciencia science; **ciencias naturales**

natural sciences (P); **ciencias políticas** political science (P); **ciencias sociales** social sciences (P)
científico/a scientist (9B); *adj.* scientific
cierto/a certain; true
cifra number, figure
cigarrillo cigarette
cima top
cinco five (1A)
cincuenta fifty (2A)
cine *m.* movie theater (2A); the movies; **ir** (*irreg.*) **al cine** to go to the movies
cinta cassette
cintura waist
cinturón *m.* belt; **abrocharse el cinturón** to fasten one's seatbelt
circulación *f.* circulation; traffic
círculo circle
circunstancia circumstance
cirugía surgery
cirujano/a surgeon
cita appointment; date (5A)
ciudad *f.* city (2A)
ciudadano/a citizen (8B)
cívico/a civic; **responsabilidad** (*f.*) **cívica** civic duty (8B); **reunión** (*f.*) **cívica** town meeting (8B)
civil: ingeniería civil civil engineering (P); **ingeniero/a civil** civil engineer (9B)
civilización *f.* civilization
clarificación *f.* clarification
claro/a clear; light
clase *f.* class (P); **clase media** middle class; **clase turística** tourist class (6A); **compañero/a de clase** classmate; **primera clase** first class (6A); **¿qué clases tienes este semestre/trimestre?** what classes do you (*fam. s.*) have this semester/quarter? (P); **sala de clase** classroom (P); **tengo una clase de…** I have a(n) … class (P); **tomar una clase** to take a class (1A)
clasificación *f.* classification
clasificar (qu) to classify
clave *f.* key
clic: hacer (*irreg.*) **clic** to click (5A)
cliente *m., f.* customer (2B)
clima *m.* climate
clínica clinic
club *m.* club
coágulo clot
cobrar to charge (*a fee*) (8A)
coche *m.* car
cocido/a cooked (3B); **cereal** (*m.*) **cocido** cooked cereal (3B)
cocina kitchen; cooking (4B)
cocinar to cook (4A)
cocinero/a cook (6A)
codiciado/a coveted

código code
codo elbow (7A)
coexistir to coexist
cognado cognate
coincidencia coincidence
coincidir to coincide
cola tail (*of an animal*); line (*of people*); **hacer** (*irreg.*) **cola** to wait (stand) in line (6A)
colaboración *f.* collaboration
colaborar to collaborate (9A)
colección *f.* collection
coleccionar to collect; **coleccionar estampillas** to collect stamps (4A); **coleccionar monedas** to collect coins (4A)
colega *m., f.* colleague (9A)
colegio high school
colesterol *m.* cholesterol
colgar (ue) (gu) to hang; to hang up (*phone*)
coliflor *f.* cauliflower (3B)
colina hill (6B)
colocar (qu) to place
colombiano/a *n., adj.* Colombian
colonia colony
colonizar (c) to colonize (5B)
color *m.* color
colorear to color (5A)
columna column
comandante commander
combatir to fight
combinación *f.* combination
combinar to combine; **combinar bien** to go well with (*clothing*) (2B)
combustibles (*m.*) **fósiles** fossil fuels (6B)
comedia comedy (8B)
comedor *m.* dining room (4B)
comentar to comment, make comments on; to discuss
comentario comment; remark; *pl.* commentaries
comenzar (ie) (c) to begin
comer to eat (1B); **dar** (*irreg.*) **de comer** to feed (9A)
comercial: centro comercial shopping center, mall (2A)
comercio business (P); **libre comercio** free trade; **Tratado de Libre Comercio (TLC)** North American Free Trade Agreement (NAFTA)
comestible *m.* food item (8A)
cometer to commit
cómico/a funny, comical (1B); **tiras cómicas** comics (5A)
comida food; meal; **comida chatarra** junk food; **comida rápida** fast food (3B)
comienzo *n.* beginning
comisión *f.* commission (8A)
como as, like; **tan pronto como** as soon as (9B)

¿cómo? how (1B); **¿cómo es?** what is he/she/it like? what are you (*form. s.*) like? (3A); **¿cómo se llama (él/ella)?** what's his/her name? (P); **¿cómo se llega a… ?** how do you get to.. .? (6A); **¿cómo te llamas?** what's your (*fam. s.*) name? (P)
cómoda dresser, chest of drawers (4B)
comodidades *f. pl.* amenities, conveniences
cómodo/a comfortable
compañero/a companion; **compañero/a de casa** housemate (4B); **compañero/a de clase** classmate; **compañero/a de cuarto** roommate (4B)
compañía company; **servir (i, i) de compañía** to give, keep company (9A)
comparación *f.* comparison
comparar to compare
compartir to share
compasión *f.* compassion
competición *f.* competition
competidor(a) competitive (9A)
competir (i, i) to compete (4A)
complemento *gram.* object
completar to complete
completo/a complete; **pensión** (*f.*) **completa** room and all meals (6A)
comportamiento behavior (9A)
comportarse to behave, act
composición *f.* composition
comprar to buy (2B); **comprar recuerdos** to buy souvenirs (6B)
compras purchases; **de compras** shopping (2B)
comprender to understand (1B); to encompass
comprensivo/a understanding (7B)
comprometer to compromise; to involve; **comprometerse (con)** to get engaged (to) (7B)
compuesto/a *adj.* compound
compulsivo/a compulsive
computación *f.* computer science (9B)
computadora computer (P); **computadora portátil** laptop computer (5A)
común *adj.* common
comunicación *f.* communication; **medios** (*pl.*) **de comunicación** media (8B); *pl.* communications (P)
comunidad *f.* community
con with (P); **con baño privado** with a private bathroom (6A); **con frecuencia** frequently; **con tal (de) que** provided (that) (7B)
concentración *f.* concentration
concentrar to concentrate; to focus; **concentrarse en** to concentrate; to be focused

concepto concept, idea
concierto concert; **ir** (*irreg.*) **a un concierto** to go to a concert (6B)
conclusión *f.* conclusion
concordancia *gram.* agreement
concurso contest; game show (8B)
condición *f.* condition
condicional *m. gram.* conditional
condimentos condiments
condominio condominium (4B)
conducir *irreg.* to drive; **sacar (qu) la licencia de conducir** to get a driver's license (5A)
conducta conduct, behavior
conductor(a) driver
conectar to connect (5A)
conejo rabbit (9A)
conexión *f.* connection
confesar (ie) to confess
confiable trustworthy
confiado/a trusting (1B)
confianza trust
confiar (confío) (en) to trust (in) (7B)
confidente confident
confirmar to confirm
conflicto conflict; **resolver (ue) conflictos** to resolve conflicts (9A)
confrontación *f.* confrontation
confrontar to confront
confundido/a confused (7A)
confundir to confuse; *refl.* to get confused (7A)
confusión *f.* confusion
confuso/a confusing
congelación *n. f.* freezing
congelado/a frozen
congelador *m.* freezer
congelar to freeze; **congelarse** to freeze up (*the screen*) (5A)
conjunto outfit; entirety
conmigo with me
conocer (zc) to know, be familiar with (*someone, something*) (3A)
conocido/a *n.* acquaintance
conocimiento awareness; *pl.* knowledge
conquista conquest (5B)
conquistar to conquer (5B); to succeed in seducing someone (7B)
consecuencia consequence
conseguir (i, i) (g) to get, obtain (4B); **conseguir + inf.** to succeed in (*doing something*) (4B)
consejo piece of advice; *pl.* advice
consenso consent
consentido *n.* whim, fancy
consentido/a indulged, spoiled
conservación *f.* conservation
conservador(a) conservative (1B)
conservar to preserve, conserve (6B)
consideración *f.* consideration

considerar to consider
consistir en to consist of
consolar (ue) to console
consonante *m.* consonant
constante *adj.* constant
constitución *f.* constitution
constituir (y) to constitute
construir (y) to build (6B)
consultar to consult
consultorio doctor's office (7A)
consumidor(a) *n.* consumer
consumir to eat; to use up
consumo consumption
contabilidad *f.* accounting (P)
contacto contact
contador(a) accountant (9B)
contaminación *f.* pollution;
    contaminación del agua water
    pollution (6B); **contaminación del aire**
    air pollution (6B)
contaminar to contaminate (6B)
contar (ue) to count (2A); to tell (2A);
    contar chismes to gossip (9A)
contener (*like* **tener**) to contain
contenido *s.* contents
contento/a happy (7A)
contestador (*m.*) **automático** answering
    machine (5A)
contestar to answer
contexto context
contigo *fam. s.* with you
continente *m.* continent (6B)
continuación *f.* continuation; **a
    continuación** following
continuar (continúo) to continue
continuo/a continuous
contra: en contra opposed
contraer (*like* **traer**) to contract
contrario *n.* opposite, contrary
contraseña password (5A)
contraste *m.* contrast
contratar to hire
contrato lease (4B); contract
contribución *f.* contribution
contribuir (y) to contribute
controlar to control (8B); to inspect
controvertido/a controversial (8B)
convencer (z) to convince
conversación *f.* conversation
convertir (ie, i) to change; **convertirse en**
    to turn into
coordinación *f.* coordination
copa (wine) glass (6A)
copiar to copy (5A)
coqueto/a flirtatious (7B)
corazón *m.* heart (7A)
corbata necktie (2B)
cordillera mountain range (6B)
coreano/a *n., adj.* Korean
correcto/a correct
corregir (i, i) (j) to correct

correo mail (2A); post office; **correo
    electrónico** e-mail (5A); **correo de voz**
    voicemail
correr to run (1B); to extend (*mountain
    range*)
correspondencia correspondence
corresponder to correspond
correspondiente *adj.* corresponding
corriente *n. f.* current; *adj.* current,
    present; **agua** (*f.* [*but* **el agua**])
    corriente running water; **cuenta
    corriente** checking account (8A); **estar**
    (*irreg.*) **al corriente** to be caught up
    (*with current events*) (8B)
corrupción *f.* corruption (8B)
cortar(se) to cut (oneself) (7A)
cortés courteous, polite (9A)
corto/a short (*except height*) (3A);
    de corto plazo short term (2B);
    pantalones (*m. pl.*) **cortos**
    shorts (2B)
cosa thing; **poner** (*irreg.*) **las cosas en
    orden** to put things in order (4B)
cosecha harvest
coser to sew
cosmético/a: cirugía cosmética
    cosmetic (plastic) surgery
cosmopolita *adj. m., f.* cosmopolitan
costa coast (6B)
costar (ue) to cost (2A)
costilla rib
costo cost, price
costumbre *f.* custom
cotidiano/a daily
creación *f.* creation
creador(a) creative (1B)
crear to create
creativo/a creative
crecer (zc) to grow
creciente *adj.* growing
crecimiento growth
crédito credit (1A); **tarjeta de crédito**
    credit card (2B)
creencia belief
creer (y) (que) to believe (that) (1B)
crema cream; **queso de crema** cream
    cheese (3B)
crianza upbringing
criar (crío) to raise (*child, pet*)
crimen *m.* crime; **crimen violento** violent
    crime (8B)
crisis *f.* crisis
cristiano/a *n., adj.* Christian
criticar (qu) to criticize (8B)
crítico/a critic
cronológico/a chronological
crucero cruise ship
crudo/a raw (3B)
cruel cruel (7B)
cruzar (c) to cross (6A)
cuaderno notebook

cuadra (city) block (6A)
cuadrado/a squared; **metros cuadrados**
    square meters (4B); **pies** (*m.*)
    cuadrados square feet (4B)
cuadro painting (4B); statistical chart; **de
    cuadros** plaid
cual: tal cual just as
¿cuál(es)? what? which? (1B); **¿cuál es
    su apellido?** what's his/her last name?
    (P); **¿cuál es tu apellido?** what's your
    (*fam. s.*) last name? (P); **¿cuál es tu
    campo?** what's your major? (P)
cualquier(a) any
cuando when(ever) (9B); **de vez en
    cuando** once in a while (3B)
¿cuándo? when? (1B)
cuanto: en cuanto as soon as (9B); **en
    cuanto a** with regard to; **en unos
    cuantos días** in a few days (1B)
cuánto *pron.* **¿a cuánto sale?** how much
    is it?; **¿cuánto hay de aquí a...** how far
    is it from here to ... ? (6A)
¿cuántos/as? how many? (1B); **¿cuántos
    años cumples?** how many years old
    are you (*turning*) (*fam. s.*)? (4A);
    ¿cuántos años tiene... ? how old is ...
    ?; **¿cuántos años tienes?** how old are
    you (*fam. s.*)?
cuarenta forty (2A)
cuarto *n.* quarter (*of an hour*); fourth;
    room (4B); **compañero/a de cuarto**
    roommate (4B); **menos cuarto** a
    quarter to (*hour*) (1A); **servicio de
    cuarto** room service (6A); **y cuarto** a
    quarter past (*hour*) (1A)
cuarto/a fourth (4A)
cuatro four (1A)
cuatrocientos/as four hundred (2B)
cuatrocientos/as mil four hundred
    thousand (5B)
cubano/a *n., adj.* Cuban
cubanoamericano/a no, *adj.* Cuban-
    American
cubierto/a (*p.p. of* **cubrir**) covered
cubiertos *pl.* silverware (6A)
cubrir (*p.p.* **cubierto/a**) to cover
cuchara spoon (6A)
cuchillo knife (6A)
cuello neck (7A)
cuenta bill (6A); check; **cuenta corriente**
    checking account (8A); **cuenta de
    ahorros** savings account (8A); **darse**
    (*irreg.*) **cuenta de** to realize
cuento story
cuerda cord; **saltar la cuerda** to jump
    rope
cuerno horn; **ponerle** (*irreg.*) **los cuernos (a
    alguien)** to be unfaithful to (some- one)
cuero leather
cuerpo body; **partes** (*f. pl.*) **del cuerpo**
    parts of the body (7A)

cuestión *f.* question
cuidado care
cuidar (de) to take care (of) (9A)
culpa fault; **echar(le) la culpa (a alguien)** to blame (someone) (9A)
cultivación *f.* cultivation
culto devotion (*to a god or belief*)
cultura culture
cumbre *f.* summit
cumpleaños *m. inv.* birthday (4A)
cumplido compliment
cumplir (con) to fulfill, carry out; **¿cuántos años cumples?** how many years old are you (*turning*) (*fam. s.*)? (4A); **cumplir... años** to be ... old (*on a birthday*) (4A); **cumplir las promesas** to keep one's word (9A)
cuñado/a brother-in-law, sister-in-law; *pl.* siblings-in-law
curandero/a healer
curar to cure
cursi tacky (8B); cheesy
cursivo/a: letra (*s.*) **cursiva** italics
curso course
cuy *m.* guinea pig (9A)
cuyo/a/os/as whose

D

dama lady; **dama de honor** bridesmaid
dañar to hurt, harm (8B)
dañino/a harmful
daño damage, hurt
dar *irreg.* to give (3B); **dar consejos** to give advice (3B); **dar de comer** to feed (9A); **dar la vuelta a** to go around (*something*); **dar las gracias** to thank; **dar un paseo** to take a walk (4A); **dar una fiesta** to throw a party (4A); **darle escalofríos a alguien** to give someone chills (7B); **darle miedo a alguien** to scare someone (5A); **darle rabia (a alguien)** to make (someone) angry; **darse cuenta de** to realize; **darse la mano** to shake hands (7B)
dato piece of information; *pl.* data, facts
de *prep.* of (P); from (P); **de compras** shopping (2B); **de corto/largo plazo** short/long term (9B); **de cuadros** plaid; **¿de dónde eres?** where are you (*fam. s.*) from? (P); **de estatura mediana** of medium height (3A): **de hecho** in fact; **de ida** one-way (6A); **de ida y vuelta** round-trip (6A); **de la mañana** in the morning (A.M.) (1A); **de la noche** in the evening (night) (P.M.) (1A); **de la tarde** in the afternoon (1A); **de las... hasta las...** from ... (*hour*) to (*hour*) (1A); **de lunares** polka-dotted; **de nada** you're welcome; **¿de qué tamaño es... ?** what size is ... ? (4B); **de rayas**

striped; **de repente** suddenly; **de venta** for sale (4B); **de vez en cuando** once in a while (3B); **es de...** it's made of ... (2B); **soy de...** I'm from ... (P)
debajo de under, below (2A)
debate *m.* debate
deber *n. m.* duty (8B)
deber + *inf.* ought to, should (*do something*); to owe (8A)
debido a due to
débil weak
década decade (5B)
decidido/a decisive
decidir to decide
decir *irreg.* (*p.p.* **dicho/a**) to say (2A)
decisión *f.* decision
declaración *f.* statement
declarar to declare
dedicación *f.* dedication
dedicarse (qu) a to dedicate oneself to
dedo finger (7A); **dedo del pie** toe (7A)
deducción *f.* deduction
deducir (*like* **conducir**) to deduct; to infer
defecto defect
defender (ie) to defend
defensor(a) *n.* defender; *adj.* defensive
definición *f.* definition
definir to define
definitivo/a definitive
deforestación *f.* deforestation (6B)
degustar vinos to go wine tasting (6B)
dejar to leave; **dejar de** + *inf.* to stop (*doing something*); **dejar en paz** to leave alone; **dejar perplejo/a (a alguien)** to leave (someone) perplexed; **dejar (una) propina** to leave a tip (6A)
del (*contraction of* **de** + **el**) of/from the
delante de in front of (2A)
delgado/a thin (3A)
delicado/a delicate
delicioso/a delicious
demandar to demand
demás: los/las demás others (4A); **dirigir (j) a los demás** to lead others (9B)
demasiado *adv.* too, too much
demasiado/a *adj.* too much; *pl.* too many
democracia democracy
democrático/a democratic
demostrar (ue) to demonstrate; to show
demostrativo/a demonstrative
denotar to denote; to indicate
densidad *f.* density
denso/a heavy
dentista *m., f.* dentist
dentro (de) in, within, inside; **dentro de poco** in a little while (1B); **por dentro** within, (on the) inside
depender de to depend on
dependiente/a salesperson (2B)
deporte *m.* sport; **practicar (qu) un**

deporte to practice a sport (1A)
deportivo/a *adj.* sport; **programa** (*m.*) **deportivo** sports show (8B)
depositar to deposit (8A)
depresión *f.* (**económica**) (economic) depression (5B)
deprimido/a depressed (5B)
deprimir(se) to depress, become depressed (7A)
derecha *n.* right-hand side; **a la derecha (de)** to the right (of) (2A); **doblar a la derecha** to turn right
derecho *n.* right (*legal*) (8B); law (9B); **derechos humanos** human rights (8B); **seguir (i, i) (g) derecho** to continue straight ahead (6A)
derramar to spill
derrocar (qu) to defeat
derrochador(a) wasteful (8A)
derrotar to defeat
desafío *n.* challenge
desafortunadamente unfortunately
desagradable unpleasant
desahogarse (gu) con to take it out on
desaparecer (zc) to disappear
desarrollado/a developed; **país** (*m.*) **desarrollado** developed country (8A)
desarrollar to develop
desarrollo (sustenable) (sustainable) development; **país** (*m.*) **en vías de desarrollo** developing country (8A)
desastre *m.* (**natural**) (natural) disaster (5B)
desastroso/a disastrous
desaventajado/a disadvantaged
desayunar to eat/have (for) breakfast (3B)
desayuno breakfast (3B)
descafeinado/a decaffeinated (3B); **café** (*m.*) **descafeinado** decaffeinated coffee
descansar to rest (1A)
descapotable convertible
descargar (gu) to download (5A)
descendiente *m., f.* descendant
descomponer (*like* **poner**) decompose (6B)
desconectar to unplug, disconnect
desconfiado/a untrusting (1B)
desconocido/a unknown
describir (*p.p.* **descrito/a**) to describe (1B)
descripción *f.* description
descubierto/a (*p.p. of* **descubrir**) discovered
descubrimiento discovery (5B)
descuento discount
descuidar to neglect
desde *prep.* from; **desde la(s)... hasta la(s)...** from ... until ... (*time*)
desear to want, desire (1A)

desechable disposable; **producto desechable** disposable product (6B)
desechos *pl.* wastes
desempleo unemployment; **tasa de desempleo** unemployment rate (8A)
deseo *n.* wish, desire (9B)
desierto desert (6B)
designar to designate
desilusionado/a disillusioned
desleal disloyal (1B)
desobedecer (zc) to disobey (3A)
despacio/a slow
despedirse (i, i) to say good-bye
despegar (gu) to take off (*plane*)
despejado/a clear; **está despejado** it's clear (*weather*) (1B)
desperdiciar to waste (6B)
desperdicios *pl.* waste (6B)
despertador *m.* alarm clock
despertarse (ie) to wake up (2A)
despreciar to despise (7B)
después *adv.* after; **después de** *prep.* after; **después (de) que** *conj.* after (9B)
destacado/a outstanding
destacar (qu) to stand out
destino destination; destiny, fate
destrucción *f.* destruction
desvelarse to stay up late
detalle *m.* detail
detallista *adj. m., f.* detail-oriented (7B)
detergente *m.* detergent (4B)
determinar to determine
detestar to detest (7B)
detrás de *adv.* behind (2A)
deuda debt (8A); **amortizar (c) una deuda** to pay off a debt (8A)
devoción *f.* devotion
devolver (ue) (*p.p.* **devuelto/a**) to return (*something*)
devoto/a devout
devuelto/a (*p.p. of* **devolver**) returned
día *m.* day (1A); **buenos días** good morning (P); **cada día** every day; **Día de Acción de Gracias** Thanksgiving (4A); **Día de la Madre (del Padre)** Mother's (Father's) Day; **Día de los Enamorados** St. Valentine's Day (4A); **Día de los Reyes Magos** Epiphany (January 6), Day of the Magi; **Día de San Patricio** St. Patrick's Day (4A); **Día de San Valentín** St. Valentine's Day (4A); **día del santo** saint's day; **Día del Trabajo** Labor Day; **día festivo** holiday (4A); **¿en qué día cae… ?** what day is … ?; **hoy en día** now a days; **¿qué día es hoy?** what day is it today? (1A); **todos los días** every day (1A)
diabetes *f.* diabetes
dialecto dialect
diálogo dialogue
diario *m.* newspaper

diario/a *adj.* daily
dibujar to draw (4A)
dibujo drawing; **dibujo animado** cartoon
diccionario dictionary
dicho/a (*p.p. of* **decir**) said
diciembre *m.* December (1B)
dictador(a) dictator
dictadura dictatorship
diecinueve nineteen (1A)
dieciocho eighteen (1A)
dieciséis sixteen (1A)
diecisiete seventeen (1A)
diente *m.* tooth; **lavarse los dientes** to brush one's teeth (4B)
dieta *n.* diet
dietético/a: refresco dietético diet soft drink (3B)
diez ten (1A)
diez mil ten thousand (5B)
diferencia difference; **a diferencia de** unlike
diferenciar (de) to be different (from)
diferente (de) different (from/than)
difícil difficult (5B)
dificultad *f.* difficulty
difundirse to diffuse, spread
digestivo/a digestive
digital: cámara digital digital camera (5A)
Dinamarca Denmark
dinamismo dynamism, quality of being dynamic
dinero money (2B); **sacar (qu) dinero** to withdraw money (8A)
dinosaurio dinosaur
dios(a) god, goddess; **Dios** *m.* god
diplomático/a diplomat
dirección *f.* direction; address (4B)
directo/a direct; straight; **pensar (ie) de manera directa** to think in a direct (linear) manner (9B); **vuelo directo** direct flight (6A)
director(a) director (9B)
dirigir (j) to direct; **dirigir a los demás** to lead others (9B); **dirigirse a** to direct oneself toward
disco: disco compacto compact disc; **disco duro** hard drive (5A)
discoteca discotheque (2A)
discreto/a discreet (1B)
discriminación *f.* discrimination (8B)
disculpar to excuse
disculpas: pedir (*irreg.*) **disculpas** to apologize
discusión *f.* discussion
discutir to discuss; to argue (7B)
diseñador(a) designer; **diseñador(a) de sitios** Web site designer (9B)
diseñar to draw; to design
disfrutar to enjoy
disponible available

disposición *f.* disposition
dispositivo device
dispuesto/a ready, willing
disquete *m.* diskette (5A)
distancia distance; **mando a distancia** remote control (5A)
distante distant; far away
distinción *f.* distinction
distinguir (g) to distinguish
distinto/a different, distinct
distorsionado/a distorted (8B)
distorsionar to distort
distraer (*like* **traer**) to distract (8B)
distribución *f.* distribution
distrito (federal) (federal) district
diversidad *f.* diversity
diversión *f.:* **ir** (*irreg.*) **a un parque de diversiones** to go to an amusement park (6B)
diverso/a diverse
divertido/a fun (1B)
divertir (ie, i) to entertain (4A); **divertirse** to enjoy oneself (5B)
dividirse to divide
divinidad *f.* divinity, god-like being
divorciado/a divorced (3A)
divorciarse to divorce, get divorced (5B)
divorcio divorce (5B)
doblar to turn (6A); **doblar a la derecha/izquierda** to turn right/left
doble double
doce twelve (1A)
doctor(a) doctor
doctorado doctoral degree (9B)
documental *m.* documentary (8B)
documento document; **guardar documentos** to save documents (5A)
dólar *m.* dollar
doler (ue) to hurt, ache (7A)
dolor *m.* pain; **dolor de cabeza** headache
doméstico/a domestic; **aparato doméstico** household appliance (4B); **quehaceres** (*m.*) **domésticos** household chores (4B); **violencia doméstica** domestic violence (8B)
dominación *f.* domination
dominante dominant
dominar to dominate
domingo Sunday (1A)
dominicano/a *n., adj.* of or from the Dominican Republic
dominio *n.* control
don *m.* gift, skill; *title of respect used with a man's first name;* **tener** (*irreg.*) **don de gentes** to have a way with people (9B)
¿dónde? where? (1B); **¿de dónde eres?** where are you (*fam. s.*) from? (P);
doña *title of respect used with a woman's first name*
dormir (ue, u) to sleep (2A); **dormirse** to fall asleep (4B)

dormitorio bedroom

dos two (1A); **los dos** both

dos mil two thousand (5B)

dos millones two million (5B)

doscientos/as two hundred (2B)

doscientos mil two hundred thousand (5B)

drama *m.* drama (8B)

drástico/a drastic

droga drug

drogadicción *f.* drug addiction (8B)

ducha shower (4B)

ducharse to shower, take a shower (4B)

duda doubt; **sin duda** without a doubt

dudar to doubt (8B)

dudoso/a doubtful

dueño/a owner (4B)

dulce *adj.* sweet (3B); *n. pl.* candy (3B); **pan** (*m.*) **dulce** sweet bread (*Mex.*) (3B)

duración *f.* duration

durante during

durar to last

durmiente: la Bella Durmiente Sleeping Beauty

duro/a hard; firm; **disco duro** hard drive (5A)

DVD: reproductor (*m.*) **de DVD** DVD player (5A); **sacar (qu) un DVD** to rent a DVD (4A)

E

e and (*used instead of* **y** *before words beginning with* **i** *or* **hi**)

echar to throw out (6B); **echar un vistazo** to look over; **echar una siesta** to take a nap; **echar(le) la culpa (a alguien)** to blame (someone) (9A)

ecología ecology

ecológico/a ecological

economía economy (8A); *s.* economics (P)

económico/a economic; **depresión** (*f.*) **económica** economic depression (5B); **nivel económico** economic level

ecoturismo ecotourism

ecoturista *m., f.* ecotourist

ecoturístico/a *adj.* ecotourist

ecuatoriano/a *n., adj.* Ecuadorean

edad *f.* age (2A); **edad adulta** adulthood

edición *f.* edition

edificio building (P)

educación *f.* education

educar (qu) to educate (8B)

educativo/a educational

efectivo: en efectivo cash (money) (2B)

efecto effect; **efecto invernadero** greenhouse effect (6B)

eficaz (*pl.* **eficaces**) effective

egoísta *adj. m., f.* selfish, egotistical (1B)

ejecutivo/a executive

ejemplificar (qu) to exemplify

ejemplo example; **por ejemplo** for example

ejercer (z) to exercise (*a right*)

ejercicio exercise; **hacer** (*irreg.*) **ejercicio** to exercise (4A); **hacer** (*irreg.*) **ejercicio aeróbico** to do aerobics (4A)

ejército army

el *def. art. m.* the (P); **el/la mayor** the oldest (3A); **el/la menor** the youngest (3A)

él *sub. pron.* he (P); *obj. of prep.* him

elección *f.* election (3B)

electricidad *f.* electricity

eléctrico/a electric; **ingeniería eléctrica** electrical engineering (P); **ingeniero/a eléctrico/a** electrical engineer (9B)

electrónico/a electronic (8A); **agenda electrónica** electronic organizer, PDA (personal digital assistant) (5A); **aparato electrónico** electronic device (5A); **correo electrónico** e-mail (5A)

elegante elegant; **cenar en un restaurante elegante** to eat in a fancy restaurant (6B)

elegir (i, i) (j) to choose; to elect

elemento element

elevar to elevate, raise

eliminar to eliminate (8B)

ella *sub. pron.* she (P); *obj. of prep.* her

ellos/as *sub. pron.* they (P); *obj. of prep.* them

embargo: sin embargo *conj.* however

emborracharse to get drunk

emergencia emergency

emocionado/a moved

emocional emotional (7B)

emocionante exciting (5B)

empanada turnover pie or pastry

emparejar to match

emperador(a) emperor, empress

empezar (ie) (c) to begin (2A); **empezar a** + *inf.* to begin to (*do something*)

empleado/a employee (9A)

empleador(a) employer

emplear to use

empleo job; **anuncio de empleo** job ad

empresa company; **administración** (*f.*) **de empresas** business administration (P)

empresarial of or related to business

en in (2A); **en cambio** on the other hand; **en caso de que** in case (7B); **en cuanto** as soon as (9B); **en cuanto a** with regard to; **en marcha** on the move; **en punto** on the dot (*time*) (1A); **¿en qué día/mes cae... ?** what day/month is . . . ?; **en unos cuantos días** in a few days (1B)

enamorado/a *n.* lover; **enamorado/a** *adj.* **(de)** in love (with) (7A); **Día** (*m.*) **de los Enamorados** St. Valentine's Day (4A)

enamorarse (de) to fall in love (with) (5A)

encantado/a nice to meet you

encantador(a) delightful, charming (7B)

encantar to love (5A); **encantarle** to charm, delight (*someone*); to love (*thing*)

encargarse (de) to take charge (of)

encender (ie) to turn on (5A)

enchufe *m.* connection

encima de on top of (2A)

enclave *m.* enclave

encontrar (ue) to find (2B); **encontrarse con** to get together (meet) with

encuentro *n.* get-together; (chance) meeting (5B)

encuesta survey

energía energy (8A)

enérgico/a energetic (1B)

enero January (1B)

enfermarse to get sick (7A)

enfermedad *f.* sickness; disease

enfermero/a *n.* nurse (7A)

enfermo/a *n.* sick person; *adj.* sick; **estar** (*irreg.*) **enfermo/a** to be sick (7A)

enfoque *m.* focus

enfrentarse a to face, confront

enfrente de across from (2A); in front of (2A)

engañador(a) deceitful (7B)

engañar to deceive (7B); to cheat on (7B); **engañarse** to fool oneself

engañoso/a deceitful

enlace *m.* link (5A)

enlatado/a canned

enojado/a angry (5B)

enojarse to get mad (7A)

enorme enormous

ensalada salad; **ensalada mixta** tossed salad (3B)

ensayo essay

enseñanza teaching (9B)

enseñar to teach (1A)

entender (ie) to understand (2A)

enterarse de to find out about

entero/a entire, whole; **limpiar la casa entera** to clean the whole house (4B)

enterrar (ie) to bury

entonces then

entrada entrance; ticket

entrante: la semana entrante next week (1B)

entrar (en + *place*) to enter (*a place*)

entre between (1B)

entregar (gu) to hand in

entrelazar (c) to intertwine

entrenamiento training

entrenar to train (9A)

entretanto meanwhile

entretener (*like* **tener**) to entertain (8B)

entretenido/a amused, entertained, fun (8B)

entretenimiento entertainment, amusement

entrevista interview; **programa** (*m.*) **de entrevistas** talk show (8B)

entrevistar to interview

entrometerse to meddle

entrometido/a meddlesome

entusiasmado/a enthusiastic; excited

enumerar to number

enviar (envío) to send (5A)

envidia envy; **tenerle** (*irreg.*) **envidia (a alguien)** to be envious (of someone) (7A)

envidioso/a envious

episodio episode

época era, age

equilibrado/a well-balanced

equipado/a equipped

equipaje *m.* luggage (6A); **facturar el equipaje** to check luggage (6A)

equipo team (4A); **trabajar en equipo** to work as a team (9A)

equivalente equivalent

equivaler (*like* **valer**) to be equivalent; to be equal

equivocarse (qu) to be mistaken

error *m.* error, mistake

erupción *f.* eruption

escala scale; ladder; layover; **hacer** (*irreg.*) **escala** to make a stopover (6A)

escalada: practicar (qu) la escalada to rappel

escalar montañas to go mountain climbing

escalofríos *pl.* chills; **darle** (*irreg.*) **escalofríos a alguien** to give someone chills (7B)

escandaloso/a scandalous (8B)

escapar (de) to escape (from) (8B)

escasez (*pl.* **escaseces**) *f.* scarcity

escena scene

esclavo/a slave

escoba broom

escoger (j) to choose

escoliosis *f.* scoliosis

esconder to hide

escondite (*m.*): **jugar (ue) (gu) al escondite** to play hide and seek (5A)

escorpión *m.* scorpion

escribir (*p.p.* **escrito/a**) to write (1B)

escrito/a (*p.p. of* **escribir**) written

escritor(a) writer

escritorio desk (P)

escuchar to listen (to) (1A)

escuela school (2A); **escuela secundaria** high school

escultor(a) sculptor (9B)

escultura sculpture

escurrir to drain

ese/a *adj.* that (2B); *pron.* that (one) (2B)

eso *neut. pron.* that (2B)

esos/esas *adj.* those (2B); *pron.* those (ones) (2B)

espacio space; **respetar el espacio personal** to respect personal space (9A)

espaguetis *m. pl.* spaghetti (3B)

espalda back (*of a person*) (7A); **hablar a espaldas de alguien** to talk behind someone's back

espantoso/a scary

español *n. m.* Spanish (*language*) (P)

español(a) *n.* Spaniard; *adj.* Spanish; **tortilla española** *omelette made of eggs, potatoes, and onions* (3B)

espárragos *pl.* asparagus (3B)

especial special

especialidad *f.* specialty

especialista specialist (9B)

especialización *f.* specialization, major

especie *f. s.* species; **especies en peligro de extinción** endangered species (6B)

específico/a specific

espectáculo spectacle, sight; show; **mundo de los espectáculos** entertainment industry (8A); **ver** (*irreg.*) **un espectáculo** to see a show (6B)

espejo mirror (4B)

espera: sala de espera waiting room (6A)

esperanza hope (7B)

esperar to hope; to wait for

espinacas *pl.* spinach

espíritu *m.* spirit

esponja sponge

espontáneo/a spontaneous (7B)

esposo/a husband, wife (3A); *pl.* married couple

espuma foam

esquí *m.* skiing (*sport*)

esquiar (esquío) (en el agua) to (water) ski (4A)

esquina corner (*street*)

estable *adj.* stable (5B)

establecer (zc) to establish (5B)

establecimiento establishment

estación *f.* season (1B); station; **estación del tren** train station (2A)

estacionar to park

estacionario stationary; **hacer** (*irreg.*) **ciclismo estacionario** to ride a stationary bike (4A)

estadio stadium (2A)

estadística *s.* statistics

estado *n.* state; condition; **estado de ánimo** state of mind; **estado físico** physical condition (7A); **Estado Libre Asociado** Free Associated State, Commonwealth; **Estados Unidos** United States; **jefe** (*m.*) **de estado** head of state

estadounidense *n., adj.* of or from the United States

estallar to explode

estampilla stamp; **coleccionar estampillas** to collect stamps (4A)

estanco tobacco shop (2A)

estante *m.* bookshelf (4B)

estantería *s.* shelves, bookcase

estar *irreg.* to be (P); **está despejado** it's clear (*weather*) (1B); **está lloviendo** it's raining (1B); **está nevando** it's snowing (1B); **está nublado** it's cloudy (1B); **estar a buen precio** to be a good price; **estar a nombre de...** to be in ... 's name; **estar al corriente** to be caught up (*with current events*) (8B) **estar celoso/a** to be jealous (7A); **estar de acuerdo** to agree; **estar en (buena) forma** to be in (good) shape (4A); **estar enfermo/a** to be sick (7A); **estar listo/a** to be ready; **estar por** + *inf.* to be about to (*do something*); **estar seguro/a de** to be sure of (8B)

estatua statue

estatura: de estatura mediana of medium height (3A)

estatus *m.* status

este *m.* east; **al este de** to the east of (2A)

este/a *adj.* this (2B); *pron.* this (one) (2B); **esta noche** tonight (1B)

este... uh ... (*pause sound*)

estelar: hora estelar prime time

estéreo stereo (5A)

estereotipado/a stereotyped

estereotipo *n.* stereotype

estilo style

estimar to think highly of (7B)

estimulante stimulating (1B)

estimular to stimulate

estímulo stimulus

esto *neut. pron.* this (2B)

estómago stomach (7A)

estos/as *adj.* these (2B); *pron.* these (ones) (2B)

estrategia strategy

estratégico/a strategic

estrecho *n.* strait

estrecho/a close

estrella star

estrenar to debut

estreno debut

estrés *m.* stress; **sufrir de estrés** to suffer from stress

estresado/a stressed

estricto/a strict

estrofa verse

estructura structure

estructural structural

estudiante *m., f.* student (P)

estudiantil *adj.* student; **centro estudiantil** student center/union (2A); **residencia estudiantil** dormitory (P)

estudiar to study (1A); **estudio...** I study.., I'm studying ... (P); **¿qué estudias?** what are you (*fam. s.*) studying?

estudio study; *pl.* studies, schooling; **estudios de posgrado** graduate studies (9B); **estudios interdepartamentales** interdisciplinary studies (P); **estudios latinos** Latino studies (P); **estudios sobre el género** gender studies (P)

estudioso/a studious

estufa stove (4B)

estupendo/a stupendous

estupidez *f.* (*pl.* **estupideces**) stupid thing

etapa step, stage

ética *s.* ethics

etiope *adj. m., f.* Ethiopian

etiqueta etiquette

etnicidad *f.* ethnicity

étnico/a ethnic

etnografía ethnography, study of the races of people

Europa Europe (6B)

europeo/a *adj.* European

evaluación *f.* evaluation

evaluar (evalúo) to evaluate

evento event

evidencia evidence

evidente evident

evitar to avoid

evolucionar to evolve

exacto/a exact

exageración *f.* exaggeration

exagerado/a exaggerated (8B)

exagerar to exaggerate (8B)

examen *m.* test; **examen médico** medical exam (7A)

examinar to examine (7A)

excavación *f.* excavation

excelencia excellence

excelente excellent

excéntrico/a eccentric (1B)

excepción *f.* exception

excepcional exceptional

excepto *adv.* except

excesivo/a excessive

excluir (y) to exclude

exclusivo/a exclusive

excursión *f.* excursión; **ir** (*irreg.*) **de excursión** to go on a hike, go hiking (6B)

excusa excuse

exhibir to exhibit

exigencias *pl.* demands

exigente demanding

exigir (j) to demand

exilado/a exiled

exilio exile

existir to exist

éxito success (5B); **tener** (*irreg.*) **éxito** to be successful (5B)

exitoso/a successful

exótico/a exotic; strange

expandir to expand

expansión *f.* expansion

expectativa expectation

expedir (i, i) to expedite; to issue

experiencia *n.* experience

experimentar to test, try out; to experience

experimento experiment

experto/a *n., adj.* expert

explicación *f.* explanation

explicar (qu) to explain

exploración *f.* exploration (5B)

explorador(a) explorer

explorar to explore (5B)

explosión *f.* explosion

explosivo/a explosive (1B)

explotar to exploit

exponer (*like* **poner**) to expose, report

exportación *f.* exportation; **productos de exportación** export products (8A)

exportador(a) exporter

exportar to export (8A)

expresar to express

expresión *f.* expression

expulsado/a expelled; thrown out

expulsar to eject

exquisito/a exquisite

extender (ie) to extend

extendido/a extended; **familia extendida** extended family (3A)

extensión *f.* extension

exterior *m.* exterior

extinción *f.* extinction; **especies** (*f. pl.*) **en peligro de extinción** endangered species (6B)

extranjero *n.* abroad; **ir** (*irreg.*) **al extranjero** to go abroad (6A)

extranjero/a *n.* foreigner; *adj.* foreign

extrañar to miss (*someone*) (7B); to be strange

extraño/a strange

extraordinario/a extraordinary

extraviar (extravío) to lose (*something*)

extremista *n., adj. m., f.* extremist

extremo *n.* extreme

extrovertido/a extroverted (1B)

F

fábrica factory (6B)

fabricado/a manufactured; **bienes** (*m. pl.*) **fabricados** manufactured goods (8A)

fabricar (qu) to make

fácil easy

facilidad *f.* ease; facility

facilitar to facilitate, make easy

factor *m.* factor, cause

facturar el equipaje to check luggage (6A)

facultad *f.* department (P)

falda skirt (2B)

falla error

falsificado/a falsified

falso/a false

falta *n.* lack (6B)

faltar to be missing, lacking

fama fame

familia family (3A); **familia extendida** extended family (3A); **visitar a la familia** to visit one's family (1A)

familiar *adj. pertaining to a family*

famoso/a famous

fanático/a fan, enthusiast

fantástico/a fantastic

farmacéutico/a *n.* pharmacist (7A); *adj.* pharmaceutical; **producto farmacéutico** pharmaceutical product (8A)

farmacia pharmacy (2A)

fascinante fascinating

fascinar to love, be fascinated by (5A)

fatal awful

fatiga fatigue

favor *m.* favor; **hacerle** (*irreg.*) **un favor a alguien** to do someone a favor; **por favor** please

favorecer (zc) to favor

favorito/a favorite

fax *m.*: **máquina fax** fax machine (5A)

febrero February (1B)

fecha date (*calendar*) (5B)

federal: distrito federal federal district

felicidad *f.* happiness

felicitación *f.* congratulations; **tarjeta de felicitación** greeting card

felicitar to congratulate

feliz (*pl.* **felices**) happy (5B)

femenino/a feminine

fenómeno phenomenon

feo/a ugly (3A)

fertilizante *m.* fertilizer

festivo: día (*m.*) **festivo** holiday (4A)

fiar (fío) to trust; **(no) ser** (*irreg.*) **de fiar** to be (un)reliable

ficción *f.* fiction; **ciencia ficción** science fiction

fiebre *f.* fever; **tener** (*irreg.*) **fiebre** to have a fever (7A)

fiel faithful (7B)

fiesta party (4A); **dar** (*irreg.*) **una fiesta** to throw a party (4A); **Fiesta de las Luces** Hanukkah (4A); **fiesta de sorpresa** surprise party (4A)

fiestero/a fond of parties

figura figure

fijar to arrange, set up; **fijarse en** to take note of, notice

fijo/a fixed; **precio fijo** fixed price (2B)
filete *m.* fillet
filmación *f.* filming
filmar to film
filosofía philosophy (P)
filosófico/a philosophical
fin *m.* end; **con fines de lucro** for profit; **fin de semana** weekend (1A); **poner** (*irreg.*) **fin a** to end; **por fin** finally
final *m.* end; *adj.* final
finalizar (c) to finalize
financiero/a financial
finanzas (*pl.*) **personales** personal finances (8A)
firmar to sign (4B)
física *s.* physics (P)
físico/a physicist (9B); **estado físico** physical condition (7A)
flagrante flagrant
flan *m.* flan (*baked custard*) (3B)
flexible flexible (9A)
flor *f.* flower
florecer (zc) to flourish
florido/a flowery; **Pascua Florida** Easter (4A)
fluvial *adj. related to rivers*
fólico: ácido fólico folic acid
folleto brochure
fondo fund
forestal *adj.* forest
forjar to create
forma form, shape; **estar** (*irreg.*) **en (buena) forma** to be in (good) shape (4A)
formación *f.* formation
formar to form
formato format
foro forum
fortalecer (zc) to strengthen (4A)
fortuna luck
forzado/a forced
fósil *m.* fossil; **combustibles** (*m.*) **fósiles** fossil fuels (6B)
foto picture; **sacar (qu) fotos** to take pictures
foto(grafía) photo(graph); photography
fotografiado/a photographed
fotógrafo/a photographer (9B)
fracasar to fail (5B)
fracaso failure (5B)
frágil fragile
francamente frankly
francés *m.* French (*language*) (P)
francés, francesa *n., adj.* French
franja strip (*of land*)
frase *f.* phrase
frecuencia frecuency; **con frecuencia** frequently
frecuente frequent
fregar (ie) (gu) to clean

frente a *prep.* in the face of; versus; facing
fresco/a fresh cool; **hace fresco** it's cool (*weather*) (1B)
frijol *m.* bean
frío *n.*: **hace (mucho) frío** it's (very) cold (*weather*) (1B)
frío/a *adj.* cold
frito/a (*p.p. of* **freír**) fried; **huevo frito** fried egg (3B); **papas fritas** French fries (3B)
frontera border
frustración *f.* frustration
frustrado/a frustrated (7A)
frustrar(se) to frustrate (7A)
fruta fruit (3B); **barra de frutas** fruit bar (3B)
frutería fruit store
fuego fire; **arma** (*f.* [*but* **el arma**]) **de fuego** firearm
fuente *f.* source; fountain
fuera de outside (of); **por fuera** (on the) outside
fuerte strong (4A)
fuerza strength
fumar to smoke
función *f.* function
funcionar to function, work (*machines*) (5A)
fundación *f.* foundation; founding (5B)
fundamental basic
funicular *m.* funicular, railway
furioso/a furious (7A)
fusilamiento shooting
fútbol *m.* soccer (4A); **fútbol americano** football (4A)
futbolista *m., f.* soccer player
futuro *n.* future
futuro/a *adj.* future

G

gallego Galician (*language spoken in the region of Galicia in northwest Spain*)
galleta cookie (3B); **galleta salada** cracker (3B)
gallina: ponérsele (*irreg.*) **la piel de gallina a alguien** to get goose bumps (7B)
gamba shrimp (*Sp.*)
ganador(a) winner
ganancias *pl.* earnings
ganar to win (4A); to earn (8A)
ganas *pl.*: **tener** (*irreg.*) **ganas de** + *inf.* to feel like (*doing something*)
ganga bargain (2B)
garaje *m.* garage (4B)
garantizar (c) to guarantee
garganta throat (7A)
gárgaras *pl.*: **hacer** (*irreg.*) **gárgaras** to gargle

gasolina gasoline
gastar to spend (2B)
gastos *pl.* expenses (8A)
gastronomía gastronomy, cuisine
gato/a cat (3A)
gemelo/a twin (3A)
gemir (i, i) to groan, moan; to howl
genealógico/a genealogical; **árbol** (*m.*) **genealógico** family tree
generación *f.* generation
general: en general in general
generalización *f.* generalization
generar to generate
genérico/a generic
género gender; genre; **estudios sobre el género** gender studies (P)
generoso/a generous (7B)
gente *f. s.* people; **rozarse (c) con la gente** to mingle with people (4A); **tener** (*irreg.*) **don de gentes** to have a way with people (9B)
geografía geography
geográfico/a geographical
geometría geometry
gerente *m., f.* manager
gesto gesture
gimnasia: hacer (*irreg.*) **gimnasia** to work out (4A)
gimnasio gymnasium (2A)
globalizado/a globalized
gobernador(a) governor
gobierno government (8B)
golf *m.* golf (4A)
golfo gulf (6B)
gordito/a chubby (3A)
gordo/a fat
gorra baseball cap (2B)
gozar (c) de to enjoy
grabar to record (5A)
gracias thank you; **dar** (*irreg.*) **las gracias** to thank; **Día** (*m.*) **de Acción de Gracias** Thanksgiving (4A)
gracioso/a funny (8B)
graduación *f.* graduation (5B)
graduarse (me gradúo) to graduate (5B)
gráfico/a graphic
gramática grammar
gran, grande large, big (1B); great (1B); **Gran Bretaña** Great Britain
granola: barra de granola granola bar (3B)
grasa *n.* fat
grasoso/a greasy
gratis *adv. inv.* free (*of charge*)
grave serious
greco/a *n., adj.* Greek
gregario/a gregarious (1B)
grifo tap, faucet; **agua** (*m.*) **del grifo** tap water
gris gray (2B)

gritar to yell, shout (9A)
grosero/a rude
grueso/a thick
grupo group
guagua bus (*Cuba*)
guapo/a handsome (3A); good-looking (3A)
guaraní *m.* Guarani (*indigenous language of Paraguay*)
guardar (documentos) to keep, save (documents) (5A); **guardar(le) rencor (a alguien)** to hold a grudge (against someone) (7B)
guatemalteco/a *n., adj.* Guatemalan
guerra war (5B); **guerra civil** civil war; **Guerra Fría** Cold War
guía *m., f.* guide (*person*); *f.* guidebook
guiar (guío) to guide
guisante *m.* pea
guitarra guitar; **tocar (qu) la guitarra** to play the guitar (1A)
gustar(le) to be pleasing (*to someone*) (3B); **me gusta…** I like … (1A); **te gusta…** you (*fam. s.*) like … (1A)
gusto taste; pleasure; **mucho gusto** pleased to meet you (P)

H

haber *irreg.* to have (*aux.*)
habichuela bean
hábil skillful; proficient; **ser (*irreg.*) hábil para (las matemáticas, las ciencias)** to be good at (math, science) (9B)
habilidad *f.* ability; skill
habitación *f.* (dorm) room (2A)
habitante *m., f.* inhabitant
habitar to live
hablante *m., f.* speaker
hablar to speak (1A); **hablar a espaldas de alguien** to talk behind someone's back
hacer *irreg.* (*p.p.* **hecho/a**) to make (2A); to do (2A); **hace** + *time* time ago (7A); **hace** + *time* + **que** + *present* it's been (*time*) since … ; **hace (mucho tiempo)** (a long time) ago; **hace… años** … years ago; **hace buen/mal tiempo** it's good/bad weather (1B); **hace (mucho) calor/frío** it's (very) hot/cold (1B); **hace fresco** it's cool (*weather*) (1B); **hace sol** it's sunny (1B); **hace (mucho) viento** it's (very) windy (1B); **hacer autostop** to hitchhike; **hacer camping** to go camping (6B); **hacer ciclismo estacionario** to ride a stationary bike (4A); **hacer clic** to click (5A); **hacer cola** to stand in line (6A); **hacer ejercicio** to exercise (4A); **hacer ejercicio aeróbico** to do aerobics

(4A); **hacer el salto bungee** to bungee jump (6B); **hacer escala** to make a stopover (*on a flight*) (6A); **hacer gárgaras** to gargle; **hacer gimnasia** to work out (4A); **hacer kayak** to kayak (6B); **hacer la cama** to make the bed (4B); **hacer la maleta** to pack a suitcase (6A); **hacer las paces con** to make up with (7B); **hacer novillos** to skip/cut school (5A); **hacer rafting** to go rafting (6B); **hacer trucos** to do tricks; **hacer un viaje** to take a trip (6A); **hacer una búsqueda** to do a search (5A); **hacer** *zapping* to channel surf (5A); **hacerle un favor a alguien** to do someone a favor; **hacerse cargo de** to take charge (*of something*); **¿qué carrera haces?** what's your (*fam. s.*) major? (P)
hacia toward
hambre *f.* (*but* **el hambre**) hunger (8B); **tener (*irreg.*) hambre** to be hungry
hamburguesa hamburger (3B)
hámster *m.* hamster (9A)
hasta *prep.* until; **de las… hasta las…** from (*hour*) to (*hour*) (1A); **hasta luego** until (see you) later; **hasta que** *conj.* until (9B)
hay (*from* **haber**): **(no) hay** there is/are (not) (P); **hay que** + *inf.* it's necessary + *inf.* (2B)
hechicero/a *adj.* magic; bewitching
hecho *n.* fact; **de hecho** in fact
hecho/a (*p.p. of* **hacer**) made; done
helado *n.* ice cream (3B); **té (*m.*) helado** iced tea (3B)
hemisferio hemisphere
hepatitis *f.* hepatitis
heredar to inherit
herencia heritage; inheritance
herida *n.* wound
hermanastro/a stepbrother, stepsister (3A)
hermandad (*f.*) **de mujeres** sorority
hermano/a brother, sister (3A); **medio/a hermano/a** half brother, half sister (3A); *m. pl.* siblings
herramienta tool
hídrico/a of or related to water
hierba herb; grass
hígado liver (7A)
hijastro/a stepson, stepdaughter (3A)
hijo/a son, daughter (3A); **hijo/a único/a** only child (3A); *m. pl.* children
hipertensión *f.* hypertension
hipoteca mortgage (8A); **amortizar (c) una hipoteca** to pay off a mortgage (8A)
hipotético/a hypothetical
hispano/a *n., adj.* Hispanic
Hispanoamérica Latin America
hispanohablante *m., f.* Spanish speaker
historia story; history (P)

histórico/a historical
historieta anecdote; short story; tale
hogar *m.* home (4B)
hoja leaf; sheet of paper; **hoja de papel aparte** separate piece of paper
¡hola! hello! hi! (P)
hombre *m.* man (P); **hombre de negocios** businessman (9B)
hombro shoulder (7A)
homenaje *m.* homage
homicidio homicide
homogéneo/a homogeneous
honesto/a honest, sincere (1B)
honor *m.* honor
hora hour; time; **a la misma hora** at the same time (1A); **¿a qué hora… ?** at what time … ? (1A); when … ? (1A); **con dos horas de anticipación** two hours ahead of time; **¿qué hora es?** what time is it? (1A); **¿tiene Ud. la hora?** do you (*form. s.*) have the time? (1A); **¿tienes la hora?** do you (*fam. s.*) have the time? (1A)
horario schedule (1A)
hormiga ant
horno stove (4B); **al horno** baked (3B)
horrible terrible, horrible
hospital *m.* hospital (2A)
hostilidad *f.* hostility
hotel *m.* hotel (2A)
hoy en día nowadays; **¿qué día es hoy?** what day is today? (1A)
hueso bone (7A)
huésped(a) guest
huevo egg (3B); **huevo frito** fried egg (3B); **huevos revueltos** scrambled eggs (3B)
humanidades *f., pl.* humanities (P)
humano human
humano/a *adj.* human; **derechos humanos** human rights (8B)
húmedo/a humid
humilde humble (1B)
humillación *f.* humiliation
humo smoke
humor *m.* humor; mood; **estar (*irreg.*) de buen/mal humor** to be in a good/bad mood
huracán *m.* hurricane (5B)

I

Ibérico/a: península Ibérica Iberian Peninsula
ida: de ida one-way (6A); **de ida y vuelta** round-trip (6A)
idea idea; **es buena idea** it's a good idea (2B)
identificar (qu) to identify; **identificarse con** to identify with
idioma *m.* language (P)
iglesia church (2A)
igual equal; **al igual que** just like

igualmente likewise, same here (P)
ilegal illegal
imagen *f.* (*pl.* **imágenes**) image (8B)
imaginar to imagine
imaginario/a imaginary
imaginativo/a imaginative (1B)
impaciente impatient (5A)
impactar to have an impact
impacto *n.* impact
imperfecto *gram.* imperfect (tense)
imperio empire
impermeable *m.* raincoat
importado/a *n.* imported
importancia importance
importante important
importar to matter; to be important (5A);
    importarle un pito not to care about
imposible impossible; **es imposible** it's
    impossible (8B)
impresión *f.* impression
impresionante impressive
imprimir to print
impuesto *n.* tax (8B)
impulsivo/a impulsive
impulso impulse
inadecuado/a inadequate
inanimado/a inanimate
inapropiado/a inappropriate (8B)
inca *n. m., f.* Inca
incaico/a *n., adj.* Incan
incendio fire; **seguro contra incendios**
    fire insurance (8A)
incertidumbre *f.* uncertainty
incluir (y) to include
incluso/a including
incompleto/a incomplete
incontrolable uncontrollable
inconveniente inconvenient
incorporar to incorporate
increíble incredible, unbelievable
indefinido/a indefinite
independencia independence (5B)
independiente independent
independizarse (c) to become
    independent
indicador *m.* indicator
indicar (qu) to indicate
indiferencia indifference
indiferente indifferent (1B)
indígena *n. m., f.* indigenous (person);
    adj. m., f. indigenous, native
indigenismo indigenism
indio/a *n.* Indian
indirecto/a indirect
indiscreto indiscreet (1B)
indispensable essential
indómito/a untamed
indudablemente undoubtedly
industria industry
inesperado/a unexpected
inestabilidad *f.* instability

inestable unstable
infarto (cardíaco) heart attack
infiel *adj. m., f.* unfaithful
infierno hell
infinitivo/a *gram.* infinitive
inflación *f.* inflation (8A)
inflexión *f.* inflection
influencia influence
influir (y) en to influence
información *f.* information
informado/a informed
informarse to inform oneself (8B)
informática computer science (P)
informativo/a informative (8B)
informe *m.* report
infraestructura infrastructure
infringir (j) to infringe
infundado/a unfounded
ingeniería (civil/eléctrica/mecánica)
    (civil/electrical/mechanical)
    engineering (P)
ingeniero/a (civil, eléctrico/a,
    mecánico/a) (civil, electrical,
    mechanical) engineer (9B)
ingenuo/a naive (1B)
Inglaterra England
inglés *n. m.* English (*language*) (P)
inglés, inglesa *adj.* English
ingresos *pl.* income (8A)
inicial *adj.* initial
iniciar to initiate, begin
inmediatamente immediately
inmigración *f.* (**ilegal**) (illegal)
    immigration (8B)
inmigrante *m., f.* immigrant (5B)
inmobiliaria: agente (*m., f.*) **de**
    inmobiliaria real estate agent
inmóvil unmoving
inmunodeficiencia: SIDA (síndrome (*m.*)
    de inmunodeficiencia adquirida) AIDS
    (Acquired Immune Deficiency
    Syndrome) (8B)
inodoro toilet (4B)
inolvidable unforgettable
inquieto/a restless
inquilino/a tenant (4B)
insecto insect
inseguridad *f.* insecurity
inseguro/a insecure
insistir en to insist on (8B)
insolación *f.* heat stroke
inspirar to inspire
instalaciones *f. pl.* facilities
instalar to install; **instalarse en** to settle
    into (*a house*) (9B)
instantáneo/a: mensajero instantáneo
    instant messenger
instituto institute
instrucción *f.* instruction
insuficiente insufficient
integración *f.* integration

integridad *f.* integrity
inteligencia intelligence
inteligente intelligent (1B)
intención *f.* intention
intenso/a intense
intentar to try
interacción *f.* interaction
intercambiar to exchange
intercambio *n.* exchange
interdepartamental: estudios
    interdepartamentales interdisciplinary
    studies (P)
interés *m.* interest; *pl.* interest (*finance*)
    (8A); **tipos de interés** interest
    rates (8A)
interesante interesting (1B)
interesar to interest, be interesting (5A)
interior *adj.* interior (6B)
internacional international; **noticias** (*pl.*)
    internacionales international news (8B)
internar to confine
internauta *m., f.* Internet user
Internet *m.* Internet (5A)
interno/a internal; **órgano interno**
    internal organ (7A)
interpretación *f.* interpretation
interpretar to interpret, explain
interrogativo/a interrogative
intimidad *f.* intimacy
íntimo/a intimate, private; close
    (*relationship*) (7B)
intoxicante poisonous; intoxicating
introducir (zc) to introduce
introvertido/a introverted (1B)
inundación *f.* flood (5B)
invadir to invade (5B)
invasión *f.* invasion (5B)
inventar to invent
invernadero greenhouse; **efecto**
    invernadero greenhouse
    effect (6B)
inversión *f.* investment (8A)
invertir (ie, i) to invest (8A)
investigación *f.* research
investigador(a) researcher
investigar (gu) to research
invierno winter (1B)
invitado/a guest
invitar to invite
inyección *f.* injection; **ponerle** (*irreg.*)
    una inyección (a alguien) to give
    (someone) a shot (7A)
ir *irreg.* to go (1B); **ir a** to go to (1B); **ir a**
    un concierto to go to a concert (6B);
    ir a un parque de diversiones to go to
    an amusement park (6B); **ir al cine** to
    go to the movies; **ir al extranjero** to
    go abroad (6A); **ir de excursión** to go
    on a hike, go hiking (6B); **irse** to go
    away, leave
irresponsable irresponsible (8A)

irritado/a irritated (7A)
irritante irritating, annoying
irritar(se) to irritate (get irritated) (7A)
isla island (6B)
istmo isthmus (*strip of land that joins two others*)
italiano/a *n., adj.* Italian
izquierda *n.* left-hand side; **a la izquierda de** to the left of (2A); **doblar a la izquierda** to turn left

J

jabón *m.* soap (4B)
jamás never, not ever (3B)
jamón *m.* ham (3B)
japonés, japonesa *n., adj.* Japanese
jarabe *m.* **(para la tos)** (cough) syrup
jardín *m.* garden (4B)
jefe/a boss, chief; **jefe de estado** head of state
jerga slang, jargon
jitomate *m.* tomato (*Mex.*)
jornada work day; **de media jornada** part-time
joven *n. m., f.* (*pl.* **jóvenes**) young person (5A); *adj.* young
joya jewel
joyería jewelry store
jubilado/a retired
jubilarse to retire (9B)
judías verdes green beans
judío/a: Pascua de los judíos Passover (4A)
juego game (4A); **juego de charadas** charades
jueves *m. inv.* Thursday (1A)
juez(a) (*m. pl.* **jueces**) judge (9B)
jugador(a) player
jugar (ue) (gu) to play (2A); **jugar a los videojuegos** to play video games (5A); **jugar al escondite** to play hide and seek (5A)
jugo juice (3B)
julio July (1B)
junio June (1B)
juntarse to get together
junto/a together
jurado panel of judges
jurar to swear (*an oath*) (9B)
justificar (qu) to justify
justo/a *adj.* fair (9A)
juvenil *adj.* youth
juventud *f.* youth (5A)
juzgar (gu) to judge

K

kayak: hacer (*irreg.*) **kayak** to kayak (6B)
kilo(grama) *m.* kilogram
kilómetro kilometer (4A)

L

la *f. def. art.* the (P); *d.o.* her, it, you (*f. form. s.*); **a la una** at one o'clock (1A); **es la una** it's one o'clock (1A)
labio lip
laboratorio laboratory
lacio/a: pelo lacio straight hair (3A)
lácteo/a dairy; **producto lácteo** dairy product (3B)
lado *n.* side; **al lado de** beside (2A)
ladrillo brick
lago lake (6B)
lamer to lick
lámpara lamp (4A)
lana wool
langosta lobster (3B)
lanza: punta de lanza spearhead
lanzar (c) to throw, fling; **lanzarse** to break into (*career*)
lápiz *m.* (*pl.* **lápices**) pencil (P)
largo/a long (3A); **a lo largo de** throughout; **de largo plazo** long-term
las *f. pl.* the (P); *d.o.* you (*f. form. pl.*); them; **a las...** at ... o'clock (1A)
lástima compassion; shame; **lástima que...** too bad that ...
lastimar(se) to hurt (oneself) (7A)
lata de aluminio aluminum can (6B)
latín *m.* Latin (*language*)
latino/a *adj.* Latino, Latina; **estudios latinos** Latino studies (P)
Latinoamérica Latin America
latinoamericano/a *n., adj.* Latin American
lavabo sink (bathroom) (4B)
lavadora washing machine (4B)
lavaplatos *m. inv.* dishwasher (4B)
lavar to wash (4B); **lavarse los dientes** to brush one's teeth (4B)
le *i.o. s.* to/for him, her, it, you (*form. s.*)
leal loyal (1B)
lealtad *f.* loyalty
lección *f.* lesson
leche *f.* milk (3B); **café** (*m.*) **con leche** coffee with milk
lechuga lettuce (3B)
lector(a) reader
lectura *n.* reading
leer (y) to read (1B)
legalmente legally
legítimo/a legitimate
lejano/a distant, far
lejía *n.* bleach (4B)
lejos de *adv.* far away from (2A)
lengua tongue; language (P); **lengua extranjera** foreign language; **sacar (qu) la lengua** to stick out one's tongue (7A); **trabársele la lengua a alguien** to get tongue-tied (7B)
lenguaje *m.* language

lentes *m. pl.* glasses (*vision*)
lento/a slow
les *i.o. pl.* to/for you (*form. pl.*), them
letra letter (*of the alphabet*); handwriting; lyrics; **letra cursiva** italics; *pl.* humanities
levantar to lift, raise up; **levantar pesas** to lift weights (4A); **levantarse** to get up (4B)
léxico vocabulary
ley *f.* law (8B)
leyenda legend
liberal liberal (1B)
libertad *f.* liberty, freedom (8B)
libertino/a libertine
libra pound (*weight*)
libre free (unfettered); **al aire libre** outdoor (s) (6B); **Estado Libre Associado** Free Associated State, Commonwealth; **libre comercio** free trade; **ratos libres** free time (4A)
librería bookstore (P)
libro book (P)
licencia license; **sacar (qu) la licencia de conducir** to get a driver's license (5A)
licor *m.* liquor
ligarse con to get together with; to be tied to
ligero/a *adj.* light
limitar to limit; **limitarse** to limit oneself
límite *m.* limit
limón *m.* lemon (3B)
limonada lemonade
limpiar to clean; **limpiar la casa (entera)** to clean the (whole) house (4B)
limpieza *n.* cleaning; cleanliness; **producto de limpieza** cleaning product (4B)
lindarse con to border
lindo/a pretty
línea line; **línea aérea** airline; **patinar en línea** to inline skate (4A)
lingüístico/a linguistic
lío problem; **meterse en líos** to get into trouble (5A)
lista list
listo/a ready (1B); clever, smart (2B); **estar** (*irreg.*) **listo/a** to be ready; **ser** (*irreg.*) **listo/a** to be clever
literatura literature (P)
llamada *n.* (telephone) call
llamar to call (1A); **¿cómo se llama (él/ella)?** what's his/her name? (P); **¿cómo te llamas?** what's your (*fam. s.*) name? (P); **llamar por teléfono** to call on the telephone (1A); **llamarse** to be called; **me llamo...** my name is ... (P)
llanura flatland, prairie (6B)
llave *n. f.* key
llegada arrival

llegar (gu) to arrive; **¿cómo se llega a… ?** how do you get to … ? (6A); **llegar a tiempo** to arrive on time (1A)

llenar to fill

lleno/a full

llevar to take, carry (1A); to wear (*clothing*) (2B); **llevar al / a la veterinario/a** to take to the veterinarian (9A); **llevar… créditos** to have … credits (1A); **llevarse bien/mal con** to get along well/poorly with (5A)

llorar to cry (7A)

llover (ue) to rain; **está lloviendo** it's raining (1B); **llueve** it's raining (1B)

lluvia rain

lluvioso/a rainy; **bosque** (*m.*) **lluvioso** rainforest (6B)

lo *d.o.* him, it, you (*m. form. s.*); **lo que** what, that which (1B)

local local; **noticias locales** local news (8B)

localizador *m.* pager

localizarse (c) to be located

loco/a mad, crazy

lógico/a logical

lograr + *inf.* to succeed (*in doing something*) (9B)

lomo loin

longitud *f.* duration

loro parrot (9A)

los *def. art. m. pl.* the (P); *d.o.* them, you (*form. pl.*); **los años veinte (treinta)** the twenties (thirties) (5B); **los/las demás** others (4A)

lucha *n.* fight; struggle

luchar to fight; to struggle

lucro: con fines de lucro for profit

luego then, next; **hasta luego** until (see you) later

lugar *m.* place (2A)

lujo luxury; **hotel** (*m.*) **de lujo** luxury hotel (6A)

lunar *m.*: **de lunares** polka-dotted

lunes *m. inv.* Monday (1A); **el (los) lunes** on Monday(s) (1A)

luz *f.* (*pl.* **luces**) light (P); electricity; **Fiesta de las Luces** Hanukkah (4A)

M

madera wood (8A)

madrastra stepmother (3A)

madre *f.* mother (3A); **madre soltera** single mother (3A)

madrina godmother

madrugada early morning hours

maestría *n.* mastery, skill; master's degree (9B)

maestro/a (de primaria, secundaria) (elementary, high school) teacher (9B)

---

magia *n.* magic

magos *pl.*: **los Reyes** (*m.*) **Magos** the Magi (Three Wise Men); **Día** (*m.*) **de los Reyes Magos** Epiphany (January 6), Day of the Magi

maíz *m.* corn (3B); **palomitas de maíz** popcorn (3B); **tortilla de maíz** corn tortilla (3B)

mal, malo/a *adj.* bad (1B); sick (2B); **caerle** (*irreg.*) **mal a alguien** to dislike someone (5A); **hace mal tiempo** it's bad weather (1B); **llevarse mal con** to get along poorly with (5A); **manejar mal** to manage poorly (8A); **pasarlo mal** to have a bad time (4A); **portarse mal** to misbehave (5A); **quedarle mal** to fit poorly (2B)

maldad *n. f.* evil

maleta suitcase; **hacer** (*irreg.*) **la maleta** to pack a suitcase (6A)

maletero skycap, porter (6A)

maletín *m.* briefcase

malgastar to waste

malicioso/a malicious (1B)

mamá mom; mother

mandar to send; to order (5A)

mandato *n.* command

mando a distancia remote control (5A)

mandón, mandona bossy (7B)

manejar (bien/mal) to manage (well/poorly) (8A)

manera manner, way; **pensar (ie) de manera directa** to think in a direct (linear) manner (9B)

manifestación *f.* demonstration (8B)

manifestar(se) (ie) to manifest, show

manipular to manipulate (8B)

mano *f.* hand (7A); **darse** (*irreg.*) **la mano** to shake hands (7B)

mansión *f.* mansion

mantel *m.* tablecloth

mantener (*like* **tener**) to maintain; to support; **mantenerse a raya** to keep (*something*) away

mantequilla butter (3B); **mantequilla de cacahuete** peanut butter (3B)

manual *m.* workbook

manufacturado/a manufactured

manzana apple (3B); city block (6A)

mañana *n.* morning; *adv.* tomorrow (1A); **de la mañana** in the morning (A.M.) (1A); **hasta mañana** until (see you) tomorrow; **pasado mañana** the day after tomorrow (1B); **por la mañana** in the morning (1A)

mapa *m.* map (6A)

máquina machine; **máquina fax** fax machine (5A)

mar *m., f.* sea, ocean (6B)

maravilloso/a marvelous

marca brand name (2B)

---

marcar (qu) to mark

marcha: en marcha on the move

mareado/a nauseated, dizzy

marearse to get nauseated, sick (*boat, car, plane*) (6A)

marido husband (3A)

marino/a *adj.* marine

mariscos *pl.* shellfish (3B); seafood (3B)

marrón *adj. m., f.* brown (2B)

martes *m. inv.* Tuesday (1A); **Martes de Carnaval** Mardi Gras (4A)

marzo March (1B)

más *adv.* more (P); plus; **cada vez más** more and more; **es más** what's more; **más… que** more … than (3A)

mascota *n.* pet (3A)

masculino/a masculine

matar to kill

matemáticas mathematics (P)

materia subject (*school*) (P)

material *m.* material

materialista *m., f.* materialist

materno/a maternal (3A)

matrícula tuition

matrimonial: cama matrimonial queen bed (4B)

matrimonio matrimony, marriage (5B)

mayo May (1B)

mayor older (3A); **el/la mayor** the oldest

mayoría majority

me *d.o.* me; *i.o.* to/for me; *refl. pron.* myself; **me gusta…** I like … (1A); **me llamo** my name is (P); **me parece(n)…** it/that seems … to me; **¿me podría traer… ?** could you (*form. s.*) bring me… ? (6A)

mecánico/a mechanic; **ingeniería mecánica** mechanical engineering (P); **ingeniero/a mecánico/a** mechanical engineer (9B)

media *n.* average

mediano/a *adj.* medium; average (2B); **de estatura mediana** of medium height (3A)

medianoche *f.* midnight (1A); **a medianoche** at midnight

medias *pl.* stockings; pantyhose

medicación *f.* medication

medicina medicine (7A)

médico/a *n.* doctor (7A); *adj.* medical; **examen** (*m.*) **médico** medical exam (7A); **seguro médico** medical insurance (8A); **servicios médicos** medical services (9B)

medidas *pl.* measures

medio *n. s.* means, middle; **medio ambiente** environment (6B); **medios de comunicación** media (8B)

medio/a *adj.* half; middle; **clase** (*f.*) **media** middle class; **media pensión** room and one other meal (usually breakfast)

(6A); **medio/a hermano/a** half brother/sister (3A); **y media** half past (*hour*) (1A)
medioambiental environmental
mediodía *m.* noon, midday (1A); **a mediodía** at noon
meditar to meditate (4A)
mediterráneo/a *adj.* Mediterranean
mejillas cheeks (3A)
mejor better (3A)
mejorar to improve
melodrama *m.* melodrama
membresía membership
memoria memory
memorizar (c) to memorize (1A)
mencionar to mention
mendigo/a beggar
menonita *n. m. f.; adj.* Mennonite
menor younger (3A); **el/la menor** the youngest
menos less; least; **a menos que** *conj.* unless (7B); **menos cuarto** a quarter to (*hour*) (1A); **menos… que** less … than (3A); **por lo menos** at least
mensaje *m.* message (5A); **mensaje de texto** text message
mensajero/a messenger; **mensajero instantáneo** instant messenger
mensual monthly; **presupuesto mensual** monthly budget (8A)
mentalidad *f.* mentality
mente *f.* mind
mentir (ie, i) to lie (4B)
mentira lie
mentiroso/a liar (5A)
mentón *m.* chin (3A)
menú *m.* menu (6A)
menudo: a menudo often
mercadeo marketing (9B)
mercado market (2A)
mercancías *pl.* goods
merecer (zc) to deserve (3A)
merendar (ie) to snack (3B)
meridional southern
merienda *n.* snack (3B)
mérito merit; **atribuirse (y) todo el mérito** to take all the credit (9A)
mermelada jam (3B)
mes *m.* month (1B); **cada mes** each month; **¿en qué mes cae… ?** ¿what month is … ?; **una vez al mes** once a month (1B)
mesa table (P); **poner** (*irreg.*) **la mesa** to set the table
mesero/a waiter, waitress (6A)
meseta plateau (6B)
mesita end table (4B)
mestizaje *m.* mixing of races
mestizo/a *n.* mixed-race person
meta goal (9B); **alcanzar (c) una meta** to reach a goal (9B)

metales (*m.*) **preciosos** precious metals (8A)
meteorológico/a meteorological
meterse to pick a fight (9A); to enter; **meterse en líos** to get into trouble (5A)
metódico/a methodical (1B)
metro meter (4A); **metros cuadrados** square meters (4B)
mexicano/a *n., adj.* Mexican
mexicanoamericano/a *n., adj.* Mexican-American
mezcla mixture
mezquita mosque
mí *obj. of prep.* (4B)
mi(s) *poss.* my (4B); **mi apellido es…** my last name is … (P); **mi nombre es…** my name is … (P)
microondas *m. s.* microwave (4B)
microscopio microscope
miedo fear; **darle miedo a alguien** to scare someone (5A); **tener(le)** (*irreg.*) **miedo (a alguien)** to be afraid (of someone) (7A)
miembro/a member
mientras *adv.* meanwhile (5B); **mientras que** *conj.* while
miércoles *m. inv.* Wednesday (1A)
migración *f.* migration (5B)
migratorio/a migratory
mil thousand, one thousand (2B)
militar *adj.* military
milla mile (4A)
millón *m.* **(de)** million (5B)
millonario millionaire
mina *n.* mine
miniserie *f.* miniseries
ministro /a minister
minoría minority
minoritario/a *adj.* minority
minuto minute
mío/a/os/as *poss.* my, (of) mine (2B)
mirar to look (at), watch (1A)
misceláneo/a miscellaneous
misión *f.* mission
mismo/a same; self; **a la misma hora** at the same time (1A)
misterio mystery
mitad *f.* half
mito myth
mitología mythology
mixto/a mixed; **ensalada mixta** tossed salad (3B)
mochila backpack (P)
moda fashion (2B); **de moda** in style
modelo model; *m., f.* model (*fashion*)
módem *m.* modem (5A)
modernización *f.* modernization
moderno/a modern
modesto/a modest
mojado/a wet
molestar to bother (3A)

momento moment, instant
monarquía monarchy
moneda currency; coin; **coleccionar monedas** to collect coins (4A)
monitor *m.* monitor (5A)
monótono/a monotonous
montaña mountain (6B); **escalar montañas** to go mountain climbing (6B)
montar a caballo to go horseback riding (6B)
morado/a purple (2B)
mórbido/a morbid
morder (ue) to bite (9A)
moreno/a dark-skinned (3A)
morir(se) (ue, u) (*p.p.* **muerto/a**) to die (4B); **ya murió** he/she already died (3A)
moro/a *n.* Moor; *adj.* Moorish
morrón *m.* blow, bang, hit
mortalidad *f.* mortality
mosca fly (*insect*)
mosquetero: los Tres Mosqueteros The Three Musketeers
mostrador *m.* counter (*kitchen, etc.*)
mostrar (ue) to show (*something to someone*)
motivo motive, reason
motor *m.* engine, motor
mover (ue) to move (around); **moverse** to move (*houses*)
móvil: teléfono móvil cell phone
movimiento movement
mozo bellhop
MP3: el reproductor de MP3 MP3 player (5A)
muchacho/a boy, girl
mucho *adv.* a lot, much (1A)
mucho/a *adj.* much, a lot (of); **hace mucho calor** it's very hot (1B); **hace mucho frío** it's very cold (1B); **hace mucho viento** it's very windy (1B); **mucho gusto** pleased to meet you (P); **pasar mucho tiempo** to spend a lot of time (1A)
mudanza move (5B)
mudarse to move (*to another house*) (5B)
mueble *m.* piece of furniture (4B)
muerte *f.* death (4A); **pena de muerte** death penalty
muerto/a (*p.p. of* **morir**) dead
muestra example
mujer *f.* woman (P); wife (3A); **hermandad** (*f.*) **de mujeres**, sorority; **mujer de negocios** businesswoman (9B); **mujer policía** policewoman; **mujer político** (female) politician (9B); **mujer química** (female) chemist (9B); **mujer soldado** (female) soldier (9B)
mujeriego *n.* womanizer
muleta crutch

multa fee, fine
multinacional multinational
mundial *adj.* world; worldwide
mundo world; **mundo de los espectáculos** entertainment industry (8A)
muñeca wrist; doll (5A)
muro wall
músculo muscle
museo museum; **visitar un museo** to visit a museum (4A)
música music (P)
músico/a musician
musulmán, musulmana *n., adj.* Muslim
muy very (1A)

N

nacer (zc) to be born (5B)
nacido/a born; **recién nacido/a** newborn baby (5B)
nacimiento birth (5B)
nación *f.* nation
nacional national; **noticias** *(pl.)* **nacionales** national news (8B); **producto nacional bruto** gross national product
nada nothing; none (3B); **de nada** you're welcome
nadador(a) swimmer
nadar to swim (4A)
nadie nobody, not anybody (3B)
náhuatl *m.* Nahuatl *(language of the Aztecs)*
náranja orange *(fruit)* (3B)
nariz *f.* nose (3A); **tener** *(irreg.)* **la nariz tapada** to have a stuffed-up nose (7A)
narración *f.* narration
narrar to narrate
natación *f.* swimming (4A)
nativo/a *adj.* native, indigenous
natural *adj.* natural; **ciencias naturales** natural sciences (P); **desastre** *(m.)* **natural** natural disaster (5B); **recursos naturales** natural resources (6B)
naturaleza nature (6B)
navegar (gu) (la red) to navigate; to surf (the Web) (1A); **navegar en barco** to sail (4A)
Navidad *f.* Christmas (4A)
navideño/a *adj.* Christmas
necesario/a necessary; **es necesario** it's necessary (2B)
necesidad *f.* necessity
necesitar to need (1A); **necesitar** + *inf.* to need to *(do something)*
neerlandés, neerlandesa *adj.* Dutch
negación *f.* negation
negar (ie) (gu) to deny (8B)
negativo/a *adj.* negative
negocio business (9B); **hombre** *(m.)* **de**

negocios businessman (9B); **mujer** *(f.)* **de negocios** businesswoman (9B)
negrita: en negrita in boldface type
negro/a *adj.* black (2B)
nervioso/a nervous (5B)
nevar (ie) to snow; **está nevando** it's snowing (1B); **nieva** it's snowing (1B)
nevera freezer (4B)
ni... ni neither ... nor
nieto/a grandson, granddaughter (3A); *pl.* grandchildren
ningún, ninguno/a *adj.* no, not any (3B)
ninguno/a *pron.* none, not any (3B)
niñero/a baby-sitter; nanny (5A)
niñez *f. (pl.* niñeces) childhood (5A)
niño/a child; boy, girl (5A)
nivel *m.* level; **nivel económico** economic level
no no; not; **no aguantar** not to be able to stand, put up with (7B); **no es cierto** it's not true (8B); **no es posible** it's not possible (8B); **no es seguro/a** it's not sure (8B); **no es verdad** it's not true (8B); **no obstante** nevertheless; **no ser de fiar** to be unreliable (9A); **todavía no sé** I still don't know (P); **ya no** no longer
noche *f.* night; **buenas noches** good night (P); **de la noche** in the evening (night); **esta noche** tonight (1B); **Noche Vieja** New Year's Eve (4A); **por la noche** in the evening (night); **todas las noches** every night (1A)
Nochebuena Christmas Eve (4A)
nocivo/a unhealthy, noxious
nocturno/a *adj.* nighttime
nombrar to name
nombre *m.* name; **estar** *(irreg.)* **a nombre de...** to be in ...'s name; **mi nombre es...** my name is ... (P)
nominar to nominate
norma norm
norte *m.* north; **al norte de** to the north of (2A)
Norteamérica North America (6B)
norteamericano/a *n., adj.* North American *(from the United States or Canada)*
nos *d.o.* us; *i.o.* to/for us; *refl. pron.* ourselves; **nos vemos** see you around
nosotros/as *sub. pron.* we (P); *obj. of prep.* us
nostálgico/a nostalgic (7B)
nota note
notable good
notar to note, notice
noticia piece of news; *pl.* news (8B); **noticias (internacionales, locales, nacionales)** (international, local, national) news (8B)
noticiero newscast, news show (8B)

novecientos/as nine hundred (2B)
novecientos mil nine hundred thousand (5B)
novedoso/a *adj.* novel
novela *n.* novel (1B)
novelista *m., f.* novelist
noventa ninety (2A)
noviazgo engagement (7B)
noviembre November (1B)
novillos: hacer *(irreg.)* **novillos** to skip/cut school (5A)
novio/a boyfriend, girlfriend; bride, groom (5B)
nube *f.* cloud
nublado/a cloudy; **está nublado** it's cloudy (1B)
nublar to darken
nudista *adj. m., f.* nudist
nuestro/a/os/as *poss.* our (1A)
nueve nine (1A)
nuevo/a new
nuez *(pl.* nueces) nut
número number (1A)
numeroso/a numerous
nunca never, not ever; **casi nunca** almost never

O

o or; **o... o** either ... or
ó or *(used between two numbers to avoid confusion with zero)*
obedecer (zc) to obey (3A)
obediencia obedience
obediente obedient (5A)
objetividad *f.* objectivity
objetivo/a objective (8B)
objeto *n.* object
obligación *f.* obligation
obligar (gu) to obligate, require
obligatorio/a required
obra *n.* work (of art)
observación *f.* observation
observador(a) observer
obsesión *f.* obsession
obstáculo obstacle
obstante: no obstante nevertheless
obtener *(like* tener) to obtain, get
obvio/a obvious
ocasión *f.* occasion
ocasionar to cause
occidental *adj.* western
océano ocean (6B); **océano Pacífico** Pacific Ocean
ochenta eighty (2A)
ocho eight (1A)
ochocientos/as eight hundred (2B)
ochocientos mil eight hundred thousand (5B)
ocio leisure time
octubre October (1B)

ocultar to cover up (*deeds*); **ocultar(le) secretos (a alguien)** to hide secrets (from someone) (7B)
ocupación *f.* occupation
ocupado/a busy
ocupar to occupy
ocurrir to occur
odiar to hate (4B)
odio hatred
oeste *m.* west; **al oeste de** to the west of (2A)
ofender(se) to offend (get offended) (7A)
ofensivo/a offensive
oferta *n.* offer
oficina office (P)
oficio job, profession; trade
ofrecer (zc) to offer (3A)
oír *irreg.* to hear (2A)
ojalá que I hope, wish that (7B)
ojo eye
oleada *n.* wave
oliva: aceite (*m.*) **de oliva** olive oil
olvidar to forget
once eleven (1A)
opción *f.* option
operación *f.* operation
opinar to think, believe
opinión *f.* opinion
oponerse (*like* **poner**) **a** to oppose
oportunidad *f.* opportunity
optativo/a optional
optimista *n. m., f.* optimist; *adj.* optimistic (1B)
opuesto/a opposite
oración *f.* sentence
orden *m.* order (*chronological*); **poner** (*irreg.*) **las cosas en orden** to put things in order (4B)
ordenador *m.* computer (*Sp.*)
ordenar to order, put in order (6A)
orejas (outer) ears (3A)
orgánico/a organic
organismo organism
organización *f.* organization
organizado/a organized (1B)
organizar (c) to organize
órgano organ; **órgano interno** internal organ (7A)
orgullo pride
orgulloso/a (de) proud (of) (5B)
orientación *f.* orientation, direction
orientarse to orient oneself
origen *m.* (*pl.* **orígenes**) origin; **¿de qué origen es/son… ?** what is/are … 's (national) origin?
os *d.o.* you (*fam. pl. Sp.*); *i.o.* to/for you (*fam. pl. Sp.*); *refl. pron.* yourselves (*fam. pl. Sp.*)
oscurecer (zc) to get dark
oscuro/a dark (5B)
oso *n.* bear

otoño fall (*season*) (1B)
otorgar (gu) to award, grant
otro/a other; another (1B)
oyente *m., f.* listener
ozono ozone; **capa de ozono** ozone layer (6B)

P

paciencia patience
paciente *m., f.* patient (7A); *adj.* patient (5A)
pacífico/a peaceful (5B); **océano Pacífico** Pacific Ocean
padecer (zc) de to suffer from (7A)
padrastro stepfather (3A)
padre *m.* father (3A); *pl.* parents; **padre soltero** single father (3A)
padrino godfather; **padrino de boda** groomsman
pagar (gu) to pay (for) (1A); **pagar a plazos** to pay in installments (8A); **pagar de una vez** to pay off all at once (8A)
página page; **página web** Web page (5A)
pago payment
país *m.* country (2A); **país desarrollado** developed country (8A); **país en vías de desarrollo** developing country; **País Vasco** Basque country; **los Países Bajos** The Netherlands
paisaje *m.* landscape (6B)
paisajista *adj. m., f.:* **arquitectura paisajista** landscape architecture
pájaro bird (9A)
palabra word
palabrota swear word
palomitas (*pl.*) **de maíz** popcorn (3B)
pampa pampa, prairie
pan *m.* bread; **pan dulce** sweet bread (*Mex.*) (3B); **pan tostado** toast (3B)
pana corduroy
panadería bakery
panceta *Arg.* bacon
panqueque *m.* pancake (3B)
pantalla screen (*movie, computer*) (P)
pantalón, pantalones *m.* pants (2B); **pantalones cortos** shorts (2B)
papa potato; **papas fritas** French fries (3B); **puré** (*m.*) **de papas** mashed potatoes (3B)
papá *m.* dad, father; daddy
papel *m.* role, part; paper; **hoja de papel aparte** separate piece of paper; **toalla de papel** paper towel (4B)
papitas *pl.* potato chips (3B)
paquete *m.* package
par *m.* pair; **un par de** a couple of
para for; in order to (1B); **para** + *inf.* in order to (*do something*) (2B); **para que** so that (7B)

parabrisas *m. s.* windshield
paraíso paradise
paracaidismo skydiving; **practicar (qu) el paracaidismo** to skydive (6B)
parada de autobuses bus stop (2A)
paráfrasis *f.* paraphrase
paraguayo/a *n., adj.* Paraguayan
paraíso paradise
parapente *m.:* **practicar (qu) el parapente** to hang glide
parar to stop
parcial biased (8B); **ser** (*irreg.*) **parcial** to be biased (8A)
parcialidad *f.* bias
parecer (zc) to look; to seem (like) (5A); **me parece(n)…** it/that seems … to me; **parece ser** it seems to be, he/she seems … (1B); **parecerse (a)** to resemble (3A)
parecido/a (a) similar (to)
pared *f.* wall
pareja couple (7B); mate; partner; *pl.* pairs
paréntesis *m. inv.* parenthesis
pariente *m., f.* relative (3A)
parlamentario/a parliamentary
parque *m.* park (2A); **ir** (*irreg.*) **a un parque de diversiones** to go to an amusement park (6B)
párrafo paragraph
parte *f.* part; **partes del cuerpo** parts of the body (7A)
participar to participate (8B)
particular particular; private; **casa particular** private residence (4B)
partido game (4A); **partido político** political party
pasa raisin
pasado/a *adj.* past; spoiled (*food*) (3B); **pasado mañana** the day after tomorrow (1B)
pasajero/a *n.* passenger (6A)
pasaporte *m.* passport (6A)
pasar (mucho) tiempo to pass, spend (a lot of) time (1A); **pasar a ser** to become; **pasar la aspiradora** to vacuum (4B); **pasar por la aduana** to go through customs (6A); **pasar por seguridad** to go through security (6A); **pasarlo bien/mal** to have a good/bad time (4A)
pasatiempo pastime
Pascua: Pascua (de los judíos) Passover (4A); **Pascua (Florida)** Easter (4A)
pasear to walk, stroll; **sacar (qu) a pasear** to take for a walk (9A)
paseo *n.* walk, stroll; **dar** (*irreg.*) **un paseo** to take a walk (4A)
pasión *f.* passion
paso step

pastel *m.* pastry; cake (3B); *pl.* pastries (3B); **porción** (*f.*) **de pastel** slice of cake (3B)

pastilla pill (7A)

patata potato (*Sp.*)

paterno/a paternal (3A)

patinar (en línea) to (inline) skate (4A)

patio courtyard, patio (4B)

patria homeland

Patricio: Día (*m.*) **de San Patricio** St. Patrick's Day (4A)

patrio/a patriotic

pavo turkey (3B)

paz *f.* (*pl.* **paces**) peace; **dejar en paz** to leave alone; **hacer** (*irreg.*) **las paces** to make up with (7B)

peaje *m.* toll (*fee*)

peca *n.* freckle (3A)

pecado *n.* sin

pecho chest (7A); **tomarse algo muy a pecho** to take something to heart (7A); to feel something intensely (7A)

peculiaridad *f.* peculiarity

pedagogía pedagogy; education

pedazo piece

pediatra *m., f.* pediatrician

pedir (i, i) to ask for, request (2B); to order (*restaurant*) (6A); **pedir ayuda** to ask for help; **pedir disculpas** to apologize (*to someone*); **pedir prestado/a** to borrow (8A)

pegado/a stuck on; close together

peinado hairdo

peinar to comb

pelar to peel

pelearse to fight (5A)

película movie (1A); **ver** (*irreg.*) **una película** to watch a movie

peligro danger; **especies** (*f. pl.*) **en peligro de extinción** endangered species (6B)

peligroso/a dangerous

pelirrojo/a red-headed (3A)

pelo (canoso/lacio/rizado/rubio) (gray/straight/curly/blond) hair (3A)

pelotero/a: ser (*irreg.*) **pelotero/a** to be a kiss-up (9A)

pena shame; penalty; sorrow; **pena de muerte** death penalty

península Ibérica Iberian Peninsula

pensar (ie) to think (2A); **pensar de** to think of; **pensar de manera directa** to think in a direct (linear) manner (9B); **pensar en** to think about

pensión *f.* boardinghouse (6A); **media pensión** room and one other meal (usually breakfast) (6A); **pensión completa** room and all meals (6A)

peor worse (3A)

pepino (de mar) (sea) cucumber

pequeñeces *f. pl.* little things

pequeño/a little, small (2B)

per cápita: renta per cápita per capita income

perder (ie) to lose (2A); **perder peso** to lose weight

pérdida loss; **pérdida de tiempo** waste of time (8B); **pérdida de valores tradicionales** loss of traditional values (8B)

perdón *m.* forgiveness

perdonable forgivable

perdonar to forgive (7B); to pardon, excuse

perezoso/a lazy (9A)

perfeccionista *m., f.* perfectionist

perfecto/a perfect

perfil *m.* profile

periférico peripheral device

periódico newspaper (1B)

periodista *m., f.* journalist (9B)

permiso permission

permitir to allow (8B)

pero but (1A)

perpetuar (perpetúo) to perpetuate

perplejo/a perplexed (7A); **dejar perplejo/a (a alguien)** to leave (someone) perplexed

perro dog (3A)

persistente persistent

persona person (1B)

personaje *m.* character (*fictional*)

personal personal; **finanzas personales** personal finances (8A); **respetar el espacio personal** to respect personal space (9A)

personalidad *f.* personality (1B)

perspectiva perspective

pertenecer (zc) to belong

peruano/a *n., adj.* Peruvian

pesa weight; **levantar pesas** to lift weights (4A)

pesado/a heavy

pesar(se) to weigh (oneself); **a pesar de** *prep.* in spite of, despite

pescado fish (*food*) (3B)

pescar (qu) to fish (6B)

pesimista *n. m., f.* pessimist; *adj.* pessimistic (1B)

peso weight; **bajar de peso** to lose weight; **perder (ie) peso** to lose weight

pesquero/a *adj.* fishing

pesticida *m.* pesticide (6B)

petróleo petroleum (oil) (6B)

pez *m.* (*pl.* **peces**) fish (*alive*) (9A)

piano piano; **tocar (qu) el piano** to play the piano (1A)

picante hot, spicy (3B)

picar (qu) to bite (9A); to nibble (4A)

picoso/a spicy (3B)

pie *m.* foot (7A); **a pie** on foot; **dedo del pie** toe (7A); **pies cuadrados** square feet (4B)

piedra rock; stone

piel *f.* skin (3A); **ponérsele** (*irreg.*) **la piel de gallina a alguien** to get goosebumps (7B)

pierna leg (7A)

pijama *m. s.* pajamas

pila (recargable) (rechargeable) battery

piloto/a pilot

pinchado/a: rueda pinchada flat tire

pintar to paint (4A)

pintor(a) painter (9B)

pintoresco/a picturesque

pirámide *f.* pyramid

piscina swimming pool (4A)

piso floor (4B); flat, apartment (*Sp.*) (4B); **barrer el piso** to sweep the floor (4B)

pista track (4A); clue

pito: importarle un pito not to care about

pizarra chalkboard (P)

pizza pizza (3B); **porción** (*f.*) **de pizza** slice of pizza (3B)

placer *m.* pleasure

plancha iron (4B)

planchar (la ropa) to iron (the clothes) (4B)

planear to plan

planeta *m.* planet

planificación *f.* planning

plano city map (6A)

planta plant (4B); floor (*of a building*) (*Sp.*) (4B)

plástico plastic; **botella de plástico** plastic bottle (6B)

plátano banana

plato plate (6A); prepared dish; *pl.* dishes (4B); **primer (segundo, tercer) plato** first (second, third) course (6A)

playa beach (6B)

plaza square, plaza (2A)

plazo term; **de corto/largo plazo** short/long term (9B); **pagar (gu) a plazos** to pay in installments (8A)

pluma pen

plumero feather duster

población *f.* population

poblado/a populated

pobre *adj.* poor (1B)

pobreza poverty (8A); **umbral** (*m.*) **de la pobreza** poverty line

poco/a *adv.* little (1B); *adj.* little; *pl.* few; **dentro de poco** in a little while (1B); **un poco** a little (1B)

poder *m.* power

poder *irreg.* to be able to, can (2A); **¿me podría traer... ?** could you (*form. s.*) bring me ... ? (6A)

poema *m.* poem

poemario collection of poetry

poesía poetry
poeta *m., f.* poet
polémico/a controversial
policía *f.* police force; *m.* policeman;
  mujer (*f.*) **policía** policewoman
poliéster *m.* polyester
poliomielitis *f.* polio
politeísta *adj. m., f.* polytheist (*believing
  in more than one god*)
política *s.* politics (8B)
político, mujer (*f.*) **político** politician (9B)
político/a political; **ciencias políticas**
  political science (P); **partido político**
  political party
pollo chicken (3B)
polvo *n.* dust; **quitar el polvo** to dust (4B)
poner *irreg.* to put (2A); **poner alto el
  volumen** to turn the volume up high;
  poner fin a to end; **poner las cosas en
  orden** to put things in order (4B);
  ponerle los cuernos (a alguien) to be
  unfaithful (to someone); **ponerle una
  inyección (a alguien)** to give
  (someone) a shot (7A); **poner la mesa**
  to set the table; **ponerse** to get,
  become (*emotion*); **ponerse de
  acuerdo** to come to an agreement;
  ponérsele la piel de gallina a alguien
  to get goosebumps (7B)
poniente *m.* west
por for (4B); because of (4B); by, through,
  around; **estar** (*irreg.*) **por** + *inf.* to be
  about to + *inf.*; **llamar por teléfono** to
  call on the telephone (1A); **pasar por
  la aduana** to go through customs (6A);
  por ciento percent; **por dentro** within,
  (on the) inside; **por ejemplo** for
  example; **por favor** please; **por fin**
  finally; **por fuera** (on the) outside; **por
  la mañana/tarde/noche** in the
  morning/afternoon/evening (night)
  (1A); **por lo menos** at least; **por
  primera vez** for the first time; **¿por
  qué?** why? (1B); **por supuesto** of
  course
porcentaje *m.* percentage
porción *f.* **(de pastel, pizza)** slice (of
  cake, pizza) (3B)
porfiado/a persistent (7B)
porque because (1B)
portada home page (*Web*); cover (*book*)
portarse bien/mal to behave well/
  badly (5A)
portátil portable; **computadora portátil**
  laptop computer (5A)
portero/a doorperson (4B); building
  manager (4B)
portugués *m.* Portuguese (*language*)
portugués, portuguesa *n., adj.*
  Portug-uese
poseer (y) to possess portuguese

posesión *f.* possession
posesivo/a possessive (7B)
posgrado/a graduate; **estudios de
  posgrado** graduate studies (9B)
posibilidad *f.* possibility
posible possible
posición *f.* position
positivo/a positive
postre *m.* dessert (3B)
potable: agua (*f.* [*but* **el agua**]) **potable**
  drinking water
práctica *n.* practice
practicar (qu) to practice (1A); **practicar
  el alpinismo de rocas** to rock climb
  (6B); **practicar la escalada** to rappel;
  practicar el paracaidismo to skydive
  (6B); **practicar el parapente** to hang
  glide; **practicar el yoga** to do yoga
  (4A); **practicar un deporte** to practice
  a sport (1A)
pragmático/a pragmatic
precavido/a cautious (5A)
precio (fijo) (fixed) price (2B); **estar**
  (*irreg.*) **a buen precio** to be a good
  price
precioso/a precious; valuable; **metales**
  (*m.*) **preciosos** precious metals (8A)
preciso/a precise (1B); **es preciso** it's
  necessary (8B)
precolombino/a pre-Columbian (before
  Columbus)
predeterminado/a predetermined
predicción *f.* prediction
predominar to dominate
preferencia preference
preferir (ie, i) to prefer (2A)
pregunta *n.* question
preguntar to ask (questions)
preliminar preliminary
premio award; prize
prenda article of clothing (2B)
prender (las luces) to turn on (the lights)
prendido/a turned on (*lights, appliances*)
prensa *n.* press (8B)
preocupación *f.* worry (8B); concern (8B)
preocupado/a worried (7A)
preocuparse (por) to worry (about) (7A)
preparar to prepare (1A)
preparativo preparation
preparatoria high school
preposición *f.* preposition
presencia presence
presentación *f.* presentation;
  introduction (P)
presentador(a) anchorman,
  anchorwoman (8B)
presentar to present; to introduce; to
  show (*a film*)
presente *n. m., adj. m. f.* present (*time*)
preservar to preserve, maintain
presidencia presidency

presidencial presidential
presidente/a president
presión *f.* pressure; **presión arterial**
  blood pressure (7A)
presenciar to witness
prestado/a borrowed; **pedir (i, i)
  prestado/a** to borrow (8A)
préstamo *n.* loan (8A); **sacar (qu) un
  préstamo** to take out a loan
prestar to loan, lend (8A)
presumido/a conceited
presupuesto (mensual) (monthly)
  budget (8A)
pretérito *gram.* preterite (tense)
pretexto pretext, excuse
prevalente prevalent
preventivo/a: señales (*f. pl.*) **preventivas**
  warning signs
previo/a previous
prima de seguro insurance premium
primaria: (escuela) primaria elementary
  school; **maestro/a de primaria**
  elementary school teacher (9B)
primavera spring (*season*) (1B)
primer, primero/a first; **por primera vez**
  for the first time; **primer (segundo,
  tercer) plato** first (second, third)
  course (6A); **primera clase** first
  class (6A)
primo/a cousin (3A); *pl.* cousins
principal *adj.* main, principal
principio beginning
prisa: tener (*irreg.*) **prisa** to be in a hurry
privacidad *f.* privacy
privado/a private; **casa privada** private
  residence (4B); **con baño privado** with
  a private bath (6A)
privilegiado/a privileged
probabilidad *f.* probability
probable probable; **es probable** it's
  probable (8B)
probador *m.* dressing room
probar (ue) to try; **probarse** to try on (2B)
problema *m.* problem
problemático/a problematic
procesar to process
proceso process
producción *f.* production
producir *irreg.* to produce
producto product; **producto
  biodegradable** biodegradable product
  (6B); **producto de limpieza** cleaning
  product (4B); **producto desechable**
  disposable product (6B); **producto
  farmacéutico** pharmaceutical product
  (8A); **producto lácteo** dairy product
  (3B); **producto nacional bruto** gross
  national product; **productos de
  exportación** export products (8A)
productor(a) producer (9B)
profesión *f.* profession (9B)

profesional *adj.* professional
profesor(a) professor (P)
profundo/a deep
programa *m.* program, **programa de entrevistas** talk show (8B); **programa deportivo** sports show (8B); **programa televisivo** television program (8B)
programación *f.* programming
programador(a) (computer) programmer (9B)
prohibir (prohíbo) to prohibit (8B)
prólogo prologue
promedio *n.* average
promesa promise; **cumplir las promesas** to keep one's word (9A)
prometer to promise (9B)
promiscuo/a promiscuous
promocionar to promote
promover (ue) to promote
pronombre *m.* pronoun
pronóstico del tiempo weather report (8B)
pronto soon; **tan pronto como** as soon as (9B)
pronunciación *f.* pronunciation
pronunciar to pronounce
propiedad *f.* property
propina tip (6A); **dejar (una) propina** to leave a tip (6A)
propio/a own
proporcionar to give
propósito purpose; aim; intention; **a propósito** by the way
prosperidad *f.* prosperity (8A)
próspero/a prosperous
protección *f.* protection
proteger (j) to protect (6B)
proteína protein
protestar to protest (8B)
provecho: buen provecho enjoy your meal
provincia province, region
provocar (qu) to provoke
proximidad *f.* proximity
próximo/a next (1B)
prueba *n.* quiz, test
psicología psychology (P)
psicólogo/a psychologist (9B)
psiquiatra *m., f.* psychiatrist (9B)
publicación *f.* publication
publicar (qu) to publish
publicitario/a: anuncio publicitario commercial (8B)
público *n.* public; audience; **teléfono público** public telephone (P)
público/a *adj.* public
pueblo small town; people, population
puerro leek
puerta door (P)
puerto (sea)port
puertorriqueño/a *n., adj.* Puerto Rican

pues... well ...
puesto *n.* stand; **puesto que** given that
pulir to polish
pulmón *m.* lung (7A)
pulsar to click
punta de lanza spearhead
punto point; period; **en punto** on the dot (*time*) (1A); **punto de vista** point of view
puntual punctual; **ser (irreg.) puntual** to be punctual (1A)
puntualidad *f.* punctuality
puré (m.) de papas mashed potatoes (3B)
púrpura purple

Q

que that, which; than; **creer que** to think that (1B); **hasta que** *conj.* until; **lo que** what, that which (1B); **más + adj. + que** more + adj. + than; **tener (irreg.) que + inf.** to have to (*do something*)
¿qué? what? (1B); **¿a qué hora... ?** at what time ... ?, when ... ? (1A); **¿por qué?** why? (1B); **¿qué carrera haces?** what's your (*fam. s.*) major? (P); **¿qué clases tienes este semestre/trimestre?** what classes do you (*fam. s.*) have this semester/quarter? (P); **¿qué día es hoy?** what day is today? (1A); **¿qué estudias?** what are you (*fam. s.*) studying? (P); **¿qué hora es?** what time is it? (1A); **¿qué trae... ?** what comes with ... ? (6A)
quechua *m.* Quechua (*language*)
quedar to be located; **quedarle bien/mal** to fit well/ poorly (2B); **quedarse** to stay (*in a place*) (6A) (2B)
quehacer *m.* chore; **quehaceres domésticos** household chores (4B)
queja complaint
quejarse (de) to complain (about)
quemar to burn; **quemar calorías** to burn calories (4A)
querer *irreg.* to want (2A); to love (7B); **quiere decir** it means
queso cheese (3B); **queso de crema** cream cheese (3B)
quien(es) who, whom
¿quién(es)? who? whom? (1B)
química chemistry (P)
químico / mujer (f.) química chemist (9B)
quince fifteen (1A)
quinientos/as five hundred (2B)
quinientos mil five hundred thousand (5B)
quiosco kiosk
quitar to remove, take away; **quitar el polvo** to dust (4B); **quitarse** to take off (*clothing*)
quizá(s) perhaps

R

rabia rage; **darle (irreg.) rabia (a alguien)** to make (someone) angry
racismo racism
radio *f.* radio (*medium*)
rafting: hacer (irreg.) rafting to go rafting (6B)
raíz *f.* (*pl.* **raíces**) root; **bienes** (*m. pl.*) **raíces** real estate (8A)
rama branch
ramo bouquet
rápido *adv.* fast
rápido/a *adj.* fast, quick; **comida rápida** fast food (3B)
raro/a strange; rare; **raras veces** infrequently, rarely
rascacielos *m. s.* skyscraper (2A)
rasgar (gu) to tear, rip
rasgo feature, trait (3A)
rasguñar to scratch
rato *n.* while, short time; **ratos libres** free time (4A)
ratón *m.* mouse (*animal*) (9A); mouse (*computer*) (5A)
raya stripe; **de rayas** striped; **mantenerse (like tener) a raya** to keep (*something*) away
rayo ray; **rayos X** X-rays (7A)
raza race (*people*)
razón *f.* reason
razonable reasonable
reacción *f.* reaction
reaccionar to react (7A)
real real; royal
realidad *f.* reality
realista *adj. m., f.* realistic
reality *m.* reality show (*TV*) (8B)
realizar (c) to attain, achieve (9B)
realmente really
rebaja sale (2B)
rebelde rebellious
recargable rechargeable; **pila recargable** rechargeable battery
recargar (gu) to recharge
recepción *f.* reception
recesión *f.* recession (8A)
receta recipe; prescription (7A)
rechazar (c) to reject
recibir to receive (1B)
recibo receipt (8A)
reciclaje *m.* recycling (6B)
reciclar to recycle (6B)
recién recently; **recién nacido/a** newborn baby (5B)
reciente recent
recipiente *m.* container
recíproco/a reciprocal
recitar to recite
reclutar to recruit
recoger (j) to pick up

recomendable recommendable
recomendación *f.* recommendation
recomendar (ie) to recommend (8B)
reconocer (zc) to recognize (3A)
reconocido/a renowned
recordar (ue) to remember (2A)
recorrido trip, journey
recorte *m.* clipping (*of a magazine*)
recreación *f.* recreation
recreo recess (5A)
recuerdo memory; souvenir; **comprar recuerdos** to buy souvenirs (6B)
recuperación *f.* recuperation (8A)
recuperarse to recuperate
recurrir a to turn to
recurso resource; **recursos naturales** natural resources (6B)
red *f.* net; Internet; **navegar (gu) la red** to surf the Web (1A)
redacción *f.* composition
reducir *irreg.* to reduce
reembolso reimbursement
reemplazar (c) to replace
reenviar (reenvío) to forward
referencia reference
referir(se) (ie, i) (a) to refer (to)
refinado/a refined
reflejar to reflect
reflexivo/a reflexive
refrán *m.* chorus (*of a song*)
refresco soft drink (3B); **refresco dietético** diet soft drink (3B)
refrigerador *m.* refrigerator (4B)
regalar to give (*as a gift*) (3B)
regalo gift (4A)
regatear to bargain (2B)
regateo bargaining
régimen *m.* diet
región *f.* region
regla rule
regresar to return (*to a place*); **regresar a casa** to go home (1A)
regulador(a) regulator
regular to regulate
reinado *n.* reign
reírse (i, i) to laugh (7A)
relación *f.* relationship
relacionado/a (con) related (to)
relacionarse to relate, be related to
relajado/a relaxed (7A)
relajante *adj.* relaxing
relajarse to relax
relatar to relate, tell
relato tale, story
religión *f.* religion
religioso/a religious
rellenar to fill
relleno/a (de) stuffed (with)
reloj *m.* clock (P); watch (P)
remar to row; **remar en canoa** to go canoeing (6B)

remedio remedy
remolino pinwheel
Renacimiento Renaissance
rencor *m.* anger; **guardar(le) rencor (a alguien)** to hold a grudge (against someone) (7B)
renovar (ue) to renew
renta per cápita per capita income
renunciar a to quit (*a job*); to give up (9A)
repartir to distribute
repasar to review (1A)
repaso review
repente: de repente suddenly
repentinamente suddenly
repetir (i, i) to repeat (2B)
repleto/a overflowing
reportaje *m.* report (8B)
reportar to report
reportero/a reporter (8B)
represa dam
representante *m., f.* representative (9B)
representar to represent
represivo/a repressive
reproductor (*m.*) **de CD/DVD/MP3/ vídeo** CD/DVD/MP3/ video player (5A)
república republic; **República Dominicana** Dominican Republic
requerir (ie, i) to require
requisito requirement
res *f.*: **carne** (*f.*) **de res** beef (3B)
resaltar to highlight
resentido/a resentful
reserva reserve; reservation (*hotel*)
reservación *f.* reservation (6A)
reservado/a reserved (1B)
resfriado *n.* cold (*sickness*); **tener** (*irreg.*) **un resfriado** to have a cold (7A)
resfriarse (me resfrío) to catch a cold
residencia estudiantil residence hall, dormitory (P)
resolución *f.* resolution
resolver (ue) (*p.p.* **resuelto/a**) **(conflictos)** to resolve (conflicts) (9A)
respectivo/a respective
respetar to respect (7B); **respetar el espacio personal** to respect personal space (9A)
respeto respect (7B)
respetuoso/a respectful
respirar to breathe (7A)
responder to respond, answer
responsabilidad *f.* responsibility; **responsabilidad cívica** civic duty (8B)
responsable responsible (8A)
respuesta response, answer
restaurante *m.* restaurant (2A); **cenar en un restaurante elegante** to eat in a fancy restaurant (6B)
resto rest, remainder; *pl.* remains; remnants
restricción *f.* restriction

resuelto/a (*p.p. of* **resolver**) resolved (7B)
resultado result
resultar to turn out, result
resumen *m.* summary
resumir to sum up
retirar to withdraw
retrasar to delay, retard
retroproyectora projector
reunión *f.* **(cívica)** (town) meeting (8B)
reunirse (me reúno) to get together
revelar to reveal
revisar to check, inspect
revista magazine (1B)
revolución *f.* revolution (5B)
revuelto/a (*p.p. of* **revolver**): **huevos revueltos** scrambled eggs (3B)
rey *m.* king; **Día** (*m.*) **de los Reyes Magos** Epiphany (January 6), Day of the Magi
rico/a rich, wealthy (2B); delicious (2B)
ridículo/a ridiculous (8B)
rincón *m.* corner
riñón *m.* kidney
río river (6B)
ríoplatense *adj.* pertaining to the **río de la Plata** (*Platte River*)
riqueza *s.* riches, wealth (8A)
ritmo rhythm
rito rite; ceremony
rivalidad *f.* rivalry
rizado/a curly (3A); **pelo rizado** curly hair (3A)
robar to rob, steal
robo break-in
roca rock; **practicar (qu) el alpinismo de rocas** to rock climb (6B)
rodear to surround
rodilla knee (7A)
rogar (ue) (gu) to beg
rojo/a red (2B)
románico/a *adj.* Romance (*language*)
romano/a *n., adj.* Roman
romántico/a romantic (7B)
romper (*p.p.* **roto/a**) to break; **romper con** to break up with (7B); **romperse** to break (a bone) (7A)
roncar (qu) to snore
ronda *n.* round
ropa clothing (2B)
rosado/a pink (2B)
rosario rosary
rosbif *m.* roast beef (3B)
rosquilla bagel (3B)
rostro *n.* face
roto/a (*p.p. of* **romper**) broken
rozarse (c) con la gente to mingle with people (4A)
rubí *m.* ruby
rubio/a blond(e) (3A); **pelo rubio** blond hair (3A)
rueda wheel; **rueda de andar** treadmill (4A); **rueda pinchada** flat tire

ruido noise
rumano/a *n., adj.* Romanian
rumor *m.* rumor
ruso/a *n., adj.* Russian
ruta route

S

sábado Saturday (1A)
saber *irreg.* to know (*facts, information*) (3A); to find out (*about something*); **saber** + *inf.* to know how to (*do something*) (3A); **todavía no sé** I still don't know (P)
sabio/a wise (1B)
sabor *m.* taste, flavor
sabroso/a savory, tasty
sacar (qu) to take out; **sacar a pasear** to take for a walk (9A); **sacar dinero** to withdraw money (8A); **sacar fotos** to take pictures; **sacar la basura** to take out the trash (4B); **sacar la lengua** to stick out one's tongue (7A); **sacar la licencia de conducir** to get a driver's license (5A); **sacar un préstamo** to take out a loan; **sacar un vídeo/DVD** to rent a video/DVD (4A); **sacarle sangre** to draw blood (7A)
sacerdote *m.* priest
sacrificarse (qu) to sacrifice oneself
safari *m.* safari
sagrado/a sacred
sal *f.* salt
sala family room (4B); **sala de clase** classroom (P); **sala de espera** waiting room
salado/a salty (3B); **galleta salada** cracker (3B)
salchicha sausage (3B)
salida exit; way out
salir *irreg.* to leave; to go out (2A); **¿a cuánto sale?** how much is it?; **salir a bailar** to go dancing; **salir con** to go out with (7B)
salsa salsa (3B)
saltar to jump; **saltar la cuerda** to jump rope
salto leap, jump; **hacer** (*irreg.*) **el salto bungee** to bungee jump (6B)
salud *f.* health (7A)
saludable healthy
saludar to greet (7B)
saludo greeting
salvar to save (6B)
san *apocopated form of* **santo**
sandalia sandal (2B)
sándwich *m.* sandwich (3B)
sangre *f.* blood; **sacarle (qu) sangre** to draw blood (7A)
sanguíneo/a *adj.* blood

santería *religion of African origin practiced in the Caribbean*
santo/a *n., adj.* saint
se *refl. pron.* herself, himself, itself, yourself (*form. s.*), themselves, yourselves (*form. pl.*)
se alquila for rent (4B)
secadora dryer (4B)
sección *f.* section
seco/a dry
secreto *n.* secret; **ocultar(le) secretos (a alguien)** to hide secrets (from someone) (7B)
secundario/a secondary; **escuela secundaria** high school; **maestro/a de secundaria** high school teacher (9B)
seda silk
sedentario/a sedentary
sediento/a thirsty
seducir (zc) to seduce (7B)
seductor(a) seductive (7B)
seguida: en seguida right away
seguir (i, i) (g) to follow (2B); **seguir derecho** to continue straight ahead (6A)
según according to
segundo/a *adj.* second; **segundo plato** second course (6A)
seguramente surely
seguridad *f.* safety; **pasar por seguridad** to go through security (6A)
seguro insurance; **prima de seguro** insurance premium; **seguro antirrobo** antitheft insurance (8A); **seguro contra incendios** fire insurance (8A); **seguro de automóvil** automobile insurance (8A); **seguro de vida** life insurance (8A); **seguro de vivienda** homeowner's insurance (8A); **seguro médico** medical insurance (8A)
seguro/a *adj.* sure; safe; **estar** (*irreg.*) **seguro/a de** to be sure of (8B)
seis six (1A)
seiscientos/as six hundred (2B)
seiscientos mil six hundred thousand (5B)
selección *f.* selection; national team (*soccer*)
seleccionar to select, choose
sello seal, stamp
selva (tropical) (tropical) jungle (6B)
semáforo signal; traffic light
semana week (1A); **fin** (*m.*) **de semana** weekend (1A); **semana entrante** next week (1B); **semana pasada** last week
semanal weekly
semejante similar
semejanza similarity
semestre *m.* semester
semilla seed
senador(a) senator (9B)

sencillo/a simple (1B); **cama sencilla** twin (single) bed (4B)
sendero path
seno breast (*of a person*)
sensación *f.* sensation
sensacionalista *m., f.* sensationalist (8B)
sensible sensitive (7B)
sentarse (ie) to sit down
sentido *n.* sense; **sentido de dirección** sense of direction; **sentido del humor** sense of humor
sentimental sentimental (7B)
sentimiento feeling, emotion (7B)
sentir(se) (ie, i) to feel (4B); **sentirse** + *adj., adv* to feel + *adj., adv.*
señal *f.* sign; signal; **señales preventivas** warning signs
señalar to point out
señor (Sr.) man; Mr.
señora (Sra.) woman; Mrs.
señorita (Srta.) young woman; Miss, Ms.
separación *f.* separation
separado/a separated (3A)
septentrional northern
septiembre September (1B)
ser *irreg.* to be (P); **¿cómo es?** what is he/she/it/like? what are you (*form. s.*) like? (3A); **¿cuál es su apellido?** what's his/her last name? (P); **¿cuál es tu apellido?** what's your (*fam. s.*) last name? (P); **¿de dónde eres?** where are you (*fam. s.*) from (P); **era** he/she/it was, you (*form. s.*) were (1B); **es buena idea** (2B); **es imposible** it's impossible (8B); **es la una** it's one o'clock (1A); **es necesario** it's necessary (2B); **es preciso** it's necessary (8B); **es probable** it's probable (8B); **mi apellido es...** my last name is ... (P); **mi nombre es...** my name is ... (P); **parece ser** it seems to be; he/she seems ... (1B); **pasar a ser** to become; **¿qué hora es?** what time is it? (1A); **ser aficionado/a** to be a fan (4A); **(no) ser de fiar** to be (un)reliable; **ser hábil para (las matemáticas, las ciencias)** to be good at (math, science) (9B); **ser parcial** to be biased (8A); **ser pelotero/a** to be a kiss-up (9A); **ser puntual** to be punctual (1A); **soy de...** I'm from ... (P)
serie *f.* series
serio/a serious (1B); **en serio** seriously
serpiente *f.* snake (9A)
servicio service; **servicio de cuarto** room service (6A); **servicios médicos** medical services (9B); **servicios sociales** social services (9B)
servilleta napkin (6A)
servir (i, i) to serve (2B); **servir de compañía** to give, keep company (9A)

sesenta sixty (2A)

sesión *f.* session

setecientos/as seven hundred (2B)

setecientos mil seven hundred thousand (5B)

setenta seventy (2A)

sexenio period of six years

sexo sex

si if (1B)

sí yes; **sí, por supuesto** yes, of course

SIDA (síndrome [*m.*] **de inmunodeficiencia adquirida])** AIDS (Acquired Immune Deficiency Syndrome) (8B)

siempre always (3B)

siesta nap; **echar una siesta** to take a nap

siete seven (1A)

siglo century (5B); **siglo XXI** twenty-first century (5B)

significado meaning

significar (qu) to mean

significativamente significantly

signo *n.* sign (*horoscope*)

siguiente following; next

silencioso/a silent, quiet

silla chair (P)

sillón *m.* armchair (4B)

simbolizar (c) to symbolize

símbolo symbol

simbología symbology

similitud *f.* similarity

simpático/a friendly, nice (1B)

sin without (4B); **sin duda** without a doubt; **sin embargo** *conj.* however; **sin que** without (7B)

sincero/a sincere

sincretismo syncretism (*consolidation of different religious doctrines*)

síndrome *m.* syndrome; **síndrome de inmunodeficiencia adquirida (SIDA)** Acquired Immune Deficiency Syndrome (AIDS) (8B)

sino but (rather)

sinónimo synonym

sinopsis *f.* synopsis

síntoma *m.* symptom

sinuoso/a winding

siquiera: ni siquiera not even

sistema *m.* system; **analista** (*m., f.*) **de sistemas** systems analyst (9B)

sitio place, location; site; **diseñador(a) de sitios** Web site designer (9B)

situación *f.* situation

situar (sitúo) to situate

sobras *pl.* leftovers (3B)

sobre about; on, on top of (4B)

sobrepasar to exceed

sobresaliente excellent

sobrino/a nephew, niece (3A)

sociable sociable (9A)

social social; **ciencias sociales** social sciences (P); **servicios sociales** social services (9B); **trabajador(a) social** social worker (9B)

sociedad *f.* society (8B)

socio/a associate; partner

socioeconómico/a socioeconomic

sociolingüístico/a sociolinguistic

sociología sociology (P)

sofá *m.* sofa (4B)

sofisticado/a sophisticated

soja soy(bean) (3B)

sol *m.* sun; **hace sol** it's sunny (1B); **tomar el sol** to sunbathe (1B)

solamente only (1A)

solas: a solas alone (1B)

soldado, mujer (*f.*) **soldado** soldier (9B)

soler (ue) + *inf.* to be in the habit of / be accustomed to (*doing something*) (2A)

sólido/a solid

solitario/a solitary

sólo (solamente) *adv.* only

solo/a alone

solución *f.* solution

solucionar to solve

sombrero hat

sonar (ue) to ring

soneto sonnet

sonido sound

sonreír (i, i) to smile

sonrisa smile

sonrojarse to blush (7B)

soñador(a) dreamer (1B)

soñar (ue) (con) to dream (about) (5A)

sopa soup (3B)

soplo breeze; breath

soporte *m.* support

sorprendente surprising

sorprender to surprise

sorpresa surprise; **fiesta de sorpresa** surprise party (4A)

sospechar to suspect

sospechoso/a suspicious (1B)

sostener (*like* **tener**) to hold up, support

sótano basement

su(s) *poss.* his, her, its, their, your (*form. s., pl.*) (1A); **¿cuál es su apellido?** what's his/her last name? (P)

subdivisión *f.* subdivision; subsection

subida rise (8A)

subir to rise, go up (8A); **subir a** to board (6A); **subirse a los árboles** to climb trees (5A)

subjuntivo *gram.* subjunctive (mood)

sublevarse to revolt

subrayar to underline

subsecuente subsequent

suburbio suburb

suceder to happen

sucesión *f.* succession

suceso event, happening

sucio/a dirty

sudadera sweatshirt (2B)

Sudamérica South America (6B)

sudamericano/a *n., adj.* South American

sudar to sweat (4A)

suegro/a father-in-law, mother-in-law (3A)

sueldo (mínimo) (minimum) wage, salary (8A)

suelo floor

sueño *n.* dream; **tener** (*irreg.*) **sueño** to be sleepy (7A)

suerte *f.* luck; **tener** (*irreg.*) **suerte** to be lucky

suéter *m.* sweater (2B)

suficiente sufficient, enough

sufrir to suffer

sugerencia suggestion

sugerir (ie, i) to suggest (4B)

suicidio suicide

sujeto *n.* subject

sumar to add

superar to exceed

supermercado supermarket (2A)

supuesto/a (*p.p. of* **suponer**) supposed; **por supuesto** of course

sur *m.* south; **al sur de** to the south of (2A)

surfear to surf (6B)

suroeste *m.* southwest

suspender to suspend

sustancia substance

sustancial substantial

sustantivo noun

sustentable: desarrollo sustentable sustainable development

sustitución *f.* substitution

sustituir (y) to substitute

suyo/a/os/as *poss.* your, of yours (*form. s., pl.*); his, of his; her, of hers (2B)

T

tabaco tobacco (8A)

tacaño/a greedy, stingy (7B)

tacón *m.* heel (*shoe*); **zapatos de tacón alto** high-heeled shoes

tal such, such a; **con tal de que** *conj.* provided that (7B); **¿qué tal?** how's it going?; **tal vez** perhaps

talento talent

talentoso/a talented

talla size (*clothes*) (2B)

tamaño size (4B); **¿de qué tamaño es...?** what size is ... ? (4B)

también too, also (P)

tampoco neither, not either (3B)

tan so; **tan... como** as ... as (3A); **tan pronto como** as soon as (9B)

tanto *adv.* so much

tanto/a *adj.* so much; such; *pl.* so many; **tanto/a/os/as… como** as much/many … as (3A)

tapada: tener (*irreg.*) **la nariz tapada** to have a stuffed-up nose

tarántula tarantula (9A)

tardar to take time (*to do something*)

tarde *n. f.* afternoon, evening; **buenas tardes** good afternoon/evening (P); **de la tarde** in the afternoon, evening (P.M.) (1A); **por la tarde** in the afternoon/evening (1A)

tarde *adv.* late (1A)

tarea homework (2A); task

tarifa rate, price, fare

tarjeta card (4A); **tarjeta de crédito** credit card (2B); **tarjeta de felicitación** greeting card

tasa rate, level; **tasa de alfabetización** literacy rate; **tasa de desempleo** unemployment rate (8A)

taxista *m., f.* taxi driver

taza cup (*coffee*) (6A)

tazón *m.* bowl

te *d.o.* you (*fam. s.*); *i.o.* to/for you (*fam. s.*); *refl. pron.* yourself (*fam. s.*); **¿cómo te llamas?** what is your (*fam. s.*) name? (P); **te gusta…** you (*fam. s.*) like … (1A)

té (*m.*) **(caliente/helado)** (hot/iced) tea (3B)

teatro theater

teclado keyboard (5A)

técnica technique

técnico/a *n.* technician (9B); *adj.* technical

tecnología technology

tecnológico/a technological

tejido/a woven

tela fabric

telecomunicaciones *f.* telecommunications

telefónica telephone company

teléfono telephone; **llamar por teléfono** to call on the telephone (1A); **teléfono celular** cell phone (5A); **teléfono público** public telephone (P)

telenovela soap opera (8B)

telepático/a telepathic

televidente *m., f.* television viewer

televisión *f.* television (*medium*); **canal** (*m.*) **de televisión** television channel; **ver** (*irreg.*) **la televisión** to watch TV

televisivo/a *adj.* television; **programa** (*m.*) **televisivo** television program (8B)

televisor *m.* television (*set*) (P)

tema *m.* theme, topic

temer to fear

temperatura temperature; **tomar(le) la temperatura** to take (*someone's*) temperature (7A)

templado/a moderate (*climate*)

temporada season (*sports*)

temprano early (1A)

tendencia tendency

tender (ie) to tend to

tenedor *m.* fork (6A)

tener *irreg.* to have (2A); **tener… años** to be … years old (2A); **tener celos** to be jealous; **tener don de gentes** to have a way with people (9B); **tener éxito** to be successful (5B); **tener fiebre** to have a fever (7A); **tener ganas de** + *inf.* to feel like (*doing something*); **tener (la) gripe** to have the flu; **tener hambre** to be hungry; **tener la nariz tapada** to have a stuffed-up nose (7A); **tener prisa** to be in a hurry; **tener que** + *inf.* to have to (*do something*); **tener que ver (con)** to have to do (with); **tener sueño** to be sleepy (7A); **tener suerte** to be lucky; **tener tos** to have a cough; **tener un resfriado** to have a cold (7A); **tenerle cariño a alguien** to be fond of someone (7B); **tenerle envidia (a alguien)** to be envious (of someone) (7A); **tenerle miedo (a alguien)** to be afraid (of someone) (7A); **tengo una clase de…** I have a(n) … class (P); **¿tiene Ud. la hora?** do you (*form. s.*) have the time? (1A)

tenis *m.* tennis (4A); **cancha de tenis** tennis court (4A); **zapatos de tenis** tennis shoes (2B)

tensión *f.* tension; **tensión arterial** blood pressure

tenso/a tense (7A); stressed

tentación *f.* temptation

terapeuta *m., f.* therapist (9B)

tercer, tercero/a third; **tercer plato** third course (6A)

terco/a stubborn

terminación *f.* ending

terminar to finish (7B); to end

término term

termostato thermostat

terraza terrace

terremoto earthquake (5B)

terrenos *pl.* lands

terrestre terrestrial

territorio territory

terrorismo terrorism (8B)

terrorista *n. m., f.* terrorist

testigo *n. m., f.* witness (8B)

testimonio testimony

textiles *m., pl.* textiles (8A)

texto text; **libro de texto** textbook; **mensaje** (*m.*) **de texto** text message

ti *obj. of prep.* you (*fam. s.*) (4B)

tibio/a warm

tiburón *m.* shark

tiempo weather, time; **a tiempo** on time;

¿cuánto tiempo hace que… ? how long has it been since … ?; **hace buen/mal tiempo** it's good/bad weather (1B); **hace** + *time* ago; **llegar (gu) a tiempo** to arrive on time (1A); **pasar (mucho) tiempo** to spend (a lot of) time (1A); **pérdida de tiempo** waste of time (8B); **pronóstico del tiempo** weather report (8B)

tienda store, shop (2A)

tierra earth, land; **tierras altas** highlands

tijeras *pl.* scissors

timbre *m.* bell; **tono de timbre** ringtone

tímido/a timid (1B)

tinto/a: vino tinto red wine (3B)

tío/a uncle, aunt (3A); *pl.* aunts and uncles

típico/a typical

tipo type; **tipos de interés** interest rates (8A)

tiras cómicas comics (5A); cartoons

tirar to throw out (6B)

titular *m.* headline (8B)

titularse to be titled

título title

tiza chalk (P)

toalla (de papel) (paper) towel (4B)

tocar (qu) (el piano / la guitarra) to play (the piano / the guitar) (1A); to touch

tocino bacon (3B)

todavía still, yet; **todavía no sé** I still don't know (P)

todo/a all; every; **todas las noches** every night (1A); **todos los días** every day (1A)

tolerante tolerant (9A)

tomar to take (1A); to drink (1A); **tomar apuntes** to take notes (1A); **tomar café** to drink coffee (1A); **tomar cerveza** to drink beer (1A); **tomar el sol** to sunbathe (1B); **tomar una clase** to take a class (1A); **tomar(le) la temperatura** to take (*someone's*) temperature (7A); **tomarse algo muy a pecho** to take something to heart (7A); to feel something intensely (7A)

tomate *m.* tomato (3B)

tono de timbre ringtone

tontería foolish thing

tonto/a silly, foolish (1B)

topacio topaz

torbellino whirlwind

tormentoso/a stormy

toronja grapefruit (3B)

torpe clumsy (5A)

torre *f.* tower (2A)

torta cake

tortilla (de maíz) *flat bread* (*made of cornmeal*) (3B); **tortilla española** *omelette made of eggs, potatoes, and onions* (*Sp.*) (3B)

tortuga turtle (9A)

tos *f.* cough; **jarabe** (*m.*) **para la tos** cough syrup

tostada de pan a la francesa French toast (3B)

tostado/a toasted; **pan** (*m.*) **tostado** toast (3B)

toxicológico/a toxicological

trabajador(a) *adj.* hardworking (1B); *n.* worker; **trabajador(a) social** social worker (9B)

trabajar to work (1A); **trabajar en equipo** to work as a team (9A)

trabajo job; **Día** (*m.*) **del Trabajo** Labor Day

trabársele la lengua a alguien to get tongue-tied (7B)

tradicional traditional; **pérdida de valores tradicionales** loss of traditional values (8B)

traducir (*like* **conducir**) to translate

traer *irreg.* to bring (2A); **¿me podría traer... ?** could you (*form. s.*) bring me ... ?; **¿qué trae... ?** what comes with ... ? (6A)

tráfico traffic

tragedia tragedy

traicionar to betray (7B)

traje *m.* suit (2B); **traje de baño** bathing suit (2B)

trama plot (*of a story*)

tranquilo/a calm, peaceful

transacción *f.* transaction

transición *f.* transition

tránsito traffic

transmitir to transmit

transparente transparent

transporte *m.* transportation (6A)

trapo rag

tras *adv.* behind, after

tratado treaty; **Tratado de Libre Comercio (TLC)** North America Free Trade Agreement (NAFTA)

tratamiento treatment

tratar to treat; to deal with; **tratarse de** to be about (8A)

través: a través de through, by means of

travieso/a mischievous (5A)

trece thirteen (1A)

treinta thirty (1A); **los años treinta** the thirties (2A)

treinta y dos thirty-two (2A)

treinta y uno thirty-one (2A)

tren *m.* train; **estación** (*f.*) **del tren** train station (2B)

tres three (1A)

tres mil three thousand (5B)

trescientos/as three hundred (2B)

trescientos mil three hundred thousand (5B)

tribu *f.* tribe

trimestre *m.* quarter (*school*)

triste sad (1B)

triunfo triumph (9B)

tropical: selva tropical tropical jungle (6B)

trotar to jog (4A)

trozo piece, chunk

truco trick; **hacer** (*irreg.*) **trucos** to do tricks

tú *sub. pron.* you (*fam. s.*) (P)

tu(s) *poss.* your (*fam. s.*) (1A); **¿cuál es tu apellido?** what's your (*fam. s.*) last name? (P)

tumultuoso/a tumultuous (5B)

turista *n. m., f.* tourist

turístico/a *adj.* tourist; **clase** (*f.*) **turística** tourist class (6A)

tutearse *to address each other as* **tú**

tuyo/a/os/as *poss.* your, of yours (*fam. s.*) (2B)

U

u or (*used instead of* **o** *before words beginning with* **o** *or* **ho**)

ubicación *f.* location

ubicarse (q) to be located

último/a last

umbral (*m.*) **de la pobreza** poverty line

un, uno/a *indef. art.* a, an; one (P); *pl.* some, any; **a la una** at one o'clock (1A); **es la una** it's one o'clock (1A); **un poco de** a little (of) (P); **una vez al mes** once a month (1B)

único/a only; **hijo/a único/a** only child (3A)

unificador(a) unifying

unión *f.* union

unir to unite, join

universidad *f.* university (P)

universitario/a of or pertaining to the university

uno one (1A); **cada uno** each one

urbano/a urban

uruguayo/a *n., adj.* Uruguayan

usar to use; to wear (*clothing*)

uso *n.* use

usted (Ud.) *sub. pron.* you (*form. s.*) (P); *obj. of prep.* you (*form. s.*)

ustedes (Uds.) *sub. pron.* you (*form. pl.*) (P); *obj. of prep.* you (*form. pl.*)

usuario/a user

útil useful

utilizar (c) to utilize, use

uva grape

V

vaca cow

vacación *f.* vacation; **de vacaciones** on vacation

vacilar to hesitate

vacío/a empty

vainilla vanilla

Valentín: Día (*m.*) **de San Valentín** St. Valentine's Day (4A)

válido/a valid

valiente brave

valle *m.* valley (6B)

valor *m.* value; **Bolsa de valores** stock market (8A); **pérdida de valores tradicionales** loss of traditional values (8B)

valorar to value

vano/a vain

vapor steam; **al vapor** steamed (3B)

vaqueros jeans (2B)

variación *f.* variation

variar (varío) to vary

variedad *f.* variety

varios/as *pl.* various

vasco Basque (*language*); **País** (*m.*) **Vasco** Basque country

vascuence *m.* Basque (*language*)

vaso glass (*water*) (6A)

vecindad *f.* neighborhood (4B)

vecindario neighborhood

vecino/a neighbor (4B)

vegetal *m.* vegetable

vegetariano/a vegetarian (3B)

vehículo vehicle

veinte twenty (1A); **los años veinte** the twenties (5B)

veinticinco twenty-five (1A)

veinticuatro twenty-four (1A)

veintidós twenty-two (1A)

veintinueve twenty-nine (1A)

veintiocho twenty-eight (1A)

veintiséis twenty-six (1A)

veintisiete twenty-seven (1A)

veintitrés twenty-three (1A)

veintiún, veintiuno/a twenty-one (1A)

velo veil

velocidad *f.* speed

vencer (z) to conquer

vendaje *m.* bandage

vendedor(a) salesperson; vendor

vender to sell (2B)

vengativo/a vengeful (7A)

venir *irreg.* to come (2A)

venta sale; **de venta** for sale (4B)

ventaja advantage

ventana window (P)

ver *irreg.* (*p.p.* **visto/a**) to see (1B); **nos vemos** see you around; **ver la televisión** to watch TV; **ver un espectáculo** to see a show (6B); **ver una película** to watch a movie

verano summer (1B)

veras: de veras really

verbo verb

verdad *f.* truth

verdadero/a true

verde green (2B); unripe; **judías verdes** green beans

verdura vegetable (3B)

vergüenza shame

verificar (qu) to check, verify

verso line (of poetry)

vestido *n.* dress (2B)

vestir (i, i) to dress (2B); **vestirse** to get dressed (2B)

veterano/a veteran

veterinario/a veterinarian; **llevar al / a la veterinario/a** to take to the veterinarian (9A)

vez *f.* (*pl.* **veces**) times; **a veces** sometimes; **cada vez** each time; **cada vez más** more and more; **de vez en cuando** once in a while (3B); **la próxima vez** the next time; **la última vez** the last time; **muchas veces** often; **pagar (gu) de una vez** to pay off all at once (8A); **raras veces** infrequently, rarely; **tal vez** perhaps; **una vez (al mes)** once (a month) (1B)

vía way; path; **país** (*m.*) **en vías de desarrollo** developing country (8A)

viajar to travel, take a trip (1A)

viaje *m.* trip; **agencia de viajes** travel agency (6A); **agente** (*m., f.*) **de viajes** travel agent (6A); **hacer** (*irreg.*) **un viaje** to take a trip (6A)

viajero/a traveler (6A); **cheque** (*m.*) **de viajero** traveler's check (8A)

vida life; **seguro de vida** life insurance (8A)

vídeo video; **reproductor** (*m.*) **de vídeo** video player (5A); **sacar (qu) un vídeo** to rent a video (4A)

videocámara camcorder (5A)

videojuego video game; **jugar (ue) (gu) a los videojuegos** to play video games (5A)

vidrio glass; **botella de vidrio** glass bottle (6B)

viejo/a *n.* elderly person; **Noche** (*f.*) **Vieja** New Year's Eve (4A)

viento wind; **hace (mucho) viento** it's (very) windy (1B)

viernes *m. inv.* Friday (1A)

vigilar to watch (over); to supervise

villano/a villain; antagonist

vino wine (3); **degustar vinos** to go wine tasting (6B); **vino blanco** white wine (3B); **vino tinto** red wine (3B)

viña vineyard

violencia violence; **violencia doméstica** domestic violence (8B)

violento/a violent (8B); **crimen** (*m.*) **violento** violent crime (8B)

virtud *f.* virtue

virus *m.* virus (*computers*)

visitar to visit (1A); **visitar a la familia** to visit one's family (1A); **visitar un museo** to visit a museum (4A)

víspera eve; day before

vista view (4A); **punto de vista** point of view

vistazo glance; **echar un vistazo** to look over

vitalicio/a for life

viticultural wine-producing

viudo/a widowed (3A); widower, widow

vivienda housing (4B); **seguro de vivienda** homeowner's insurance (8A)

vivir to live (1B)

vivo/a alive (3A)

vocabulario vocabulary

vocal *f.* vowel

volante *m.* steering wheel

volar (ue) to fly (9A)

volcán *m.* volcano (6B)

volcánico/a volcanic

vólibol *m.* volleyball (4A)

volumen *m.* volume; **bajar el volumen** to lower the volume; **poner** (*irreg.*) **alto el volumen** to turn the volume up high

voluntario/a volunteer (8B); **trabajar de voluntario/a** to volunteer

volver (ue) (*p.p.* **vuelto/a**) to return (*to a place*) (2A); **volver a** + *inf.* to (*do something*) again

vos *fam. s.* you (*used instead of* **tú** *in certain countries of Central and South America*)

vosotros/as *sub. pron.* you (*fam. pl. Sp.*) (P); *obj. of prep.* you (*fam. pl. Sp.*)

votante *m., f.* voter

votar to vote (8B)

voto: derecho al voto right to vote

voz *f.* (*pl.* **voces**) voice; **correo de voz** voicemail; **en voz alta** aloud

vuelo (directo) (direct) flight (6A); **asistente** (*m., f.*) **de vuelo** flight attendant (6A)

vuelta *n.* turn; **dar** (*irreg.*) **la vuelta a** to go around (*something*); **de ida y vuelta** *adj.* round-trip (6A)

vuelto/a (*p.p. of* **volver**) returned

vuestro/a/os/as *poss.* your (*fam. pl. Sp.*), of yours (*fam. pl. Sp.*) (1A)

W

web Web (World Wide Web); **página web** Web page (5A)

X

X: rayos X X-rays (7A)

Y

y and (P); **y cuarto** quarter past (*hour*) (1A); **y media** half past (*hour*) (1A)

ya already; **ya murió** he/she already died (3A); **ya no** no longer

yeso cast (*for a broken bone*)

yo *sub. pron.* I (P)

yoga *m.* yoga; **practicar (qu) el yoga** to do yoga (4A)

yogur *m.* yogurt (3B)

Z

zanahoria carrot (3A)

zapatería shoe store

zapatilla slipper

zapato shoe (2B); **zapatos de cuero** leather shoes; **zapatos de tacón alto** high-heeled shoes; **zapatos de tenis** tennis shoes (2B)

zapping: **hacer** (*irreg.*) *zapping* to channel surf (5A)

zona zone

zumo juice (*Sp.*)

INDEX

This index is divided into two parts: Part I (Grammar) covers topics in grammar, structure, and usage. Part II (Topics) lists cultural topics, maps, countries, and vocabulary topics treated in the text. Other general topics appear alphabetically.

Part I: Grammar

Part II: Topics

Vocabulary

CREDITS

ABOUT THE AUTHORS

BILL VANPATTEN is Professor of Applied Linguistics and Second Language Studies at Texas Tech University. His areas of research are input and input processing in second language acquisition, sentence processing in a second language, and the effects of formal instruction on acquisition processes. He has published widely in the fields of second language acquisition and second language teaching and is a frequent conference speaker and presenter. His publications include *Making Communicative Language Teaching Happen* (with James F. Lee, 2003, McGraw-Hill), *From Input to Output: A Teacher's Guide to Second Language Acquisition* (2003, McGraw-Hill), *Processing Instruction: Theory, Research, and Practice* (2004, Lawrence Erlbaum Associates) and most recently, *Theories in Second Language Acquisition: An Introduction* (with Jessica Williams, 2007, Lawrence Erlbaum Associates). In addition to being lead author of *Sol y Viento*, he is also the lead author of *¿Sabías que... ?* and *Destinos*, as well as the designer for the *Destinos* telecourse. He has recently published his first work of fiction, a collection of short stories titled *Chicago Tales*, published by Outskirts Press (2007).

Dr. VanPatten is the 2007 recipient of the Anthony Papalia Award for Excellence in Teacher Education, awarded jointly by the American Council on the Teaching of Foreign Languages and the New York State Association of Foreign Language Teachers.

MICHAEL J. LEESER is Assistant Professor of Spanish in the Department of Modern Languages and Linguistics at Florida State University, where he is also Director of the Spanish Basic Language Program. Before joining the faculty at Florida State, he taught a wide range of courses at the secondary and post-secondary levels, including courses in Spanish language and Hispanic cultures, teacher preparation courses for secondary school teachers, and graduate courses in communicative language teaching and second language acquisition. He received his Ph.D. in Spanish (Second Language Acquisition and Teacher Education) from the University of Illinois at Urbana-Champaign in 2003. His research interests include input processing during second language reading as well as second language classroom interaction. His research has appeared in journals such as *Studies in Second Language Acquisition* and *Language Teaching Research*. He also co-authored *Sol y viento: En breve* (2008, McGraw-Hill).

GREGORY D. KEATING is Assistant Professor of Linguistics and Second Language Acquisition in the Department of Linguistics and Asian/Middle Eastern Languages at San Diego State University. Before joining the faculty at San Diego State, he taught courses in communicative language teaching and Spanish teacher education at the University of Illinois at Chicago, where he received his Ph.D. in Hispanic Linguistics and Second Language Acquisition. His areas of research include Spanish sentence processing, the role instruction plays in language acquisition, psycholinguistics, and the acquisition of Spanish syntax and vocabulary. He is a recipient of several teaching awards, including one from the University of Notre Dame, where he received his M.A. in Spanish Literature. In addition to teaching and research, he has supervised many language courses and teaching assistants and has assisted in the coordination of technology-enhanced lower-division Spanish language programs. He is also a co-author of *Sol y viento: En breve* (2008, McGraw-Hill).